# Hospitality Services

## Third Edition

by

## Johnny Sue Reynolds, Ph.D., CFCS

Educational Specialist and Professor Emeritus
Merchandising and Hospitality Management, University of North Texas
Denton, Texas

## Dorothy Chase, Ph.D.

Professor, Recreation and Tourism, Central Washington University
Co-Chair, Department of Family and Consumer Sciences
Ellensburg, Washington

Publisher
**The Goodheart-Willcox Company, Inc.**
Tinley Park, Illinois
www.g-w.com

# Introduction

*Hospitality Services* introduces you to careers in hospitality. The hospitality industry offers careers in five areas: foodservice, lodging, travel, tourism, and recreation. The textbook is organized into six parts. Part One provides an overview of the entire industry, including the essential role of customer service.

Part Two presents the foodservice industry. You will be introduced to the artistry of food preparation and service. You will also learn the essentials of food safety and sanitation. The basics of running a restaurant, including purchasing and receiving, are presented. You will also get to see how hotel foodservice works.

Part Three presents all aspects of the lodging industry. You will learn about the front office, housekeeping, security, and engineering.

Part Four brings three distinct segments of hospitality to life. You will learn the basics of travel and tourism and explore the world of recreation. You will also discover career options in each segment.

Part Five looks at the business behind the glamour. The basics of business structures and management principles are presented. An overview is provided of each of these support areas: human resources, marketing and sales, and accounting. A chapter on safety and emergency procedures shows you how to keep yourself and your guests safe. A chapter on legal and ethical considerations tackles these important issues in the industry.

Which hospitality career is right for you? Part Six helps you relate your talents and interests to the various careers in hospitality. Skills for success are presented to ensure your personal success in your chosen career. If you want to run your own business, the concluding chapter points you in the right direction.

# About the Authors

Johnny Sue Reynolds is well known and admired among high school hospitality teachers in Texas. She has master's and doctorate's degrees and certification in Foodservice Management. Johnny Sue is Professor Emeritus at the University of North Texas and former Associate Dean and Hospitality Management Department Chair. She is currently an educational consultant who enjoys teaching and developing online courses, developing FCS assessment , and mentoring student teachers. Reynolds has taught family and consumer sciences courses in Texas middle schools and high schools, as well as adult education courses. She earned a B.S. degree from the University of Mary Hardin-Baylor, M.S. degree from the University of North Texas, and Ph.D. from Texas Woman's University.

Dorothy Chase, Ph.D., is a professor of Recreation and Tourism at Central Washington University and co-chair of the Department of Family and Consumer Sciences. Dr. Chase earned a bachelor's degree in English from the University of Winnipeg, a master's degree in Education Administration from Lakehead University, and a doctorate in Parks, Recreation and Tourism Management from Clemson University. She spent a year as an exchange professor in Korea and has visited more than 50 countries for business or leisure. She has worked in retail travel and tours, and has also consulted in community tourism development. She served on provincial and national boards of the Canadian Institute of Travel Counselors for several years.

# Acknowledgments

The author and publisher are grateful to the following people who provided valuable input to this edition.

## Contributing Author

**Marcus Kieltyka**
Instruction and Outreach Librarian
Central Washington University
Ellensburg, Washington

## Industry Reviewers

**Nancy A. Haley**
General Manager
Wyndham Cleveland Hotel
Cleveland, Ohio

**Douglas Heath**
President, Group Communications
Institute, Inc.
Formerly Executive Vice President/CEO,
Meeting Planners International
Keller, Texas

**Costas Katsigris**
Director Emeritus, Food and Hospitality
Services
El Centro Community College
Dallas, Texas
Adjunct Lecturer
University of North Texas
Denton, Texas

**Paul Ramirez**
Director of Human Resources
Holiday Inn Select
Houston, Texas

## Teacher Reviewers

**Sharon Boyd**
Teacher/Coordinator
Grand Prairie High school
Grand Prairie, Texas

**Cheryl Hirni**
Career and Technical Education Teacher
Nashua High School
Nashua, New Hampshire

**Susan W. Kee**
Teacher of Marketing Education
Jackson Central-Merry High School
Jackson, Tennessee

**Barbara S. Lasko**
Family and Consumer Sciences Teacher
York Community High School
Elmhurst, Illinois

**Nancy Wanamker McIver**
Family and Consumer Sciences Teacher
Lin-Wood Public School
Lincoln, New Hampshire

# Contents in Brief

# Contents

## Part One
## Welcome to Hospitality

# Part Five

# Going Green

# Hospitality Ethics

# Profiles

# Promotes Successful Learning

## Chapter Titles

Introduce the topics covered in each Part of the text.

### Part Two
### The Foodservice Industry

## Chapter Objectives

Summarize the learning goals for each chapter.

## Before You Read

Questions what you already know before reading chapter content.

### Chapter 15
#### Travel

**Chapter Objectives**

After studying this chapter, you will be able to
- list the two major segments of the travel industry.
- identify the agencies and professions associated with travel planning.
- list the five Ws of travel planning.
- identify the major reasons for travel.
- compare and contrast the five major modes of transportation.
- assess the influence that new technologies have on transportation and the travel industry.
- identify various career opportunities in the travel industry.

**Before You Read**

Try to answer the following questions before you read this chapter.
- What are the two major segments of travel?
- What are the different modes of travel?

**Terms to Know**

## Terms to Know

Present the new terms you will learn in the chapter to expand your vocabulary.

# Enhances and Extends Learning

## Chapter Summary

Provides a quick overview and reinforcement of chapter content.

## Review

Provides an opportunity to review basic concepts and evaluate understanding of content.

---

## Chapter *16* *Review*

### Chapter Summary

- Tourism significantly impacts local economies.
- Terrorism had a significant impact on tourism that lead to additional security and protection for travelers.
- Technology continues to significantly influence tourism, especially for traveler security.
- Travel and health documentation are vital for international travel.
- Seasonality is an important influence for tourism destination areas.
- Destination marketing organizations (DMOs) work with local tourism officials to help promote area tourism.
- Several types of tour options are available that vary in structure to meet traveler needs.
- Tourism can influence community development, social factors, and environmental concerns.
- As tourism continues to grow, many career options are promising.

### Review

1. Compare and contrast a *domestic tourist* with an *international tourist*.
2. How does spatial context relate to sense of place?
3. Name two ways tourism affects economies.
4. What is a *national tourism* office and why is it important?
5. Describe three travel documents needed by international travelers.
6. What information about travel requirements can citizens obtain from the U.S. Department of State?
7. What is seasonality and why can it be a challenge for tourism?
8. List segments of the tourism industry.
9. What does ecotourism seek to accomplish?
10. What is unique about the voluntourism segment of the tourism industry?
11. Name three major types of tours.
12. What is the difference between a *docent* and an *interpreter*?
13. Name three operations and travel career areas that large tourism companies offer.

### Critical Thinking

14. **Predict.** Predict the consequences of failure to procure personal identification documents when traveling from country to country.

Discuss reasons why such documentation is *more* or *less* important today.

15. **Draw conclusions.** Draw conclusions about the benefits of smart identification technology to travelers and countries and discuss in class.
16. **Assess.** What are examples of biometric identifiers? Assess what privacy issues might be linked to such identifiers. Are the benefits greater than the privacy issues? Cite the text and reliable Internet or print resources to support your responses. Write a summary.
17. **Infer.** Suppose the hospitality company you work for primarily focuses on tours to the Caribbean Islands (see the map in Appendix B). Since you will be guiding tours, you decide to investigate sustainable developments in the area. Use the text and at least three reliable Internet resources to research and make inferences about sustainable developments, including economic, environmental, and cultural and social. Write a summary of your findings. How would you use this information in your work?
18. **Analyze.** Imagine you want to be a Certified Tour Professional (CTP). Analyze ways you might act as a peace ambassador when interacting with other travelers. Discuss your actions with the class.

#### Common Core

**College and Career Readiness**

19. **Speaking.** Use text and reliable Internet resources to research the process for obtaining a passport or visa to a country of your choice. Summarize your findings in an oral presentation.
20. **Writing.** Suppose you have been hired by a U.S. hospitality company that has many TDAs around the globe. You will spend your first year traveling to countries in

Central and South America. Use the CDC and the U.S. Department of State websites to investigate information you need for travel health. Identify diseases and health conditions common to the areas, vaccination requirements, and what to do if you should become sick abroad. Write a summary of your findings for each category.

21. **Reading.** Use at least three reliable Internet or print resources to research the categories of seasonal TDAs. For each category, identify one popular tourist destination. What attractions draw tourists to the area? What factors impact the profitability of each area? Write a summary for each category to share with the class. Cite your resources.
22. **Writing.** Visit the National Park Service website and research parks that focus on heritage tourism. Choose one site to research. Then write a public service announcement (PSA) about the tourism area, highlighting its key heritage features.
23. **Writing.** Suppose you are interested in working in cruise ship tours. Write an essay explaining your interest in the cruise industry. Cite the text and other reliable resources to support your explanation.
24. **Speaking.** Talk with your school counselor to identify nearby community colleges or universities that offer programs in tourism. Arrange a tour of one of the schools. Note key aspects of the program to share in an oral report in class.
25. **CTE Career Readiness Practice.** To learn more about the voluntourism segment, use reliable Internet, print, and interview resources to further investigate aspects of voluntourism. Summarize your findings in writing. When evaluating the reliability of information, remember to
    - identify author/writer/speaker credibility
    - verify the details
    - identify bias

---

## Critical Thinking

Challenges the use of higher-level critical thinking skills when reviewing chapter concepts.

## Common Core

For college and career readiness, these activities link chapter content to various academic areas such as writing, reading, speaking, and listening.

# Encourages Exploration of Chapter Topics

## Profiles

Fascinating and inspiring industry leaders share their hospitality experiences. Time lines summarize their career paths.

### Elaine Grossinger Etess— First Woman President of AH&LA

Elaine Grossinger Etess knows quite a bit about hospitality. She grew up at a world-famous resort in the Catskills of New York. Her parents and grandparents owned Grossinger's, a resort that started as a boarding house. The resort welcomed wealthy and famous guests from around the world.

The Grossingers' approach to hospitality is what made the resort so popular. They created an atmosphere of warmth and comfort. To the Grossingers, guests were more like extended family members than customers. Guests enjoyed their stay at Grossinger's, and the word soon spread.

As a young person, Elaine had no interest in working at the hotel, even though her mother wanted her to join the family business. Instead, Elaine's life took a different turn, and she attended Russell Sage College and Syracuse University. Elaine then married her childhood sweetheart and raised three children. Elaine, her husband, and their children moved to Grossinger's after her husband finished his medical residency and a tour in the service. They lived in a new home on the hotel grounds.

A few years later, Elaine became involved with the hotel. The use of weather stripping the interior design of the hotel and hiring the youth activities director. Her responsibilities and interest in the hotel grew from there. She began to handle special sales accounts and guest relations. This led her into an administrative and managerial role. Upon her mother's death in 1972,

Elaine became executive vice president. She continued in this role until the sale of Grossinger's in 1985.

Elaine is well known for her leadership. She started her own company and serves as its president. Called Elaine G. Etess Associates, this consulting firm helps other companies in the hospitality field. In 1989, she became the first woman president of the American Hotel & Lodging Association (then the American Hotel & Motel Association). In 2002, Elaine was inducted into the Hospitality Hall of Honor of the Conrad Hilton College of Hotel and Restaurant Management.

*Photo courtesy of Elaine G. Etess*

#### Elaine G. Etess's Career Path

| | |
|---|---|
| 1927: | Born in New York City, New York |
| 1972: | Became executive vice president of Grossinger's |
| 1982: | Earned her Certified Hotel Administrator (CHA) designation |
| 1985: | Founded her own company, Elaine G. Etess Associates |
| 1989: | Elected as first woman president of AH&LA (then AH&MA) |
| 1990: | Became hospitality director at Forest Trace resort retirement community |
| 2002: | Inducted into the Hospitality Hall of Honor at the Conrad Hilton School of Hotel and Restaurant Management |

Part Three   The Lodging Industry

## Going Green

Focuses on green and sustainable concepts and practices in the hospitality industry.

Chapter 15   Travel

### Going Green

#### Green Airports

Because of their size, airports impact the environment. Since its opening, the Denver International Airport has used a large solar energy system capable of providing 3.5 million kilowatt-hours of energy per year. The Fort Lauderdale-Hollywood International Airport (FLL) is recognized for pursuing environmentally friendly actions. The FLL is implementing the Green Airport Initiative (GAI), which seeks to improve environmental quality and efficiency. The GAI plan is to reduce the overall environmental footprint by addressing factors related to air, water, energy, and waste disposal.

The Alaska ferry system is 50 years old. Older ships will gradually be replaced by Alaska Class Ferries that are more environmentally friendly and fuel efficient.

#### Air Travel

Today, most people in the United States have flown on commercial airlines. Once reserved for wealthy individuals, air travel has become an affordable means of quick transportation, 15-10.

##### Booking a Flight

Passengers can book flight reservations with a travel agent or with the airline itself, by phone or online. A traveler will have needs and preferences for a specific airline based on the following:

- airports served
- scheduled time of flights
- reputation for service and quality
- nonstop versus connecting flights
- frequent flier benefits
- aircraft used

##### Flight Scheduling

Flying often means leaving one time zone and landing in another. On all transportation schedules, the times listed are local times. Schedulers must take the different time zones into account. Therefore, it is useful to be familiar with time zones when traveling. (See Appendix A for a map of the world's time zones.)

15-10 Many people choose flying for its speed and convenience.

279

Part Three   The Lodging Industry

256   238

In recent years, the cost of fuel has risen dramatically. Keeping a hotel or restaurant warm in winter and cool in summer requires a great deal of fuel. Therefore, proper control over the temperature is very important. The temperature in a hotel should be closely watched and regulated based on the number of guests and the outside temperature. Proper insulation in the walls of the hotel is essential in keeping the cost of heating and cooling down.

Windows and doors have a direct effect on the cost of heating a hotel. The use of weather stripping around the doors reduces the amount of heat that is lost. Features such as double doors, double-paned windows, and thermopane glass can also decrease the amount of heat that is lost. Some hotels use solar heat as a way to conserve fuel.

Water is another expensive resource that hotels use in large quantities. Leaky faucets and toilets waste large amounts of water. The engineering department can make sure these are repaired quickly. In addition, many of the new plumbing fixtures, such as low-flow toilets and showers, use less water. Some hotels have replaced old fixtures with these water-conserving fixtures. Many hotels encourage their guests to reuse towels in order to conserve the water and fuel used to wash towels.

In some hotels, guests must use their key card to activate the air conditioning and lighting system when they enter the room. When the guest

leaves the room, the air conditioning and lighting automatically reset to an energy-efficient level.

Resource management requires cooperation from all hospitality employees. The engineering department often works with management to educate employees about ways to conserve resources. For example, ovens need to be preheated for baking. However, preheating for an hour or leaving an oven on all day uses up a great deal of fuel. Engineering can work with the executive chef to determine that ten minutes of preheating is enough. The executive chef can then make sure that everyone who bakes only preheats the oven for ten minutes.

#### Emergencies

The engineering department is usually in charge of all safety issues, including fire safety, 14-7. maintenance of fire safety systems, and when emergencies occur, engineering plays a major role.

The engineering staff knows the location of firefighting and emergency equipment in the hotel. They also know the location of all equipment that could possibly explode or experience other emergencies. All staff must know the safest emergency routes. The engineering staff works closely with the security staff, kitchen staff, and municipal emergency services during an emergency.

### Hospitality Ethics

#### Ethics and Absenteeism

Ethical employees arrive at work on time, ready to perform their duties competently. In return for meeting this obligation, employees receive wages and the satisfaction of knowing they have performed their jobs well. Hospitality managers report, however, that *absenteeism*—or frequent absence from work—is a problem in the industry.

What happens when employees fail to show up for work? The burden of doing their work is shifted to others in the department and sometimes to other departments. This upsets work plans and lowers employee morale. Any worker with an absenteeism problem will be out of a job quickly. No employer can allow a worker's behavior to negatively impact guests, coworkers, and the reputation of the business.

## Hospitality Ethics

Gives real-life information to provide insight on issues that arise in the workplace.

# Presents Concepts Simply

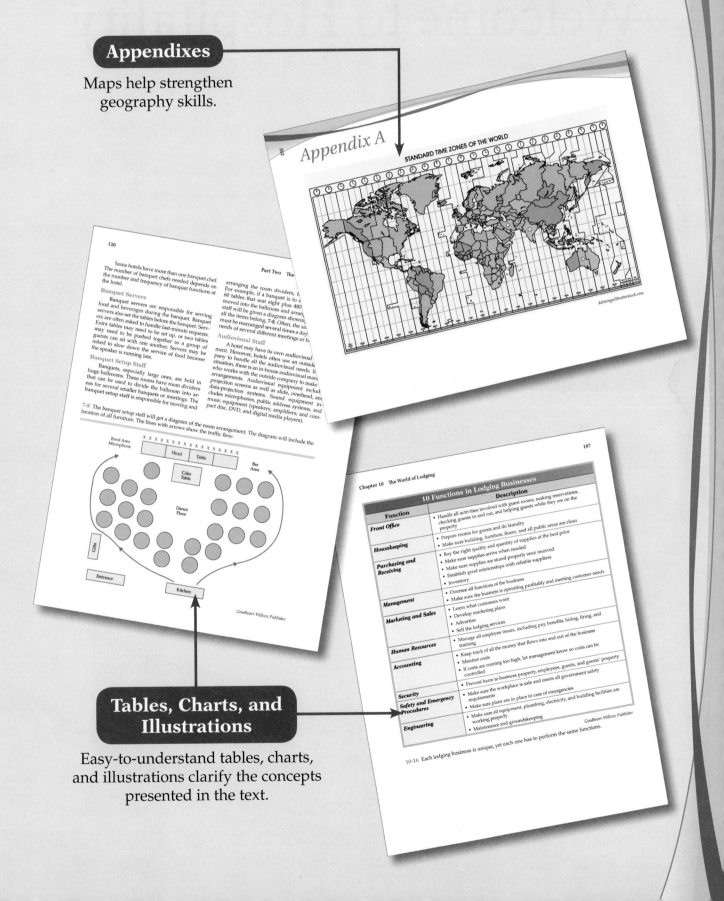

## Appendixes

Maps help strengthen geography skills.

## Tables, Charts, and Illustrations

Easy-to-understand tables, charts, and illustrations clarify the concepts presented in the text.

# Part One
# Welcome to Hospitality

3

4

# Chapter *1*
## The World of Hospitality

## Chapter Objectives

After studying this chapter, you will be able to

- **explain** the importance of the hospitality industry to the economy.
- **describe** the diversity of the hospitality industry.
- **differentiate** among the five segments and **give** an example of one business in each.
- **explain** why all segments of the hospitality industry should aim to satisfy the customer.
- **describe** the ways in which chains differ from franchises.
- **explain** the purpose of professional organizations and career and technical student organizations.

## Before You Read

Try to answer the following questions before you read this chapter.

- What segments make up the hospitality industry?
- Why are professional associations important to the hospitality industry?

## Terms to Know

hospitality
hospitality industry
foodservice industry
lodging
accommodation
lodging industry
travel industry
tourism industry

travel package
recreation
recreation industry
single-unit business
independent business
multi-unit business
chain

brand
franchise
franchisor
franchisee
professional association
career and technical student
    organization (CTSO)

What do you picture when you hear the word *hospitality*? Here's an example. Think of the hospitality extended by a friend's family. You stayed with them for a week while your parents were away on business. They provided you with a comfortable, friendly place to stay, good meals, and good company. You felt safe and happy. The word *hospitality* comes from the Latin word *hospes*, which means *host* or *guest*. **Hospitality** has come to mean *meeting the needs of guests with kindness and goodwill*.

The **hospitality industry** provides services to people away from home. These services include food, lodging, travel, tourism, and recreation. Hospitality is a "people-serving-people business" and service is at the heart of the hospitality business. Hospitality workers are dedicated to creating positive experiences for their guests, **1-1**. The goal of the hospitality industry is to make sure that guests feel safe and happy as a result of using the products and services offered by its many different businesses.

**1-1** Creating positive guest experiences is the goal of the hospitality staff.

*David Gilder/Shutterstock.com*

# Size and Economic Impact

According to the World Travel and Tourism Council (WTTC), travel and tourism is the world's largest industry and one of the most important. It has been one of the leading growth industries since the WTTC first started measuring the economic impact of the industry 20 years ago. The hospitality industry has a major impact on national economies around the world.

In the United States, about 14 million people work in the hospitality industry. It is the second largest employer. (Health care is the largest.) Worldwide, over 235 million people are employed in the industry. Jobs in hospitality include servers, chefs, travel agents, room attendants, hotel managers, meeting and event planners, restaurant managers, tour operators, convention and visitor bureau workers, theme park and national park employees, and recreation directors.

The hospitality industry is important to the U.S. economy because it generates more than $1 trillion each year. Whenever people buy food away from home to eat right away, they are spending money on a hospitality product or service. Whenever people travel, they spend money on transportation as well as food, lodging, and entertainment. They may even buy gifts for themselves and others. All these dollars become the wages of hospitality workers, profits of hospitality businesses, and taxes paid to federal, state, and local governments. Figure **1-2** shows how the money that travelers spend flows through the economy.

International visitors to the United States insert over $150 billion directly into the U.S. economy. For example, each international visitor to the United States spends an average of $4,300 per visit. This includes expenditures for

- lodging
- foodservice
- entertainment
- retail, such as clothes, gifts, and souvenirs
- local transportation

The hospitality industry impacts the economies of other countries. For example, Cuba has relied on its hospitality industry as one way to lift its poor economy. Tourism has provided a source of international investment since the early 1990s.

# HOW TOURISM DOLLARS ARE SPENT

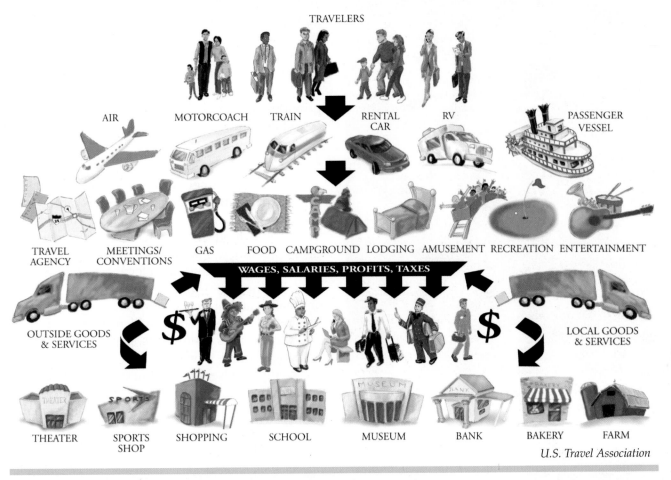

1-2 The money that tourists spend supports the economy.

## Industry Diversity

When something is *diverse*, it includes many different elements. The hospitality industry is very diverse. Some businesses in the hospitality industry are small; some are large. Some provide food, while others provide a place to sleep. Yet others provide entertainment or transportation.

Think about the times you have used a hospitality business. Possibilities could include eating lunch at a restaurant, staying at a hotel, seeing a movie, and taking a plane to visit relatives. Restaurants, hotels, movie theaters, and airplanes are all hospitality businesses. Other kinds of businesses in the hospitality industry include cruise ships, casinos, and theme parks, 1-3.

The people who use hospitality businesses are also diverse. A hospitality business may serve guests from throughout the United States and the world. Consequently, these guests represent many ages, cultures, and religions. Some guests may have disabilities and need special help.

Hospitality employees are also diverse. They may come from different countries and have different languages, religions, abilities, levels of education, and interests. Many new immigrants to the United States find their first jobs in the hospitality industry. Hospitality workers also vary in age—from high school students on their first jobs to retired persons working part-time.

## Industry Complexity

*Complex*, another word used to describe the hospitality industry, means *made of two or more*

*Georgia Department of Economic Development*

**1-3** Theme parks such as Six Flags Over Georgia are part of the hospitality industry.

*parts*. The hospitality industry consists of five parts or segments: food, lodging, travel, tourism, and recreation. This text will use the term *hospitality* to refer to the whole industry.

The hospitality industry is complex because many parts of the industry work together and are hard to separate. For example, many lodging businesses also offer food and beverages. Figure **1-4** provides an overview of these five segments of the hospitality industry.

## Food

The food segment of the hospitality industry consists of businesses that prepare food and beverages for customers. It is also called the **foodservice industry**. A foodservice business can range from casual to fancy. For example, both a sidewalk hot dog vendor and an elegant restaurant are food businesses, **1-5**. The business can be large or small. The hot dog vendor is a small business. McDonald's Corporation, which owns and operates McDonald's restaurants, is one of the largest businesses in the world.

Many foodservice businesses are located in another business. For example, foodservice businesses are often located in movie theaters, malls,

| \multicolumn{3}{c}{**Segments of the Hospitality Industry**} | | |
|---|---|---|
| **Segment** | **Categories in Segment** | **Examples** |
| *Food and Beverage* | Quick-service restaurants, full-service restaurants, street vendors, carryout, cafeterias | McDonald's, Olive Garden, Good Humor trucks, Taco Bell, your school cafeteria |
| *Lodging* | Hotels, motels, inns, bed-and-breakfasts, hostels, campsites | Hilton Hotels, Budget Suites, Holiday Inn, KOA Kampsites |
| *Travel* | Rental cars, buses, trains, airplanes, cruise ships, travel agents | Avis Rent a Car, Greyhound Bus, Yellow Cab, Amtrak, Southwest Airlines, Princess Cruises, Adventure Travel |
| *Tourism* | Tour companies, tourism offices, convention and visitors bureaus | Vermont Bike Tours, Indiana Tourism Council, Chicago Convention and Visitors Bureau |
| *Recreation* | Amusement parks, theme parks, nature parks, museums, movie theaters, sports arenas, concert halls, participatory sports | Six Flags, Disneyland Resort, Grand Canyon National Park, The Art Institute of Chicago, Sony Movie Theaters, Conseco Field House, Carnegie Hall, Blue Mountain Ski Area |

*Goodheart-Willcox Publisher*

**1-4** Identify two segments of the hospitality industry and discuss how they relate to each other.

1-5 Fine-dining restaurants are one part of the food and beverage segment.

*Omni Hotels & Resorts*

1-6 This luxury hotel is part of the lodging segment.

and airports. Because people eat out more often today than they did 50 years ago, much more money is spent at restaurants and other foodservice businesses.

The foodservice industry is the largest and most varied part of the hospitality industry. It may be the world's most well-known industry. It employs over 10 million people and is one of the nation's leading employers.

## Lodging

**Lodging** is a place to sleep for one or more nights. **Accommodation** is another word often used to mean *a place to sleep*. The **lodging industry** consists of businesses that provide overnight accommodations. A business that provides overnight accommodations is often called a *lodging property*.

Lodging facilities vary widely from expensive resort hotels to budget motels. Accommodations can be found to fit any price range and level of service. Some lodging properties pamper visitors with special services, **1-6**. Others concentrate on

convenience and low price. Examples of lodging businesses range from the elegant Ritz-Carlton Hotel in New York City and the reasonably priced Embassy Suites Hotels to the inexpensive Motel 6. A bed-and-breakfast in a private home is also part of the lodging industry. There are almost five million guest rooms in approximately 52,000 different properties throughout the United States. There are about 13 guest million rooms worldwide. Campgrounds are also part of the lodging industry.

## Travel

The **travel industry** consists of businesses that physically move travelers from one place to another. These businesses include car rentals, taxi and ferry services, train and bus services, and airlines. Travel includes trips of varying lengths—from overnight stays to round-the-world vacations involving several destinations and weeks of travel.

Travel for pleasure has changed in recent decades. Previously, Americans took week-long vacations and stayed with relatives or friends. Now a shorter weekend vacation taken more often is preferred. These travelers usually stay in a hotel or motel.

What types of vacations do people take? Some travel to visit historical sites or natural wonders. Some take trips for romantic reasons, such as a honeymoon. Others travel somewhere to rest, read, ski, snorkel, or go backpacking. Families often like to travel to visit relatives or pursue hobbies such as mountain biking or fishing, **1-7**.

Because travel is often necessary for business success, most companies budget a certain amount of money for travel every year. The amount budgeted may increase or decrease depending on economic factors. Business travel, including business conferences and events, is responsible for nearly 23 percent of all travel conducted in the United States.

## Tourism

The **tourism industry** consists of businesses that organize and promote travel for business, leisure, and other purposes. Businesses in the tourism industry include travel agencies, tour operators, cruise companies, meeting and convention planners, convention and visitors bureaus, and travel and tourism offices.

One of the main functions of tourism businesses is to plan various types of trips. A vacation, for example, might involve several different hospitality businesses. Suppose you want to attend a Detroit Tigers baseball game at Comerica Park in Detroit, Michigan, **1-8**. This trip might involve the following: transportation by bus to Detroit and back home, two nights stay at a motel, meals at several restaurants, tickets to the baseball game,

**1-8** A travel planner can arrange a weekend package to see a major league baseball game in another city.

Travel Michigan

**1-7** A bike ride is one way to enjoy a vacation in a scenic area.

Dan Koeck, North Dakota Tourism

and transportation within the city. If you planned the trip yourself, you would need to contact at least four different hospitality companies.

On the other hand, a professional travel planner could contact all the hospitality companies and make all the arrangements. The planner would then offer a package trip to Detroit. A **travel package** includes trip arrangements for several segments of the hospitality industry, such as transportation, lodging, meals, and entertainment. One fee is charged for the total package that covers all arrangements.

Many cities, states, and countries have offices that promote tourism, which helps their economies grow. Tourism offices advertise their location as a great place to visit. They develop brochures, print and Internet ads, and radio and TV commercials to encourage tourists to visit. Large U.S. cities often have a convention and visitors bureau that advertises the unique heritage and ecology sites, festivals, attractions, and recreational facilities in the region. The brochure helps potential visitors understand the products and services available. It also connects potential visitors to the businesses that will serve them when they arrive.

Each state has a government office or agency that promotes the state as a tourist destination. Examples include the Texas Economic Development & Tourism Department, and the Indiana Office of Tourism Development. One of the most famous and successful state advertising campaigns was developed in New York. The 1970s "I LOVE NEW YORK" campaign marketed tourism and vacations in the state of New York. The slogan and its logo are still recognized around the world.

## Recreation

**Recreation** is any activity that people do for rest, relaxation, and enjoyment. The goal of recreation is to refresh a person's body and mind. Different people enjoy different forms of recreation. You might enjoy seeing a movie, but your friend might prefer visiting a museum or going to a ball game.

The **recreation industry** consists of providers of activities for rest, relaxation, and enjoyment. Types of recreation operations include entertainment, spectator and participatory sports, and attractions. *Entertainment businesses* provide a show for you to watch. Examples include movies, live theater, and concerts. *Spectator sports* are sports that you watch others play, such as a professional football game. *Participatory sports* are sports you take part in yourself, such as golf or skiing.

*Attractions* are temporary or permanent places of special interest to visit. Attractions such as amusement parks are entertainment businesses. Other attractions are nonprofit operations, often sponsored by local or state governments. Examples include festivals, state fairs, museums, and zoos, **1-9**. The U.S. National Park Service has almost

**1-9** Zoos are one type of attraction that families love to visit.

*Fort Worth, Texas Zoo*

400 national parks that provide countless opportunities for outdoor recreation. Other attractions provided by the National Park Service are historic sites, museum collections, and national landmarks and monuments. Figure **1-10** gives you an idea of the size of the hospitality industry's recreation segment.

# A Customer Focus

All segments of the hospitality industry—food, lodging, travel, tourism, and recreation—must successfully meet customer needs. Imagine you are taking a vacation to New York City. What hospitality workers would you encounter on your trip? Who is responsible for making your trip to New York City exciting?

To get ready, you will need to reserve a flight and a room by communicating with reservation agents on the phone or through each company's website. To plan activities for each day of the trip, you then visit the official website of New York City. There you find maps, tips on things to do, restaurant recommendations, and more.

On the day of your trip, you arrive at the airport. You may interact with reservation agents, security officers, and flight attendants. After arriving in New York City, a taxi driver takes you to your hotel, **1-11**. At the hotel, you are greeted by the hotel staff and checked into your room. During your visit to New York City, you are served by servers at restaurants, waited on by sales associates at stores, and greeted by ushers in theaters. At museums and other attractions, tour guides provide explanations.

A huge number of hospitality workers affect your impression of New York City. They all help make your trip to New York City fun, exciting, and safe. Their goal is to make your trip totally satisfying.

# Business Categories

The Census Bureau defines and maintains statistics on U.S. businesses. It identifies *single-unit* and *multi-unit* as the two categories for classifying all existing businesses.

## Single Unit

A **single-unit business** has only one establishment. An *establishment* is a single physical location

| Number of Visits per Year for Recreation Providers ||
| --- | --- |
| **Recreation Type** | **Number of Visits in a Year** |
| Theme and Amusement Parks | 309 million |
| National Park Service | 275 million |
| Casinos | 131 million |
| Major League Baseball | 51 million |
| Golf Players | 26 million |
| Major League Football | 16 million |
| Broadway Show | 12 million |
| NASCAR Races | 10 million |

Goodheart-Willcox Publisher

**1-10** Millions of people visit recreational venues yearly.

**1-11** Taxi services are an important part of the hospitality industry.

Blend Images/Shutterstock.com

where business transactions take place and payroll records are kept. A single-unit business is also called an *independent business*. An **independent business** is not connected legally or by contract to any other business. The owner of an independent business is responsible for all business decisions and does not need to follow any other guidelines. (Of course, all businesses must follow local, state, and federal laws.)

An example of an independent business is Amore's Italian Restaurant, owned by Antonio Amore. He came to the United States in 1984 from Milan, Italy, and had a dream to open his own restaurant specializing in authentic Italian food. He uses his mother's recipes for most of the menu items. Antonio makes all the decisions about the restaurant. He decides on the decor, what menu items to serve, what to charge, and what the servers will wear.

## Multiple Unit

A **multi-unit business** has two or more establishments. These units function as part of a chain or part of a franchise. The business itself may consist of a chain of units, franchised units, or a mix of both.

### Chain

A **chain** is a business that has more than one establishment under the same name and the same ownership. For example, suppose Antonio Amore decides to open two more Amore restaurants. Amore's would now be a chain. An example of a restaurant chain is the Olive Garden Restaurants. All 780 Olive Garden Restaurants are owned by a company called Darden Restaurants, Inc. This is the largest casual dining restaurant company in the world, employing more than 185,000 people. Employees at Darden's headquarters in Orlando, Florida, make all the decor, menu, and customer-service decisions for the restaurants.

The most important aspect of a chain is its name, which becomes its brand. A **brand** is a name, logo, tagline, or any combination of these that distinguishes a product from its competitors, **1-12**. When customers see the brand, they associate a certain product and type of service with that particular brand. For example, McDonald's is a chain restaurant. The McDonald's brand consists of the McDonald's name, The Golden Arches (a logo), and the tagline "I'm lovin' it." Wherever people see the McDonald's brand, they know exactly what they will get. The McDonald's brand tells

*Romano's Macaroni Grill*

**1-12** This logo helps brand Romano's Macaroni Grill, a casual dining restaurant.

the customer that he or she will get McDonald's selections in a clean restaurant with quick service. Another example is the Four Seasons luxury hotel chain. When customers see a hotel with the name Four Seasons, they expect to find a luxury hotel.

### Franchise

The second type of multi-unit business is the franchise. A **franchise** is the right to do business using the brand and products of another business. The term *franchise* also refers to the business that is set up. Opening a new business unit takes a great deal of money. Sometimes the chain owner does not have enough money to open another unit. However, someone who is outside the chain might want to open a unit of the chain. The chain owner can give that outside person the right to use the chain's name and sell the chain's products.

The legal document that sets up a franchise is called a *franchise agreement*. The franchise agreement includes the rules and standards that the outside person must follow in running the franchise. In exchange for the right to use the chain's brand name and sell the chain's products, the outside person pays a certain amount of money to the chain owner. This money is called a *franchise fee*, which is also stated in the franchise agreement.

The person who owns the chain and the brand is called the **franchisor**. The person who buys the right to use the brand is the **franchisee**. The franchisee actually owns the franchise business, but is connected legally by the franchise agreement to the franchisor. All franchises are part of a chain, but not all chains have franchises.

For example, suppose that Antonio Amore wants to expand his business. Suppose Mary Green wants to open an Italian restaurant. Antonio can decide to grant a franchise to Mary. Antonio is the franchisor. Mary is the franchisee. The franchise agreement would say that Mary may open a restaurant called Amore's, using Antonio's mother's recipes. The franchise agreement would include how much Mary would pay for the franchise (the franchise fee) and the ways in which Antonio is required to help her start the business. The franchise agreement would also include the requirement that Mary run the business however Antonio wants. Mary might have to pay a certain percent of the profits to Antonio. The advantage to Mary is that Amore's is already famous for its excellent food. Mary will also get help from Antonio to start and run her restaurant. It would be more difficult for Mary to start her Italian restaurant from scratch. Mary will own her unit of Amore's, but she will be part of the Amore's chain. As a franchise of the Amore's chain, she must follow the rules set by Antonio, **1-13**.

One of the most famous restaurant franchise operations is McDonald's. Burger King, Wendy's, and Subway are other well-known restaurant franchises.

The lodging industry also has independents, chains, and franchises. An example of an independent would be a bed-and-breakfast run by a single family. Hotel chains include Holiday Inn and Hilton Hotels. Many hotel chains also sell franchises.

For example, some Hilton Hotels are owned by Hilton; others are franchises.

# Professional Associations

A **professional association** is a group of people organized to improve themselves, their profession, and their industry. Professional associations are also called *professional organizations*. Professional associations provide a way to meet others in the profession, learn about the latest trends, and make friends. The hospitality industry has over 50 professional associations. The major association in the foodservice industry is the National Restaurant Association (NRA). In the lodging industry, the major association is American Hotel & Lodging Association (AH&LA). The major association in the travel industry is the U.S. Travel Association.

Professional associations work to benefit the professionals and better the profession. Members have the opportunity to learn more about the profession. Professional associations also act on behalf of the industry when it must be represented at a governmental level.

| Antonio's Business Expands | | |
|---|---|---|
| *Independent* | Antonio is sole owner of one unit. | |
| *Chain* | Antonio is sole owner of three units. | |
| *Franchise* | Antonio is owner of three units and the Amore's brand. | Mary, as a franchisee, owns one unit. |

*Goodheart-Willcox Publisher*

**1-13** Antonio's business expands from an independent business to a chain. He then franchises a restaurant to Mary.

## Activities

Professional associations work in five areas: professional development, standards and ethics, networking, public relations, and government relations.

### Professional Development

*Professional development* is the process of continuing your education in your profession after you leave school. It is also called *continuing education*. Most professional organizations provide professional development opportunities, such as educational workshops and web-based seminars on the latest developments. This education often takes place at the organization's annual meeting. These are major gatherings at which the profession showcases the latest trends in technology, supplies, and products. Many professional organizations publish journals, newsletters, and books. For example, the AH&LA publishes *Lodging Magazine*. These publications also help professionals keep up-to-date on changes in their profession.

### Standards and Ethics

Professional organizations also develop standards for the practice of their profession. The NRA has developed industry standards for food safety and sanitation. Many organizations also have certificate programs. Members can go through an educational program and take a qualifying exam. If they pass the exam, they receive a certificate that confirms their qualifications to handle specific jobs. Professional organizations often develop a *code of ethics*, which is a statement of proper, professional behavior for members of the profession.

### Networking

*Networking* is the process of meeting people in your profession. People working in the same profession often share similar interests. Professional organizations often have social gatherings at their meetings that allow attendees to network, **1-14**. Networking provides the opportunity to meet others to problem solve, share new ideas, and learn

# *Hospitality Ethics*

## Learning About Ethics

**Ethics** is a discipline consisting of principles of conduct that govern the behavior of an individual or group. These principles deal with right and wrong behavior and with moral duty and legal obligation.

In the field of hospitality and all areas of life, you will face ethical challenges from time to time. How can you tell if the decisions you make conform to principles of good behavior? Here are some questions to ask yourself before you take action.

### *On the Job*

- Does my plan follow employee rules and my employer's code of ethics and/or code of professional conduct?
- Have I discussed my plans with my supervisor in cases of unusual or special situations?

### *On and Off the Job*

- Is my plan of action honest, fair, respectful of others, and legal?

professional organizations develop environmental guidelines for the business they serve. However, they also release the guidelines to the general public to emphasize the industry commitment to responsible use of environmental resources.

### Government Relations

*Government relations* involves informing local, state, or national governments about the issues that are important to the profession. Sometimes a profession wants to make sure its point of view is considered when public policy is made. Many associations have offices that monitor legislation affecting the industry. Associations also have staff members who communicate with lawmakers about issues affecting the industry and profession.

## Value of Involvement

There are many advantages to being involved in professional organizations. Many professional organizations offer scholarships to students planning to enter the profession. Also, employers know that job candidates involved in their professional organizations are usually more up-to-date in their knowledge. An employer might choose a person who is active in a professional organization over a person who is not.

Involvement in a professional organization helps you stay informed and, therefore, do a better job. Attending meetings and conventions can be fun and keep you excited about your career. Many professional organizations provide help to job seekers by posting job openings in their messages to members.

Professional organizations also give you an opportunity to develop your abilities and leadership skills. There are many volunteer positions that need to be filled in a professional organization. The president and vice president lead the organization, which helps them develop their leadership skills. The treasurer handles the finances of the organization and gets experience in finances. The program chair organizes and plans programs for monthly meetings. Through planning such programs, the program chair gets to meet important people in the field.

Yuri Arcurs/Shutterstock.com

**1-14** Networking can help professionals share information and ideas.

about career opportunities. Networking can also be fun.

### Public Relations

*Public relations* involves providing information about the industry to the general public. There are two purposes for public relations. One is to inform the public about the profession to attract new professionals. Another is to build a positive image of the profession and industry. For example, many

## *Career and Technical Student Organizations*

Students can become involved with professional development through career and technical student organizations. A **career and technical student organization (CTSO)** is an organization for students with an interest in a career area, such as hospitality or business. The purpose of a CTSO is to give students the opportunity to develop interpersonal, leadership, career, and technical skills. Most CTSOs work closely with professionals in industry and give students an opportunity to meet them. Many CTSOs provide scholarships. Some of these scholarships are sponsored by major businesses in the industry.

A CTSO will usually have a school chapter for students to join. Students then participate in chapter meetings as well as civic, service, social, and fundraising activities, **1-15**. In addition, many CTSOs have competitive events that enable students to demonstrate their career and technical skills. Participating in competitive events at the local, state, and national levels is a motivating experience for students.

Two CTSOs for students interested in hospitality are Family, Career and Community Leaders of America (FCCLA) and SkillsUSA. Both

Goodluz/Shutterstock.com

1-15 Working with group members on CTSO projects can help you build leadership skills.

organizations have a culinary arts competitive event. The Future Business Leaders of America (FBLA) and DECA—An Association of Marketing Students are two CTSOs that focus on the business and marketing aspects of hospitality. There are also CTSOs for many other career areas.

# *Going Green*

## Sustainability

You may have heard the term *sustainability* used in connection with environmental issues. However, *sustainability* refers to more than the environment. It also means not having a negative social or economic effect. Something that is sustainable does not deplete the environmental resources of future generations, negatively affect their communities, or cause economic loss.

# Chapter 1
## Review

## Chapter Summary

- Hospitality is the world's largest industry.
- The hospitality industry includes many different businesses.
- The hospitality industry is composed of five segments: food, lodging, travel, tourism, and recreation.
- The foodservice industry is the segment of the hospitality industry that people experience most often.
- All segments of the hospitality industry must work together to successfully meet customer needs.
- Businesses are classified as single-unit, meaning they are independent, or multi-unit, meaning they are chains, franchises, or a blend of both.
- Professional associations work to benefit their members and the profession.
- Career and technical student organizations are a great way to develop interpersonal, leadership, career, and technical skills.

## Review

1. What does the hospitality industry contribute to an economy?
2. Why is the hospitality industry considered diverse and complex?
3. Describe and give an example of each of the five segments of the hospitality industry.
4. Name two businesses within which a foodservice operation exists.
5. What is the role of travel in the hospitality industry?
6. Explain the difference between the travel industry and the tourism industry.
7. Give two examples each of a recreation business and a nonprofit source of recreation.
8. Why is it important for all the segments of the hospitality industry to work to satisfy the customer? Give an example.
9. What are the differences among an independent business, a chain, and a franchise?
10. Describe the five basic activities of professional associations.
11. What are the benefits of joining a professional organization?

# Critical Thinking

12. **Organize.** Make a list of at least 12 hospitality businesses that you have used or would like to use. Organize those 12 businesses into the five segments of the hospitality industry. Using this information, make an electronic presentation explaining the segments of the hospitality industry.

13. **Compare and contrast.** Describe a pleasure trip and a business trip. Then compare and contrast the two.

14. **Choose.** Imagine you want to open your own restaurant. Would you rather start your own independent business or buy a franchise? Explain your reasons.

15. **Predict.** Imagine you are a professional in the hospitality industry. Explain why you would join a professional organization.

16. **Create.** Create a poster illustrating the diversity of the hospitality industry in your local area. Share the presentation with your class.

## Common Core

### College and Career Readiness

17. **Math.** Select a hotel franchise and research its website. How many units does the franchise own? How much does it cost to purchase a unit in the franchise? What is involved in purchasing a business unit in the franchise? What other information did you find about the franchise on this website? Create a spreadsheet or a graphic presentation organizing your findings.

18. **Reading.** Read a magazine, newspaper, or online article about the impact of the economy on the travel and tourism industry. Determine the central ideas of the article and review the conclusions made by the author. Provide an accurate summary of your reading, making sure to identify the who, what, when, where, why, and how of the article's central idea.

19. **Writing.** Write an essay on how tourism affects the economy in your area or state.

20. **Speaking.** Research the different types of career and technical student organizations. What types of opportunities do these organizations provide students? Why are they important? Give an oral report to the class on your findings.

21. **Writing.** Visit a local lodging property, such as a hotel, motel, or bed-and-breakfast. Write an essay about your visit, describing the lodging property in detail.

22. **Speaking.** Contact your closest visitor's bureau to ask about recreation opportunities in your area. Give an oral report to your class about your findings.

23. **CTE Career Readiness Practice.** Imagine it is five years in the future and you are starting your first full-time job. Your new employer is a meeting, event, and convention planning agency, and you know the work is fast-paced and demanding. You have watched some family members and friends suffer the effects of workplace stress on their health and wellness over the years. Your goal is to maintain health and wellness by developing a plan for handling workplace stress. Investigate and evaluate the resources on the *National Institute for Occupational Safety and Health* link on the Centers for Disease Control (CDC) website. Then write your plan for preventing job stress.

20

# Chapter 2
## Service: The Heart of Hospitality

## Chapter Objectives

After studying this chapter, you will be able to

- **analyze** why customers are important to the hospitality business.
- **describe** the needs that hospitality businesses satisfy.
- **explain** the importance of quality service.
- **describe** the two types of hospitality employees.
- **list** the six characteristics of customer-focused employees.
- **distinguish** the 11 critical moments in customer service.
- **assess** the importance of good communication skills.
- **describe** methods of handling customer complaints.

## Before You Read

Try to answer the following questions before you read this chapter.

- How does consistent quality service help a business gain and keep customers?
- When does a customer's experience make the biggest impact on customer satisfaction?

## Terms to Know

service
customer service
customer
guest
empathy
customer satisfaction

quality service
consistent quality service
service encounter
word-of-mouth publicity
front-of-the-house

back-of-the-house
front-of-the-house employees
back-of-the-house employees
customer-focused employee
critical moment

**Service** is an activity that is done for another person. In hospitality, *service* often refers to the act or manner of serving food and drink. However, the hospitality industry does more than just serve food and drink. Hospitality is the business of satisfying people's needs. **Customer service** in a hospitality business is the total customer experience with that business. The total customer experience includes the performance of the staff, the courtesy of the staff, the cleanliness of the property, and the way customers are treated during their visit.

## Customers

A **customer** is someone who purchases products or services from a business, such as a department store or a hotel. Hospitality customers are often referred to as *guests*. A **guest** is a customer who purchases products or services from a hospitality business. In this text, these terms will be used interchangeably.

The customer is the main reason for the hospitality industry, **2-1**. If there were no customers, there would be no business and no profits. The customers are the ones who actually provide the money for the business, including the salaries. The success of any hospitality business depends on *return* customers. Service is a critical part of the hospitality industry because poor service is the number one reason that customers do not return to a business.

Customers come in all shapes and sizes, abilities and personalities, ethnic backgrounds, and religions. People from all over the world are traveling everywhere. A resort in California might have

**2-1** Hospitality-business success depends on customer satisfaction.

*Blend Images/Shutterstock.com*

guests from all 50 of the United States, Japan, Europe, Asia, and Africa. A NASCAR race may have spectators from all over the world. These travelers have different languages, customs, and expectations. Many have special needs. For example, a person with diabetes has certain dietary needs. A person using a wheelchair may need help getting around. A person who has been traveling a long time may be very tired and unable to think clearly. Hospitality workers need to develop the ability to understand and relate to all different people.

The best way to understand people is to develop empathy. **Empathy** is the ability to put yourself in someone else's shoes and know how that person feels. Empathy helps you figure out what customers need.

# Customers' Needs

When people are hungry, they look for a place to eat. When they are hot, they look for a place to get a cool drink. Tired travelers look for a place to sleep. However, people need more than good food, cold beverages, or a comfortable place to sleep.

Customers also look for a place where they feel welcome. People often return to the same restaurant where the servers recognize them. In fact, the quality of feeling welcome is often more important than the quality of the food or the comfort of a hotel room.

Hospitality businesses satisfy both the physical and psychological needs of customers. Abraham Maslow developed a method to describe how human needs are met. He ranked human needs in order from most basic needs to higher needs. This ranking, called *Maslow's hierarchy of needs*, is shown in **2-2**.

The hierarchy of needs is shown as a pyramid. The most basic needs are at the bottom of the pyramid: physical needs and safety needs. These needs must be at least partially filled before a person has the energy to pursue the higher needs. The higher needs are mostly psychological needs. Psychological needs include the need to feel accepted, the need for self-esteem, and the desire for self-actualization. *Self-actualization* means expressing your true self through reaching personal goals and helping others. People who are hungry usually do not have the physical energy to participate

**Levels of Human Needs**

*Goodheart-Willcox Publisher*

**2-2** Maslow organized human needs into a pyramid. The needs at the bottom must be at least partially met before a person can work to meet needs at the higher levels.

in activities that will fill their acceptance, esteem, and self-actualization needs.

Most hospitality businesses fill customers' basic physical and safety needs. Restaurants provide food. Hotels provide overnight lodging for tired travelers. Cruise ships have medical facilities on board. Some hotels have small boutiques or gift shops where travelers can purchase clothing. Most hotels provide electronic key systems for security.

Many hospitality businesses also provide ways for customers to meet needs for acceptance, esteem, and self-actualization. For example, acceptance needs can be fulfilled by eating with friends at a restaurant, attending a convention, and going to family reunions. Esteem needs can be met through staying at luxury hotels or a fancy resort. Self-actualization needs can be met through travel to foreign countries or taking educational tours, **2-3**.

Hospitality businesses can also meet customers' acceptance and esteem needs through the way they treat their customers. Treating all customers with respect and dignity fulfills some of these needs. Remembering a customer's name and using it when you see him or her also builds esteem and a feeling of acceptance.

Ariwasabi/Shutterstock.com

2-3  This woman is meeting her self-actualization needs by traveling to foreign countries and taking photographs.

# Satisfying Customer Needs

**Customer satisfaction** is the positive feeling customers have about a business that meets their needs. Hospitality companies meet the needs of their customers through quality service. Quality service is achieved by thoroughly training employees in the art of customer service.

## Quality Service

**Quality service** is service that meets or exceeds customer expectations. Customers' expectations change with the situation. For example, customer expectations at a fast-food restaurant will probably be different from expectations at a fancy restaurant. However, certain customer expectations are universal. All customers expect

- to be treated with dignity and respect, **2-4**
- their requests to be handled accurately and efficiently
- honesty in product descriptions and answers to questions
- money transactions to be handled honestly and accurately

Quality service is the key to establishing and maintaining a successful business. Service always depends on people—the employees who provide the service. Customers frequently compliment the following service elements:

- cleanliness and attractive appearance of facilities and grounds

2-4  Why is treating people with degnity and respect an important part of quality service?

* employees who respond quickly to requests
* employees who anticipate customer needs
  Each of these service elements is based on good training and the attitude of employees.

## Consistent Service

Quality service is necessary in today's competitive hospitality market. Even more important is consistent quality service. **Consistent quality service** is providing the same good service and products to customers each and every time they come to your business. Making sure that customers receive quality service is often difficult. However, all hospitality professionals know that delivering consistent quality service is the key to success. McDonald's is an example of consistent quality service. McDonald's major goal is to ensure consistency at all McDonald's restaurants. No matter where in the world you buy a McDonald's hamburger, it is of the same quality, served with the same good service, in a clean and cheerful restaurant.

Quality service depends on the interactions that take place between customers and staff. An interaction between a customer and a staff member is called a **service encounter, 2-5.** Service encounters are the basic building blocks of quality hospitality service. They occur before, during, and even after the customer's visit.

The first service encounter could be a telephone conversation between a guest and a hotel reservations agent. If the agent is not friendly and helpful, the guest will have a negative service encounter. Customers develop a sense of satisfaction

Dmitrijs Dmitrijevs /Shutterstock.com

2-5  How does a service encounter influence customer satisfaction?

based on the combined effect of their service encounters. Hospitality employees must be at their best at all times to ensure good service encounters. Hospitality businesses often fail or succeed based on the quality of service.

## Importance of Service Quality

Quality service is important because people often talk about their experiences at restaurants and hotels. People often choose restaurants and hotels based on recommendations from friends and coworkers. This type of publicity is called *word-of-mouth*. **Word-of-mouth publicity** is the informal conversation people have about their experiences with a business. In the hospitality industry, word-of-mouth publicity is one of the major ways that people learn about a hospitality business. Word-of-mouth can give a business good or bad publicity.

For example, a hospitality consultant claims that 90 percent or more of unhappy customers do not return to the business. Even worse, he claims that each of those unhappy customers will describe their bad experience to at least nine other people. Suppose a restaurant has 100 customers. If service is poor, 90 of them will not come back. Those 90 customers will each tell 9 (or more) of their friends about their bad experience. As a result, more than 810 people will hear about the poor service at the restaurant. Those 810 people will probably never even try the restaurant!

Conversely, positive word-of-mouth publicity can have a huge positive effect on a business. A restaurant owner once described the financial benefit of positive word-of-mouth. Suppose one customer spends $150 a year at his restaurant. That customer is pleased and tells two friends. Those friends go to his restaurant and each spends $150. Those two friends then tell two friends, and they each spend $150 a year at the restaurant. If this pattern continues over 10 years, it would result in over $600,000 in sales.

# Hospitality Employees

The people who provide quality service are the hospitality employees, who are organized into two groups: front-of-the-house employees and back-of-the-house employees.

The **front-of-the-house** is the area in a hospitality business that guests usually see. In a restaurant, the front-of-the-house includes the entrance and the dining room. In a hotel, the front-of-the-house includes the entrance and the lobby area. The back-of-the-house is the area in a hospitality business that guests usually do not see. The **back-of-the-house** is also called the *heart-of-the-house*. In a restaurant, the back-of-the-house includes the kitchen and the receiving and storage areas. In a hotel, the back-of-the-house includes the laundry, boiler room, receiving and storage areas, and offices.

**Front-of-the-house employees** are employees whose main function is to interact with customers. In the food and beverage business, front-of-the-house employees include servers, cashiers, hosts and hostesses, and parking attendants. In lodging businesses, front-of-the-house employees include bell attendants, front desk staff, reservations agents, and security officers.

**Back-of-the-house employees** are employees whose work rarely involves interacting with customers. In the food and beverage business, back-of-the-house employees include chefs, cooks, dishwashers, and receiving clerks, **2-6**. In the lodging business, back-of-the-house employees include housekeepers, building engineers, grounds attendants, and laundry attendants. The types of hospitality employees are listed in **2-7**.

You might think that only front-of-the-house employees need to worry about customers, but that is not the case. All employees are responsible for making sure that customers receive the best service possible. Every interaction that a customer has with any employee makes an impression. Back-of-the-house employees occasionally interact with customers. If the engineer is the person that a customer sees in the hall when she has a question, she will ask the engineer. That engineer's appearance, behavior, and response will influence that customer's impression of the business. The engineer must be as customer-focused as the bell attendant who carried her bags.

The first requirement of quality service is a sincere desire to please the customer. An employee with a sincere attitude remembers that the customer is the reason for the business. This attitude develops from being customer-focused.

2-6 A chef is a back-of-the-house employee.

*Bonefish Grill*

| Types of Hospitality Workers | | | | |
|---|---|---|---|---|
| | **Food and Beverage** | | **Lodging** | |
| ***Front-of-the-House*** | Banquet server<br>Bartender<br>Busser<br>Cashier | Host or hostess<br>Room service server<br>Servers | Bell attendant<br>Cashier<br>Concierge<br>Door attendant<br>Front desk agent | Parking attendant<br>Reservations agent<br>Security officer<br>Sales staff |
| ***Back-of-the-House*** | Chef<br>Cook<br>Dishwasher<br>Food preparation staff | Receiving clerk<br>Setup staff<br>Steward | Accounting staff<br>Engineering staff<br>Executive housekeeper<br>Human resources staff | Housekeeper<br>Laundry attendant<br>Marketing staff<br>Room attendant |

*Goodheart-Willcox Publisher*

**2-7** Front-of-the-house employees work mainly with customers. Back-of-the-house employees only occasionally interact with customers.

## Customer-Focused Employees

Quality service occurs when customers do not have to ask for anything. All of their needs are anticipated and provided. A **customer-focused employee** is an employee who can anticipate customer needs. Customer-focused employees have the following six characteristics:

- They make immediate eye contact.
- They have good posture.
- They smile warmly.
- They respond quickly to requests.
- They use the customer's name whenever possible.
- They are clean and well groomed.

### Eye Contact

As a hospitality employee, you should make eye contact with the customer as soon as he or she enters your area, such as when you open the door for the customer. By making eye contact, you show a willingness to serve. Eye contact communicates that you are giving the customer your total attention, **2-8**.

### Posture

Good posture is an important trait of all employees. Employees that customers see, such as door attendants, servers, concierges, housekeepers, and front desk staff, should pay particular attention

*Levent Konuk/Shutterstock.com*

**2-8** Customers appreciate a smile and eye contact.

to their posture. Your posture should be relaxed but alert. Your head should be up. Do not stare at the ground or look off into space. Avoid slumping your shoulders or stooping your back. Your face should look interested and lively, not bored. Project an attitude of enthusiasm.

### Smile

A smile is part of the uniform of all hospitality employees. A warm smile communicates respect for the customer and readiness to help. It also invites friendliness while showing that you enjoy your job.

### Quick Response

When a customer asks a question or makes a request, respond quickly. Your attitude should be positive and businesslike. Your response should show your competency, concern for the customer, and willingness to help.

### Use of Customer's Name

When possible, call customers by their names. In a restaurant, guests' names are often listed on the waiting list. Call guests by their names as they are being seated. Bell attendants in a hotel can learn guests' names from the front desk staff. The attendant can then refer to the guests by name, especially while escorting them to their rooms. Some coffee shops encourage their servers to remember their regular customers' names. When customers hear their own names, they feel important and welcome. This makes them more likely to return to your business.

### Good Grooming

The image of a hospitality business comes from the impression that is made by its staff. It is extremely important that all employees who are seen by the public have a good appearance and good grooming. Companies often have strict grooming and uniform regulations that employees must follow.

Have you ever been to a restaurant where the servers were wearing dirty aprons? How do you feel about restaurant employees who have tongue, lip, and eyebrow piercings? Have you been served food by a server with badly chipped nail polish? How did you feel? It may have made you feel uncomfortable about eating there. That is why good grooming is so important.

# Critical Moments

All service encounters are important. However, certain service encounters have a greater impact on customer satisfaction than others. These encounters are called *critical moments*. A **critical moment** is a time when the customer's experience makes a bigger impact on customer satisfaction than at other times. Figure **2-9** lists 11 critical

## Eleven Critical Moments

- First phone call to the business
- First view of the building entrance
- Interaction with the greeter
- Wait for a table or room
- First moments at the table or in the hotel room
- First encounter with bussers and servers
- Encounter with the manager
- Arrival of food
- Visit to the restroom
- Presentation of the check or bill
- Last interaction with server or front office staff

*Goodheart-Willcox Publisher*

**2-9** Proper responses at critical moments reflect quality customer service. Name a positive response to each critical moment listed above.

moments in hospitality services. Hospitality employees must make sure the critical moments leave a positive impression.

## *Phone Calls*

Guests often form impressions about your hospitality business long before they even enter the building. They may first call your business for information or to make a reservation. They form an impression based on the way the person answering the phone treats them. If the person answering the telephone treats them rudely, they may never come to your business. Figure **2-10** lists some tips for making a good telephone impression.

## *The Building Entrance*

Imagine walking up to an elegant hotel. What would you think of the hotel if there were cigarette butts on the floor all around the entrance? What would you think if the glass doors were dirty? You might wonder how clean the other parts of the hotel are, especially those that you do not see, such as the kitchen or the laundry department. Some customers will never enter your front door if they get the feeling from the outside that the business has poor housekeeping.

How do you keep customers from forming a bad impression of your business? Before and

## Telephone Tips for Good Impressions

**Smile when you answer the phone.** Smiling automatically makes your voice sound more pleasant no matter what mood you are in.

**Know answers to the most frequently asked questions.** Common questions concern hours the business is open, special promotions that are being advertised, parking, special events, the type of menu items that are served in the restaurant, and check-in and checkout times.

**Know directions to the business from other parts of town.** Determine the top five areas from which most of your customers will ask directions. These areas might include airports, hotels, convention centers, major highways, or local neighborhoods. Post the directions next to your telephone.

**If a caller must be put on hold, check back within 30 seconds.** If you do not check back quickly, the customer might become frustrated and hang up. If you say, "It's really busy here right now. Can you call back?" you might also lose your customer. In either case, the customer is very likely to call another business that has the time for him or her.

*Goodheart-Willcox Publisher*

**2-10**  Answering the telephone in a friendly, professional manner is part of quality service.

during every shift, employees should inspect and clean the parking lot, sidewalks, lobby, planters, and other places that might collect trash or become dirty. Get in the habit of picking up any trash that you come across. Check for burned-out lights, spills or gum, chipped paint, dirty or torn carpets, and posters or menus that are out-of-date. If you observe a problem that you cannot correct, such as a bad odor outside the building or a burned-out neon sign, inform the proper person of the problem. The building entrance must be spotless to create a good impression on customers, **2-11**.

### The Greeter

The greeter is the first person guests meet when they enter a hospitality business. Greeting is often a formal part of a person's job, such as a hotel bell attendant or the host or hostess in a restaurant. Sometimes the task of greeting falls on whomever the guest sees first. The greeting a customer gets when first entering a business makes a very strong impression.

As a greeter, open the door for every guest that you can. Greet all guests whenever possible within 30 seconds of their entrance. If you are really busy, look at the guest, smile, and say, "I will be right with you." The guest will feel acknowledged and less uncomfortable about waiting. Make all guests feel welcome and valued the minute they enter your front door.

*DavidXu/Shutterstock.com*

**2-11**  A pristine, beautifully decorated entrance will create a good impression on customers.

### The Wait

Nobody likes to wait. However, waiting is a reality at many restaurants. The greeter's behavior can determine whether the guest has a pleasant wait or becomes angry.

In a restaurant, the "Please Wait To Be Seated" sign often makes guests nervous when the greeter is not present. Guests stand around with nothing to do and feel uncertain about when the greeter is going to return. If you are a server and you see a guest waiting by one of these signs, acknowledge the guest with a smile and say, "The greeter (or host or hostess) will be right with you."

If there is a waiting list, try to "sell" the wait. Make the customers feel welcome by greeting them warmly. Then take down their information, and make them comfortable. You might say, "Four for dinner? May I please have your name? There is a 20-minute wait, but you are welcome to have a seat in the bar. I will come get you as soon as your table is ready. The server in the bar or on the patio can make you comfortable with one of our great appetizers or specialty drinks." When the table is ready, use the customer's name. For example, say, "Mr. Davis, your table is ready."

## The Table or Hotel Room

Showing guests to their table or hotel room leads to another critical moment. The physical aspects of a restaurant table or a hotel room make a big impression on guests. In order to have a successful critical moment, employees should check for cleanliness of the table or room.

In a restaurant, check the table. Is it steady or does it rock? Clear plastic wedges that are designed to stabilize a table are a good way to remedy this annoying problem. Some tables are equipped with stabilizers. Also make sure that everything on the table is clean and not sticky, including menus and condiments.

In a hotel, make sure the hotel room is clean and smells fresh. Look around to make sure everything that should be in the room is there and in the proper spot, **2-12**.

The way guests are taken to their table or hotel room can contribute to a positive critical moment. In a restaurant, the greeter should carry the guests' drinks to the table, hang up their coats, and pull out their chairs. The greeter should recommend a food item or a beverage special when seating their guests. An example of an appropriate welcome is, "Tonight I recommend the Fajita Nachos with chicken and our popular Raspberry Tea. I hope you enjoy your meal."

In a hotel, unlock the guest room for your guests, turn on the lights, and place their luggage

**2-12** A clean, fresh hotel room makes a positive first impression.

LI CHAOSHU/Shutterstock.com

and hanging clothes in the proper places. Show your guests the important features and amenities of the room, the location of the ice machine, and emergency exits. Ask your guests if they have any questions about the room or the hotel. At many hotels, a front desk agent calls guests 15 minutes after they have checked in. The agent asks the guests if everything is satisfactory and if they need anything else.

## The Busser and Servers

Your guests are now sitting at a steady table with clean condiment containers and spotless menus. Their next experience will probably be with the busser, who will arrive to remove extra place settings or to deliver water. What impressions are your guests getting now?

Bussers have their own critical moments for good customer service. They are an important part of the total sales team and should know the restaurant's food and beverage items as well as a server does. They should be able to answer questions that guests commonly ask, such as, "Where are the restrooms?" The busser's personal appearance is also significant. Is he or she wearing a clean uniform? Is the towel clean? Is the bus tub clean?

Servers spend more time with guests than any other member of the restaurant staff. They should strive to create a good experience for everyone they wait on, **2-13**. They should know everything about the menu, including daily specials and policies about substitutions. Some customers may have food allergies, so it is important for the servers to know the recipe ingredients and the ways the food is prepared. Servers should also be knowledgeable about vegetarian meals, special healthful items on the menu, and children's selections.

Servers should acknowledge and greet each customer promptly, no more than two minutes after the guests have been seated. The server should introduce himself or herself by name and ask for the beverage orders. Suggesting specific appetizers before turning in the beverage order will save time and extra steps.

Get the first beverage order to the guests no longer than five minutes after taking the order. Learn and use guests' names when possible. Make specific suggestions at every step of the meal. For example, recommend drinks, appetizers, main courses, side dishes, wine, desserts, and after-dinner drinks. Using language such as "It's my pleasure" to

Golden Pixels LLC/Shutterstock.com

**2-13** How does server knowledge enhance the guest experience?

respond to requests is more positive than saying "No problem."

Check your appearance. Is your uniform clean? Is your hair combed and restrained so your hair does not get into the guests' food? Are your perfume, cologne, and makeup appropriate and not overbearing? Are there any food stains on your apron or clothes? What about your breath? Do you have visible piercings or tattoos? Again, first impressions are important.

## The Manager

Interacting with the manager can create a positive critical moment for a guest. A hospitality business cannot be managed from an office in the back of the hotel or restaurant. Restaurant managers should try to greet every guest in the dining room. They should watch the guests' faces as they receive their food. Hotel managers should frequently walk around the lobby, smiling and making eye contact with the guests. They can then introduce themselves, learn guests' names, and briefly talk with them to make them feel welcome.

## The Arrival of Food

In a restaurant, the moment the customers wait for is the arrival of their food, **2-14**. How long did it take before their food arrived? Does the food look appetizing? Have the necessary condiments, such as ketchup, mustard, and crackers, been delivered to the table? Check back within two bites (NOT two minutes) to be certain that the food tastes the way the customers expected. Ask if your customers need anything else.

## The Restroom

At some point during their visit, customers may visit your public restroom. Does it look like your restroom at home would look if you were having company? Does it have a pleasant odor? Is it stocked with soap, toilet paper, and towels? The restroom should be checked for cleanliness every 30 minutes throughout each shift. Report any plumbing problems immediately to the engineering department. The person responsible for the restrooms should wipe up water and soap residue around the sinks, pick up any paper on the floor, and clean the toilets.

## The Check or Bill

In a restaurant, guests will sit leisurely at a table during lunch or dinner, sometimes for hours. However, once they decide to leave, they are ready to leave. You can succeed with the previous critical moments, but then destroy the entire experience by taking too long to deliver the check. Most servers realize it is important to deliver the check. However, they often leave the check on the table and then disappear. Have you ever seen guests with cash or credit card in hand looking for someone to take their payment?

After delivering the check, take a few steps; then turn around and look at your guests. See if they have already placed their payment on the table. If they have not, return to the table within two minutes to see if they are ready to pay, **2-15**.

In a hotel, the checkout process is also a critical moment. Guests are packed and ready to leave. They may be in a hurry to catch a taxi or a plane. Make sure their checkout process goes smoothly and quickly. The front desk agent should ask guests if they had a pleasant stay. The agent should confirm that the bill is correct and can also offer to make reservations for a future stay. Many hotels have automated checkout to make the checkout process smoother and faster.

**2-15** After delivering the check, why is it important to return within two minutes to see if guests are ready to pay?

**2-14** When food is presented, plates should be clean and food should be beautifully displayed and appealing.

MN Studio/Shutterstock.com

kovtynfoto/Shutterstock.com

# Hospitality Ethics

## What Is a Strong Work Ethic?

According to Webster, *work ethic* is the belief that work has a moral benefit and an ability to strengthen character. Having a strong work ethic in today's competitive workplace is key to achieving success on the job. Employees display a strong work ethic by keeping a positive attitude, interacting well with others, respecting timeliness, and doing the best job possible. When things do not go as planned, these employees still control their emotions, act fairly, and show respect for others—all of which builds character. Besides receiving payment for their work, employees with a strong work ethic receive the internal reward of feeling pride in their accomplishments.

## *The Goodbye*

The goodbye is the last critical moment that employees can influence. Make sure guests have a positive last impression of their visit. Any employees who see guests leaving should smile and thank them for staying at their hotel or restaurant. Thank your guests by name if possible and invite them back for another visit. When you smile at departing guests, they smile back, and arriving guests will see departing guests leaving with a big smile. The message they receive is, "These people must have had a great time here."

# Customer Relations Techniques

Customer relations skills are the skills necessary to provide good customer service. They include communication skills and the ability to handle customer complaints.

## *Communication Skills*

Communication is crucial for every employee at every level in the hospitality industry. Communication begins at the top of a business, with managers. Managers must communicate the rules of the company, standards of customer service, and information about the business to their employees. This can be accomplished through regular staff training sessions and employee handbooks.

Front-of-the-house employees must communicate effectively with customers. For example, a concierge must be able to give guests clear directions to a nearby museum. Front-of-the-house employees must also be able to communicate with their coworkers to make sure things run in a quiet and orderly fashion.

Back-of-the-house employees must communicate with each other and outside suppliers to create a smooth and efficient operation. For example, orders for supplies must be correctly given to suppliers. Supervisors and staff members must use good communication skills when planning, organizing, and completing work orders and production schedules, **2-16**.

Three methods of communication are commonly used in all areas of the hospitality industry. They are verbal, written, and nonverbal communication skills.

### Verbal Communication

Verbal communication includes the tone of voice you use and the way you speak. Use proper grammar at all times, not slang. Never use profanity in a hospitality business. Profanity shows that a person has a lack of manners, a lack of respect for the business that employs them, and an "I don't care" attitude toward the customers. Remember that you represent your hospitality business. Never discuss one customer with another customer or employee.

CandyBox Images/Shutterstock.com

2-16 Restaurant employees must be able to communicate clearly with one another.

## Written Communication

Hospitality employees must be able to communicate in a written form. For example, food servers must write menu orders clearly so the kitchen staff can read them. If the orders are unclear, the staff may prepare the wrong food. Front desk staff in a hotel must be able to enter correct information into the computer system. If the information is incorrect, guests will have problems checking out.

Never use an informal style of writing such as that used in texting. Capitalize words at the beginning of sentences. Use capital *I*s in sentences such as, "Please let me know if there is anything I can do to make your stay more enjoyable."

## Nonverbal Communication

Nonverbal communication is the message you communicate with your body language. Facial expression, hand gestures, posture, and eye contact are ways that we communicate nonverbally. The way you look when communicating with a customer tells a great deal about how you feel about that person. If you keep looking away from the person, you indicate impatience or annoyance. When you ignore a customer, you send a nonverbal message of "you are not important" or "we don't care about you." As a hospitality worker, you are always on display. Make sure your nonverbal actions communicate warmth and concern for your customers.

## Handling Customer Complaints

There will always be customer complaints. The key is to resolve these complaints to the customer's satisfaction. The following seven techniques will help you resolve customer complaints in almost any situation:

- Listen with empathy.
- Allow the customer to vent.
- Be supportive.
- Do not blame someone else.
- Have a positive attitude.
- Offer solutions.
- Follow through on the solution.

### Listen with Empathy

The best way to handle customer complaints is to have empathy for the customer's feelings. Listen carefully to the customer. Attempt to understand and feel what the customer is feeling. Try to see the situation from the customer's point of view. In most cases, customers want to know that someone has listened to them, their feelings have been understood, and someone is willing to help.

An apology is one of the best ways to let your customer know that you have heard and understood the problem. The best words to use are simply "I am so sorry." The value of an apology is often underestimated. It can make the difference between an angry customer who will never return to your business and a satisfied customer who will return.

The customer who discovers a hair in his or her omelet has a justifiable complaint. The server should use words and tone of voice that express empathy. For example, the server might say, "Oh, that's terrible. I am so sorry! I will tell the chef about this problem so it does not happen again. Let me bring you a fresh omelet, or would you prefer something else? I will be right back with your order." The server should quickly bring the new order to the customer and apologize once again. If it is possible, ask the manager to discount or "comp" (pay for) the customer's meal. By taking quick action, the server may have made a loyal customer.

### Allow the Customer to Vent

Often, customers need only to vent their feelings about the complaint, 2-17. Give customers the time to completely vent their feelings. Evaluate all ideas and all sides of the situation carefully. Separate yourself from the complaint. The customer has a problem with the situation, not with you. You may think that the customer is wrong. However, because the customer feels that he or she has a legitimate complaint, you must listen and try to resolve the problem.

### Be Supportive

Express your concern for and support of the customer. Let the customer know that you want to find a solution for the problem. If the customer is angry, let the customer know that he or she has the right to be angry. Let the customer talk about the situation. Just listen and show your support. It is often helpful to take notes. Some hospitality businesses have forms that you or the customer can fill out. Putting the complaint in writing often helps the customer feel heard. It also helps the business keep track of complaints and solve them.

### Do Not Blame Someone Else

Avoid placing the blame on someone else and making excuses for the problem. Customers do not want to hear about it. When you blame someone for the problem, it only makes you look bad. The discussion should be about what can be done about the situation, not who is to blame. If you are at fault, admit your mistake and apologize to the customer.

### Have a Positive Attitude

Express a positive attitude about the customer and the relationship the customer has with the business. Do not be negative at any time during the complaint process. Often a customer may be so pleased with the way a problem is resolved that he or she becomes a loyal customer.

Have a positive attitude about customer complaints. Look at the complaint as a way to better help the customer. Also consider the complaint as a way to learn more about doing your job better. A

*Alexander Raths/Shutterstock.com*

**2-17** Why is listening with empathy benficial to resolving a customer complaint?

complaint may enable you to make a change that will avoid the problem in the future.

### Offer Solutions

Offer the customer one or more solutions to the complaint. If none of the solutions is acceptable, ask the customer what it would take to satisfy him or her. It is important for you to know your company's policies on customer complaints so you know the options. Ask your manager about solutions that you can use.

Agree on a solution that pleases everyone involved. The manager may have to authorize some of the requests.

### Follow Through

Follow through personally to make sure the solution is carried out correctly and quickly. Most customer complaints can be settled with an apology and quick action. If the complaint is handled poorly, the customer will probably never come back. If a complaint is handled in a positive way, you may gain a loyal customer.

# Chapter *2*
## *Review*

## Chapter Summary

- Customers are the reason for the hospitality business.
- Hospitality businesses meet the physical and psychological needs of customers.
- Quality service is service that meets or exceeds customer expectations.
- The two categories of hospitality employees are front-of-the-house and back-of-the-house.
- A customer-focused employee is an employee who can anticipate customer needs.
- A critical moment is a time when the customer's experience makes a bigger impact on customer satisfaction than at other times.
- Good communication skills are necessary for good service.
- The best way to handle customer complaints is to listen and have empathy for the customer's feelings.

## Review

1. What is customer service in a hospitality business?
2. Explain why customers are important to a hospitality business.
3. How can a hospitality business meet the physical and psychological needs of a customer?
4. What can a hospitality worker do to ensure quality service?
5. How can bad word-of-mouth publicity harm a hospitality business?
6. Explain the difference between front-of-the-house and back-of-the-house employees.
7. List the six characteristics of customer-focused employees and explain the importance of each characteristic.
8. List the 11 critical moments in customer service and explain why they are critical.
9. List and give an example of each of the three types of communications skills that hospitality workers use.
10. List and describe seven techniques that are useful in handling customer complaints.

# Critical Thinking

11. **Draw conclusions.** With a classmate, role-play a situation in which one of you is a server and the other is a restaurant customer with a complaint. Conclude with a discussion of the pros and cons of the techniques that were used in the role play.

12. **Identify.** Create a flowchart that shows how to handle customer complaints.

13. **Predict.** Make a chart showing how poor word-of-mouth publicity can result in a huge loss of customers for this business.

14. **Assess.** Describe which human needs are fulfilled by going on a family trip to a luxurious resort.

15. **Predict.** What could happen if servers do not know which ingredients and preparation techniques are used in the restaurant's menu?

16. **Evaluate.** Describe the one critical moment you believe is most important when you are dining at a restaurant.

## Common Core

### College and Career Readiness

17. **Writing.** Write an essay describing a recent experience you had as a customer at a hotel or restaurant. How did you feel about the quality of the service you received? Would you go back there again? Would you recommend that hotel or restaurant to others? What were the service encounters that made a difference during your visit?

18. **Speaking.** In small groups, search the Internet for information about Abraham Maslow, the psychologist who developed the Hierarchy of Needs. Create an electronic presentation and present your findings to the class.

19. **Writing.** Customer-focused employees have six characteristics. Write a story about a restaurant server who has these six characteristics. Be sure to give examples.

20. **Speaking.** Eat a meal at a full-service restaurant. While dining, take notes about the 11 critical moments. Give a presentation about your experience to the class.

21. **CTE Career Readiness Practice.** Presume you are a front desk manager at a hotel. Your interpersonal skills—your ability to listen, speak, and empathize—are a great asset in working with customers. A hotel guest comes to the front desk to complain that her room was not cleaned until after 4:00 p.m. In addition, she felt the cleaning that was done was poor quality. What do you say to the guest? Why? What do you recommend as a solution?

# Chapter 3
# Hospitality Past, Present, and Future

## Chapter Objectives

After studying this chapter, you will be able to

- **name** three countries that played an important role in the early days of the hospitality industry.
- **name** five contributions to the hospitality industry by the United States.
- **associate** the relationship of the change in transportation and the growth of the hospitality industry.
- **assess** four challenges that the hospitality industry faces today.
- **list** four factors that affect the hospitality industry that people cannot control.
- **determine** how knowing trends helps the hospitality manager.
- **list** and give an example of the four types of trends that affect the hospitality industry.

## Before You Read

Try to answer the following questions before you read this chapter.

- How did the invention of new modes of transportation influence the development of the hospitality industry?
- What types of trends affect the future of hospitality?

## Terms to Know

| | | |
|---|---|---|
| souvenir | accessible | globalization |
| cruise | peak seasons | transnational corporation |
| hotelier | off-peak seasons | trend |
| motel | recession | demographic trend |
| amenity | contraction | social trend |
| diversity | expansion | lifestyle trend |

Hospitality is one of the oldest businesses. The first written records of travel were recorded on cave walls about 6,000 years ago. Human beings had just invented money, writing, and the wheel. These inventions made it easier to conduct business and to travel. As more people traveled, more hospitality businesses developed.

# Early History

The hospitality industry probably began with the Sumerians. In 4000 B.C., the Sumerians lived in a region near the Persian Gulf that was then called Mesopotamia. They grew grains that they turned into alcoholic beverages. The Sumerians built taverns and served beer to people in the surrounding areas. These taverns were some of the very first hospitality businesses.

Early traders traveled from region to region to trade their spices, gold, and other exotic goods. They needed places to eat and sleep while they were traveling. People built inns and taverns along the trade routes to serve tired, hungry, and thirsty travelers.

Three countries played important roles in the early days of the hospitality industry: Egypt, Greece, and the Roman Empire. Ancient Egypt began the tourism trade. In 2700 B.C. the pharaohs built elegant burial tombs, called pyramids. The beauty and majesty of the pyramids started attracting visitors, **3-1**. The Egyptians began encouraging citizens to visit the pyramids. The base of the pyramids also became great locations to hold large festivals. As more and more people started visiting Egypt, these visitors needed places to eat and sleep. The Egyptians developed places to meet these needs. Souvenir collecting also became popular because tourists visiting the pyramids wanted to take home a reminder of their visit. (A **souvenir** is an item that reminds you of a place you visited.) People began setting up booths around the pyramids and started selling souvenirs to tourists. The Egyptians also organized the first cruises. A **cruise** is a pleasure trip taken by boat or ship.

The ancient Greeks, who loved to travel, also played an important role in the development of the hospitality industry, **3-2**. They traveled all over Europe and established many colonies. Greece

**3-1** The pyramids of Egypt started attracting tourists in 2700 B.C. How did the Egyptians meet visitor needs?

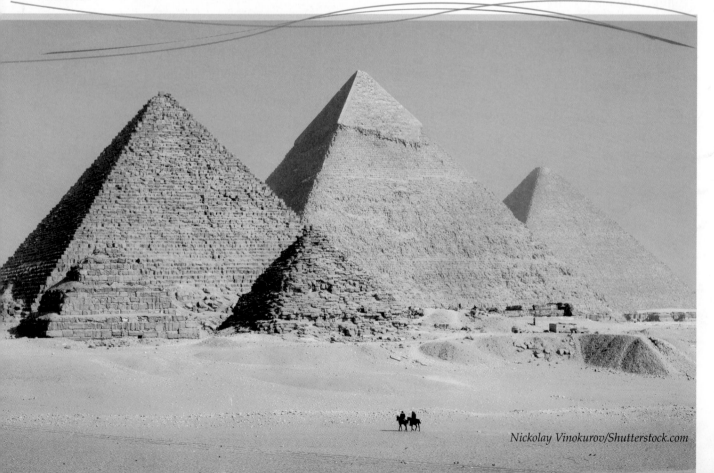

*Nickolay Vinokurov/Shutterstock.com*

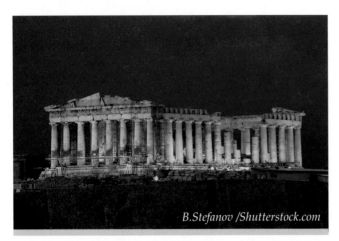

B.Stefanov /Shutterstock.com

3-2 The Parthenon was built by the Greeks in 438 B.C. as a temple to the goddess Athena. Tourists today visit Greece to see this incredible building.

made two major contributions to the hospitality industry. The first contribution was language, as Greek became the universally accepted language of international trade. Second, Greek money became the standard of exchange for monetary transactions. Common language and common currency made travel and business easier. As the amount of travel increased, so did the need for more hospitality services.

In 146 B.C., the Greeks were defeated by the Romans. The Roman Empire then became the major power in the world. The Romans developed a road system throughout their empire, which made travel throughout Europe quicker and easier.

After the fall of the Roman Empire, there were many wars and invasions throughout Europe. Travel was dangerous, and travel and tourism virtually stopped during this period. During the Middle Ages, the churches in Europe offered food and a place for travelers to rest. This period was followed by the Renaissance, which saw a rebirth of travel and artistic interests. Travel again became popular and safe. Taverns and inns were once again opened for tourists.

# Development in the United States

The United States has made great contributions to the hospitality industry. Grand hotels, motels, restaurant chains, fast-food businesses, and

franchises all originated in the United States. The hospitality business grew along with new modes of transportation. As each new mode of travel developed, hospitality businesses developed along the route or at the stations. These new modes of transportation include the stagecoach, railroads, the automobile, and commercial airlines.

## Inns for Stagecoach Travelers

Stagecoach routes were established in the United States in the 1600s. Inns where travelers ate and slept soon developed all along these routes. Large inns kept hundreds of horses on hand to supply the stagecoaches with rested horses in exchange for tired ones. Switching horses took about 30 minutes, giving passengers and drivers enough time to eat a meal.

The stagecoaches usually arrived at a set time. The innkeeper would have everything prepared for the passengers when they arrived. The servers stood at the door to take each guest's hat and coat. The innkeepers led the guests to a table set with dishes full of food. Good service was very important at these inns. The travelers were thirsty, hungry, and very dusty from their trip, 3-3. They were hot and sweaty in the summer months and freezing cold in the winter. The innkeepers tried their best to take care of the travelers' needs.

Inns and taverns were popular gathering places. These were the places where people met to discuss politics and problems of the day. Much of the planning and recruiting of soldiers for the American Revolutionary War was carried out in colonial inns and taverns.

The first building designed specifically as a hotel was probably New York City's City Hotel. This five-story hotel was built in 1794. Guests paid

3-3 Travel by stagecoach was long and difficult.

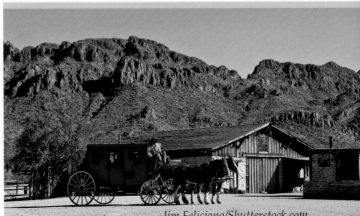

Jim Feliciano/Shutterstock.com

two dollars (which was a lot of money in 1794) to stay in one of the hotel's 73 rooms. For their two dollars they also received meals: breakfast, lunch, 6:00 p.m. tea, and dinner.

## Grand Hotels for Railroad Travelers

During the 1800s, railroad travel developed and spread, 3-4. Travel by railroad was much more comfortable than stagecoach travel had been. Trains also greatly decreased the length of travel time. For example, a 110-mile trip had taken a long 11 hours by stagecoach. Now the same trip took only two-and-a-half hours by train. Travel over long distances became possible for more people. Inns, saloons, and restaurants were built close to the railway stations.

It was during this railroad boom that the first grand hotel was built in America. A *grand hotel* offers luxury accommodations. The Tremont House in Boston was constructed in 1828. At the same time, a new hospitality profession began: hotelier. A **hotelier** is the owner or manager of a hotel.

The Tremont House was a grand hotel because of its many special features. These features included 170 private rooms, a lobby with a rotunda (similar to the one in the U.S. Capitol), six large meeting rooms, a 200-seat dining room serving French cuisine, and a reading room full of newspapers from countries all over the world.

**3-4**  As trains became the most convenient mode of travel, inns were often built near train stations.

*Faded Beauty/Shutterstock.com*

The Tremont House was four stories tall. At this time elevators had not yet been invented, which caused problems for the guests. Tremont's hotelier created a new position: bellhop. When the bellhop heard the bell ring, he had to "hop to it" to help guests. The bellhop's job was to help guests carry their heavy luggage upstairs. This same position is now called a *bell attendant*. The Tremont House set the standard for America's grand hotels and started a revolution of luxury hotels in Europe.

Hotels were often the first places where new technology was used. The first public building heated by steam heat was a hotel. Hotels were among the first places to have elevators and electric lights.

In Europe, Cesar Ritz was raising the standards of luxury hotels. At the Savoy Hotel in London, Ritz established high standards of excellence and luxury. He also put Auguste Escoffier in charge of the kitchen. Escoffier created the modern organization of a hotel kitchen and developed new and exciting dishes. Ritz and Escoffier made dining at the Savoy a luxurious and elegant experience. The elite of society, politics, and the arts gathered at the Savoy. Ritz and Escoffier made hotel restaurant dining socially important. In 1898, Ritz built the world-famous Ritz Hotel in Paris. He was the first hotelier to give each guest room a private bath, built-in closets, and telephones.

Back in the United States, hotel industry pioneers were developing something new: the hotel chain. In the early 1900s, Ellsworth Statler developed his chain of Statler hotels. Statler was the first to develop uniform standards for hotels. His hotels featured telephones in every room, modern plumbing, full-size closets with lights, radios, and free morning newspapers. He also developed a list of service rules, called *The Statler Service Code*. Each employee had to memorize the code and follow it.

## Motels for Automobile Travelers

A **motel** combines basic hotel services with convenience for the automobile traveler. A motel is located near the highway. Parking is free and located right outside the motel rooms, 3-5. The first motels were small and simple, with fewer than 20 guest rooms. They were often called *tourist courts* or *motor courts*. Motels did not have the facilities of a hotel such as restaurants, room service, and bell attendants. Guests had to carry their own luggage.

Tyler Olson/Shutterstock.com

3-5 A motel is usually a one-story building with rooms accessible from the parking lot.

In 1952, a Memphis businessman named Kemmons Wilson took his family on a vacation to Washington, D.C. He was disappointed by the shortage of accommodations to meet his family's needs. They could either stay at an expensive downtown hotel or a small motor court along the road. The hotels charged extra for children. The motor courts were often dirty and small, and did not have air conditioning, swimming pools, or a restaurant. As a result of this trip, Wilson decided to develop his own chain of hotels that would meet a traveling family's needs.

Wilson developed the Holiday Inn, with the name taken from the 1942 movie of that name. The Holiday Inn was designed as a roadside motel that had extra amenities to meet the needs of traveling families. These extras included a children-stay-free policy, a swimming pool, and a restaurant. Wilson also guaranteed reliably clean and comfortable rooms. He developed a large, distinctive sign, which people could easily see from the road. Holiday Inns are now one of the most recognized hotel chains in the world.

Motels soon became larger and began to offer more services. Business travelers liked having coffee shops, cocktail lounges, and meeting rooms. Swimming pools were important to traveling families, 3-6. Telephones in each room, usually present in hotels but not available in motels, became a basic amenity in motels. An **amenity** is an extra item or service that adds to a traveler's comfort or convenience. Hotels offered coin-operated radios and television sets during this period, but motels provided free televisions. These amenities were usually advertised on the motel's outdoor sign.

Motels were usually built at the edge of towns. Land costs were much lower there than downtown, where most hotels were built. Most motels are one or two stories tall. This simple construction is inexpensive to build compared with downtown high-rise hotels built on expensive real estate. The savings in construction costs are usually passed on to the guests in the form of lower rates. Today, it is often difficult to tell the difference between some motels and full-service hotels. The amenities and level of service vary based on the location and price of the property.

## Airport Hospitality for Air Travelers

Hospitality choices grew again when commercial jets began operating in 1958. Hotels that were located in the downtown areas of the cities began to decline. Airports became the new center for hotel, motel, and restaurant development. Industry leaders such as J.W. Marriott opened hotels near airports. New vacation areas were developed in locations that were easily accessible by air.

Jet airline service also decreased the time and inconvenience of international travel. Because it was easier and more convenient to travel between countries, international travel grew. Large corporations began opening offices around the world. Now corporations conduct business all over the world and rely on jets for transportation.

As air travel became more common, airports became the location of new hospitality businesses. Hotels, motels, foodservices, and restaurants were designed to meet the needs of air travelers. Airline

3-6 Swimming pools are an attractive amenity to traveling families.

Studio 1One/Shutterstock.com

catering became a major hospitality business. Airport hotels developed meeting rooms to serve the needs of the many business meetings held near airports, **3-7**. Airport shuttle services developed to transport guests from hotels to nearby airports.

# Hospitality Today

The hospitality industry has several major challenges. These challenges include

- delivering consistent service
- diversity of the workforce
- accommodating special needs
- impact of seasons

## *Delivering Consistent Service*

In the eyes of guests, hospitality businesses fail or succeed based on the quality of service they receive. Guests must receive the same good service each and every time they come to your business. Making sure that guests receive quality service is often difficult to do. Delivering consistent quality customer service is even more challenging.

Delivering quality service always involves people. Remember, hospitality is a people-serving-people business, **3-8**. Managers have two ways to ensure good service: procedures and training. They can develop procedures that ensure good service and then train all employees in the procedures. They must also train employees to be customer-focused.

## *Diversity of the Workforce*

The face of the hospitality industry is changing because the world is changing, particularly in the United States. In the past, white males made up the largest part of the workforce. However, women and people of many different backgrounds continue to enter the workforce in greater numbers, making the workplace more diverse. **Diversity** is the word used to describe a group of people from a variety of backgrounds, cultures, religions, beliefs, and languages.

In order to be successful, the hospitality business must learn how to meet the various needs of these employees. They must develop ways to help all employees succeed. They must help everyone

**3-7**  This hotel meeting room is designed for conventions and large meetings.

*Renaissance-Worthington Hotel, Fort Worth, Texas*

*Famous Dave's*

**3-8** Delivering consistent service is a challenge that a hospitality business must meet.

learn to work successfully together. Many programs help hospitality businesses support their employees. Some of these programs include

- opportunities for education, career, and professional development
- transportation to and from work
- assistance in learning English
- accessibility, career development, and opportunities for advancement for employees with disabilities
- retraining in job skills for older employees
- child care referrals or assistance
- flexible schedules

## Accommodating Special Needs

People with special needs are traveling more, and hospitality businesses are working to meet their needs. In addition, more people with special needs are in the workforce. Special needs include medical conditions, physical disabilities, and cognitive disabilities. For example, a guest with diabetes may need a special diet.

A guest who uses a wheelchair may need a room with special features. An employee with cognitive disabilities may need special training and supervision. Many older workers also have special needs due to physical and medical conditions, **3-9**. They may need some workplace accommodations, such as increased lighting, lifting restrictions, and training programs.

Special needs also include needs and preferences based on religion, health, or circumstances. Hospitality workers must use problem-solving and communication skills to meet these needs. For example, some religions do not allow the use of electricity on certain holy days. At these times, elevators and phones cannot be used. The hospitality worker may have to show the guest where the stairs are. Many people have food preferences based on health, taste, or religious restrictions. For example, many people do not want salad

Copyright Amtrak 2001. Photo courtesy of Amtrak

**3-9** Amtrak provides a wheelchair and an attendant (called a Red Cap) to help passengers with special needs.

dressing on their salads. A customer-focused server will ask if the customer wants salad dressing on the side and follow instructions carefully. Children traveling alone also have special needs. Airlines in particular have developed procedures for ensuring the safety and well being of children traveling alone.

The *Americans with Disabilities Act* was passed to make sure that people with disabilities are treated fairly. This law requires that public buildings be **accessible**, or able to be entered and used by a person with a disability. Most hospitality businesses have developed special accommodations for people with disabilities. For example, features such as ramps, automatic doors, and special bathroom facilities enable people using wheelchairs to easily enter and use a business. Another example is signs in *Braille*, a special language for those who are visually impaired. It is read by touching raised dots. Most elevators have Braille numbers for each floor. Special telephones enable those who are hearing impaired to communicate with hospitality businesses. Many hotels also have special fire alarms that use strobe lights to alert people who are hearing impaired in case of fire.

## Impact of Seasons

The demand for hospitality services varies with the seasons. **Peak seasons** are those seasons with the highest demand, **3-10**. During peak

seasons, hospitality businesses are the busiest. **Off-peak seasons** are those seasons with the lowest demand. During off-peak seasons, the number of customers is very low.

The timing of the peak and off-peak seasons depends on the location of the business. During the winter, demand in cold, snowy Chicago is lowest. However, in warm, sunny Ft. Lauderdale, the demand is highest in the winter. The timing of peak seasons also depends on the type of business. Hotels that serve mainly families are often busiest during the December holidays and the summer vacation season. Hotels that serve mainly business customers are often slowest during the December holidays.

Hospitality businesses must find ways to deal with the changes in demand. A major problem is knowing how to staff the business. For example, a restaurant with 10 servers might function very well during off-peak seasons. However, during the peak season, it would not have enough servers. Conversely, suppose the restaurant hires 20 servers for the peak season. During the off-peak season, the 10 extra servers have nothing to do. Most businesses cannot afford to keep employees who have nothing to do.

Hospitality managers have to design methods to cope with peak seasons and off-peak seasons. Some hospitality businesses hire temporary staff during the peak season. Some lower their prices or offer coupons during the off-peak season to

**3-10** Summer is the peak season for many family vacation destinations because children are out of school.

Andresr/Shutterstock.com

# Hospitality Ethics

## Ethical Leadership

Ethical leadership inspires, guides, and encourages employees to act on principles that promote right and good actions. An ethical leader values all employees, which in turn encourages them to be respectful, just, and fair when dealing with challenging issues.

As global travel and tourism increase, so does the potential for hospitality workers to face various ethical dilemmas. When their leaders strictly adhere to a code of ethical conduct, it motivates employees to stay true to their employer's and their own core values—using them as tools to solve ethical dilemmas.

lure guests to stay at their properties or eat at their restaurants. Good marketing strategies can help increase customers during off-peak seasons by enticing travelers to visit during slower times of the year.

## Factors Affecting Success

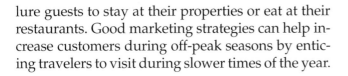

There are many factors that affect the hospitality industry, but the following four factors are *not* under a manager's control:

- weather
- political conditions
- economic conditions
- globalization

Each of these factors is subject to change. The change can be sudden and unpredictable. For example, on the day of a huge outdoor festival, it suddenly rains. Visitors leave, and the businesses earn half of what was expected. Although these four factors are not under a manager's control, hospitality managers must learn how to cope with their effects.

### *Weather*

The weather has a major impact on many hospitality businesses, **3-11**. From a local thunderstorm to a huge hurricane, bad weather can cause major damage to hospitality businesses. For example, a seaside resort may lose customers when it starts raining. Many resorts have developed policies to protect themselves from the impact of bad

weather. When a guest leaves early, it is very hard to find another guest to take his or her place. As a result, some hotels do not refund the cost of the room if a guest leaves early.

The Caribbean Islands are a popular vacation destination. They are located in an area that is affected by hurricanes and have suffered the effect of many hurricanes in the past. The hospitality industry on the islands is devastated each time a hurricane hits. So far, there is no protection from the effect of a hurricane. After each hurricane, hospitality businesses must rebuild.

**3-11** Bad weather, such as tropical storms, is a factor that cannot be controlled.

B747/Shutterstock.com

## Political Conditions

Hospitality businesses thrive under good conditions. Bad or dangerous political conditions discourage travel. Countries that suffer from war or unstable political conditions lose hospitality customers. For example, Europe has always been a prime tourist destination. However, during World War II, no one traveled to Europe for pleasure.

In more recent times, the terrorist attacks on New York City and Washington, D.C. on September 11, 2001 had a devastating effect on the U.S. hospitality industry and the hospitality industry worldwide. No airplanes flew in the United States for almost three days. Flights around the world were rerouted. For months afterwards, travel by air was greatly reduced. Many hospitality businesses in New York City, including the world-famous Windows on the World Restaurant, were destroyed. Cities that depend on tourists and business travelers, such as Las Vegas and New York City, suffered major economic losses. The hospitality industry as a whole lost billions of dollars. Fortunately, Europe's hospitality industry recovered after World War II, and the U.S. hospitality industry continues to receover from 9/11.

One of the major effects of 9/11 was an increase in concern about airplane and transportation security. As a result, the U.S. Congress passed the *Aviation and Transportation Security Act* on November 19, 2001. This law makes airport security a federal responsibility. It increases the amount of security at airports, increases the qualification and training requirements for baggage and passenger screeners, and includes measures to improve security for people who travel by bus and train.

## Economic Conditions

Many hospitality businesses rise and fall with the economy. When the economy is good, these businesses do well, **3-12**. When the economy is bad, these businesses do poorly. The U.S. economy rises and falls in irregular cycles. The falling times are called *recession* or *contraction*. A **recession** or **contraction** is a period when the economy is slowing down and doing poorly. People lose jobs during a recession and, as a result, have less money. One of the first things they cut out is spending on travel, recreation, and restaurants. The hospitality industry is one of the first industries hurt during a recession. It is also one of the last industries to recover when the economy starts picking up.

Photo Courtesy of Carnival Cruise Lines

**3-12** What effects do recession and expansion have on hospitality businesses?

The rising times are called **expansion**. An expansion is a period when the economy is growing and doing well. During an expansion, people have more money to spend. They often spend this extra money on travel, recreation, and restaurants. During the 1990s, the United States experienced the longest economic expansion in its history. During this period, hospitality businesses did extremely well.

## Globalization

Globalization is having a major impact on the hospitality industry. **Globalization** is the process in which the economies of different nations become interconnected. The term *global economy* is used to refer to the worldwide economy composed of the interconnected economies of all the nations.

Before globalization, each country's economy was mostly separate from the others. An economic problem in one country usually had little effect on another country. With globalization, each country's economy is dependent on the economies of other countries. An economic problem in one country can affect the economies of countries around the world. An example of the effect of globalization occurred in 2009. During this global recession, people stopped traveling for pleasure. Instead, they stayed close to home and took "staycations." Businesspeople traveled less, and many conventions and meetings were canceled. People ate out at restaurants less and cooked more meals at home.

Another aspect of globalization is the transnational corporation. A **transnational corporation** is a corporation that has major operations in several countries. Before globalization, corporations had their main operations in one country. They might import or export products, but most of their employees and offices were in one country. With globalization, many big corporations have major offices and many employees in countries around the world.

A sign of the hospitality industry's economic health is the continuing development of tourism facilities both nationally and internationally. Hotels, theme parks, shopping centers, restaurants, resorts, and golf courses are continuing to be built and expanded worldwide.

# Trends for the Future

No one can predict the future with 100 percent accuracy. However, if you study trends, you can make fairly good predictions. A **trend** is a general direction in which something is moving. Information that you gather from newspapers, professional organizations, the Internet, and professional colleagues can keep you up-to-date on the trends. Trends help hospitality managers decide which services to offer.

A trend in the hospitality business refers to the direction in which customer preferences are moving. For example, a current food and beverage trend is that more people are drinking specialty coffees, **3-13**. A trend is different from a fad. A *fad* is something that is extremely popular, but for a very short amount of time. Examples of food fads include frozen yogurt, smoothies, and cupcakes.

Trend research is often called *consumer research*. It is performed by marketing research professionals. Trend researchers count how many people are buying specific goods and services at a specific point in time. Six months later, they count again. If more people are buying, the trend is up. If fewer people are buying, the trend is down. Based on the trends, hospitality managers can decide which services to offer customers. For example, trend researchers noticed that each year, more business travelers were taking their laptop computers with

Kzenon/Shutterstock.com

**3-13** In addition to specialty coffees, what are some other current food and beverage trends?

them. When these travelers arrived at a hotel, they wanted to connect to the Internet. As a result of this research, most hotel managers decided to add Internet connections in their hotel rooms. The hotel managers then advertised this amenity. In turn, this amenity attracted more business travelers to these hotels. In order to remain competitive, many hotels now offer free wireless Internet service.

There are four types of general trends that affect all kinds of businesses, including hospitality businesses:

- demographic trends
- social trends
- lifestyle trends
- technology trends

## Demographic Trends

*Demographics* is the study of the characteristics of a population of people. These characteristics include age, income, and ethnic origin. A group of people can be studied based on one or more of these characteristics. The group can then be divided into subgroups based on characteristics. For example, the age characteristic can be used to divide a group into subgroups based on age, **3-14**. An example of subgroups based on age includes: babies (0 to 2), children (2 to 12), teenagers and young adults (13 to 21), adults (21 to 65), and older adults (over 65). A **demographic trend** is the increase or decrease over time in the number of people in a demographic subgroup.

A major demographic trend is the increase in the number of people over 65. The aging of the American population is not news. Because of better

Monkey Business Images/Shutterstock.com

3-14 Teenagers are a demographic subgroup.

nutrition and better health care, Americans are living longer. The baby boomers (the large group of people who were born between the years of 1946 and 1964) are entering the age of retirement. Retired people like to travel and have the time to travel, and many can afford to travel. Retirees are the fastest-growing segment of the hospitality market. The hospitality industry is responding to this increase. For example, many retirees like to travel in recreational vehicles (RVs). The RV industry and RV campgrounds are growing. The Elderhostel organization, now known as Road Scholar, is popular with older travelers. These programs offer adults ages 55 and older the opportunity to exchange ideas, share experiences, and explore the world together. Hostels offer low cost and unique learning opportunities to older adults.

Another demographic trend is the increase in the number of young people (ages 18 to 24) who travel. Young people usually travel in small groups. Their needs are very different from the needs of older adults. Young people are usually very conscious of travel costs. They often look for the lowest prices in airfare and lodging.

Some cruise lines have profited from meeting the needs of the different age groups on the same cruise. These cruise lines attract young adults, families, singles, and older travelers by offering specific activities for each age group. For example, after dinner, older passengers may go to a lounge to listen to a piano player. Teens may play basketball on the top deck. Parents may head to a variety show to watch performers sing and dance. Passengers who are in their 20s may go to the dance club. Other guests may watch a movie or sit in a quiet lounge.

## Social Trends

A **social trend** is a change in the structure or beliefs of the society. One social trend is the change in family structure. Years ago, the typical family had a biological mother and father and one or more children. Now there are many different kinds of families. Examples include one-parent families, families with adopted children, stepfamilies, and households with just one person.

Another social trend is the change in attitude toward gaming. For many years the gaming industry was seen as corrupt. In recent years, this type of entertainment has gained social acceptance. More and more people are going to casinos to try their luck at gambling. Hospitality companies have taken advantage of the shift in the social perception of casinos to make money in the gaming industry. Large casinos cater not only to the gambler, but also to their families. Many casinos offer dining facilities and hotel accommodations. Communities are taking advantage of the economic benefits that gaming businesses can bring to a local economy. People who work at casinos must be 21 years or older and receive special training. Casinos are also regulated by the government.

## Lifestyle Trends

A **lifestyle trend** is a change in the way people live their lives. A major lifestyle trend is the concern for health. As a result, many people want low-fat, low-calorie meals or vegetarian meals, even when they dine out. They also want to be able to exercise. Most hotels and cruise ships now have workout facilities and classes to meet this need, **3-15**.

Another trend is impulse buying. People even buy travel on impulse. Travel plans are often last-minute decisions. Business travelers sometimes change their schedules until the moment they leave on a trip. In response to this trend, many hospitality businesses have made it easier to make last-minute travel plans. Many websites combine ease of reservations with low fares. Some websites make it easy to book airfares and hotel rooms at the last minute. These services encourage people to travel on impulse, but they also help businesses fill guest rooms and airline seats that otherwise might have gone empty. On the other hand, the airline industry has not made it convenient to

3-15 This cruise ship includes basketball courts and walking tracks for people who want to incorporate physical activity into their vacation.

make last-minute travel changes. They usually charge a "change fee."

Another lifestyle trend is the desire to learn and have new experiences. In travel, this lifestyle trend results in the demand for experiences that include education or adventure. Many tour companies have developed packages around an educational theme. For example, many universities sponsor theater trips and trips to study the history and culture of a foreign country. Some organizations, such as Earthwatch, organize trips around researching and learning about natural phenomena. Other tour businesses organize adventure trips, such as river rafting.

## Technology Trends

The way people use technology affects many aspects of their lives. The invention of the railroad, automobile, and airplane changed life and the hospitality business in the United States and around the world. The development of electricity, elevators,

indoor plumbing, and air conditioning were also major changes. Nowadays these technologies are taken for granted. The focus is on new technologies, such as wireless communications.

The Internet has had a large impact on the hospitality industry. Using the Internet, customers can research many kinds of hospitality businesses. Customers can visit the website of a specific hospitality business. Many businesses also provide apps for digital tablets and smart phones. (*Apps* are software applications, most commonly for mobile devices.) For example, if you are looking for an airline flight, you can visit the website of a specific airline or use the airline's app. Once at the site, you can get information, make reservations, and buy tickets. Tickets to movies and concerts can be purchased online or with apps as well. Some businesses will allow you to show the digital ticket on your mobile device's screen instead of printing out the ticket.

The website of a restaurant usually provides information on the menu, location, hours, and any other special information about the restaurant. Hotel websites usually include beautiful photos of the property and provide information about the hotel, room rates, and location. Websites and apps are also valuable for marketing and for communicating with customers. Many company websites include information on available jobs with the company. In addition, the Internet is used for research and education in the field of hospitality.

Some websites and apps enable you to research several hospitality businesses at once. For example, some sites give you choices on flights, lodging, cars/rail, vacations, cruises, and deals. Some websites enable you to search for the lowest prices. Others allow travelers to compare pricing from several online travel companies. The Internet has also changed how people make decisions about the hospitality businesses they use and the places they visit. The primary function of some websites is to provide customers a forum for rating and recommending various locations and services. This information is then available to anyone who searches for it.

Customers are using more mobile computer technology in their daily lives, and they want that technology available when they travel. To meet these needs, hotels and restaurants may offer free wireless connections. Airplanes are equipped with telephones, and airports have computer workstations and charging stations. Some airlines offer on-board Internet service to their passengers for a fee.

In the lodging industry, computers have made a huge difference in the way information about guests, employees, and finances is handled, **3-16**. Computer software called a *property management system* keeps track of all this information on the computer. Before computers, all this information was recorded by hand and kept in paper files. The computer system makes it much easier to keep track of and use the information. Lodging businesses that have more than one property can use software called an *enterprise system*. This system combines information from the property management system for each property. Information for all the properties is then available on one computer system. This information is used to run the business more efficiently.

The food and beverage industry uses a computer system called a *point-of-sales system*. Basically, this system replaces the handwritten check. Servers can use a touch screen or a handheld device to record the orders. The system then sends orders to the kitchen, calculates the charges and taxes, and keeps track of items sold and inventory used. The system also records the payment and generates a customer check. Some systems have a vibrating pager that lets the server know when the order is ready to be picked up in the kitchen.

Technology can also help with sanitation. Dishwashing machines and laundry washers come equipped with computerized systems. These systems keep track of water temperatures and instruct the machines to use exactly the amount of detergent needed. High-tech thermometers also help food preparers make sure that foods are kept at proper temperatures.

# Hospitality Trends

Hospitality professionals keep up with trends because when they know what the "next big thing" is, they can better serve their customers' needs and wants. Sometimes it is hard to tell what will be a trend. Sometimes something that looked like a trend turns out to be a fad. Trends also change over time. Figure **3-17** shows some of the hospitality trends at the beginning of the twenty-first century.

**3-16** These front desk agents are using computers to manage information about guests.

*Photo courtesy of Kenwood Communications*

## Hospitality Trends

### Food and Beverage Trends

**Dining Out:** Dining out is part of the American way of life. Many Americans eat half or more of their meals away from home.

**Convenience Foods:** When Americans eat at home, they want easy-to-prepare or already prepared foods. Carryout, even from fine-dining restaurants, continues to grow.

**Quality:** Whether eating at home or away, Americans are demanding high-quality ingredients.

**Global Choices:** Americans want variety. New ethnic cuisines grow in popularity, such as Nuevo Latino and Tapas. Fusion, a creative mix of ethnic cuisines, is also popular.

**Entertainment:** Restaurants make eating an event, with special themes, decor, and activities. An example is the Rainforest Cafe. This restaurant is decorated with lifelike tropical animals, huge aquariums, and artificial jungle plants.

**Coffee:** Specialty coffees and coffee bars continue to grow in popularity.

**Healthful but Tasty:** Americans are more health conscious and want healthful foods. Examples include Asian and Mediterranean cuisines, low-fat foods, and vegetarian foods. People also want to know what ingredients are used and how their food is prepared.

**Beef:** For special occasions, beef is still king. Steakhouse chains such as Morton's of Chicago are expanding.

**Grocery Stores:** Delis, salad bars, and food-to-go are popular for busy Americans.

### General Trends

**Security:** Security continues to grow in importance for the entire hospitality industry.

**Service:** Lodging businesses continue to emphasize service over gimmicks. Instead of adding one more item to the toiletries basket, they focus on genuine hospitality through smiles, customer appreciation, and overall kindness.

**Older Adult Travel:** The number of older adults traveling is growing.

**Family Travel:** The number of adults traveling with children is growing.

**Impulse Travel:** Pleasure travelers will continue to make last-minute travel plans, including lodging.

**Internet Use:** Most travelers use the Internet to research and compare lodging and other hospitality businesses. The number who make reservations and buy tickets online continue to grow.

**Women Business Travelers:** More and more women are traveling for business.

**Internet Connections:** Most businesspeople take their laptops with them and expect Internet connections at hotels and travel centers. As a result, many full-service and most limited-service hotels have added free wireless Internet connections.

**Frequent Short Vacations:** Instead of one long vacation, people are taking more frequent short vacations. The long weekend (Friday through Sunday or Monday) vacation is very popular. Often people stay close to home and take stay-cations.

*Goodheart-Willcox Publisher*

**3-17** Hospitality managers consider trends when planning new restaurants and hotels.

# *Chapter* 3
## *Review*

## Chapter Summary

- Hospitality is one of the oldest businesses.
- Egypt, Greece, and the Roman Empire played important roles in the early days of the hospitality industry.
- The United States made significant contributions to the hospitality industry.
- The hospitality industry grew along with new modes of transportation.
- Four challenges to hospitality today are delivering consistent service, diversity of the workforce, accommodating special needs, and the impact of seasons.
- There are four factors that affect the success of the hospitality industry and that managers cannot control: weather, political conditions, economic conditions, and globalization.
- Trends help hospitality managers decide which services to offer.
- Four types of trends affect the hospitality industry: demographic trends, social trends, lifestyle trends, and technology trends.

## Review

1. When and how did the hospitality industry probably begin?
2. Describe the contributions of ancient Egypt, Greece, and the Roman Empire to the development of the hospitality industry.
3. List five major contributions to the hospitality industry by the United States.
4. In the United States, transportation developed from stagecoach to railroad to automobile to commercial airline. How did the hospitality industry change along with these transportation developments?
5. List the four major challenges to the hospitality industry and give an example of each.
6. What is the purpose of the *Americans with Disabilities Act*?
7. Give three examples of how hospitality businesses can meet the special needs of people with disabilities.
8. List the four factors that affect the hospitality industry that managers cannot control and give an example of each.
9. Why do hospitality businesses do poorly during an economic recession?

10. Why do hospitality businesses do research about trends?

11. List the four types of general trends and show how each one might affect the hospitality industry.

12. Give one example of a food and beverage trend and one example of a lodging trend.

# Critical Thinking

13. **Analyze.** Imagine that you live in prehistoric times. What problems would your restaurant have if money and a form of written communication did not exist?

14. **Identify.** In small groups, brainstorm examples of factors that affect success in the hospitality industry. Report the results to the class.

15. **Predict.** Imagine you are the owner of a national chain of restaurants. You want to be aware of the latest food trends so your restaurants can stay up-to-date. What trends do you anticipate will be most popular in the next five years?

16. **Analyze.** How does the trend of impulse buying impact the travel industry?

17. **Predict.** How will the demographic trend of the aging population affect the hospitality industry in the next 20 years?

18. **Determine.** Research the *Americans with Disabilities Act*. Give examples of accommodations that can be made in each of the following areas: quick-service restaurants, fine-dining restaurants, hotels, cruise ships, trains, airports, and airplanes.

19. **Identify.** List ten ways computers are used in the hospitality industry.

# Common Core

### College and Career Readiness

20. **Reading.** Create a time line that shows the development of the hospitality industry. Provide the sources you used for your research.

21. **Writing.** Research and write a brief history on the Road Scholar organization. When and how did the program begin? How is this concept similar to youth hostels?

22. **Reading.** Read several articles about how global recession affected the hospitality industry. What started the recession? How did it affect the travel and tourism industries? How did it affect the lodging industry? Did it affect the restaurant industry? How did hospitality companies manage to survive the recession?

23. **Math.** Identify a destination of your choice and plan a trip using two major modes of transportation. Make a table showing the distance, time, and cost per mile for each option.

24. **Writing.** Research the diversity policy of a large, well-known hospitality company. Does this company have a diversity policy? How easy is it is to find? How would you suggest that they improve their diversity policy? Write a report summarizing your findings.

25. **CTE Career Readiness Practice.** One trend in lodging is to create a resort based on a theme, such as the jungle or a famous city. Analyze the possibility of this trend continuing. Do you think it will become predominant? What evidence supports your view? Share your findings with the class.

# Part Two
# The Foodservice Industry

58

# Chapter 4

## The World of Food and Beverages

## Chapter Objectives

After studying this chapter, you will be able to
- **describe** the types of commercial foodservice.
- **describe** the types of noncommercial foodservice.
- **distinguish** between commercial and noncommercial foodservice.
- **list** the functions that all foodservices must perform.
- **analyze** how a restaurant concept distinguishes one restaurant from another.
- **assess** the importance of customer feedback.

## Before You Read

Try to answer the following questions before you read this chapter.
- What is the difference between commercial and noncommercial foodservice?
- What is a restaurant concept?

## Terms to Know

foodservice
commercial foodservice
quick-service restaurant
fast-food restaurant
cafeteria
buffet

carryout restaurant
full-service restaurant
fine-dining restaurant
catering
in-house foodservice
contract foodservice

restaurant concept
theme
ambiance
market
market segment
target market

According to the National Restaurant Association, there are over 945,000 foodservice businesses in the United States. **Foodservice** is the business of making and serving prepared food and drink. It includes restaurants, hotels, clubs, catering, healthcare facilities, transportation centers, and cruise lines. Foodservice is a service industry that generates billions of dollars a year in sales and employs millions of workers.

Foodservice operations range from small to large. A small business might consist of one person who sells ice cream from a small freezer on wheels. A large business might be a restaurant that serves 1,000 meals a day. Foodservice operations are also found in hotels, cruise ships, schools, hospitals, airplanes, trains, and employee cafeterias, **4-1**. Even some grocery stores provide foodservice in the form of soup and salad bars and prepared meals.

**4-1** This chef is preparing breakfast on an Amtrak Superliner train.

*Copyright Amtrak 2012. Photo courtesy of Amtrak.*

# Types of Foodservice Operations

There are many ways to categorize foodservice operations. Customers tend to categorize them by price, from budget to very expensive. Customers also categorize foodservice operations by type of service offered, such as self-service and sit-down service. From an industry perspective, there are two basic types of foodservice operations: commercial and noncommercial.

# Commercial Foodservice

**Commercial foodservice** consists of food and beverage businesses that compete for customers. The main goal of these businesses is to make a profit. Examples include Macaroni Grill, Olive Garden, and Dunkin' Donuts. Most commercial foodservice businesses are restaurants or restaurant-like operations.

Commercial foodservice operations can be organized into four categories: quick-service restaurants, full-service restaurants, catering, and hotel and club foodservices.

## Quick-Service Restaurants

A **quick-service restaurant** provides customers with convenience, speed, and basic service at low prices. A major feature of quick-service restaurants is self-service. The customers help themselves, usually by carrying their food to their tables. Quick-service restaurants generally have few employees in relation to the number of people served. Quick-service restaurants include fast-food restaurants, cafeterias, buffets, and carryout restaurants.

### Fast-Food Restaurants

A **fast-food restaurant** generally has a counter where you place your order and wait for it. You then pick up your order, pay for it, and either carry it to a table or take it with you. Fast-food restaurants often have drive-through windows that provide faster service for people who are in a hurry or want to stay in their cars. Fast-food restaurants generally have the following characteristics: a small number of menu items (usually fewer than 20), items that can be prepared in three to five minutes, a small dining area, and high-tech foodservice equipment.

## Cafeterias

A **cafeteria** is foodservice in which the food is displayed along a counter called a *serving line*. The customers take trays and walk along the serving line, where servers are stationed. When they see a food they want, they ask the server, who serves them the food, **4-2**. The customer then puts the dishes on the tray and takes it to a table. A cafeteria is not all-you-care-to-eat. Cafeterias are often large and capable of serving many customers at once. There is little or no table service. This type of foodservice is very common in schools and hospitals, but there are some commercial cafeterias.

## Buffets

A **buffet** consists of food displayed on tables. Servers keep the displays of food stocked with food items. Customers walk around and serve themselves. They then take their food to their table. Sometimes servers will serve coffee and beverages and remove dirty dishes. Most buffets are all-you-care-to-eat. Buffets are often large and capable of serving many customers at once.

## Carryout Restaurants

A **carryout restaurant** specializes in preparing food for customers to take with them to eat at home or elsewhere, **4-3**. Carryout restaurants may provide some seating, but the major focus is food to carry out. Some carryout restaurants also offer delivery services. Delicatessens, grocery stores, and some full-service restaurants provide carryout meals. Often these meals are higher in quality than the typical meal at a fast-food restaurant. The restaurants are usually located in cities where people work long hours and have little time to cook. The restaurants make eating at home convenient because the food is already prepared. Some grocery stores also specialize in carryout foods.

## Full-Service Restaurants

A **full-service restaurant** is a restaurant in which customers sit at a table and give their orders to a server, who brings their food to the table. There are many kinds and varieties of full-service restaurants. Some have quick-service features such as carryout service and drive-through windows. Others offer buffet service at specific meals, such as Sunday brunch. However, the major feature of a full-service restaurant is table service—food brought to the customer at a table. The two major categories of full-service restaurants are fine dining and casual.

**4-2** Cafeterias have food arranged along a serving line.

CandyBox Images/Shutterstock.com

**4-3** Many carryout restaurants offer carry out and delivery services. Why is this a popular trend with today's conusmers?

Monkey Business Images/Shutterstock.com

# Richard Chamberlain—
## *Pioneer of American Alpine Cooking*

*Photo courtesy of
Chef Richard Chamberlain*

After initially enrolling in a cooking course to meet girls, Richard Chamberlain found himself embarking on a long and prosperous career in the restaurant business. He studied culinary arts at El Centro College in Dallas and interned at the luxury hotel restaurant Rosewood Mansion on Turtle Creek. He first gained recognition by working as executive chef of San Simion Restaurant in Dallas, Texas. He was honored for his work by being named one of *Food & Wine Magazine's* "Rising Stars to Watch."

Chamberlain gained further attention while working as executive chef for Little Nell hotel in Aspen, where he developed the concept of American Alpine cooking. This earned him a nomination for "The Best Chef in the Northwest" award by the James Beard Foundation. Chamberlain has also worked as executive chef at Rattcliff's in Dallas and as executive sous chef at Hotel Bel-Air in Los Angeles.

In 1993, he opened his first restaurant, Chamberlain's Steak and Chop House, in Dallas. The establishment was named one of the top new restaurants by *Bon Appetite* magazine. Other honors awarded over the years include *Gourmet's* "One of America's Top Tables" and *Zagat Guide's* "One of America's Top Restaurants."

Chamberlain has opened several more restaurants throughout his career: Chamberlain's Fish Market Grill in Dallas; Tarragon at Elk Mountain in Montrose, Colorado; and Envy Steakhouse in Las Vegas. He also has appeared several times on NBC's *Today Show* and on Discovery Channel's *Great Chefs* program. He is now a board member of the American Heart Association's Dallas chapter.

## Richard Chamberlain's Career Path

**1960:** Born in Dallas, Texas

**1975:** First job at Hardee's Hamburgers

**1978:** Studied at El Centro College, Dallas, Texas

**1980:** First real job at the Mansion on Turtle Creek, Dallas, Texas

**1986:** Began serving as executive chef at San Simeon Restaurant in Dallas

**1992:** Nominated for "The Best Chef in the Northwest" award by the James Beard Foundation

**1993:** Opened Chamberlain's Steak and Chop House in Dallas

**1999:** Chamberlain's named one of "America's Top Restaurants" by *Zagat*

**2000:** Chamberlain's received "Award of Excellence" by *Wine Spectator*

**2001:** Opened Chamberlain's Fish Market Grill in Dallas

**2003:** Opened Envy Steakhouse in Las Vegas (in partnership with The Renaissance Las Vegas)

**2006:** Received National Restaurant Association's Restaurant Neighbor Award for extensive charity work

### Fine-Dining Restaurants

A **fine-dining restaurant** emphasizes the highest quality in service, ingredients, décor, and atmosphere. Service is lavish, with a relatively large number of employees per customer. Prices are very high. These restaurants are usually small, with seating for fewer than 100 customers. Most fine-dining restaurants hire professional chefs with years of culinary training and experience, **4-4**. Only about one percent of full-service restaurants are considered fine-dining restaurants.

### Casual Dining Restaurants

The rest of the full-service restaurants fall into the category of casual dining. These include the affordable restaurants that many people frequent, such as McDonald's and Denny's. The many types of casual dining restaurants range from budget to expensive, and from very casual to somewhat formal. Types of casual dining restaurants include single-item, ethnic, and family restaurants.

A common casual restaurant is the single-item restaurant. These restaurants choose to specialize in a single item of food. Examples include pizza, steak, pancakes, and seafood. These restaurants may serve a few other types of food, but their strength is a single food.

Another popular casual restaurant is one that specializes in ethnic cuisine. Italian, Greek, Mexican, and Chinese restaurants have always been popular. More recently, Ethiopian, Indian, Japanese, Spanish, and Thai restaurants have also become popular, **4-5**.

Family restaurants cater to the needs of families and emphasize variety and comfort. Family restaurants usually serve breakfast, lunch, and dinner and have an extensive menu. They may offer salad bars, breakfast bars, and dessert bars,

4-4  Professional chefs prepare meals with the highest quality ingredients in fine-dining restaurants.

*Yuri Arcurs/Shutterstock.com*

4-5  Asian restaurants are a popular type of casual dining. What types of casual dining are most popular in your community?.

*Golden Pixels LLC/Shutterstock.com*

and almost everything is prepared to order. (In a quick-service restaurant, the food is made ahead of time.) Home cooking is popular in family restaurants. *Home cooking* refers to comfort foods and traditional American dishes such as meatloaf, mashed potatoes, and apple pie. Many family restaurants are independent family-owned businesses, but many chains also have a family-dining concept.

## Hotel and Club Foodservice

Hotels provide a wide array of food and beverage services. For example, a hotel may have a bar in the lobby, a family-style restaurant, an elegant fine-dining restaurant, a soft-serve ice cream shop, sandwich service by the swimming pool, room service, catering services, and vending machines near guest rooms.

There are more than 12,000 private clubs in the United States. Private clubs were developed to meet the social and leisure needs of their members. Families and individuals join clubs to enjoy the companionship of friends in a comfortable environment. The many types of clubs in operation include country clubs, city clubs, yacht clubs, health clubs, military clubs, tennis clubs, beach clubs, faculty clubs, and hunt clubs. Membership is often by invitation and membership dues are required. Most clubs operate at least one dining room, **4-6**. They usually have extensive catering facilities. Members commonly hold weddings, reunions, and other social events in these facilities.

## Catering

**Catering** is the provision of food and service for a special event. Catering usually involves feeding a large number of people at one time. Guests either all eat the same menu items or have a limited selection.

Special events can be either business events or social events. Catered business events include conventions, business meetings, receptions, awards dinners, and company holiday parties. Catered social events include birthday parties, weddings, proms, anniversaries, holiday celebrations, graduations, reunions, festivals, and charity events. Catering can also include civic functions, such as a city summer festival or an art fair. Some caterers

4-6 Most clubs have a dining room and catering facilities.

*The Downtown Club at Plaza, Houston, Texas. A ClubCorp Property*

specialize in one food, such as preparing fancy appetizers or baking beautiful wedding cakes. Other caterers prepare complete meals and supply serving equipment and workers for the event.

The catering service may be on-premise or off-premise. *On-premise catering* takes place at the caterer's place of business. The caterer may have a banquet hall with an attached kitchen. On-premise catering also takes place at the hotels and restaurants that offer catering services, **4-7**. Other organizations, such as private clubs, may provide on-premise catering.

*Off-premise catering* occurs when the function is held away from the caterer's place of business, such as picnics, clubs, and private homes. Caterers of off-premises events must have special trucks or vans that can transport foods safely to the location of the event.

4-7  Hotels and banquet halls often have on-premise catering. How do customers benefit from such venues?

erwinova/Shutterstock.com

Caterers can operate from their own homes or from a separate business location. Some caterers have large businesses with many employees, while other caterers work alone. Caterers must serve each function according to a preset timetable. They must work closely with the event coordinator, decorator, entertainment manager, and customer. Above all, caterers must be flexible enough to handle last-minute changes. These include people who arrive late, changes in the weather, and performances that end early or run late.

## Recreation Businesses

Often foodservice is offered as part of a recreation business. Examples include sports arenas, zoos, movie theaters, and museums, **4-8**. With foodservice within the zoo, a hungry family does not have to leave the zoo to find food. One wildlife center in Texas is complete with a hilltop restaurant where diners can watch hundreds of rare and endangered animals roam. Most ballparks have the traditional hot dogs and peanuts, but sports arenas offer many popular foods, such as burgers, salads, burritos, and ice cream.

Some sports and entertainment facilities offer fine-dining services. For example, the Levy Restaurants organization provides restaurant-quality foodservice at a variety of sports and entertainment venues.

## Shopping Centers and Stores

A foodservice business may be located within another business. For example, many brand-name commercial chains provide foodservice within shopping malls and stores.

4-8  Concessions such as popcorn, candy, and drinks are popular treats at movie theaters.

Deklofenak/Shutterstock.com

## Going Green

### Creating a Food Waste and Recovery Program

Food waste is costly for foodservice businesses. Costs include payments for solid waste pickup, water and sewage, and electricity used by waste-disposal equipment. A foodservice business can reduce these costs by creating a waste reduction and recovery program. The U.S. Environmental Protection Agency (EPA) provides guidance in "Putting Surplus Food to Good Use: A How-to Guide for Food Service Providers." The following list includes methods of reducing food waste in order from the most to the least important:

- Reduce the amount of food waste produced.
- Donate extra food to feed the hungry.
- Donate food scraps to local farmers or zoos for animal feed.
- Investigate industrial uses for waste oils and scraps.
- Consider food composting.
- Send food waste to landfills or incinerators only as a last resort.

The guide gives managers suggestions as to how each method can be implemented. This resource and others can be accessed at the EPA's website.

You have probably seen fast-food restaurants clustered in one area of your local mall. They are designed for convenience and quick service for hungry shoppers. Many upscale department stores have nicer restaurants in their stores. Foodservices are also found in bookstores, grocery stores, and convenience stores.

### Transportation Centers

Foodservice in transportation centers include restaurants at airports, railroad stations, and bus terminals. Foodservice in the station is designed for travelers. Some travelers need food quickly and others have time between trains or flights to enjoy a relaxing meal. Most foodservices in airports, bus terminals, and railroad stations are commercial quick-serve restaurants. However, foodservice operations can range from candy shops to fine dining in large transportation centers. For example, O'Hare Airport in Chicago has over 75 restaurants and foodservice businesses including Starbucks Coffee, Great American Bagel, Burrito Beach (Mexican), and Wolfgang Puck (fine dining).

Transportation centers also include highway plazas and truckstops for motorists and bus passengers, **4-9**. Highway plazas usually include a food court with several quick-service options, a

4-9 Restaurants at truckstops and plazas are usually casual restaurants where motorists can eat quick meals.

*Steve Simzer/Shutterstock.com*

gas station for refueling, and a convenience store. Truckstops are provided for people who make their living driving freight trucks. Restaurants at truckstops are geared to offering homestyle meals quickly so truckdrivers can eat and get back on the road. Many of these are open 24 hours and serve breakfast foods all day.

## In-Transit Foodservice

Examples of foodservice on the transportation itself include airplane food, dining cars on long-distance trains, and a wide selection of foodservices on cruise ships.

Most *domestic flights* (flights within the United States) do not serve meals, but snacks for purchase are usually offered to passengers. International flights, however, still serve complete meals. Food served on an airplane is usually not prepared on the airplane. An airplane's kitchen is called a *galley*, and it is very small. Food is prepared in a large kitchen near the airport terminal and transported to the airplane in a special truck. The fully prepared food is loaded onto the airplane, ready to be served to passengers. Some large jet liners that fly international flights have chefs on board who prepare meals for passengers.

Amtrak, America's intercity train service, provides a variety of dining options. Most trains have a lounge car that serves fast foods, snacks, and beverages from 6 a.m. until midnight. Long-distance trains have dining cars that serve breakfast, lunch, and dinner.

Cruise ships are known for making a wide variety of food available 24 hours a day. Dinners are often formal affairs, with gourmet food served by expert servers. Cruise ships often have extravagant midnight buffets, **4-10**.

# Noncommercial Foodservice

Noncommercial foodservice is a foodservice operation that is supported or subsidized by a host company or organization. The foodservice provider must please the guests as well as the host or client. These foodservice operations exist for the convenience of certain audiences, some of which may be captive audiences. The operations are found in schools, hospitals, other health care facilities, and places of employment.

*Photo courtesy of Carnival Cruise Lines*

4-10  Cruise ships often provide lavish buffets.

## Schools

Schools include all types of educational institutions, such as child care centers, public schools, colleges, universities, technical schools, and summer camps. School foodservice contributes to students' health and well-being.

Many elementary, middle, and high schools serve breakfast and lunch. Children in preschool through kindergarten also receive a morning snack. In addition, school foodservice staff may cater special school functions such as receptions and athletic banquets. Residential schools such as universities serve all student meals on-site. School foodservice programs usually use the cafeteria style of service, **4-11**.

Many educational institutions have arrangements with well-known fast-food resturants to offer foodservice within their institution. For example, some schools have outlets of Pizza Hut and Taco Bell.

Schools may have **in-house foodservice**, which means it is run by the institution itself. For example, many colleges have a dining hall in each dormitory that is operated by its own foodservice department. That department is responsible for purchasing and maintaining all equipment, food, and supplies. It is also responsible for hiring, training, supervising, and paying all foodservice staff.

In **contract foodservice** the school hires an outside company to run its food operation. For example, instead of having a foodservice department, the college can hire Aramark, a company that specializes in providing foodservice to schools.

Monkey Business Images/Shutterstock.com

4-11 School cafeterias are a type of noncommercial foodservice.

## Health Care Facilities

Hospital patients must eat all their meals at the institution. Foodservice in health care settings is an integral part of the health services offered to patients. The food served must provide all the calories and nutrients that patients need to restore and maintain health. Many of the patients require special diets, **4-12**.

The residents of assisted-living facilities and retirement communities live in their own apartments, townhomes, or single-family residences. Most of the residents in this type of housing are able to take care of themselves. As a service to the residents, the facilities usually provide a communal dining room where residents can have one or more of their daily meals.

## Employers

Some employers provide foodservice as a convenience to their employees. An example is the employee cafeteria in an office building. Usually the time allotted for lunch is quite brief, so having foodservice on-site is a time-saver. Federal and state government buildings and municipal buildings in large cities also provide foodservice.

Foodservice must be affordable for workers, yet be of good quality and variety. Employers know that worker morale can be positively affected by offering quality meals in an attractive setting. The employer often subsidizes the foodservice to make it more affordable for the employees.

4-12  A hospital patient's meals are planned according to their dietary needs.

## Others

Noncommercial foodservice is provided to individuals in an institution, such as the military or a prison. These type of foodservices mainly serve people who are not able or do not have time to seek a commercial food and beverage business.

In fact, the United States Department of Defense, which oversees all military foodservice operations, prefers that military personnel eat on-base rather than go off-base to find meals. For this reason, it must ensure that all military bases offer quality foodservice. The Department of Defense estimates that it spends close to $5 billion on military foodservice each year. Over 23,000 individuals are employed in this industry, including managers, supervisors, preparation and service workers, and cooks. In order to become a military foodservice worker, individuals must first complete about 20 weeks of training, including instruction in food preparation in addition to Basic Combat Training. Workers in this industry have the challenge of offering foods that taste good and are reminiscent of home, but also provide the nutrition needed for military personnel to perform their jobs well.

## Functions in Foodservice

Each foodservice operation is unique, yet each one has to perform the same functions. Figure **4-13** lists and describes the 12 common functions. In a small business, one person may perform several of these functions.

## Restaurant Concepts

The concept of the restaurant distinguishes one restaurant from another. A **restaurant concept** is the whole idea of the restaurant or the restaurant chain. It includes the theme, target market, location, décor, ambiance, and service style of a restaurant.

A **theme** is a specific idea around which something is organized. In a restaurant, the theme organizes everything the restaurant does. The theme is carried out in the décor of the restaurant, the uniforms of the servers, the type of food served, and the look of the menu. For example, the theme of the Hard Rock Cafe restaurants is rock and roll music and musicians, **4-14**. Each Hard Rock Cafe plays rock and roll music and displays memorabilia from rock and roll musicians.

Ambiance is also a part of the restaurant concept. **Ambiance**, or *atmosphere*, is the feeling or mood associated with a particular place. Examples of ambiance include romantic, elegant, casual, homelike, fun, and sporty. Ambiance is created by the décor of the restaurant and the menu, table setting, music, and lighting. For example, the Hard Rock Cafe creates an atmosphere of high energy with the music it plays and its décor. Mexican restaurants often use colorful plates, servers in colorful uniforms, and Mariachi music to create a Mexican fiesta atmosphere. Barbeque restaurants may use red-and-white checked tablecloths to create a picnic-like feeling.

## 12 Functions in Foodservice Business

| Function | Description |
|---|---|
| *Menu Planning* | Select food and beverages that will meet customers' needs and make a profit. |
| *Production* | Make food and beverages. Make sure food is ready when needed and looks attractive. Avoid waste. Retain nutrients. Ensure that food is safe and wholesome. |
| *Service* | Serve food to customers. Make sure servers are trained in the style of service the business uses. Make sure that servers and all employees practice good customer service. |
| *Purchasing and Receiving* | Buy the right quality and quantity of food at the best price. Make sure food and supplies arrive when needed. Make sure food is stored properly once received. Establish good relationships with reliable suppliers. Inventory. |
| *Food Safety and Sanitation* | Make sure procedures are followed to ensure that all food and beverage products are safe to eat. |
| *Management* | Oversee all functions of the business. Make sure the business is operating profitably and meeting customer needs. |
| *Marketing and Sales* | Learn what customers want. Develop marketing plans. Advertise. Sell the food and beverage services. |
| *Human Resources* | Manage all employee issues, including pay, benefits, hiring, firing, and training. |
| *Accounting* | Keep track of all the money that flows into and out of the business. Monitor costs. If costs are running too high, let management know so costs can be controlled. |
| *Security* | Make sure the money handled is safe from theft. Make sure customers and their property are safe from harm. |
| *Safety and Emergency Procedures* | Make sure the workplace is safe and meets all government safety requirements. Make sure plans are in place in case of emergencies. |
| *Engineering and Maintenance* | Make sure all equipment, plumbing, electricity, and building facilities are working properly. Make sure building, furniture, floors, and all public areas are clean. |

*Goodheart-Willcox Publisher*

**4-13** Each foodservice business must perform these 12 functions. What consequences may occur from failing to perform one or more functions?

**4-14** The Hard Rock Cafe is an example of a theme restaurant.

*Hard Rock Cafe, International*

The restaurant concept also includes the types of customers that the restaurant wants to attract. A **market** consists of all the people who could potentially buy what you are selling. In the foodservice industry, the market consists of everyone who eats and drinks. It is more useful, however, to divide the market into subgroups with similar needs. These subgroups are called *market segments*. A **market segment** is a subgroup of a larger market; a market segment has similar needs and wants for the product you are selling. The foodservice market can be segmented in many different ways. One way is by age. Market segments based on age would include children, teenagers, young adults, and mature adults. Another way to divide the market into segments is to group customers based on interests and activities. These might include shoppers, sports fans, and couples on a date, **4-15**. Your **target market** is the market segment whose needs you strive to meet.

The choice of target market is a major part of the restaurant concept. For example, the target market for the Hard Rock Cafe is people who love rock music. The owners of the Hard Rock Cafe make all their decisions with this target market in mind.

# Customer Feedback

All foodservice managers need to know if their customers are satisfied. If customers are *not* satisfied, the manager needs to know why. Then the business can work to improve customer satisfaction. There are many ways to test customer satisfaction with the dining experience. The dining experience is not only the food that is being served.

It also includes the ambiance, the friendliness and courtesy of the staff, and the cleanliness of the restaurant.

Many foodservice operations use guest comment cards to obtain information about customer satisfaction. However, comment cards cannot always be used. Comment cards work well in family and fast-food restaurants, but they are often out of place in fine-dining restaurants.

Many fine-dining restaurants use the mystery shopper technique instead. *Mystery shoppers* are persons who are hired to dine at a restaurant. They do not reveal their true identity to the restaurant staff. Mystery shoppers are asked to prepare detailed reports on the restaurant's facilities, food and beverage quality, service, and staff. This method usually gives objective information about how the restaurant is perceived by customers.

There is another way to find out about guest satisfaction. Managers can walk around the restaurant and talk with their guests. They can ask the guests what they think about the food and service.

**4-15** Shoppers are an example of a target market in foodservice.

Blend Images/Shutterstock.com

# Chapter 4
## Review

## Chapter Summary

- A foodservice business makes and serves prepared food and drink.
- The foodservice industry categorizes foodservice operations into two main groups: commercial and noncommercial.
- Commercial foodservice operations can be organized into several categories: quick-service restaurants, full-service restaurants, and hotel and club foodservices, catering, recreation businesses, shopping centers and stores, transportation centers, and in-transit foodservice.
- Noncommercial foodservice includes foodservice provided at school, at health care facilities, by employers, and by other institutions.
- All food and beverage businesses must accomplish the same 12 common functions.
- The concept of a restaurant makes one restaurant different from another.
- Managers need customer feedback so they can improve customer satisfaction.

## Review

1. What is the difference between a commercial foodservice and noncommercial foodservice?
2. List the four types of quick-service restaurants.
3. Explain how a full-service restaurant is different from a quick-service restaurant.
4. Describe three types of casual restaurants.
5. What is the difference between on-premise catering and off-premise catering?
6. Give three examples of foodservice found at a recreation business.
7. Give three examples of noncommercial foodservice.
8. Why do employers offer foodservice?
9. List the 12 functions that all food and beverage businesses must perform.
10. What is a restaurant concept?
11. How does a restaurant's concept make it different from another restaurant?
12. How can food and beverage managers get customer feedback?

# Critical Thinking

13. **Organize.** Create a poster that shows the structure of the foodservice industry. Use pictures from magazines, photographs, or illustrations to show the different categories.

14. **Design.** Create a restaurant concept that includes the target market, theme, ambiance, décor, and menu. Prepare a display that describes your restaurant concept.

15. **Predict.** Imagine you are the manager of a foodservice business. Choose one of the 12 functions of foodservices. Describe what would happen to your business if this function were not performed.

16. **Make inferences.** Describe the target market for the following restaurants: Olive Garden, Famous Dave's, Cici's Pizza, McDonald's, and Starbucks. You may use the Internet to find information.

17. **Identify.** Develop a detailed chart that shows the foodservice businesses within your school's zip code.

18. **Produce.** Research a country whose cuisine you have never tried before. Find and prepare an appealing recipe from that country and take pictures of the resulting food. Give a report to your class describing the country, its culture, its food, and the food you prepared. What is your opinion about this particular cuisine?

# Common Core

**College and Career Readiness**

19. **Speaking.** Give a presentation on why the choice of a target market is a major part of the restaurant concept.

20. **Listening.** Interview a parent or another adult on their experiences at fine-dining restaurants.

21. **Writing.** Write an essay explaining why customer feedback is important to a food and beverage operation.

22. **CTE Career Readiness Practice.** Imagine you work for a local restaurant with a 1950s concept. Your supervisor tells you and your team that the restaurant is losing business because the theme is no longer appealing to the target market—adults aged 21 to 40. Your team assignment is to develop a creative and innovation plan for solving this problem. Use the following process to produce your plan:

- **Analyze the problem.** Look at the problem from all potential angles.

- **Apply past learning/brainstorm possible options.** What similar problems has your team dealt with in the past? What aspects of past learning might you use to solve this problem? Brainstorm a list of possible solutions without passing judgment on *any* options. Accept all ideas—including those that seem impossible—and piggyback off the ideas of others.

- **Gather new information for solving the problem.** Examine recent research and data. What costs (both financial and human) are involved in solving the problem?

- **Organize data and compare all the options.** What research best offers the best possible options for solving the problem? What new and unique alternatives can you identify? What risks are involved with each solution? How can each solution benefit the employer and solve the problem? What impact will each solution have on customers and others?

- **Choose an option for solving the problem.** Identify the option that has the best potential value.

- **Summarize the actions necessary to solve the problem.** Write a proposal identifying the creative actions your team would take for solving the problem. Note the data that supports your actions. What is the cost involved in implementing the solution? How long will it take to implement the solution and determine its impact?

# Chapter 5
## Food Preparation and Service

## Chapter Objectives

After studying this chapter, you will be able to

- **analyze** how the menu functions as the restaurant's game plan.
- **describe** six factors to consider when planning a menu.
- **explain** the role of standardized recipes in food production.
- **give** examples of food preparation and cooking methods.
- **list** and **describe** the three aspects of food presentation.
- **list** and **contrast** the five basic styles of service.
- **relate** four techniques for serving food.

## Before You Read

Try to answer the following questions before you read this chapter.

- What is the focus of a restaurant's concept?
- How are standardized recipes helpful in a foodservice business?

## Terms to Know

| | | |
|---|---|---|
| menu | combination pricing | plating |
| fixed menu | party | portion control |
| cycle menu | nutrients | garnish |
| market menu | food production | serving |
| hybrid menu | consistency | flatware |
| appetizer | recipe | glassware |
| entrée | yield | plateware |
| side dish | standardized recipe | condiment |
| à la carte pricing | beverage | bussing |
| table d'hôte pricing | food presentation | sidework |

# The Menu

A **menu** is a list of food and beverage items served in a foodservice operation. A menu is most commonly printed on paper and given to guests as they are seated, **5-1**. Menus can also be written on a board. In quick-service restaurants, the menu is often posted on a display board behind the cash registers.

However, a menu is more than just a list of food and beverages. The menu is the basic game plan for a restaurant. It is the tool used to meet the needs and wants of customers. Before the menu is developed, the owners of the business determine the market segment they will serve. They find out what customers in that market segment need and want. They then develop the restaurant's concept and theme. These are expressed through the menu and the restaurant's décor (inside and out), service style, and server uniforms.

The menu expresses the concept and theme through the choice of foods on the menu, the prices, and the design of the menu itself. For example, a fine-dining restaurant serves people who want the best in food and service and are willing to pay for it. The menu will include elegantly prepared dishes, high-quality foods, and prices to match. The menu may be printed in script-style print on paper that looks like parchment. The paper of the menu may be presented in a folder that looks like a leather-bound book.

The menu is also the main way a foodservice business communicates with its customers, **5-2**. The menu serves as a type of contract between the foodservice establishment and the customer. It represents the food items the guest will later see and eat. As a result, the menu must correctly reflect the type, form, style, amount, condition, and method of preparation of the food items on the menu.

Consumer groups, governmental regulatory bodies, and even industry self-regulatory bodies ensure that what is seen on the menu is what the customers get on their plates. The menu must accurately describe the food that is being served. Many states have truth-in-menu laws that require this accuracy. Some cities require that restaurants have the calorie content and a listing of all ingredients used in the food preparation process. In addition, the federal Food and Drug Administration requires that any health claims meet FDA standards.

## Types of Menus

Menus are classified according to how frequently the same foods are offered. The four classifications of menus are fixed, cycle, market, and hybrid.

In a **fixed menu** the same foods are offered every day. Once a fixed menu is developed, it hardly ever changes. Fixed menus are typically found in fast-food restaurants, ethnic restaurants, and steakhouses.

In a **cycle menu** foods change daily for a set period of time; at the end of that period of time, the menu repeats itself. Common cycle lengths are every week, every two weeks, or every month. For example, in a weekly menu cycle, there is a

5-1 A menu is a communication tool used between customers and the foodservice operation to help meet customer needs.

*AVAVA/Shutterstock.com*

## Old Hickory Steakhouse
### est. 1977

### Appetizers

**BEEF TENDERLOIN CARPACCIO**
THINLY SLICED WITH
ARUGULA-PARMESAN SALAD AND
ROASTED SHALLOT VINAIGRETTE ...12

**SHRIMP COCKTAIL**
JUMBO GULF SHRIMP WITH OUR
HORSERADISH "PINK SAUCE" ...14

**APPLEWOOD SMOKED BACON**
ACCOMPANIED WITH
APPLE RUM CHUTNEY ...13

**ESCARGOT ENCROUTE**
GARLIC AND HERB SAUTÉED SNAILS
WITH BOURSIN CHEESE AND
WILD MUSHROOMS ...13

**JUMBO LUMP CRAB CAKES**
ACCOMPANIED WITH
NAPA MUSTARD SAUCE ...15

**FOIE GRAS**
ACCOMPANIED WITH HOT APRICOT JAM
AND PRICKLEY PEAR COULIS ...18

### Artisanal Cheeses
YOUR MAITRE FROMAGER WILL PRESENT A VARIETY OF ARTISINAL CHEESE
FROM AROUND THE WORLD

THREE SELECTIONS ...15                  SIX SELECTIONS ...24

### Soup

**SOUP OF THE DAY**
PREPARED DAILY ...8

**LOBSTER BISQUE**
MAINE LOBSTER CROSTINI ...10

### Salads

**BC FARMS ORGANIC GREENS**
BELGIAN ENDIVE, ARUGULA AND
WATERCRESS WITH FRESH PEARS,
CANDIED PECANS, FETA CHEESE,
AND CITRUS VINAIGRETTE ...10

**HEIRLOOM TOMATOES & MOZZARELLA**
SLICED TOMATOES AND
BUFFALO MOZZARELLA WITH
BASIL INFUSED VIRGIN OLIVE OIL ...9

**CAESAR SALAD**
ROMAINE HEARTS WITH
CREAMY GARLIC DRESSING,
PARMIGIANO REGGIANO WITH
ANCHOVY TAPENADE CROUTONS ...8

**BLT WEDGE**
BUTTER LETTUCE WEDGE WITH
APPLE SMOKED BACON, TOMATOES
AND MAYTAG BLUE CHEESE DRESSING ...9

GENERAL MANAGER, BERESFORD WALL

EXECUTIVE CHEF, JOANNE BONDY

GRATUITY OF 20% ADDED TO PARTIES OF 6 OR MORE.

### Ala Carte Entrees

SAUTEED LEMON SCENTED
ATLANTIC SCALLOPS
TH LOBSTER BUERRE BLANC ...26

FOOD MARKET
GHT'S FEATURED
ARY CREATION ...MP

**WINDY MEADOWS GARLIC
ROASTED ORGANIC CHICKEN**
WITH ROASTED SHALLOT JUS ...25

**SCOTTISH SALMON**
FRESH HERBS AND
MAPLE MUSTARD GLAZE ...24

### 1855 Premium Black Angus
OF BLACK ANGUS BEEF IS CONSIDERED OUTSTANDING ENOUGH TO EARN THE
1855 PREMIUM RATING. IT IS THE FINEST BLACK ANGUS BEEF IN THE WORLD.
R STEAKS ARE HAND SELECTED AND AGED A MINIMUM OF 14 DAYS.

**T-BONE**
25 OZ. ...41

**RIBEYE**
16 OZ. ...35

**BONE-IN FILET**
16 OZ. ...65

### Steaks & Chops

**VEAL CHOP**
16 OZ. ...36

**DOUBLE CUT LAMB CHOPS**
14 OZ. ...35

TURAL" ANGUS NEW YORK STRIP AU POIVRE
12 OZ. ...38

### Lobster Tail
AIL OR HALF TAIL ... MP

WITH HALF LOBSTER TAIL
LEMON BUERRE BLANC ...MP

### The Table
OVEN ROASTED WILD MUSHROOMS ...9
SHALLOT & BACON SKILLET POTATOES ...9
GARLIC TRUFFLE FRIES ...8
SAUTEED BABY SPINACH ...8
HEARTS OF ARTICHOKES AU GRATIN ...10

### Sauces
BÉARNAISE ...4
COGNAC PEPPERCORN ...4
PORT WINE SHIITAKE MUSHROOM ...4
HORSERADISH CREAM ...4

### Steak Toppings
FOIE GRAS ...16
CRAB OSCAR ...15
BLUE CHEESE CRUST ...8
LOBSTER OSCAR ...20

*Gaylord Texan*

5-2  How does a menu serve as a type of contract? Why?

different menu for every day of the week—one menu is used on Monday, a different menu is used on Tuesday, and so on. The menus then repeat starting on Monday. Some cycle menus are written on a seasonal basis. A new menu is used for each season to take advantage of the availability of fresh foods. Cycle menus provide some variety for people who eat in the same place every day, such as schools, hospitals, and other institutions.

A **market menu** changes with the availability of food products. It takes advantage of foods that are in season, inexpensive, and easy to get. Market menus are becoming more popular with chefs and customers. Market menus challenge the chef's creativity to use fresh and seasonal products, **5-3**. This type of menu changes frequently because the availability of the food products changes frequently. As soon as a product is no longer available, it is removed from the menu. Market menus often change each day.

**5-3** Alice Waters, the founder of Chez Panisse restaurant, always uses the freshest local ingredients.

*Photo by Franklin Avery, Courtesy of Chez Panisse*

A **hybrid menu** is a combination of two types of menus. A popular combination is the fixed menu with a cycle menu or a market menu. Part of the menu remains the same, and part of the menu changes. For the fixed plus cycle menu, part of the menu changes regularly. For example, a restaurant might have a different soup for every day of the week. For the fixed plus market menu, part of the menu changes with the availability of food products. For example, a restaurant may have a special every night that features fresh foods in season, such as seafood and vegetables.

## Parts of the Menu

The parts of the menu vary with the type of restaurant. However, there are seven classic parts of the menu. These parts correspond to the parts of a meal eaten during a full dinner. These parts are appetizers, soups, salads, entrees, side dishes, desserts, and beverages, **5-4**. An **appetizer** is a small portion of food served before a meal. The purpose of an appetizer is to stimulate the appetite. Examples include chips and salsa, spinach-artichoke dip, and fried cheese sticks. Another term for appetizer is *hors d'oeuvre*. An **entrée** is the main course of a meal. A **side dish** is usually a portion of food that goes with the entrée, such as vegetables. Examples of side dishes include potatoes, rice, green beans, and asparagus.

### Seven Classic Parts of a Menu

| Parts | Examples |
|---|---|
| • Appetizers | • Stuffed Mushrooms |
| • Soups | • Broccoli Cheese Soup |
| • Salads | • Spinach and Mandarin Orange Salad |
| • Entrées | • Glazed Ham |
| • Side Dishes | • Cornbread Stuffing and Steamed Carrots |
| • Desserts | • Chocolate Mousse |
| • Beverages | • Iced Tea |

*Goodheart-Willcox Publisher*

**5-4** How might menu consistency benefit customers and restaurants?

## Pricing

There are three methods of pricing menu items: à la carte, table d'hôte, and combination. In **à la carte pricing** every food and beverage item on the menu is priced and ordered separately. For example, suppose you order a cup of soup, fried chicken, mashed potatoes, green beans, and iced tea. Each of these items would be priced separately. À la carte pricing is very common in cafeterias, delicatessens, and many fine-dining restaurants.

In **table d'hôte pricing** a complete meal is offered at a set price. Another term for this type of pricing is *price fixe*. In English, it is often called *fixed price*. The term *table d'hôte* is French for *host's table*. The term came from the innkeeper's practice of seating all guests at one large table and serving them all the same meal. Table d'hôte menus are often offered at very elegant fine-dining restaurants.

In **combination pricing** some food items are priced and ordered separately, and other food items are grouped together and priced as a group. The entrée is often grouped with bread, soup or salad, a potato, and a vegetable, and one price is charged for this combination of food. Appetizers, beverages, and desserts are often priced separately. This type of pricing is very common in full-service restaurants. For example, suppose you want a cup of soup, fried chicken, mashed potatoes, green beans, a piece of pie, and coffee. The pie and coffee would be priced separately. The soup, chicken, mashed potatoes, and beans would be offered at one price.

## Menu Planning

Many factors must be considered when planning a menu, including taste, variety, appearance, nutrition, production methods, and price. While making decisions on these factors, the menu planner must always keep the customer in mind.

### Taste

Taste is a major reason that customers go to restaurants, **5-5**. You need to know what tastes your customers like in order to plan an appropriate menu. Different cultures have different taste preferences. Each individual perceives taste differently. However, you should be able to develop a menu that will appeal to your target market.

Foods should be selected that taste good together. A variety of flavors make a meal more enjoyable. The chef is usually the person who plans a dish so the flavors work well together.

Photo courtesy of Princess Cruises

5-5  Most people select food based on its taste.

It is also important to offer textures in a menu. An example of a menu with different textures is crisp fried chicken paired with a cream-style soup and a firm vegetable such as broccoli.

### Variety

When a group of people goes out to eat, each person has his or her own tastes and preferences. A group of people who go out to eat together is called a **party**. Restaurants need to provide enough variety to please the target market, plus the one or two members of the party who are not part of the target market. Some restaurants excel at offering variety.

For example, T.G.I. Friday's has a very extensive menu with over a hundred menu items. Other restaurants specialize. For example, Red Lobster specializes in seafood. However, someone in a party going to Red Lobster might not like fish. Popeyes Chicken specializes in fried chicken. However, someone in a party going to Popeyes might not want fried food. A restaurant that specializes has to decide how much variety to offer. Red Lobster offers some chicken and steak choices. Popeyes offers some nonfried sandwiches and seafood options.

## Appearance

When planning a menu, think about how the foods will look together on a plate or next to each other on the table. Meals should have a variety of colors. One-color meals can look unappetizing, **5-6**. For example, a meal of macaroni and cheese, corn, and applesauce is basically one color. The look of this meal might be improved by changing the corn for carrots and the applesauce for green beans.

Using different shapes of food in a meal will make the plate even more interesting to the eye. For example, green beans can be left long and skinny and carrots can be cut into circles.

## Nutrition

People eat to satisfy their hunger. However, the reason they are hungry is because their bodies need nutrients. **Nutrients** are chemical substances in food that help maintain the body. Some nutrients supply energy to the body. Some nutrients provide the building blocks for the body's cells and tissues, such as skin, bones, and muscle. Some nutrients are necessary for the chemical reactions that take place in the body.

The food people eat has a major impact on their health. The U.S. Department of Agriculture and the U.S. Department of Health and Human Services have developed guidelines for healthy eating. For a healthful diet, a person must eat a variety of foods. A variety is more likely to include all the nutrients a person needs to stay healthy. To help people make wise choices, MyPlate was developed. *MyPlate* is a plan that organizes food into groups that have similar nutrients, **5-7**. Learn more about MyPlate at www.Choose**MyPlate**.gov. In addition, the *Dietary Guidelines for Americans* suggest actions that promote health, **5-8**.

People who eat in commercial foodservice operations have a wide choice of what to eat. They can eat one meal in a restaurant and the rest of the meals at home. If they want to, they can eat all their meals at one restaurant. However, they have the choice. For this reason, commercial foodservice operations are mostly concerned with taste and appearance. However, they do try to provide offerings from each part of MyPlate.

Institutional foodservices are much more concerned with nutrition. In many cases, people who eat in institutional foodservices have no other choice about where to eat. For example, patients in a hospital, soldiers on an army base, and prisoners in a prison facility have no choice about where to eat. Therefore, institutional foodservices pay close attention to the nutritional content of each meal they serve.

## Production Methods

When a foodservice business is first planned, the target market, concept, theme, type of food, and type of service are chosen. Once these decisions are made, the kitchen facilities are built. The

**5-7** MyPlate suggests how much food a person should eat from each group each day.

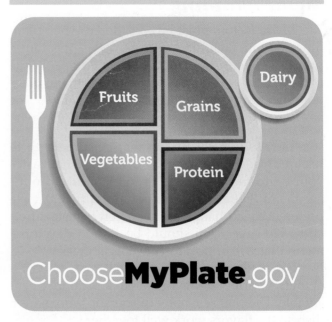

*USDA*

**5-6** Eggs Benedict by themselves are very bland in color. Adding green asparagus and a sprinkle of paprika makes the dish appear more appetizing.

*Glenn Price/Shutterstock.com*

---

## Recommendations from the Dietary Guidelines for Americans

**Balance calories to achieve and manage a healthful weight.**
- Control calorie intake to maintain or reduce weight.
- Increase physical activity and decrease sedentary activities.

**Consume nutrient-dense foods and beverages.**
- Reduce intake of calories from solid fats, *trans* fats, added sugars, and refined grains.
- Consume less than 2,300 mg of sodium each day.
- At least half of the grains consumed each day should be whole grains.
- Increase intake of fruits, vegetables, fat-free or low-fat milk products, and seafood.
- Replace high-fat protein foods with sources that are lower in fat or are sources of oils.
- Replace solid fats with oils whenever possible.

*U.S. Department of Health and Human Services/USDA*

5-8  The Dietary Guidelines for Americans promote health and good nutrition.

---

kitchen staff must be able to prepare the foods on the menu in the kitchen facilities at the restaurant.

The kitchen must have the equipment needed to cook the type of food the restaurant will serve. For example, a restaurant that specializes in fried chicken must have deep fat fryers. A fine-dining restaurant that never serves fried chicken may not need such fryers.

The kitchen staff must also be capable of preparing the food on the menu in the time available. A menu item that is complicated and takes a long time to prepare will not be a good choice for a quick-service restaurant. If a fine-dining restaurant chooses a complicated food item, it must make sure that the kitchen staff knows how to prepare it, **5-9.**

A variety of food production methods should be used in menu planning. A menu of fried chicken, french fries, cheese sticks, and fried fish relies on only one method of food preparation—frying. In order to offer variety in preparation, a restaurant can offer fried foods, baked foods, sautéed foods, raw foods (such as salads), and steamed foods. This makes the menu much more interesting.

### Price

Menu items should vary in price so guests have a choice among less expensive, moderate, and more expensive items. For example, hamburgers, chicken, and steaks could be offered on the menu. Hamburgers are inexpensive, chicken is moderately priced, and steaks are expensive.

Setting prices for menu items is an important part of the foodservice business. The price charged for a menu item must take into account the cost of preparing the item. This includes the costs of the ingredients, labor involved in preparing the item, rent or mortgage, utilities, and hidden costs (salt, pepper, cream, sugar, sauces, jellies). The price must also include a reasonable amount for profit. The restaurant manager will use a formula or a computer program to figure out how much to add for profit. In addition, the price of menu items must be in the range expected by customers.

## Food Production

**Food production** is the process of changing raw foods into menu items. The major difference

5-9  Kitchen staff must be trained to make special dishes.

*ClubCorp, Inc.*

between food production in your home and food production in a foodservice operation is quantity. Most foodservice operations serve large numbers of people every day.

## Standardized Recipes

A major challenge in the foodservice business is consistency. **Consistency** is the quality of producing the same result every time. Every time a food item is made, the result is exactly the same in terms of quality and quantity (amount produced).

The major tool for achieving consistency is the standardized recipe. A **recipe** is a set of instructions for preparing a food item. It includes information about ingredients, equipment, cooking methods, and yield. **Yield** is the amount of food that a recipe produces. For example, the yield of

a cookie recipe is how many cookies (of a specific size) the recipe makes. Yield is usually given as the number of portions or servings that the recipe makes. For example, a cookie recipe might make two dozen two-inch cookies.

A **standardized recipe** is a recipe that has been tested for consistency. The standardized recipe includes detailed instructions so anyone with basic cooking skills can make the recipe, **5-10**. Cooks should use these recipes exactly as they are written. A standardized recipe should include the following items:

- each ingredient, including spices
- precise amounts of each ingredient
- preparation instructions in detail
- portion size
- yield (number of portions)

## Standardized Recipe

RECIPE FOR:   Snickerdoodles

| COOKING INSTRUCTIONS: Bake at 325°F for 10 to 12 minutes or until light brown. | PORTION SIZE: two 3-inch cookies |
|---|---|
| EQUIPMENT NEEDED: Scale, quart measure, cup measure, scraper, measuring spoons, mixer w/paddle, mixing bowl, 18" × 24" × 1" cookie sheet pans (4), #40 dipper, small bowl | YIELD: 200 3-inch cookies OR 100 servings |

| INGREDIENTS | WEIGHTS | MEASURES | DIRECTIONS |
|---|---|---|---|
| Butter | 4 lbs | | 1.  Cream together butter & sugar with paddle. |
| Sugar | 6 lbs | | 2.  Add eggs & vanilla, cream. |
| Eggs | | 3 qts | 3.  In a bowl, combine flour, cream of tartar, baking soda, salt, & cinnamon. |
| Vanilla | | 3 1/3 c | |
| Flour | 6 lbs | | 4.  Add dry ingredients to creamed mixture with a paddle. |
| Cream of Tartar | | 5 T + 1 t | 5.  Using a #40 dipper, form balls and dip in cinnamon-sugar topping mixture. Pat lightly. |
| Baking Soda | | 2 T + 2 t | |
| Salt | | 1 T | 6.  Place on cookie sheet pans. |
| Cinnamon | | 1 T + 1 t | 7.  Bake. |

CINNAMON-SUGAR TOPPING MIXTURE

| INGREDIENTS | WEIGHTS | MEASURES | DIRECTIONS |
|---|---|---|---|
| Sugar | | 1/2 c | Combine sugar and cinnamon in a small bowl. |
| Cinnamon | | 1 T | |

*Goodheart-Willcox Publisher*

**5-10**  A standardized recipe has been tested for consistency. It also provides detailed instructions so anyone with cooking skills can follow it.

## Preparation

Items are prepared for final cooking in the preparation area. The food preparation area is often divided into six areas: meat/fish/poultry, vegetable, salad, sandwich, bread, and dessert. In smaller foodservice operations, the vegetable and salad or the salad and sandwich preparation areas are often placed together. The goal of these preparation areas is to prepare quality items in quantities that can meet customer demands. Preparing too much can be expensive if the extra food must be thrown away.

Preparation often consists of measuring and processing. *Measuring* is using a measuring tool to get the correct amount of an ingredient. Measuring tools include measuring spoons and cups. *Processing* means cleaning and changing the form of the food and includes chopping, slicing, pureeing, and dicing, **5-11**. Knives, slicers, food processors, and choppers are used for processing. Processing also includes breading, marinating, and battering items.

Some foodservice operations purchase preportioned items. *Preportioned items* are items that have already been washed and cut or measured. The use of preportioned items has been a growing trend in foodservice operations for a number of years. For example, many restaurants use prewashed, precut, and preportioned salad greens. This saves labor costs as well as preparation time and space. Facilities that use these convenience items need less space for preparation areas. The use of frozen and canned fruits and vegetables has also reduced the need for space to wash, cut, and chop food items.

Good cooks know that it is important to have everything ready before beginning to cook. All cooking utensils and equipment should be clean and easy to reach. Ingredients should be washed, measured, processed, and within easy reach. The process of getting everything ready is called *mise en place*, a French term that means *to put in place*. Good cooks also keep their workspace neat and clean up as they go along.

## Cooking Methods

The standardized recipe will specify the type of cooking method to use. Cooking methods are chosen that produce the desired menu item. There are three basic cooking methods: moist heat, dry heat, and dry heat with fat. Microwaving refers to the use of a specific tool (microwave oven) rather

*Karlova Irina/Shutterstock.com*

**5-11** Good knife skills are part of food preparation.

than to a cooking method. Both dry and moist heat methods can be used in a microwave.

*Moist heat* uses liquid such as water or broth to conduct heat to the food. Examples of moist heat methods include boiling, simmering, stewing, and steaming. The *dry heat* method uses no liquids; heat is conducted to the food by air alone. Examples of dry heat methods include baking, broiling, grilling, and roasting. The *dry heat with fat* method requires the use of a fat, such as butter or corn oil. Methods include sautéeing, pan frying, and deep frying.

## Beverage Preparation

A **beverage** is a liquid that is drinkable. Beverages include coffee, tea, cocoa, soft drinks, milk, fruit drinks, and alcoholic drinks. Beverage service is a significant part of any meal or snack. Sometimes people go to a restaurant just to get something to drink. Beverages can be served before, during, and after a meal.

Coffee has been recognized as a symbol of hospitality for many years, **5-12**. Some customers rate a restaurant based on the quality of the coffee. People like its rich smell. Coffee must be made with great care. The equipment must be clean, and the proportions of coffee and water must be exact. Coffee tastes best right after it has been brewed. Brewed coffee should not be served if it has been sitting for more than an hour.

Tea is also a very popular beverage. Tea can be served either hot or cold. If cold tea is served,

CandyBox Images/Shutterstock.com

5-12  Coffee is a favorite beverage. It must be prepared properly.

it should be iced. If hot tea is served, it should be very hot. Some customers prefer tea with lemon; others like it with milk.

Alcoholic drinks include wine, beer, liquor, and cocktails. *Cocktails* are iced drinks of wine or

distilled liquor that are mixed with flavoring ingredients. The United States government and state governments regulate the sale and consumption of alcohol. The federal Uniform Drinking Age Act of 1984 pressured all states to raise the minimum drinking age to 21. Each state has an agency that regulates the sale and consumption of alcohol and enforces those regulations. All stores and restaurants that sell alcohol must get a liquor license from the state liquor agency.

## Presentation

**Food presentation** is the art of making food look attractive and appetizing. Many of the design concepts in food presentation are from the study of graphic art. When food is arranged on a plate, it should have balance, proportion, and contrast. When a guest sees attractive food, it causes the digestive system to get ready for eating by secreting digestive juices. This reaction to food is summarized in the expression, "The food looked so good, it made my mouth water." Food presentation consists of three aspects: plating, portion control, and art.

## Going Green

### Energy-Efficient Ice Machines

A foodservice operation can cut costs by replacing an older commercial ice machine with a newer ENERGY STAR model. According to the U.S. Environmental Protection Agency (EPA), annual water usage can be reduced by 2,500 gallons. Utility costs can also be cut by $110 per year. The EPA's ENERGY STAR program identifies and promotes products that are energy efficient.

The machines are air-cooled and use less water than standard water-cooled machines. Since many are programmable, managers can choose how much ice to make based on demand. Some machines detect the hardness level of water and remove minerals to speed up the ice-making process. A number of machines require fewer labor hours for cleaning because they have built-in antimicrobial protection.

Foodservice operations must weigh the advantages and disadvantages of buying energy-efficient ice machines. Paying lower utility bills and using less water may offset a higher purchase price.

## Plating

**Plating** is the placing of food on a plate. The plate is like a canvas for a painter. The food is like the paint, **5-13**. However, there is more to plating than painting with food. The cook or chef must take care that the food is handled properly. Portion control is also an important part of plating.

Food is not the ideal artistic medium. Food is usually moist and greasy. If wet and greasy foods are put on a plate, the liquids run together. As a result the food becomes soggy, and the appearance is unappetizing. Therefore, food must be removed from the cooking utensil in a way that drains as much liquid as possible. Slotted spoons are often used for this reason. The plate itself should also be dry. In addition, hot foods should be served on hot plates. Cold foods should be served on cold plates.

Plate rims must be clean. There should be no drips or spots. The food on the plate should look

5-13 Plating is arranging the food on the plate.

*Alistair Cotton/Shutterstock.com*

neat. Many restaurants have someone who performs quality control. This person looks at each plate before it is served to make sure the food looks good and the plate rim is clean. Any plates not meeting the standard are sent back to the kitchen.

## Portion Control

Portion control is another important part of food presentation. **Portion control** is making sure that each portion of a food item is always the correct size. Portion control is important for two reasons: customers and cost control. Each customer must be served the same amount of food. If you see that another customer is getting a larger portion, you will feel cheated.

Portion control also helps the foodservice operation control its costs. If the portion sizes vary, then the amount of food used in each portion varies. It is difficult to control costs if portion sizes vary.

Serving utensils include large serving spoons, long-handled serving spoons, salad tongs, spatulas, and chafing dishes. Some serving utensils are designed to give predetermined portion sizes, and the sizes are marked on the handle of the utensil.

## Art

Once the preparation and portion issues are settled, the chef or cook can work on the artistic appearance of the food. The shapes, sizes, textures, and colors of the food on the plate should balance each other, **5-14**. When planning the menu, the chef has to think about how the foods will look on the plate. It is always appealing to have something colorful. However, many foods are not that interesting in color. For example, the traditional meat and potatoes are brown and white. Chefs often add a colorful vegetable, such as carrots or broccoli, to make the plate more colorful and appetizing.

Another way to add color and interest to a plate is to add a garnish. A **garnish** is a decoration, so to garnish means to decorate a food or a plate of food. Garnishes should always be edible. The garnish should also harmonize with the taste of the food.

Colorful fruits and vegetables are popular garnishes. Popular fruit garnishes include strawberries, grapes, cherries, and slices of orange, lemon, peach, kiwi, apple, and pineapple. Popular vegetable garnishes include parsley, tomatoes, green and red peppers, radishes, and olives. Often the garnishes are cut into interesting shapes. Radishes

5-14 The balance of shapes, sizes, textures, and colors of food on a plate create an artistic appearance.

and carrots are often cut to look like roses. Fruit slices are often arranged to resemble a fan. Nuts are also used to provide variety in texture and color. Almonds, walnuts, sesame seeds, and sunflower seeds are popular nut garnishes.

Herbs and seasonings are often used to add color to food. Paprika is sometimes sprinkled over mashed potatoes to add a little color.

# Serving

In the foodservice business, **serving** is delivering food to a guest. Serving consists of four parts: setup, serving food, bussing, and sidework. Before you learn about the four parts, you should first understand the different styles of service.

## Styles of Service

There are five basic styles of service: over-the-counter, drive-through, cafeteria, buffet, and seated.

### Over-the-Counter

Over-the-counter service is a style that is used mainly in quick-service and fast-food restaurants. Customers place their orders at a long counter that has cash registers. Meals are paid for and received at this counter. Customers either take the meal with them or carry their food to a table.

### Drive-Through

Drive-through service is a style of service that many quick-service restaurants offer. Customers stay seated in their cars for the whole process of

# Alice Waters— *The Delicious Revolution*

David Liittschwager

Alice Waters had revolutionary ideas about food. In the 1960s and 70s, fast food and frozen TV dinners were becoming very popular. Fine dining trends focused on very fancy dishes with lots of sauces. Alice wanted to open a restaurant that served simple dishes made from locally grown produce and foods so the natural essence of each food could shine. She wanted the atmosphere of her restaurant to feel like a dinner party with friends.

Alice developed her ideas while spending a year in France. She was very impressed with a meal at a French country restaurant that included trout freshly caught from a nearby stream and fresh-picked raspberries from the garden.

With financial help from family and friends, Alice opened her restaurant Chez Panisse in Berkeley, California, in 1971. Alice and the staff of Chez Panisse are committed to serving the freshest food in season from local sources. Chez Panisse serves one set menu that changes daily. The changes reflect foods that are in season. Her restaurant is one of the first to have a "forager" on staff. A *forager* is a person who seeks the best ingredients and establishes a relationship with the farmers growing them.

Alice introduced her ideas about food to schoolchildren through a project called *The Edible Schoolyard*. Through this program, students plant, harvest, and cook their own food. They learn the importance of food in their lives and the values of respecting others and the planet.

Many people say that Alice changed the way Americans think and feel about food. Alice helped spark a nationwide interest in organic foods and farmers' markets. She is one of the most recognized and influential chefs in America, and many well-known chefs trained in her kitchen. She was ranked as one of the world's best chefs by the prestigious magazine *Cuisine et Vins du France*. In 2001, the magazine *Gourmet* named Chez Panisse the best restaurant in America. Alice is the author of eight cookbooks, most recently *The Art of Simple Food*.

## Alice Water's Career Path

**1944:** Born in Chatham, New Jersey

**1962:** Studied early childhood education at the Montessori School in London

**1963:** Spent a year living in France

**1967:** Graduated from the University of California, Berkeley

**1971:** Opened Chez Panisse

**1982:** Alice's first cookbook, Chez Panisse Menu Cookbook, published

**2000:** Awarded *Bon Appetit* magazine's Lifetime Achievement Award

**2001:** Chez Panisse named best restaurant in America by Gourmet magazine

**2004:** Received James Beard Foundation Lifetime Achievement Award

**2008:** Received Global Environmental Citizen Award

ordering, paying, and being served. Customers drive up to an order window or speaker and order their food. They then drive to a service window. At the service window, they pay for their meal and pick up their food. There may be a separate pay window and service window. Customers then take the food with them, **5-15**.

## Cafeteria

Cafeterias are very popular in institutional foodservice. In the cafeteria style of service customers are given a tray with silverware and a napkin. Food items are displayed along a counter called a *serving line*. Servers stand behind the serving line. Customers carry their trays along the serving line and request food they want. The server serves the food and hands the customer the plate. The customer places the plate on the tray and continues walking down the serving line. At the end of the serving line is a cashier. The customer pays the cashier and then carries the tray to a table.

## Buffet

In buffet service, food is arranged on tables throughout the dining area. The presentation of food on the buffet tables is very important. Servers keep the displays of food stocked with food items. At some of the tables, a server may be available to serve you. For example, some buffets have a meat-carving station. Breakfast buffets often have a station where omelets are made to order. Customers walk around and serve themselves. They then take their food to a table.

## Seated

Seated service is service in which the customers are seated at a table. A server comes to the table to take the order. The server then brings the food to the table. There are three popular styles of seated service: American, French, and Russian.

Many restaurants use *American service*. The food is plated in the kitchen. This type of service is also called *plate service*. It is the fastest of all types of service. American service requires the least amount of skill to wait on customers.

Some fine-dining restaurants use *French service*. In French service the meal is partially prepared in the kitchen. Then the server finishes the cooking, carving, or flaming of the food in front of the customer. The partially prepared food is brought to the table on a cart. This cart is called a *gueridon*. The gueridon has a small heating utensil on it called a *rechaud*. The rechaud is used to complete the cooking in front of the customer. An example of French service is the preparation of crêpes suzette. The crêpes are prepared on the gueridon. Then a cherry mixture is placed on the crêpes. A liqueur mixture is poured on the crêpes and lighted. The crêpes will begin to flame as the guests watch. After the flame goes out, the crêpes will be served.

In *Russian service*, the food is cooked and divided into portions in the kitchen. The portions of food are placed on trays. The server carries the tray of food to the table. The server uses a special serving spoon and fork to place a portion on each guest's plate. This style of service is often used at banquets, when a large number of people are served similar food items.

## *Setup*

Setup involves preparing the table for service. The first step is to make sure the table itself is stable and does not wobble. Wobbling can be controlled with special table-levelers. The next step is to cover the table, if that is the restaurant's style. Tables may be covered with cloth tablecloths or placemats made of paper, cloth, or straw.

The next step is setting the table. Each guest gets a place setting. Items included in a place setting depend on the style of service, restaurant concept and theme, and meal being served, **5-16**. General categories of items included in a place setting are napkins, flatware, glassware, and plateware.

In a fine-dining restaurant and for many catered events, napkins are folded in special ways. **Flatware** consists of the knives, forks, and spoons that guests will use during a meal. It is also called *silverware* or *cutlery*. **Glassware** includes all the drinking glasses. There may be as many as three

**5-15** When using drive-through service, customers pick food up at the window.

## Place Setting

| Menu Item | Flatware | Glassware | Plateware |
|---|---|---|---|
| *Fresh berries* | Teaspoon | | |
| *Salad with dressing* | Salad fork | | |
| *Sirloin steak* | Dinner knife<br>Main course fork | | |
| *Potatoes au gratin* | | | |
| *Green beans* | | | |
| *Rolls and butter* | | | Bread and butter plate |
| *Ice cream* | Teaspoon | | |
| *Coffee* | Teaspoon | | Cup and saucer |
| *Water* | | Water glass | |

### Arrangement on Table

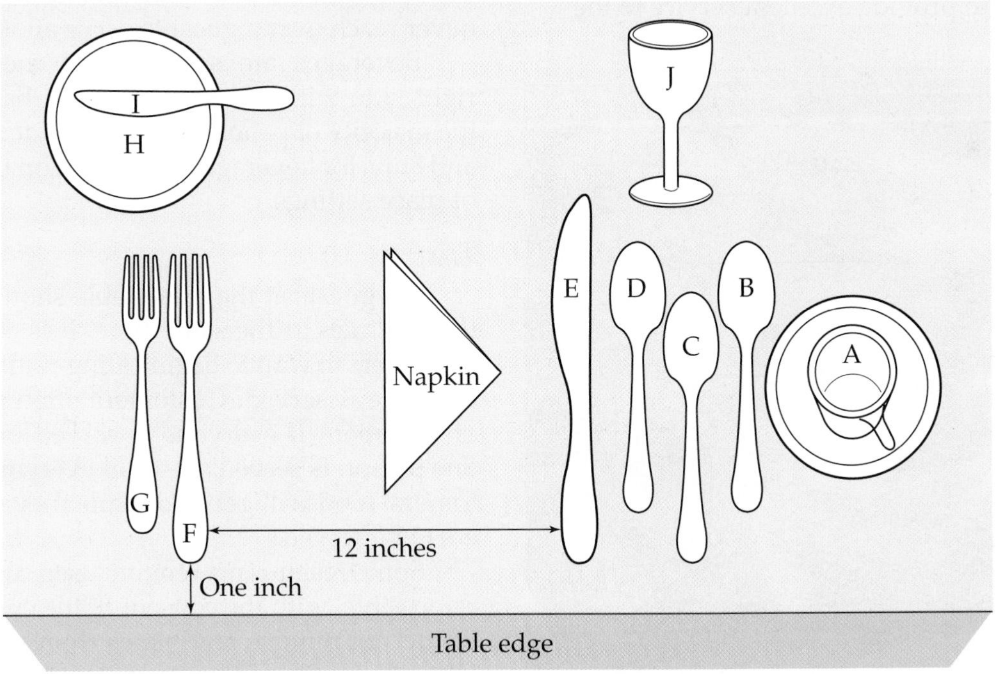

12 inches
One inch
Napkin
Table edge

A  Coffee cup and saucer
B  Fruit spoon
C  Coffee spoon
D  Dessert spoon
E  Dinner knife
F  Main course fork
G  Salad fork
H  Bread and butter plate
I  Butter knife
J  Water glass

*Goodheart-Willcox Publisher*

**5-16**  The items included in a place setting depend on the menu and the style of service. This meal will be served American service. Therefore, plateware for the berries, salad, steak and side dishes, and ice cream are not needed on the table.

glassware items per setting: a water glass, a juice glass, and a wine glass. **Plateware** includes all dishes, such as plates and soup bowls, plus coffee cups and saucers. Plateware is also called *china*.

The final step is to add any additional accessories or condiments to the table. Accessories can include flowers, candles, napkin dispensers, and menu or advertisement holders. A **condiment** is something that is added to food to make it taste better. Condiments often placed on the table include salt, pepper, syrup, sugar, soy sauce, hot sauce, ketchup, mustard, and cream. All condiments and accessories should be checked regularly to make sure they are clean, fresh, and full.

## Serving Food

Regardless of service style, service should be excellent, **5-17**. Staff must always be attentive to customer needs. Each restaurant has its own

**5-17** No matter what the setting, servers must be prepared to provide excellent service to the customers.

*Eric Limon/Shutterstock.com*

standards. However, the most important thing is the comfort and safety of the customer. If you have to serve from the "wrong" side for the customer's comfort or safety, do it. The following are generally recommended serving techniques.

### Sequence

Female customers should be served before male customers. If the server can easily determine which female is the oldest, she should be served first. If children are in the party, they should be served first to help keep them occupied and happy. This allows the adults at the table to enjoy their meals without fussy children. The host or hostess of the party should be served last.

### Direction

Food is served from the customer's left side with the server's left hand. A good way to remember this is by the saying, "leave (the food) with the left." Some use the saying "lead with the left." The left hand is used to serve the food gracefully. It helps to avoid the possibility of bumping into the customers with the server's elbow. You should never reach over a guest to serve another guest.

Beverages are served from the customer's right side with the server's right hand. Because the majority of people are right-handed, the glasses and cups for beverages are placed on the right side of place settings.

### Timing

All guests at the same table should be served their entrées at the same time. It is courteous for customers to wait to begin eating until everyone at the table is served. Customers often get annoyed or impatient if everyone is served but one, or if one person is served ahead of everyone else. Customers' food will get cold while they wait for others to be served.

Some restaurants remove used dishes as soon as possible, with the consent of the customer. Others do not remove any plates from the table until all customers have finished eating their meals. You never want to rush people who have not finished eating. Sometimes customers may suggest that they want their plate to be cleared from the table. Take that plate away even if the other customers have not finished their meals.

### Clearing Dishes

Dirty dishes are cleared from the customer's right side with the server's right hand. A good

# Hospitality Ethics

## Reporting Tip Income

According to the *Internal Revenue Service (IRS)*, any employees who receive tips must report tip income to the federal government. Employees who receive more than $20.00 in tips during a calendar month are required to give a written statement to their employers that includes the

- employee's name, address, and social security number
- name and address of the employer
- total amount of tip income
- period for which and the date on which the statement is given to the employer

Employers can furnish employees with special forms for reporting tip income. Employees can also use forms furnished by the IRS. For more information on tip reporting, see the IRS website. Do a search using the key words *reporting tip income*.

way to remember this is by the saying, "Remove with the right." The right hand is used to remove dishes gracefully and to avoid the possibility of bumping into the customer. Dishes should be removed from the table in a counterclockwise pattern, **5-18**. Never stack or scrape dirty plates by a customer's table. It is very unappetizing to see food being scraped off a plate. Wait until you get in the kitchen or out of the sight of the customers before scraping food off plates.

The server should "crumb the table" before serving the dessert. A side towel or a crumbing device can be used to brush crumbs from the table into a small plate.

### Bussing

Bussing is an essential part of excellent service. **Bussing** consists of setting the place settings, clearing dirty dishes from the table, and taking the dirty dishes to the kitchen. Sometimes the servers also do the bussing. However, often a separate person, the busser, performs these tasks. When there are one or more bussers, the bussers also help the servers. They can pour beverages, refill condiment containers, and help with heavy trays of food.

### Sidework

**Sidework** consists of duties that servers must perform other than serving guests. These duties

include preparing the dining room, learning the menu, folding napkins, replenishing condiments, and leaving the work area in good order when the shift is completed.

**5-18**  Remove dishes in a counterclockwise pattern.

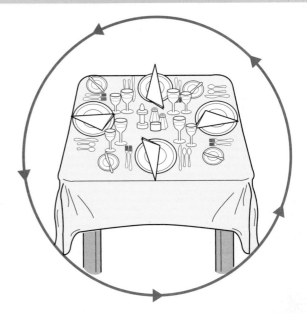

*Goodheart-Willcox Publisher*

# Chapter 5
## Review

## Chapter Summary

- The menu is the basic game plan for a restaurant.
- Many factors must be considered when planning a menu.
- Standardized recipes help restaurants maintain consistency.
- Food preparation includes measuring and processing.
- The three basic cooking methods are wet heat, dry heat, and dry heat with fat.
- The three aspects of food presentation are plating, portion control, and art.
- The five basic styles of service are over-the-counter, drive-through, cafeteria, buffet, and seated.
- Leave with the left; remove with the right.

## Review

1. How does the menu function as the basic game plan for a restaurant?
2. List and describe each of the four types of menus.
3. List the seven classic parts of a menu.
4. Explain the difference between à la carte pricing and table d'hôte pricing.
5. List six factors to consider in menu planning and describe how you would use them to plan a menu.
6. Explain how restaurants use standardized recipes to achieve consistency.
7. Describe two food preparation techniques.
8. Describe the three cooking methods and give an example of each.
9. Why is portion control important?
10. What can a chef do to make a plate of food look appealing?
11. Describe the five basic styles of service and give an example of a restaurant where each style is used.
12. Describe three popular styles of seated service.
13. Why should children be served first?
14. Explain why food is served from the left and removed from the right.
15. From which side are beverages served?

# Critical Thinking

16. **Compare and contrast.** Compare the three different ways of pricing menu items: à la carte, table d'hôte, and combination. Which restaurants in your area use these types of pricing?

17. **Create.** Design a menu using the following factors: taste, variety, appearance, nutrition, production, and price.

18. **Analyze.** Analyze reasons that the menu is a type of contract between the foodservice establishment and the customer.

19. **Determine.** Imagine you are a server in a restaurant. Make a list of all the sidework items that need to be completed during your shift.

20. **Identify.** Create a list of restaurants that have less expensive items and more expensive items on the same menu. What type of restaurants tend to have these choices?

# Common Core

### College and Career Readiness

21. **Writing.** Using magazines, find pictures of food that look attractive and appetizing. Write detailed descriptions of ways the food was plated in order to make it attractive.

22. **Reading.** Find a recipe for chocolate chip cookies. Locate and label these items on the recipe: yield, portion size, ingredients, measurements, directions, baking temperature, and baking time.

23. **Speaking.** Investigate the science facts behind MyPlate at www.Choose**MyPlate**.gov. Create an electronic presentation to organize and relate your findings.

24. **Speaking.** Develop a presentation discussing the five basic styles of service: over-the-counter, drive-through, cafeteria, buffet, and seated. Provide examples of at least two local restaurants per style of service.

25. **CTE Career Readiness Practice.** Use the Internet to contrast the educational requirements for two or more careers in food preparation and service. What is different about the job responsibilities and expertise? Under which career pathways do you find these careers? How much time, effort, and experience does it take to become proficient in these careers? How does this information fit with your career goals? Find the answers by searching such professional association websites as the National Restaurant Association. Write a summary or prepare a digital presentation to share your findings with the class.

# Chapter 6

## Front- and Back-of-the-House

## Chapter Objectives

After studying this chapter, you will be able to

- **describe** the responsibilities of the general manager.
- **list** the six functions of the front-of-the-house.
- **contrast** the members of the front-of-the-house staff and the back-of-the-house staff.
- **describe** the responsibilities of the restaurant manager.
- **list** the seven functions of the back-of-the-house.
- **describe** the responsibilities of the executive chef.
- **assess** the importance of the work of the steward and dishwashing crew.

## Before You Read

Try to answer the following questions before you read this chapter.

- What is the difference between front-of-the-house staff and back-of-the-house staff?
- What employees work in the back-of-the-house?

## Terms to Know

| | | |
|---|---|---|
| seating | point-of-sales system (POS) | sous-chef |
| reservation | culinary | kitchen manager |
| walk-ins | pass-through | steward |
| open seating | restaurant manager | dishwasher |
| booking a reservation | server | chef |
| overbooking | busser | cook |
| residence time | executive chef | expediter |
| call-ahead seating | | |

Restaurants are divided into two areas: the front-of-the-house and the back-of-the-house. Each area has its own responsibilities. Both areas must work closely together to make the restaurant a success. Figure **6-1** shows the organization of a typical restaurant. The general manager is in charge of the entire restaurant. The left half of the figure shows the employees of the front-of-the-house. The right half of the figure shows the employees in the back-of-the-house.

# General Manager

The *general manager* is responsible for the overall operation of the entire restaurant, including the front-of-the-house and the back-of-the-house employees. Often he or she is also the owner of the restaurant. The general manager hires and supervises managers to assist in the operation of the restaurant, **6-2**. If the restaurant is part of a chain, the general manager will be responsible for communications with the corporate headquarters.

## Responsibilities of the General Manager

- Optimizing profit
- Supervising the managers
- Safety and sanitation
- Quality and consistency
- Purchasing and receiving
- Guest relations
- Employee relations
- Marketing and sales
- Human resources
- Accounting
- Security
- Engineering and maintenance

*Goodheart-Willcox Publisher*

6-2  The general manager of a restaurant is responsible for the entire operation.

6-1  Each restaurant has its own organization. However, many restaurants follow the organization in this figure.

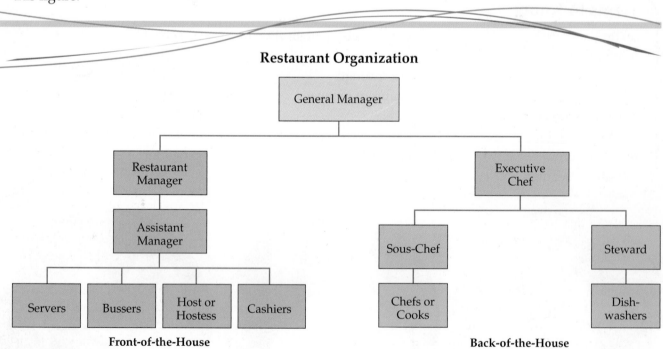

**Restaurant Organization**

Front-of-the-House

Back-of-the-House

*Goodheart-Willcox Publisher*

# Front-of-the-House Functions

*Front-of-the-house* refers to the area in a hospitality business that guests usually see. In a restaurant, the front-of-the-house usually includes the lobby or entrance, the host/hostess stand, and the dining room. Front-of-the-house employees are those who work directly with guests. The front-of-the-house is responsible for the following six functions: seating guests, selling food, transmitting orders to the kitchen, serving customers, bussing tables, and obtaining payment from customers.

## Seating

**Seating** is the process of finding seats for customers in a restaurant. When customers enter a restaurant, they are seated by a host or hostess. Customers should be seated as soon as possible after they enter the restaurant. They should be seated so they will be served in the most efficient way. Many restaurants organize the tables into stations. A specific server is responsible for the tables in his or her station. The host or hostess must evenly distribute the guests so one station is not filled while another one is empty.

Many restaurants have a computerized table management system. If there are no tables available when guests arrive, the hostess gives them a *pager*. The pager is about the size of a coaster. It has the capacity to flash or vibrate when it receives a signal from the hostess. The hostess has a computer terminal and monitor that keeps track of each table in the restaurant, **6-3**. It tells which tables are occupied, how long customers have been at each table, and which tables are empty. When the hostess finds a table for the waiting guests, she sends a signal to the pager. The pager flashes or vibrates, signaling the guests to return to the hostess stand. The hostess then seats the guests.

A **reservation** is a promise to hold something for a customer until the customer needs it. In the foodservice industry, a *reservation* is the promise of a table in a restaurant. Customers call ahead to reserve a table for a specific number of people for a particular date and time. **Walk-ins** are customers who arrive at a restaurant but have not made a reservation. These customers walk in the door and expect to be seated. Many casual restaurants do not take reservations. This approach is called

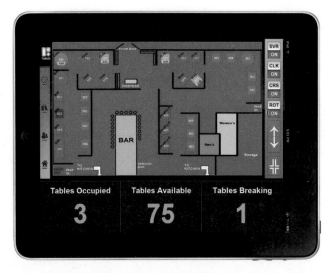

*Photo courtesy of JTECH Communications, Inc.*

**6-3** A computerized table management system helps employees monitor each table.

open seating. Customers are seated on a first come, first served basis.

The process of taking a reservation is called **booking a reservation**. Reservations have advantages and disadvantages. The main advantage to customers is that the table is ready when they arrive. A reservation will hold a table for a party, even if a walk-in comes in first. However, restaurants will only hold a reservation for a certain length of time. If the party with the reservation does not come in within about 15 minutes, the table will be given to a walk-in customer.

The advantage to the restaurant is that the manager knows how many customers to plan for and when they will arrive. Reservations also make the customers happy. There are some disadvantages, though. Guests may not show up for their reservations, and as a result the restaurant may lose money. To avoid this problem, some restaurants make more reservations than there are tables. This is called **overbooking**. Guests with reservations whose tables are not available due to overbooking can become very unhappy.

**Residence time** is the time that it takes a party to eat a meal, pay the bill, and leave the restaurant. Ninety minutes are usually needed for a party of four people to eat a complete meal that includes appetizers, beverages, the main course, and dessert, **6-4**. Reservations should be scheduled two hours apart. This leaves enough time to clean and

bikeriderlondon/Shutterstock.com

6-4 The residence time for a party of four is usually 90 minutes.

reset the table. For example, suppose a party of four makes a reservation for 6 p.m. The next reservation for that table can be made at 8 p.m. Larger parties usually take longer. Therefore, the residence time will be longer for large groups.

**Call-ahead seating** is a fairly new seating method. It is also called *priority seating*. Its purpose is to reduce long waits for a table. Customers call the restaurant and have their names added to the waiting list. Call-ahead seating does not guarantee that the guest will have a table at a certain time, but it does guarantee a place in line. With this method, the customer can wait somewhere other than in the restaurant. This system keeps the waiting time in the restaurant to a minimum.

## Sales

The sales function occurs when the server takes the customer's food order. Often, customers know exactly what food they want. Sometimes

they cannot decide. If they have not made up their minds, they may need some help. Servers use a process called *suggestive selling*—recommending menu items that the customer might like. Suggestive selling increases sales for the restaurant and usually increases tips for the server. The more a server sells, the higher their tips can get.

Some restaurants include wineglasses in the place setting or place a bottle of unopened wine on each table to encourage purchase. Other restaurants sell two-ounce wine samples.

Desserts are another way servers can increase their sales. Many restaurants display their desserts so customers can view them before beginning their meals. This suggestive selling technique has been used successfully by many restaurants. Another excellent way to highlight desserts is to bring out a sample tray of all the desserts that are offered. This sample tray often tempts people into purchasing desserts and after-dinner drinks.

## *Transmitting Orders*

A critical part of the restaurant business is getting the customers' orders to the kitchen and then getting the correct orders back to the correct customers. Each restaurant develops its own system for the process. The steps in this process are an important part of the training of a new server.

This process can be broken into five steps: taking the order, transmitting the order, preparing the order, checking the order, and retrieving the order. Three of the steps are done by the server. The other two are usually done by kitchen staff. It is essential that the servers and the kitchen staff work together as a team.

### Taking Orders

The server takes the orders from the guests. In many restaurants the server has a tablet that consists of paper checks, **6-5**. This is called a *guest check*. Each table in the restaurant has a number. For each new party, a new check is filled out with the date, table number, name of the server, and the number of guests in the party. Each restaurant develops its own way of filling out guest checks.

When there is more than one guest at a table, the server must note which person gets each order. There are many ways to do this. One way is to give each seat at the table a number. Each order can then be identified by the seat number.

Then, each person's order must be clearly recorded. A restaurant will usually have a list of abbreviations to use on the guest checks. Servers must make sure that each order is recorded accurately. A good way to ensure accuracy is to repeat each person's order back to him or her.

Many restaurants are using a point-of-sales system to improve the process of taking orders and transmitting them to the kitchen. A **point-of-sales system (POS)** is a computerized system for recording an order at the place where the order is taken (at the point where the sale is made). Point-of-sales systems are used in many retail sales settings.

Some restaurant POS systems have wireless handheld units with touch screens. Instead of writing down the order, the server can immediately enter the order into the POS. Many restaurants do not yet have handheld units. These restaurants have computer terminals near the tables instead. Once the server has written down the orders, he or she enters the order at a terminal using a touch screen, **6-6**.

*wavebreakmedia/Shutterstock.com*

**6-5** How many local restaurants can you name that still use paper checks?

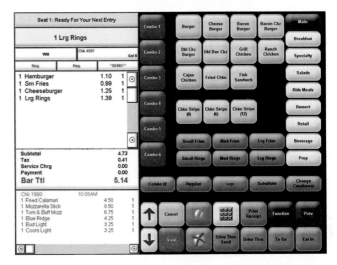
*MICROS Systems*

**6-6** This is an example of a touch screen for recording guest orders. This touch screen is part of a restaurant POS (point-of-sale system).

## Transmitting Orders to the Kitchen

Once the orders are accurately recorded, they must be transmitted to the kitchen. There are two basic methods of transmission: noncomputerized and computerized. In the noncomputerized method, the server goes to the kitchen and places the check on a spindle. The person preparing the orders then picks up the check from the spindle and prepares the orders.

In a computerized system, there is at least one printer in the kitchen. The orders are sent to the proper printer. For example, some kitchens will have a printer at the hot food station, another printer at the cold food station (pantry), and another printer in the dessert station. The cook goes to the printer and picks up the work order, **6-7**. This system saves the server the time it takes to walk to the kitchen to deliver an order.

The POS improves ordering and transmission accuracy. A POS also calculates and prints out the checks, **6-8**. Many POS systems have additional capabilities that make it easier to manage a restaurant. These include keeping track of the number of menu

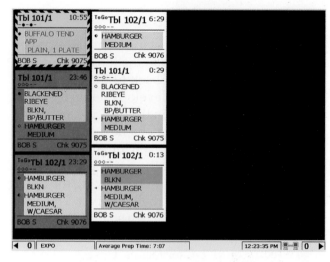

*MICROS Systems*

6-8  This screen shows two restaurant bills—one for table 101 and one for table 102.

items sold, alerting servers to items that have sold out, keeping track of inventory, and credit/debit card processing. In addition, a POS can handle the employee time clock, employee scheduling, payroll, accounting, frequent diner loyalty programs, and sales reports.

## Preparing Orders

Once the orders are in the kitchen, the culinary staff takes over. **Culinary** means related to kitchens and cooking. The culinary staff consists of the chefs, cooks, and other staff involved in preparing food. While the main course is being prepared, the server can serve appetizers, soups, and salads.

Timing of food preparation is a critical skill in the restaurant business. All guests in the same party should be served their main courses at the same time. However, different courses take different amounts of time to prepare. For example, a well-done 18-ounce T-bone steak and a seafood alfredo on the same check would be started at different times. The well-done T-bone steak should be started first because it takes about 30 minutes to prepare. The seafood alfredo only takes about ten minutes to prepare. Each restaurant develops a system for ensuring that the meals are ready at the same time. In some restaurants, the server would put in the steak order before the alfredo order. In other restaurants, a member of the culinary team organizes and monitors the timing of the orders. This team member is often called an *expediter*.

6-7  This is a point-of-sale system that shows the customer's order being transmitted to the kitchen.

*MICROS Systems*

### Checking Orders

After an order is done but before it is picked up and served, it should be checked for accuracy and appearance. First the order should be checked against the actual order, either on the guest check or in the POS. Then the order must be checked to make sure it meets the restaurant's standards. The portion sizes must be correct, and the food must be properly cooked and arranged on the plate. This is also the time when garnishes are added. A member of the culinary team usually checks the orders, but in some restaurants the server does the checking.

### Retrieving Orders

Food should be served as close to the time that it is finished cooking as possible. Hot foods must often be kept for a short time before they are picked up. Most restaurants will have a special area equipped with heat lamps to keep the food hot until served. This area is usually called the **pass-through** or the *window*.

Most restaurants have a system for alerting servers when their orders are ready. A noncomputerized restaurant might have a neon number board. Each server will be assigned a number. When the server's number is lit, his or her order is ready. A POS may post an alert on the terminal.

Some restaurants have a wireless server-paging system, **6-9**. The chef punches the server's code into the system, which pages the server. The server then goes to the pass-through to pick up the order.

## Serving

Serving food and beverages is a major function of the front-of-the-house. Regardless of style of service, quality service is the primary responsibility of the front-of-the-house staff. Quality service takes place when guests in a restaurant never have to ask for anything. For example, when guests reach for their coffee cups, the handle is placed right where their thumb and fingers naturally go. The water glasses are always filled. The main entrée is placed on the plate closest to the customer. A piece of pie should be served with the point facing the customer. Guests do not have to ask for ketchup, butter, or more bread. A second cup of coffee is poured before the customer requests it. The guest check is correct and is presented to customers before they ask for it. The server thanks the guests for coming to the restaurant. Guests often do not realize they have received excellent service until after they have left the restaurant.

## Bussing

Bussing is setting the place settings on the table, clearing the dirty dishes from the table, sweeping under the table, and assisting the servers whenever needed. Quality service depends on efficient work by the bussers.

### Wireless Server-Paging System

Chef pages server.

Pager alerts server that order is ready.

Server picks up order at pass-through.

*Redi-Call Inc. www.redi-callusa.com*

6-9  A wireless server paging system enables the chef to page the server as soon as the order is ready.

## Payment

After dessert and additional beverages are served, the check should be given to the customer. If the server cannot determine who is the host of the party, the check should be placed facedown in the center of the table. After the bill is paid, the customers should be thanked for coming to the restaurant and encouraged to return.

The actual handling of payment is done in several different ways. In many restaurants, the customers take the check and payment to a cashier at the front of the restaurant. In other restaurants, the server takes the payment. The server then either handles the payment or takes the payment to a cashier.

Some restaurants only accept cash. Others will accept credit and debit cards, **6-10**. Restaurants within a hotel often allow hotel guests to charge restaurant bills directly to their room. In that case, payment for the meals will be made when the room bill is paid.

# Front-of-the-House Staff

Front-of-the-house staff consists of one or more managers, host or hostess, servers, bussers, and cashiers. Restaurants that serve alcoholic beverages will have bartenders. Large restaurants will often have *trainers*, workers whose major responsibility is to train new employees. The exact job titles and responsibilities often vary from restaurant to restaurant.

## Managers

The front-of-the-house usually has a manager called the restaurant manager. The **restaurant manager** is responsible for everything that happens in the front-of-the-house. A major responsibility is hiring the rest of the front-of-the-house staff, and then training and supervising them. The restaurant manager schedules all staff, handles guest relations, and oversees quality of service. In addition, the restaurant manager is responsible for front-of-the-house cleanliness, cash management, and coordination with the back-of-the-house. In

**6-10** Ask what forms of payment a restaurant accepts before being seated.

RTimages/Shutterstock.com

a small restaurant, the general manager and the restaurant manager are often the same person.

A large restaurant may have an assistant restaurant manager. In some restaurants, the front-of-the-house management is divided between a service manager and a sales manager. The service manager is responsible for all matters pertaining to servers, service, and the dining room. The sales manager is responsible for the bar staff and beverages, host or hostess, carryout staff, and cashiers. The sales manager will also handle all cash and accounting duties.

A successful restaurant manager must know the different types of service, when to use them, and how to serve properly. The manager must also know the correct methods of beverage service. Restaurant managers are responsible for reducing costs and waste. All managers are responsible for ensuring communication among all employees in the restaurant. The restaurant manager must have excellent interpersonal skills for dealing with customers and supervising and training staff. He or she must have the ability to stay calm when under pressure. The manager must be in good physical condition as the hours are long and often stressful.

## Host or Hostess

The major responsibility of the host or hostess is to manage the flow of customers in the dining room, **6-11**. The host or hostess must make customers feel welcome and ensure that they are promptly seated. He or she must also manage customers when there are not enough tables and they must wait. The host or hostess keeps track of which tables are occupied, which ones are ready, and which ones are almost ready. He or she is also responsible for spreading the customers throughout the dining room so one server is not overloaded. There are many table management computer programs that help manage the dining room. Wireless systems also help the host or hostess communicate with servers and other staff concerning available tables.

In many restaurants the host or hostess has additional tasks. In some, the host or hostess is also the cashier. He or she may also serve the beverages and bread.

## Servers

Servers used to be called *waiters* and *waitresses*. Today, **servers** get their name based on what

Blend Images/Shutterstock.com

6-11 The host or hostess is the first employee a guest sees in a restaurant.

they do: serve customers. To serve the customer means to meet all his or her needs, and even to anticipate the customer's needs and respond before the customer asks.

The responsibilities of servers usually vary only a little from restaurant to restaurant. First, they are the representatives of the restaurant to the customer. Second, they sell the dining experience to the customer, including both food and beverage items. Third, they are responsible for delivering the dining experience to the customer. In addition, in many restaurants the servers are responsible for collecting payment from customers.

The servers are also the ones who hear complaints from guests. It is important that servers know how to be patient, kind, and good listeners. In addition, servers must have physical stamina and be able to lift and carry heavy trays or plates of food.

## Bussers

One of the most important employees in a restaurant is the **busser**. This person is an assistant to the servers. The busser is responsible for setup, clearing, and resetting of tables. The busser keeps the area under and around the table clean and helps the servers in any other way necessary.

## Cashiers

Cashiers handle payments for the meals. The restaurant cashier has the same duties as any retail cashier. The cashier prepares a *change fund*. This fund contains a certain amount of money that is used to make change. The cashier also reports the receipts. Sometimes the cashier prepares the bank deposit.

In some restaurants, the cashier has a station at the front of the restaurant. The guests bring the guest check and payment to the cashier. In other restaurants, the cashier will have a station in the bar or in the kitchen. The server takes the payment from the guest and brings it to the cashier.

# Back-of-the-House Functions

The *back-of-the-house* is the area in a hospitality business that guests usually do not see. It is also called the *heart-of-the-house*. In a restaurant these areas include the kitchen, receiving and storage areas, and business offices. Back-of-the-house employees include all employees whose work does not directly involve interaction with guests. The

# Going Green

## Reducing Employee Turnover

Employee turnover is high across much of the foodservice industry—and it is costly. Foodservice operations spend millions of dollars a year training new employees. After an employee leaves, the business must often pay their remaining employees higher overtime wages to work longer hours and pick up extra shifts.

Another key is a focus on employee retention. Many foodservice operators find inexpensive and creative ways to retain employees and keep them happy. Some ideas include

- providing employee mentoring programs and improved training
- offering flexible work schedules
- interviewing employees to find out what they like about their jobs and what employers can work to improve
- rewarding employees for achieving sales and productivity targets with prizes, such as electronic devices or gas cards
- creating employee newsletters to boast about employee accomplishments
- celebrating employee birthdays and work anniversaries
- conducting team-building activities, such as after-hours bowling contests or barbeques

Better screening of job candidates is also key to reducing turnover.

back-of-the-house is responsible for the following seven functions: food production; purchasing and receiving; marketing and sales; human resources; accounting; security; and engineering and maintenance. In some restaurants, the general manager is responsible for the marketing and sales, human resources, accounting, security, and engineering and maintenance.

This part of the chapter focuses on the back-of-the-house functions related to the kitchen and food production. The kitchen is the center of all food preparation and production. The ovens and other cooking equipment are located in the kitchen, **6-12**. Food and other items are received, stored, prepared, and plated for service there. Servers go to the kitchen to place orders, pick up food that is ready to be served, and return dirty dishes for cleaning. Dishes and other items are cleaned and stored in the kitchen.

# Back-of-the-House Staff

The back-of-the-house staff consists of one or more managers; staff responsible for cleaning and maintaining plateware, flatware, glassware, and utensils; and food production staff. The exact job titles and responsibilities often vary from restaurant to restaurant.

## *Managers*

There are two general areas that need to be managed in the kitchen: menus and operations. The menu area includes everything involved in planning menus, developing standardized recipes, and creating new recipes. The operations area includes kitchen safety and sanitation; hiring, training, and supervising all back-of-the-house staff; food quality; food quantity; coordination with the front-of-the-house; and cost controls. Purchasing, receiving, and inventory are often part of the kitchen operations area.

**6-12** What equipment can you identify in this kitchen?

*atm2003/Shutterstock.com*

# Walter Cotta—
## *Executive Chef Cooks Up Rave Reviews*

*Photo courtesy of Martinez Productions International*

As a small boy in El Salvador, Walter Cotta ate many dishes unique to his culture. He enjoyed eating dishes flavored with fruits and Latin spices and dreamed of a career involving food. When he started his first job at the age of nine years as a bricklayer, Walter's dream couldn't have seemed farther away. At that time, Walter could only imagine he would create dishes and menus around the flavors and ingredients of his culture.

For Walter, a turning point was a 1989 vacation to the United States during which he took a job as a dishwasher at a small Italian restaurant. Watching the chefs prepare dishes in the kitchen fascinated Walter. He chose to stay in the United States and work toward becoming a chef. He began reading cookbooks and taught himself the basics of cooking. As he learned more, Walter started creating his own recipes. After working as a dishwasher, Walter held several other restaurant jobs and gained more responsibility with each job.

In 1993, Walter was appointed executive chef of Alegría Cocina Latina in Long Beach, California. His job is to plan the menu, create recipes, and do the inventory and paperwork for the kitchen operations. Walter takes a more "hands-on" approach than a typical executive chef. He often works in the kitchen alongside the 2 sous-chefs and 20 workers he supervises to make certain each plate is perfect for the customers.

Walter's recipes are well known for their Latin flavor and artistry. The food earns rave reviews and draws crowds to eat at Alegría Cocina Latina every night. As an expert on Latin cooking, Walter serves on judges' panels for Latin cuisine award programs and contests. His genius has found creative and cost-cutting ways to source his cutting-edge, fresh organic ingredients in local markets while maintaining quality.

## Walter Cotta's Career Path

**1966:** Born in Santa Ana, El Salvador

**1974:** Worked as a bricklayer

**1989:** Vacationed to the United States; first restaurant job as a dishwasher

**1992:** First job as a cook at Sostanza

**1993:** Accepted job as sous-chef at L'Opera

**1994:** Hired as executive chef at Alegría Cocina Latina, Long Beach, California

**2002:** Featured chef for U.S. Potato Board Web site and spokesperson for Sparkletts Water

**2005:** Created Latin desserts for Lactaid®

**2009:** Named Executive Chef for L'Opera, an award-winning fine-dining Italian restaurant in Long Beach, California

In an independent restaurant, one manager is usually responsible for both the menu and the operations area. This manager is called the *executive chef*. The executive chef may have an assistant, called the *sous-chef*. A unit of a chain restaurant usually has a kitchen manager.

## Executive Chef

The **executive chef** is the top manager in a restaurant or hotel kitchen. He or she is responsible for everything related to the kitchen and food preparation. The following lists the nine responsibilities that an executive chef often has:

- coordinate kitchen activities
- direct the kitchen staff's training and work, **6-13**
- plan menus
- create recipes
- set and enforce nutrition requirements
- set and enforce safety and sanitation standards
- participate in the preparation and presentation of menu items
- ensure that quality standards are maintained
- purchase food items and equipment

In addition, many executive chefs participate in designing the printed menu, developing the look of the dining room, and designing the layout of the kitchen.

Some executive chefs coach the dining room staff so they can correctly answer questions about the menu. Many executive chefs work with food vendors to learn about new food items and products that are available. Executive chefs often work with equipment vendors, food stylists, restaurant consultants, public relations specialists, sanitation engineers, nutritionists, and dietitians.

## Sous-Chef

The **sous-chef** is the second-in-command in the kitchen. (In French, *sous* means *under*.) The sous-chef has similar training but less experience than the executive chef. The sous-chef's primary responsibility is to make sure the food is prepared, portioned, garnished, and presented according to the executive chef's wishes. The sous-chef may be responsible for producing menu items and supervising the kitchen. When the executive chef is absent or off duty, the sous-chef performs the duties of the executive chef.

**6-13** The executive chef helps train the other chefs in the kitchen staff.

*CandyBox Images/Shutterstock.com*

Sous-chefs may also be responsible for scheduling employees and may take over for other chefs as needed. The sous-chef often serves as the expediter or announcer who accepts the orders from the dining room staff. He or she relays the orders to the station chefs and then reviews the dishes for corrections before they are served to the customers.

### Kitchen Manager

In a chain restaurant, the person responsible for the menu is the *corporate executive chef*. He or she is located at the corporate headquarters. The corporate executive chef is responsible for the menu development for all the units of the chain. Sometimes a team of corporate executive chefs will work on the menus.

As a result, there will not be an executive chef in each unit of the chain. Instead each unit will have a kitchen manager. A **kitchen manager** is the top manager in the kitchen of a unit of a chain restaurant. He or she is responsible for kitchen operations. This manager may be called the *kitchen professional* or the *culinary manager*.

## Steward

Every restaurant must have clean glassware, silverware, and plateware. Every kitchen must have clean utensils and equipment. These items must be not only clean, but also sanitary. The people who take care of this area are the steward and the dishwashing crew, **6-14**. Without them, the restaurant would come to a complete standstill.

The **steward** supervises the dishwashing, pot washing, and cleanup. The steward usually does the purchasing of the glassware, flatware, and plateware. This includes selecting products, management of inventory, bidding of products, receiving products, inspections, and storing of products. This person also keeps track of the china, glassware, and flatware in the restaurant. The steward must make sure the restaurant never runs out of clean dishes. He or she is also responsible for the general cleanliness of the kitchen.

The **dishwasher** has the responsibility of operating the dishwashing machine. He or she also hand washes large items like pots and heavily soiled items in large sinks called *pot sinks*. The dishwasher has major responsibility for keeping all dishes and utensils sanitary. If dishes and utensils are not sanitary, diseases could be spread to customers.

Julie Flavin Photography/Shutterstock.com

**6-14**  A steward is in charge of all a restaurant's plateware.

## Food Preparers

Food preparers include chefs, cooks, and expediters. The exact titles and organization of the kitchen vary from restaurant to restaurant.

### Chefs

A **chef** is a professional cook. To become a chef requires a considerable amount of training and experience. The traditional titles and responsibilities of chefs in fine-dining and hotel kitchens were developed by the great French chef Auguste Escoffier (1846-1935). He organized the kitchen into stations and created specific positions with specific tasks at each station. The original name for each position was in French. Many of these positions are still called by their French names. The general name for the various chefs is *station chefs* or *line cooks*. In French the name is *chefs de partie*. Escoffier's system for organizing the kitchen is called the *kitchen brigade*, **6-15**.

| Escoffier's Kitchen Brigade | | |
|---|---|---|
| **Title in English** | **Title in French** | **Tasks** |
| Station Chefs | *Chefs de partie* | |
| Sauté Chef | *Saucier* | Sautéed items and their sauces |
| Fish Chef | *Poissonier* | Fish dishes and their sauces |
| Roast Chef | *Rôtisseur* | Roasted foods and their sauces |
| Grill Chef | *Grillardin* | Grilled foods |
| Fry Chef | *Friturier* | Fried foods |
| Vegetable Chef | *Entremetier* | Hot appetizers, soups, vegetables, starches, pastas, eggs |
| Pantry Chef | *Garde Manger* | Cold foods, such as salads, cold appetizers, pâtés, salad dressings, sandwiches |
| Pastry Chef | *Pâtissier* | Baked items, pastries, desserts |
| Baker | *Boulanger* | Breads, rolls |
| Butcher | *Boucher* | Butcher meats, poultry |
| Swing Cook | *Tournant* | Works where needed |

*Goodheart-Willcox Publisher*

**6-15** The great French chef Auguste Escoffier organized the kitchen into separate stations and created a chef position in charge of each station.

Today, most fine-dining and hotel restaurants use a simplified version of Escoffier's kitchen brigade. For example, very few restaurants have their own pastry chef and bakers. Many commercial bakeries can meet the needs of restaurants. In addition, restaurant chains and commercial bakeries have developed frozen baked products. These products are quick and easy to prepare, as well as delicious.

## Cooks

A **cook** is a person who prepares food for eating. Casual restaurants usually have one or more cooks who prepare the meals. These cooks may be called *line cooks*, *station cooks*, or *short-order cooks*. They are often organized into two groups: hot food cooks and cold food cooks. There may also be a prep cook.

## Expediter

Most casual, fine-dining, and hotel restaurants have an expediter. The **expediter** is the member of the culinary staff who gets the orders from the servers, gives them to the station chefs or line cooks, and checks the orders before they are picked up.

# Chapter 6 Review

## Chapter Summary

- The general manager is responsible for the overall operation of the restaurant.
- The front-of-the-house is responsible for the following six functions: seating guests, selling food, transmitting orders to the kitchen, serving customers, bussing tables, and obtaining payment from customers.
- A critical part of the restaurant business is getting the customers' orders to the kitchen and then getting the correct orders back to the correct customers.
- Front-of-the-house staff consists of one or more managers, host or hostess, servers, bussers, and cashiers.
- The restaurant manager is responsible for everything that happens in the front-of-the-house.
- The back-of-the-house is responsible for the following seven functions: food production; purchasing and receiving; marketing and sales; human resources; accounting; security; and engineering and maintenance.
- The back-of-the-house staff consists of one or more managers; staff responsible for cleaning and maintaining plateware, flatware, glassware, and utensils; and food production staff.
- The executive chef is responsible for the menu and the kitchen operations.
- Without the steward and the dishwashing crew, a restaurant would come to a complete standstill.

## Review

1. Describe the front-of-the-house of a restaurant.
2. List six responsibilities of the general manager.
3. List and explain each of the six functions of the front-of-the-house.
4. List and explain the five steps in transmitting an order.
5. Describe the role of the POS in transmitting orders to the kitchen.
6. List six responsibilities of the restaurant manager.
7. List the seven functions of the back-of-the-house.
8. List five responsibilities of the executive chef.
9. Explain the difference between an executive chef of an independent restaurant and a kitchen manager in the unit of a chain restaurant.
10. Why is the work of the steward and dishwashing crew important?

# Critical Thinking

11. **Identify.** Discuss ways that servers can use suggestive selling.

12. **Analyze.** What are the advantages to wireless paging systems in both the front- and back-of-the-house?

13. **Predict.** How would the business be affected if the front-of-the-house and the back-of-the-house do not work together? How might guests be affected?

14. **Debate.** As a class, debate the following question: Who has the more difficult job in a foodservice operation—front-of-the-house servers or back-of-the-house cooks?

15. **Draw conclusions.** Discuss advantages and disadvantages of restaurants that require reservations.

16. **Compare and contrast.** Interview one front-of-the-house employee and one back-of-the-house employee from a local restaurant of your choice. Ask them about their job responsibilities. Summarize your interviews in a report to the class. After all students have given their reports, discuss the similarities and differences apparent in positions from each category.

## Common Core
### College and Career Readiness

17. **Writing.** Imagine you are the general manager of a restaurant. You need a new executive chef. Write a description of the ideal person for the job.

18. **Speaking.** Investigate the types of call-ahead seating methods offered in five local restaurants. How do these methods help keep waiting time in the restaurant to a minimum? Give an oral report on your findings.

19. **Writing.** Imagine you are a restaurant manager in the days before computer systems. Write a detailed procedure for getting the orders of a party of four to the kitchen. Then write a detailed procedure for getting the correct order to the correct customer.

20. **Listening.** Interview a restaurant manager about the use of a POS system. Prepare questions in advance.

21. **Writing.** Investigate environmentally friendly procedures that restaurant employees could use. Write a summary of your findings, including advantages and disadvantages of each.

22. **CTE Career Readiness Practice.** Suppose you work for a popular restaurant. Your supervisor gives you the following problem to solve: the restaurant is consistently overbooking, and customers with reservations are finding long waits for tables. Some customers leave rather than wait for a table, and word-of-mouth about the restaurant is becoming negative. Your first effort to creatively solving the problem is to ask questions. Create a mind map like the following to dig deeper into the problem.

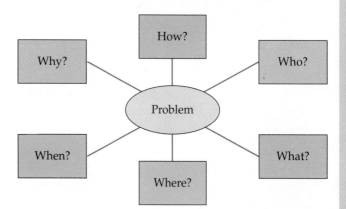

# Chapter 7

## Hotel Food and Services

## Chapter Objectives

After studying this chapter, you will be able to

- **describe** the role of the food and beverage director.
- **explain** how a banquet is booked.
- **list** the responsibilities of each member of the banquet staff.
- **contrast** the four styles of banquet service.
- **explain** the role of the banquet manager during the banquet.
- **describe** the functions of the room service department.
- **describe** the role of the bartender and servers in monitoring alcohol consumption.

## Before You Read

Try to answer the following questions before you read this chapter.

- What hotel staff members are involved in banquet planning?
- What types of services are included in hotel beverage service?

## Terms to Know

food and beverage director
banquet
convention
function
clients
banquet event order
banquet manager
banquet chef
banquet servers
banquet setup staff

station
passed-items function
seated buffet
seated banquet
skirting
break down
room service
room service manager
bar

front bar
service bar
special-purpose bar
beverage manager
hospitality suite
minibar
bartender
beverage server
bar back

Most lodging properties offer some kind of food and beverage service. Such service can range from a simple offering of coffee and sweet rolls in the lobby to a full-service fine-dining restaurant, **7-1**. Examples of lodging foodservice include full-service dining rooms, coffee shops, cafes, snack bars, room service (in-room dining), carryout service, and banquets. Examples of lodging beverage services include cocktail lounges, bars, service bars, banquet bar service, and minibars in guestrooms.

## Organization

The organization of foodservices in a lodging property depends on the size and number of foodservices offered. Some hotels have a full-service restaurant that is independent of the hotel. Such restaurants are organized and managed in the same way as an independent restaurant. The restaurant just happens to be located within a hotel.

Many hotels manage their own foodservices. A typical hotel will have a cocktail lounge, a full-service dining room, a banquet department, and room service. Many hotels have more than one restaurant. For example, a hotel might have a coffee shop, an ethnic restaurant, a snack shop, and an elegant fine-dining restaurant.

The manager in charge of all the food and beverage services in the hotel is called the **food and beverage director**. He or she reports to the hotel's general manager. The food and beverage director is usually responsible for five departments: beverages, dining room, kitchen, banquets, and room service. Each of these departments has a manager who reports to the food and beverage director: the beverage manager, the dining room manager, the executive chef, the banquet manager, and the room service manager, **7-2**.

Two of the departments, dining room and kitchen, are organized and managed in ways very similar to an independent restaurant. One of the major differences between an independent restaurant and a hotel dining room is that the hotel dining room usually offers three meals a day and is open seven days a week. An independent restaurant might serve only lunch and dinner or only dinner and be closed one day a week. In an independent restaurant, the executive chef is responsible for that one restaurant. In a hotel, the executive chef will be responsible for all the foodservices in the hotel, including all dining rooms, coffee shops, snack shops, banquets, and room service.

The rest of this chapter will focus on three departments: the banquet department, room service, and the beverage department.

7-1   This lodging property includes a coffee bar in the lobby.

*zhu difeng/Shutterstock.com*

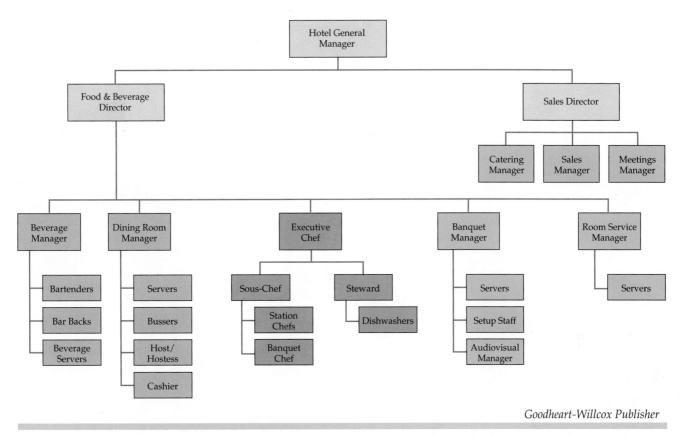

Goodheart-Willcox Publisher

**7-2** Each hotel has its own organization. Many hotels follow the general organization in this figure.

# Banquet Department

The banquet department handles all special food events at a hotel. A **banquet** is food served in honor of a special occasion. Usually, large numbers of people eat at the same time at a banquet. There are two types: business banquets and social banquets. These categories are basically the same as the two types of catering. The term *banquet* includes receptions.

Business banquets are often planned during conventions and business meetings. A **convention** is a large meeting, usually sponsored by a group for its members. Many industries and professions have professional associations. Professional associations often hold conventions for their members, **7-3**. For example, the following groups hold conventions: teachers, physicians, hospitality professionals, automobile manufacturers, technology businesses, and air conditioning equipment representatives. In addition, career and technical student organizations hold conventions. During a convention, banquets are held for business meetings, awards ceremonies, receptions, networking,

and socializing. Business banquets are often held for holiday celebrations and other business-related special events.

Social banquets are held for a variety of celebrations. Weddings, bar and bat mitzvahs, special birthdays, and anniversaries are commonly celebrated by a banquet at a hotel. Other occasions include graduations, school and family reunions, proms, and charity events. **Function** is another term for a special event.

## Booking the Banquet

A banquet is booked through the sales department. (The sales department is sometimes called *Sales and Marketing* or *Sales and Catering*.) The sales department separates banquets into two categories. The first category is the *single event banquet*, where the purpose of the event is the banquet. Single events can be business or social. Business examples would include an office party or a company awards dinner. Social examples would include a wedding or a charity ball. These events usually do not require sleeping rooms, although some of them may. For example, a wedding might require some

Multicultural Foodservice & Hospitality Alliance

**7-3** These college students, who are studying hospitality, are attending the convention of National Society of Minorities in Hospitality (NSMH).

sleeping rooms for out-of-town guests and the bride and groom. These single events are booked by the catering manager. The catering manager works with the client to reserve the banquet and to arrange all the details, **7-4**. Banquet customers are often called **clients**.

The second category is the *meeting banquet*, in which the banquet is just part of a larger event. The larger event requires a block of sleeping rooms and meeting rooms, as well as one or more banquets. Meeting banquets are usually part of a business convention. Examples include the Annual Convention of the American Medical Association and the National Leadership Meeting of the Family, Career, and Community Leaders of America. There are also social conventions for social groups and fan clubs. For example, there are several Official Star Trek Conventions every year. The

convention and the meeting banquets are booked by sales managers. Once the group has decided to book their convention, the sales manager turns the client over to the meetings and banquets manager. The meetings and banquets manager works with the client to arrange all the details of both the convention and the banquets.

One of the jobs of the sales department is to sell the hotel's meeting and banquet services to professional associations and to the general public. When a person or association decides to hold an event or convention at a hotel, they contact someone in the sales department. The catering manager or the meetings and banquets manager will help the client make important decisions about the details that are necessary for a successful event. Some large conferences are booked five years in advance. This advance booking is done to make

7-4 Clients may call the catering manager to discuss the details of a wedding banquet.

*zulufoto/Shutterstock.com*

sure there is enough space for the meetings and banquets. Some conventions attract thousands of attendees. For example, the National Restaurant Association's Annual Restaurant and Hotel Show attracts over 50,000 attendees.

In order for a banquet to take place, the hotel needs to know all the details of what the client wants. The catering manager (for single events) and the meetings and banquets manager (for conventions) meet with their clients to work out all the details. The details include number of people attending the event, time of banquet, type of service, choice of foods, bar and beverage needs, timing of courses, room setup and decor, and audiovisual needs. Once these details have been agreed upon, the catering manager and the meetings and banquet manager write up a banquet event order for each banquet.

The **banquet event order** is a written record of all the decisions that have been made about what the client wants during the banquet. The banquet event order contains instructions for the kitchen, the banquet manager, and the audiovisual department. A copy of this order is then sent to the food and beverage director, the executive chef, the beverage manager, and the banquet manager. All the members of the food and beverage division must work together to make the banquet a success. Many hotels hold daily "BEO" meetings to go over the banquet event orders, plan, and handle changes.

The banquet manager also continues to work with the sales department as necessary. The sales staff is the major link between the client and the banquet manager. The banquet manager is the key person in charge of making sure all the details get accomplished. The banquet manager works with the catering manager or the meetings and banquets manager to make sure that the arrangements meet the clients' needs.

On the day of the banquet, the staff member with whom the client has been working (either the catering manager or the meetings and banquets manager) is there at the beginning of the function to make sure everything meets the client's needs. The client is then introduced to the banquet manager, who takes over from that point and is responsible for everything that happens during the rest of the banquet, **7-5**.

## Banquet Department Staff

Once the banquet event order is submitted to the banquet manager, the banquet department is

7-5 Good communication with the banquet manager will help ensure that a client's banquet requirements are met.

*Deklofenak/Shutterstock.com*

responsible for making sure that all the details are handled and the banquet runs smoothly. Everyone who works in the banquet department must be very detail-oriented. The staff includes the banquet manager, servers, setup staff, and audiovisual staff. The banquet chef is a critical part of the banquet team; however, he or she is technically part of the kitchen staff.

## Banquet Manager

The **banquet manager** is responsible for making sure that all aspects of each banquet run smoothly. The banquet manager is also responsible for making sure the instructions from the sales department and clients are carried out.

One of the major responsibilities of the banquet manager is to hire and schedule workers. The number of workers needed varies with the number of banquets and conventions scheduled. During a week with no conventions, few workers are needed. However, there are weeks when several conventions and banquets are scheduled for each day. The banquet manager must be sure to schedule enough workers and often hires temporary or part-time banquet workers when more are needed, **7-6**.

The banquet manager supervises the banquet staff and all banquets that are in progress. The main job of the banquet manager is to make sure the client does not have to worry about anything related to the event. When a banquet function is being set up and while it is taking place, the banquet manager supervises many different employees. The banquet manager will see that the function runs smoothly.

One of the major tasks of the banquet manager is to prepare a timeline for the event, **7-7**. The timeline is helpful to make sure that all tasks are performed in a punctual manner. It also serves as a checklist to make sure everything that needs to be done gets done.

7-6 Many workers are needed to staff a large banquet.

| | | Banquet Setup Timeline | |
|---|---|---|---|
| **Start** | **Complete** | **Task** | **Staff** |
| 5:00 | 5:00 | Report to Grand Ballroom | All |
| 5:00 | 5:15 | Staff Meeting; setup assignments given out | All |
| 5:15 | 5:30 | Tablecloths on tables | Anthony, Juan |
| | | Knives on tables | Emily, Tamika |
| | | Forks on tables | Maria, Courtney |
| | | Spoons on tables | Jake, Grace |
| 5:30 | 5:45 | Table numbers on tables | Anthony, Juan |
| | | Napkins on tables | Anthony, Juan |
| | | Butter knives on tables | Emily, Tamika |
| | | Dessert forks on tables | Maria, Courtney |
| | | Dessert spoons on tables | Jake, Grace |
| 5:45 | 6:00 | Water glasses on tables | Anthony, Juan |
| | | Champagne glasses on tables | Emily, Tamika |
| | | Coffee cups and saucers on tables | Maria, Courtney |
| | | Bread and butter plates on tables | Jake, Grace |
| 6:00 | 6:20 | Skirt head table | Emily, Tamika, Courtney, Maria, Jake, Grace |
| | | Butters on table | Anthony, Juan |
| 6:20 | 6:50 | Fruit cocktail and creamers on tables | Anthony, Juan, Jake, Grace |
| | | Pour water into each glass | Emily, Tamika, Maria, Courtney |
| 6:50 | 7:00 | Pour champagne | All |
| | 7:00 | Room completely set up | |

*Goodheart-Willcox Publisher*

7-7 The banquet manager prepares a timeline to make sure everything is done on time.

## Banquet Chef

The banquet chef is a member of the kitchen staff. However, he or she works closely with the banquet manager. The **banquet chef** is responsible for feeding all large groups in the hotel. Food trays for a buffet and showpieces, such as ice sculptures, are also the banquet chef's responsibility.

The banquet chef makes sure the kitchen is ready for the food preparation for banquets.

Banquet sizes can range from 30 to 3,000 people. The average banquet size is 250. The banquet chef supervises the organization, preparation, and timing of the banquet service. For large banquets, plating the food is a major undertaking. The banquet chef will create an example of how the plate should look. He or she will then set up an assembly line, using all available workers, to plate the food.

Some hotels have more than one banquet chef. The number of banquet chefs needed depends on the number and frequency of banquet functions at the hotel.

### Banquet Servers

**Banquet servers** are responsible for serving food and beverages during the banquet. Banquet servers also set the tables before the banquet. Servers are often asked to handle last-minute requests. Extra tables may need to be set up, or two tables may need to be pushed together so a group of guests can sit with one another. Servers may be asked to slow down the service of food because the speaker is running late.

### Banquet Setup Staff

Banquets, especially large ones, are held in huge ballrooms. These rooms have room dividers that can be used to divide the ballroom into areas for several smaller banquets or meetings. The **banquet setup staff** is responsible for moving and arranging the room dividers, tables, and chairs. For example, if a banquet is to serve 480 people, 60 tables that seat eight plus 480 chairs must be moved into the ballroom and arranged. The setup staff will be given a diagram showing them where all the items belong, **7-8**. Often, the same ballroom must be rearranged several times a day to meet the needs of several different meetings or banquets.

### Audiovisual Staff

A hotel may have its own audiovisual department. However, hotels often use an outside company to handle all the audiovisual needs. In that situation, there is an in-house audiovisual manager who works with the outside company to make the arrangements. Audiovisual equipment includes projection screens as well as slide, overhead, and data-projection systems. Sound equipment includes microphones, public address systems, and music equipment (speakers; amplifiers; and compact disc, DVD, and digital media players).

**7-8** The banquet setup staff will get a diagram of the room arrangement. The diagram will include the location of all furniture. The lines with arrows show the traffic flow.

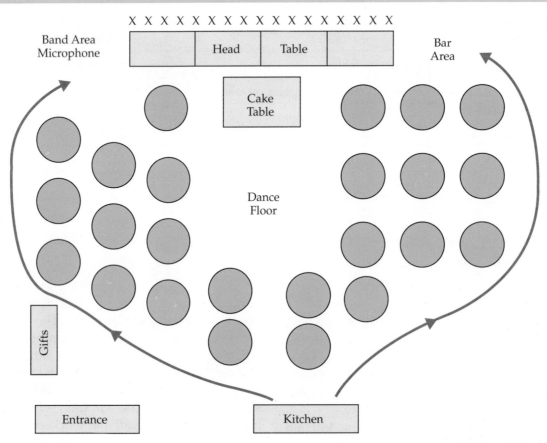

# Roberto Alicea— *Young Chef with Flavor*

*David Carlson*

Roberto Alicea was passionate about food from a young age. As the son of a Puerto Rican father and an Italian mother, he was exposed to flavors from both cultures. Roberto's family gathered around the table three times a day for his mother's home-cooked meals. Italian dinners at his grandmother's house were a Sunday tradition.

In his teen years, Roberto's job as a cook at the Hyatt Regency Chicago hotel helped him escape from the violence of his inner-city Chicago neighborhood. Roberto got an early start on his career by graduating ahead of his class. Roberto's parents hoped he would go to college, but instead Roberto chose to train as a chef. His parents encouraged him to do his best, and he has done just that. Today, Roberto is the chef de cuisine at The Park Grill and executive chef of the Park Hyatt Hotel Los Angeles.

Despite being young, Roberto has an impressive résumé. His career path has been short but fast-paced. In less than 10 years, Roberto went from training to becoming an acclaimed executive chef. In between, he worked at several restaurants, including three Hyatt hotel restaurants in Chicago. Most recently, Roberto was the demi chef de cuisine at Nomi, located in the Intercontinental Los Angeles Century City hotel.

Roberto's menus are well liked because of his focus on natural flavors. He starts with quality meats and produce combined with unique sauces to create unforgettable flavors. Guests enjoy his one-of-a-kind style and culinary flair.

## Roberto Alicea's Career Path

**1975:** Born in Chicago, Illinois

**1990:** Worked at Little Caesar's Pizza restaurant

**1993:** Prep cook, All Seasons Restaurant, Hyatt Regency Hotel Chicago

**1994:** Graduated from Roberto Clemente High School

**1995:** Studied at La Coquina in Orlando, Florida

**1997:** Worked at One Sixty Blue restaurant as a sauté cook

**2000:** Demi chef de cuisine at Nomi restaurant

**2002:** Executive chef of The Park Grill in Los Angeles, California

**2010:** Opened Andaz on 5th Avenue in New York City; noted for supporting local farmers and purveyors

# Banquet Service

Planning, organizing, and running a banquet requires coordination among many departments and staff members.

## *Types of Service*

The banquet department offers several different styles of service. There are four popular styles of banquet service: standing buffet, passed-items function, seated buffet, and seated banquet. *Buffet* is the general term used for meal service in which the food is set out on tables and guests help themselves. The location in the room where food or beverage is available is called a **station**. Sometimes there are servers at a station. For example, at a brunch, there might be an omelet station with a chef to make the omelets to order.

### Standing Buffet

Standing buffets are designed so people will socialize. The food served is *finger food*, or food that is easy to eat with your fingers. Examples include cheese and crackers, sliders, vegetables and dip, and cocktail hot dogs. Usually the food stations are scattered around the room to encourage mingling. These stations are also called *kiosks*. Beverage service is provided. Guests walk around the tables and help themselves. Usually, there are no tables and chairs, or maybe only a few scattered around the edges of the room. Dirty dishes are placed on trays that are provided. Standing buffets are popular for cocktail parties and receptions.

### Passed-Items Function

The **passed-items function** is a type of standing buffet. Instead of food on buffet tables, servers walk around the room with food and beverages on trays, **7-9**. Guests take items from these trays as the servers walk around. The food served is also finger food. Sometimes the food is fancier than the food at a standing buffet. Examples include miniature quiches, shrimp skewers, and fancy hors d'oeuvres. This style of service is also used to encourage people to socialize and is popular for cocktail parties and receptions.

### Seated Buffet

At a **seated buffet**, tables are set and guests choose or are assigned a place at a table. Guests serve themselves from a buffet table and then return to

Eric Limon/Shutterstock.com

**7-9** Appetizers such as these are easy for guests to eat during a passed-items function.

their seats to eat. There is also a beverage station. Servers clear dirty dishes. The food can be anything from a simple lunch to an elaborate dinner. Sometimes beverages or some parts of the meal are served by servers. For example, guests may serve themselves everything except beverages. Servers would serve beverages and clear the tables. Sometimes the first course, often the salad course, is set on the table before guests arrive.

### Seated Banquet

At a **seated banquet**, tables are set and guests choose or are assigned a place at a table. Servers serve all parts of the meal. The food is usually plated in the kitchen and brought to guests by servers. Sometimes Russian service is used for a seated banquet. Everyone eats at the same time. Beverages are also served, although sometimes there is a bar station in the room. Often, everyone is served the same food, **7-10**. Sometimes there may be a choice of main course. The servers also clear dirty dishes.

### Selecting Type of Service

When the client and the banquet manager choose the style of service, they must consider the number of guests and the cost. Most clients have a budget, and what they decide to do often depends on that budget. A seated banquet is usually less expensive than a buffet. In a seated banquet, you know the exact number of guests and each guest is served the same amount of food.

## Décor and Table Settings

Décor and table settings are a very important part of banquet service. They set the mood and the ambiance of the event. The theme of the event

**7-10** Seated banquet guests are often served the same food, which is plated in the kitchen.

*Eric Limon/Shutterstock.com*

and the color scheme are usually chosen by the client, with advice from the catering or meetings and banquet staff. Different rooms in the hotel are often decorated in different ways to accommodate various types of events. One room might be smaller with more modern decor. The large ballroom is often decorated with many fancy chandeliers, mirrors, and wallpaper with golden colors.

Buffet tables and food stations are decorated to make the food look appetizing. Flowers, fruits, vegetables, ice sculptures, and food sculptures can be used as decorations. Often great effort is devoted to the table décor. Many banquets have elaborate centerpieces that match the theme of the event.

Table linens such as tablecloths, napkins, and table skirting also add to the ambiance of the room. Table linens are available in a wide variety of colors and fabrics. **Skirting** is a table linen placed around buffet tables to hide the table legs and make the table look elegant. The skirting can help set the theme of the event. White skirting is used for weddings, silver skirting is used for anniversaries and New Year's celebrations, and colorful skirting is used for holiday and birthday parties, **7-11**. Linens must be cleaned and properly ironed. Wrinkled and stained linens detract from an appealing and well-set table.

Place settings are designed based on the menu that will be served. Flatware, glassware, and plateware should be chosen to match the food that will be served. For example, if soup will be served, each place setting must have a soupspoon. Napkin folds should match the theme of the function. Because so many people must be served at once, the food must be served quickly and efficiently. In order to serve guests quickly, the utensils are set on the table before the banquet begins.

## Setup

Setup for a banquet is more than just setting the tables. Before the tables can be set, the room must be set up with appropriate tables, chairs, service equipment, and audiovisual equipment. Different types of events require different types of setups.

The amount of time needed for the setup depends on the type of banquet. For example, a reception can be set up more quickly than a served sit-down meal. If the banquet room will be empty several days or hours before the event begins, the

*Goncharuk/Shutterstock.com*

7-11 Décor and table settings create the ambiance of a banquet.

setup can be scheduled during slow time periods. However, if the banquet room is occupied until 5:00 p.m. and you need to set up the room for a 7:00 p.m. reception, time becomes critical. This type of schedule requires an adequate number of workers, so the banquet manager must be sure to schedule enough. In many hotels, members of other departments often pitch in and help when time is limited.

## Room Arrangement

Identify the type of room setup that is best suited for the event. Meeting rooms require different setups from banquet and reception rooms. There should be enough space for all guests to sit or stand comfortably and room for the servers to walk around and serve. Space should also be allowed for any additional activities. For example, some banquets require a dance floor and a band. Others require a speaker's podium and a raised

area for speakers or important guests. Some require audiovisual equipment.

A diagram will be made to show the setup staff how to arrange the room. The banquet manager usually prepares this diagram. The diagram should show where each guest would sit and the flow of traffic for both guests and servers. Refer again to Figure 7-8. The diagram should also indicate space for special service equipment, audiovisual equipment, and any special activities.

Meeting rooms have several standard room arrangements. The two most commonly used are the theater style and the schoolroom style, **7-12**.

## Audiovisual Equipment and Lighting

Many banquets, both business and social, require audiovisual equipment. Many business banquets feature a speaker or a panel of speakers. Speakers require microphones, and many require an electronic presentation system. Social banquets

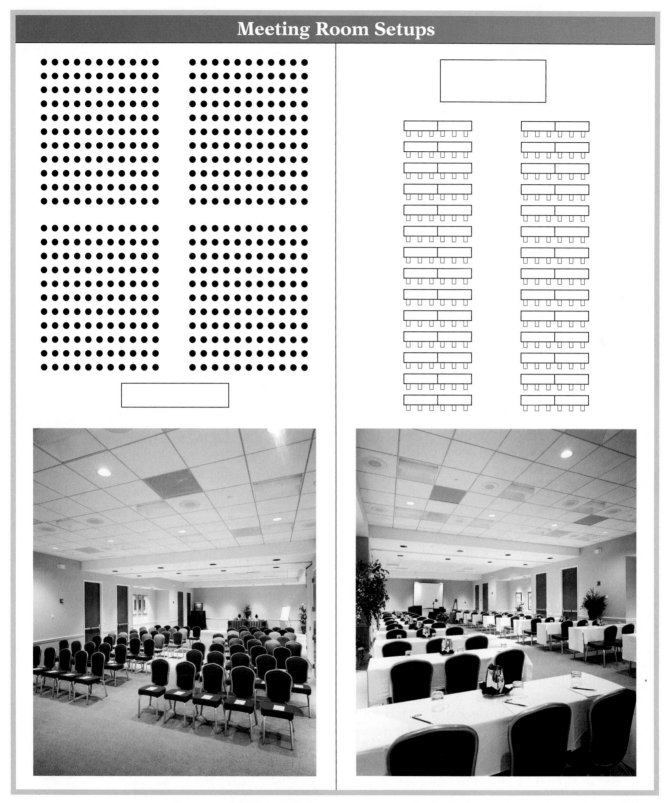

**Meeting Room Setups**

*Diagrams by Goodheart-Willcox Publisher. Photos courtesy of The Speedway Club, Texas Motor Speedway*

**7-12** Meeting rooms are often arranged theater style or schoolroom style.

may also have speakers. It has become popular to show electronic presentations during the banquet for weddings, anniversaries, and other special social events. When arrangements are being finalized for a banquet, clients indicate on a form any audiovisual equipment they might need. It is important to select the proper equipment. Larger rooms require more powerful sound and visual systems.

The lighting for a function is extremely important. Lighting that is too harsh can ruin the atmosphere. Too little lighting could prevent guests from seeing each other and their beautifully prepared meals. Lighting for functions generally includes dimmers, chase or rope lights, and spotlights. A spotlight can be used to highlight a speaker or a bride and groom as they dance. Dimmer lights are used to make the lighting lower when a video is being shown or brighter to accentuate a speaker. Most hotels can also provide a variety of special effects, including fireworks, falling balloons, fog, thunder, rain, and even imitation snow.

All equipment must be placed in such a way that no one will trip over the equipment or the cords. Electrical cords are taped to the floor. Brakes are set on rolling carts so they do not roll. Guest and server safety is very important during a banquet.

### Temperature

The temperature of a room should be comfortable for guests. If a room is too cold, the guests will be miserable because they are cold. If a room is too warm, the guests will get sleepy. Check with your guests to make sure the room temperature is pleasant.

## Breakdown

After the function is over, the banquet or meeting room must be broken down. To **break down** a banquet room means to clear dishes and food, clean tables and chairs, put away all furniture and equipment, and clean the floor.

All silverware, glassware, and plateware that were not removed during the banquet should be removed. All must be washed, dried, and put away. The special service equipment must be removed. Equipment should be removed carefully to avoid accidents. For example, the hot water that was used to heat chafing dishes could spill and cause serious burns.

Dirty linens must be taken to the laundry. Tables and chairs must be wiped down and dried before they are stored. Storing dirty chairs and tables can attract insects and rodents. Storing wet wooden tables can cause permanent watermarks to form. Audiovisual and other equipment must be carefully removed and properly stored to prevent breakage. Floors should be swept and mopped. The banquet room is now ready for the next event.

# Room Service

**Room service**, or *in-room dining*, is the delivery of food and beverages to guests in their hotel rooms, **7-13**. The room service department manages room service deliveries. The amount of room service offered varies. Some hotels offer 24-hour room service while others have limited hours. The room service department is usually located in the hotel kitchen.

Guests order room service from a menu in the hotel room. The guest calls room service on the phone and places the order. In some hotels, the guests may be able to order room service through an interactive menu on the television. Many hotels use a doorknob menu for ordering breakfast. Each room gets a menu that contains a breakfast menu/order form. Guests select the breakfast items they want and the time they want it to be delivered. Guests must hang the menus on the outside doorknob of the room, usually before 1 a.m. A room service representative will pick up the menu/order forms during the night and deliver them to the kitchen.

7-13 Most full-service hotels have room service for their guests' convenience.

ampyang/Shutterstock.com

The menus let the kitchen know how many breakfasts are needed and by what time. Breakfast will be delivered at the designated time to the proper room the next morning. This is a great customer service feature.

In some hotels, meals are delivered on fancy carts. Guests can use these carts as their dining table. In other hotels, room service meals are delivered on trays. The food is covered by a plate cover to keep hot food hot and cold food cold.

## Room Service Staff

The size of the room service staff depends on the size of the hotel, room service hours, and the number of guests who usually order room service. The room service staff usually consists of a room service manager and room service servers.

The **room service manager** supervises all room service operations. He or she usually has an office or work area in the kitchen. The manager usually takes the room service orders over the phone. The manager also coordinates with the kitchen so guests will receive their meals promptly. If the hotel has a POS, room service will use the same system.

The employees who deliver the food to guest rooms are called the *room service servers*, **7-14**. They are responsible for delivering the food and collecting payment from the guests. The guests can pay by cash or credit card, or they can sign the guest check to charge the meal to the room. The guests will pay their room service bill when they pay their hotel room bill.

When guests finish their room service meals, they place the cart or tray outside the guest room. Room service servers occasionally check the halls of the hotel for room service carts and trays. Some hotels ask the guests to call room service when they want their carts or trays to be picked up. Then the servers will return to the room to collect the carts and trays.

# Beverage Department

The beverage department includes all of the bars in the hotel. A **bar** is a place that serves alcoholic beverages as well as nonalcoholic beverages. The three types of bars are front bars, service bars, and special-purpose bars. A **front bar** has one or more bartenders. The bartenders serve the public

erwinova/Shutterstock.com

**7-14**  Room service servers carry meals to the guests' rooms.

face-to-face. In a **service bar**, servers take customer orders and give them to the bartender. The bartender makes the drinks, which the servers then serve to the customers. Service bars are found in cocktail lounges. A cocktail lounge is usually an attractive and comfortable room where people can sit, relax, and have a beverage and snacks.

A **special-purpose bar** is usually set up for one particular event, such as a banquet, **7-15**. Portable bars are placed in the hall outside the banquet room to serve guests while they wait. Portable bars are sometimes placed inside of the banquet room to provide beverage service for guests during an event. The portable bar is taken away when the event has ended.

7-15 A special-purpose bar might be used to serve guests at a wedding reception.

## Beverage Department Staff

The beverage department usually has four types of employees: the beverage manager, bartenders, bar backs, and beverage servers. The beverage manager reports to the food and beverage director.

The **beverage manager** usually oversees the hotel's front bars, service bars, special-purpose bars, room service beverage deliveries, hospitality suite bars, and minibars. The job description of the beverage manager is similar to that of the executive chef. They both supervise departments that create finished menu products and serve them to guests. The finished products of the beverage department are alcoholic and nonalcoholic drinks.

A **hospitality suite** is a special room in a hotel that is reserved by a group for the purpose of serving refreshments to the group. Hospitality suites are usually stocked with snack foods and have bar service.

A **minibar** is a small cabinet containing small bottles of alcoholic beverages and snacks. The minibars are located in guest rooms and are locked. If guests want to use the minibars, they use the key they are given at check-in. They can select their beverages and snacks from the minibar. A

beverage staff member checks each minibar each day, notes what was taken, charges those items to the guest, and restocks the minibar. The guests are charged for all their minibar purchases when they check out of the hotel.

The beverage manager oversees all the bars, hires and trains the staff, and does all the purchasing and inventory in order to control beverage costs. The banquet department works with the beverage manager to develop beverage menus for special events. They also work together to evaluate products and services.

The **bartender** concentrates on alcoholic-beverage production and service to guests. He or she prepares the cocktails and other beverages such as beer, wine, coffee, tea, and soft drinks that are served in the bars. In some hotels, the same person who prepares drinks also serves them. That person is the bartender. When a service bar is used, the preparation of drinks and serving are separated. A **beverage server** takes orders for beverages and gives the orders to the bartender. The server then serves the drinks and takes payment.

Bartenders are sometimes assisted by bar backs. A **bar back** is responsible for making sure the bar is stocked with liquor, ice, glassware, and supplies. The bar back works in the back of the bar.

# Going Green

## Growing Popularity of Boxed Wines

In the United States, most wines come in glass bottles. However, in many European countries, wine—even high-end wines—also come in cartons. These boxed wines are beating bottled wines in international wine competitions. Given the many advantages of the box packaging format over bottle, the sales of boxed wines is becoming a trend in the United States.

Boxes are more economical because the packaging costs less to manufacture and transport. Box packaging is also environmentally friendly. It requires less energy to produce and less fuel to transport than heavier bottles. The boxes are made of recyclable materials and can easily be folded flat and stored until recycled. Unlike glass containers, the lightweight boxes are easy to handle and store, and they do not shatter. Boxed wines have a longer shelf life than bottled wines.

The quality and taste of boxed wines can sometimes surpass that of bottled wines. Wine can degrade in bottles because glass does not fully protect the wine from UV light, which affects its quality and taste. Also, once opened and poured, a bottle fills with oxygen, which can also degrade the wine. Boxed wine is held in an inner bag inside the box. When wine is dispensed, the bag collapses on itself, leaving little room for oxygen to enter. Although more high-end wines are being sold in cartons, aged wines must still be sold in bottles.

One of the major responsibilities of bartenders and beverage servers is to monitor the alcohol consumption by guests and to prevent alcohol-related problems, **7-16**. Places that serve alcohol usually develop an alcohol service policy. The goal of this policy is to prevent alcohol-related problems from occurring. The policy usually includes enforcing local and state liquor laws, checking identification for anyone who looks younger than 30, keeping track of how much alcohol guests have consumed, and suggesting that guests eat something along with their alcoholic beverages. The policy usually also includes how to handle guests who are showing signs of being affected by alcohol. Many restaurants and bars encourage designated driver programs. They also often have a relationship with a dependable cab company and post its phone number in many places. All bartenders and beverage servers should be trained to prevent problems before they occur. They must learn how to handle situations in ways that do not create more problems and do not embarrass guests.

7-16  Bartenders and beverage servers should be trained to prevent alcohol-related problems.

*Hyatt Hotels Corporation*

# Chapter 7
## Review

## Chapter Summary

- The manager in charge of all the food and beverage services in the hotel is called the food and beverage director.
- A banquet is booked through the sales department.
- The staff includes the banquet manager, servers, setup staff, and audiovisual staff.
- The banquet chef is a critical part of the banquet team; however, he or she is technically part of the kitchen staff.
- There are four popular styles of banquet service: standing buffet, passed-items function, seated buffet, and seated banquet.
- The banquet manager is responsible for making sure all aspects of each banquet run smoothly.
- The room service department manages room service deliveries.
- One of the major responsibilities of bartenders and beverage servers is to monitor the alcohol consumption by guests and to prevent alcohol-related problems.

## Review

1. List the managers who report to the food and beverage director.
2. Describe the difference between a single event banquet and a meeting banquet.
3. Explain the importance of the banquet event order.
4. Describe the responsibilities of each member of the banquet staff.
5. Explain the differences among the four popular banquet styles.
6. Which banquet style is usually the least expensive? Why?
7. Describe the setup and breakdown for a banquet.
8. What is another term used for *room service*?
9. Explain how a guest can get room service for breakfast.
10. List the four types of employees in the beverage department and describe their responsibilities.

# Critical Thinking

11. **Determine.** Describe the detailed information that is needed on a banquet event order.

12. **Create.** Develop a room setup diagram for a standing buffet. Be sure to note the locations of all food and beverage stations.

13. **Draw conclusions.** What foods would you suggest serving at a standing buffet for participants at a technology conference? Justify your responses.

14. **Design.** Using colored markers or pencils, create a complete banquet tablesetting for eight. Develop a theme or occasion for the banquet and make your tablesetting fit that theme.

15. **Assess.** Imagine you are a businessperson who is meeting with the catering manager to plan a banquet for 300 people. Make a list of questions you will ask the catering manager in order to make sure that your banquet is successful.

16. **Organize.** Plan a banquet. Decide the occasion for the banquet, such as a wedding or prom. Select the style of banquet, select a menu, and plan the place setting to match the menu. Develop a timeline for preparing and serving the banquet.

# Common Core

**College and Career Readiness**

17. **Speaking.** Role-play the interaction between a meeting and banquets manager and the president of a student career organization who is planning an annual convention.

18. **Speaking.** Use the Internet to find information on creating fancy napkins folds. If possible, find and view demonstration videos. Practice making three different types of napkin folds and demonstrate your techniques to the class.

19. **Writing.** Summarize and describe the responsibilities of catering managers.

20. **Reading.** Research how ice sculptures are created. Answer questions such as the following:
    - Why is some ice cloudy and other ice crystals clear?
    - How is salt used? What effect does it have on the sculpture, and why?
    - What is aluminum welding? How can ice be welded?

21. **CTE Career Readiness Practice.** Presume you are in charge of decorations for banquets and receptions at a hotel. You have a staff of creative-thinking employees who are dedicated to beautiful decorations at reasonable prices. Get together with your staff (two or more classmates) and brainstorm a list of several possible ideas for creating elegant, affordable wedding reception decorations. Then narrow the list to the three best options. How would you implement one of these options? What roles would the employees play? What criteria will you use to determine how well goals are met?

# Chapter *8*
## Purchasing and Receiving

## Chapter Objectives

After studying this chapter, you will be able to
- **describe** the role of the purchaser.
- **list** the five main tasks of purchasing.
- **explain** the purpose of a specification.
- **outline** the process of selecting a supplier.
- **relate** how a purchase order is used.
- **describe** the three tasks of receiving.
- **determine** why proper storage is important in restaurants.
- **describe** the two main tasks of inventory.

## Before You Read

Try to answer the following questions before you read this chapter.
- Why must all deliveries received be carefully checked according to a restaurant's procedures?
- How are products stored properly to avoid spoilage?

## Terms to Know

| | | |
|---|---|---|
| purchasing | cost-effective buying | credit memorandum |
| receiving | supplier | repackaged foods |
| storage | bid | FIFO |
| inventory | order | issuing |
| purchaser | purchase order | requisitioning |
| specification | receiving dock | requisition form |
| in stock | shipment | inventory control |
| par stock | invoice | physical inventory |
| reorder point | delivery slip | perpetual inventory |
| perishable | | |

**Purchasing** is the buying of goods and services for use in a business. Before a restaurant can make menu items, it must purchase raw foods, equipment, and utensils. A hotel must have guest room furniture and linens to meet guests' needs. In addition, many items get used up or worn out and must be replaced on a regular basis, **8-1**. Raw foods are used up when menu items are made and sold. Guest room linens wear out and must be replaced. Cleaning supplies are needed for daily maintenance of a hotel or restaurant. The businesses from whom goods and services are purchased are called *suppliers*.

**Receiving** is the process of making sure the items delivered are the items that were ordered. Usually, more items are purchased and received than can be used immediately. The items that are not used immediately must be stored. **Storage** is a safe, secure place in which items are placed until they are needed. Once you start storing items, you need to know how much you have in storage. **Inventory** is the process of counting and keeping track of all the items in storage. The word *inventory* also refers to the items that are in storage.

Most businesses perform purchasing, receiving, storage, and inventory. However, the demand on food and beverage businesses is especially high. Foods are used up at a higher rate than many other products that businesses purchase. Food items also have a higher risk of being delivered spoiled or in unusable condition. Therefore, the rest of this chapter will focus on purchasing, receiving, storing, and inventory in foodservice businesses. The general concepts apply to all businesses.

## Staff

In small operations, the owner or manager handles the purchasing role along with other management responsibilities. In larger properties, the owner or manager assigns purchasing to individual department heads. For example, the executive chef or kitchen manager may do the food purchasing, **8-2**.

**8-1** Before a hotel can serve guests, it must have all the things it needs, such as lightbulbs, cleaning supplies, toiletries for guest rooms, and linens.

*prietZone/Shutterstock.com*

Hilton Hotels Corporation

8-2 What are some advantages of the executive chef purchasing the food for a restaurant?

In a hotel, the executive housekeeper may order all supplies for the housekeeping division. Most large businesses have a separate purchasing department. Some businesses have separate departments for purchasing, receiving, and inventory. Sometimes purchasing, receiving, and storage are handled by one department. Inventory is often handled by the accounting department.

Regardless of who does the purchasing, the responsibility of the purchaser is to make sure the operation has everything it needs in the right amounts at the right time. A **purchaser** is an expert in buying goods and services for a business. The purchaser also makes sure to get the best prices for all items purchased. The purchaser's job is to minimize costs and maximize the quality of the supplies.

There are usually several other purchasing positions. The receiving clerk is responsible for the receiving process. The storeroom clerk is responsible for issuing items and sometimes for inventory. There is usually an inventory manager responsible for inventory.

# Purchasing

The goal of purchasing is to make sure that supplies, equipment, and services are available to the operation in amounts needed. This section focuses on the purchase of supplies, particularly food products. Purchasing consists of five main tasks: developing specifications, determining quality, determining quantity, selecting suppliers, and ordering.

## Developing Specifications

Purchasing is a process in which the purchaser orders products from the supplier. In order to meet the purchaser's needs, the supplier has to know exactly what the purchaser wants. If you have ever gone grocery shopping for another person, you know that there are many choices for each food item. For example, consider bananas. Some people like bananas slightly green. Others want bananas that are all yellow. Someone who is making banana bread will want bananas that are starting to get brown speckles. If someone sends you shopping for bananas, he or she will probably specify what kind of bananas are desired.

In the same way, the purchaser must have a detailed description for each food product ordered. A **specification** is a detailed description of the product that is needed. Specifications should include the name of the product, the quality desired, package size, a general description, and any other information that will help the supplier give you exactly what you want, **8-3**. Specifications are sometimes called *specs* for short. The purpose of specifications is to make sure you get the exact

| Food Specification ||
| --- | --- |
| Product Name | Canned Peaches |
| Menu Item | Peach Cobbler |
| General Description | Yellow cling peaches, sliced, in light syrup |
| Grade | U.S. Grade B |
| Brand | Del Monte |
| SKU | NAMP/IMP # PeachS13796 |
| Supplier | Ben E. Keith |
| Packaging | #10 can |
| Pricing Unit | Case |
| Items per Unit | 6 cans per case |
| Special Instructions | |

*Goodheart-Willcox Publisher*

8-3 A specification is a detailed product description.

items you need. Specifications must be detailed and accurate. Specs that are too brief or sloppy may result in the wrong products being purchased.

To develop specifications, the purchaser works with the person or department that needs the products. For example, the chef is usually the person who decides what food products are needed. The chef will work with the purchaser to develop the specifications for each food item needed.

## Determining Quality

Quality is one of the main characteristics that must be indicated on a food specification. Most products are available in a variety of quality levels. Food purchasers must know what quality of products they need for the recipes that will be prepared. In order to make sure that everyone is using the same quality standards, the U.S. Department of Agriculture (USDA) has developed standards called U.S. Grade Standards, 8-4. The department of the USDA that develops these grade standards is the Agricultural Marketing Service (AMS). It is totally separate from the USDA's Food Safety and Inspection Service, which is mandatory and ensures the wholesomeness of food. The U.S. Grade Standards are voluntary. Their purpose is to provide a common vocabulary for evaluating the quality of food. All grade levels are safe and wholesome to eat.

The U.S. Grade Standards cover the characteristics of the food such as the following: size, color, shape, blemishes, uniformity, aroma, tenderness, and texture. Each food product has its own grades and grade requirements. There are grade standards for 235 agricultural products. In general, there are three basic grades: A, B, and C. U.S. Grade A is the top grade. It is the most appealing, most nearly perfect, and usually the most expensive. U.S. Grade B is almost as good as Grade A. The food may not be uniform in shape or color. U.S. Grade C, also called *standard quality*, is still good, but may not be as attractive or flavorful.

The grade of product needed depends on the use. For example, U.S. Grade A whole canned tomatoes must be 80 percent whole. U.S. Grade C whole canned tomatoes are less than 70 percent whole. In a recipe for antipasto, the tomatoes must be whole, and U.S. Grade A would be required. In a recipe for chili or stew, the tomatoes will be broken up during cooking. For the chili recipe, U.S. Grade C tomatoes will be fine and will be cheaper.

## Determining Quantity

No restaurant likes to be embarrassed. Not having enough food in stock to meet the demands of guests can result in guest complaints and embarrassment. **In stock** means on hand, either in the kitchen or in the storeroom, 8-5.

### Quantity Needed

Determining the quantity that is needed is a complex task. Purchasing and inventory must work together. Inventory must let purchasing know when the supply of a product is running low. Inventory can do this by developing a *par stock*

| U.S. Grade Standards: Basic Grades | |
|---|---|
| *Grade A:* | Top grade. Most appealing. Most nearly perfect. Usually the most expensive. |
| *Grade B:* | Almost as good as Grade A. May not be uniform in shape or color. |
| *Grade C:* | Also called *standard quality*. May not be as attractive or colorful. |

*Goodheart-Willcox Publisher*

8-4 All grades are wholesome and safe. Grades are based on factors that affect appeal, such as color and shape. Each food has its own grading standards.

8-5 This warehouse manager is checking the food in stock in the storeroom of a school cafeteria.

*Photo by Ken Hammond for U.S. Department of Agriculture*

and *reorder point* system. This system is based on knowing how much of each product is used during a specific time period.

**Par stock** is the maximum amount of a particular item that is allowed to be in storage at any one time. As the item is used, the amount of the item goes down. The **reorder point** is the minimum amount of an item in storage, or the point at which more of the item must be ordered. When the amount of an item reaches the reorder point, that item must be reordered to bring the amount back to par stock. For example, the par stock for canned peaches is five cases. The reorder point is two cases. The purchaser will check the stock to see how many cases are on hand. If there are only two cases remaining, three more must be ordered to bring the number up to par stock.

One of the purposes of a par stock system is to make sure the business does not keep too much inventory. Products cost money to buy. Products that are used up and sold to customers earn money for the business. Products that sit on the shelf in storage do not earn money for the business. Products in storage actually cost the business money. Therefore, purchasing and inventory managers have to figure out just the right amount of each product to keep in stock. Enough must be in stock to meet customer demand. However, the goal is to keep the smallest amount in stock and still meet customer demand.

## Perishability

Several other factors affect the quantity of an item purchased. If you order frequently, you can buy smaller quantities. If you order infrequently, you may have to buy larger quantities. Some suppliers will deliver only at certain times, so restriction must be considered. Another factor is whether the products are perishable. A **perishable** is a product that can spoil quickly. Perishables include milk, meat, fresh fruits and vegetables, and bakery products such as bread, **8-6**. You must buy perishables in quantities you can use before they spoil. Perishables are usually ordered daily.

Nonperishable products such as napkins do not have to be ordered daily. Nonperishable products can be ordered once a week or once every two weeks. Even though nonperishable products will not spoil, you do not want to keep too much on hand. When products sit on the shelf, they do not earn money for the restaurant.

Sergii Figurnyi/Shutterstock.com

8-6  A perishable product, such as fruit, can spoil quickly.

## Cost-Effective Buying

**Cost-effective buying** is buying the most products at the best quality for the least amount of money. Many suppliers offer price discounts if a large amount of a product is ordered. Buying in quantity can be cost effective. However, if the item is perishable, you have to be able to use it up before it spoils. If the item is nonperishable, you have to have space to store it.

It is also more cost effective to buy food products in season. For example, watermelons and strawberries are abundant and inexpensive during the months of May and June. These same items become scarce and expensive during the winter months. There have been times when lettuce has been too expensive for restaurants to use. Menus have to be adjusted to take into consideration the cost and availability of food products.

When food items are purchased, the delivery cost must also be considered in the purchase price of the item, **8-7**. It costs the same for a supplier to deliver one case of a product as it does to deliver ten cases. For example, if the cost of a delivery is $75, and ten cases are delivered, the delivery cost is only $7.50 per case. If only one case is delivered, the delivery cost is $75 per case. The total cost of the product to the restaurant includes the delivery costs.

## Selecting Suppliers

A **supplier** is a business from whom supplies are purchased. Suppliers are also called *vendors*.

**8-7** Ordering multiple items at one time can help save delivery costs.

*Yuri Arcurs/Shutterstock.com*

Suppliers of food are often called *purveyors*. There are suppliers for every possible product a restaurant could need. Examples include suppliers of vegetables, fruits, meats, flour, desserts, equipment, linens, and temporary banquet workers.

Before selecting suppliers, you must know something about them. Many suppliers regularly send sales representatives to call on restaurants. The purpose of these sales calls is to introduce the supplier and its products. Suppliers are constantly developing new products to meet restaurant needs. For example, a popular new product is preportioned cheesecake. These cheesecakes can be purchased in many different flavors and come sliced and ready to serve. Another purpose is to establish a good working relationship between the supplier and the restaurant.

One of the major ways of selecting a supplier is through the bidding process. A **bid** is a document that states what the supplier will charge for a specific product. The purchaser researches suppliers for a specific product. The purchaser then will select a few suppliers of the product. Each supplier receives the specifications for the product and then sends back a bid. The bid includes the price for the specific product and any other services or considerations the supplier will offer. For example, the supplier might offer free delivery. The purchaser evaluates the bids and selects the best one.

## Ordering

*Ordering* is giving the supplier instructions concerning what is to be purchased. An **order** is a list of products that a business wants to purchase. The products are often called *items*. A **purchase order** or *P.O.* is the form used for submitting orders to a supplier, **8-8**. Almost every business that buys products uses purchase orders. The forms should include the purchase order number, purchase order date, delivery date, item name, quantity of each item, unit price, and total price per item.

A paper purchase order is usually a three-part form. The reason for having three copies is that several different people need to know exactly what was ordered. The top copy is sent to the supplier, who uses it to fill the order. The second copy goes to the person who will receive the order at the restaurant. The third copy goes to the accounting department for the payment process. Most purchase orders are now sent by e-mail.

# Going Green

## Produce Calculator

Almost 30 percent of the garbage generated by restaurants consists of food waste. Much of it results from inefficient purchasing. Sometimes restaurants estimate that they will need more produce for service than they really do. The leftover produce often rots and is thrown away.

The Oklahoma Farm to School produce calculator is an online resource that helps foodservice managers better estimate their produce needs. For instance, if fresh tomatoes are needed, a manager enters the number of meals being served into a spreadsheet. The calculator determines the amount of tomatoes to order. Managers also enter costing data to determine price per pound and price per serving. To learn more about the produce calculator, visit the Oklahoma Farm to School website.

8-8  How is this purchase order set up to avoid confusion for the supplier?

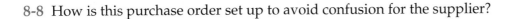

**The Walnut Hill Restaurant**
**2417 Walnut Hill Street**
**Oakmont, TN 78203**
**555-666-7777**

**PURCHASE ORDER**
**NUMBER 1450**
**Please put this purchase order number on all invoices, bills of lading, or correspondence relating to this order.**

**To:** Town Foods
     204 Seventeenth Street
     Oakmont, TN 78203

**Purchase Order Date:** March 18

**Delivery Date:** March 20

| Quantity | Item | Unit Price | Total Price | Received | Comments |
|---|---|---|---|---|---|
| 15 dozen | hot dog buns | 1.85/doz | 27.75 | | |
| 1 case | all meat hot dogs | 6.50 | 6.50 | | |
| 10 lbs | cheddar cheese | 3.00/lb | 30.00 | | |
| 2 cans (#10) | chili without beans | 2.50/can | 5.00 | | |

*Goodheart-Willcox Publisher*

Purchase orders provide documentation for what was ordered. A completed purchase order helps to protect both the purchaser and the supplier from any misunderstandings about the order. Purchase orders should always contain a purchase order number. This number helps both the supplier and the restaurant purchaser keep records and follow up. The purchase order number is used to track the order. For example, if an item is not delivered, the purchaser can refer to the purchase order number when asking for credit on that undelivered item.

In some situations, a purchase order is not needed every time a product is ordered. One situation is the daily purchase of perishables. Many restaurants order the same amount of perishables every day. Instead of writing purchase orders for these items every day, a standing order is written. A *standing order* is an order that does not change and should be filled at regular time intervals, such as every day. For example, a restaurant may have a standing order with a bakery for three dozen muffins and two dozen Danish every day for breakfast, **8-9**.

Another situation in which purchase orders are not used is contract buying. In *contract buying*, a contract is written that specifies which products are to be delivered for a guaranteed price. Contract buying is used for products that are purchased in large quantities over a fairly long time period, from three months to a year. Items often purchased on a contract basis are paper goods and cleaning supplies. Food items can also be purchased on a contract basis. The supplier guarantees the price during this period.

In some cases, contracts might be written allowing for small price changes during that period. Government, chain, and institutional foodservices often purchase on a contract basis.

# Receiving

After products have been ordered, the supplier delivers them. Receiving is the process of making sure the items delivered are the items that were ordered. The receiving process includes three tasks: delivery, checking, and documentation.

**8-9** Restaurants often have a standing order with a bakery for breads and other baked goods.

val lawless/Shutterstock.com

## Delivery

The first step in receiving is the delivery. Deliveries are usually received on a **receiving dock**, **8-10**. The receiving dock is usually located near where the items will be stored. During delivery, the products are unloaded from the truck and placed in the receiving area. All of the items delivered from one supplier at one time are often called a **shipment**. The receiving staff must be ready when the deliveries arrive. In order for the receiving staff to be ready, delivery times are often limited to specific days and times. The ideal time for most restaurant deliveries is early in the day, but never during busy mealtimes.

## Checking

The checking process consists of examining the delivered items to make sure they are the items ordered and they are in good condition, **8-11**. Checking is performed while the items are being unloaded. Checking usually involves comparing the items received against the items ordered on the purchase order. This process is necessary because the items delivered are sometimes not the items ordered. The supplier may not have had the items you ordered, or perhaps the person who filled the order made a mistake. Sometimes the items delivered are spoiled. In order to avoid paying for items not received or spoiled items, the receiving department checks each delivery.

An invoice is usually delivered along with the items. An **invoice** is a bill that includes a complete

Photo by Ken Hammond for U.S. Department of Agriculture

**8-11** This warehouse supervisor is checking a delivery of celery for a school lunch program.

listing of what was delivered along with the quantity and price for each item. The invoice is prepared by the supplier. The items on the invoice should be the same as the items on the purchase order, and both should be the same as the items in the shipment. In cases where an invoice is not used, a delivery slip is used. A **delivery slip** contains the same information as an invoice, except prices are not included.

Most restaurants have a list of checking procedures. These procedures are usually written down and taught to all receiving staff, **8-12**.

## Documentation

The process of documentation begins during checking. When any error or spoiled, damaged, or otherwise unacceptable item is found, it is noted on the invoice or delivery slip. The delivery driver initials the note. The delivery driver's initials serve as proof of the errors or problems. Spoiled, damaged, or otherwise unacceptable items are not accepted by the restaurant. The delivery driver puts them back on the truck.

The delivery driver then prepares a credit memorandum. A **credit memorandum** lists the products that were returned. A credit memorandum is also called a *credit slip*. The credit memorandum is stapled to the invoice. At the end of each day, all the invoices or delivery slips plus all credit memos are sent to accounting.

**8-10** Receiving is the first step of the delivery process. Items are usually received at the receiving dock.

Photo courtesy of IGA, Inc.

## Procedure for Checking Received Items

1. Count or weigh the items. For example, the number of cases of canned peaches received can be counted. The amount of ground beef received can be weighed.

2. Compare the amount received with the amount listed on the invoice or the delivery slip.

3. If there is any difference, record the difference on the invoice or delivery slip. For example, if the invoice says three cases of peaches were delivered, but you counted only two, cross out *three* and write *two* on the invoice next to canned peaches.

4. Compare the quality of the item received with the quality specified on the invoice. For example, you ordered U.S. Grade B peaches, but you were sent U.S. Grade A peaches, which are more expensive. Note errors in quality on the invoice or delivery slip.

5. Check the temperature of refrigerated and frozen foods. Refrigerated foods should be below 41°F. Frozen foods should be 32°F or colder. Foods that are too warm should be returned.

6. Look for any damage. For example, if one of the cases of tomatoes was torn, and several cans were dented, note damage on the invoice or delivery slip.

7. Stamp the invoice or the delivery slip with a receiving stamp. The receiving stamp should be initialed in the appropriate spots to show that the checking process has been completed.

*Goodheart-Willcox Publisher*

8-12  What can happen if checking procedures are not followed?

# Storage

After products have been received, they should be stored properly. Improperly stored foods and other items can spoil and become unusable. Spoiled items must be replaced at added cost to the restaurant. As soon as the receiving process is completed, all items should be placed in appropriate storage areas. Frozen items and items that need refrigeration should be put away first. Food should never be stored in passageways, restrooms, or utility rooms. Food and utensils used to prepare and serve food must be protected from dust, insects, rodents, toxic materials, and unclean equipment and utensils. Food and food-related items should never be stored in the same room as chemicals such as cleaning supplies.

## Storage Facilities

There are three basic types of storage facilities: refrigerators, freezers, and storerooms. Refrigerators, also called *coolers*, are used to keep foods cold. Refrigerators must be kept at a temperature below 41°F. Freezers are for foods that must remain below 32°F. (The freezing point of water is 32°F.) Storerooms are used for both nonperishable and perishable items that do not require refrigeration. Ideally the climate in storerooms should be controlled to keep the temperature cool and dry. Nonperishable items include canned foods, flour, sugar, oil, paper products, and spices. Perishable items that do not require refrigeration include onions and potatoes.

Cleanliness is a must for all food storage facilities. Refrigerators must be cleaned regularly to remove any food that might have spoiled. All storage areas must be cleaned regularly. In addition, a professional exterminator should be brought in on a regular basis. Even if the floor is clean and there are no insects or rodents, no food items should be stored on the floor, 8-13. If large items must be stored on the floor, they should be placed on a raised platform.

Whenever possible, store foods in their original packaging. If food is removed from its original packaging, repackage it carefully for storage. **Repackaged foods** are those foods that have been partially used and not stored in their original containers after opening. Examples of foods that are often repackaged are cooking oil, syrup, salt, sugar, and flour. These items are usually placed in special bins or storage containers that give easy access when cooking. Clearly label repackaged foods. Prevent contamination by keeping repackaged food items covered in clean, nonabsorbent containers until they are needed for food preparation.

*Baloncici/Shutterstock.com*

8-13 No food items should ever be stored on the floor. Canned food items are stored off the floor on shelving in this warehouse.

Some items are packaged in unsealed packaging. Unsealed packaging includes paper bags, boxes, and sacks. For example, carryout containers are purchased in unsealed packaging. Products purchased in unsealed packaging should be transferred to tightly sealed, insect-proof containers. These containers keep them fresh and free from contamination.

A key concept in usage of stored foods is **FIFO**: *first in, first out*. FIFO means that the first food item received should be the first food item used. In other words, food items should be used in the order in which they are received. When each food item is received, write the date on the package. In storage areas, place new food products behind the older food products and use the older food products first.

## Reducing Theft

Unfortunately, theft by employees is often a problem. To eliminate the temptation of theft, all purchased items should be moved from the receiving area to locked storage as quickly as possible. Once foods are stored, appropriate security methods must be maintained at all times.

Storerooms should be open at certain times and locked at all other times. All employees should follow a specific process for obtaining needed items from the storerooms. This process is called *issuing* or *requisitioning*.

# Inventory

All the items that you need to run your restaurant or hotel have been purchased, received, and stored. The two main tasks of inventory are issuing and inventory control. The first is to make items available to employees as they need them. The second is to keep track of the items used so more can be ordered when needed.

The process of making items available to employees is called **issuing** or **requisitioning**. Items that are needed are listed on a requisition form. A **requisition form** is a form used to request items from inventory, **8-14**. The manager approves the items requested on the requisition form. The requisition form is taken to the storeroom and given to the storeroom clerk. The storeroom clerk gets the requisitioned items. The clerk then issues (gives) the items to the employee. Requiring requisition forms for all items taken from inventory helps keep track of the items. It also discourages

theft because no items can be removed without a signed requisition form.

For example, suppose you are making peach cobbler for dessert. According to the standardized recipe, you need three cans of peaches. You list three cans of peaches on a requisition form. You take the form to the executive chef, who approves your request by placing her initial on the form. You take the form to the storeroom clerk. The clerk issues three cans of peaches to you.

The storage areas are very active places. New items are constantly being received. Items in inventory are constantly being requested and given out. Inventory staff members need to know what is in inventory at all times. They also need to know when items are being used up and must be reordered. The process of keeping track of items in inventory is called **inventory control**. Computers and point-of-sales systems have made inventory control much easier.

There are two types of inventory: physical and perpetual. A **physical inventory** consists of actually

8-14 Chefs must use a requisition form to obtain items they need for making dishes. The requisition form enables the storeroom manager to keep track of what has been used and what needs to be ordered.

Hilton Hotels Corporation

going into the storage areas and counting every item, **8-15**. Physical inventory is time-consuming but necessary.

**Perpetual inventory** consists of keeping a record (usually on computer) of the total number of each item in inventory, then adding whenever new items are received and subtracting whenever items are issued. For example, when the new shipment of three cases of peaches arrives, the three cases will be added to the two already in inventory. Since there are six cans per case, the total number of cans will be updated to 30. When you requisition three cans for the peach cobbler, the storeroom clerk will subtract the three cans from the 30 in inventory. The computer record for the perpetual inventory will show that there are now 27 cans of peaches in inventory.

The perpetual inventory can be used for ordering. The computer will be programmed to send a notice when the reorder point is reached on each item. The purchaser will then know to order more of the item. Perpetual inventory also helps identify when theft has occurred. If the physical inventory shows many fewer items than are recorded in the perpetual inventory, it is possible that someone has stolen the missing items.

# Relationships with Suppliers

One of the most important things that purchasers do is create good relationships with suppliers. A restaurant needs suppliers it can trust and depend on.

The purchasing department should establish ground rules for the business relationship with each supplier. These rules should be communicated to the suppliers and their sales representatives so a good business relationship can be established. For example, sales representatives must make appointments to see the purchaser.

The purchaser's relationship with suppliers should follow business ethical standards. For example, purchasers should not make personal

*Golden Pixels LLC/Shutterstock.com*

**8-15** Why is a physical inventory necessary even when a perpetual inventory is kept in computer software?

purchases or take any gifts from suppliers. The relationship between purchaser and supplier is a professional one. Just as a restaurant or hotel has guests as their customers, the restaurant or hotel is the customer of the supplier.

# Chapter 8
## Review

## Chapter Summary

- The responsibility of the purchaser is to make sure that the operation has everything it needs in the right amounts at the right time.
- Purchasing consists of five main tasks: developing specifications, determining quality, determining quantity, selecting suppliers, and ordering.
- The purpose of specifications is to make sure you get the exact items you need.
- One of the major ways of selecting a supplier is through the bidding process.
- Purchase orders provide documentation for what was ordered.
- The receiving process includes three tasks: delivery, checking, and documentation.
- Improperly stored foods and other items can spoil and become unusable.
- The two main tasks of inventory are issuing and inventory control.

## Review

1. Why is the role of purchaser important?
2. Describe the five main tasks of purchasing.
3. How is a specification used to get the food item you want?
4. What is the purpose of the U.S. Grade Standards?
5. How does the bidding process work?
6. List the information that should be included in a purchase order.
7. Describe the three tasks of receiving.
8. Describe the process for checking received items.
9. Why is proper storage of food items important?
10. Describe the two main tasks of inventory.

# Critical Thinking

11. **Assess.** What skills does a purchaser need to have?

12. **Determine.** List the steps in the process of receiving. Then describe how you would implement the steps to receive an order for 50 pounds of ground beef.

13. **Identify.** In a Mexican restaurant, which food items would be considered perishable? Which would be considered nonperishable?

14. **Analyze.** What are some ways that purchasing over the Internet helps the environment?

15. **Compare and contrast.** List the purchasing staff in large operations. How is this different from the purchasing staff found in small operations?

## Common Core

### College and Career Readiness

16. **Writing.** Prepare specifications for lettuce for a salad.

17. **Listening.** Interview a food and beverage purchaser of an Italian restaurant to find out the par stock and reorder points for canned tomatoes.

18. **Speaking.** Role-play the process of ordering hot dogs for a school picnic.

19. **Writing.** Imagine you are the purchaser for a family restaurant. Write a description summarizing your responsibilities.

20. **CTE Career Readiness Practice.** Your manager at the restaurant where you work overheard you explaining the directions for cooking a low-cost chicken dish to a coworker. The manager asks you to demonstrate your dish to the kitchen staff. She said the restaurant will supply your ingredients. You need to supply the recipe and prepare a cost list showing the total cost and cost-per-portion. Your chicken dish is a one-dish meal that uses chicken, broccoli, whole-grain noodles, and grated low-fat cheese topping and makes eight portions. Think about the following as you prepare your demonstration:

    - thrifty substitutions to make that are equally nutritious and utilize foods from every food group
    - ways to save time during preparation
    - methods for keeping food safe

# Chapter 9
## Food Safety and Sanitation

## Chapter Objectives

After studying this chapter, you will be able to
- **list** the three types of food contaminants.
- **determine** why restaurant managers are most concerned about bacteria.
- **evaluate** the two main ways to prevent food contamination.
- **appraise** practices that prevent foodborne illness.
- **contrast** cleaning and sanitizing.
- **describe** the role of government in preventing foodborne illness.
- **explain** HACCP.
- **describe** the role of the manager in preventing foodborne illness.

## Before You Read

Try to answer the following questions before you read this chapter.
- What are the sources of foodborne illness?
- What steps can hospitality employees take to help prevent foodborne illness?

## Terms to Know

contaminant
foodborne illness
contaminated food
physical contaminant
chemical contaminant
biological contaminant
pathogen
microorganism
potentially hazardous foods
temperature danger zone

room temperature
virus
transmit
parasite
personal hygiene
sanitation
cleaning
sanitizing
food contact surface
equipment

utensils
food handling
holding unit
thermometer
thermostat
cross-contamination
holding
Hazard Analysis Critical Control Point (HACCP)
critical control point (CCP)
critical limit

A group of friends went to Jan's favorite restaurant for her birthday dinner. After two days, Jan got very sick. Her friends later found out that Jan had been taken to the hospital along with a dozen other restaurant guests. Luckily, everyone recovered within a few days. The local department of health investigated the situation and found that all the sick people had eaten a hamburger cooked rare. Further investigation showed that the hamburger was contaminated with bacteria named *E. coli*, which had caused the guests to become ill. This particular type of bacteria lives in the intestinal system of human beings. Further investigation showed that one employee had prepared the hamburger patties. This employee had failed to use proper handwashing procedures after using the toilet. The bacteria were transmitted from the employee's hands to the hamburger patties and then to the guests.

A major cause of foodborne illness is careless employees who do not wash their hands or do not handle food properly. The typical symptoms of foodborne illness are nausea or vomiting, diarrhea, fever, and cramps. Some types of foodborne illness can even cause death. In addition, certain people are more likely to become ill from foodborne illness. These groups include infants, young children, older adults, pregnant women, and people with certain illnesses, **9-1**.

**9-1** Older people and children, as well as pregnant women and people with certain illnesses, are more likely to become sick from contaminated food.

*wong sze yuen/Shutterstock.com*

An incident of foodborne illness may not only result in the discomfort of illness, but it can also ruin a foodservice business. Would you want to eat at a restaurant where people had gotten sick from eating the food? Restaurant managers must make sure that every employee knows proper sanitation procedures. Each employee is responsible for following safe sanitation procedures. Even one instance of not washing hands can cause hundreds of people to become ill. Federal, state, and local governments also want to make sure that restaurant food is safe to eat. These governments have established laws and regulations to ensure that food in restaurants is safe.

# Sources of Foodborne Illness

A **contaminant** is a substance in food that does not belong in the food. Contaminants in food can cause illness or death. A **foodborne illness** is a disease that is caused by eating contaminated food. **Contaminated food** is food that contains something that does not belong and can cause illness. There are three types of contaminants: physical, chemical, and biological.

## *Physical Contaminants*

A **physical contaminant** is an item that accidentally gets into food. Examples include hair, jewelry, chips of glass or china, bits of metal, wood splinters, insect parts, bandages, and fingernails. Some of these contaminants, such as a hair or insect part, are unpleasant but not necessarily dangerous. However, if customers find these items in their soup, they might never eat in your restaurant again.

Other physical contaminants can cause serious injury, including glass chips or bits of metal. A customer could suffer cuts to the mouth and digestive system. For example, a customer was served a plate of spaghetti. When he took a mouthful, he bit into a metal screw and broke a tooth. It was later discovered that the screw had fallen from the warming unit in the kitchen.

## *Chemical Contaminants*

A **chemical contaminant** is a chemical that is toxic or not usually found in food. There are several types of chemical contaminants: pesticides, cleaning agents, and metals in solution. Pesticides are sometimes left on foods that grew in the fields. Cleaning agents include bleach, ammonia, and silver polish. Metals such as copper, lead, and cadmium occur in cooking pots and utensils. They are not a problem unless the metals are dissolved off during cooking. (A solid bit of metal would be a physical contaminant.)

Chemical contaminants can get into food when cleaning supplies are not properly marked and stored, 9-2. A thick, clear yellow cleaning solution might look like cooking oil. A white powdery cleaning agent might look like powdered sugar. Any cleaning chemical accidentally used in a food would cause immediate and severe illness.

Other chemical contaminants can affect health in the long term. This is especially true of chemical contaminants that enter foods in small amounts, such as pesticides and metals. These contaminants can cause cancer and nervous disorders. Restaurants must make sure that all utensils and equipment

9-2 Cleaning agents should be clearly marked so they are not confused with food ingredients.

Lana Langlois/Shutterstock.com

used in cooking and food preparation do not leach chemicals into the food. Following government regulations for utensils and equipment will protect customers from this potential danger.

## Biological Contaminants

Biological contaminants are responsible for most cases of foodborne illness. A **biological contaminant** is a microscopic living substance that accidentally gets into food. Types of biological contaminants include bacteria, parasites, viruses, molds, and fungi. A biological contaminant that causes disease is called a **pathogen**. Pathogens are sometimes called *disease-causing microorganisms*. A **microorganism** is a living substance so small that you must use a microscope to see it. Not all microorganisms cause disease or are biological contaminants. Many microorganisms are used to create tasty and healthful foods. Yeast, a type of fungus, is widely used as an ingredient in bread to make it rise.

Three groups of pathogens are responsible for most foodborne illnesses. They are the bacteria, the viruses, and the parasites, 9-3. The five main symptoms of foodborne illness caused by pathogens are nausea, vomiting, diarrhea, cramps, and fever.

### Bacteria

Of all the pathogens, restaurant managers are most concerned about bacteria. Bacteria are the most common cause of foodborne illnesses. *Bacteria* are single-celled, microscopic organisms. Hundreds of thousands of bacteria could fit on the period at the end of this sentence. Bacteria are everywhere. A small number of bacteria are usually not harmful. Human beings have a variety of natural protective mechanisms that fight harmful bacteria.

Not all bacteria cause disease. Right now, millions of bacteria are living on your skin and in your body. These bacteria are not harmful to you. In fact, the bacteria that live in your intestines actually help digest your food. Problems can occur if bacteria travel from your hands to the food you are handling. Bacteria also live in the intestines of healthy cattle. These bacteria can also accidentally contaminate meat and cause problems.

One of the characteristics of bacteria is that they reproduce very rapidly under ideal conditions, which are often found in food. Some bacteria populations double every 20 minutes. Under ideal conditions, one bacterium might produce over a

## Examples of Biological Contaminants

| Type | Organism Name | Incubation Period* |
|------|---------------|---------------------|
| **Bacteria** | Clostridium botulinum | 12 to 36 hours |
| | Escherichia coli (E. coli) | 2 to 5 days |
| | Salmonella | 6 to 48 hours |
| | Staphylococcus aureus | 2 to 4 hours |
| **Virus** | Hepatitis virus A | 10 to 50 days |
| | Norwalk virus | 1 to 2 days |
| **Parasite** | Cryptosporidium parvum | 2 to 10 days |
| | Cyclospora cayetanesis | 7 days |
| | Trichinella spiralis | 4 to 28 days |

*Note: The incubation period is the length of time between ingesting the pathogen and the appearance of symptoms.

*Goodheart-Willcox Publisher*

9-3 Bacteria, viruses, and parasites are responsible for most foodborne illnesses.

## Potentially Hazardous Foods

| Raw and Cooked | Cooked |
|----------------|--------|
| Dairy products | Casseroles |
| Eggs | Custard |
| Fish | Fish salads |
| Meat | Meat salads |
| Poultry | Potatoes |
| Shellfish | Rice |

*Goodheart-Willcox Publisher*

9-4 Foods in which bacteria grow well are called *potentially hazardous foods*.

billion bacteria. The goal of foodservice workers is to kill bacteria or to keep bacteria from reproducing. Two of the conditions necessary for bacteria to grow are food and warm temperatures.

Bacteria grow best in certain kinds of foods called **potentially hazardous foods**. Potentially hazardous foods can be raw or cooked meat, poultry, fish, shellfish, eggs, and dairy products, **9-4**. Many foods become potentially hazardous after they are cooked. For example, bacteria do not grow in raw rice and potatoes, but after being cooked, these become potentially hazardous foods. Casseroles, custard, meat and fish salads, stuffing, and potato salad made with mayonnaise are all potentially hazardous cooked foods.

However, food alone is not enough for bacteria. They also need the proper temperature.

Bacteria reproduce fastest at temperatures between 41°F and 135°F. Below 41°F, bacteria are alive but do not reproduce. Below 0°F, most bacteria die (although some survive). At temperatures above 135°F, most bacteria die. Therefore, the temperatures between 41°F to 135°F are called the **temperature danger zone, 9-5**. **Room temperature** is a temperature around 70°F, so it is in the danger zone. Many kitchens are much warmer than room temperature.

Time is also a factor. If a food is at room temperature for a few minutes, not enough bacteria will grow to cause harm. However, if a food is left at room temperature for two or more hours, enough bacteria may grow to cause illness. Special care must be taken to make sure that potentially hazardous foods are not left in the temperature danger zone for more than four hours total during the entire "life" of the food.

### Viruses

A **virus** is a microorganism that reproduces in the cells of other living things. Viruses are much, much smaller than bacteria. Foods can transmit viruses to people. **Transmit** means to carry from one place to another. Foods give viruses a way to get into the human body when a person eats the food that contains the virus. Once the virus is in the body, it can reproduce and make a person sick.

Food can also transmit viruses from one person to another. For example, suppose you have a cold. You might sneeze on a salad. The salad, which is carrying your cold viruses, is then served

## Temperature and Bacterial Growth

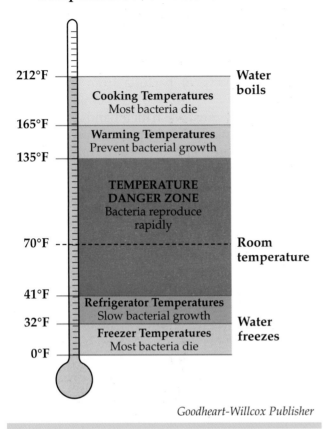

*Goodheart-Willcox Publisher*

**9-5** The speed at which food bacteria reproduce depends on the temperature of the food.

to a customer. When the customer eats the food, your cold viruses get into the customer and makes him or her sick. The best way to prevent the transmission of viruses is good personal hygiene and proper food handling.

### Parasites

A **parasite** is an organism that must live in another living thing in order to survive. The living thing that a parasite lives in, called a *host*, can be a person, animal, or plant. The parasite gets nourishment from the host. Parasites can range in size from an amoeba, which has one cell, to a tapeworm, which can grow to 30 feet. Parasites can live inside some of the animals that humans eat as food (poultry, cattle, pigs, and fish). They are usually passed to humans through an animal host. Many parasites cause serious illness in humans. Good personal hygiene and proper food handling can prevent contamination by parasites.

# Preventing Foodborne Illness

There are three main ways to prevent foodborne illness: personal hygiene, sanitation, and proper handling of food. **Personal hygiene** consists of the actions a person takes to keep his or her body and clothing clean and to remove pathogens. Sanitation consists of the actions taken to prevent and control disease. **Sanitation** includes the processes of cleaning and sanitizing. **Cleaning** is the physical removal of dirt and food from surfaces. **Sanitizing** is the treatment of a clean surface with chemicals or heat to reduce the number of pathogens to safe levels. Proper handling of food includes proper storage and cooking. The following discussion on preventing foodborne illness is organized into four sections: employee practices; food sources and storage; equipment, utensils, and surfaces; and food handling.

## Employee Practices

One of the most common sources of food contamination is the hospitality employee. At the same time, hospitality employees are the best people to prevent food contamination, **9-6**. Of the many things hospitality employees can do to prevent foodborne illness, the most important is handwashing. Employee practices that prevent foodborne illness are generally called good personal hygiene. These practices include staying home when sick, keeping fingernails short, washing hands properly and frequently, bathing daily, wearing clean clothing, avoiding wearing jewelry, keeping hair restrained, controlling sweat, using gloves when directed, and using sanitary serving methods. The goal of all these actions is to prevent contaminants and pathogens from getting into food.

### Stay Home When Sick

Everyone who handles food should be healthy. Foodservice employees should never be on duty when they have diseases that can be transmitted through direct contact with food or other persons. Employees who show signs of illness should be reassigned or sent home. Signs of illness include fever, sneezing, coughing, vomiting, diarrhea, or oozing burns and cuts. Employees should not return to work until they are no longer sick and do not risk passing along their diseases.

Family, Career and Community Leaders of America, Inc.

**9-6** This student is a future hospitality employee. She is learning safe food handling as well as cooking techniques.

People who are not sick can carry disease-producing microorganisms. They may never show the symptoms or they may have recovered. However, they can pass on the pathogens that could make your customers ill. The foodservice manager must educate employees and communicate with them about their health status.

### Keep Fingernails Short

Fingernails should be trimmed, filed, and maintained so handwashing will effectively remove soil and bacteria from under and around them. No nail polish should be worn in food production areas. Artificial nails should also not be worn, as they could fall off into the food. Bacteria hide under artificial nails as well. Fake nails may look attractive, but they are dangerous in a foodservice operation.

### Wash Hands Properly

Most contaminants that cause foodborne illness enter food from the hands of foodservice workers. Hands easily pick up contaminants, such as bacteria from unclean surfaces, chemicals from cleaning products, or bacteria from the nose or mouth.

Employees must wash their hands thoroughly, **9-7**. The workplace should provide proper handwashing stations. Hot and cold running water must be available at all times. An adequate supply of soap or detergent must be available. Forced-air blowers and single-use paper towels must be used for hand drying.

For thorough handwashing, wet hands and forearms with hot water. Use approved cleaning soaps or detergents. Vigorously rub the surfaces of hands, wrists, and forearms for at least 20 seconds. Clean under and around fingernails using a brush. Clean between fingers. Soap, water, and friction are all needed to adequately clean skin. Thoroughly rinse under clean running water. Dry hands using a single-use paper towel or an electric hand dryer. Do not dry hands on your apron or a dish towel.

### Wash Hands Frequently

Wash your hands whenever you touch an unclean surface. Hands should be washed after

**9-7** Hand washing is the best action you can take to prevent the spread of disease.

hxdbzxy/Shutterstock.com

using the toilet, sneezing, nose blowing, wiping away sweat, touching hair, working with raw food products, and touching any dirty surface.

## Bathe Daily

Personal cleanliness is important. Lack of personal cleanliness can offend customers, cause illnesses, and contaminate food or food-contact surfaces. It is very important to bathe every day.

## Wear Clean Clothing

Employees should always wear clean work clothes. Dirty clothing presents two problems: odor and contamination by bacteria. Every effort must be made to reduce the risk of passing contamination from clothing to others. Dirt can enter the business on an employee's shoes or clothing. Ordinary dirt contains many microorganisms from sewage, fertilizer, or street dirt. Employees should especially change dirty aprons after working with raw foods such as poultry, seafood, beef, or pork, **9-8**.

## Do Not Wear Jewelry

Jewelry should never be worn during food production or dishwashing. Rings, watches, bracelets, necklaces, earrings, and other body-part adornments can collect bacteria that causes foodborne illnesses. Jewelry or parts of the jewelry can fall off and enter the food. Jewelry can also be a safety hazard by getting caught in equipment.

## Keep Hair Restrained

Caps, nets, or other hair restraints should be worn to prevent hair from falling into food. Hair must also be kept clean. Dirty hair harbors pathogens and microorganisms.

## Control Sweat

Another common source of contamination is sweat. Food handlers should be careful not to drip sweat onto equipment or into food products. Wear a sweatband or hat. Do not wipe off sweat with your hands and then touch food. Do not use wiping cloths that are used on food contact surfaces to wipe off sweat. A **food contact surface** is a surface that comes in contact with food. A disposable towel or napkin should be used to wipe away sweat and then thrown away. Then hands should be thoroughly washed.

## Use Gloves When Directed

Many foodservice operations require the wearing of disposable gloves during food preparation or

*Yuri Arcurs/Shutterstock.com*

**9-8** Employees who wear aprons should change them when they become dirty.

service. Bare hands often harbor bacteria. Gloves provide a barrier between bacteria on bare hands and food. Gloves are often required during the preparation of cold food such as sandwiches and salads. However, gloves provide no protection if they become contaminated. For example, gloves become contaminated if a person touches a contaminated surface while wearing the gloves. Examples of contaminated surfaces include the person's mouth, the floor, and money. Gloves should be changed after every possible contamination. Hands must also be washed before gloves are put on.

## Use Sanitary Serving Methods

All tableware and serving utensils must be handled in a sanitary way, **9-9**. Make sure your hands are clean before handling tableware and utensils. Do not touch the eating surfaces of tableware when setting tables or when handling and storing utensils. Hold plates by the bottom or by the edge. Hold cups by the handle or the bottom. Hold knives, forks, and spoons by the handle. Never touch the food contact surfaces. Tableware and utensils must be handled this way at all times, including before, during, and after serving food.

When storing silverware in drawers or holders, place each piece so it can be picked up by its handle. Never carry glasses or cups by putting your fingers inside the glass. After you handle dirty tableware, wash your hands.

Dispense ice only with scoops, tongs, or other appropriate equipment. Do not use your hands, cups, or glasses to scoop ice. A glass should *never* be used to scoop ice! If the glass breaks, you will not be able to tell what is glass and what is ice. A customer may then swallow glass. The handle of the scoop should never touch the ice. The scoop should not be stored inside the ice machine. Your hands should never touch the surface of the ice. Handle ice just as carefully as you would handle food.

*Hilton Hotels Corporation*

**9-9** Servers contribute to food safety by using sanitary serving methods.

# *Going Green*

## Using Information Technology to Reduce Food Waste

At many foodservice operations, large amounts of food are thrown out. Many operations do not realize how much waste is generated. This is when a computerized food waste management system can help. It can allow businesses to track and manage their food waste more efficiently, thereby reducing costs.

In operations using such a system, employees weigh the waste. They enter the item name, weight, loss reason, type of container, and service area into a preprogrammed touch screen system. The system tracks whether the food is pre-customer waste or uneaten by the customer. It also records whether the food will be thrown out, donated, or composted. Then it estimates the value of the lost food. The data from a computerized food waste management system helps identify trends and problem areas that result in costly food waste.

## Food Sources and Storage

Food and beverage businesses buy food products from many different sources. For example, a restaurant might buy fresh vegetables from a local farmer's market and fresh lobsters from a special source in Maine. Each of these places is a food source. Once the food is purchased, it must be shipped to the restaurant and then stored.

### Sources

Today, food is transported all over the world. You may have eaten a banana from Costa Rica with your cereal this morning. The beef you ate last night may have come from New Zealand. Each food source (supplier) has workers who handle food. Each of these places might cause contamination in the food they sell. It is important that the food sources are reliable. Suppliers should be chosen who sell clean, fresh, and uncontaminated food products. Suppliers should be able to provide verification that they follow standard sanitary practices.

Generally, food that is prepared in a private home cannot be used or offered for sale in a foodservice business, **9-10**. The only way that food produced in a private home can be used is if the health department inspects the kitchen and approves it.

### Shipping

Reliable suppliers keep food products separate from general supplies during shipping. General supplies are items such as cleaning agents. Reliable suppliers also protect food packages from becoming damaged or torn during shipping.

Food products should be shipped in vehicles that are clean and in good repair. These vehicles also keep potentially hazardous foods at safe temperatures during shipping. Receiving clerks should be instructed to occasionally inspect delivery vehicles. When shipments of food are received at the restaurant, they must be inspected for spoilage and other contamination.

Food often spoils during shipping. Spoiled food may not be harmful, but it looks bad and smells unpleasant. Spoilage is detected by the senses. For example, you can see mold, smell sour milk, and feel slimy produce. On the other hand, contamination cannot usually be seen, tasted, smelled, or felt. Because contamination cannot be detected by the senses, it is especially important to work with reliable suppliers and practice good sanitation and food handling procedures.

*Ariwasabi/Shutterstock.com*

**9-10** No matter where it is prepared, food that is offered for sale in a foodservice business must be approved by the local health department.

### Storage

Once food is received, it must be properly stored to prevent spoilage and contamination. The most important rule of storage is *first in, first out (FIFO)*, **9-11**. When each food item is received, write the date on the package. In storage areas, place new food products behind the older food products. Use the older food products first.

Store food only in approved areas. Food should never be stored in passageways, restrooms, or in utility rooms. Protect food from dust, flies, rodents and other pests, toxic materials, and unclean equipment. Foods should never be stored in the same area as cleaning supplies. Cleaning supplies and other chemicals should be in a separate, marked storage area. Foods should never be stored on the floor or next to walls. Whenever possible, store foods in their original packaging. If food is removed from its original packaging, repackage it carefully for storage.

Foods must be stored at the proper temperatures. Refrigerators should be kept at temperatures below 41°F. Freezers should be kept at a temperature of 32°F or below. When freezer or refrigerator doors are opened, the temperature inside rises. For this reason, the temperatures inside freezers and refrigerators must be regularly checked to make sure the proper temperature is being maintained.

9-11  Place new food products behind the older products so the older products are used first. Food products should have the date received written on the package.

Blend Images/Shutterstock.com

9-12  Good housekeeping is one of the best ways to prevent pests from entering a restaurant.

### Rodent and Insect Control

Pests such as rodents and insects can cause serious problems for restaurants. Customers can be scared away if they see insects and rodents. These pests can contaminate food, spread diseases, and destroy your property. The best pest control method is to prevent pests from getting into the business at all. This requires a continuous program to get rid of any pests that actually do invade the business.

The major ways to control pests are through good housekeeping and preventing entry. Good housekeeping includes all the usual cleaning and sanitizing, **9-12**. It also includes prompt and proper disposal of trash and garbage. Pests can enter a business with deliveries, through open doors and windows, and through cracks and holes in walls and floors. All deliveries should be checked for signs of infestation. Doors and windows should be tight-fitting and kept closed. All cracks and holes should be fixed.

Pesticides can be as deadly to people as they are to rodents and insects. Use them only as a last resort. These products should be used only by a licensed pest control operator. The use of chemicals to control pests is only recommended in combination with the other control procedures of good housekeeping and preventing entry.

## Equipment, Utensils, and Surfaces

**Equipment** includes all the devices used to prepare food. Examples include mixing machines, pots, and ovens. **Utensils** are all the small pieces of equipment used in the kitchen, plus all the items used to serve food to guests, including plates, glasses, and silverware.

### Construction

The Food and Drug Administration (FDA) has set standards for equipment and utensils. The purpose of the standards is to make sure the equipment and utensils are easy to clean and sanitize and safe to use, **9-13**. These standards require that the equipment and utensils be smooth and seamless, easy to clean, and easy to take apart and

erwinova/Shutterstock.com

9-13 Federal standards require that equipment and utensils be easy to clean and sanitize and safe to use.

reassemble. For safety, the equipment and utensils should have rounded corners and edges, except for knives and other cutting edges.

Materials used for the construction of utensils and food contact surfaces of equipment must be nontoxic. They cannot transfer colors, odors, or tastes to foods. Stainless steel is the preferred material for food contact surfaces because it can be easily sanitized. It is used for tabletops, sinks, dish tables, dishwashers, and ventilation hood systems. Other types of surfaces that can be sanitized for use in kitchens include plastics and marble.

## Cleaning Versus Sanitizing

Cleaning and sanitizing are two different processes. *Cleaning* is the physical removal of soil and food residues from surfaces of equipment, utensils, tables, and floors. *Sanitizing* is the treatment of a surface with chemicals or heat to reduce the number of disease-causing organisms to safe levels. A surface must be cleaned before it can be sanitized.

Bacteria and viruses on equipment can be killed by cleaning them with a sanitizing solution such as bleach. Bleach solutions are mixtures of water and chlorine bleach. Other types of sanitizers include iodine and quaternary ammonium compounds (quats).

## Dishwashing

Dishwashing is one of the most important jobs in the food and beverage business. The purpose of dishwashing is to clean and sanitize equipment, dishware, and utensils. Dishwashing is a two-part operation: first clean and then sanitize.

Cleaning and sanitizing kitchen equipment and utensils can be done manually or by machine. Most food establishments will use manual dishwashing methods to clean and sanitize pots, pans, and utensils used to prepare and serve food. Mechanical dishwashers are normally used for glasses, plates, and flatware. In both manual and mechanical methods, hot water and sanitizing solutions are used to sanitize.

## Food Handling

**Food handling** most often refers to procedures that prevent the growth of bacteria in foods. The main way to prevent the growth of bacteria is to keep foods out of the temperature danger zone. The two basic rules of safe food handling are *keep cold foods cold* and *keep hot foods hot*, **9-14**. Sometimes you cannot avoid letting foods pass through the temperature danger zone, such as when cooling down a hot food. In these cases, the goal is to have the food pass through the danger zone as quickly as possible.

The tools to help you handle food properly include freezers, refrigerators, ranges, ovens, holding units, ice, thermometers, and thermostats. A **holding unit** is a piece of equipment that holds food at a specific temperature. A **thermometer** is

a tool for measuring temperature. Temperature in the United States is measured in degrees Fahrenheit (°F). In other countries, the Celsius scale is used (°C). Thermometers are used to check and monitor temperatures of

- foods during cooking
- foods in holding units
- foods when they are delivered, to make sure they are at safe temperatures
- freezers, refrigerators, and holding units
- solutions used for cleaning and sanitizing

If the temperature in a piece of equipment is not correct, the thermostat must be adjusted. A **thermostat** is an automatic device that regulates the temperature of a piece of equipment.

The preparation of food has six processes during which safe food handling is important. These processes are preparing raw food, cooking, cooling, thawing, reheating, and holding.

### Preparing Raw Food

Raw food often has small amounts of pathogens and other contaminants. For example, raw fruits and vegetables often have soil on them. Soil contains many microorganisms. In another example, *salmonella* bacteria are often found on raw chicken.

## Basic Rules of Food Handling

Keep cold foods cold.     Keep hot foods hot.

*Kellis/Shutterstock.com*     *anekoho/Shutterstock.com*

**9-14** The main way to prevent the growth of bacteria is to keep foods out of the temperature danger zone.

One of the major dangers when handling raw food is cross-contamination. **Cross-contamination** is the transfer of microorganisms from one food item to another. Cross-contamination can occur when a raw food is placed on the same surface as a cooked food. The bacteria from the raw food get into the cooked food. These bacteria can then reproduce quickly to harmful levels in the cooked food. Cross-contamination can take place between one food item and another, one surface and another, one food item and a surface, or a surface and a food item. The main rules to prevent cross-contamination are to keep raw foods away from cooked foods and to always wash your hands after handling raw foods, **9-15**.

## Cooking

The first goal of cooking food is to make it appetizing. However, appetizing food will not please customers if it makes them sick. The second goal of cooking is to destroy pathogens or reduce them to safe levels. For this reason, the FDA has developed temperature recommendations for cooking foods.

The FDA temperature recommendations are not cooking instructions. These are the temperatures to which the cooked food must be brought and held in order to be safe. The FDA temperature recommendations state a minimum temperature and an amount of time that the food must be held at that temperature, **9-16**. An accurate thermometer is essential for measuring the temperatures of foods to make sure that they have reached these requirements.

## Cooling, Thawing, and Reheating

Cooling, thawing, and reheating are processes that take time and require food to go through the

### Procedures to Prevent Cross-Contamination

- Thoroughly clean raw food. Wash all fresh fruits and vegetables, including lettuce and other salad ingredients. Wash your hands when finished.
- Prepare raw seafood, poultry, and meat on surfaces and with utensils that can be sanitized. After preparation, sanitize all surfaces. Wash hands.
- Do not handle raw foods, including eggs, and then touch cooked foods or foods that will not be cooked. Always wash your hands after handling raw foods. For example, a person who is preparing fried chicken can cross-contaminate by touching the raw chicken, then touching the cooked fried chicken before washing hands.
- Do not let raw foods drip on cooked foods in the refrigerator.

*Goodheart-Willcox Publisher*

**9-15** To prevent cross-contamination, keep raw foods separate from cooked foods.

temperature danger zone. For this reason, these processes must be done as quickly as possible. Special precautions must be taken to reduce the growth of bacteria during cooling, thawing, and reheating, **9-17**. An accurate thermometer must be used during all these steps to ensure safety. Improper reheating is one of the most common causes of foodborne illness.

| FDA Minimum Internal Food Temperatures | | |
|---|---|---|
| **Food** | **Minimum Internal Temperature** | **Minimum Holding Time** |
| Beef, pork, fish, lamb | 145°F | 15 seconds |
| Ground meats, sausage | 155°F | 15 seconds |
| Poultry, stuffed meats, stuffed pasta, stuffing, casseroles | 165°F | 15 seconds |

*Source: FDA 2009 Food Code, www.fda.gov*

**9-16** The FDA temperature recommendations are not cooking instructions. They are temperatures to which the cooked food must be brought and held in order to be safe.

## Safe Cooling, Thawing, and Reheating

| Process | Precautions | Steps |
|---------|-------------|-------|
| *Cooling* | Cool as quickly as possible. | 1. Place food in a clean stainless steel container. <br> 2. Place container in cold water or ice bath. <br> 3. Stir food during cooling. <br> 4. Cool until food reaches 41°F. |
| *Thawing* | Keep food from reaching and staying in the temperature danger zone. | *Options* <br> • Thaw in original wrapper in the refrigerator. <br> • Thaw in original wrapper under cold running water in a sink. <br> • Thaw in microwave. |
| *Reheating* | Bring to 165°F as quickly as possible. | 1. Reheat only enough food to meet needs. <br> 2. Reheat liquids over direct heat. <br> 3. Reheat solid foods in a convection oven. <br> 4. Small portions can be reheated in a microwave. <br> 5. Never use a steam table to reheat foods. Reheat first and then transfer to the steam table. |

*Goodheart-Willcox Publisher*

9-17 Growth of bacteria occurs most often during cooling, thawing, and reheating.

## Holding

**Holding** is keeping potentially hazardous foods out of the temperature danger zone during the period while the food is waiting to be served to guests. The main rule of holding is keep hot foods hot and cold foods cold.

Safe holding of cold foods requires that they be kept below 41°F. Examples of foods that must be served cold are salads and shrimp cocktail. Ice is used to keep cold foods on salad bars and buffets below 41°F. The ice used to cool food cannot be served to customers, but it still must be clean and sanitary.

Safe holding of hot foods requires that they be kept above 135°F after cooking. The temperature of these foods must be checked regularly. If the temperature of the food falls below 135°F, the food may become unsafe to eat.

In order to make sure that foods are being held at the proper temperature, the temperature of the foods must be checked regularly. One critical step in safe food handling is to make sure someone is assigned the task of checking the temperatures of all held foods. Many companies have developed noncontact, infrared digital thermometers to make temperature checking easier, **9-18**.

9-18 The chef is using a noncontact, infrared, digital thermometer to check the temperature of the soup.

*Raytek Corporation*

# Government Regulations

Federal, state, and local government agencies have laws that regulate food safety and sanitation in foodservice businesses. They are responsible for enforcing food safety.

## Federal Agencies

Five federal agencies have a major responsibility for food safety: the Food Safety and Inspection Service (FSIS), the Food and Drug Administration (FDA), the Animal and Plant Health Inspection Service (APHIS), the Centers for Disease Control and Prevention (CDC), and the Environmental Protection Agency (EPA), **9-19**.

## State Agencies

Most states have a public health agency responsible for the regulation of foodservice businesses. Many states have used the FDA Model Food Code to create their own food codes. For example, the state of Texas has developed the Texas Food Establishment Rules, which are based on the FDA food code. This code was developed by the Texas State Health Services.

| Federal Agencies Responsible for Food Safety | | |
|---|---|---|
| **Name** *Agency* | **Abbreviation** | **Responsibilities** |
| **Food Safety and Inspection Service** *U.S. Department of Agriculture* | FSIS | The FSIS is responsible for the safety of meat, poultry, and eggs. The agency carries out inspections of meat, poultry, and egg processing plants. |
| **Food and Drug Administration** *U.S. Department of Health and Human Services* | FDA | The FDA is responsible for all foods not covered by the FSIS. The FDA is responsible for making sure that these foods are pure, safe to eat, and properly labeled. Also, the FDA develops a model food code. This food code lists all the recommended procedures for making a foodservice safe and sanitary. Many state and local governments and restaurants use the code to help them develop appropriate and safe facilities and procedures. |
| ***Animal and Plant Health Inspection Service*** *U.S. Department of Agriculture* | APHIS | The main responsibility of APHIS is to protect food, plants, and animals from disease. |
| **Environmental Protection Agency** *Independent Agency* | EPA | The EPA is responsible for making sure that toxic chemicals do not enter the air and water supply. The EPA also protects the public health and the environment from risks from pesticides. |
| **Centers for Disease Control and Prevention** *U.S. Department of Health and Human Services* | CDC | The CDC aids the other departments by investigating causes of foodborne illness outbreaks. It helps educate people on proper sanitation and is responsible for inspecting cruise ships. |

*Goodheart-Willcox Publisher*

9-19 Five federal agencies are important in preventing foodborne illness.

As part of the food code, many states require each foodservice to have at least one person on staff who has a food safety certification. In addition, most states require that foodservice establishments obtain a permit before they are allowed to open. In order to receive the permit, the foodservice establishment has to meet specific food safety and sanitation requirements.

## *Local Health Departments*

Local health departments, run by a city, municipality, or county, are usually responsible for enforcing state food codes. The local health departments often administer the food safety exams and issue restaurant permits. Local health departments periodically inspect restaurants to make sure they continue to meet food safety and sanitation requirements. Local health departments are also responsible for investigating any reported incidents of foodborne illness.

The outbreak of foodborne illness is a serious situation. Because it takes a while for symptoms to develop, it may take a few days for the outbreak to become known. Usually, people will start calling the local health department to complain about becoming ill after eating food at a certain restaurant. The health department will then visit the restaurant and inspect it thoroughly for food safety and sanitation violations. Health department inspectors will also take samples of food to determine the cause of the illness. If the violations are serious, the health department will close the restaurant until the violations are corrected.

## HACCP

The **Hazard Analysis Critical Control Point (HACCP)** is a system of assuring food safety. This system was developed by the Pillsbury Company in the 1960s for the National Aeronautics and Space Administration (NASA). Space program officials realized that if an astronaut developed a foodborne illness in space, it could become a life-threatening situation. In the environment of space, food had to be absolutely safe, and the risk of foodborne illness could not be allowed.

HACCP (pronounced hass´ ip) sets up control points to ensure the proper handling of food from the moment it enters the restaurant until it is fully prepared and served. In other words, HACCP is a

way of organizing and documenting all the rules of safe food handling so they are followed.

HACCP consists of seven steps, **9-20**. During the hazard analysis, each food and menu item is analyzed for potential hazards while it is in the foodservice. Examples of hazards include employees who do not wash their hands after using the toilet, cold foods held at room temperature for too long, and reheated foods that are not heated to a hot enough temperature. A **critical control point (CCP)** is a point when a hazard can be prevented. Critical control points usually occur during receiving, storage, preparation, holding, and serving. For example, potato salad is potentially hazardous if it is held at too warm a temperature, so one critical control point is during holding.

Each critical control point is given a critical limit to prevent hazards. A **critical limit** is an action or a temperature required for food safety. Critical limits usually involve time and temperature or human contact with food. For example, a critical control point for potato salad occurs when it is put into the cooler. The hazard is that any bacteria in the potato salad will grow to dangerous levels if the temperature in the cooler is too high. The critical limit is a cooler temperature below 41°F. A monitoring system must be set up to check the temperature of the cooler every four hours. If the temperature is found to be over 41°F, then corrective action is taken. When the seven steps of HACCP are completed for each food or menu item, you will have a flowchart for each food and menu item. This flowchart will indicate all the CCPs, critical limits, and corrective actions. These flowcharts should be posted where employees can easily refer to them.

## Role of the Manager

The general manager of a restaurant and the food and beverage manager in a hotel are responsible for the safety and sanitation of their operations. Most states require that at least one employee have certification in safety and sanitation. That employee is often the manager. Managers are responsible for identifying risks in the day-to-day operation of a foodservice business. A foodservice manager should develop and maintain standards aimed at preventing foodborne illness. Often, this involves establishing a HACCP program. Food and beverage managers have the ultimate responsibility for serving food that is safe to eat, **9-21**.

| Seven Steps of HAACP | | |
|---|---|---|
| | **Step** | **Action** |
| 1 | Conduct a hazard analysis | Identify and assess potential hazards in the food that you serve. A careful study should be made of each menu item. All potentially hazardous foods should be identified. Estimate the amount of risk that is present. Focus on the most hazardous foods on your menu. |
| 2 | Identify critical control points | Study the path of each food and menu item from the time it enters the foodservice to the moment it is served. Identify the critical control points. |
| 3 | Set critical limits | Set critical limits for each CCP. The critical limits are usually based on FDA recommendations. However, you can set stricter limits based on your specific situation. For example, the FDA standard requires ground beef to be cooked to 155°F for 15 seconds. You can set the limit at 160°F for 15 seconds. An important critical limit is to specify handwashing at the critical points. The critical control points and limits should be recorded in flowcharts and recipes, which are located where employees can easily check them. |
| 4 | Establish monitoring procedures | Someone must monitor each CCP to assure that the limits are followed. The manager should set up a system of monitors to check each CCP and limit. For example, one worker can be given the responsibility to check the cooler temperature every four hours. |
| 5 | Take corrective action | For each critical limit, decide what must be done if the limit is not met. Take steps to meet the limit. Decide when food must be thrown out. |
| 6 | Establish record-keeping procedures | Set up a system for keeping records on the critical points and limits. When the critical points are checked, the results must be recorded. For example, records must be kept on equipment repair, thermostat regulations, and temperature checks. All documentation must be maintained. |
| 7 | Evaluate the HACCP plan regularly | The manager should evaluate the plan regularly to see if HACCP is working. Changes should be made as necessary to ensure food safety and sanitation. |

*Goodheart-Willcox Publisher*

**9-20** The Hazard Analysis Critical Control Point (HACCP) is a system of assuring food safety.

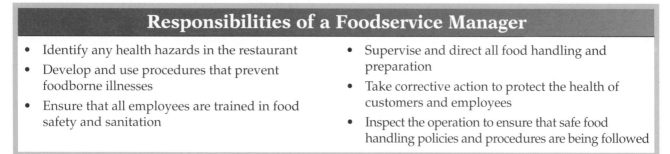

**Responsibilities of a Foodservice Manager**

- Identify any health hazards in the restaurant
- Develop and use procedures that prevent foodborne illnesses
- Ensure that all employees are trained in food safety and sanitation
- Supervise and direct all food handling and preparation
- Take corrective action to protect the health of customers and employees
- Inspect the operation to ensure that safe food handling policies and procedures are being followed

*Goodheart-Willcox Publisher*

**9-21** According to the National Assessment Institute, a food and beverage manager is responsible for all actions to ensure safe food and sanitary conditions.

# Chapter 9
## Review

## Chapter Summary

- An incident of foodborne illness can result not only in the discomfort of illness, but it can also ruin a foodservice business.
- There are three types of contaminants: physical, chemical, and biological.
- Bacteria are the most common cause of foodborne illnesses.
- There are three main ways to prevent foodborne illnesses: personal hygiene, sanitation, and proper handling of food.
- Sanitation and personal hygiene procedures can be organized into four areas: employee practices; food sources and storage; equipment, utensils, and surfaces; and food handling.
- Cleaning is the physical removal of soil and food residues from surfaces. Sanitizing is the treatment of a surface that has been previously cleaned to reduce the number of disease-causing microorganisms to safe levels.

- Federal, state, and local government agencies have laws that regulate food safety and sanitation in foodservice businesses.
- The Hazard Analysis Critical Control Point (HACCP) is a system of ensuring food safety.
- The general manager of a restaurant and the food and beverage manager in a hotel are responsible for the safety and sanitation of their operations.

## Review

1. Why is food safety and sanitation so important to foodservice?
2. List and give an example of each of the three types of food contamination.
3. What are the three types of pathogens that are most responsible for foodborne illness?
4. What are the five main symptoms of pathogen-caused foodborne illness?
5. Describe the temperature danger zone.
6. List eight employee practices that prevent foodborne illness and give a reason for each.
7. Why is proper food storage important?

8. Summarize ways to discourage insects and pests from coming into your business.
9. Why is dishwashing important?
10. How can you prevent cross-contamination?
11. What are the two purposes of cooking food?
12. Describe the procedures for safely cooling, thawing, and reheating food.
13. When you hold foods, how can you keep them out of the temperature danger zone?
14. List four responsibilities of the local public health department for food safety and sanitation.
15. List and explain the seven steps of HACCP.
16. Describe the role of the manager in preventing foodborne illness.

# Critical Thinking

17. **Design.** Create a poster that shows the 11 ways employees can prevent foodborne illness.
18. **Develop.** Choose a menu item that you like to prepare. Develop a HACCP chart for that item.
19. **Analyze.** Imagine you are the manager of the Coffee Cup Deli, and you are inspecting your kitchen during the lunch period. You notice salad ingredients and raw chicken on the same counter top. You also notice that your employees are wearing dirty aprons, which they are using to dry their hands.
    A. What sanitation hazards do you notice during your inspection?
    B. Which hazards could cause an outbreak of foodborne illness?
    C. What other areas of the restaurant should the manager check for hazards?

# Common Core

### College and Career Readiness

20. **Reading.** Research information on how rodents contaminate food service operations. Include current press releases that reported about rodent-infested restaurants.
21. **Speaking.** Bring a can or package of food from home. Demonstrate proper storage procedures and labeling with this food item.
22. **Writing.** Use the Internet to research proper handwashing techniques. The U.S. Food and Drug Administration website is one suggested resource. Write a report on your findings.
23. **Speaking.** Prepare an electronic presentation on the pathogens discussed in this chapter. Include images to display to the class.
24. **CTE Career Readiness Practice.** The ability to read and interpret information is an important workplace skill. Presume you work for a restaurant that serves Japanese food. The restaurant is considering adding sushi to its menu, but the manager wants you to evaluate and interpret some research on a HACCP system for sushi. You will need to locate three reliable sources of the latest HACCP information related to sushi. Read and interpret the information. Then write a report summarizing your findings.

# Part Three
# The Lodging Industry

168

169

Anna Azimi/Shutterstock.com

170

# Chapter 10

## The World of Lodging

## Chapter Objectives

After studying this chapter, you will be able to

- **describe** the characteristics of full-service hotels, limited-service properties, and specialty accommodations.
- **list** the three types of hotel ownership.
- **explain** what a hotel management company does.
- **explain** what an affiliation group is and what it does.
- **describe** the three size categories of lodging properties.
- **assess** the relationship between level of service and price of a hotel room.
- **contrast** the six major market segments in the lodging industry.
- **describe** the role of foodservice in many lodging properties.

## Before You Read

Try to answer the following questions before you read this chapter.

- What is the difference between a room rate and a rack rate?
- What are some examples of specialty accommodations?

## Terms to Know

| | | |
|---|---|---|
| full-service hotel | suite | hotel management |
| concierge | limited-service property | referral system |
| convention hotel | continental breakfast | affiliation group |
| trade show | limited-service hotels | consortium |
| exhibit hall | budget hotels | rack rate |
| convention center | specialty accommodations | room rate |
| luxury hotel | conference center | guest mix |
| resort hotel | bed-and-breakfast (B&B) | meal plan |
| resort | hostel | lodging concept |

The lodging industry consists of all businesses that provide overnight accommodations. A business that provides overnight accommodations is often called a *lodging property*. Lodging properties range from campgrounds to luxury hotels. Many lodging businesses offer food and beverages as part of their services.

# Types of Lodging Businesses

Lodging businesses can be organized in many ways. Guests often think of lodging businesses in terms of price, location, or services offered. Business analysts think of lodging businesses in terms of ownership and affiliation. **10-1**, Level of service, which relates to price, is one way the lodging industry can be organized. Usually, the higher the level of service, the higher the price charged for the accommodations.

Lodging businesses can be organized into categories based on level of service: full-service hotels, limited-service properties, and specialty accommodations. Both full-service hotels and limited-service properties provide guest rooms with private baths, telephones, and televisions. Specialty accommodations vary in their levels of service, but usually provide less than full-service hotels. This category includes bed-and-breakfasts, hostels, and campgrounds.

If you look up the word *hotel* in the phone book, you will see many lodging properties listed. The names of the properties will include words

| Lodging Industry Organization Based on Service | |
|---|---|
| **Categories** | **Examples** |
| *Full-Service Hotels* | |
| Full-Service | Wyndham Hotels, Hilton Hotels, Holiday Inn Select |
| Convention | Hyatt Regency McCormick Place |
| Luxury | Ritz-Carltons, Four Seasons |
| Resort | Kauai Coconut Beach Resort (Hawaii) |
| Extended-Stay | Residence Inns by Marriott, Homewood Suites by Hilton |
| Condominium | Kona by the Sea Condominiums (Hawaii) |
| *Limited-Service Properties* | |
| Limited-Service Hotels | Holiday Inn Express, La Quinta Inns, Courtyard by Marriott |
| Budget Hotels | Motel 6, Microtel, Super 8 |
| *Specialty Accommodations* | |
| Conference Centers | Hickory Ridge Conference Center (Illinois) |
| Lodges | Buccaneer Country Lodge (Vermont) |
| Bed-and-Breakfast Operations | The Chateau Tivoli (California) |
| Hostels | Miami Beach International Hostel |
| Campgrounds | KOA Kampgrounds |

*Goodheart-Willcox Publisher*

**10-1** The lodging industry can be organized in many ways. A common way is to group lodging properties based on level of service.

such as *hotel*, *inn*, *motel*, *motor inn*, *lodge*, *resort*, and *bed-and-breakfast*. The word *hotel* may refer to any type of lodging, so you often cannot tell the type of lodging property from its name. In addition, the types of services offered by a lodging business can change. Therefore, the differences among the categories are often blurred.

## Full-Service Hotels

Even though the word *hotel* is often used to refer to any type of lodging, the most common association with the word *hotel* is the full-service hotel. This image of the hotel developed during the age of the grand hotels: an elegant building, rich guests in fancy clothing, hotel staff in colorful uniforms to cater to the guests' every need, lavish banquets, and room service.

A **full-service hotel** is large and provides many services. The first distinguishing feature of a full-service hotel is its architecture. Hotels are usually two or more stories high, **10-2**. Many hotels are huge—over 3,000 rooms. Guest rooms are arranged along shared inside hallways.

The second distinguishing feature is the level of service. Full-service hotels usually provide a full range of services, including luggage assistance, one or more restaurants, one or more bars or cocktail lounges, room service, meeting and banquet facilities, spa services, recreational facilities, and concierge services. A **concierge** is a hotel staff member who helps guests make arrangements, such as dinner reservations. A concierge also

*Doubletree Hotel Dallas-Lincoln Center. Hilton Hotels Corporation*

10-2  This hotel is distinguished by its architecture. The guest rooms are set along shared inside hallways.

advises guests on what to do and see in the area around the hotel. Full-service hotels pride themselves on their high level of service and usually charge the highest prices. Examples of full-service

# *Hospitality Ethics*

## Ethics and Civility

In the hospitality industry (and in all walks of life), expressing *civility* is an ethical action not to take lightly. Civility is politeness and courtesy in behavior and speech. People who are polite and courteous show good manners and respect for others. They go the extra mile to provide excellent customer service in an honest and fair way. Through their actions, they help build a positive reputation for their employers and the industry. In contrast, those who mistreat customers or spread harmful gossip about coworkers show a lack of respect for those they serve.

hotels include Marriott Hotels, Hilton Hotels, and Hyatt Hotels.

In addition to the general category of full-service hotels, there are five subcategories: convention, luxury, resort, extended-stay, and condominium.

## Convention Hotels

A **convention hotel** is designed to provide for the special needs of conventions and trade shows. A *convention* is a large meeting, usually sponsored by a group for its members. A wide variety of groups hold conventions, from professional associations to student career organizations to social organizations and clubs. The number of people attending a convention can range from 50 to over 50,000. Trade shows are often held along with a convention or by themselves. A **trade show** is an exhibit during which people show the goods and services they have to sell. For example, the National Restaurant Association (NRA) holds an annual convention. In 2012, over 61,000 people from all over the world attended this convention. The NRA has a trade show along with the convention in which over 2,000 companies that sell to restaurants and hotels showed their goods and services. The space where a trade show is held is called an **exhibit hall, 10-3**.

Convention hotels usually provide sleeping rooms for 200 or more people, banquet space for groups over 100, many meeting rooms, an exhibit hall, and business services such as voice mail, Internet access, mailing services, and copying services. Convention hotels usually have large lobbies to accommodate large groups when they

arrive. Convention hotels also have many *double-occupancy rooms*—rooms for two or more people.

Convention hotels are often located near a convention center. A **convention center** is a large building designed specifically to hold large meetings, conventions, and trade shows. There are no sleeping accommodations in a convention center. A convention center is often developed by the city in which it is located. Often, the convention center staff works with the convention hotels in the area to make sure there are enough rooms for all convention participants.

McCormick Place in Chicago is considered North America's largest convention center. It has more than 2.2 million square feet of exhibit space. McCormick Place is a short ride from several convention hotels, which accommodate the enormous conventions that take place there. The National Restaurant Show is one of the many annual conventions that are held at McCormick Place.

## Luxury Hotels

A **luxury hotel** provides the highest level of amenities, service, room furnishings, public spaces, and technology. These hotels provide more services, more personal attention to guests, and more elegance than a typical full-service hotel. These hotels charge higher prices to cover their higher level of services and amenities. Some of the best-known luxury hotels are the Four Seasons Hotels, the W Hotels, and the Ritz-Carlton Hotels.

## Resort Hotels

A **resort hotel** caters to the vacationer or leisure traveler. A **resort** is a place that provides entertainment, recreation, and relaxation for vacationers, **10-4**. Many locations are considered resorts because of their climate or scenery. Many resort areas are located near seashores, mountains, and hot springs. Famous resort locations include Saratoga Springs, New York, for the hot springs; Vail, Colorado for the mountains; and the Hawaiian Islands for the beaches. Many resort hotels are found in resort locations.

However, resort hotels are also found in nonresort locations, such as the suburbs or rural areas. In order to make these hotels into resort hotels, special facilities are built to attract pleasure-seeking guests. Special facilities include spas, saunas, swimming pools, and physical fitness equipment. Many resort hotels have a golf course, tennis courts, and a pro shop on the property. Because of their many

**10-3** This photo shows an exhibit hall at the National Restaurant Association's national convention and trade show.

*Photo courtesy of the National Restaurant Association*

nikolpetr/Shutterstock.com

**10-4** Resorts, such as this ski lodge in Italy, provide recreation as well as lodging.

amenities, resort hotels often attract executive and corporate meetings.

Guests often spend a week or more at a resort hotel. Some resort hotels provide the highest level of services and amenities and are considered luxury resorts, such as the Carmel Valley Ranch.

### Extended-Stay Hotels

A significant number of people need lodging for five or more days. Guests who stay for 5 to 29 days are called *extended-stay guests*. *Long-stay guests* stay for 30 days or more. Extended- and long-stay guests are often businesspeople who must spend an extended amount of time in a city that is not their home.

A variety of types of hotels meet the needs of these guests: extended-stay hotels, all-suite hotels, and residential hotels. The major characteristic of these hotels is that they provide kitchen facilities and more than one room for each accommodation. Some also provide the same amenities as other hotels, including daily housekeeping service, laundries, restaurants, cocktail lounges, and room service. Since these hotels provide kitchen facilities and more space, families and other groups that need more space often stay in extended-stay, all-suite, and residential hotels.

A **suite** is a hotel accommodation that consists of more than one room. In a full-service hotel, suites are usually quite expensive. All-suite hotels were developed to provide more space at a lower cost. All-suite hotels offer only suites, which are usually two hotel rooms joined together, **10-5**. The suite is sold for approximately the price of one hotel room. These suites combine living space with kitchen facilities. In some all-suite hotels, the kitchen facilities are basic: a small refrigerator, an electric coffeemaker with a supply of coffee, a microwave oven, and a wet bar. To keep rates low, many all-suite hotels have small lobbies and no meeting rooms. Some do not have a restaurant or bar. However, some all-suite hotels have lounges, meeting rooms, and limited foodservice. Some also provide amenities such as a free breakfast, free wireless Internet access, a pool, and a health club.

LI CHAOSHU/Shutterstock.com

10-5  This suite has two rooms—a living area and a separate bedroom.

Extended- and long-stay suites provide a full kitchen with dishes and utensils. Some provide a grocery shopping service for guests. Guests can turn in a shopping list to staff members, who will take care of the shopping and have the groceries delivered.

Residential hotels cater to long-stay guests. A typical guest might be an executive who has been relocated from another state. The executive may not be able to move into a house or apartment until his or her home is sold. Residential hotels offer many hotel amenities, including daily housekeeping, restaurants, and room service. The décor is usually more like a home with a kitchen, living area, and bedroom.

## Condominium Hotels

Condominium hotels offer many amenities. They have multiroom apartments with full kitchens. Some have on-site food and beverage service. The units are usually owned by individual owners.

The overall property is operated by a management company. Condominium hotels are usually located in resort areas or downtown areas of cities. However, many new, upscale hotels are being built with condos above them. For example, the Park Hyatt in Chicago has condominiums above the hotel. The owners of the condos make use of many of the hotel amenities, such as room service and housekeeping.

There are two types of condominium ownership. In one type, an individual owns the unit. The other type is called *time-share ownership*. A time-share owner owns the right to use the unit for a specific time of the year. Other time-share owners own the right to use the unit at different specific times. For example, a time-share owner could purchase two weeks in a time-share condo located in South Padre Island, Texas. He or she owns the right to use the condo during the same two weeks each year. Sometimes time-share owners trade with each other. These trades are arranged through time-share trading organizations, such as RCI or Interval International. The South Padre Island owner might arrange to trade his Texas time-share for two weeks in a condo in Florida.

## Limited-Service Properties

A **limited-service property** focuses on charging lower prices, which it is able to do by providing fewer services than a full-service hotel. Limited-service properties are smaller, too. The first limited-service hotels were called *motels*. A motel is distinguished from a hotel by its architecture and level of service. A traditional motel was one or two stories high, with no interior corridors and no elevators. Parking was located close to the rooms, and all the rooms were entered from the outside. To increase guest security, most new motels now have central corridors, with a lobby and breakfast room. A room key must be used to enter the property from all exterior doors except the main entrance. Some limited-service properties provide only the room and housekeeping in order to charge the lowest price.

Motels offer minimal services. There are no bell attendants to assist with luggage. Rooms are small but adequate room with beds, TV, phone, free Internet access, private bath, and daily housekeeping, but no foodservice, bar, or recreational facilities. As a result, motels can charge a lot less per night than hotels.

As time went on, people wanted something between the full service and expense of a hotel and the no-frills economy of a motel. Motels got a little bigger and started offering more amenities. For example, many motels offer swimming pools and a continental breakfast. A **continental breakfast** consists of breakfast foods that do not need to be cooked, **10-6**. A continental breakfast can be as simple as coffee and sweet rolls. It can also be more elaborate and include fruit juices; coffee and tea; cold cereal and milk; bread and a toaster; fruit; bagels and cream cheese; and a variety of sweet rolls. Some even have breakfast items such as eggs, waffles, and sausage. A continental breakfast can be served in a building that does not have a full kitchen.

During the same period, some hotels got a little smaller and offered fewer amenities. Many of these smaller hotels use the word *inn* in their names. The bigger motels and the smaller hotels merged into a category of properties that offer a

Iakov Filimonov/Shutterstock.com

**10-6** A free continental breakfast is a popular hotel amenity.

medium level of services at a midrange price. This category is called *limited-service hotels*.

Limited-service properties can be organized into two categories: limited-service hotels and budget hotels.

### Limited-Service Hotels

The **limited-service hotels** offer a medium level of service and a midrange price. The typical limited-service hotel is three or four stories tall, has the word *inn* as part of its name, and offers more services than a motel but fewer than a hotel. They are often located near business parks or highways. Limited-service hotels usually do not have a restaurant or bell attendants. Some offer a continental breakfast in the lobby. Many have an indoor pool. Some have a few meeting rooms. Most offer Internet access in each room. Usually at least one brand-name restaurant is located nearby. La Quinta Inns, Hampton Inns, Fairfield Inns, and Comfort Inns are examples of limited-service hotels.

### Budget Hotels

The category of budget hotels is also called *economy hotels*, *budget motels*, or *economy motels*. **Budget hotels** have the lowest rates and the least service. The goal of these businesses is to focus on offering a comfortable, clean place to sleep at the lowest rate. One of the first businesses in this category was Motel 6, which offered rooms for $6 a night in the 1960s. Microtel is typical of newer properties in this category. They offer rooms with 30 percent less space.

## Specialty Accommodations

The category of **specialty accommodations** includes a variety of accommodations that provide less personal service than a full-service hotel, but more than a motel. Some provide a unique experience, such as a bed-and-breakfast, **10-7**. Some specialty accommodations provide guest rooms with private baths, telephones, and televisions. However, many provide shared accommodations and shared bathrooms. For example, a bed-and-breakfast sometimes has only one bathroom to serve several rooms of guests. Many, such as youth hostels and campgrounds, include some of the least expensive and lowest service accommodations. Some campgrounds provide only a shared bathroom with cold running water and a space to pitch a tent.

The specialty accommodations category can be divided into five groups: conference centers, lodges, bed-and-breakfast operations, hostels, and campgrounds.

### Conference Centers

A **conference center** is a lodging facility where 60 percent or more of the total occupancy is generated by conferences. The term *conference center* usually refers to smaller facilities located in suburban or rural areas or on college campuses. These conference centers specialize in offering sleeping rooms, meeting rooms, and meals for smaller conferences. Usually, everyone attending one of these conferences goes to the same meeting and eats all their meals together. Conference centers usually offer a complete package of sleeping rooms, meeting rooms, and meals. The staff is trained to serve meeting planners and attendees. Some very large corporations such as General Motors operate their own conference centers to provide facilities for training their own employees. Other conference centers are operated by universities.

### Lodges

Lodges provide rooms and housekeeping for those guests who want to participate in a recreational activity. Activities include hunting, skiing, fishing, or horseback riding. Lodges are usually small, ranging from 10 to 100 rooms. They are usually located in areas where the activity is done. Some lodges are designed to offer peace and serenity to the guests, **10-8**.

**10-7** A bed-and-breakfast may offer rooms decorated with charming Victorian appointments.

*Marcin Sylwia Ciesielski/Shutterstock.com*

Timothy Michael Morgan/Shutterstock.com

**10-8** Lodges are often located in beautiful natural areas.

## Bed-and-Breakfast Operations

Guests looking for personal service and charming locations are often interested in bed-and-breakfast operations. A **bed-and-breakfast (B&B)** is a private home offering one or more guest rooms. They originated from the European tradition of people opening their homes to travelers. Today's B&Bs combine as much of that historic charm and personal touch as possible. Many B&Bs include a home-cooked breakfast and an opportunity to meet the host family and the other guests. Some bed-and-breakfasts are much larger and are more like a small inn. These larger B&Bs are sometimes called *bed-and-breakfast inns*.

Some business travelers who choose B&Bs are tired of impersonal hotel rooms. Many vacationers are looking for a friendly, family-like atmosphere. Guests often say that arriving at a B&B at the end of the day is like coming home after a hard day's work. Eating breakfast with the hosts and other guests adds to that warm feeling. Each B&B is as unique as its owner from beautifully restored Victorian homes in New England to simple stucco dwellings in New Mexico.

## Hostels

A **hostel** is an inexpensive place to stay where sleeping rooms, bathrooms, and kitchen facilities are shared. No linens, toilet articles, or housekeeping services are provided. Guests usually bring their own linens or rent them from the hostel. In some hostels, guests perform chores as part of their payment. Guests may be allowed to prepare their own food in the kitchen. The limited services and features keep the price low and encourage guests to get to know each other. Many people stay in hostels for the sense of adventure and the opportunity to meet a variety of people.

### Campgrounds

Campgrounds started out as places to pitch a tent with bathrooms nearby. Today, campgrounds have a range of facilities. The most basic have just cold running water and an outhouse. The more luxurious have hot showers and modern plumbing, hookups for recreational vehicles, and swimming pools, **10-9**. Campgrounds are usually located in natural areas where people go to hike and enjoy the scenery. Many are located in or near national and state parks.

# Location

Another way to categorize lodging properties is based on location. There are five main locations: center city, suburban, highway, airport, and resort.

## Center City

Many hotels are located in a city's downtown business district. Downtown properties have many advantages. They are near large office buildings and retail stores. They are also usually close to the city's entertainment center, which gives guests places to go for fun at night. Many downtown properties are full-service hotels. Limited-service properties and occasionally a hostel can also be found in the center city. Center city properties usually attract corporate business travelers during the week and leisure travelers and families

**10-9** Many campgrounds have hook-ups for recreational vehicles.

*Jim Perkin/Shutterstock.com*

on the weekends. Social events, such as weddings and reunions, are often held in downtown hotels on the weekends.

## Suburban

As the suburbs developed, so did the demand for lodging there. Many businesses moved to the suburbs and large housing developments and shopping centers were built. Accommodations were needed for business meetings, conventions, individual business travelers, and social events. Full-service, limited-service, and specialty accommodations can be found in the suburbs.

## Highway

As the highway system developed, the demand rose for lodging along the highways. Most accommodations along the highways are limited-service hotels and budget hotels.

## Airport

As airports developed, the demand grew for nearby lodging including full-service, limited-service, and specialty accommodations, **10-10**. Airport development also led to the development of businesses and industrial parks in the same area.

## Resort

Resort locations are very popular places to build lodging properties of all types. Examples of resort locations include the Caribbean Islands for their beautiful beaches and water sports and the Rocky Mountains for the majestic mountains and skiing. Luxury hotels, full-service hotels, limited-service properties, and specialty accommodations are all found in resorts.

# Ownership and Management

Lodging properties can also be classified by the type of ownership. Like restaurants, lodging properties can be independent, chains, or franchises. An independent lodging property is a single-unit business not connected with any other business. Most bed-and-breakfasts are independent and usually have one owner. However, that owner could be a single person, partnership, or corporation.

Pavel L Photo and Video/Shutterstock.com

**10-10** Hotels near an airport can be a major convenience for busy travelers.

## Hotel Chains

Chains are multiple-unit businesses that have the same brand name and the same ownership. Again, that one owner could be a single person, partnership, or corporation. A franchise is a unit of a chain that has been purchased by an outside owner. The outside owner runs the franchise in the way required by the chain owner.

One of the main advantages of a chain is the brand name. The chain owner develops and maintains brand identity through advertising, public relations, and other promotions. All the units of the chain, including franchises, benefit from a strong brand identity. The chain owner also works to develop brand loyalty. One way to develop loyalty is through frequent guest programs. Whenever you stay at a unit of the chain, you earn points. The more points you earn, the more benefits you receive. Examples of benefits include free health club privileges and the opportunity to cash in points for free nights.

Another advantage of a chain is the ability to save money by purchasing supplies in large quantities. When the chain buys towels, it buys towels for every hotel in the chain. A chain can have anywhere from 3 to over 5,000 units. A chain can also provide centralized and specialized services, such as training, site selection, and information systems. In fact, one of the greatest advantages of a chain is a central reservations center. A central reservations center is one office that handles the reservations for all the units in the chain. A guest can call one toll-free number to reserve a room at any hotel in the chain anywhere in the world.

Figure **10-11** shows 10 of the largest hotel chains in the world. When you look at this table, keep in mind that the hotel industry is dynamic. The number of hotels owned by each chain changes often. The rankings of these chains changes from year to year. The companies themselves change, either by merging or selling their hotel businesses. However, this chart will give you a good idea of the major world hotel chains.

## Hotel Management

There is one other arrangement in hotel ownership, which occurs when the owner does not manage the hotel. Ownership and management are not the same thing. **Hotel management** is the day-to-day running of the hotel. Hotel management is often called *hotel operation*. The same person or company does not have to own and manage a hotel. One person or company can own the hotel, and another person or company can manage it.

For example, a company that has no experience with hotels may buy or build a hotel. The owner will then hire a hotel management company to run the hotel. Many of the companies that manage hotels are part of a well-known hotel chain. For example, the Hilton Hotels Corporation also manages hotels. Suppose you want to own a Hilton Hotel. However, you do not want to buy a Hilton franchise because you do not want to run the hotel yourself. Instead, you build the hotel yourself and then hire the Hilton Hotels Corporation to run the hotel for you. Your hotel has the Hilton name on it, even though you own it. The Hilton Hotels Corporation takes care of all the day-to-day responsibilities of running your hotel according to the standards set by the Hilton Hotels Corporation. As a result, your hotel is very successful because it has the Hilton name and is run like a Hilton Hotel.

There are also hotel management companies that are not part of a major chain. For example, you could buy a Hilton franchise. Then you could hire a hotel management company to manage the hotel for you. Because of these different ownership and management arrangements, it is often difficult to know who actually owns the hotel. As far as customers are concerned, they identify the owner with the brand name on the hotel. If the hotel says *Hilton*, the customer will assume that it is owned or operated by the Hilton Hotels Corporation. However, the hotel could actually be owned

| Hotel Chain Rankings, 2012 | | | |
|---|---|---|---|
| **Rank** | **Company Name** *Headquarters* | **Number of Rooms** | **Number of Hotels** |
| 1 | IHG (InterContinental Hotels Group) *Windsor, England* | 658,348 | 4,480 |
| 2 | Hilton Hotels Corp. *Beverly Hills, CA* | 633,238 | 3,843 |
| 3 | Marriott International *Washington, DC* | 617,837 | 3,537 |
| 4 | Wyndham Hotel Group *Parsippany, NJ* | 613,126 | 7,205 |
| 5 | Accor *Paris, France* | 531,714 | 4,426 |
| 6 | Choice Hotels International *Silver Spring, MD* | 502,460 | 6,203 |
| 7 | Starwood Hotels & Resorts Worldwide *White Plains, NY* | 315,346 | 1,077 |
| 8 | Best Western International *Phoenix, AZ* | 311,598 | 4,078 |
| 9 | Home Inns & Hotels *Shanghai, China* | 176,562 | 1,077 |
| 10 | Carlson Hotels Worldwide *Minneapolis, MN* | 165,802 | 1,426 |

*MKG Group*

**10-11** The rankings of the top hotel chains may change from year to year. This table provides a snapshot of the top chains in 2012.

by a person, partnership, corporation, or nonprofit corporation that has no ownership connection with Hilton.

# Affiliation

An independent hotel often has a hard time competing against the hotel chains. A major challenge is how to let potential guests know about your hotel. An independent hotel does not have the money for national advertising or a national reservations center. In the 1940s and 50s, independent hotels started referring guests to each other. These informal groups developed into a formal referral system. Today, a **referral system** is a group of independent hotels that creates a central office for reservations and marketing, **10-12**. A referral system is also called an **affiliation group** or a **consortium**. (The plural of *consortium* is *consortia*.) Consortia vary in size. Best Western International is one of the largest. At last count, it had over 4,200 hotel members in 80 countries. Preferred Hotels & Resorts Worldwide is another consortium. It has over 110 hotel members in 20 countries. An independent hotel becomes a member of a consortium by meeting the membership requirements and paying dues.

*wavebreakmedia/Shutterstock.com*

**10-12**  A central reservations system is one of the major benefits of an affiliation group.

Best Western markets itself as "The World's Biggest Hotel Family®." However, an affiliation group is not a chain in the sense that has been defined here. Each member of an affiliation group is an independent hotel. Each member owns and operates its own property, which can have its own name. The people who run the affiliation group have limited control over the members. The chain owner decides on the décor and operating requirements for each chain member. The chain owner has a great deal of control over members and franchisers of the chain. In an affiliation group, each member makes its own decisions, except in areas required by the affiliation group. For example, in order to be a member of an affiliation group, the owner may have to agree to meet certain design and operating standards. A member of an affiliation group can leave the group if it becomes dissatisfied. The affiliation group can also ask a member to leave if the member does not meet the group's requirements or pay its dues.

Best Western is a chain in the sense that hotels carrying the Best Western name meet Best Western's standards of quality. When customers see the Best Western name and logo on a hotel, they know they will be getting a certain standard of services and amenities. Best Western is also a chain in the sense that it provides its member hotels with many services. These services are similar to those that a chain owner provides to its members and fall into two categories: marketing the hotel and managing the hotel.

In the area of marketing, Best Western provides advertising, sales, and special promotions. Best Western conducts a national advertising campaign on television and in print. It has 22 sales offices around the world. The *Best Western's Travelers' Guides and Road Atlases* contain color photographs, maps, and information about all the Best Western hotels. More than 1.5 million guides are distributed annually. Best Western's website provides complete information on all member hotels and enables guests to book reservations online. The company makes sure that all member hotels are listed in the major online hotel distribution and reservation systems. Best Western also provides member hotels with their global frequent traveler's program, called *Gold Crown Club International*®. One of the most valuable services that Best Western provides is a worldwide reservations system, located in its Phoenix headquarters.

In the area of hotel management and operations, Best Western provides training and assistance. The company provides comprehensive training, general manager training, and specialized workshops for hotel staff. Best Western also has a professional staff to coordinate buying so members can get the same purchasing power as the large chains. The company provides professionals to help with facilities design, operations, and revenue management.

## Size and Price

Lodging properties can also be grouped based on size. A small property has 1 to 50 rooms. A midsize property has 51 to 200 rooms. A large property has 201 or more rooms.

Another way to categorize lodging properties is by price. Sometimes three price categories are used: premier, moderate, and budget. Sometimes five categories are used: luxury, first-class, midrange, economy, and budget. These categories also indicate the level of service. Figure **10-13** shows how lodging properties can be categorized by price with levels indicated by the number of dollar signs. Prices for hotel rooms vary by location. In general, all levels of lodging accommodations are more expensive in a big city. Part of the reason is that the cost of real estate is much, much higher in a city. For example, in New York City, a room in a luxury hotel might be $700 a night, a first-class

| Lodging Properties, Categorized by Price and Service Level | | | |
|---|---|---|---|
| **Price Type** | **Price Level** | **Service Level** | **Examples** |
| Luxury | $$$$$ | Full service, extra attention to service and guest needs | Ritz-Carlton, Waldorf-Astoria®, Four Seasons, some bed & breakfasts |
| First-Class (also called Upscale) | $$$$ | Full service | Marriott Hotels, Wyndham Hotels |
| Midrange | $$$ | Limited service | Holiday Inn Express, Courtyard by Marriott |
| Economy | $$ | Very limited service | Econo Lodge, Super 8 |
| Budget | $ | Self-service | Hostels, Campgrounds |

*Goodheart-Willcox Publisher*

**10-13** The actual prices of a room vary by geographic location of the hotel. However, the relationship among the price types remains the same.

might be $400 a night, a midrange might be $250 a night, an economy might be $150 a night, and a budget might be $80 a night.

## Room Rates

The **rack rate** is the official rate for one night's lodging at a lodging property. However, the actual rate charged to a specific guest varies. The **room rate** is the price actually charged to a guest for one night's lodging. The rack rate is the rate usually used when someone classifies lodging properties based on their room rates.

A lodging property wants to charge room rates that will generate profit. However, rates have to be competitive with rates of similar hotels and appropriate for the type of traveler who stays there. Rates are usually established by the top manager or a team of managers. These managers study the economic situation of the hotel and the general economy. Hotel rates often vary from day to day.

Hotels also usually offer special rates in specific situations and for specific types of guests. For example, rates in the off-peak season will be lower than rates during the peak season.

A group that makes reservations for a large number of people at one time may get a special lower rate. Hotels often offer discounts to older

adults and the military. Hotels also offer discounts to members of travel clubs. One of the largest travel clubs is the AAA, the American Automobile Association.

## Lodging Market

A *market* consists of all the people who could potentially buy what you are selling. In the lodging industry, the market consists of everyone who travels. The goal of every lodging business is to meet the needs of the market. However, it is very difficult to meet the needs of such a diverse and large market. It is more useful to divide the market into subgroups with similar needs, called *market segments*. A market segment is a subgroup of a larger market; the market segment has similar needs and wants for the product you are selling. A large market can be segmented in many different ways.

### Market Segments

The lodging market can be divided into six major segments: business, conventions and meetings, leisure, budget, extended-stay, and special. A lodging property will usually select one or two of these segments, **10-14**. It will then focus on meeting the specific needs of that segment.

## Segments of the Lodging Market

| | |
|---|---|
| **Business** | Business Travelers |
| **Conventions and Meetings** | Groups of People |
| **Long-Stay** | Need Accommodations for Five or More Days |
| **Leisure** | Traveling for Personal Reasons |
| **Budget** | Traveling as Cheaply as Possible |
| **Special** | Personnel from the Airlines, Military, and Government |

*Goodheart-Willcox Publisher*

**10-14** A lodging property usually chooses one or two segments to target.

### Business

The business segment consists of people traveling for business. The company that sends them pays all their travel expenses. Business travelers are usually individual adults or small groups of adults. Business travelers want services that will help them accomplish their business goals. They want their sleeping room to have a desk, phone, and Internet access. They may need access to business services, such as mailing services, copy machines, and fax machines. They might also prefer a restaurant, lounge, and room service. Lodging properties that cater to the business segment include full-service hotels and limited-service hotels.

### Conventions and Meetings

The conventions and meetings segment consists of people traveling to a specific convention or meeting. These travelers are usually groups of adults and may vary in size from 50 to over 50,000. Some meetings are business related. For example, a business may organize a meeting to train its employees. Other conventions are sponsored by professional and social organizations. Convention hotels and conference centers specialize in serving the conventions and meetings segment.

### Leisure

The leisure segment consists of people traveling on vacation or for personal reasons, such as visiting family and friends, and social events

such as a wedding. Leisure travelers often travel in groups of one or two adults with children. All types of lodging properties serve leisure travelers. In particular, resort hotels, limited-service hotels, condominium hotels, and bed-and-breakfasts serve this market segment.

### Budget

The budget segment consists of people looking for the cheapest accommodations. Families and students are a large part of this segment. This segment may overlap with the leisure segment. Some business travelers are also budget-minded. This market segment is served by limited-service properties, hostels, and campgrounds.

### Extended-Stay

The extended-stay segment consists of people who need accommodations for five or more days. Many of these people are relocating for business reasons. They need a more homelike atmosphere, kitchen facilities, laundry facilities, and more closet space. This market segment is served by extended-stay hotels, all-suite hotels, and residence hotels.

### Special

The special segment includes groups who have made special arrangements with the lodging business for low rates. The main groups in this category are the airlines, government, and military. Limited-service hotels and budget hotels serve this market segment.

## Target Market and Guest Mix

Many businesses find that they are more successful when they focus on meeting the needs of one market segment, a process called *target marketing*. A *target market* is the market segment the lodging business focuses on. For example, convention hotels select the conventions and meetings segment as their target market, **10-15**. A bed-and-breakfast might select leisure travelers looking for a homelike experience as its target market.

Many full-service and limited-service hotels must attract guests from more than one market segment to be successful. The hotel might specialize in serving one market segment yet also attract guests from other market segments. For example, a hotel that caters to business travelers during the business week might offer a special low-cost deal on weekends to attract leisure travelers. The **guest mix** is the percentage of each segment that is staying at

Anton Gvozdikov/Shutterstock.com

10-15 The target market for convention hotels are the people who are attending meetings.

a lodging property. Some properties might specialize in leisure guests. They might have a guest mix of 60 percent leisure, 30 percent business, and 10 percent conventions and meetings. Other properties might specialize in business travelers and have a guest mix of 60 percent business, 30 percent convention, and 10 percent leisure.

## Functions in Lodging

Each lodging business is unique, yet each one has to perform the same functions. Figure **10-16** lists and describes the functions. In a small business, one person may perform several of these functions. In a large business, there is usually a separate department for each function.

## Lodging and Foodservice

In many lodging properties, providing food and beverages is an essential part of the lodging's services. Almost every property has vending machines for soft drinks or snacks. Full-service hotels have at least one restaurant. Many full-service hotels have a fine-dining restaurant plus casual dining restaurants, snack shops, room service, and cocktail lounges. Banquets and catering are also an important part of the offerings at a full-service hotel.

Limited-service properties often provide a continental breakfast and coffee in the lobby. Some

limited-service hotels have a coffee shop. Specialty accommodations also often provide at least one meal. Many bed-and-breakfasts are famous for their home-cooked breakfasts.

Foodservice is such an important part of a hotel's offerings that many hotels have room rates that include meals. These arrangements are especially popular at resorts where people stay for a week or more. A room rate that includes meals is called a **meal plan**. The *Full American Plan* includes three meals a day. The *Modified American Plan* includes only two meals, usually breakfast and dinner. The *Continental Plan* includes a continental breakfast. When rates are listed as *European Plan*, no meals are included.

## Lodging Concepts

What makes one lodging property different from another? The concept of the property distinguishes one from another. A **lodging concept** is the whole idea of the lodging property or chain. The lodging concept includes the theme, target market, décor, ambiance, and level of service.

Many limited-service chains focus on providing clean, comfortable, safe accommodations at reasonable prices. Many luxury hotels focus on elegance and the best service for their wealthy target market.

Many hotels have a lodging concept based on a theme. One example is the Hyatt Regency Tamaya Resort and Spa in New Mexico. The theme of the resort is the culture of the Tamayame, the native people who lived in the area. Guests are greeted by a sculpture of the Tamayame welcoming guests with outstretched arm. The architecture is reminiscent of a historic Southwestern Pueblo community. Cultural treasures and artwork are showcased throughout the resort. Rooms are decorated with artwork and furnishings in the southwest theme. There is a Tamaya Cultural Museum and Learning Center at the resort. Bread baking and traditional pueblo singing and dancing are regular features.

Many independents and some units of chains strive to create a unique lodging experience. For example, at the Jumbo Stay near Stockholm, Sweden, you can stay in a retired 747 jumbo jet that has been converted into a hostel. Vacationers who want to experience life aboard a vintage train can stay at the Aurora-Express in Fairbanks, Alaska.

| 10 Functions in Lodging Businesses | |
|---|---|
| **Function** | **Description** |
| *Front Office* | • Handle all activities involved with guest rooms, making reservations, checking guests in and out, and helping guests while they are on the property |
| *Housekeeping* | • Prepare rooms for guests and do laundry<br>• Make sure building, furniture, floors, and all public areas are clean |
| *Purchasing and Receiving* | • Buy the right quality and quantity of supplies at the best price<br>• Make sure supplies arrive when needed<br>• Make sure supplies are stored properly once received<br>• Establish good relationships with reliable suppliers<br>• Inventory |
| *Management* | • Oversee all functions of the business<br>• Make sure the business is operating profitably and meeting customer needs |
| *Marketing and Sales* | • Learn what customers want<br>• Develop marketing plans<br>• Advertise<br>• Sell the lodging services |
| *Human Resources* | • Manage all employee issues, including pay, benefits, hiring, firing, and training |
| *Accounting* | • Keep track of all the money that flows into and out of the business<br>• Monitor costs<br>• If costs are running too high, let management know so costs can be controlled |
| *Security* | • Prevent harm to business property, employees, guests, and guests' property |
| *Safety and Emergency Procedures* | • Make sure the workplace is safe and meets all government safety requirements<br>• Make sure plans are in place in case of emergencies |
| *Engineering* | • Make sure all equipment, plumbing, electricity, and building facilities are working properly<br>• Maintenance and groundskeeping |

*Goodheart-Willcox Publisher*

10-16 Each lodging business is unique, yet each one has to perform the same functions.

# Chapter *10*
## Review

### Chapter Summary

- Lodging businesses can be organized into categories based on level of service: full-service hotels, limited-service properties, and specialty accommodations.

- There are five subcategories of full-service hotels: convention, luxury, resort, extended-stay, and condominium.

- Limited-service properties can be organized into two categories: limited-service hotels and budget hotels.

- The types of lodging ownership are independent, chain, and franchise.

- A referral group (also called an *affiliation group* or *consortium*) is a group of independent hotels that creates a central office for reservations and marketing.

- A small property has one to 50 rooms. A midsize property has 51 to 200 rooms. A large property has 201 or more rooms.

- Properties that provide more service usually charge higher prices.

- The lodging market can be divided into six major segments: business, conventions and meetings, leisure, budget, long-stay, and special.

### Review

1. Describe the differences among the categories of businesses in the lodging industry.
2. What is a convention hotel?
3. Why is a guest room in a limited-service property less expensive than a room in a full-service hotel?
4. Give two examples of specialty accommodations and describe their level of service.
5. What is the difference between an independent, chain, and franchise lodging property?
6. What does a hotel management company do?
7. Why does an independent hotel sometimes have a hard time competing against the chains?
8. What are the five price categories of lodging properties?
9. What are the six major segments of the lodging market?
10. List the functions in lodging businesses.
11. List four types of foodservice found in lodging properties.

# Critical Thinking

12. **Compare and contrast.** Make a poster or a chart that shows the differences among full-service hotels, limited-service properties, and specialty accommodations.

13. **Organize.** Choose a large U.S. city and use the Internet to find listings of its lodging properties. Organize these properties into three categories: full-service hotel, limited-service property, and specialty accommodation.

14. **Evaluate.** Imagine that you are responsible for planning the four-day state conference for your student career organization. Five hundred students and two hundred adults will be attending. Describe the kind of lodging property you would choose and explain your reasons for choosing it.

15. **Identify.** Pretend you are a business person working on a long-term contract for six weeks in another state. While working in this location, you will be staying in an extended-stay hotel. Describe the services that you will need while living in this hotel.

16. **Design.** Using the Internet, find five unique or unusual hotels. Make a poster showing the unique characteristics of these lodging properties.

# Common Core

### College and Career Readiness

17. **Writing.** Imagine that you are an independent owner and operator of a hotel in your hometown. Write an essay describing the advantages and disadvantages of belonging to an affiliation group, keeping your property's location in mind.

18. **Speaking.** Use the Internet to research a convention hotel. Give an oral report on your findings answering the following questions:
    - Where is it located?
    - How large is the exhibit space?
    - What conventions and trade shows are held here?
    - How many guest rooms does the hotel have?
    - What services does this convention hotel offer?
    - What other hotels are available for the convention attendees?

19. **Speaking.** Give an oral report on the differences among convention hotels, luxury hotels, and resort hotels. Include examples of the types of hotels.

20. **Reading.** Research lodging properties that focus on being environmentally friendly. Describe the specific steps they take in order to be classified this way. Include the way these steps affect the environment.

21. **Listening.** Interview someone who lives in a condominium hotel. Why did he or she choose this option? Present a short report to your class. Include a description of the condominiums available and what they offer.

22. **CTE Career Readiness Practice.** Search the Internet for new technologies in the lodging industry. Choose one of interest and determine the following: What are the benefits of using the technology to enhance productivity? What are some disadvantages or risks of using the new technology? What actions could you take to mitigate the disadvantages or risks? In your opinion, for what applications will this new technology most likely be used? Create a digital report to share your findings with the class.

190

# *Chapter 11*
## Front Office

## Chapter Objectives

After studying this chapter, you will be able to
- **describe** the functions of the rooms division.
- **explain** the functions of a property management system (PMS).
- **state** the functions of the front office.
- **identify** the main duties of staff in the reservations, uniformed services, and telecommunications departments.
- **outline** the main duties of the front desk agent.
- **explain** the two tasks of particular importance that the front office manager does.
- **list** and **describe** the steps in the hotel guest cycle.

## Before You Read

Try to answer the following questions before you read this chapter.
- How do lodging properties keep track of information related to guests and rooms?
- What responsibilities are fulfilled by the front desk?

## Terms to Know

| | | | |
|---|---|---|---|
| sleeping room | front office manager | room inventory | registration |
| guest room | nonguaranteed reservation | bell captain | registration record |
| function room | guaranteed reservation | door attendant | guest folio |
| rooms division | reservations agent | bell attendant | account settlement |
| director of rooms | reservation record | wake-up call | guest history record |
| property management system (PMS) | central reservations center | front desk agent | forecasting |
| front office | | check-in | work shift |
| | | checkout | hotel guest cycle |

The main business of a lodging property is selling sleeping rooms. Notice that the hotel industry makes a distinction between sleeping rooms and function rooms. A **sleeping room** is a room where guests sleep for one or more nights, **11-1**. A sleeping room is also called a **guest room**. A **function room** is a room that customers rent for an activity, such as a meeting, wedding, or banquet.

The major source of income for lodging properties is sales of sleeping rooms. The many tasks involved in selling sleeping rooms include taking reservations, assigning rooms, giving out room keys, helping guests with luggage, cleaning rooms, and washing linens. These tasks and others are handled by the rooms division.

# Rooms Division

The **rooms division** is the part of the hotel that handles all tasks involved in preparing and selling sleeping rooms. The main functions of the rooms division are to sell rooms, help guests while they are in the hotel, and clean rooms. The manager in charge of the rooms divisions is the **director of rooms**. In a small hotel, a few people carry out all the tasks of the rooms division.

In a larger hotel, the tasks of the rooms division are divided into departments. Each department has several employees to handle various tasks. The two main departments in the rooms division are the front office and housekeeping. The front office department takes care of selling rooms and helping guests. The housekeeping department takes care of cleaning rooms.

Sometimes security and engineering are part of the rooms division; sometimes they are a separate division. Figure **11-2** lists the departments of the rooms division and summarizes the functions.

## Racking System

The rooms division must keep track of a great deal of information. Examples of the kind of information include the following:
- How many guests are in the hotel?
- Which rooms are occupied?
- Who is in each room?
- When are new guests expected, and which rooms have they reserved?
- How many rooms are available to sell?
- Which rooms are ready to be cleaned?
- Have the guests in certain rooms checked out yet?

Many different workers in different parts of the hotel need this information.

In the days before computers, all the record keeping in a hotel was done by hand. The major system for keeping track of room reservations, guests, and metal keys was called a *racking system*. The major tool of the racking system was a rack, a type of shelving system that had a place for each room in the hotel. Some racks had a metal file pocket for each room. These were often used to store index cards containing information about each room, such as its status and the name of the guest in the room. Other racks had hooks designed to hold the metal keys for each room. Other racks were made of wood and had a cubbyhole for each room. These racks were used to hold mail and messages for guests in each room. The term *rack rate* comes from the days when racking systems were used.

## Property Management System

Today, computers can keep better records than a racking system can. A hotel might have a racking system to hold messages and mail for guests, but the rest of the information is kept electronically. Very few lodging properties use racking systems for room reservations and room status. Only properties such as bed-and-breakfast inns with metal keys use key racks. Properties with valet parking will have a racking system to keep track of guests' cars and their keys.

**11-1** A guest room is where the guest sleeps and stores personal items while staying at the hotel.

*Omni Hotels & Resorts*

## Organization and Functions of the Rooms Division

| ROOMS DIVISION | | | |
|---|---|---|---|
| *Rooms Director*<br>Prepare and sell rooms; help guests | | | |
| **FRONT OFFICE DEPARTMENT** | **HOUSEKEEPING DEPARTMENT** | **SECURITY DEPARTMENT** | **ENGINEERING DEPARTMENT** |
| *Front Office Manager*<br>Sell rooms, interact with guests, provide information | *Executive Housekeeper*<br>Keep hotel and rooms clean and sanitary | *Director of Security*<br>Protect people, property, and cash | *Chief Engineer*<br>Keep equipment and building in good repair |
| **Reservations**<br>Take reservations over phone, fax, and Internet<br>**Uniformed Services**<br>Help with luggage and transportation, provide information<br>**Telecommunications**<br>Answer phones, direct calls, take messages<br>**Front Desk**<br>Check-in and checkout, answer questions and requests, help guests | **Guest Rooms**<br>Clean and sanitize guest rooms<br>**Public Areas**<br>Clean public areas such as lobbies and hallways; clean and sanitize public restrooms<br>**Laundry**<br>Wash laundry, take care of linens<br>**Special Cleaning**<br>Deep cleaning (such as carpet cleaning) and special projects such as outside window washing<br>**Contract Services**<br>Obtain outside companies for special cleaning tasks such as washing exterior windows | **Structural Security**<br>Make sure all security equipment and systems are functioning<br>**Security Policies**<br>Set policies and make sure they are followed<br>**Surveillance**<br>Observe people and places; be alert for problems<br>**Safety and Emergency Procedures**<br>Develop safety policies and emergency procedures; handle emergencies<br>**Records and Investigations**<br>Keep required records of incidents and emergencies | **Building Systems**<br>Keep electrical, plumbing, and other systems in good repair<br>**Building and Equipment**<br>Maintain building, parking lot, elevators, escalators, and kitchen and laundry equipment<br>**Guest Rooms and Public Areas**<br>Handle maintenance problems in these areas<br>**Recreational Equipment**<br>Maintain swimming pools, hot tubs, and exercise equipment<br>**Grounds**<br>Maintain landscaping and golf courses |

*Goodheart-Willcox Publisher*

**11-2** The rooms division is the part of the hotel that handles all tasks involved in preparing and selling sleeping rooms. Often, security and engineering are included in the rooms division. Sometimes they are separate divisions.

The computer software and hardware used to run lodging properties is called a **property management system (PMS)**, 11-3. A PMS keeps all the information for all departments in one computer system. This information can be accessed from computers anywhere on the property. For example, the guest in room 1104 checks out at the front desk. The front desk agent (also called a *front desk clerk*) uses the PMS to check out the guest. The PMS records the information in the computer file for room 1104. This file will say that the guest in room 1104 checked out at 11 a.m. on April 26. The housekeeper has an office at the other end of the hotel. She needs to know if room 1104 is empty so someone can clean it. She goes into the PMS through the computer on her desk and looks at the file for room 1104. She can tell immediately that the guest checked out at 11 a.m. and the room can be cleaned.

*Pressmaster/Shutterstock.com*

11-3  A property management system (PMS) is used to keep track of all information for the hotel.

The PMS can also be used for the electronic key system, guest records, accounting, inventory, purchasing, and receiving. Most PMSs include e-mail. The PMS enables all departments of the hotel to communicate with one another and share information.

# The Front Office

The **front office** handles everything related to selling sleeping rooms and interacting with guests. The manager of the front office is usually called the **front office manager**. In a large hotel, the responsibilities of the front office are divided among four or more departments. Each department has a supervisor and several workers to do the department's tasks. In a smaller property, the front office may not be divided into departments and the staff of the front office performs all the tasks.

The front office can be divided into four departments: reservations, uniformed services, telecommunications, and front desk, **11-4**. Some front offices are also responsible for the hotel gift shop and the recreational facilities, such as the health club and swimming pool.

# Reservations Department

In the lodging industry, a *reservation* is a promise to hold a room for a specific guest for a specific date or set of dates. The date on which a guest arrives is called the *arrival date*. The date on which the guest leaves is called the *departure date*.

Two types of reservations are nonguaranteed and guaranteed. A **nonguaranteed reservation** expires at a specific time (usually 6 p.m.) on the reserved date. If the guest does not arrive by 6 p.m., the hotel is free to sell the room to another guest. The guest who did not use the reservation is not billed for the room.

Many guests prefer to guarantee the reservation. A **guaranteed reservation** holds the room until the guest arrives, whatever time that is. In order to guarantee the room, the guest pays in advance, usually by credit card. If the guest does not show up at all, the guest is billed for the room. On the other hand, if the guest shows up and there is no room available, the hotel will find a room at another hotel for the night. The hotel may pay for the cost of one night's lodging and transportation to the other hotel. This process is called *walking the guest* to another hotel.

## *Taking Reservations*

Guests make reservations by mail, phone, fax, and Internet. Most guests make reservations by phone or Internet. When guests call to make a reservation, a **reservations agent** takes the call. The agent finds out what type of accommodations the guest wants and asks a number of other questions: How many guests are in the party? How many beds do you require? When are your arrival and departure dates? Do you have any special requests? A common special request is for a handicapped-accessible room.

### Selling the Property

An important part of the reservations agent's job is selling the hotel. For this reason, these agents

## Organization of Front Office

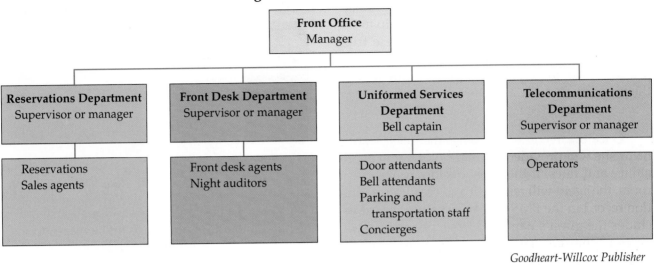

**Front Office**
Manager

| **Reservations Department** Supervisor or manager | **Front Desk Department** Supervisor or manager | **Uniformed Services Department** Bell captain | **Telecommunications Department** Supervisor or manager |
|---|---|---|---|
| Reservations Sales agents | Front desk agents Night auditors | Door attendants Bell attendants Parking and     transportation staff Concierges | Operators |

*Goodheart-Willcox Publisher*

**11-4** The front office handles everything related to selling sleeping rooms and interacting with guests.

are often called *reservations sales agents*. The reservations agent must be able to answer the guest's questions. When the reservations agent describes the hotel with enthusiasm, the caller is encouraged to make a reservation.

The reservations sales agents must know the properties they are selling, **11-5**. They need to know the differences in the rooms and what amenities are offered at each property. They need to know about the entertainment and other activities at the property and nearby. Many reservations agents are in a *central reservations center*, which makes reservations for the entire hotel chain. They may be located in an office far from the properties

**11-5** The reservations sales agents must be able to answer questions about the property, such as what show is being performed and if the property is wheelchair accessible.

*Photos courtesy of Princess Cruises*

themselves. Because of this need, these reservations agents are often sent on *fam tours*, or *familiarization tours*. This is an all expenses-paid trip to the hotel properties to learn about them. These trips are also offered to travel agents, travel writers, and tour directors to help them become familiar with the property.

### Making the Reservation

Once the agent knows what the guest wants, he or she will provide information on room availability and rates. If the guest decides to reserve a room, the agent will reserve it and create a reservation record in the PMS. The **reservation record** includes the guest's name, address, phone number, dates of the reservation, type of room assigned, and any special requests. The reservation record is generated in the PMS when the agent inputs the information. If the guest wants to guarantee the reservation, the agent will record the credit card number and give the guest a confirmation number. In some small properties, the reservation record will be written by hand, usually on a card of some type. The reservation cards will be kept in a racking system.

Hotel chains and affiliation groups have central reservations centers. A **central reservations center** is an office that handles reservations for all the hotels in the chain or affiliation group. The central reservations center has a toll-free number, which guests can call to make reservations for any hotel in the system. The hotel chains and affiliation groups will have a multiple-unit PMS. This PMS will link each hotel in the chain or affiliation group to the central reservations center. When a reservation is made in the central reservations center, the information can be immediately accessed at the specific hotel through the PMS.

When a reservation is made by fax, the reservations agent enters the information into the PMS. The confirmation number is faxed back to the guest.

Guests often like to make reservations over the Internet, **11-6**. At the hotel's website, guests can see photos of the property and the guest rooms. Some hotels also offer a virtual tour of the property. Guests can use the website to select arrival and departure dates and type of room.

A number of Internet search engines are available to assist guests in making their hotel reservations. These search engines can compare prices of different lodging properties.

*Hyatt Hotels Corporation*

**11-6**  A hotel website provides information about the hotel and allows guests to make reservations.

## Room Inventory

The reservations manager is responsible for keeping an accurate room inventory. **Room inventory** is a count of the number of rooms sold and the number of rooms available each day. Every time a reservation is made, the PMS subtracts that room from the total number of rooms available on that day. In some smaller properties, this count is done by hand. The room inventory lets the reservations agents know how many and which rooms are available at all times. It lets the reservations agents know exactly how many rooms are left to sell on any given day. If agents did not have this information, they might sell more rooms than the hotel has available.

The proper handling of reservation information can be critical to the success of a lodging property. A good reservations system correctly monitors available rooms. By knowing exactly how many rooms are left to sell, managers can determine what rate to charge for a room. For example, when the hotel is almost sold out, rates are at their highest. When many rooms are available, the rate will be lower to encourage guests to stay at the hotel.

## Reservations Staff

If the lodging property has a reservations department, it is usually staffed by a reservations manager and several reservations sales agents. If the property is too small to have a separate reservations department, reservations may be handled by front desk staff or telecommunications staff. Room inventory may be handled by the reservations manager, the front desk manager, or the sales manager.

# Uniformed Services Department

The uniformed services department got its name because most of its staff wear uniforms, **11-7**. This department is also called *guest services*. The uniformed services department was developed in 1828 for the Tremont House in Boston. This hotel was four stories tall and was built before the invention of the elevator. A bellhop helped guests carry their heavy luggage to the fourth floor. Today, these staff members are called *bell attendants*. They have been a vital part of all luxury and first-class lodging properties ever since. Limited-service properties do not have uniformed services.

A member of the uniformed service is usually the first hotel employee that guests see. These are the people who open car doors, unload baggage, and open the hotels' doors for people. The uniformed services team includes door attendants, bell attendants, parking and transportation staff, and concierges. This team begins the hospitality link between the hotel and the guest. The **bell captain** supervises the uniformed services staff. The tasks of the uniformed services can be divided into four areas: door services, bell services, parking and transportation services, and information and arrangements.

## Door Services

A **door attendant** takes care of all guest needs as guests arrive at a hotel. The door staff are generally considered the "coordinators" of the front drive. They coordinate the activities of the front door of the hotel to ensure a professional, organized appearance. They are the first and last impression the guest has of the hotel.

The major responsibility of door attendants is to help guests with their luggage. Door attendants open car doors and help guests from their cars, taxis, or shuttles. They then unload luggage and place it on a luggage cart. Bell attendants are usually nearby to help with the next step. Door attendants usually leave guests in the care of bell attendants, who escort guests to the front desk.

Door attendants also hail cabs. Often, door attendants work with parking and transportation staff to park cars and arrange transportation for guests.

## Bell Services

A **bell attendant** is responsible for helping guests with luggage in the hotel, **11-8**. Bell attendants usually coordinate with the door attendants to escort guests and their luggage into the hotel and to the front desk. Once a guest is registered, the bell attendant takes the luggage and the guests to their rooms. The bell attendant will make sure the room is in order. He or she will often describe the hotel's amenities and features and encourage guests to take advantage of them. When guests check out of the hotel before they are ready to depart, the bell attendant will take their luggage and put it in a safe place until they are ready.

**11-7**  In many properties, door attendants and bell attendants wear elegant uniforms.

*Raffles International Hotels & Resorts*

**11-8**  A bell attendant's main function is to help guests transport luggage to their rooms.

*Swissôtel Dalian, China. Raffles International Hotels & Resorts*

Many hotels provide guests with laundry facilities and dry cleaning services. If the hotel offers shoe shining and repair, the bell attendant will take care of these services for guests. A company outside the hotel will do the laundry, dry cleaning, or shoe repair. The bell attendant will take the items from the guest, deliver them to the outside company, pick them up, and return them to the guest.

## *Parking and Transportation*

Many luxury and first-class hotels provide valet parking and drivers for airport shuttles. The staff in parking and transportation also arrange for taxis, limousines, and other transportation.

## *Information and Arrangements*

The concierge provides information about entertainment, sports, amusements, transportation, tours, and babysitting. A large hotel may have two or more concierges. They must be familiar with the area where the hotel is located. Guests will often ask the concierge many questions during their stay, such as directions to certain locations in the area. The concierge is also available to make arrangements for dining, entertainment, and transportation. For example, guests can ask the concierge to make them reservations for the theater. The concierge is usually stationed at a visible desk in the lobby of the hotel.

Some hotels have a special floor called a *concierge floor*, which includes its own guest rooms, a lobby, a lounge and a concierge available to help only the guests on the floor, **11-9**. Often access to the concierge floor is limited to those guests with rooms on that floor. The concierge lounge usually offers continental breakfast, afternoon snacks, evening desserts, and beverages all day.

# Telecommunications Department

*Telecommunications* consists of the telephone system, the computer software that runs it, any communication services provided to the guests, and the telecommunications staff. The telecommunications system is often connected to the PMS. Hotels use telecommunications in running the

*Photo courtesy of John Q. Hammons Hotels*

**11-9** The concierge floor has guest rooms, a lobby, and one or more concierges.

business, as do all businesses. In addition, most lodging properties provide telecommunications services to guests. Full- and limited-service hotels have at least one phone in every room. Some specialty properties and institutional lodging services do not have a phone in each room.

Many luxury and full-service hotels have telephone operators. These operators are sometimes called PBX operators. PBX stands for *private branch exchange*, the part of the telephone system that handles calls within the hotel. Hotel operators answer incoming calls. The operator then directs the call to the proper person. Some hotel operators take messages for guests, although most lodging properties have automated phone systems with voice mail. Operators will also handle emergency calls.

Hotel operators often handle wake-up calls. A **wake-up call** is a phone call placed by the hotel to the guest's room at a specific time requested by the guest. There is usually an alarm clock in each guest room, but many guests prefer to get a wake-up call. Many properties have an automated wake-up call system.

In smaller hotels, the reservations staff performs operator duties. In limited-service properties, front desk staff often perform operator duties, **11-10**.

Stamford Hotel

11-10  In small or limited-services properties, the front desk agent will also perform the tasks of reservations agent and telephone operator.

# Front Desk Department

Whether the lodging property is small or large, the front desk is command central. The front desk is one of the first areas that a guest sees, and its appearance sets the mood for the rest of the hotel. Neatness, organization, beauty, and efficiency are just a few of the characteristics that a front desk should communicate to the guest. The first impression the front desk gives will help create a good image for the hotel.

A person who works at the front desk is called a **front desk agent**. Front desk agents may also be called *guest service agents* or *front desk clerks*. The main responsibilities of front desk agents are guest check-in and checkout. **Check-in** is the process of registering guests, assigning rooms, and distributing keys. **Checkout** is the process of paying for rooms and returning keys. Front desk agents also answer questions and handle problems. When guests do not know whom to ask, they ask the front desk agent. Front desk agents also coordinate guest services and guest information. When a lodging property is small, the front desk agents also handle the tasks of reservations, uniformed services, and telecommunications.

Front desk tasks can be organized in many ways. Six possible categories include greeting, check-in, checkout, financial tasks, guest security, and guest services.

## Greeting

Front desk agents are the hotel's ambassadors. They are often the first hotel employees that guests meet, **11-11**. Guests may have had a hard, exhausting day of work or travel by the time they arrive at the hotel. The front desk agent's pleasant disposition can make the guest feel comfortable and welcome. Using the guest's name whenever possible also makes guests feel welcome.

Guests who arrive without reservations are called *walk-ins*. Walk-ins give front desk agents the opportunity to sell guest rooms. The front desk agents must be very familiar with the hotel's room types, rates, and guest services to successfully sell a guest room. They must be able to describe these features in a positive way.

## Check-In

Check-in consists of many tasks. Typical tasks include registration, determining method of payment, and room assignment.

### Registration

A lodging property needs to know who is in the hotel at all times. **Registration** is the process of keeping a list of everyone who is staying at the hotel. When guests arrive at the hotel, they register at the front desk. The front desk agent creates a registration record in the PMS for each guest. The **registration record** contains information about the guest's method of payment, the arrival and departure dates, automobile model and license plate number, and any special requests. Special requests can include a rollaway bed, a child's crib, or a preferred room location. The registration record usually includes the guest's billing address and telephone number. If the guest has made a reservation, the reservation record becomes the registration

Blend Images/Shutterstock.com

11-11  A warm welcome from the desk agent sets a positive mood for the rest of the guest's stay.

record. The front desk agent will go over the information in the reservation record to make sure it is still correct.

Most states require the guest's signature on a registration card. This signature establishes the innkeeper-guest relationship. The registration card is essentially a contract between the hotel and guest. The hotel agrees to provide certain services. The guest agrees to the rate and dates of occupancy and to pay for all charges.

## Method of Payment

Once a guest agrees to rent a room, the front desk agent must confirm the guest's method of payment. Methods of payment include cash, personal check, debit card, and credit card. The front desk agent must take steps to make sure payment will be made.

If cash or a check is used, the guest is usually required to pay for the entire stay at check-in. Most hotels also ask for a refundable deposit to cover any phone calls, food taken from the guest-room minibar, or movie rentals. Guests who pay by cash or check are usually not allowed to charge anything to their rooms. For example, if these guests order room service, they will have to pay cash when the food arrives.

If a guest wants to pay by check, the desk agent will use a check authorization service that will guarantee the check for payment. If the service does not approve the guest's check, the guest cannot use a check and must use another form of payment.

Today's business and pleasure travelers usually pay for their hotel visits by credit card. They present their credit cards when they check in, **11-12**. The desk agent uses a credit authorization

Swissôtel Chicago. Raffles International Hotels & Resorts

**11-12** Most travelers today pay by credit card.

service to find out whether the guest has enough credit to pay for their stay at the hotel. The use of a credit card makes the process of check-in quicker and easier. In addition, once the guest has established credit, the guest can charge a variety of services to the room.

### Room Assignment

Once the guest has registered and payment method has been confirmed, a room can be assigned. The front desk agent uses the information in the registration record to assign a room and a room rate for each guest. When assigning guest rooms, the agent must know what each guest room is like. The types of hotel rooms can range from a standard single guest room to a luxurious suite. Furnishings, amenities, and the room's location within the hotel will make rooms different, even though they may be the same type. The PMS can quickly give the agent all the information he or she needs to make room assignments. The PMS will also show which rooms are available on each date.

Front desk agents must know about the hotel's accommodations for guests with physical disabilities. The *Americans with Disabilities Act* requires new and renovated properties to be barrier-free. *Barrier-free* means that the rooms are designed to meet the needs of people with disabilities, **11-13**. Barrier-free features include extra-wide doorways for wheelchairs, extra-large bathrooms, grab bars

beside the toilet and inside the bathtub area, lowered bathroom vanity countertops, and handles on door and bathroom fixtures instead of knobs. A feature for people who are hearing impaired is smoke and fire detection systems with strobe lights as well as sound.

Once the room is assigned, the agent gives the guest the room key.

## Financial Tasks

The front desk also handles many important financial tasks. These tasks include recording guest transactions and performing the night audit.

### Guest Transactions

A *financial transaction* is the process of buying and paying for something. There are many activities that cost a hotel guest money. For example, there is a charge for every phone call made from the guest room. If the room is equipped with a

**11-13** This barrier-free shower is especially designed for easy access by people who use wheelchairs or crutches.

*Photo courtesy of Princess Cruises*

minibar, the guest is charged for all the contents that have been taken. Guests who have established credit with a credit card may charge expenses to their rooms. For example, if a guest orders room service, the charge for the meal is due when it is brought to the room. The guest can pay cash for the meal, but if the guest has established credit when he or she checked in, the guest can charge the meal to the room. The charge is added to the day's room charge. Meals at the hotel's restaurants, movie rentals, health club and spa charges, and gift shop purchases can all be charged to the room.

One of the major responsibilities of front desk staff is to keep track of charges to guests and payments by guests. The record of charges and payments is called the **guest folio**. A guest folio is also called a *guest account*. The guest folio is usually started when the guest checks in. In a PMS, the guest folio is part of the registration record. Because the PMS is used throughout the hotel, hotel staff can input charges to each guest folio from many different places. For example, staff can input charges from the front desk, telephone system, restaurants, health club, beauty salon, and gift shop. In some small properties, the guest folios are kept by hand.

Many guests charge their food and beverage expenses to their guest rooms, **11-14**. The front desk relies on the food and beverage departments to correctly make these charges to the guest's folio through the PMS. Before the computer age, food and beverage workers had to manually transfer these charges to the front desk. Today, the PMS automatically performs this task.

At the end of each shift, the front office staff must perform cash-handling tasks similar to those of any worker who handles cash in a retail setting. The desk agent must make sure the cash on hand matches the amount of cash recorded by the PMS or the cash register.

## Night Audit

An *audit* is a careful examination of the financial records of a person or company. Every night, an audit must be done of the hotel's financial transactions for the day. A hotel's night audit is an accounting procedure that is performed every night on the hotel's financial transactions. The person who does the night audit, the *night auditor*, is usually a desk agent on the night shift (11 p.m. to 7 a.m.). The night auditor may report to someone in the accounting department.

*Photo courtesy of Swissôtel Hotels and Resorts*

**11-14** It is very convenient for guests to charge food and beverage expenses, such as in-room dining, to their room.

The night auditor performs several tasks as part of the night audit. One task is balancing the daily financial transactions. The auditor will compare the cash, checks, and credit card receipts on hand with the records in the PMS. The two amounts should match. The purpose is to make sure no money was lost or stolen. While balancing the transactions, the auditor may discover errors or problems. It is the auditor's job to correct the errors and solve the problems.

Another important task is to post room charges and taxes. Each night that a guest stays in the hotel, he or she is charged the room rate and taxes. These charges must be entered into each guest's folio. Entering these charges into the guest folio is called *posting the charges*. The night auditor posts these charges using the PMS.

# Valerie Ferguson— *Achieving the American Dream*

*Photo courtesy of Loews Hotels*

Valerie Ferguson's first job in the hospitality industry was as a night clerk at a hotel. Today, she is the vice president of brand management for Loews Hotels. She knows that hospitality is an industry where a person can start from humble beginnings and end up a success.

Valerie graduated with a degree in government from the University of San Francisco and moved to Atlanta to attend law school. However, she changed her mind and decided she would return to San Francisco for law school. To earn money for the move, Valerie took a job as night clerk at the Atlanta Hyatt Regency. She worked the front desk from 11 p.m. to 7 a.m. for $2.90 an hour. She loved working in a hotel. Every day was a challenge. What Valerie saw as a 3-month job turned into an 18-year career with Hyatt Hotels.

She quickly worked her way up the career ladder. She held positions as director of rooms, rooms executive, assistant director of housekeeping, and front office manager. In 1985, Valerie became general manager of The Lodge, a Hyatt hotel owned by McDonald's Corporation. It was her first of five general manager positions. In 1998, she was elected chair of the American Hotel & Lodging Association, the leading national association that represents hotel professionals. She was the first African-American and the second woman to hold this position.

The road to success has not always been easy. Valerie has faced racism and sexism, but despite these experiences, Valerie has never felt limited. Her response has been to work hard and be professional. She also found that you must set strong goals and ask for advancement.

## Valerie Ferguson's Career Path

**1953:** Born in Philadelphia, Pennsylvania

**1977:** Graduated from the University of San Francisco with a bachelor of arts degree in government; became a night clerk at Hyatt Regency Atlanta

**1985:** Hired as general manager of The Lodge Hotel

**1990:** Named by Ebony magazine as one of the Top 100 Black Women in Corporate America

**1991, 1993:** Nominated by Hyatt Hotels as general manager of the year

**1998:** Hired as regional vice president of Loews Hotels and managing director for the Loews Philadelphia hotel

**1998:** Chaired the American Hotel & Lodging Association (then known as the American Hotel & Motel Association)

**2010:** Became senior vice president of operations of Loews Hotels, overseeing operations of Loews Atlanta Hotel and properties along the U.S. East Coast

**2012:** Became vice president of brand management

The night auditor will also prepare a night audit report. This report will show the financial activities for each department for the day. It will also show total sales and total expenses. These reports will help managers with their financial planning.

# Checkout

The checkout process is one of the front desk agents' responsibilities. The type of process depends on the level of service and amount of computerization. Luxury hotels may emphasize personal service. Many hotels offer express checkout services. All checkout processes consist of typical tasks such as bill presentation, account settlement, keys collection, payment processing, and room status update, **11-15**.

## Bill Presentation

The first step in checkout is to give the guest a final copy of the bill. The guest can then review the charges and make sure they are correct. Before computers became common in hotels, guests had to call the front desk before checking out. The front desk agent would prepare the bill while the guest was packing. The guest would then come to the front desk to review and pay the bill. If many guests were checking out at the same time, this process might take a while.

**11-15** When guests check out, front desk agents have several tasks.

*Hyatt Hotels Corporation*

Computers speed up the entire checkout process. The front desk agent can have the PMS prepare a bill the evening before the guest's departure date. During the night, the bill is slipped under the guest's door. In the morning, the guest can review the bill and call with any corrections. A new bill can then be quickly prepared by the time the guest gets to the front desk to pay. In some hotels, guests can use the TV to review their bills and check out.

Some hotels offer express checkout. Guests can use express checkout if they received approval for their credit cards when they checked in. If the bill is correct, the guest does not have to stop by the front desk before he or she leaves the hotel. The charges will automatically be charged to the credit card used to check in.

## Account Settlement

**Account settlement** is the term used for the process of correcting any errors in the bill and taking payment from the guest. Some or all of account settlement can be done by computer and phone. In hotels with express checkout, the guest does not need to stop by the front desk to settle his or her account.

If there are problems, the guest might prefer to settle the account at the front desk. Some guests prefer to talk to the desk agent while settling the account. Sometimes, guests want to use a method of payment different from the one they specified during check-in. For example, the guest may want to use a different credit card, a personal check, or cash.

## Key Collection

Once the bill is settled, the front desk agent must collect the keys. The guest may have a room key, minibar key, and safe deposit box key. The agent should also check to make sure that the guest has collected any items placed in the hotel's safe deposit box.

## Payment Processing

After the guest has paid, the payment must be processed. Payment processing involves recording the payment and showing that all charges have been paid. The front desk agent enters the payment information into the guest folio, which then shows that the guest has paid. The balance owed by the guest shows as zero. This process is sometimes called *zeroing out the account*. The agent can then give the guest a copy of the bill showing that the bill has been paid.

Checkout and payment also result in the creation of a guest history record. When the night audit is done, the PMS updates the guest folio and shows that the guest has paid and left the hotel. The registration record and the guest folio then become part of that guest's history record. The **guest history record** is a record kept by a lodging property that records information about each guest each time he or she stays at the property. The guest history record is usually kept in the PMS. This information can help the reservations agents and front desk agents when the guest returns to the property. They can check the PMS and find out what room the guest has been in, how long the guest stayed, and what special requests the guest made. This information will help the agents better meet this guest's needs. The sales and marketing department also uses guest history records to learn about guests and develop promotions.

### Room Status Update

The last major task of the checkout process is updating room status for housekeeping. When a guest is using a room, the room status is *occupied*, **11-16**. When the guest checks out, the room status changes to *vacant*. The PMS system automatically changes the room status when a guest checks out. The room status information is then always up-to-date and available on the PMS. In some small properties, the room status is recorded by hand and transmitted by hand or by phone to the housekeeping department.

## Guest Security

Guest security is another major responsibility of front desk agents. Security tasks include key control, guest privacy, surveillance, safe deposit boxes, and emergencies.

### Key Control

Front desk agents are responsible for all guest room keys. They issue guest room keys, minibar keys, and safe deposit box keys; collect keys; and handle lost or stolen keys.

Guests often come to the front desk when they have lost their keys or gotten locked out of

**11-16** When a guest is using a room, the room status is *occupied*.

their rooms. The front desk agent is responsible for making sure that only the guest actually assigned to the room gets a key. When asked to replace a lost key, the agent must ask the guest to show identification, such as a driver's license. A convention name tag is not sufficient since it could easily be picked up by a dishonest person and used as identification.

If a guest is locked out of his or her room, he or she may not have identification. One way to verify the guest's identification is to ask for name, address, and phone number and check them against the registration record. Another possibility is to arrange for the guest to be taken to the room to get identification.

### Privacy

Front desk agents are responsible for protecting guests' privacy. Agents are instructed not to give out guest room number or information about who is staying in the hotel. If someone enters the hotel looking for a particular guest, the agent can take a message or call the guest room for the visitor. If someone calls the hotel, the caller should not be given the guest's room number. The operator or front desk agent can connect the caller to the guest's room. In addition, room service charges, movie rentals, and special requests are to remain private transactions.

### Surveillance

*Surveillance* is the process of closely observing what is going on in an area. All employees at a lodging property must be alert to unusual people or events. However, the front office staff, especially front desk agents, are particularly responsible. The front desk agent is located in the lobby, **11-17**. The lobby is the area where guests enter and leave the property. The front desk agent must be alert to any suspicious people or unusual behavior in the lobby.

In addition, guests will call the front desk when they have security concerns. Front desk agents need to know how to handle security issues. Front desk agents usually work closely with the security staff to resolve security issues.

### Safe Deposit Boxes

Many hotels offer guests the use of safe deposit boxes to protect jewelry and other valuable items. Two keys are required to open each box—one kept by the front desk agent and the other kept by the guest. The guest and the front desk agent must both be present to open the box.

*Raffles International Hotels & Resorts*

**11-17** The people working at the front desk have a good view of everything going on in the hotel lobby. In this hotel, the front desk is along the wall on the left.

### Emergencies

When guests have emergencies, they usually call the front desk for help, so front desk agents must be trained to handle these situations safely and efficiently. These employees may also be responsible for announcements during emergencies such as a fire alarm. During emergencies, front desk agents will work closely with security.

## Guest Services

Front desk agents are responsible for providing a number of guest services. These services include information, requests, and problem solving.

### Information

Whenever guests have questions about anything, they usually call the front desk. The front desk agent must be able to answer these questions, **11-18**. If the agent does not know the answer, he or she should know who can answer the question. For example, suppose a guest calls the front desk and asks for a restaurant suggestion. The agent may refer the guest to the concierge.

### Requests

Guests often call the front desk when they need something. For example, a guest may need extra towels. A family may decide they need a crib for a baby. The front desk agent is responsible for making sure that guests get what they request. Agents must often communicate and cooperate with other departments to meet guests' needs. For example, the extra towels must be obtained through the housekeeping department.

11-18 Front desk agents must be prepared to answer a variety of questions.

### Problem Solving

Guests also call the front desk with any problems. Common problems involve heating, lighting, air conditioning, and plumbing. The guest room may be too hot or too cold. There may not be any hot water. The desk agent will have to solve these problems. Usually the agent will refer the problem to the proper department. Heating, cooling, and plumbing problems are referred to the engineering department.

When guests check out at the desk, the front desk agent should try to find out if they had any problems. The agent should ask if the guests enjoyed their stay and listen carefully to the responses. Any current problems should be solved as quickly as possible. Other problems should be reported to the appropriate department.

## Traits of Front Office Staff

Successful front office staff have certain characteristics. They must have the ability to solve problems and be friendly, energetic, and detail oriented, **11-19**. Good grooming and a pleasant appearance are important. Excellent interpersonal and communication skills are also necessary. Guests should be greeted by a person with a friendly smile and welcoming manner. A grumpy front desk agent would not make a very good first impression on a guest.

Front office staff must also be calm and patient. Often front office workers are confronted with several guests at once. Each guest has a different and urgent problem. You may be asked to find a special room for a guest. You may be asked

Conrad Hotel, Singapore. Courtesy of Hilton Hotels Corporation

**11-19** The front office team must have excellent interpersonal and communication skills.

to split the hotel bill in half between two guests so they can each pay their part of the bill. There may be a fire alarm or a storm warning. During each of these situations, you must remain pleasant and figure out how to efficiently handle the situation.

# Role of the Front Office Manager

The front office manager has many responsibilities. This person is in charge of all front office staff and activities, as well as the front office budget. The front office manager has the usual responsibilities of a manager: hiring, training, supervising, evaluating, and motivating all front office staff. The front office manager must also know how to use the PMS and is responsible for selling rooms and training staff to sell rooms.

# *Hospitality Ethics*

## Using Bias-Free, Gender-Neutral Language

Seeking ways to deliver spoken and written messages with sensitivity and respect is an example of living out your ethical principles. Using bias-free, gender-neutral language shows others you care for their identity as people. It gives you credibility with guests, coworkers, friends, and family. When choosing words, pay attention to the country or culture in which you work and live. Although there are ethical ways to speak and write that transcend all cultures, you want to be sensitive to culture-specific ways of communicating. Here are a few guidelines to remember for choosing words wisely.

- **Gender.** Look for general words that are inclusive of all people regardless of gender. For instance, instead of using *mankind* as a reference to all people, use *humanity*. Use *bell attendant* instead of *bellman*.

- **Ethnicity or culture.** Refrain from using words that identify people by race, ethnicity, or cultural group. In this way, you will avoid accidently perpetuating any stereotypes.

- **Disability.** Because an individual is a person first, refer to the person first and not the disability (*a person who uses a wheelchair*, not *wheelchair user*; *a person who has low or no vision*, not *a blind person*).

- **Age.** People of any age should be treated with respect and dignity. Unless age is pertinent to the context of a message (such as those related to child care or age-related discounts), avoid references to age.

There are two tasks of particular importance for the front office manager: forecasting and scheduling.

## Forecasting

Many different managers and departments need to know how many guests are expected at the hotel. The front office manager is responsible for **forecasting**, or predicting the number of guests who will stay at the hotel. The front office manager will use the PMS to forecast the number of rooms occupied during the upcoming week.

First, the manager collects information. The manager gets the number of guests who have reserved rooms for each day. Information for each guest's length of stay is also gathered. Based on past experience, the manager estimates the number of walk-ins and no-shows. A *no-show* is a person who made a reservation but never shows up.

The manager then gets the number of guests who are already registered in the hotel and uses this information to calculate the forecast (the number of guests expected to check in and check out each day during the next week). The forecast is sent to all the managers in the hotel to help them determine how many workers they will need.

## Scheduling

The process of assigning staff to work at specific times is called *scheduling*. At a hotel, there are three work shifts. A **work shift** is a regular period of time during which work is done. The *day shift* is from 7 a.m. to 3 p.m. The *afternoon shift* is 3 p.m. to 11 p.m. The *night shift* is 11 p.m. to 7 a.m. A manager must make sure there are enough workers assigned to each shift. The manager can use the PMS to help with scheduling.

Good shift planning helps to make the front office workload manageable when a full house is checking out. *Full house* is a term used when the hotel is full or when all rooms have been sold. Suppose all 350 guests at a convention want to check out at the same time. Even with express checkout, the lines at the front desk might be long. This can be irritating when guests are in a hurry. With proper scheduling, enough staff will be available to quickly take care of a large group.

# The Hotel Guest Cycle

The goal of the front office staff is to make the guests' stay as comfortable and pleasant as possible. In order to achieve this goal, every staff member in the front office must work together as a team. In a small property without separate departments, there may be only one or two people working the front office. In these properties, fewer services are offered, and guests usually help themselves with luggage and other tasks. No matter what the size of the front office, the team must work together to impress guests, meet their needs, and make them want to return to the hotel.

To understand how the front office team works, it helps to look at a guest visit as stages in a cycle. The stages of a guest visit are called the hotel guest cycle. The **hotel guest cycle** has four stages: prearrival, arrival, occupancy, and departure, **11-20**.

## Prearrival Stage

The *prearrival stage* includes everything the guest does before arriving at the property. The two main tasks are choosing a property and making a reservation.

**11-20** The hotel guest cycle has four stages.

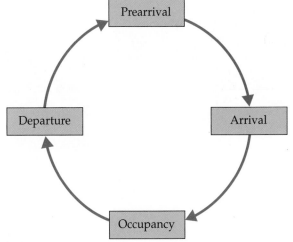

**Stages in the Hotel Guest Cycle**

*Goodheart-Willcox Publisher*

Guests select hotels for many reasons. Some of these reasons are related to how successful the marketing and sales departments are in promoting the property. Location and room rate may also determine which hotel a guest chooses. Other reasons are personal. For example, the guest may have stayed at the hotel before and had a good experience. Friends may have suggested the hotel. The guest may be tired and choose the closest property.

When guests make reservations over the phone, they interact with one or more front office staff. They may speak to the hotel operator, a reservations sales agent, or a front desk agent. The way these staff members interact with the guest often creates the impression the guest has of the entire property.

## Arrival Stage

The *arrival stage* includes everything that occurs when the guest first arrives at the property, **11-21**. The tasks of this stage include arriving at the property, unloading the luggage, getting the

**11-21** The arrival stage includes everything that the guest does and experiences from the moment he or she arrives to the moment he or she is settled in the room.

Conrad Hotel, Istanbul. Courtesy of Hilton Hotels Corporation

luggage into the property, parking the car, and registering. The front office staff with whom guests interact include door attendants, bell attendants, parking valets, and front desk agents. The staff must all work together smoothly to get guests registered and comfortably settled in their rooms.

For guests who have not made reservations, this will be their first encounter with the property and its staff. Good first impressions are the responsibility of the front office staff.

## Occupancy Stage

The *occupancy stage* includes everything the guest does while staying at the hotel. Guests use room service, rent movies, eat at hotel restaurants, buy drinks in the lounge, and use recreational facilities, **11-22**. During this stage, guests ask questions about the hotel and the surrounding area. They call to request wake-up calls and extra towels. They enter and leave through the hotel lobby.

Front office staff with whom guests interact during this stage include door attendants, bell staff, concierge, valet parkers, van drivers, telephone operators, and front desk agents. During this stage, guests also interact with members of many other hotel divisions and departments. For example, guests will see the housekeeping, security, and maintenance staff. They will also interact with hotel food and beverage staff. Every staff member whom the guest sees makes an impression.

## Departure Stage

The *departure stage* includes all activities involved with leaving the hotel and settling the bill. The guest will pack up, review the bill, correct any errors, arrange transportation to the airport, and pay the bill. Guests are often in a hurry during this stage. Many have planes to catch. It is very important for front office staff to be efficient during this stage.

Front office staff with whom guests interact during this stage include door attendants, bell staff, valet parkers, van drivers, operators, and front desk agents.

**11-22** The occupancy stage includes everything that the guest does and experiences while staying at the hotel.

# Chapter 11
# Review

## Chapter Summary

- The rooms division is the part of the hotel that handles all tasks involved in preparing and selling sleeping rooms.
- The computer software and hardware used to run lodging properties is called a property management system (PMS).
- The front office can be divided into four departments: reservations, uniformed services, telecommunications, and front desk.
- The main responsibilities of front desk agents are guest check-in and checkout.
- Front desk tasks can be organized into six basic categories: greeting, check-in, checkout, financial tasks, guest security, and guest services.
- There are two tasks of particular importance for the front office manager: forecasting and scheduling.
- The hotel guest cycle has four stages: prearrival, arrival, occupancy, and departure.

## Review

1. What is the main function of a lodging property?
2. What are the functions of the rooms division?
3. What are the four main departments of the front office department in larger hotels?
4. Describe the main duties of the reservations staff.
5. What are the four main areas of the uniformed staff's tasks?
6. Describe the main duties of the telecommunications staff.
7. Name the two main responsibilities of front desk agents.
8. Why are front desk agents described as the hotel's ambassadors?
9. What is the purpose of registration?
10. How do front desk agents keep track of guest financial transactions?
11. Describe the checkout process.
12. List four ways front desk agents ensure guest security.
13. Describe the responsibilities of the front office manager.
14. Describe the stages in the hotel guest cycle.

# Critical Thinking

15. **Identify.** Role-play a scenario of a guest checking in at a hotel. Discuss ways that the front desk agent can be an ambassador for the hotel during this process.

16. **Make inferences.** What types of information do hotel concierges need to know in order to meet the needs of their guests? What are the responsibilities of their position?

17. **Create.** Make a poster that illustrates the steps in the hotel guest cycle.

18. **Analyze.** Why is forecasting important for a hotel?

# Common Core

## College and Career Readiness

19. **Speaking.** Explain how record keeping in a hotel was done prior to having computers. Demonstrate the process along with your oral report.

20. **Writing.** Investigate the career options in the front office of a hotel. Choose at least one career area of the front office that interests you. What are the educational and training requirements for this position? What is the salary range? What is the outlook for this position in the future? Write a brief report on your findings.

21. **Listening.** With another classmate, take turns role-playing a potential hotel guest and a hotel reservations agent. List the questions that you would ask the guest who is calling for a reservation. As you role-play, answer the questions you have developed.

22. **Math.** Select a destination city and dates for a trip you would like to take. Using the Internet, locate hotel rooms and room rates for that location and dates. Make a spreadsheet comparing the costs of the available options.

23. **CTE Career Readiness Practice.** Create a one-act play for two persons that depicts a positive interaction between a front desk agent and a hotel guest who uses a wheelchair checking into the hotel. Be sure to include notes to the actors about body language and facial expressions. Do the same to illustrate a negative interaction on the same topic. What is the essential difference between the two plays/interactions? How does the way you say something influence whether it will be received negatively or positively?

214

# Chapter *12*

## Housekeeping

## Chapter Objectives

After studying this chapter, you will be able to

- **describe** the three major functions of the housekeeping department.
- **contrast** between the meanings of *clean* and *sanitary*.
- **list** the six groups of tasks for cleaning a guest room.
- **describe** the public areas of the hotel that require cleaning.
- **list** the three major tasks of the laundry department.
- **describe** the role of the executive housekeeper.
- **describe** the communications between the housekeeping department and the front office.

## Before You Read

Try to answer the following questions before you read this chapter.

- What is the difference between something that is *clean* and something that is *sanitized*?
- What tasks are involved in cleaning a lodging property guest room?

## Terms to Know

housekeeping department
clean
sanitary
mildew
linens
laundry
room attendant
inspector
assistant housekeeper
executive housekeeper

cleaning cart
consumables
turndown service
public areas
house attendants
house staff
laundry supervisor
laundry attendants
seamsters

mending
linen room
in-house housekeeping services
contract housekeeping services
outside contractors
scheduling
occupied
vacant
out-of-order room

Housekeeping is the second major department in the rooms division, but it is just as important as the front office department. The **housekeeping department** is responsible for keeping the hotel clean, **12-1**. Without clean rooms, a hotel would go out of business. Guests will not stay in or pay for a dirty room. If guests are given a dirty room, they will probably complain and are unlikely to use the hotel again. The housekeeping department is responsible for protecting guests from infection and illness.

The housekeeping department has the largest staff in the hotel. It can consist of about 75 percent of the total permanent hotel staff. In large convention hotels, the percentage of housekeeping employees will be about one-third of the total staff.

The three major functions of the housekeeping department are to keep the hotel clean, sanitary, and attractive. Housekeeping departments are often organized into four areas: guest rooms, public areas, laundry, and contract services, **12-2**.

# Cleanliness and Sanitation

Guest rooms and public washrooms must be both clean and sanitary. **Clean** is the state of being free of dirt and bad odors. **Sanitary** is the state of being free from disease-causing pathogens or having a safe level of pathogens.

## *Cleanliness*

A major goal of housekeeping is to prevent the growth of mildew. **Mildew** is a type of fungus that grows on damp surfaces. Mildew causes a bad odor and often turns surfaces such as bathroom grout black. It also stains linens. Mildew can grow on towels, shower curtains, sheets, bathroom fixtures, and floors. Housekeeping must make sure mildew does not grow by cleaning surfaces and taking linens to the laundry. Following proper washing procedures when laundering linens will prevent mildew.

**12-1** Housekeeping is responsible for keeping guest rooms, the lobby, and other common areas clean.

*Diego Cervo/Shutterstock.com*

## Organization of a Housekeeping Division

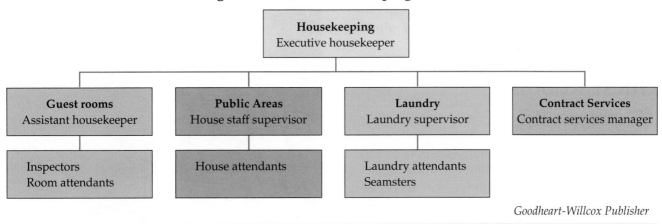

```
                        Housekeeping
                    Executive housekeeper
```

| Guest rooms | Public Areas | Laundry | Contract Services |
|---|---|---|---|
| Assistant housekeeper | House staff supervisor | Laundry supervisor | Contract services manager |
| Inspectors Room attendants | House attendants | Laundry attendants Seamsters | |

*Goodheart-Willcox Publisher*

**12-2** Housekeeping departments are often organized into four areas.

Another major cause of dirty rooms is dust. Dust looks bad and can irritate the eyes, noses, and throats of guests. Some guests are allergic to dust. Dust can be controlled by daily dusting of all surfaces and vacuuming of all carpets, **12-3**.

## Sanitation

A *pathogen* is a living substance that can cause disease. Pathogens include bacteria, viruses, fungi, and parasites. Guest rooms often provide good places for pathogens to grow. Many different people use guest rooms and hotel facilities every day. These people can bring pathogens with them, even when the guests themselves are not sick.

*Sanitation* consists of the actions taken to prevent and control disease. Sanitation includes the processes of cleaning and sanitizing. *Cleaning* is the physical removal of dirt from surfaces. *Sanitizing* is the treatment of a clean surface with heat or chemicals to reduce the number of disease-causing microorganisms to safe levels.

The items that must be sanitized are the bathrooms and the linens. In the bathroom, the sink, toilet, tub, and floor must be sanitized by washing them with a sanitizing solution.

Linens are sanitized in the laundry department. **Linens** consist of all the items in the guest room made of cloth. Linens that need to be washed or have just been washed are called **laundry**. Laundry may include sheets, pillowcases, pillow protectors, towels, and washcloths. Mattress pads, shower curtains, and bedspreads are also washed on a regular basis. The term *Laundry* is often used

for the place where these linens are washed. Linens also include draperies, blankets, and pillows. These items are usually dry cleaned.

**12-3** Dust can be controlled by daily dusting of all surfaces and vacuuming of all floors.

*erwinova/Shutterstock.com*

Laundry is cleaned in a washing machine using hot water, which helps kill pathogens. However, hot water is not enough. Laundry must be washed in a sanitizing solution.

# Guest Rooms

The staff who are responsible for the guest rooms are the executive housekeeper, assistant housekeeper, inspectors, and room attendants.

A **room attendant** is the person who cleans the guest rooms. In the past, these workers were called *housekeepers* or *maids*. The **inspector** is the member of the team who checks the room after it is cleaned. Inspectors are also called *floor housekeepers*, *floor supervisors*, or *checkers*. The inspector makes sure the room has been properly cleaned and is ready for the next guest. If the room is not up to standards, the inspector works with the room attendant to prepare the room. The **assistant housekeeper** manages the inspectors and the room attendants. The **executive housekeeper** is the top manager of the housekeeping department. The executive housekeeper may also be called the *director of housekeeping*. The executive housekeeper is responsible for keeping the rooms clean and sanitary. He or she is also responsible for the linens, guest room supplies, cleaning supplies, and housekeeping staff. In a small property, the executive housekeeper may perform all the tasks of the assistant housekeeper and the inspectors.

The room attendant has the major responsibility for the cleanliness and sanitation of the guest rooms. The tasks of the room attendant can be divided into six groups: entering the guest room, cleaning the guest room, providing guest supplies, reporting problems, limiting guest room access, and turndown service.

## *Entering Guest Rooms*

Room attendants should do their jobs without bothering guests. There is often a conflict between when the room attendants work and when guests are in their rooms, **12-4**. Since guests often stay in a room more than one night, the guest's belongings will be all around the room when the room is cleaned. Room attendants must learn how to properly enter guest rooms and how to work around guest belongings.

*Photo Courtesy of ~~~~ival Cruise Lines*

**12-4** If guests are still in their room when the room attendant is ready to clean, the attendant may have to return at a later time.

The assistant housekeeper gives the attendant a list of rooms to clean. The room attendant should knock on the door and say, "Housekeeping." If there is no answer, the attendant should repeat these actions. If there is still no answer, the attendant should unlock the door and slowly enter the room while again announcing himself or herself. The attendant should quickly check to see if anyone is in the room. If there are guests still in the room, the attendant should apologize for coming in. Then he or she should ask the guests when would be a good time to return.

Guests are given a doorknob hanger or a card to stick in the door's key card slot with the words *Do Not Disturb* or *Privacy Please*. When the room attendant sees this sign on the door, he or she knows not to enter the room.

## *Cleaning Guest Rooms*

The heart of the room attendant's job is cleaning the room. It is the room attendant's responsibility to maintain the hotel's standards of cleanliness, sanitation, and appearance. A room attendant cleans an average of 15 to 20 rooms a day. Approximately 18 to 25 minutes are allowed for cleaning each room. Within this short amount of time, attendants must perform the following tasks:

- empty trash
- dust all furniture
- clean mirrors
- change sheets and make beds
- vacuum carpet

- clean and sanitize the bathroom
- provide guest room supplies

Attendants must be efficient and organized. Following a specific order and procedure helps room attendants maintain standards of cleanliness, sanitation, and appearance. Figure **12-5** shows a procedure for cleaning a guest room.

## Procedure for Cleaning a Guest Room

1. Knock on door and say "Housekeeping"
2. If no answer, repeat.
3. If no answer, unlock door.
4. Enter room slowly and say "Housekeeping." Check for guests.
5. Place cleaning cart across doorway.
6. Turn on lights, open drapes, set air conditioner.
7. Gather items guests have left behind. Place on cart to be turned in.
8. Clean ashtrays, mirrors, and furniture.
9. Dust and clean furnishings.
10. Empty trash.
11. Vacuum.
12. Make beds.
    A. Place bedspreads, pillows, blankets on a chair.
    B. Remove sheets and pillowcases.
    C. Place new sheets and pillowcases on bed.
    D. Make bed.
13. Clean bathroom.
    A. Empty trash.
    B. Remove dirty towels.
    C. Clean and sanitize floor, tub, sink, toilet.
    D. Restock supplies and towels.
14. Inspect room.
15. Record comments on worksheet.
16. Close drapes, set air conditioner, spray air freshener.
17. Turn off lights.
18. Leave room and lock door.

*Goodheart-Willcox Publisher*

**12-5** Following a specific order and procedure helps room attendants maintain standards of cleanliness, sanitation, and appearance.

The cleaning cart helps attendants be efficient. A **cleaning cart** is a doorway-sized cart that holds cleaning supplies, equipment, guest room supplies, and linens. Enough supplies are in the cart for a half-day's work. The cart reduces the need to run back to the linen room and the supply room, which might be at the other end of the building or on another floor. The cart also has a small basket for carrying all the cleaning sprays, sponges, and small supplies into the guest room. The basket reduces the need to run back to the cart while cleaning the room.

Cleaning carts also have a trash bag and a laundry bag for collecting trash and dirty linens from each room. Plastic trash liners make trash bag maintenance easier. Laundry bags are usually made of fabric and can be washed when they become dirty. The cleaning cart should be cleaned with a sanitizing solution at the end of each shift. Then the cart should be restocked.

## *Providing Guest Supplies*

There are a variety of supplies that guests use up during their stay. Products that get used up are called **consumables**, and they must be replaced regularly. Most properties supply the following consumables: toilet paper, facial tissue, small bars of soap, shampoo, hair conditioner, moisturizing lotion, and a notepad and pen by the phone. The notepad and pen usually have the property's name on them. Guest rooms with coffeemakers are often supplied with packets of ground coffee, sugar, and powdered creamer.

Most full-service hotels and many limited-service hotels provide guests with additional bathroom supplies. These may include mouthwash, disposable shower cap, sewing repair kit, and shoe shine cloth. These grooming supplies are often called *toiletries*, **12-6**.

**12-6** Consumable toiletries such as these are replaced by housekeeping every day.

*Phill Danze/Shutterstock.com*

## Reporting Problems

Since room attendants are in the guest rooms every day, they are responsible for noticing problems. A common problem is finding belongings that guests leave behind, which are referred to as *lost and found*. The attendant should put the items on the cart and take them to the appropriate department. Lost and found items are turned in to a supervisor in housekeeping, the front office, or security. The supervisor logs the date and room in which the item was found. All lost and found items should be kept in a locked room or closet. When a guest calls, the supervisor can consult the log and find the item by date and room. The hotel can then return the item to the guest.

Room attendants also check the rooms for damaged items or items that need repair. Common problems are burned out lightbulbs, broken air conditioners, and dripping faucets. The items that the attendant can fix should be fixed, such as changing lightbulbs, **12-7**. Other problems should be reported to the executive housekeeper. Attendants must also report any missing items. Unfortunately, many guests want things from the hotel as souvenirs. Common items stolen include pillows, towels, blankets, bedspreads, and pictures. Some hotels charge the guest's credit card for any missing room items.

Room attendants sometimes encounter a guest who is ill or needs help. The attendant should call for help immediately. If the attendant cannot enter a room, he or she should inform the executive housekeeper.

The room list that the attendant gets indicates whether the guest has left the hotel or is staying another day. A room in which the guest has arranged to stay another day is called a *stayover*. If a stayover room appears vacant, the attendant should notify the executive housekeeper immediately. Sometimes a guest will *skip*. This means that the guest left without paying the bill. When the guest's credit card information is taken at check-in, this rarely occurs. However, room attendants and the executive housekeeper should be aware of this possibility and remain alert when cleaning rooms.

## Limiting Guest Room Access

The room attendant is responsible for making sure no unauthorized people enter a guest room. The only people who should enter a guest room are the room attendant assigned to clean it; housekeeping managers on duty; engineering, maintenance or security staff assigned to check out something in that room; and the assigned guest.

If someone asks you to open a guest room door, explain your property's policy. Refer him or her to the front desk for assistance. If a guest asks to enter a guest room you are working in, ask for his or her key. Make sure the key works in the lock before allowing the person to enter the room.

Room attendants must make sure strangers do not enter the room while they are working. A stranger could steal guest property while the attendant is working in the bathroom. A stranger could also attack the room attendant. In some hotels, the attendant places the cart so it completely blocks the room's doorway. A guest room should never be left open and unattended.

## Turndown Service

**Turndown service** is housekeeping work that is performed in the evening. Turndown service includes straightening up the room and restocking guest supplies. The attendant then turns down the bedding and places a chocolate on the pillow. The attendant may also leave a doorknob hanger with a menu for ordering breakfast room service. This service is common in luxury hotels.

# Public Areas

The **public areas** include hallways, stairs, lobby, lounges, public restrooms, restaurants, meeting rooms, banquet halls, and recreation areas, **12-8**.

**12-7** Housekeeping can perform minor repairs, such as replacing lightbulbs. Major repairs will require the engineering department.

*Christian Delbert/Shutterstock.com*

12-8   Hallways are part of the public areas of the hotel.

12-9   Floors and railings in the public areas are polished daily at this hotel.

Retail stores and the offices of the hotel staff are also considered public areas. The public areas are also known as *the house*, and the workers responsible for cleaning them are known as **house attendants** or **house staff**. These workers may also be known as *public area attendants*, *public area housekeepers*, or *lobby attendants*. The house attendants are assigned daily cleaning tasks in the public areas. In addition, they are responsible for deep cleaning projects in the public areas and the guest rooms.

Some house attendants work along with the room attendants. They gather dirty linens from the carts and take them to the laundry. They also empty the carts' trash bags and vacuum cleaner bags. Some house attendants are responsible for keeping the cleaning supplies in stock in the storeroom.

Other house attendants clean the public areas. For example, they will vacuum hallways during the day, clean and supply the public restrooms, clean windows, and polish metal or wood surfaces such as railings, **12-9**. Often, meeting and banquet rooms must be cleaned between events. Some public areas are cleaned at night when fewer people are around. This type of cleaning is sometimes called *night service*.

Most hotels have a deep cleaning program for both guest rooms and public areas. The manager assigns special cleaning projects so each guest room or public area is deep cleaned once a quarter (every three months). Guest room deep cleaning includes many tasks such as flipping mattresses and removing drapes and bedspreads for cleaning. All furniture is moved away from the walls for thorough cleaning underneath and behind. High dusting removes cobwebs from the ceiling and elsewhere. Lampshades, light fixtures, walls, and carpets are cleaned. Furniture is steam cleaned. In addition, someone from engineering checks the room and performs needed structural or mechanical repairs.

Similar deep cleaning projects are performed in the public areas. Examples include carpet cleaning, high dusting, cleaning of drapes, and steam cleaning of furniture.

# Laundry

The laundry department, which is responsible for the cleaning and maintenance of all linens, is part of housekeeping. The staff of the laundry usually includes the laundry supervisor, laundry attendants, and seamsters. The **laundry supervisor** supervises the attendants and seamsters. The supervisor is also responsible for keeping track of all linens and replacing linens when necessary. In a small property, the executive housekeeper performs the duties of the laundry room supervisor. The **laundry attendants** perform all the tasks involved in washing laundry. The **seamsters** repair worn or torn linens. Seamsters used to be called *seamstresses*.

The laundry department has three major tasks: washing laundry, care of linens, and inventory of linens.

## Washing Laundry

Washing laundry includes five tasks: sorting, washing, drying, folding, and storing. The purpose of washing laundry is to make it clean, sanitary, and attractive. In large hotels, one laundry attendant may sort laundry all day. Another laundry attendant may operate only the washing machines, **12-10**. Others may have single responsibilities for drying, folding, or storing linens. Small properties are not able to have laundry attendants who do only one task. Laundry attendants in these properties may be responsible for all five laundry tasks throughout their shift.

### Sorting

Before laundry can be washed, it must be sorted. Different items require different treatment. Sorters should separate laundry into piles of regular, damp, stained, and torn or damaged items. Damp linens should be separated from dry linens. Damp linens are washed as soon as possible to prevent the formation of mildew. Stained linens require pretreatment. Torn and damaged linens either require repair or must be discarded.

Linens often get dirty and stained or torn and damaged, and they wear out from normal use. In addition, careless actions by guests and staff also damage linens. Linens may be dragged

**12-10** In large hotels, laundry is washed around the clock.

*Vasily Smirnov/Shutterstock.com*

along floors, have things spilled on them, or be used to clean up spills. Linens should never be used to wipe up spills, and staff should not use washcloths or towels for cleaning tasks because the cleaning solutions can ruin them. Linens also get torn by nails or splinters in carts, baskets, and linen chutes.

Linens that are stained or very dirty should be treated with a stain remover as soon as possible. Pretreatment must be done before washing. The pretreatment depends on the type of fabric and the type of soil or stain. There are three basic treatment methods for stains: soaking in a stain removal solution, applying a detergent paste to the stain, and using special treatment methods listed on a stain removal chart.

Linens that are torn or damaged need to be repaired before they are washed. If they are washed first, they may ravel and tear during the washing process. If the item cannot be mended immediately, it should be stored in a locked cabinet until it can be repaired. Damaged linens are placed in a locked cabinet so they do not get mixed in with the good linens or with the cleaning cloths. Linens that cannot be repaired must be discarded and deleted from inventory.

### Washing and Drying

Cleaning and sanitizing occur during washing and drying. These tasks require washing machines and dryers. Hot water and sanitizing solutions are used in the washing machine for both cleaning and killing pathogens. Damp linens provide a good environment for pathogens and mildew to grow, so laundry must be thoroughly dried before folding. Laundry is dried in the dryer, where pathogens often thrive in the lint trap. Therefore, the lint trap must be regularly cleaned with a sanitizing solution.

### Folding and Storing

After linens are dried, they must be ironed and folded. Flatwork presses and flatwork irons are used to iron sheets. Some hotels have machines that automatically fold sheets. Once linens are folded, they are stored in the linen room.

## Care of Linens

Linens that receive poor treatment will wear out quickly. Worn out linens are not attractive, and they do not make a good impression on hotel guests. New linens are expensive, so efforts

# Going Green

## Towel Laundering

Hotels use a great deal of water, detergent, energy, and labor to process guest room laundry. Most hotels now post signs in guest bathrooms encouraging guests to help protect the environment by reusing their towels. If guests place their towels on the floor, it is a signal to the housekeeping department to replace the towels. Otherwise, the guests can reuse their towels during their stay.

are made to make them last. Linens should last at least three years before they require repair. Careful handling and proper washing help them last longer, **12-11**. When linens are torn or damaged, they should be repaired if possible.

Repairing linens is also called **mending**. The mending job must look professional. A seamster repairs the linens, drapes, curtains, and other linen products for the hotel. Seamsters are trained to mend linens so you cannot see where they were damaged.

**12-11** Linens must be handled carefully to help them last as long as possible.

stefanolunardi/Shutterstock.com

## Inventory of Linens

The **linen room** is where clean linens are stored. The executive housekeeper usually has an office in or next to the linen room. The storage rooms for guest room cleaning supplies and extra linens are also located in that area.

The linen room supervisor or the executive housekeeper is responsible for the linen inventory. Ideally, the hotel should have five times the daily amount of laundry used. This amount provides one set in the guest rooms, one set in the laundry, one set in the room attendants' floor closet, one set in the linen room, and one set in transit from one place to another. Very few hotels can afford to have that much linen. Most hotels have three or four times the daily amount of linen used.

Linens need to be replaced periodically for four reasons: normal wear and tear, improper use, losses in the laundry, and theft. Ideally, linens should only have to be replaced because of normal wear and tear. Repeated washings will eventually wear them out. The quality of the linens will help determine how long they will last, **12-12**.

The second reason that linens need to be replaced is because of carelessness or incorrect use. Careless employees may drag linens so they tear or use linens as cleaning rags, which will wear them out quickly. The third reason is losses in the laundry. For some reason, a certain amount of laundry just disappears during the laundry process. This situation is similar to your laundry at home: one sock always mysteriously disappears in the dryer.

The fourth reason is theft. Unfortunately, both guests and employees take linens. Theft by guests should be reported as soon as it is noticed. Careful

**12-12** High-quality linens are a good investment for a lodging property because they will last longer.

senkaya/Shutterstock.com

supervision of the linen room can help cut down on employee theft.

An effective inventory system will help reduce employee theft. The PMS can be used to keep the linen inventory records. The linen room must be locked, and only authorized employees should be admitted. Items cannot be taken without a requisition form that is approved by the supervisor. A perpetual inventory should be kept showing linens that have been issued, purchases of linens, discarded linens, and the total number of linens on hand. Twice a year, a count should be made of every linen item in stock and compared with the perpetual inventory. Someone from the accounting department should assist and supervise the count.

# Contract Services

There are two types of housekeeping services: in-house housekeeping services and contract housekeeping services. Hotels use the type of service that best fits their budget, staffing, and available space.

## In-House

**In-house housekeeping services** are done by housekeepers who are employees of the hotel. Hotel facilities, equipment, and supplies are used. Housekeeping employees are scheduled and supervised by the executive housekeeper.

### Advantages

The main advantage of in-house housekeeping services is that the employees work for the hotel, **12-13**. They have to follow the hotel's rules and standards, wear the hotel's uniforms, and maintain the hotel's image. The employees are responsible to the hotel management, and the hotel management has authority over the employees.

### Disadvantages

In-house laundry services can be expensive to operate. Costs include equipment, equipment maintenance, employee recruitment and training, employee benefits, linens, and laundry supplies. It also takes a great deal of space to set up a hotel laundry facility. Some hotels do not have the space that is required to have their own laundry facility.

An in-house housekeeping department must fill all positions. Night cleaning positions are often hard to fill and supervise. In addition, there are

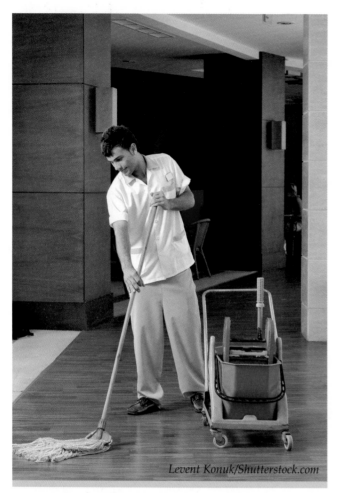

12-13 The employees of in-house housekeeping services work for the hotel.

certain tasks that require specialized knowledge, experience, and equipment. Examples include tasks that require hazardous cleaning chemicals and cleaning the outside windows of high-rise buildings. Most in-house housekeeping services do not have the specialized knowledge, experience, and equipment required.

## Contract

**Contract housekeeping services** are services performed by a company that is not part of the hotel. The outside company hires the staff and owns the equipment used. The outside company provides all supplies needed. These services are often called **outside contractors**.

### Advantages

Some hotels have found that it is more cost-effective to have certain housekeeping tasks done by outside contractors. These tasks include laundry services, night cleaning, cleaning of public areas, cleaning of hotel offices, and cleaning of retail stores. Cleaning that requires special knowledge, equipment, and experience is also contracted out, **12-14**. One example is exterior window cleaning.

Laundry services are often contracted to a company that specializes in commercial laundry. The contract laundry service picks up the laundry from the hotel. The laundry is taken to the commercial laundry facility. The laundry is then sorted, washed, dried, folded, and brought back to the hotel. There are advantages in using contract laundry services. They often give 24-hour turnaround service. They pick up and deliver every day except Sundays and holidays. Hotels that use contract laundry services do not have to pay for employee salaries, benefits, and training. They pay the contract laundry service on a *per piece basis*. This means the hotel is charged for each piece of laundry that is cleaned.

### Disadvantages

Disadvantages of using contract services could include security problems, the possibility of poor quality cleaning, and the lack of flexibility when emergency cleaning needs occur.

Contract laundry services often do not return all the linens that are expected. As a result, the hotel could run out of clean linens. Sometimes the linens are not properly cleaned or folded. Major problems occur when the hotel and the laundry service count different numbers of pieces delivered. The hotel must take special care to accurately count all linens sent to the outside laundry.

# Role of the Executive Housekeeper

The executive housekeeper is the manager in charge of the housekeeping department and its budget. He or she is in charge of all housekeeping-related tasks in the hotel. The executive housekeeper also has the usual responsibilities of a manager: hiring, training, supervising, evaluating, and motivating all housekeeping staff.

There are five areas of particular importance for the executive housekeeper: training, scheduling staff, supplies and equipment, room status, and contact with the front desk.

*Levent Konuk/Shutterstock.com*

**12-14** Carpet cleaning and other cleaning tasks that require special equipment are often contracted out.

*Photo courtesy of John Q. Hammons Hotels*

## Training

Housekeeping staff are a critical part of the hotel's success. They are responsible for the cleanliness, sanitation, and attractiveness of the guest rooms. They also often interact with guests. For these reasons, training is extremely important. The executive housekeeper must make sure that each member of the housekeeping staff is well trained. Training must include how to properly perform work tasks. Staff also need to be trained in proper ways to interact with guests.

## Scheduling Staff

The executive housekeeper is responsible for making sure rooms are ready when they are needed, **12-15**. In order to have rooms cleaned, there must be enough staff on duty. The process of assigning staff to work at specific times is called **scheduling**. The executive housekeeper must know how many rooms are forecasted to be occupied each day. The number of rooms occupied will determine how many room attendants are needed. The executive housekeeper uses the PMS to plan schedules.

The executive housekeeper gets the number of rooms occupied per night from the front office or from the PMS. The number of rooms occupied for a specific night is called a *house count*. The executive housekeeper uses the house count to determine how many housekeeping staff are needed the next day. For example, suppose that 208 rooms are forecasted to be occupied tonight. If each room attendant cleans 16 rooms a day, then the executive housekeeper will need to schedule 13 room attendants to clean rooms tomorrow.

Blend Images/Shutterstock.com

12-15 Rooms must be clean so they are ready for occupancy upon the guest's arrival.

## Supplies and Equipment

The executive housekeeper must make sure the housekeeping department has all the supplies it needs. Supplies include linens, consumables, and cleaning supplies. The executive housekeeper is also responsible for the laundry equipment. He or she must make sure the equipment is regularly inspected and maintained.

## Room Status

The executive housekeeper must keep track of the occupancy and cleanliness status of each room. There are two basic occupancy status categories: occupied and vacant. **Occupied** means that a guest is registered to the room and that the guest or the guest's belongings or both are in the room. **Vacant** means that no guest is registered for that room and no guest or belongings are in the room. There are two basic cleanliness status categories: clean and dirty. An occupied room or a vacant room can be clean or dirty. All dirty rooms must be cleaned. Another category of room status is out-of-order. An **out-of-order room** is being renovated or repaired. It does not need to be cleaned and is not available to sell. The executive housekeeper must make sure that the room status files in the PMS are correct and up-to-date.

The executive housekeeper prepares an assignment sheet for each room attendant, **12-16**. The housekeeper has to determine how many rooms each attendant can clean. He or she has to

# *Hospitality Ethics*

## Ethics—A Commitment to Excellence

When striving for excellence, employees show they are striving for quality. In the hospitality industry, this means giving guests the best possible service. A commitment to excellence is the *value* employees bring to the guest—value for the money and time the guest spends. A commitment to excellence is not limited to just certain employees. Excellence should be a common thread throughout an organization from top management to entry-level employees.

| Housekeeping Assignment Sheet, Room Attendant 1 | | | | | | | |
| --- | --- | --- | --- | --- | --- | --- | --- |
| DATE: 04/26/XX | | | | | | | |
| Room number | Size | Status | Occupancy (blanks indicate vacant rooms) | Arrival | Departure | Number of People | VIP |
| 0401 | 1 | dirty | occupied | 04/14 | 04/27 | 1 | ✓ |
| 0402 | 1 | dirty | occupied | 04/25 | 04/28 | 1 | |
| 0403 | 1 | dirty | | | | | |
| 0404 | 1 | dirty | | | | | |
| 0406 | 1 | dirty | occupied | 04/25 | 04/28 | 1 | |
| 0413 | 1 | dirty | ◊ occupied | 04/25 | 04/26 | 1 | |
| 0414 | 1 | dirty | ◊ occupied | 04/24 | 04/26 | 1 | |
| 0417 | 1 | dirty | | | | | |
| 0418 | 1 | dirty | | | | | |
| 1406 | 1 | dirty | • | 04/26 | 04/30 | 1 | |
| 1407 | 1 | dirty | | | | | |
| 1409 | 1 | dirty | | | | | |
| 1410 | 3 | dirty | occupied | 04/23 | 04/29 | 1 | |
| ◊ Departure expected today<br>• Arrival expected today<br>✓ VIP guest; requires extra amenities | | | | | | | |

Goodheart-Willcox Publisher

12-16  An assignment sheet such as this one is prepared for each room attendant.

keep in mind that a three-room suite will take longer to clean than a standard room. The assignment sheet lists each room to be cleaned. It also indicates whether the guest is departing or staying another night. If the guest is departing, the room attendant will wait until the guest has left to clean the room. Once the room is clean, the room's status must be changed in the computer. Some hotels have the ability to change the status right from the guest room with wireless handheld communication devices. The room status is updated in the PMS.

Each room is physically checked every day—even the vacant rooms. The purpose of the physical check is to make sure the status listed in the housekeeper's report matches the actual physical status of the room. The executive housekeeper sends the housekeeper's room status report to the front desk. Then, one of the front desk staff will check the housekeeper's room status report against the list in the PMS for every guest in the house. The purpose of this check is to make sure that a guest has not left the hotel but is still registered in the computer. In this case, either the guest left without paying or the computer record is inaccurate. This check will also show a room that has a guest in it, but the computer does not show the guest registered. This situation indicates an error in the computer record.

## Contact with Front Office

Throughout the day, the front office departments and housekeeping regularly communicate with each other, **12-17**. They communicate about house counts, room status, security concerns, and guest requests for amenities and supplies. The PMS makes it much easier for the front desk and housekeeping to keep each other up-to-date on room status.

### House Counts

The front office manager is responsible for forecasting the number of rooms that will be occupied each night. The executive housekeeper will obtain this forecast from the front office manager. The executive housekeeper will then use this information to schedule employees. The executive housekeeper will also check the house counts each day to see if any adjustments in staffing are needed.

### Room Status

Reservations agents, front desk agents, and housekeeping staff need to know the status of each room. Reservations and front desk agents need to know which rooms are available to sell to guests. Housekeeping needs to know which rooms are ready to be cleaned. This information is recorded in the PMS. The housekeeping staff and the front office staff can use the PMS to check the status of individual rooms at any time.

### Security Concerns

The front desk depends on the housekeeping staff to report any unusual situations that could indicate a security problem for guests. Some situations that housekeeping staff might notice include

*Kenwood Communications*

**12-17** Members of the housekeeping staff often use wireless communicators to keep in touch with the front office staff.

unregistered guests on the floor, fire exit door propped open, sounds of domestic violence, or a vandalized guest room.

These potential threats to security should be reported to the front desk. The front desk agents will send a message about the situation to the appropriate person.

### Guest Requests

When guests have requests, they usually contact the front desk. Many of the requests concern items provided by housekeeping. Examples include extra blankets, towels, soap, shampoo, toilet tissue, and facial tissue. The front desk must efficiently relay these requests to housekeeping, who can then quickly respond to the guest requests. Quick responses to requests make a good impression on guests.

# Chapter 12
## Review

## Chapter Summary

- The three major functions of the housekeeping department are to keep the hotel clean, sanitary, and attractive.
- Clean is the state of being free of dirt and bad odors. Sanitary is the state of being free from disease-causing pathogens or having a safe level of pathogens.
- The tasks of the room attendant can be divided into six groups: entering the guest room, cleaning the guest room, providing guest supplies, reporting problems, limiting guest room access, and turndown service.
- The public areas of the hotel that require cleaning include hallways, stairs, lobby, lounges, public restrooms, restaurants, meeting rooms, banquet halls, recreation areas, retail stores, and the offices of the hotel staff.
- The laundry department has three major tasks: washing laundry, care of linens, and inventory of linens.
- The executive housekeeper is in charge of all housekeeping-related tasks in the hotel.
- The housekeeping department and the front office communicate about house counts, room status, security concerns, and guest requests for amenities and supplies.

## Review

1. List the three major functions and four areas of the housekeeping department.
2. Contrast a clean surface with a sanitary surface.
3. Describe the main responsibility of each of the following: room attendant, inspector, assistant housekeeper, and executive housekeeper.
4. List the procedures for cleaning a guest room.
5. How is a cleaning cart used?
6. List two ways a room attendant can limit access to a guest room.
7. Describe the tasks of the house staff.
8. What does a seamster do?
9. List and describe the five tasks that are involved in washing laundry.
10. List the four reasons linens need to be replaced.
11. Explain the difference between contract housekeeping and in-house housekeeping.
12. List the five areas of particular importance for the executive housekeeper.
13. Name the two basic occupancy status categories.
14. Why do housekeeping and the front office need to communicate with each other?

# Critical Thinking

15. **Design.** Imagine you are the executive housekeeper of a large hotel. Develop a room assignment sheet for Room Attendant 2. Use Figure 12-16, "Sample Housekeeping Assignment Sheet," as your model. Use room numbers 0501 through 0520.

16. **Draw conclusions.** How can Figure 12-5, "Procedures for Cleaning a Guest Room," help you when you are cleaning your own space at home? Which of the procedures would work and which would not work in your own space? How can you implement the procedures that are practical?

17. **Identify.** What items are usually contained on a housekeeping cleaning cart? What function do these items serve?

18. **Assess.** Explain what a room attendant should do when the need for a repair in a guest room occurs?

## Common Core

### College and Career Readiness

19. **Writing.** Brainstorm with two of your classmates about the importance of the housekeeping department. Write a one-page report summarizing your brainstorming session.

20. **Reading.** Research mildew and its effect on human health. How does it reproduce and spread? Why is the elimination of mildew a major goal of housekeeping?

21. **Listening.** Interview the executive housekeeper at a local hotel on the positions and responsibilities of the housekeeping department. Ask questions such as the following:

- How many employees are in the housekeeping department? How is the department organized?
- What are the procedures for cleaning and sanitizing the guest rooms?
- Who is responsible for cleaning the public areas of the hotel?
- How is the linen inventory monitored?
- How is guest and employee theft monitored?

22. **CTE Career Readiness Practice.** Each employee has a stake in the profitability of the company for which he or she works. Thinking of ways to save money for your company contributes to the success of the company and perhaps your advancement in that company. How can an individual employee positively and negatively affect a company's profitability? How do positive and negative customer interactions affect profitability? How does employee productivity and attendance affect profitability?

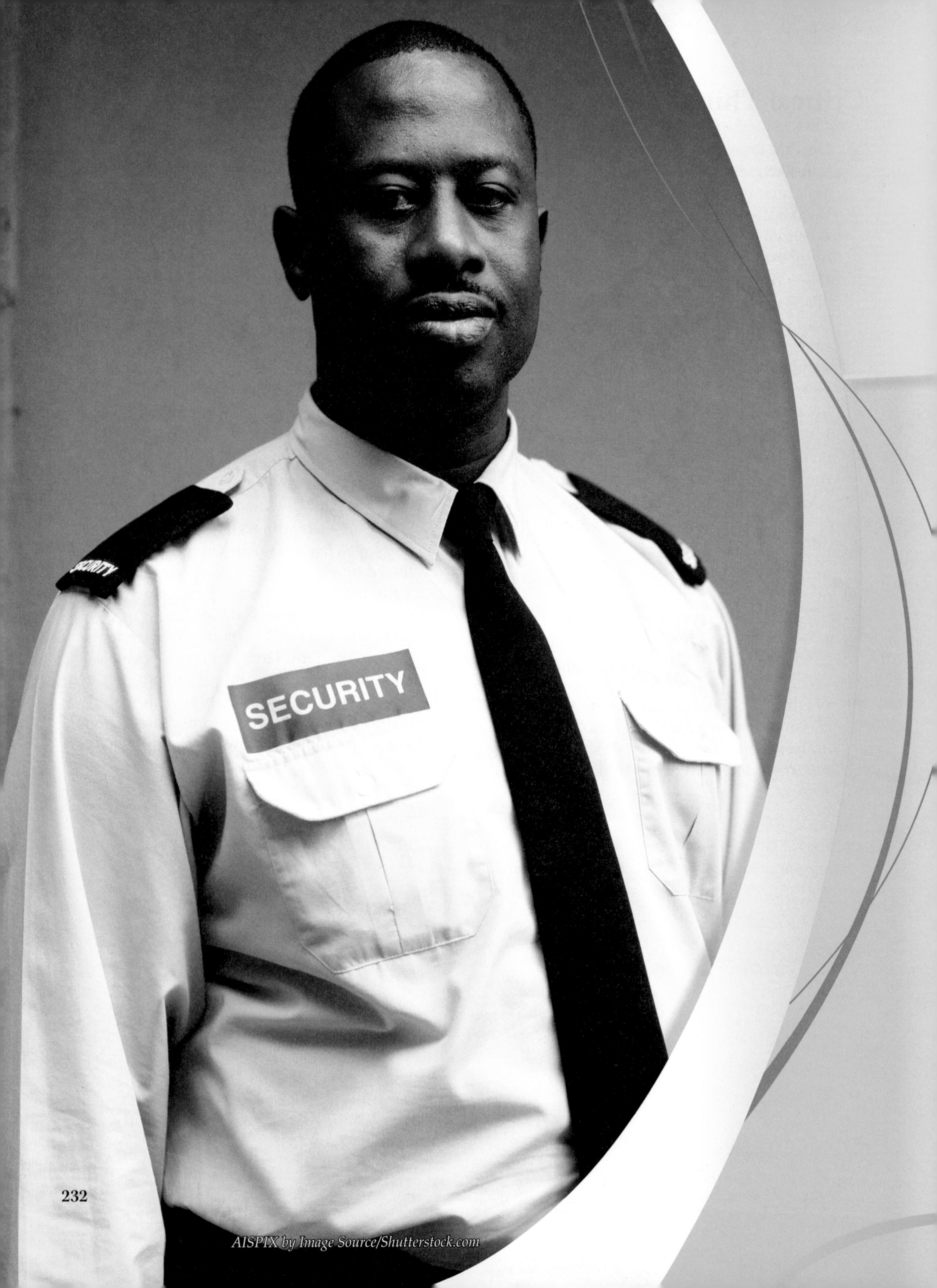


AISPIX by Image Source/Shutterstock.com

# *Chapter* 13
## Security

## Chapter Objectives

After studying this chapter, you will be able to

- **state** the major responsibility of the security department.
- **list** the four groups of security activities.
- **determine** three examples of structural security.
- **determine** three examples of security policies.
- **describe** the three basic tasks that security officers perform while on patrol.
- **describe** the relationship between the security department and the front desk.
- **assess** the role of all employees in maintaining security.
- **list** the four security-specific tasks that the director of security performs.

## Before You Read

Try to answer the following questions before you read this chapter.

- What steps do hospitality businesses take to keep customers safe?
- What roles are fulfilled by the director of security?

## Terms to Know

| | | |
|---|---|---|
| security | property insurance | security policies |
| security officers | liability insurance | key control |
| liability | crime insurance | key card |
| safe deposit box | plainclothes security officer | surveillance |
| vault | uniformed security officer | patrol |
| limitation of liability | structural security | security log |
| insurance | security system | accident report |
| insurance policy | | |

Security is critical for all hospitality businesses, which are attractive targets for criminals. Both foodservice businesses and lodging businesses have cash on the property. Both are often open late at night, and both have guests who are carrying purses or wallets or other valuables. Both have valuable materials on the premises that guests or employees may be tempted to take. Both have potentially hazardous materials that may catch fire. Both are subject to natural and human-caused disasters.

Guests expect their physical selves, property, and surroundings to be safe from harm, **13-1**. When guests are victims of crimes, the result is bad for the guest and the business. Guests have lost money, cameras, jewelry, clothing, and even their lives. Sometimes the losses cannot be repaid. Often the victim or the victim's family will sue the hospitality business, which can result in huge financial losses to the business. When word of the crime gets out, the reputation of the business suffers. The number of customers often falls greatly when a business suffers a serious crime or frequent crimes.

The best way to protect guests and the hospitality business is good security. **Security** consists of actions taken to prevent crime and protect the safety of people and property. The emphasis of security is prevention, but security staff are also responsible for handling problems and emergencies. The term *security* is also used to refer to the security department as a whole and to the staff of the security department.

Most businesses need security. However, guests stay only a short time at restaurants and other foodservice businesses. Guests at lodging properties spend one or more nights. Guests often leave their belongings in the hotel room while they are out during the day or in the evening. As a result, lodging properties need more security than restaurants. This chapter will focus on the security needs of lodging properties. However, many of the recommendations apply to foodservice businesses.

# Overview of Security

In a lodging property, especially a large one, security may be its own division. The security division will have a director of security, assistant director, supervisors, and security officers, **13-2**. **Security officers** are the staff members who carry out the actions to prevent crime and protect the safety of people and property. In a smaller property, security may be part of the rooms division. In a very small property, the general manager will be responsible for security. Some hotels hire an outside security company to provide security officers.

To some extent, all employees have a responsibility for security. Each employee must be alert to problems and know what to do in an emergency. The security department must train all employees in security procedures.

## *Protection*

The major responsibility of the security department is the protection of people and property. The security department is responsible for the safety of all the people at the hotel, including guests and employees. Guests expect to be safe in public areas, parking lots, and their rooms. Employees expect to be safe when on duty late at night and when walking to their cars.

The security department is responsible for the protection of guests' property and the hotel property. Guests should feel comfortable about leaving their belongings in the guest room and their cars in the parking lot. Security must also protect the business itself from theft.

Hotel and restaurant cashiers handle a great deal of cash, **13-3**. At the end of the day, this cash must be transferred to a vault or safe for safekeeping. At certain times the cash is transferred to a bank. It is important that cash and the employees handling it be kept safe during these times.

13-1 Guests expect their surroundings to be safe.

*Fort Worth Convention & Visitors Bureau*

## Organization of the Security Division

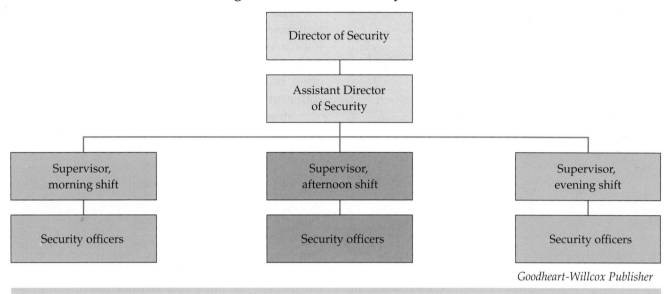

Goodheart-Willcox Publisher

**13-2** Security may be its own division or it may be part of the rooms division.

Christy Thompson/Shutterstock.com

**13-3** Cash and the employees who handle cash must be protected.

## *Threats to Security*

There are three categories of threats to security: people, hazards and accidents, and natural disasters. The major threat to security is people who intend to do harm. There are many types of people in this category. A *trespasser* is a person who is present on property where he or she has no business. An *intruder* is a person who enters an area in which he or she has not been permitted or invited, such as a closed place of business or a guest room. A *criminal* is a person who has committed a crime. A *terrorist* is a person who tortures or kills people for a political cause. A *thief* is a person who robs and steals property from people and places. An *arsonist* is someone who sets fires. A *burglar* is a person who enters a building for the purpose of committing a crime. Security departments work to keep out or catch people who intend to do harm.

Employees and guests are sometimes a threat to security. Guests sometimes steal hotel property, such as towels and blankets. Housekeeping staff members are usually the first to notice, and they work with the front desk and the security department to get the property back. Employees sometimes steal money, supplies, hotel property, and guests' property. Special procedures help to deter this type of crime. Security works with department managers to stop this type of crime or catch the criminal.

Another threat to security comes from hazards and accidents. Restaurants use fire in their work, **13-4**. Both restaurants and hotels contain many materials that could easily go up in flames and large pieces of equipment that could break down or catch fire. Accidents can happen anywhere. Hotel workers can have accidents on the job. Guests can fall and hurt themselves, or someone might become ill and need medical attention.

Dmitry Kalinovsky/Shutterstock.com

13-4  Fire is a potential hazard in restaurants and hotels. Many chefs use fire when they cook.

*Natural disasters* include hurricanes, tornadoes, floods, and earthquakes. Theses disasters often cannot be predicted. They require quick action to save lives and property.

## Liability

**Liability** means responsibility, especially responsibility to pay for damage or loss. How much financial responsibility does a hospitality business have when a guest's property is damaged or stolen?

### Limits on Liability

The degree of liability depends on the situation in which the property was stolen or damaged. If a camera is stolen because the guest left it in the lobby, the hotel is not responsible. If a guest props open the room door to let friends come in and something is stolen, the hotel is not responsible.

Most hotels provide a safe deposit box or an in-room safe for guests to place their valuables. A **safe deposit box** is a metal box that requires two keys to open. The front desk agent has one key and the guest has the other. Both parties must be present with their keys to open the box. Safe deposit boxes are usually kept in a large locked room called a **vault**. In-room safes are locked and unlocked by entering a digital combination using numbers of the guest's choice. If guest property is stolen because the guest did not use the safe deposit box or in-room safe, the hotel is not liable.

Most states have rules that protect hotels by limiting the amount of their liability for losses. These are known as Innkeeper's Laws. A **limitation of liability** is a limit on the amount of money that a hotel must pay a guest for a loss of property. Hotels must post signs that explain the limits of liability. Hotels must also provide safes for guests to place their valuables. In addition, the hotel must post signs that tell about the availability of these safes. A hotel is not liable for losses if the guest does not place his or her valuables in the hotel safe deposit box or the in-room safe.

Some states do not have a limitation of liability law. In these states, hotels are responsible for loss of guest property under common law. This means that the hotel must pay the guest the full value of the property that was lost. However, most courts limit the liability of the hotel if safe deposit boxes are available to guests.

Most foodservice operations are not responsible for guests' property. If the guest walks in and hangs up his or her own coat on the coatrack, the restaurant is not liable. If the restaurant takes your items and charges you a fee to watch them, then the restaurant is liable if the items are stolen.

### Risk of Lawsuits

Hospitality companies are always at risk for lawsuits, **13-5**. A suit can be filed at any time. However, if the company consistently follows good safety and security procedures, the company can reduce the chance of losing a lawsuit.

Junial Enterprises/Shutterstock.com

**13-5** By their nature, hospitality companies are particularly vulnerable to lawsuits.

All hospitality businesses should have an attorney available. The attorney can give legal advice and suggestions when the possibility of a lawsuit occurs. In addition, all managers should be trained on how to properly handle and document safety and security issues.

## Insurance

**Insurance** is a financial arrangement used to protect individuals or businesses against financial loss. The details of this financial arrangement are recorded in a document called an **insurance policy**.

Insurance companies sell insurance policies. For example, an individual would buy an automobile insurance policy from an insurance company. The auto insurance policy would protect the individual by providing a certain amount of money if the individual were to wreck his or her car. The individual pays a certain amount every month

for the insurance policy. This monthly payment is called a *premium*.

Hospitality businesses usually buy three types of insurance: property, liability, and crime, **13-6**. (An insurance company can customize other types of insurance to meet the needs of individual hospitality businesses.) **Property insurance** pays for loss or damage of property owned by the business. Property insurance usually covers losses due to fires, tornadoes, hail, accidents, burglary, and arson. For example, if a restaurant suffers a fire, the insurance company will pay for the cost of repairs or replacement of the building and equipment lost in the fire.

**Liability insurance** provides payment if the hospitality business is sued and the courts determine that the hospitality business is liable. Guests can sue a hospitality business if their property is lost or damaged. Guests can also sue if they suffer bodily injury or illness. Employees can sue a business if their property is lost or damaged. If the courts determine that the business is liable, then the court will usually require the business to pay damages (an amount of money) to the victim. The liability insurance will pay the damages. If employees suffer bodily injury or illness on the job, it is usually covered by *worker's compensation*, a type of insurance that a business buys to cover employee accidents, illnesses, and injuries.

**Crime insurance** pays for losses due to crimes such as theft, arson, forgery, and embezzlement. Theft and arson may be covered under property insurance. Businesses often buy a special kind

**13-6** Poperty, liability, and crime insurance are all essential to hospitality businesses.

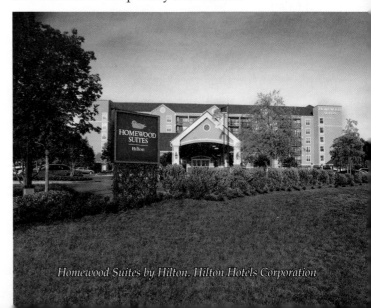

Homewood Suites by Hilton. Hilton Hotels Corporation

# Elaine Grossinger Etess—
## *First Woman President of AH&LA*

*Photo courtesy
of Elaine G. Etess*

Elaine Grossinger Etess knows quite a bit about hospitality. She grew up at a world-famous resort in the Catksills of New York. Her parents and grandparents owned Grossinger's, a resort that started as a boarding house. The resort welcomed wealthy and famous guests from around the world.

The Grossingers' approach to hospitality is what made the resort so popular. They created an atmosphere of warmth and comfort. To the Grossingers, guests were more like extended family members than customers. Guests enjoyed their stay at Grossinger's, and the word soon spread.

As a young person, Elaine had no interest in working at the hotel, even though her mother wanted her to join the family business. Instead, Elaine's life took a different turn, and she attended Russell Sage College and Syracuse University. Elaine then married her childhood sweetheart and raised three children. Elaine, her husband, and their children moved to Grossinger's after her husband finished his medical residency and a tour in the service. They lived in a new home on the hotel grounds.

A few years later, Elaine became involved with the hotel. She began by supervising the interior design of the hotel and hiring the youth activities director. Her responsibilities and interest in the hotel grew from there. She began to handle special sales accounts and guest relations. This led her into an administrative and managerial role. Upon her mother's death in 1972,

Elaine became executive vice president. She continued in this role until the sale of Grossinger's in 1985.

Elaine is well known for her leadership. She started her own company and serves as its president. Called Elaine G. Etess Associates, this consulting firm helps other companies in the hospitality field. In 1989, she became the first woman president of the American Hotel & Lodging Association (then the American Hotel & Motel Association). In 2002, Elaine was inducted into the Hospitality Hall of Honor of the Conrad Hilton College of Hotel and Restaurant Management.

## Elaine G. Etess's Career Path

**1927:** Born in New York City, New York

**1972:** Became executive vice president of Grossinger's

**1982:** Earned her Certified Hotel Administrator (CHA) designation

**1985:** Founded her own company, Elaine G. Etess Associates

**1989:** Elected as first woman president of AH&LA (then AH&MA)

**1990:** Became hospitality director at Forest Trace resort retirement community

**2002:** Inducted into the Hospitality Hall of Honor at the Conrad Hilton School of Hotel and Restaurant Management

# *Hospitality Ethics*

## Ethics and Accountability

What does it mean to be accountable? *Accountability* is accepting responsibility for your actions. All people are responsible for their actions, especially in how they treat others.

Because the focus of hospitality is serving people, accountability is a necessary employee virtue. For instance, hospitality managers are accountable for the safety and welfare of the employees they supervise. Likewise, *all* hospitality employees are accountable for treating guests respectfully. Regardless of their job tasks, employees must also protect guest health, safety, security, and welfare.

of insurance called *fidelity bonds*. In a hospitality business, many people have responsibility for the company's money and property. Sometimes dishonest employees will steal money or property, such as cash from the cash register or food from the storage closet. Fidelity bonds protect the company against losses caused by employee theft and embezzlement.

The cost of insurance depends on how likely the business is to use the insurance. The higher the chance of burglary or accidents, the more expensive the premium. For this reason, properties with good security and safety programs usually have lower premiums.

### *Security Staff*

The quality of the staff often determines the quality of the security. The most important quality is honesty. Security officers are given the responsibility for guest security, their valuables, the hotel vault, and all keys to the property. These employees will be required to undergo background checks before they are hired.

Security officers must be able to respond quickly in an emergency. Security work requires people who are problem solvers and can think on their feet. Security officers must also be able to remain calm during difficult situations.

A security officer who does not wear a uniform is called a **plainclothes security officer**. The term *plainclothes* refers to wearing regular clothing. Plainclothes give no indication that the wearer is a

member of the security staff. Many hotel managers prefer plainclothes officers because uniformed officers might give the impression that the hotel has a problem with crime. They think the sight of uniformed officers makes guests nervous.

Some hotel policies require security staff to wear uniforms and badges. Many managers think that **uniformed security officers** give the impression that everything is under control, **13-7**. Guests feel safe because there are officers around to prevent problems and to respond to emergencies.

### *Maintaining Security*

Maintaining security is a complex task. Security activities can be divided into four groups: structural security, security policies, surveillance, and safety and emergency procedures. In addition, security staff must keep records and investigate problems. All businesses must carry out these activities to ensure the safety of customers and employees and the security of property.

## Structural Security

The buildings of a business must have features that provide security. **Structural security** consists of the security features that are built into a building. Structural security should be built into the hotel, guest rooms, and any other buildings on the lodging property. Modern technology provides many features that increase security.

R. Knudsen/Photography Inc. Courtesy of Vance International Inc.

13-7 A security officer's uniform identifies him or her to those who need assistance.

should be locker rooms where staff can bring a lock and lock up their belongings.

All hospitality properties must be equipped with fire alarms, smoke detectors, and any other equipment required by local fire departments, **13-8**. It is also a good idea to have a burglar alarm system.

## Guest Rooms

Guests need to feel safe in their rooms. For this reason, most guest rooms are equipped with one or more locks. Guests also need a secure place to keep valuables when they are not in their rooms. Most lodging properties provide safe deposit boxes or an in-room safe.

Locks on guest room doors keep out intruders while guests are in their rooms. Most guest rooms have a dead bolt lock that can be locked from the inside of the guest room. An extra security feature is the privacy latch on guest room doors. The door can only be opened about two inches with this latch in place. This type of lock is convenient for receiving small supplies from housekeeping without opening the door completely. Most guest room doors also have a peephole to let the guest see who is at the door without opening it.

Many hotels provide a safe deposit box for guests' valuables. The front desk agent handles safe deposit boxes. The hotel may provide in-room safes for guests to use. An in-room safe is usually

## Buildings

Many security features can be built into a lodging property. Examples include lights, locks, alarms, and lockers for staff. New technology also provides many security features that can be built in.

Good lighting is important for both guest and employee security. Brightly lit parking lots help get rid of shadows where criminals might hide. Well-lit hallways and walkways make guests feel more secure and help keep dishonest people away. Some lights should be left on all night inside the buildings. Fire exits must be clearly marked.

All exit, entrance, and storeroom doors should have locks. Dead bolt locks are the most secure. The best deadbolt locks are those with square-headed bolts. These bolts can only be moved by a key. They are made of a type of steel that is very difficult to cut through. The longer the bolt, the better the security. Staff need a safe place for their personal belongings while they are working. There

13-8 All hospitality properties must be equipped with fire alarms, smoke detectors, and any other equipment required by local fire departments. This room has smoke detector above the beds and a sprinkler above the doorway.

drserg/Shutterstock.com

located in a guest room closet. The safe has a computerized lock or a lock and key. Guests can lock their jewelry or other valuables in this safe.

## Technology

Technology has provided many systems that help maintain security. Examples include security systems; electronic key systems; telecommunications; wireless transmittal devices; digital cameras; TV systems; and smoke, fire, and flood detection systems.

Most hospitality businesses have security systems. A **security system** is a computerized burglar detection and alarm system. Motion detectors or sensors on windows and doors detect trespassers. If a window or door is forced open or broken, a loud alarm sounds. The system is often connected by telephone lines to the police department. At the same time that the alarm sounds, a message is sent to the police department. These systems have backups in case telephone lines are cut or the electricity goes out. Some front desks have an emergency alarm that goes right to the police station in case of a robbery.

Most lodging properties use electronic key card systems, **13-9**. The major advantage of this type of system is that the key can quickly and easily be changed. A metal key system requires buying a new key and lock mechanism and the services of a locksmith. In an electronic key card system, the front desk agent can change a key card in a few minutes and a lost or stolen card can quickly be made useless.

**13-9** In an electronic key system, if a guest's key is lost or misplaced, the key and lock can quickly and easily be changed.

sixninepixels/Shutterstock.com

Some staff can always be found at their desks near a telephone. Examples include front desk agents, reservations agents, and operators. Other staff move around when they do their jobs and are rarely near a telephone. Examples include van drivers, security officers, room attendants, and managers. Two-way radios, pagers, wireless transmitters, and cell phones enable various staff members to communicate with one another when they are far from a telephone. A front desk agent may need to contact the executive housekeeper who is inspecting rooms. A bell attendant may need to contact a van driver to find out when the driver will return to the hotel. Two-way radios and wireless transmitters are especially important to security staff. They provide a quick way for security officers to contact each other, the hotel operator, and fire and police departments. In an emergency, these methods of communication can be a matter of life and death for a guest or hotel employee. For example, if a guest is having a heart attack, it is faster to radio the operator to call for an ambulance. In addition, the security officer can stay with the guest instead of looking around for a phone.

Digital camera surveillance systems are used to record areas where crimes might occur, **13-10**. The camera is permanently mounted so it records a specific area. Areas include places where cash is handled, parking lots, entrances, elevators, and stairways. The recordings are watched to find suspects and document crimes that have been committed. Signs are usually posted that say that a video camera is in use, which helps discourage crime. A person is less likely to commit a crime if he or she knows that a camera is recording his or her actions. The video and audio are recorded and saved on the hotel's computer hard drive and can be viewed from anywhere in the world.

*Closed-circuit television (CCTV)* is a TV system used to monitor the hotel on a 24-hour basis. TV monitors are set up in areas where crimes might occur. A security officer watches the television monitors for unusual activity. Guests often feel more secure in places where there are video cameras or closed-circuit TV systems. The newest CCTV systems use a hard-drive digital system for storage and monitoring.

Some hotels have sophisticated smoke, fire, and flood detection systems. These computerized systems can provide information on the safety status of each room or area of the hotel. This information is transmitted to a central control panel. When

Martin Muransky/Shutterstock.com

13-10 Surveillance cameras are often utilized in public areas such as parking lots and stairwells.

a fire is detected, the system automatically does several things. It uses the phone system to notify guests in each room that there is an emergency. It adjusts the ventilation system to push smoke out of the building. It also calls the local fire department and unlocks the fire doors located at the bottom of each stairwell. During a fire, guests will leave the building by the stairs and exit through the fire doors.

# Security Policies

Security policies are the rules that employees must follow to ensure security. Security policies are sometimes called *security procedures*. Security policies include rules concerning employee ID cards, key control, limiting entrances, lost and found, and special procedures.

## Employee ID Cards

Many hospitality businesses require employees to wear a photo ID card, 13-11. This card has a photograph of the person and identifies the wearer as an employee of the business. Photo ID cards make it easy to determine that a person is really a hotel employee and not a stranger off the street. Employees should wear these at all times while at work.

## Key Control

Room locks and keys are the single most effective way to ensure guest safety, and good key control system is a major factor in keeping a property secure. **Key control** is knowing where all hotel keys are located at all times and knowing who has each key. When the location of each key is known, it is easier to discover when a key has been lost or stolen, and immediate steps can be taken to protect the place the key unlocks.

There are two types of room key systems: the hard key system and the electronic key system. In a *hard key system*, a metal key fits into a keyhole in a lock. In an *electronic key system*, a **key card** with a magnetic strip contains the room combination. Key cards are about the size of a credit card and

Amy J. Berk

**13-11** This employee's photo ID card identifies her as a member of the staff.

sixninepixels/Shutterstock.com

**13-12** This key card unlocks the door simply by touching the sensor on the lock.

can be made of plastic, metal, or pressed paper. The key card fits into a special lock in the door where the magnetic strip is read. If the combination matches, the door is unlocked. New wireless *radio-frequency identification (RFID)* technology allows guests to walk up to their room and unlock the door by waving the key card or a bracelet in front of the door lock, **13-12**.

A hard key system is less expensive in the beginning. However, guests often forget to return keys at checkout time, and hard keys can be lost or stolen. When this happens, locks must be changed and new keys purchased. Hard key systems are often more expensive in the long run, so they are usually only used by very small or specialty properties.

An electronic system may be more expensive at the beginning, but it solves many of the problems of a hard key system. When a new guest registers, a new combination is electronically assigned to the key card and the corresponding lock on the guest room door. The guest room lock will open only when the new key card is used. If the key card is lost or stolen, the combination can be canceled electronically. Key cards do not have the room number or hotel information on them, so if a valid key card is found, the finder will not know which room it opens. New keys and combinations

are quick and easy to make. When the guest leaves, the combination is canceled. The electronic system can also run reports that will tell which keys have been used to enter a specific room. This procedure almost guarantees guest room security.

Many employees need keys to perform their jobs. For example, room attendants need keys to enter guest rooms that need cleaning. The security division is responsible for issuing keys to employees and keeping a log of all keys. Workers can be given key cards that open only those rooms to which they need access. Keys cannot be duplicated and usually must be turned in at the end of each shift.

## *Limiting Number of Entrances*

Most large lodging properties have many entrance doors. The more doors a place has, the harder it is to keep out troublemakers. As a result, a hotel will often limit the number of doors that are open. Certain doors are always locked. Other doors are locked after a certain hour. Security is responsible for checking locked doors and locking doors on time. Some properties have doors that open only with the use of the guest room key card.

## *Lost and Found Procedures*

Guests often accidentally leave behind personal items. Items that are missing may not be noticed until the guests arrive home. Most lodging properties have procedures for handling lost and found items. Often security handles these items. Each item is logged with information such as date and place found and the finder's name. When a guest calls to find an item, it can be quickly located in the lost and found document.

Foodservice businesses also have lost and found items. The items turned in are usually kept in the manager's office.

## Special Procedures

Security officers are often needed to help with special procedures involving guests. For example, if a guest does not pay the bill, the front desk will have the guest room locked. Locking a guest out of a room is called a *lockout*. If the guest does not pay a bill, the guest's luggage may be seized. Seizing luggage is called a *luggage lien*. The hotel has the right to hold guests' belongings until the bill is paid. Help from security is often needed during lockouts and luggage liens.

# Surveillance

**Surveillance**, the process of closely observing what is going on in an area, is a critical part of the security officer's job, **13-13**. Security officers regularly perform surveillance while on **patrol**, the act of walking or riding around an area for the purpose of maintaining security.

Security officers must be able to reach managers, front desk agents, and municipal police and fire departments. Officers often are equipped with pagers, two-way transmitters, or cell phones. During emergencies, this quick communication could help prevent the loss of property, money, or lives.

Security officers perform three basic tasks when on patrol: look for people who might make trouble, look for physical conditions that might lead to danger, and perform routine tasks.

## People

Security officers are trained to look for people who do not belong. Someone who does not belong in the hotel might be planning trouble. A person hiding in the shadows might be planning a burglary. A person trying a key in several doors may be trying to break in.

Security officers are also alert for any disturbances. For example, they will step in to break up a fight and keep an eye out for people in distress, **13-14**.

Security officers also watch employee entrances. The purpose is not only to protect employees, but also to prevent theft by employees. Another responsibility may be to escort people through parking lots at night or to their rooms if they request.

## Physical Conditions

Security officers look for unsafe conditions, damaged property, and broken equipment. Examples of unsafe conditions include burned out lightbulbs and shrubs that need to be trimmed. Security officers will also check the pool area to make sure safety fences are closed. Examples of damaged property include windows or doors that may have been damaged by attempted break-ins. Broken property includes an automatic door that does not work.

**13-14** Security officers will watch for suspicious people and people who might be in distress.

©REATISTA/Shutterstock.com

**13-13** All security officers perform surveillance to help ensure guests' safety.

Isantilli/Shutterstock.com

Any physical problems will be documented and reported to the proper department. Security officers are often responsible for sending requests to the engineering or maintenance department for repairs.

### Routine Tasks

Certain tasks must be done every day. For example, doors must be locked at a specific time. Certain lights must be turned off at a specific time. Security officers perform these tasks during their patrols.

# Safety and Emergency Procedures

The security division develops and implements emergency response plans. These plans should include responses for fires, tornadoes, illnesses, falls, and other emergencies. This department should conduct emergency drills to practice the emergency response plans. The security officers should be trained to give cardiopulmonary resuscitation (CPR) and first aid. There should be a person on staff at all times who is trained in these procedures.

# Records and Investigations

Security officers must document anything that requires action. The first way they document is to keep a security log. A **security log** is a book in which all security incidents are recorded. It is also a communication tool between security agents. In the security log, the officer will note what the problem was, where and when it occurred, and what action was taken.

When an accident occurs on the property, the law requires that an accident report be completed. An **accident report** contains detailed information such as the time, date, and location of the accident; names of the people involved; detailed description of the accident; and names of people investigating the accident.

# Security and Front Desk Cooperation

The security department and front desk work together to maintain guest security. Fire safety systems, emergency systems, and investigations of guest security concerns require the cooperation of these departments. When guests have security concerns, they call the front desk. Front desk agents cannot leave the front desk to help the guest, so they contact the security department and report the situation. Often, the front desk agent uses a two-way radio transmitter for faster communication with security staff, **13-15**. The security officers then take charge of the situation. In an emergency, front desk staff and security work together to make sure all guests know what to do and where they are supposed to go.

# Role of All Employees

Employees have specific security responsibilities related to their specific jobs. For example, the front desk agent is responsible for guest room keys. However, all employees are responsible for noticing and reporting problems or dangers. In general, all employees are responsible for reporting accidents and hazards, reporting suspicious people, and taking responsibility for keys. Employees are also responsible for knowing the security and safety procedures of the place where they work.

**13-15** Technology such as two-way radios helps provide faster communication between the front desk and security staff.

*Kenwood Communications*

## Report Accidents and Hazards

All employees should be alert to accidents and potentially dangerous physical conditions and know how to handle these situations. In most places, the first step is to report the situation to your manager or supervisor, who then reports the problem to the security department, **13-16**. The security department will then decide what steps need to be taken, such as whether to call the police or fire department.

## Report Suspicious People

All employees should know what to do if they see a person who looks strange or is acting in a strange or dangerous way. Especially monitor a person who is

- looking in the windows and doors
- trying the same key card in several doors
- trying to get into a room without a key card

13-16  Potential emergencies should be quickly but discreetly reported to the manager.

*Dragon Images*

- changing direction whenever another person approaches
- sitting in a car for a long time or driving a car around and around the property

Be sure to observe the person carefully. The security officer will ask you to describe the person's appearance, specific actions, and last location. If the person was in a car, you will be asked for the license plate number.

If the situation permits, ask the person if he or she needs help. You must always be polite and respectful. The person you suspect might just be lost, confused, or ill. Do not let guests' looks or customs affect how you treat them. Just because a person is different from you does not mean that he or she is dangerous.

If the person does not answer, runs away, or gives a strange answer, contact security. Continue to watch the person without being noticed until the security officer arrives. The security officer will decide whether the police should be called.

## Take Responsibility for Keys and Key Cards

Security can be maintained by all employees when they take responsibility for the keys and key cards that they are issued. First, employees should follow company rules for key control. For example, employees usually have to sign for the keys at the beginning of the shift and return the keys at the end of the shift. In addition, employees should keep the keys with them at all times. Keys and key cards should not be left on a table or other surface. Employees should not lend keys to others. If an employee loses a key, the supervisor should be informed immediately.

# Preventing Employee Theft

Unfortunately, employee theft can be a problem at hospitality businesses. Employees often steal cash, linens, guest room supplies, silverware, and food. One way to prevent employee theft is the proper storage and inventory of supplies. Supplies should be kept in a locked storeroom to which only authorized employees have keys. A requisition system should be used when items are needed. Accurate inventories should be taken to discover when items are missing. Several other policies can help reduce employee theft, **13-17**.

---

### Policies to Reduce Employee Theft

- Employees are not allowed on the property before or after work hours.
- Any package that an employee brings into or takes out of the property must be inspected.
- Employees must punch in and out with time cards. These time cards record the exact time that each employee arrives and leaves the workplace.
- Employees must enter and exit through the employee entrance. Security will be posted at this entrance during employee arrival and departure times.

*Goodheart-Willcox Publisher*

**13-17** A major way to reduce employee theft is through an inventory and requisition system. It is also helpful to have specific policies to deter theft.

# Role of the Director of Security

The director of security is responsible for maintaining the safety and security of the entire lodging property. The director must be well trained in security procedures. Directors of security in large convention hotels are often former FBI agents or high-ranking retired police officers. In addition, the director of security has the usual responsibilities of a manager: hiring, training, supervising, evaluating, and motivating all security staff. The director of security also manages the budget for the security department.

There are four security-specific tasks that the director of security must carry out: develop and implement safety and security policies, train employees, prepare staff schedules, and maintain equipment.

## Develop and Implement Policies

One of the main ways of ensuring safety and security is to have good policies. The director of security is responsible for developing and improving these policies. Policies are needed for handling emergencies, evacuations, keys, and the lost and found. Once the policies are in place, the director must make sure they are properly carried out.

## Train Employees

After the security policies are developed, employees must be trained. Each department will have specific security policies that must be learned. The director of security will work with the human resources department and the director or manager of each department to train its staff. In addition, there are general security procedures that all staff must know, such as fire and evacuation procedures. The director of security is responsible for this training as well.

## Prepare Staff Schedules

The security department operates on a 24-hour basis in many hotels. The director must make sure that each shift is staffed with a shift supervisor and security officers. The number of officers needed for each shift depends on the size of the hotel. Special events and conventions may require additional security. The director of security is responsible for hiring extra officers for these special events. Extra security officers can usually be hired from an outside security agency.

## Maintain Equipment

Security equipment must be maintained on a regular basis. The director of security is responsible for scheduling regular maintenance of equipment such as computer security systems, alarms, communication devices, and security vehicles.

# Chapter *13* Review

## Chapter Summary

- The major responsibility of the security department is the protection of people and property.
- Security activities can be divided into four groups: structural security, security policies, surveillance, and safety and emergency procedures.
- Structural security consists of the security features of a building.
- Security policies are the rules that employees must follow to ensure security.
- Security officers perform three basic tasks when on patrol: look for people who might make trouble, look for physical conditions that might lead to danger, and perform routine tasks.
- The security division develops and implements emergency response plans.

- The security department and front office work together to maintain guest security.
- All employees are responsible for security.
- There are four security-specific tasks that the director of security must carry out: develop and implement safety and security policies, train employees, prepare staff schedules, and maintain equipment.

## Review

1. Why is good security important for hospitality businesses?
2. List the three categories of threats to security.
3. What is limitation of liability?
4. Explain the difference between property insurance and liability insurance.
5. Name the two types of security officers and describe the advantages and disadvantages of each.

6. Give three examples of structural security.

7. What is the purpose of an employee ID card?

8. Why is key control important?

9. What are the three basic tasks of security officers on patrol?

10. What is the responsibility of the security department in preparing for emergencies?

11. What must a security officer do every time something occurs that requires action?

12. What is the relationship between the security department and the front office?

13. Describe the role of all employees in maintaining security.

14. How can employee theft be prevented?

15. What are the four security-specific tasks of the director of security?

# Critical Thinking

16. **Identify.** Give examples for each of the three categories of threats to security in a hotel.

17. **Assess.** List security incidents that might happen at a hotel. Summarize ways that these security problems could be avoided.

18. **Determine.** Imagine that you are the director of security of a large hotel. Suppose that one of the new room attendants thinks that he or she is not responsible for security. How would you respond?

19. **Predict.** Describe ways that a lack of security in a hospitality business can cause the business to lose customers.

20. **Draw conclusions.** Explain the reasons some hospitality businesses prefer to use plainclothes security officers while others prefer to use uniformed security officers.

# Common Core

**College and Career Readiness**

21. **Speaking.** Use the Internet to find a news story about a hotel that has had security issues. How did the management of the hotel handle the issue? Retell the story in your own words in an oral report to the class.

22. **Writing.** Prepare a one-page report about the need for hospitality businesses to have liability insurance. Share the report with your class.

23. **Listening.** Interview a member of a hotel security department about the reasons hospitality businesses are always at risk for lawsuits.

24. **CTE Career Readiness Practice.** In small teams, debate the following question: Is it better for a hospitality business to employ uniformed security officers rather than plainclothes security officers? Identify text factors that support the expression of your position and factors that interfere with the opposing team's position.

250

# Chapter *14*
## Engineering

## Chapter Objectives

After studying this chapter, you will be able to

- **state** the purpose of engineering.
- **list** the six functions of engineering.
- **describe** the three building systems for which engineering is responsible.
- **list** four examples of equipment and parts of a building that require maintenance.
- **determine** the responsibilities of engineering for guest rooms and public areas in a hotel.
- **list** eight tasks of groundskeeping.
- **distinguish between** the responsibilities of the chief engineer, skilled technicians, and maintenance staff.

## Before You Read

Try to answer the following questions before you read this chapter.

- When is nonpotable water used in a hospitality business?
- For what jobs are skilled technicians needed?

## Terms to Know

preventive maintenance
deep cleaning
potable water
nonpotable water
HVAC systems

chlorine
pH value
grounds
landscaping
groundskeeper

groundskeeping
chief engineer
plant manager
facility manager

The engineering department is responsible for the physical facilities of the hotel. The tasks of the engineering department include maintenance, repairs, deep cleaning, and groundskeeping. All facilities need engineering services. However, the number of these services depends on the size of the facility. A small restaurant needs few engineering services. It does not need a full-time engineer and can call in an engineering service when needed. A huge resort hotel that includes indoor and outdoor swimming pools, restaurants, spa facilities, and a golf course usually has a fairly large engineering staff, **14-1**. This staff will include a chief engineer, plumbers, electricians, and maintenance workers. Some engineering departments are responsible for the maintenance and repair of company vehicles, such as vans and riding lawn mowers. This chapter will focus on the engineering department in a hotel. However, many of the tasks and procedures apply to smaller lodging properties and to restaurants. In smaller businesses, the engineering department may be called *maintenance*.

**14-1** A large resort has several buildings, one or more swimming pools, a golf course, tennis courts, and other facilities. This type of property usually has a large engineering department.

*Omni Mount Washington Resort in Bretton Woods, New Hampshire, Omni Hotels & Resorts*

# Purpose

The purpose of engineering is to keep the facility in top condition for safety, guest satisfaction, and profitability.

## Safety

Much of the equipment in restaurants and hotels is potentially hazardous. Electrical systems can short circuit and cause a fire. Gas in kitchens can explode. Elevators can get stuck with guests inside. Ventilation systems can become contaminated with pathogens. Plumbing can burst and cause water damage. One of the main purposes of engineering is to prevent these kinds of disasters.

## Guest Satisfaction

The look of a hospitality business is vital to its success, **14-2**. Guests do not want to stay in a shabby hotel with leaky faucets or backed up plumbing. They do not want to eat in a restaurant that looks dirty or has a pest problem. The daily cleaning provided by restaurant servers and room attendants is not enough. Engineering is responsible for the deep cleaning tasks. In a hotel, engineering often works with housekeeping on the deep cleaning tasks. In addition, to keep the look of a business fresh, it needs to be remodeled periodically. This is especially true in hotels. Engineering will work with housekeeping and upper management on remodeling tasks.

**14-2** Guest satisfaction depends on the condition of the hospitality facility. Engineering has a major role in keeping the facility in good condition.

*handy/Shutterstock.com*

Most of the equipment in a hotel or restaurant needs regular maintenance to avoid unexpected breakdowns. Breakdowns of equipment are expensive, frustrating, and sometimes dangerous to employees and guests. Major breakdowns could force the hotel or restaurant to close until the equipment can be repaired or replaced. For example, suppose the air conditioning breaks down in a Texas hotel ballroom during a summer wedding. The guests will be extremely uncomfortable and complain. The hosts of the wedding might demand their money back. The hosts might tell others about the bad experience, and the hotel might lose future business. The hotel may also have to cancel other events until the air conditioning is repaired.

Many pieces of equipment, fixtures, and furnishings need minor repairs and maintenance due to normal wear and tear. For example, air conditioners must have their filters replaced regularly. Plumbing fixtures develop leaks. Drains get stopped up. Engineering is responsible for attending to these types of tasks.

## Profitability

The engineering department is responsible for some of the most expensive items on the property. It is less expensive to maintain the equipment regularly than to wait until it breaks down. As discussed in the air conditioning example, unexpected breakdowns result in dissatisfied customers and large repair bills. If the business must close until repairs are finished, it will lose a great deal of income.

Most of the equipment and systems require a great deal of costly energy and water, 14-3. Engineering is responsible for making sure that all the equipment runs as efficiently as possible, so this department is often required to develop ways to save energy and water.

When new equipment is needed, engineering is responsible for researching, getting bids, and choosing the best equipment for the purpose and price. There are also many engineering tasks that require specialized expertise or additional labor. Engineering is responsible for finding the best outside contractor for each task.

Because engineers are so familiar with the equipment in the facility, they also often work with insurance companies. The engineers will work with the business's manager or owner to

Lake County Indiana Convention & Visitors Bureau, Hammond, Indiana. www.alllake.org

14-3 Hotels require a large amount of electricity and water. What are some ways engineering has developed to save energy and water?

make sure that the business has the best insurance coverage for each type of equipment and system.

# Functions

Engineering has six functions: preventive maintenance, deep cleaning, repairs, remodeling, resource management, and emergencies.

## Preventive Maintenance

**Preventive maintenance** consists of the cleaning and repair of equipment that is in working order. Preventive maintenance in a business is very similar to preventive maintenance needed by cars to keep them in top running condition and prevent unexpected breakdowns. Most obviously, a car needs to be filled with gasoline as the gasoline gets used up. The levels of other fluids, such as brake fluid, transmission fluid, and coolant, need to be checked and replaced. Oil needs to be replaced at recommended intervals. Locks and hinges should be lubricated. Belts and hoses need to be checked and replaced when worn. Tires need to be checked for air, filled as needed, and replaced when worn. For best appearance, the car should be washed and waxed periodically. Similarly, all the buildings, grounds, and equipment in a hospitality business need preventive maintenance.

In a hotel or restaurant, preventive maintenance is performed on all equipment, such as boilers, washing machines, stoves, and refrigerators. Preventive maintenance on equipment includes tasks such as replacing filters, adding lubricants to moving parts, and replacing parts that show wear. Preventive maintenance is also performed on the building itself, including windows, doors, painting, brick mortar repairs, stucco repairs, and roof repairs. Preventive maintenance increases the lifetime of equipment and the building. It often catches problems before they turn into emergencies by preventing unexpected breakdowns.

Most businesses have a preventive maintenance schedule for all equipment and parts of the building, 14-4. Each item is inspected on a regular basis. Some items need to be checked daily, weekly, or monthly. Other items can be checked less often.

## Deep Cleaning

**Deep cleaning** is more thorough cleaning that involves extra time or equipment. Deep cleaning is usually done every three months in guest rooms and public areas. Deep cleaning tasks include flipping mattresses over, cleaning under and behind furniture, steam cleaning furniture, and cleaning walls and carpets. Deep cleaning is often part of the responsibility of the housekeeping department. However, in some places, engineering is responsible for these tasks. Often the two departments will work together. Engineering does preventive maintenance in the rooms while housekeeping does the deep cleaning.

| Sample Preventive Maintenance Schedule | | | |
|---|---|---|---|
| **Daily** | **Weekly** | **Monthly** | **Quarterly** |
| • Thermostats in public areas<br>• Temperature of freezers and coolers<br>• Temperature of boiler<br>• Guest rooms for maintenance problems<br>• Temperature, cleanliness, and chemical balance of swimming pool<br>• Lights<br>• Vacuum cleaners | • Equipment<br>• Landscaping<br>• Elevators and escalators<br>• Lights and light fixtures<br>• Signs<br>• Stairways and walkways<br>• Handrails | • Air conditioner filters<br>• Smoke detectors<br>• Maintenance shop<br>• Floor mats and carpets<br>• Sprinkler systems<br>• Windows<br>• Ceilings and walls | • Ice machines<br>• Guest room mattresses (rotate)<br>• Carpets (clean)<br>• Parking lots |
| | | **Every Two Months** | **Twice a Year** |
| | | • Washers and dryers<br>• Kitchen appliances<br>• Water heaters<br>• Locks<br>• Meeting rooms<br>• Housekeeping carts<br>• Cribs and rollaway beds<br>• Chipped or peeling paint | • Bathroom fan filters<br>• Hot water systems<br>• Weather stripping around doors and windows<br>• Fire extinguishers |
| | | | **Annually** |
| | | | • Swimming pool<br>• Structural cracks<br>• Woodwork<br>• Siding<br>• Gutters, downspouts, and drains |

*Goodheart-Willcox Publisher*

**14-4** This sample schedule indicates how often each item should be checked and repaired if necessary.

## Repairs

When something in a hotel or restaurant breaks down, it must be repaired. Examples include leaking faucets, broken washing machines, and nonfunctioning air conditioning. Most businesses have a system for requesting repairs. If the situation is an emergency, emergency procedures are followed. If the situation is not an emergency, the procedures for requesting maintenance are followed. The person who discovers the problem fills out a maintenance request form, **14-5**. These forms help the engineering department keep track of needed repairs and make sure they are completed in a timely manner.

## Remodeling

Remodeling is often done to enhance the looks of a property. After several years, facilities begin to look old and tired. Guests will not want to visit properties that are out-of-date. Changing furniture, plumbing, and lighting fixtures; repainting; and replacing the linens and carpet are examples of remodeling tasks. Sometimes remodeling changes the look of a business so much that it looks like an entirely different place. Other times, remodeling simply updates the property and makes it look fresh and clean.

Remodeling is sometimes needed to install the most modern equipment, such as wireless Internet, property management systems, and electrical systems. Sometimes remodeling is done to meet new laws. For example, when the *Americans with Disability Act* was passed, many hospitality businesses remodeled doors, curbs, and bathrooms to make them accessible for people with disabilities.

## Resource Management

Hospitality managers are responsible for promoting the efficient use of fuel, electricity, and water. The engineering department is responsible for implementing methods of conservation, **14-6**.

**14-6** Engineering is often responsible for conservation, such as recycling aluminum cans.

**14-5** Maintenance requests are made by filling out forms such as this.

### Example of a Maintenance Request

*Hearthstone Hotel*
*Maintenance Request*

By _____ Date _____

Location _____

Problem _____

_____

_____

Assigned to _____

Date completed_____

Time spent_____

Completed by _____

Remarks_____

*Goodheart-Willcox Publisher*

*Photo courtesy of Princess Cruises*

In recent years, the cost of fuel has risen dramatically. Keeping a hotel or restaurant warm in winter and cool in summer requires a great deal of fuel. Therefore, proper control over the temperature is very important. The temperature in a hotel should be closely watched and regulated based on the number of guests and the outside temperature. Proper insulation in the walls of the hotel is essential in keeping the cost of heating and cooling down.

Windows and doors have a direct effect on the cost of heating a hotel. The use of weather stripping around the doors reduces the amount of heat that is lost. Features such as double doors, double-paned windows, and thermopane glass can also decrease the amount of heat that is lost. Some hotels use solar heat as a way to conserve fuel.

Water is another expensive resource that hotels use in large quantities. Leaky faucets and toilets waste large amounts of water. The engineering department can make sure these are repaired quickly. In addition, many of the new plumbing fixtures, such as low-flow toilets and showers, use less water. Some hotels have replaced old fixtures with these water-conserving fixtures. Many hotels encourage their guests to reuse towels in order to conserve the water and fuel used to wash towels.

In some hotels, guests must use their key card to activate the air conditioning and lighting system when they enter the room. When the guest leaves the room, the air conditioning and lighting automatically reset to an energy-efficient level.

Resource management requires cooperation from all hospitality employees. The engineering department often works with management to educate employees about ways to conserve resources. For example, ovens need to be preheated for baking. However, preheating for an hour or leaving an oven on all day uses up a great deal of fuel. Engineering can work with the executive chef to determine that ten minutes of preheating is enough. The executive chef can then make sure that everyone who bakes only preheats the oven for ten minutes.

## Emergencies

The engineering department is usually in charge of all safety issues, including fire safety and maintenance of fire safety systems, 14-7. When emergencies occur, engineering plays a major role.

The engineering staff knows the location of all firefighting and emergency equipment in the hotel. They also know the location of all equipment that could possibly explode or experience other emergencies. All staff must know the safe exit and emergency routes. The engineering staff usually works closely with the security staff, front office staff, and municipal emergency services during an emergency.

# Hospitality Ethics

## Ethics and Absenteeism

Ethical employees arrive at work on time, ready to perform their duties competently. In return for meeting this obligation, employees receive wages and the satisfaction of knowing they have performed their jobs well. Hospitality managers report, however, that *absenteeism*—or frequent absence from work—is a problem in the industry.

What happens when employees fail to show up for work? The burden of doing their work is shifted to others in the department and sometimes to other departments. This upsets work plans and lowers employee morale. Any worker with an absenteeism problem will be out of a job quickly. No employer can allow a worker's behavior to negatively impact guests, coworkers, and the reputation of the business.

14-7 Engineering checks the functionality of all the emergency equipment on property.

14-8 Engineering is responsible for maintenance and repair of electrical systems.

The functions of engineering are performed in the following five areas: building systems, building and equipment, guest rooms and public areas, recreational equipment, and grounds.

# Building Systems

Every building has a number of systems that must function smoothly. In some ways, these systems are like the systems in the human body. For example, the building's electrical system could be compared to the human body's nervous system. The main building systems are electrical, plumbing, and heating and air conditioning.

## Electrical Systems

Electrical systems are the major source of energy in many hospitality businesses, 14-8. Electricity is used to provide heat, light, and power. Electricity can be used to heat the entire hotel and powers equipment such as vacuum cleaners, air-conditioning units, refrigerators, ventilation systems, and elevators. It is often used to generate hot water and also powers the lights, cooking equipment, bath exhaust fans, and televisions. Cut-off or interrupted electricity creates problems for hospitality businesses. The engineering department is therefore also responsible for back-up electrical generators.

Safety requirements are very important, especially in the electrical area. If you have ever had an electrical shock, you know about the dangers of electricity. The engineering department must make sure that all safety devices are in place and operating properly. For example, there are special electrical outlets located near water, such as in a bathroom or kitchen. These outlets are designed to turn off the electricity if water is detected. The engineering staff must make sure that these outlets are working properly.

## Plumbing Systems

Plumbing systems are designed to provide **potable water**, or safe drinking water. Plumbing systems are also designed to dispose of waste matter in a sanitary way. Plumbing systems have two important goals: the comfort of the guest and the maintenance of proper health precautions.

Water supply systems are regulated by the local health departments. Potable water is used for drinking, washing, laundering, and cooking. Water that is not clean enough to drink but is still usable is called **nonpotable water**. Nonpotable water may be used for toilet flushing purposes, air conditioning, and in other cases where there is no direct human contact with the water. This water must be kept separate from the potable water.

Plumbing systems require continuous maintenance to make sure the sewage flows properly without creating any sanitary problems. The plumbing system must provide proper pressure and circulation to prevent corrosion, clogged pipes, and bad odors, **14-9**.

Hot water should be kept at a temperature of about 120°F in guest rooms and 140°F in laundry rooms and kitchens. Hot water systems should be cleaned twice a year to remove lime deposit buildups. When lime deposits form, water heaters do not perform efficiently. Inefficient water heating may result in higher utility bills.

Plumbing systems frequently have problems caused by clogged pipes and drain traps. The engineering staff must use proper chemicals on a regular basis to reduce clogging. When problems do occur, mechanical equipment must be used to clear the clogged materials. Maintenance workers must also be able to repair leaking faucets, clogged drains, and stopped-up toilets.

## *Heating and Air Conditioning Systems*

Heating, ventilation, and air conditioning systems are called **HVAC systems**. HVAC systems have one main purpose: to keep guests comfortably warm in the winter and cool in the summer.

**14-9** Hot water heaters and other plumbing systems frequently require maintenance and repair.

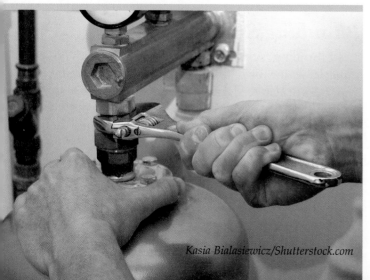

*Kasia Bialasiewicz/Shutterstock.com*

One of the major complaints of hotel guests is that their rooms are either too hot or too cold. Normally, a comfortable level of heat in a room is around 68°F. The heat level of a room should be maintained close to this temperature. Many hotels have zoned central heating and air conditioning that can be controlled with a thermostat in each room. One unit is zoned for a certain number of guest rooms and is connected to those rooms through air ducts. The guests can adjust the temperature in their own room. Air circulation is based on the need and the demand per room. The size of the unit determines how many guest rooms it will service. Other hotels have individual room air conditioners that can both heat and cool a single room. These systems can also be regulated by the guest.

HVAC systems must be regularly maintained by the engineering department to make sure the units are working properly. Regular maintenance also lengthens the life of the HVAC equipment, which can be very expensive to replace.

# Building and Equipment

Most restaurants and hotels are located in buildings. Engineering is concerned with the integrity of the building. In this context, *integrity* means *wholeness*. Engineering checks for holes, tears, or leaks in roofs, walls, floors, or parking lots. Any damage found must be repaired.

Most restaurants and hotels contain a variety of equipment. Engineering is also concerned with keeping all equipment, large and small, in good working order. Engineering provides preventive maintenance for roofs, walls, floors, parking lots, elevators, escalators, kitchen equipment, and laundry equipment.

## *Roofs, Walls, Floors*

The basic building structure must be kept in good repair, both for safety and for attractiveness, **14-10**. Repairs can include such things as fixing holes in walls, mending carpet, repairing or replacing loose tiles, and touch-up painting.

Roofs are designed to keep out water from rain and snow, decrease heat loss in the wintertime, and decrease heat gain in the summertime. Roofs must be inspected regularly. Holes, broken shingles, and other damage to the roof can result in leaks. Engineering will repair any damage.

14-10 Engineering is responsible for the maintenance and repair of the roof, walls, floors, and windows.

14-11 Elevator repair and maintenance may be contracted to an elevator service company.

## Parking Lot

Parking lots must be maintained for two basic reasons. First, the parking lot is often the initial thing that guests see when entering the property. If the parking lot and paving are well maintained, guests will not notice them. However, if there are potholes, bumps, and growing weeds, guests may form a bad impression of the business. In addition, a poorly maintained parking lot can be a safety hazard to guests and employees. People could fall and become injured if the parking lot has holes or uneven surfaces.

## Elevators and Escalators

Elevators and escalators are the main ways guests get to their rooms or to the public areas of a hotel, 14-11. The maintenance schedule and use of elevators are carefully regulated by local authorities. Elevator equipment is inspected regularly for safety. The certificate showing the date of the last inspection will be on display inside the elevator. Inspections are done quarterly in some cities and every six months in others. There are regulations that control the size and capacity of elevators, ventilation systems, and elevator safety equipment. Elevator maintenance and repair require special knowledge and skill. The engineering department usually contracts with an elevator service company for all maintenance and repairs.

Escalators are common in convention hotels. In these hotels, large groups of people travel by escalators to meeting rooms that are on different floors. Escalators are extremely expensive to maintain because objects often become stuck in the moving steps and break down the system.

## Kitchen Equipment

The kitchen equipment in a hotel or a restaurant must operate efficiently and correctly so meals can be prepared as planned. In a hotel, the engineering department may be able to do most of the kitchen equipment repairs. Sometimes hotels and restaurants have maintenance contracts with restaurant equipment repair companies to make repairs as needed. Other restaurants call a restaurant equipment repair company only as needed for repairs.

# Guest Rooms and Public Areas

The engineering department is responsible for the maintenance and repair of guest rooms and public areas, 14-12. Engineering may also be responsible for the regular deep cleaning of guest rooms and public areas. When this type of cleaning is performed, workers also look for anything that needs repair.

Hotel room attendants and house staff are always on the alert for maintenance problems. When they find problems, they fill out a maintenance request form and send it to the engineering department. Some hotels also place maintenance

Photo courtesy of Princess Cruises

14-12 Engineering is usually responsible for maintenance, repair, and deep cleaning of the public areas, such as this sun atrium lounge area on a cruise ship.

request forms in each guest room. The guests fill them out and leave them for the room attendant. Guests can also call the front desk to report any maintenance problems they find.

The engineering staff organizes all the maintenance requests and makes sure they are handled. Most of these requests involve repairs. After these repairs are made, it is important for workers to clean up any messes that have been made during the repair process. The work must be inspected to make sure that it is acceptable and looks good. Guests should never be able to tell that a repair has been made.

Keeping the guest rooms and public areas in good condition requires that the engineering department work closely with other departments of the hotel. The front desk, housekeeping, and security departments all notify the engineering department of items that need to be repaired. Guests will call the front desk when they have a maintenance request and the front desk agent notifies the engineering department.

# Recreational Equipment

Many lodging properties have recreational equipment. Many motels have a swimming pool

and hot tub. Larger hotels may have large pools, steam and sauna rooms, and exercise rooms.

## Swimming Pools

Swimming pools must have clear sparkling water in order to look inviting to guests. Pools get dirty from things that fall into them, such as leaves, grass, insects, hair, and trash. Swimming pools and hot tubs must also be maintained to prevent pathogens from causing illness. Bacteria get into the water from the people who use the pool. A microscopic water plant called *algae* tends to grow on pool surfaces. The algae create a slippery green surface that looks and feels unpleasant and may cause people to slip and fall. There are three main methods to keep a pool clean: chemicals, filtering, and scrubbing, **14-13**. Swimming pools should also be closed once a year for thorough cleaning, repainting, and repair.

### Chemicals

The main chemical used to keep swimming pool water safe is **chlorine**. When mixed in water, chlorine kills pathogens and other microorganisms. The amount of chlorine in the water must be carefully monitored. Too much chlorine will sting the eyes of swimmers, but too little will not kill pathogens and algae. Swimmers may get sick from a pool contaminated with pathogens. Pool maintenance staff usually checks chlorine levels once or twice a day.

The pH of pool water is another aspect that is controlled by chemicals. The **pH value** indicates the level of acidity or alkalinity of the water. The values of pH range from 1 to 14. Values between 1 and 7 are acid. Lemon juice and vinegar are acid. Values between 7 and 14 are alkaline. Most soap solutions are alkaline. A pH of 7 indicates *neutral water*—water that is neither acidic nor alkaline. If the water is too alkaline, the water will look cloudy and the chlorine will not work properly. If the water is too acidic, it will corrode the pool pipes. Pool maintenance staff will check pH levels once or twice a day.

If the levels of chlorine and pH are wrong, the pool must be closed for about an hour while they are corrected. The appropriate chemicals are added to the water and the pool pump is run to mix them. The chlorine and pH levels are measured again to make sure they are correct.

*Omni Hotels & Resorts*

**14-13** Chemicals, filtering, and scrubbing are three main methods to keep a pool clean and inviting.

### Filtering and Scrubbing

Pools need to be regularly vacuumed and skimmed to remove leaves and debris. *Vacuuming* should be done at least once a week to remove leaves and any debris that have fallen into the pool. If there are trees around the pool, the vacuuming must be done more often. *Skimming* is done by using a wire mesh basket at the end of a long pole. The wire mesh basket is skimmed across the surface of the water to remove leaves and other items floating on the surface. Brushes are used to clean the sides and the bottom of the pool. Every pool has lint baskets that are designed to automatically collect leaves and debris while the pump is operating. Lint baskets should be emptied regularly, and daily if possible. Any problems that are noticed by the maintenance employees should be repaired as soon as possible.

## Hot Tubs

Hot tubs should be cleaned daily. The temperature and pH of the water should also be checked daily. Sometimes water needs to be added to hot tubs, and the water temperature should be checked to make sure it is not too hot or too cool.

## Exercise Equipment

Most full-service hotels have a fitness room for their guests, **14-14**. The equipment that is commonly found in fitness rooms includes stationary

_...d Hotel, Brussels. Courtesy of Hilton Ho... Corporation_

**14-14**  This hotel has the pool, hot tub, and exercise equipment all in the same area.

bicycles, treadmills, stair-climbing machines, elliptical machines, and weight training equipment. Some fitness rooms have an area for doing warm-ups, stretching, and cooldown exercises. Fitness rooms usually contain a television that guests can watch while exercising. All equipment in fitness rooms should be properly maintained. This is done to prevent injuries from happening while guests are exercising. Fitness rooms should also be properly cleaned and sanitized to protect guests from pathogens.

# Grounds

Most restaurants and hotels have grounds. The word **grounds** refers to the outside area around a building. Many restaurants and hotels have at least a little grass and most have some landscaping. **Landscaping** is the use of trees, flowers, and shrubs in artistic ways to make a building and the grounds around it look appealing. Beautiful landscaping can be very appealing to guests. Many hotels have large grounds, and some have golf courses and other natural areas.

## Basic Groundskeeping

Large hotels have one or more groundskeepers on the engineering staff, and they might even have a separate groundskeeping department, **14-15**. A **groundskeeper** is a person responsible for the upkeep of the grounds around a building.

A groundskeeper is usually knowledgeable about plants, pesticides, landscaping, and insects. **Groundskeeping** is work that includes landscaping, watering, weed control, mowing, trimming, fertilizing, and trash removal.

The grounds department begins each day by learning what tasks need to be done that day. The head groundskeeper decides what needs to be done and assigns the work. This department should coordinate its work with other departments in the hotel. The groundskeeping department needs to know when meetings are being held so noise from mowing and trimming equipment will not disturb guests or functions that are taking place. Mowing and trimming should never begin before eight o'clock in the morning.

Any equipment that belongs to the grounds department should be regularly cleaned and maintained. This will help the equipment last longer and operate more efficiently. When equipment breaks down, it should be reported to the supervisor of the engineering department and repaired as quickly as possible.

The lawns and landscaping should be watered regularly. Most hotels have automatic sprinkler systems that are programmed to water the property on a regular basis. These systems are very similar to the systems that are found in homes. It is important to manage the amount of water that is used so water is not wasted. The grounds department should regularly check to make sure the automatic sprinkler system is working properly and that it is used only when necessary to maintain the landscape's beauty.

Safety rules and procedures must be followed at all times to help reduce or eliminate accidents. Work areas must always be cleaned after a job is completed or at the end of each day. The areas must be left in a safe condition so guests or other employees are not injured.

## Golf Courses

Golf courses require special types of maintenance, **14-16**. They are usually maintained by someone called a _golf course superintendent_. This person is responsible for making sure the golf course is always in good playing condition. The superintendent must watch the weather and the environment to make sure the golf course is protected. For example, factors such as insects, freezes, hot weather, droughts, and excessive rain can ruin a golf course very quickly.

Pavel L Photo and Video/Shutterstock.com

**14-15** A large hotel with a lot of landscaping needs a groundskeeping department.

The superintendent is responsible for making sure the golf course always looks good and is in good condition for play. The grass on golf courses varies between the fairway and the greens. Special procedures must happen at certain times of the year to keep the greens in playable condition. Golf course superintendents generally go through many years of training before they are put in charge of a course.

# Engineering Staff

Most of the tasks of engineering must be performed at all foodservice and lodging properties. If a restaurant or hotel has any of the buildings, equipment, or areas discussed, these items must be maintained.

Alistair Scott/Shutterstock.com

**14-16** Golf courses require maintenance to ensure proper playing conditions.

## Restaurants

A restaurant needs fewer engineering services than a lodging property. Restaurants usually have minimal grounds and landscaping and do not have recreational equipment, guest rooms, large public areas, elevators, escalators, or laundry equipment, **14-17**. However, most restaurants do have electrical, plumbing, ventilation systems, and heating and cooling systems. Most also have roofs, walls, floors, parking lots, and kitchen equipment.

Chain restaurants have engineering specialists who take care of these tasks. Owners of independent restaurants may do as many of these tasks themselves as possible to save money. Independent restaurant owners may hire restaurant equipment professionals to repair kitchen equipment. They may also have a landscaping service take care of outside maintenance and beautification.

**14-17** A small restaurant needs fewer engineering and groundskeeping services than a large hotel.

clearlens/Shutterstock.com

## Lodging Properties

A small bed-and-breakfast in a private home may not need engineering services. In other very small properties, the general manager might supervise all the engineering tasks. If the general manager cannot perform the tasks himself or herself, he or she will hire outside contractors.

Most hotels need the full range of services for building systems, building and equipment, guest rooms and public areas, recreational equipment, and grounds. The person in charge of engineering is often called the **chief engineer**. A small hotel may just have a chief engineer and a few maintenance staff. The chief engineer will hire outside contractors when additional expertise or maintenance staff are needed. A large hotel will have a full engineering division.

### Chief Engineer

The chief engineer is the top manager of the engineering department. The chief engineer may also be called the **plant manager** or the **facility manager**. In a smaller business, the person in charge may be called a *maintenance supervisor*, *building superintendent*, or *engineering supervisor*. This person trains, supervises, and motivates employees in the engineering department. Chief engineers keep a list of all items that need to be repaired or maintained. They assign jobs to the maintenance workers. The chief engineer may also do many of the repairs and maintenance tasks in the hotel. He or she keeps a complete inventory of parts and supplies that are needed for the hotel and orders these items as they are needed.

Each morning, the chief engineer gets a list of maintenance requests from the general manager, front desk staff, and housekeeping personnel. The chief engineer then assigns tasks to the maintenance workers. The maintenance or repair should be done as soon as possible. This quick response helps satisfy hotel guests and reduces the number of rooms that cannot be sold because they need to be repaired.

The maintenance staff prioritizes which repairs need to be done each day. Preventive maintenance tasks are also prioritized and scheduled for completion. Maintenance workers try to work in rooms that are vacant. Emergency and safety-related maintenance and repair problems will receive first priority and be corrected first.

All members of the engineering staff are responsible for maintaining the tools, equipment, and maintenance shop, **14-18**. Employees should make sure that they have extra tools and spare parts on hand for repairs. Machines and tools should be in good working order and in safe condition to operate. Flammable materials must be stored in proper containers and in the proper locations.

## Skilled Technicians

Skilled technicians perform specialized tasks in a hotel. These skilled technicians are electricians, plumbers, sound technicians, HVAC professionals, carpenters, and painters.

Although the size of the maintenance staff will vary from hotel to hotel, most hotels use the services of an in-house electrician. In most areas, only a licensed electrician is permitted to do the majority of electrical work.

Licensed plumbers do all of the major plumbing that is needed in a hotel. This includes guest room plumbing, kitchen plumbing, water fountains, and public restrooms. Sound technicians work with the catering department and special events coordinators to provide the sound systems needed for banquets, weddings, and business meetings. HVAC professionals repair heating, ventilation, and air conditioning systems. Carpenters make structural repairs to the property. Painters are responsible for repainting hallways, ceilings, and other items as needed.

## Maintenance Staff

Hotel general maintenance workers need to know how to do minor repairs, basic electrical work, basic plumbing, equipment repairs, and structural repairs. Most of these positions do not require special licensing.

Maintenance workers must be able to understand and identify common power tools and their functions, methods of operation, and safety procedures. Power tools such as saws, grinders, screwdrivers, and drills are basic tools used for making repairs. Employees must be trained to use these power tools safely before being allowed to use them.

In some hotels, all maintenance and repairs are done by the hotel's maintenance staff. Other hotels

*auremar/Shutterstock.com*

**14-18** Keeping tools and equipment in good condition is the responsibility of all engineering employees.

may find it less expensive to use outside contractors for the jobs that are only done occasionally. For example, an outside contractor may be hired to do exterior painting that is only done every three years. In smaller hotels, there may not be enough plumbing work to hire a full-time plumber, electrician, or carpenter. These hotels hire outside contractors for these jobs when it is necessary.

# Chapter 14
## Review

## Chapter Summary

- The purpose of engineering is to keep the facility in top condition for safety, guest satisfaction, and profitability.
- Engineering has six functions: preventive maintenance, deep cleaning, repairs, remodeling, resource management, and emergencies.
- The main building systems are electrical, plumbing, and heating and air conditioning.
- Engineering provides preventive maintenance for buildings and equipment.
- The front desk, housekeeping, and security departments all notify the engineering department of items that need to be repaired.
- Swimming pools and recreational equipment also need to be maintained.

- Groundskeeping includes landscaping, watering, weed control, mowing, trimming, fertilizing, trash removal, and beautification of the lawn and gardens with trees, shrubs, and flowers.
- A large hotel will have a full engineering division, including a chief engineer, skilled technicians, and maintenance staff.

## Review

1. How does the engineering department provide safety, guest satisfaction, and profitability?
2. Give two examples of preventive maintenance for equipment and two examples for a building.
3. List eight items for which engineering provides preventive maintenance.

4. What is a preventive maintenance schedule?
5. Why do restaurants and hotels remodel their buildings?
6. Why do hotels and restaurants want to conserve fuel and water?
7. List ten items in a hotel that require electricity.
8. Why is chlorine added to swimming pool water?
9. What does a groundskeeper do?
10. Describe the difference between the engineering services needed in a small restaurant and a large hotel.
11. Describe the responsibilities of the chief engineer.
12. List the six types of skilled technicians that may be in an engineering department.

## Critical Thinking

13. **Identify.** Brainstorm reasons that it is important to maintain and repair physical facilities of a hotel or restaurant. Write a short report explaining your reasons.
14. **Draw conclusions.** Why is the look of a hospitality business vital to guest satisfaction?
15. **Predict.** What are some possible negative outcomes if a parking lot is not maintained?
16. **Design.** Make a poster showing the different ways that hospitality businesses can promote the efficient use of fuel, electricity, and water.

## Common Core

**College and Career Readiness**

17. **Speaking.** Role-play an example of how future business can be lost when a customer becomes unhappy due to poor maintenance. Include ways the business can try to appease the customer to retain his or her business.
18. **Writing.** Imagine that you are the chief engineer in a large convention hotel. Make up a problem that is happening in the hotel. Then write a story describing how you learned of the problem and how you solved it.
19. **Listening.** Interview a local hotel manager about the methods of resource management used in his or her hotel. Ask about the following areas:
    - Heating and air conditioning systems
    - Water heaters and hot water temperature
    - Plumbing repairs
    - Window insulation and exterior doors
    - Solar heat
20. **CTE Career Readiness Practice.** Research cleaning products formulated specifically for fitness room equipment. Make a recommendation for a cleaning solution that disinfects, is noncorrosive to the equipment, and is environmentally friendly. Do further research to see if your recommendation eliminates methicillin-resistant *Staphylococcus aureus* (MRSA). Write a report summarizing your findings in an organized manner and cite three reliable sources.

# Part Four
# Travel, Tourism, and Recreation

269

270

# Chapter *15*
## Travel

## Chapter Objectives

After studying this chapter, you will be able to

- **list** the two major segments of the travel industry.
- **identify** the agencies and professions associated with travel planning.
- **list** the five Ws of travel planning.
- **identify** the major reasons for travel.
- **compare and contrast** the five major modes of transportation.
- **assess** the influence that new technologies have on transportation and the travel industry.
- **identify** various career opportunities in the travel industry.

## Before You Read

Try to answer the following questions before you read this chapter.

- What are the two major segments of travel?
- What are the different modes of travel?

## Terms to Know

travel
person-trip
tourism
destination
destination marketing
   organization (DMO)
travel industry
travel agent
supplier

travel planner
travel agency
commission
economy of scale
business travel
dynamic packaging
meetings, events, and incentive
   (ME&I) travel
incentive travel

leisure travel
visit friends and relatives (VFR)
frequency
carrier
elapsed flying time
hub
scheduled airlines
charter airlines

When you hear the word *travel*, you may think of tropical locations or faraway destinations, **15-1**. Methods of transportation may come to mind. You may contemplate the various tasks involved in booking a trip.

In its most basic form, **travel** is the movement of a person from one location to another location of some distance for any of several reasons. Some travelers engage in person-trips. According to the U.S. Travel Association, a **person-trip** is one person on a trip away from home overnight in paid accommodations, or on any trip to a place more than 50 miles (one way) away from home. Travelers may use several different modes of transportation when traveling.

Travel is often discussed along with tourism as part of "the travel and tourism industry." *Tourism* is a term often used for both the travel industry and recreation sectors. **Tourism** is the industry that develops and organizes destinations and then markets those destinations to travelers. A **destination** is a predetermined endpoint to which a mode of transportation travels. A destination may also be the combination of tourism components in a geographical location, such as lodging and attractions.

A broader range of businesses relate to tourism, from lodging to recreational services to destination marketing organizations. A **destination marketing organization (DMO)** is an organization that represents stakeholders in a destination's tourism industry. The DMO promotes the features of the destination to potential visitors in order to increase business.

**15-1** Many people think of seeing the world when they hear the word *travel*.

MJTH/Shutterstock.com

# The Travel Industry

The businesses that offer the products and services for people to travel are part of the **travel industry**. Travel services and regulations apply to *domestic travel*, which is the travel within one country, and *international travel*, which is travel between countries. Many of the same services associated with U.S. domestic travel are also related to international travel. Certain hotels and resorts may specialize in accommodating foreign visitors.

## *Travel Planning*

Who can help travelers plan their trips? Travel agents and travel planners are qualified to help a traveler make the best decisions, **15-2**. A **travel agent** is an individual who works at a retail business that brings travelers and travel industry suppliers together. A hospitality **supplier** is a company that creates and provides fundamental travel products. For example, a hotel supplies travelers with rooms. Travel agents may work from a brick-and-mortar location, over the Internet, or both. A **travel planner** has many of the same duties as a travel agent, but usually works in-house for a large corporation.

A **travel agency** is a private business that promotes travel sales to the public on behalf of the travel industry. The agency may sell accommodations, transportation, and tours to travelers. Travel agencies then earn money from the suppliers in the form of a commission. A **commission** is a percentage of the sale price that is paid to the seller. For example, a hotel room that costs $150 per night could earn a travel agent 10%, or $15, per night. A travel agent may also collect a service fee for professional services from the traveler.

Part of the service fee helps to pay for services to which the general public does not have access. One such service is the *Global Distribution System (GDS)*, a network that travel agents use to match the traveler's needs with available products. The travel distribution system employs computer programmers who write the software and sales staff who contract with suppliers.

Travel professionals may increase their status by working toward industry-recognized certifications. Examples include the Certified Travel Associate (CTA), Certified Travel Counselor (CTC), and CTIE (Certified Travel Industry Executive).

Franck Boston/Shutterstock.com

15-2  A travel agent can help answer travel-related questions and provide knowledge, experience, and service.

Travel experts assist travelers in determining the available options that best meet their needs. The five basic decisions that all travelers must make are known as the five Ws of travel. The answers to the five Ws will often decide what travel services will be needed, **15-3**.

Online travel agencies and travel agencies that belong to chains or consortiums are able to offer good prices to consumers because of economy of scale. An **economy of scale** in a service industry is achieved when a supplier, such as a hotel, is able to offer a reduced price because of large sales volume. For example, a travel agency will guarantee customer reservations for a specific number of room nights in exchange for a reduced rate. The agency then passes the savings on to its customers by quoting discount prices for the rooms.

## The Five Ws of Travel

- *Who* is traveling? (number of people and their ages)
- *What* type of trip is it? (business or leisure)
- *What* mode(s) of transportation will be required?
- *When* is the trip? (urgency, season)
- *Where* is the destination? (location)
- *Why* is the trip needed? (motivation)

*Goodheart-Willcox Publisher*

15-3  Asking these questions can help travelers make firm decisions about available options.

## Online Travel Agencies

Many travelers make their reservations directly with online travel agencies. Online travel agencies are growing rapidly and employ thousands of employees in positions such as customer service, reservations, sales, supplier support, marketing, information technology (IT), analysts, and managers. These agencies hire employees who have a passion for travel, know GDS, and are problem solvers. Employees must be computer literate, flexible, patient, and willing to learn in a highly dynamic area of the travel industry.

# Market Segments of Travelers

Today, people are traveling for more reasons than ever before. In fact, in 2011, there were nearly 2 billion person-trips in the United States alone. This activity accounts for $1.9 trillion in economic output and supports 14.4 million jobs. The two major segments of travel are business travel and leisure travel, **15-4**.

## Business Travel

**Business travel** is travel done for the purpose of sales, training, and functions related to work. Business travel accounted for 458 million person-trips in 2011.

Usually, one person or a small group of adults will travel for business purposes. In these situations, people may be gone for a short time. They need to find the quickest mode of travel and stay

in places that are convenient. Many larger companies have partnerships with travel agencies, while other companies employ travel planners.

Travel professionals work to arrange tickets, lodging, car rental, and other services needed by business travelers. **Dynamic packaging** is a process used by travel agents that allows travelers to build their own package of flights, hotels, and car rentals around their specific needs.

Often companies allow their employees to arrange their own travel. Many available websites assist business travelers by providing information about tracking flights and finding last-minute seats, hotels, local information, and restaurants.

There is one hidden cost associated with using websites instead of professional travel agents to book trips. That hidden cost is time. Sometimes employees can spend a long time booking their own travel online. This is time they could be using to perform their primary job functions instead.

### ME&I Travel

One type of business travel is **meetings, events, and incentive (ME&I) travel**. This is a type of tourism that includes a planned agenda for large groups with a similar work, educational, or recreational purpose. In 2011, the ME&I segment of business travel accounted for 153 million person-trips.

One example of ME&I travel is a convention. A *convention* is a large meeting or gathering of people with a common interest. The purpose of a convention is professional development for its attendees with the aim of increasing business opportunities.

Only a limited number of destination cities, such as Las Vegas or Chicago, can handle large convention groups and their needs—meeting space, exhibit halls, and lodging. A convention city should be accessible from many cities and have good on-site transportation, **15-5**.

The final aspect of business travel, **incentive travel**, has many characteristics of leisure travel. Incentive travel is a form of reward from a company to its employees for outstanding work. It is also a way to encourage excellent employee job performance, which in turn increases company profits.

## Leisure Travel

**Leisure travel**, also called *pleasure travel*, is travel for rest, relaxation, and enjoyment. In 2011, U.S. residents reported taking 1.5 billion person-trips for leisure. These trips generated 564.1 billion in spending and supported 5.3 million jobs.

15-4 Tourism is divided into these major segments.

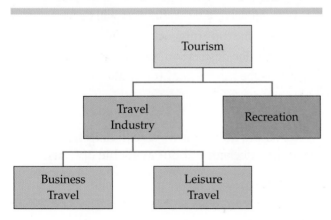

*Goodheart-Willcox Publisher*

15-5  The Las Vegas Convention Center (LVCC) has more than three million square feet of floor space for exhibits, meeting rooms, and training spaces.

Vacations to the beach or travel to attend a sporting event are examples of leisure travel. Another example is trips to **visit friends and relatives (VFR)**, a form of travel in which the specific purpose is to see people as opposed to the destination. VFR travelers may stay with their hosts, or they may require separate nearby lodging such as hotels or motels.

Unlike business travel, most domestic leisure travel is arranged by the travelers themselves purchasing tickets and reserving hotels. If domestic travelers do not use professional planners, they may not know all their options and may, therefore, pay higher prices. For international destinations, leisure travelers more routinely use travel agents.

## Modes of Travel

One of the most important decisions made by a traveler is the mode of transportation to and from a destination and throughout the stay. The five primary modes of transportation are car, rail, bus, water, and air.

### Cars

In the 1950s, a national interstate highway network was created in the United States, making it easier to use personal vehicles for travel. Today, more leisure travel is done by car than any other form of transportation. In 2011, Americans took 1.14 billion domestic leisure trips by car.

Car travel has a number of advantages. Most importantly, it provides maximum flexibility. Drivers can leave whenever they want, travel nearly everywhere, and stop whenever they want.

Another reason for the popularity of car travel is that personal vehicle ownership is nearly universal in most industrialized countries. This means a vehicle is available to most potential travelers.

Car travel can be less expensive than other forms of travel, especially for a family. Technological advancement has made cars safer, more comfortable, and more fuel efficient than ever

## *Going Green*

### Green Travel Options

Some travel agencies and websites offer green travel options to customers. These include hybrid car rentals, green hotel options, tips for responsible travel, and the opportunity to purchase carbon offsets. A *carbon offset* is a carbon reduction strategy that counterbalances the environmental impact of another event, such as air travel, that results in the emission of greenhouse gases. The money used to purchase carbon offsets goes toward funding clean energy and carbon reduction projects. For example, Expedia has partnered with TerraPass, a leading carbon offset provider, to help travelers make up for their carbon use.

before. Future technology advances will make vehicles even safer.

Various services have developed to ease the rigors of car travel. Two of the most popular services are the drive-through restaurant and highway motels. The fast-food "drive-thru" was first popularized by McDonald's in the 1940s under the name *Speedee Service System*. Drive-through restaurants offer the convenience of quickly picking up a meal or snack without taking the time to leave the vehicle. Passengers can eat while they continue on the road.

Budget motels were built near highway exits and along heavily used roads with travelers in mind. Convenient lodging helps travelers save the time they would otherwise spend hunting for accommodations away from their travel route.

One resource for car travelers is the *American Automobile Association (AAA)*, an important information and emergency service provider. The organization began by providing members with road maps. It now includes a variety of traveler services, including emergency road services, approved lodging, and discounts.

### Rental Car

A *car rental agency* is a business that rents vehicles to travelers. Car rental agencies are commonly located at airports, hotels, and downtown locations. Travelers make reservations through travel agents or directly through central reservations offices and websites, **15-6**. A traveler may choose to travel by airplane and rent a car at the destination. Therefore, many travel agencies will include the option of a car rental with the purchase of an airline ticket or hotel reservation package.

**15-6** When renting a car, read the contract carefully before signing so you understand your liability.

*Yuri Arcurs/Shutterstock.com*

Travelers may prefer renting a vehicle for car travel rather than submitting their personal cars to travel wear and tear. Families may also wish to rent a different kind of vehicle, such as a recreational vehicle (RV). An RV would provide the group not only with transportation, but also with their lodging. Travelers could reserve overnight spots along their route in commercial RV parks or state parks.

A car renter must have a valid driver's license, be eligible for insurance, and be of a minimum age (often 25 years old). The traveler and agent always inspect the vehicle for damage before the driver departs with the car rental and immediately following its return. Car rental agencies are often franchises of worldwide companies, such as Hertz, Avis, or Budget.

## Rail Travel

In 1970, the U.S. federal government passed the *Rail Passenger Service Act* creating the National Railroad Passenger Corporation, also called *Amtrak*. Using over 21,000 miles of routes, Amtrak's 317 trains stop in more than 500 cities in 46 states, serving 82,000 travelers. Although this number seems large, passenger rail travel is used less often in the U.S. than in many countries because so many Americans own personal cars.

Some of the primary rail routes in the U.S. are very long and have been in service for over 100 years. The train called the Sunset Limited takes 48 hours on its route from New Orleans through San Antonio to Los Angeles. The Coast Starlight connects Seattle and Los Angeles in 35 hours. Of course, these overnight Amtrak trains offer sleeping rooms for sale. Meals can be reserved in the dining car aboard the train. Travelers on a budget can book reclining coach seats.

### High-Speed Rail

In many advanced countries, train travel has entered the high-speed and high-tech era. High-speed rail is found in Western Europe, Japan, and China. In fact, the world's first high-speed train, the Shinkansen or Bullet Train, entered service in 1964, connecting Tokyo and Osaka in Japan.

High-speed trains travel between 120 and 300 miles per hour and connect large cities. In the U.S., the only high-speed train is the Acela Express, **15-7**. It connects cities between Washington, D.C. and Boston. In most cases, car travel of the same distance would require much more time due to heavily populated areas and congested highways.

15-7 Amtrak's Acela Express, which is a high-speed train, runs in the Northeast Corridor.

15-8 The pace of train travel allows passengers to enjoy picturesque landscapes.

## International Rail Travel

In many parts of the world, train travel is still the most popular form of long-distance travel. Some of the most famous scenic travel routes in the world are rail lines. For example, the luxurious Blue Train travels seaside to connect Pretoria to Cape Town, South Africa. VIA Rail's Canadian from Toronto needs four days to cross the forests, prairies, and Rocky Mountains of western Canada to reach the Pacific Ocean at Vancouver. Some trains offer short scenic excursions and are really classified as attractions, not transportation. For example, tourists in Alaska can sit in the dome car of the McKinley Explorer and view the scenery between Anchorage and Denali National Park.

Leisure travelers consider the train ride to be part of the trip, so they do not object to the time it takes. The long-distance trains make it possible to view scenery at a leisurely pace, 15-8. Rail travel encourages passengers to interact through family-style meals in the dining cars. Passengers are allowed more luggage than by air. Coach seat travel is not expensive, but adding on sleepers and meals generally puts the cost of a train trip higher than air travel.

A train's *porter* is a combined passenger manager and tour guide. Land-based positions include passenger service agents. Travelers make reservations directly through central reservations offices or websites, or through travel agents.

## Bus Travel

Greyhound is the largest bus service in the U.S. and Canada, connecting over 3,000 cities and towns. To give passengers a choice of times on their routes, bus lines practice frequency. **Frequency** is the offering of several departures daily or weekly by a **carrier**, a company that transports passengers. Smaller independent bus lines also operate from points within regions and connect to major lines. Bus travel is generally the safest and least expensive transportation. Because motor coaches seat about 54 passengers, one coach can replace dozens of cars used by individual travelers.

Buses offer flexibility. While Greyhound may take reservations, travelers can also board a bus at the last minute if seats are available. Travel may be direct on one bus, or passengers may be required to transfer to other busses. Passengers generally obtain a tag from a *passenger agent* for each piece of luggage. They may also carry small pieces of luggage on board. On arrival, passengers pick up their own luggage from the side of the bus. Buses have a restroom on board and also take rest stops for about 15 minutes approximately every two hours.

Some modern coaches offer electrical outlets, Wi-Fi, seat belts, and extended leg room. Passengers can use their electronic devices online during the trip. The coaches are also wheelchair accessible.

Intercity bus terminals are generally found in central locations. In some cities, the bus station is part of a transportation hub along with the train station, airport bus services, and local city bus or subway lines. Reservations and tickets are sold directly from the carrier at the terminals, from ticket agents, or online.

Airport buses (also called *airporters*, *shuttles* or *limos*) operate out of most major airports on set schedules with frequency. The vehicles used are usually premium coaches that offer service from the airport to locations such as downtown hotels. Other shuttles take passengers to towns within about 150 miles. The higher cost is offset by improved conveniences for passengers. Reservations can be made directly through the "airporter" company, travel agent, or a participating hotel.

## Ferries

A *ferry* is a boat that carries passengers and vehicles across bodies of water, between islands, or between the mainland and islands. Ferries are government run and charge reasonable fares, **15-9**. They often operate in scenic areas. Ferry and cruise passengers view the same scenery, but from different locations on board. Ferries operate in many inland states, but the largest ferry systems are operated by coastal states.

The nation's largest system, Washington State Ferries, operates 23 ferries across Puget Sound and its inland waterways from Tacoma, Washington, to Sidney, British Columbia. The system carries 23 million passengers a year, including daily commuters, commercial users, and tourists. Ferries can also transport vehicles and bicycles.

Alaska's ferry system is the only marine route that is designated a National Scenic Byway and All-American Road. It is called the *Alaska Marine Highway* for good reason. Many Alaska towns are not accessible by road the way towns in the lower 48 states are. Eleven ferry boats provide year-round connections that stretch 3,500 miles across 33 communities from Bellingham, Washington, through Prince Rupert, British Columbia, to Dutch Harbor at the end of the Aleutian chain. Connecting remote towns by ferry allows for a higher standard of living in the far north.

Some routes take several days. Passengers may take seats in reclining lounges or roll out sleeping bags on the open deck. Most passengers reserve a cabin with bathroom and use public shower facilities. Vehicles, including RVs, must be measured exactly so their space on the car deck can be reserved.

**15-9** Cyclists pay $2.00 in addition to the passenger fare to ride Washington State Ferries.

*Washington State Department of Transportation*

# Going Green

## Green Airports

Because of their size, airports impact the environment. Since its opening, the Denver International Airport has used a large solar energy system capable of providing 3.5 million kilowatt-hours of energy per year. The Fort Lauderdale-Hollywood International Airport (FLL) is recognized for pursuing environmentally friendly actions. The FLL is implementing the Green Airport Initiative (GAI), which seeks to improve environmental quality and efficiency.

The GAI plan is to reduce the overall environmental footprint by addressing factors related to air, water, energy, and waste disposal.

The Alaska ferry system is 50 years old. Older ships will gradually be replaced by Alaska Class Ferries that are more environmentally friendly and fuel efficient.

## Air Travel

Today, most people in the United States have flown on commercial airlines. Once reserved for wealthy individuals, air travel has become an affordable means of quick transportation, **15-10**.

### Booking a Flight

Passengers can book flight reservations with a travel agent or with the airline itself, by phone or online. A traveler will have needs and preferences for a specific airline based on the following:
- airports served
- scheduled time of flights
- reputation for service and quality
- nonstop versus connecting flights
- frequent flier benefits
- aircraft used

### Flight Scheduling

Flying often means leaving one time zone and landing in another. On all transportation schedules, the times listed are local times. Schedulers must take the different time zones into account. Therefore, it is useful to be familiar with time zones when traveling. (See Appendix A for a map of the world's time zones.)

15-10  Many people choose flying for its speed and convenience.

For example, on a flight leaving Seattle/ Tacoma, the departure time given will be in Pacific standard time (PST) or Pacific daylight time (PDT). The arrival time of the flight in New York will be shown in the Eastern time zone (EST or EDT). If the flight is an overnight flight, or *red-eye*, it leaves Seattle/Tacoma at 11 p.m. It arrives at New York's John F. Kennedy airport at 7 a.m. + 1. The *+1* means *the next day*.

This flight does not actually take eight hours. All times are local times, and the Eastern time zone is three hours later than the Pacific zone. This means the **elapsed flying time**, the actual length of time that passes between departure and arrival of a flight, is five hours.

## Codes

The airline industry operates with a high level of technology. Using codes in place of names is a shorthand form of communication, **15-11**.

**15-11** When taking a flight, you may notice the three-letter code of your destination airport on your baggage tag.

gh19/Shutterstock.com

Three-letter codes are used for cities, including
- *CHI* for Chicago
- *PDX* for Portland, Oregon

Three-letter codes are also used for airports, such as
- *ORD* for O'Hare Airport in Chicago
- *JFK* for John F. Kennedy International Airport in New York City

Sometimes the city code and the airport code are the same, such as *SLC* for the city of Salt Lake City and also for Salt Lake City International Airport.

Airlines are coded, too. Airline codes are two-letter designations, such as *DL* for Delta, or *BA* for British Airways.

## Airports

The U.S. has nearly 400 airports with scheduled commercial flights, making it easy to fly most anywhere in the country. About 80 of these airports handle over a million passengers a year, **15-12**.

For tourism purposes, the best way to measure the size of an airport is by the number of passengers who depart the airport (outbound) and arrive at the airport (inbound). An example of this measurement is a passenger who flies from San Diego to Las Vegas and back to San Diego. The traveler would be counted twice at San Diego International Airport and twice at McCarran International Airport.

By passenger count, Hartsfield-Jackson in Atlanta is the country's largest airport. This airport is the headquarters for Delta Airlines and also serves as its main hub. A **hub** is an airport designated by an air carrier to serve as the point for its online connections. Large numbers of airport employees are needed to provide security, foodservice, and retail services to these millions of passengers.

## Scheduled Airlines

**Scheduled airlines** offer planned flights over set routes. The airline's timetable represents the carrier's main product—its flights. **Charter airlines** only fly when they are contracted by clients, such as tour operators, travel agents, and sports teams.

| Busiest Airports in the United States | | | | | |
|---|---|---|---|---|---|
| Rank | City | City Code | Airport | Airport Code | Passenger Traffic (2011) |
| 1 | Atlanta | ATL | Hartsfield-Jackson Atlanta International | ATL | 92,389,023 |
| 2 | Chicago | CHI | Chicago O'Hare International | ORD | 66,659,709 |
| 3 | Los Angeles | LAX | Los Angeles International | LAX | 61,862,052 |
| 4 | Dallas/Fort Worth | DFW | Dallas/Fort Worth International | DFW | 57,744,554 |
| 5 | Denver | DEN | Denver International | DEN | 52,849,132 |
| 6 | New York | NYC | JFK International | JFK | 47,683,529 |
| 7 | San Francisco | SFO | SFO International | SFO | 40,810,141 |
| 8 | Phoenix | PHX | Phoenix Sky Harbor International | PHX | 40,591,948 |
| 9 | Las Vegas | LAS | McCarran International | LAS | 40,560,285 |
| 10 | Houston | HOU | George Bush Intercontinental | IAH | 40,128,953 |

*Airports Council International*

15-12  These are the 2011 top 10 U.S. commercial airports ranked by passenger traffic.

Statistics about airline size can change rapidly because carriers occasionally merge. Currently, the four largest scheduled airlines by passenger count—American, Delta, United, and Southwest— are based in the United States. Until the merger of American Airlines and US Airways, Delta Airlines was the largest scheduled carrier by passenger numbers, fleet size, and kilometers flown, in both the U.S. and the world. Delta Airlines has about 75,000 employees and operates 5,000 flights daily on all continents except Antarctica. American Airlines now employs about 100,000 workers and operates 6,500 flights per day.

## Check-In and Boarding

Once a reservation is made and paid for, a ticket is issued. Most tickets today are electronic tickets, or *e-tickets*. To board an aircraft, each passenger must have a *boarding pass*. A passenger may have printed the boarding pass from a computer ahead of time or obtain it at check-in. Check-in may take place at an automated kiosk or with customer service agents at the airline's check-in counter, **15-13**.

To further ease check-in and boarding, many airlines have adopted paperless or e-boarding passes. E-passes allow passengers to download an app to their smartphone or tablet. The apps contain a *quick response code (QR code)*, which is a digitally encrypted image. The QR codes are scanned by the gate agent at the departure gate. Airlines use QR codes to improve passenger check-in security and speed up boarding.

Darq/Shutterstock.com

**15-13** Some airports provide automated kiosks for quick, convenient check-in.

### The Flight

On board an aircraft, *flight attendants* or cabin crew act as hospitality hosts, welcoming passengers, providing beverages, and selling snacks. However, their most important function is passenger safety, **15-14**. Safety training can include first aid, CPR, and managing emergency evacuations with slides and life rafts. The U.S. Federal Aviation Administration (FAA) requires flight attendants to hold a Certificate of Demonstrated Proficiency, which is issued by the FAA. Flight attendants are normally trained in an airline's hub city for up to six months. Private schools offer similar training.

Flight attendants generally must meet a minimum educational level of high school diploma. Some airlines require a college degree, which may include the study of foreign languages. Multilingual flight attendants are in demand for international flights.

Flight crews' flying hours are limited for safety reasons, so they may have layovers at destination cities. This gives them time to spend as tourists in different locations. One of the great benefits of working for an airline is free and reduced-rate travel—not just for the employee, but also for the employee's family and traveling companions. Many airline employees have seen the world using their airline passes.

## Travel Careers—Present and Future

The travel industry is a very dynamic segment of the economy, with more people traveling to more places for more reasons. These increased demands have called for more efficient transportation means and more skilled travel assistants.

As a result of the tightened security of check-in procedures, passengers are required to be at the airport several hours before a flight is scheduled to depart. This has led to a growth in airport-based foodservice operations. Because there are more air travelers, the demand for products and services associated with air travel continue to expand.

This means that there is still a need for airplane builders, pilots, technicians, and personnel at efficient airports. The airlines will continue to need passenger agents, flight crews, customer service representatives, and plane groomers.

Many of these jobs will require some form of advanced education and training. Colleges and universities today offer programs in travel, tourism, transportation studies, leisure studies, hotel and restaurant management, and recreation.

*michaeljung/Shutterstock.com*

**15-14** Flight attendants help passengers stow carry-on luggage safely so overhead compartments do not open mid-flight.

To help meet this growing demand for travel, many new exciting technologies and professions have been created or will be created in the future. At airports and other transportation centers, increased security measures have led to a significant growth in the demand for security personnel, **15-15**. Already, security services are now using more advanced forms of security, such as face-recognition software and iris scans for identification.

**15-15** The Transportation Security Administration (TSA) supervises security procedures before passengers board planes.

*James Steidl/Shutterstock.com*

# Chapter 15
## Review

## Key Points

- The travel industry includes the businesses that offer products and services for people to travel.
- The answers to the five Ws will often decide what travel services will be needed.
- The two major purposes for travel are business and leisure.
- In the U.S., the personal car is used for leisure travel more than any other form of transportation.
- Rail travel offers the opportunity to view scenery at a leisurely pace.
- Bus travel is relatively safe, inexpensive, and flexible.
- Ferries are a unique form of transportation that connects many islands and coastal communities.
- Air travel is an affordable means of quick, scheduled transportation to airports all over the world.
- Because there are more travelers, the demand for workers, products, and services associated with travel continue to grow.

## Review

1. What is the difference between a travel agent and a travel planner?
2. What are two ways that travel agencies earn money?
3. What are the five Ws of travel?
4. What are the two major segments of travel?
5. What is the hidden cost of booking a trip without using a travel agent?
6. Name the five major modes of transportation.
7. Why is passenger rail travel used less often in the U.S. than in other countries?
8. What does frequency mean in the travel industry?
9. Why is it important to understand time zones when traveling by airplane?
10. How is the size of an airport measured?
11. What is the difference between scheduled airlines and charter airlines?
12. What is the most important function of flight attendants?
13. Why has tightened airport security resulted in a need for more airport-based service operations?

# Critical Thinking

14. **Draw conclusions.** What are some benefits of dynamic packaging?
15. **Assess.** Think of a trip you or a family member has made. Discuss how the five Ws of travel planning influenced decision making about the trip.
16. **Identify.** Describe the closest airport to your hometown, answering the following questions: How far away is it? What is the code for the airport? Which airlines serve this airport? What are their codes? Does it serve as a hub for any airlines? What types of jobs are available at the airport?
17. **Analyze.** Use Appendix A or another map to identify time zones in the continental United States. Name two cities that fall into each time zone. What time is it in New York when it is 1:00 p.m. in each of the zones? What time is it in Los Angeles when it is 2:00 a.m. in each of the zones?
18. **Make inferences.** Locate the nearest convention center to your home. Check its website and list the events held there. Which events will draw business travelers? Which ones will draw leisure travelers? How can you tell?

# Common Core

**College and Career Readiness**

19. **Speaking.** Give a slideshow presentation identifying different transportation options that serve your area.
20. **Writing.** Write a summary of three job opportunities associated with travel planning that interest you. Use the O*NET OnLine website to find detailed information about each career to include in the summary.
21. **Math.** Using an online travel service or airlines' websites, plan a trip to your favorite destination. Find information for at least two different airlines. Write itineraries showing possible airlines, departure and arrival cities, flight numbers, departure and arrival times, flight time, and prices. After comparing all the factors, choose one option and explain why you chose it.
22. **CTE Career Readiness Practice.** Create a one-act play for two persons that depicts a positive interaction between a travel agent or check-in agent and a traveler. Be sure to include notes to the actors about body language and facial expressions. Do the same to illustrate a negative interaction on the same topic. What is the essential difference between the two plays/interactions? How does the way you say something influence whether it will be received negatively or positively?

# Chapter *16*
## Tourism

## Chapter Objectives

After studying this chapter, you will be able to

- **explain** tourism and its relationship to the economy.
- **describe** the important documents needed for travel and tourism.
- **describe** the technologies used in more secure travel.
- **relate** important health and safety information to travel.
- **analyze** categories of tourism destination areas.
- **list** several segments of tourism.
- **compare and contrast** types of tours and cruises.
- **summarize** tourism factors that influence communities and climate.
- **discuss** careers associated with the tourism industry.

## Before You Read

Try to answer the following questions before you read this chapter.

- What effect does tourism have on a destination's economy?
- What is the difference between a hosted tour and an escorted tour?

## Terms to Know

United Nations World Tourism Organization (UNWTO)
spatial context
sense of place
tourism destination area (TDA)
infrastructure
national tourism office
country of origin
passport
visa

tourist card
embassy
consulates
Department of Homeland Security (DHS)
biometric identifiers
seasonality
ecotourism
heritage tourism
independent tour

domestic independent tours (DIT)
foreign independent tours (FIT)
hosted tour
escorted tour
city guide
site guide
docent
interpreter
carrying capacity

Tourism is the world's largest industry. The term *tourism* covers many kinds of services that travelers need, including transportation, lodging, attractions, and recreation of all sorts. Travel and tourism information is a service distributed at many points worldwide.

# Tourism: The World's Largest Industry

The **United Nations World Tourism Organization (UNWTO)** is a special agency of the United Nations that defines standards of tourism used in many countries, **16-1**. The UNWTO defines a *tourist* as a person who "travels to and stays in places outside the usual environment for not more than one consecutive year for leisure, business and other purposes." Tourists travel to various destinations for business or pleasure, but not to work there permanently.

Tourists traveling within their own country are *domestic tourists*. Within the U.S., *tourists* are defined as visiting a place more than 50 miles from home or staying overnight in paid accommodations. An *international tourist* travels to another country, which may be few or many miles from home. Regardless of how far you travel, you are seen as a representative of your hometown, state, and country.

## *Place*

Tourism occurs at large and small places and can be local, national, and international. A tourist may visit a memorial marker along a remote highway or a crowded foreign country. Places are the **spatial context** for tourism—the unique physical spaces that people can visit. Visitors may especially appreciate the sense of place in areas that are unique. **Sense of place** is a person's subjective orientation toward a place. Many times it is the specific sights, smells, and sounds that create a place's distinctive ambience or atmosphere.

| Acronyms Commonly Used in Tourism | | | |
|---|---|---|---|
| United Nations World Tourism Organization | UNWTO | visitor information center | VIC |
| tourism destination area | TDA | tourist information center | TIC |
| United States Travel Association | USTA | Center on Ecotourism and Sustainable Development | CESD |
| Forma Migratoria Multiple | FMM | The International Ecotourism Society | TIES |
| Department of Homeland Security | DHS | visit friends and relatives | VFR |
| Western Hemisphere Travel Initiative | WHITI | nongovernmental organization | NGO |
| Secure Electronic Network for Travelers Rapid Inspection | SENTRI | United States Tour Operators Association | USTOA |
| enhanced drivers license | EDL | American Automobile Association | AAA |
| enhanced identification | EID | domestic independent tours | DIT |
| European Union | EU | foreign independent tours | FIT |
| International Certificate of Vaccination | ICV | Certified Tour Professional | CTP |
| destination marketing organization | DMO | National Tour Association | NTA |
| convention and visitors' bureau | CVB | International Institute of Peace through Tourism | IIPT |

*Goodheart-Willcox Publisher*

**16-1** This table will serve as a reference for the many acronyms used in this chapter.

In 2012, the UNWTO recorded one billion international tourist arrivals, half of which were located in Europe. An *international tourist arrival* is a person who originates in one country and crosses an international border to reach a tourism destination area in another country. A **tourism destination area (TDA)** is a location that intentionally attracts visitors and brings in revenue through tourism, such as the Grand Canyon or South Island, New Zealand.

## Tourism and the Economy

Tourism brings new money into communities. One aspect of tourism's economic impact on the local economy is that of building **infrastructure**, the basic physical and organizational structures needed for the operation of a society or a community. Roads, bridges, airports, and hotels are examples of infrastructure. When a city or region hosts a large event such as the Olympics, there is the need to develop the infrastructure before the tourists arrive, **16-2**. Private corporations may spend hundreds of millions of dollars on venues, transportation, and power supply infrastructures. Often a region builds infrastructure rapidly in the several years prior to a major event.

Tourists who are departing are *outbound*, and those arriving are *inbound*. For example, an American vacationing in Mexico is outbound from the U.S. and is considered an international inbound arrival for Mexico. During the visit, the tourist buys lodging, food, and entertainment. The visit clearly benefits the Mexican economy.

The trip may also benefit the U.S. economy. The tourist is likely to have purchased air transportation and possibly a tour package in the U.S. When Mexican residents vacation in California, they are inbound international arrivals for the U.S. economy, **16-3**.

While many Americans enjoy travelling abroad, the United States also experiences high levels of inbound tourism. In 2011, the U.S. ranked second as the most visited country internationally, attracting 62.3 million foreign tourists. France ranked first. Also in 2011, Americans traveling abroad spent $110 billion, while foreign visitors to the U.S. spent $153 billion. Tourism contributed a $43 billion trade surplus that year for the U.S. economy.

## National Tourism Marketing

A **national tourism office** promotes tourism abroad to bring international tourists into

16-2 The Russian government is spending nearly $10.5 billion dollars for infrastructure development, expansion, and hosting of the 2014 Winter Olympic Games in Sochi.

its country. Some countries spend millions of dollars promoting tourism to attract inbound visitors because tourism brings revenue and economic development to its destinations. Tourism offices measure impacts in at least two ways: number of visitors and amount of money spent.

Where do you think most inbound visitors to the United States come from? If you said that most visitor arrivals are from the country's closest neighbors, Canada and Mexico, you are correct! Tourists whose **country of origin** (the country from which a person's trip originates) is Canada or Mexico make up over half the international visitors to the U.S. and also travel most often to the U.S. These three countries maintain close relationships in many areas of common interest.

Travelers who originate in overseas countries stay longer and spend more money. U.S. tourism officials believe that in the next decade, many inbound tourists will originate from China, Brazil, Russia, Australia, and Argentina.

The U.S. Travel Association (USTA) promotes travel to and within the United States. Another goal of the USTA is to educate Americans on the importance of tourism to the economy. An example of a marketing campaign of the USTA is Brand USA. Brand USA was established by the Travel Promotion Act of 2010 to promote the United States as a premier travel destination. Brand USA operates as a joint public and private entity. USTA and

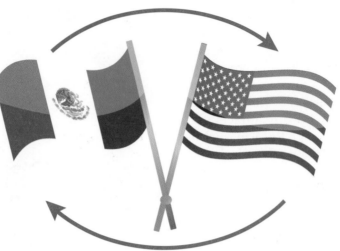

**Outbound Mexican tourists**
often purchase
• air tickets
• prepaid packages

In 2011, 13.4 million
**inbound Mexican tourists**
spent $8.7 billion on
• tourist activities, gifts
• hotels/dining/car rental

In 2011, 17.1 million
**inbound American tourists**
spent $8.9 billion on
• tourist activities, gifts
• hotels/dining/car rental

**Outbound American tourists**
often purchase
• air tickets
• prepaid packages

*alexmillos/Goodheart-Willcox Publisher*

**16-3** Tourism can benefit both the outbound and inbound countries' economies. Here are examples of inbound and outbound spending by travelers between the U.S. and Mexico in 2011.

Brand USA work closely with the travel industry and with the state travel and tourism offices, **16-4**. Other countries likewise promote travel through unique marketing campaigns.

# Documents for Travel and Tourism

While it might seem that travel documents have always been required, little or no documentation was required before World War I. After the war's conclusion in 1918, countries adopted the practice of requiring personal identification to travel across international borders at border

checkpoints. A *border crossing* or *checkpoint* is a location between two countries where travelers and goods are inspected. These checkpoints may be located in airports, at seaports, or on the actual land border. Countries also began to employ large numbers of border police and customs and immigration officers to ensure all travelers had the necessary documents.

## Passports

A **passport** is a document issued by a national government as proof of a person's identity and citizenship. It allows a traveler to leave the country of origin and return, **16-5**.

In the U.S., the State Department regulates travel by issuing passports to U.S. citizens. Minors under 16 years of age must apply for a passport in person with one or both parents. Minors who are 16 and 17 years of age can apply on their own, but they must appear in person. U.S. citizens age 18 and older can apply either in person or through the mail.

## Visas and Tourist Cards

A **visa** is a permission issued by a country to a noncitizen authorizing the holder to enter, exit, or live in a country for a specific time. For example, the U.S. State Department issues visas to inbound foreign visitors. Visas are usually stamps placed in a passport.

**16-4** Have you seen this logo for Brand USA?

DiscoverAmerica.com

*Brand USA*

16-5 The booklet is the traditional format of a passport.

*vanHurck/Shutterstock.com*

16-6 This work visa entry stamp was placed in the passport by the Department of Homeland Security, which oversees the U.S. Customs and Border Protection Agency.

Travelers planning to visit many countries could require a lot of time to obtain separate visas for each country. Therefore, many travel agencies complete this necessary work as part of their professional services.

Instead of visas, Mexico and most other Latin American countries require U.S. citizens to have a **tourist card** to enter and exit. Mexico's tourist card is the *Forma Migratoria Multiple (FMM)*. The FMM can be obtained ahead of time from an airline or travel agent, or it can be issued at the border. One section of the form is collected by immigration officials on entry into Mexico and the other upon exit.

## *Embassies and Consulates*

An **embassy** is the official office of one country in another country. The embassy is staffed by the *diplomatic mission*, the name for the group of employers who work there. The embassy, always located in the country's capital, is usually headed by an ambassador. **Consulates** are smaller diplomatic missions located in a country's regional cities.

Embassies or consulates can issue various types of visas, such as tourist or visitor, work, and student visas, **16-6**. Additionally, cities with embassies or consulates have private visa services that can obtain the required visas within a few days.

# A New World of Travel After 9/11

The terrorist attacks of September 11th, 2001, were a defining event that signaled the need for additional security and protection of travelers. One result was the creation of the **Department of Homeland Security (DHS)**, a cabinet-level agency designated to protect the United States from terrorist attacks and accidents and respond quickly to natural disasters. The DHS, with over 250,000 employees, has assumed various tasks to ensure greater protection. Some of these areas overlap with travel and tourism.

## *New Technology, New Initiatives*

While a passport booklet contains machine readable coding, many countries now issue various forms of high-tech identification. The DHS works with other countries in designing high-tech or "smart" pieces of identification. These smart IDs are not only difficult to counterfeit, but also ensure greater passenger security by including more types of personal data. This technology is designed to make mass travel safer and faster.

*Biometric technology* or *biometrics* is identification that is readable by computers and more secure. **Biometric identifiers** are unique, measurable characteristics that label or identify people. Some examples of biometric data include DNA samples, blood samples, voice recognition, fingerprints, and iris scans.

## NEXUS/SENTRI Programs

The DHS participates in the *Western Hemisphere Travel Initiative (WHITI)*. One of the initiative's goals is to facilitate faster and safer travel among Canada, the U.S., Mexico, Bermuda, and the Caribbean countries. Because of the volume of frequent travelers over the U.S.–Canada border, the NEXUS card was created.

The *NEXUS Trusted Traveler Program* allows low-risk, preapproved U.S. and Canadian citizens to use an identification card that enhances security and reduces wait times at the border. In addition to a ten-fingerprint law enforcement check, the NEXUS ID also uses iris recognition technology.

The *SENTRI (Secure Electronic Network for Travelers Rapid Inspection)* is a similar program between the United States and Mexico. Citizens of the countries submit paperwork that is reviewed in a biographical background check of criminal, law enforcement, customs, immigration, and terrorist databases.

## Passport (PASS) Card

Another development of the WHITI is that the U.S. State Department allows two new forms of smart ID for travel within the Western Hemisphere—the PASS card and enhanced drivers licenses. A *passport (PASS) card* is a less expensive, wallet-sized passport with a microchip. The microchip contains both biometric information on its holder and an RFID chip. These chips are read by a customs and border protection database, facilitating quicker and more secure border crossing, **16-7**.

**16-7** The PASSCard contains an OCR Optical Character Recognition section on the reverse side.

*U.S. Department of State*

The PASS card is not yet acceptable for air travel. It is not currently recognized by other countries as a valid form of international travel documentation.

## Enhanced Drivers License

The *enhanced drivers license (EDL)* or *enhanced identification (EID)* is a form of travel documentation that acts in the same manner as the PASS card. The EDL/EID has been created through cooperation between the DHS and various U.S. states. These cards contain an RFID microchip within a state-issued driver license or identification card.

Currently, only the states of Washington, New York, Vermont, and Michigan have activated cards. California, Arizona, and Texas agencies are also developing EDLs. Like the PASS card, EDLs can only be used at land and sea ports of entry.

Travelers need to be aware that the rules governing these new forms of documentation are subject to change. Travelers should always check documentation status with the U.S. State Department.

# A Passport-Free World?

Another idea for facilitating increased travel and tourism is the waiving of passport requirements at border checkpoints. In June 1985, representatives of five European countries met in Schengen, Luxembourg, and signed the Schengen Agreement. This treaty permitted the visual surveillance of private vehicles without their needing to stop at border crossings.

By 2005, 27 countries had signed an updated Schengen Agreement and established passport-free travel in the European Union (EU), **16-8**. Over 400 million people were allowed to move freely among member countries. Like the WHITI, this agreement is an example of international cooperation.

Overall, the EU is similar to a single country where there are no internal controls, but there are external requirements. For example, the EU expects all its citizens to be treated equally regarding visa requirements by non-EU countries. In return, these countries promise to treat an inbound traveler equally regardless of where he chooses to arrive within the EU. This means that German, French, and Italian citizens are to be treated as equals when travelling to China in regards to visa requirements. In return, a Chinese citizen would have the same entry requirements whether arriving in Berlin, Paris, or Rome.

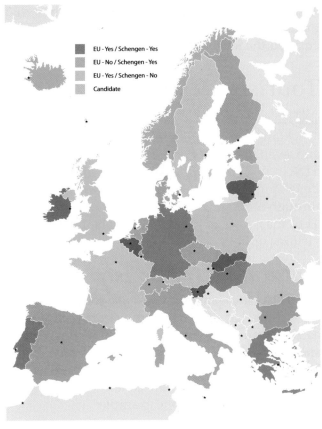

*Media Guru/Shutterstock.com*

**16-8** This map identifies the countries of the Schengen Agreement and the EU.

# Travel Information

The U.S. Department of State is the official source for information on travel requirements for U.S. citizens seeking to travel abroad or foreign tourists seeking to visit the United States. On its website, the State Department publishes a travel advisory on each country. These advisories provide tourists with information they need to know prior to and during a visit. Information is included on

- entry and exit information for U.S. citizens
- safety and security
- medical emergencies, medical facilities, and insurance
- criminal penalties and the legal system
- current political environment
- tourist attractions
- special circumstances, such as severe weather

Because Mexico is a popular spring break destination for nearly 100,000 college and high school students each year, the State Department issues a special spring break travel notice. The special notice gives would-be revelers precautions such as

- travel requirements
- general safety rules
- differences between Mexican and American law
- road regulations and hazards
- drug and alcohol laws
- possession laws for firearms and knives

## *Health*

Due to the rapid mobility of people and goods across the globe, infectious diseases are transported swiftly from one continent to another. In 2009, for example, a virus called H1N1 or swine flu spread through infected airline passengers within days to all continents. The virus caused a pandemic resulting in thousands of deaths. Due to rapid communication, many advanced countries quickly contained the outbreak by isolating sick travelers, quarantining planes and passengers, and rapidly distributing vaccines.

The *International Certificate of Vaccination (ICV)*, or "yellow card," is proof of vaccinations and other medical tests. The UN World Health Organization issues the certificate or "medical passport" to national health departments. In turn, these agencies distribute them to clinics and other medical facilities. Upon the completion of a medical test or vaccination, the certificate is signed or stamped and given to the individual, **16-9**.

**16-9** The reverse side of the "yellow card" contains the date and type of vaccination, its dosage and method, and a physician's signature.

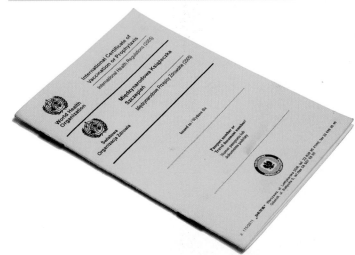

*Bjorn Stefanson/Shutterstock.com*

Travelers need to be aware that each country establishes the requirements needed to enter it. The country of origin also has requirements for reentry. As countries cooperate to limit the spread of infectious diseases, travel is encouraged and a greater degree of trust and peace between nations is reached.

### Safety

Documents and border security checks may appear to hinder travel. However, countries need to ensure that citizens are safe when they travel. If travelers feel unsafe about a region or country, they will probably not go there and instead choose another destination.

For example, on March 11, 2011, an earthquake and tsunami off the Pacific coast of Japan caused the Fukushima Daiichi nuclear power plant to fail and release radioactive material. Most people have a strong fearful reaction to any possibility of nuclear contamination. In this instance, the effect was a serious decrease in tourism in Japan. The Japan National Tourism Organization reported that over $300 million in tourist revenue was lost in the year following the accident. It also reported that tourism levels as of early 2013 had not yet equaled the levels achieved prior to the event.

# Tourism Destination Areas

Many communities, regions, states, countries, and even groups of countries set out to become TDAs. A TDA supplies tourism infrastructure development and then creates tourism demand through marketing the TDA to potential visitors. A TDA may cater to domestic visitors, international visitors, or both.

### Natural Versus Constructed

TDAs are generally created around a central attraction. That attraction may be from nature, such as the Grand Canyon, or it may be constructed, such as the Walt Disney World theme area. Often a natural place becomes popular with tourists and then planned attractions are constructed around it, **16-10**. Niagara Falls is one example.

**16-10** The Skywalk, managed by the Hualapai Tribe, allows visitors to view the Grand Canyon through a glass floor.

*jabiru/Shutterstock.com*

## Seasonality

Another way of categorizing TDAs is by **seasonality**, or fluctuations in the number of visitors, expenditures, and transportation needs. Seasonality can be based on climate, too. Seasonality categories to consider are

- all season
- winter warm
- winter cold
- summer resort

Seasonality remains a challenge in the tourism industry in terms of human resources and profitability. Seasonal variations create business risk due to imbalances in the demand from visitors and the supply of products and staff services. Today, many TDAs attempt to be all season if possible.

### All Season TDA

All season TDAs are popular year round, but they are often especially busy on school holidays when children have time off. For example, the many theme parks in central Florida have visitor numbers that exceed the visitor arrivals in many countries! Many all season TDAs include every aspect of travel, tourism, and recreation:

- transportation by bus or boat
- entertainment and education
- lodging properties
- food and beverage outlets
- retail establishments
- meetings and conventions
- youth programs

All season TDAs may be natural areas. For example, nearly five million visitors a year visit the Grand Canyon National Park. It is Arizona's top tourist attraction, most often visited in summer. The Grand Canyon is a family destination with awe-inspiring scenery and unique hiking opportunities.

### Winter Warm TDA

For Americans who live in northern states and Alaska, winter can mean six months of snow. These people may vacation in warm, sunny locations to break up the winter. Some of the popular "sun destinations" are in Florida, southern California, Arizona, Texas, and other states located along the Gulf of Mexico.

Some sunseekers travel to close international destinations in Mexico and the Caribbean Islands. Cancun is Mexico's most popular TDA. Its offerings include sun, warm temperatures moderated by the ocean, the clear warm waters of the Caribbean, newer properties, fresh foods, and authentic Mayan archeology and culture, **16-11**.

### Winter Cold TDA

Winter cold TDAs are often ski resorts. Besides skiing, these resorts also offer winter sports such as ice skating, sledding, snowboarding, and snowshoeing. Colorado is an example of a famous winter cold resort area. It has a cluster of excellent ski resorts, such as Aspen, Breckenridge, Copper Mountain, Steamboat, Telluride, and Vail.

### Summer Resort TDA

In the summer months, many people enjoy going to a lake or coastal setting. The northern states of Minnesota, Wisconsin, and Michigan are renowned for their many lakes in wooded settings. Activities are often centered on water sports, including swimming, sailing, canoeing, kayaking, and fishing. Beaches and hiking trails are usually available. Accommodations are often in the style of timber lodges or one-family cabins, with some owned by individual families. RV resorts and campgrounds are often situated near recreational lakes.

Unlike smaller lakes, the Great Lakes are usually not considered warm enough for swimming. However, other water sports are available, and their awe-inspiring size make them a popular destination.

## Destination Marketing Organizations

Local festivals, events, and sporting tournaments are often coordinated by *destination marketing organizations (DMO)*. A DMO may operate

16-11 Mexico is known for its creative resort architecture, including this Cancun property.

a convention and visitors' bureau (CVB). A CVB promotes an area to potential convention groups and visitors. Meeting planners and event planners representing businesses and organizations work with the DMOs, convention centers, and other event venues.

The CVB may operate a visitor information center (VIC) or tourist information center (TIC). Wherever you go in the world, you will likely see a similar sign for tourist information, **16-12**.

# Segments of Tourism

Making tourists happy is the goal of the tourism industry, and when tourists develop new interests, the industry provides more offerings. Some segments of tourism, for example, now focus on sustainable development or on ecotourism. Interest in heritage-related tourism is growing, while local-interest tourism remains strong. Another new interest expressed by tourists is combining their desire to volunteer with tourism.

## *Sustainable Development*

As long ago as 1987, the United Nations defined sustainability as development that "meets the needs of the present without compromising the ability of future generations to meet their own needs." For that reason, sustainable development is important to tourism. Sustainable businesses aim to promote

- economic development
- environmental protection
- cultural and social development

**16-12** The *i* for *information* is a universal symbol for tourist information. Have you ever seen this or a similar sign?

*linerpics/Shutterstock.com*

Some tourists investigate the sustainability of tourism destinations before deciding to book a trip there. Therefore, more destinations are working to make their facilities sustainable. Some tour operators and other tourism companies have based their business model on offering sustainable or green products, **16-13**. Tour operators, major airlines, and lodging establishments have green policies such as recycling and conservation of water and energy.

## *Ecotourism*

**Ecotourism** is tourism based on observing and preserving the natural environment and culture of a destination area. Ecotourism businesses seek to protect the natural environment and the culture of local people while contributing to their economy. Lodges and other facilities are built in a sustainable way using local materials. An organization such as the Center on Ecotourism and Sustainable Development (CESD) offers certifications to sustainable businesses that follow a code of conservation ethics. Voluntary membership for ecotourism businesses and destinations is offered by The International Ecotourism Society (TIES), based in Washington, DC.

## *Heritage Tourism*

Today's society is more mobile than ever before. For example, a boy who grows up in New England may move to Fort Myers, Florida, to

**16-13** Evergreen Escapes is a green tour operator that uses bio-diesel powered vans and provides their customers with bicycles to experience Pacific Northwest destinations.

*Evergreen Escapes*

attend college, and then relocate to Phoenix for career reasons. His personal heritage, though, is in New England, and he may return there many times to visit. A return home will bring back many memories. Relatives and friends from New England will also visit him in his new location, a form of travel known as *visit friends and relatives (VFR)*. Mobility leads to more mobility and, therefore, more tourism.

**Heritage tourism** involves people traveling to places that authentically represent history and culture. Often, people first visit heritage sites on school field trips or with their families. Heritage sites include monuments, statues, forts, and historically significant city and residential areas, **16-14**.

Most national historic sites are administered by the National Park Service. The National Park Service has 22,000 employees and is part of the Department of the Interior. It oversees nearly 350 historic sites and 58 national parks. The Great Smokey National Park in Tennessee and North Carolina continues to be the most visited park in the U.S. with about 9 million visitors annually. The Grand Canyon National Park is second with about 4.2 million visitors annually. Over 100 million visitors have toured the 18th-century buildings of Colonial Williamsburg since its restoration.

Many tourists seek to enhance their travel by becoming active participants or reenactors in "living history." The Civil War reenactment of 1998 commemorating the Battle of Gettysburg drew over 85,000 reenactors and observers, **16-15**.

Denton Rumsey/Shutterstock.com

16-15 Because historical reenactments include activities for men, women, and children, they have large followings among people of many ages.

16-14 Charleston, South Carolina, is a popular tourist destination. One of its many historic attractions is its famed Rainbow Row.

Beth Whitcomb/Shutterstock.com

The National Park Service also operates the national monuments. The most visited national monument in the United States is the Lincoln Memorial, which registered 5.9 million visitors in 2011. The Statue of Liberty is perhaps the most recognized national monument and was visited by 3.73 million people that year.

Many Americans are immigrants or descendants of immigrants whose roots lie in other countries. Immigrants create international VFR traffic. Descendants of people who immigrated to the U.S. in the 19th century may have an interest in visiting the country of origin, even if family ties have been lost. *Genealogy*, the study of family histories, is a popular leisure activity. It has led to a great deal of domestic and international tourism to visit people and places.

## Local Interest

Large numbers of tourists are attracted to well-known sites such as Colonial Williamsburg and Gettysburg, which are significant in U.S. history. However, many less famous historic sites are important to local areas. Most communities today are doing what they can to maximize economic development from tourism. This includes restoring, interpreting, and promoting local historic sites.

Industrial sites from past eras, such as mills, canals, or blacksmith shops, interest those who appreciate how things work. The making of traditional crafts such as candles, quilts, and pottery interest artisans. Tourists may buy souvenirs from TDAs such as these to take home with them.

### Festivals and Events

Events of all types are a major draw for visitors. Events can be public community affairs or private affairs such as weddings. Most communities hold cultural festivals, ranging from local summer fairs and parades to international festivals. One example is the annual Royal Edinburgh Tattoo in Scotland, which draws about 250,000 visitors—half of these from overseas, **16-16**.

Sports events generate tourism. Sports tourism is important locally with tournaments played for various age groups in soccer, basketball, and football. Professional sports teams may draw fans as tourists travel to the large cities where games are played. National championship events are big revenue generators for the cities hosting them.

**16-16** The Royal Edinburgh Tattoo draws visitors from all over the globe.

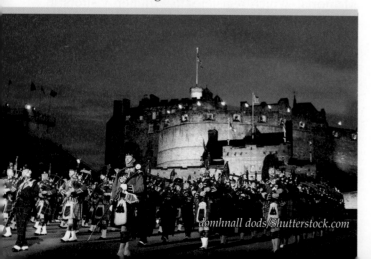

domhnall dods/Shutterstock.com

The Olympic Games have been held 48 times since the start of the modern Olympics in 1896. Each time, millions of people—athletes, staff, and spectators—from over 200 countries travel to the host city to take part. Destinations compete to host the games because they bring in such a huge amount of tourism revenue. For example, Pyeongchang in the Republic of Korea tried three times before winning the bid to host the Winter Olympics in 2018.

## Voluntourism

Perhaps you or your classmates have taken a mission trip sponsored by a religious or youth organization. Such groups commonly undertake projects related to improving the infrastructure, education, or health in locations with ongoing needs, such as in Central America.

*Habitat for Humanity* is an organization that works to build housing in areas of the U.S. and elsewhere. Programs permit high school and college student groups to be "global village" volunteers. Natural disasters such as Hurricane Katrina in 2005 and Hurricane Sandy in 2012 brought out not only official relief workers, but also American and international volunteers. These are examples of volunteerism that unintentionally included tourism.

*Voluntourism*, on the other hand, is a segment of tourism that intentionally includes volunteer activities. Tour operators or volunteer program coordinators may be involved in its planning and promotion. International tourists originate in the developed countries of the world and, when traveling abroad, see people and places in less fortunate circumstances. In addition to pursuing their own pleasure, they develop a desire to contribute something to the local area. The solution is a "volunteer vacation" in which people combine their leisure time with developmental activities such as maintaining a trail, digging a well, or tutoring children, **16-17**.

Tour operators may develop on-site projects directly, or they may partner with *nongovernmental organizations (NGOs)*. NGOs raise funds in developed countries to create projects in poorer countries where personnel is already stationed. NGOs invite participation in development and local employment. The tour operators create tour packages that combine travel and leisure with some volunteer service. Alternatively, sometimes the volunteer program is stressed and leisure is only a small part of the trip. Voluntourism is an example

(Photo by Blake Martin Courtesy of GIVE)

16-17 This volunteer is reading with children in Nicaragua.

of a force that promotes global understanding and peace. Cooperation between volunteer travelers and the local people changes both for the better.

# Tours

A *tour*, as defined by the United States Tour Operators Association (USTOA), may include products ranging from "highly structured escorted packages" to "a collection of independent components that travelers piece together themselves." A tour package includes at least two of the following elements:

- transportation
- lodging
- meals
- entertainment
- attractions
- sightseeing activities

Tours are packaged by tour operators. Tour operators may be outbound operators, inbound operators, or both. Tours are often sold to the customer by travel agents.

The term *tour* can also refer to a designed routing in a tourist destination area that a tourist could walk, cycle, or drive. These suggested routes may be designed by DMOs such as government tourist boards. For example, *Manitours* is designed and published by Travel Manitoba. Automobile associations such as the American Automobile Association (AAA) provide TripTik Travel Planner, or car rental companies may also suggest routes. These tour routes are not commercial products but an information and promotion service.

From the traveler's viewpoint, a tour may be taken independently or with a group, 16-18. People may choose to take tours for several reasons. A prearranged tour frees people from the hassle and continuous decision making of self-directed travel. Tours save passengers time and money because tour operators buy their lodging and tickets at wholesale rates. People can travel with others who have similar interests. The tour may be educational as tour guides interpret the sites. For some TDAs, there are no practical alternatives to taking a tour. For example, to travel to exotic destinations such as interior China or the Egyptian pyramids, most people choose tours.

# *Going Green*

## GIVE

Based in Seattle, Growth International Volunteer Excursions (GIVE) was started by recent college graduates who traveled the world to communities in need. GIVE's mission is to inspire growth, empower native peoples, and encourage sustainable change worldwide. GIVE's two-week tours to Tanzania, Zanzibar, and Nicaragua focus on development through leisure activities. Voluntourists work to build schools and teach English while experiencing cultural immersion abroad.

Goodluz/Shutterstock.com

**16-18** This tourist is on an independent tour in Paris using a travel guide book and an electronic tablet for guidance and interpretation.

## Types of Tours

An **independent tour** is the least structured type of tour. It includes lodging and at least one other element from a supplier. The itinerary is set by the travelers themselves. An example is two nights' accommodation with dinner and symphony tickets included. It can be reserved for any dates, although the price may vary with the season. Travelers can purchase this dynamic packaging from travel agents, online agencies, hotels, and airlines.

**Domestic independent tours (DIT)** or **foreign independent tours (FIT)** are plans that are custom-designed for particular travelers. They are created by a wholesaler or a travel agent. A **hosted tour** puts together two or more elements along with the services of a local host or guide. Travelers going independently to exotic areas or places where there are language barriers appreciate this local help.

An **escorted tour** is the most structured. The tour begins and ends on a specific date and the itinerary is preset. Everything that is included for the price is clear. An escort accompanies the travelers for the whole tour. Much of the trip is generally taken by motor coach.

While a coach driver and escort will deliver passengers to an attraction, the escort may not be able to provide detailed information about that site, and the tour operator calls in experts. For city tours, a **city guide** will "step on" the coach

and take over the guiding. A **site guide** provides interpretation at an attraction. A site guide who volunteers at a museum is called a **docent**. An **interpreter** is a mixture of a teacher and an actor. The traveler learns in a few moments the essential facts that the interpreter has researched, **16-19**.

Escorts, guides, and docents all provide interpretation that makes a trip meaningful and memorable for passengers. Volunteer docents gain valuable experience for working in tour operations. Some major operators of escorted tours are

- Abercrombie & Kent
- Adventures by Disney
- Collette Vacations
- Contiki Vacations (for 18–35 year olds)
- Globus
- Tauck
- Trafalgar Tours

**16-19** This park ranger is offering interpretation to visitors on a tour through Cliff Palace in Mesa Verde National Park, Colorado.

William Silver/Shutterstock.com

# Cruises

Cruises and life at sea often seem romantic and idealistic. Today's mass-market cruise ship is similar to a floating resort. A ship supplies cruise passengers with food and beverage, entertainment, recreation, and a high level of service from the entire staff. In addition, a typical seven-day cruise will visit four ports of call. A passenger can unpack just once, yet visit several destinations. The ports are often located in the areas of greatest interest to tourists, **16-20**.

There are over 30 major cruise lines. Many lines are headquartered in Miami, but their ships sail all over the world. Popular lines include Royal Caribbean, Carnival Cruises, Holland America Line, and Princess Cruises. The most popular cruise itinerary is in the Caribbean. Some cruise lines own private islands that are used exclusively by the lines' passengers. While Caribbean cruises operate year round, most other cruises operate in winter. In spring, some ships leave the Caribbean and travel through the Panama Canal to service the West Coast and Alaska. Alaska cruises operate only in summer.

## *Ships of Many Sizes*

Today's typical cruise liner is about 90,000 tons and carries about 2,000 passengers and 1,000 crew. Royal Caribbean Line's Oasis-class ships are the largest ships at 5,400 passengers each. However, there are not many ports large or deep enough to take these ships, **16-21**.

On the other hand, small ships of only 12 cabins are ideally suited to view areas such as the Columbia River, Prince William Sound, or the Galapagos Islands. Paddle wheelers of the American Queen Steamboat Company cruise the Mississippi River while long, narrow Viking River Cruises tour the Rhine River in Germany.

# Tourism Impacts

The countries of the world are increasing in their interdependence. The world seems smaller

16-20 Cruise ships dock close to the Aloha Tower in an old central part of Honolulu, Hawaii.

*Bruce C. Murray/Shutterstock.com*

*Ruth Peterkin/Shutterstock.com*

**16-21** The *Oasis of the Seas*, docked on the left at Phillipsburg, St. Maarten, clearly shows the size comparison of this huge ship with the typical midsize ship docked on the right.

and easier to navigate for tourists. In fact, people and places are becoming more alike. Some tourists even complain that shopping has become the same everywhere.

Because communications are instant and worldwide, crises news about a crisis spreads quickly. Crises such as disease outbreaks, natural disasters, and political turmoil may exert a negative impact on travel and tourism. The political impact of 9/11 is evident in increased security, the need for additional documentation, and longer wait times at airports. All these events affect when and where people want to travel.

## *Impacts of Travel and Tourism on Communities*

While outside events can affect tourism, tourism itself can have effects on communities. Other impacts on communities from travel and tourism may be economic, social, and environmental.

Tourism creates economic development. For many countries of the world, tourism is the top industry. Many small island nations, such as St. Lucia in the Caribbean, rely on tourism to support their economy. Economic impacts are usually positive. However, if the economy is overly dependent on tourism, a crisis may have a greater effect.

Tourism means that visitors and hosts learn about each other. Local artisans and performers thrive on the attention they get from outside

audiences. Social impacts such as pride in a place are positive, too. With visitors paying admissions, historic sites gain the economic means to be preserved.

Some places, though, can become too popular and become very crowded. When their carrying capacity is exceeded, the environment may be at risk. **Carrying capacity** is the maximum number of people that can be held in a place or on a mode of transportation. In outdoor recreation, it is the number of visitors that a park or other land area can manage without environmental degradation. Prolonged overuse of a place can result in the complete collapse of a tourism destination area, **16-22**.

## *Climate Change*

A climate change can affect a TDA's economy and marketing approach as well as its recreation and tourism. *Climate change* refers to a significant change in the measures of weather patterns over a given area. Many tourism agencies and tourism councils are studying the impact of climate change with respect to their specific areas of operation. They are drawing on the knowledge of experts from numerous fields, including meteorology and geography.

# Careers in Tourism

Because of tourism's great size and rapid growth, there are many exciting and promising career paths. Future careers that emerge are likely to be based on technological advances and a solid educational foundation.

**16-22** Carrying capacity is determined by social, physical, environmental, and ecological limitations. Would you like to be on this beach? Why?

*jan kranendonk/Shutterstock.com*

Though entry-level jobs may be available with a high school diploma, positions increasingly require a two-year or four-year college degree. Tourism programs are available at colleges throughout the country. A tourism program is linked with applied fields such as hospitality and tourism; hospitality, events, and tourism; or recreation and tourism. These programs may be offered by family and consumer sciences or business programs, or hotel and culinary schools.

Large tourism companies employ thousands of people around the globe. Operations and travel career areas offer positions in

- foodservice and culinary
- hotel lodging operations
- theme park operations
- facilities and security
- retail store operations
- travel and cruising

Seasonal TDAs may include positions such as ski instructor, lifeguard, lift operator, groomer, and rental and repair shop operator, **16-23**. Year-round jobs at seasonal TDAs are available in administration, sales and marketing.

For all types of tours, workers behind the scenes design the itineraries and packages, negotiate with suppliers, and create a product for consumers. Tour operators must plan several years in advance and project changes in tastes and trends.

People working in the tour segment can achieve a *Certified Tour Professional (CTP)* designation from the National Tour Association (NTA). The CTP's areas of specialization include leadership, marketing and sales, and financial management.

**16-23** What kind of job at a ski resort would you find most appealing?

S. Borisov/Shutterstock.com

Cruise ships offer many different types of positions. In addition, staff working aboard cruise ships have the opportunity to visit exotic ports of call, just as passengers do. Officers who navigate and sail cruise ships have special technical training and licensing. Other onboard hospitality positions include

- cruise staff
- youth recreation staff
- hotel front desk
- shore excursions desk
- party planner
- cruise director and assistant cruise directors
- entertainer

If you enjoy the idea of representing your country abroad, you might consider working for the Department of State. The Department of State needs all types of specialists to help keep its embassies and consulates working.

## *Tourism Professionals Promoting Peace*

The *International Institute of Peace through Tourism (IIPT)* capitalizes on the influence, skills, and knowledge of travel and tourism professionals. For over thirty years, the IIPT has sponsored peace conferences for tourism professionals and promoted local benefits in developing countries' tourist destinations.

In 1961, President John F. Kennedy envisioned an international citizen program known as the *Peace Corps*. Serving primarily developing countries, American volunteers seek to accomplish three primary goals of

- providing technical/development assistance
- helping other peoples better understand the United States
- educating Americans on other cultures and peoples

After three months of training, a volunteer serves abroad for 24 months. Volunteers may work with local governments, schools, and various organizations, addressing issues such as hunger, education, business, information technology, agriculture, and environment.

Peace and cooperation among nations happen through interactions between people. Beyond the economic impacts of tourism, travelers socialize and promote understanding with the local peoples being visited. Because travel and tourism is the world's largest industry, it can be a powerful force for peace.

# Chapter 16
## Review

## Chapter Summary

- Tourism significantly impacts local economies.
- Terrorism had a significant impact on tourism that lead to additional security and protection for travelers.
- Technology continues to significantly influence tourism, especially for traveler security.
- Travel and health documentation are vital for international travel.
- Seasonality is an important influence for tourism destination areas.
- Destination marketing organizations (DMOs) work with local tourism officials to help promote area tourism.
- Several types of tour options are available that vary in structure to meet traveler needs.
- Tourism can influence community development, social factors, and environmental concerns.
- As tourism continues to grow, many career options are promising.

## Review

1. Compare and contrast a *domestic tourist* with an *international tourist*.
2. How does spatial context relate to sense of place?
3. Name two ways tourism affects economies.
4. What is a *national tourism* office and why is it important?
5. Describe three travel documents needed by international travelers.
6. What information about travel requirements can citizens obtain from the U.S. Department of State?
7. What is seasonality and why can it be a challenge for tourism?
8. List segments of the tourism industry.
9. What does ecotourism seek to accomplish?
10. What is unique about the voluntourism segment of the tourism industry?
11. Name three major types of tours.
12. What is the difference between a *docent* and an *interpreter*?
13. Name three operations and travel career areas that large tourism companies offer.

## Critical Thinking

14. **Predict.** Predict the consequences of failure to procure personal identification documents when traveling from country to country.

Discuss reasons why such documentation is *more* or *less* important today.

15. **Draw conclusions.** Draw conclusions about the benefits of smart identification technology to travelers and countries and discuss in class.

16. **Assess.** What are examples of biometric identifiers? Assess what privacy issues might be linked to such identifiers. Are the benefits greater than the privacy issues? Cite the text and reliable Internet or print resources to support your responses. Write a summary.

17. **Infer.** Suppose the hospitality company you work for primarily focuses on tours to the Caribbean Islands (see the map in Appendix B). Since you will be guiding tours, you decide to investigate sustainable developments in the area. Use the text and at least three reliable Internet resources to research and make inferences about sustainable developments, including economic, environmental, and cultural and social. Write a summary of your findings. How would you use this information in your work?

18. **Analyze.** Imagine you want to be a Certified Tour Professional (CTP). Analyze ways you might act as a peace ambassador when interacting with other travelers. Discuss your actions with the class.

# Common Core

### College and Career Readiness

19. **Speaking.** Use text and reliable Internet resources to research the process for obtaining a passport or visa to a country of your choice. Summarize your findings in an oral presentation.

20. **Writing.** Suppose you have been hired by a U.S. hospitality company that has many TDAs around the globe. You will spend your first year traveling to countries in Central and South America. Use the CDC and the U.S. Department of State websites to investigate information you need for travel health. Identify diseases and health conditions common to the areas, vaccination requirements, and what to do if you should become sick abroad. Write a summary of your findings for each category.

21. **Reading.** Use at least three reliable Internet or print resources to research the categories of seasonal TDAs. For each category, identify one popular tourist destination. What attractions draw tourists to the area? What factors impact the profitability of each area? Write a summary for each category to share with the class. Cite your resources.

22. **Writing.** Visit the National Park Service website and research parks that focus on heritage tourism. Choose one site to research. Then write a public service announcement (PSA) about the tourism area, highlighting its key heritage features.

23. **Writing.** Suppose you are interested in working in cruise ship tours. Write an essay explaining your interest in the cruise industry. Cite the text and other reliable resources to support your explanation.

24. **Speaking.** Talk with your school counselor to identify nearby community colleges or universities that offer programs in tourism. Arrange a tour of one of the schools. Note key aspects of the program to share in an oral report in class.

25. **CTE Career Readiness Practice.** To learn more about the voluntourism segment, use reliable Internet, print, and interview resources to further investigate aspects of voluntourism. Summarize your findings in writing. When evaluating the reliability of information, remember to
   • identify author/writer/speaker credibility
   • verify the details
   • identify bias

306

# Chapter *17*

## Recreation

## Chapter Objectives

*After studying this chapter, you will be able to*

- **explain** the concept of leisure, including work-life balance.
- **understand** the history of public parks and recreation in the United States.
- **discuss** motivations for and benefits of parks, recreation, and leisure.
- **assess** the value of public/community agencies.
- **compare and contrast** different types of nonprofit and private agencies.
- **recognize** the benefits of volunteerism.
- **identify** different types of specialized recreation, special events, and entertainment options available in the United States.
- **list** career opportunities available to recreation professionals.

## Before You Read

Try to answer the following questions before you read this chapter.

- What are some benefits of recreation and leisure?
- Can you name some careers in the recreation field?

## Terms to Know

leisure time
quality of life (QOL)
work-life balance
log
activity stacking
National Park Service (NPS)

Civilian Conservation Corps (CCC)
motivation
Outward Bound
programming

demographics
interpretation
hybrid
secular
time-share

# Leisure

The ancient Greeks considered leisure to be the highest value in life and work the lowest. In Aristotle's time, the upper-class people of Athens did not work. Nearly all their time was free time, so they were able to pursue intellectual and cultural activities as they wished, **17-1**. The Greek word for leisure was *schole*, which sounds like *school*. Leisure time allows people the time and opportunity to educate themselves.

The word *leisure* is related to the English words *license* and *liberty*. These words and their roots mean *freedom*. A classic definition of *leisure time* is *time free from obligation*. Obligations include work and other activities related to providing for the necessities of life—food, clothing, and shelter. Leisure activities occur in nonwork time. **Leisure time**, then, is the time left over after work and other necessities. Leisure time helps improve quality of life. **Quality of life (QOL)** is a person's overall satisfaction with the conditions of his or her life. A person's quality of life may depend on many factors, including physical, social, environmental, psychological, intellectual, and emotional factors.

## Work-Life Balance

A century ago, the average workweek was about 60 hours. Today, the workweek is generally considered to be five eight-hour days, or 40 hours. Clearly, much less of a person's life is devoted to work hours than in the past. However, as a result of portable communications devices, many people today do take their work home with them.

Hourly employees who work over 40 hours are generally paid overtime. Of course, some nonhourly employees find it necessary to work much more than 40 hours to complete their work. Some workers have long commutes to and from work, which adds stress and fatigue to their day. In the United States, workers spend an average of 25 minutes each way for their jobs. This adds roughly another hour to the time taken by work and work-related activities.

In many households, everyone works. The household chores may need to be divided so no one person is overburdened. Although most people have more time for leisure than working people did a century ago, many have packed calendars. They seek out **work-life balance**, equal time spent between career or work demands and the needs of life-related activities such as home, family, friends, health, and leisure.

Workers like to have flexibility at work so they have time to care for themselves and others. Many employers recognize this and offer flexible schedules. For example, an employee may be able to start a job any time between 7:00 a.m. and 10:00 a.m. and end any time between 3:00 p.m. and 6:00 p.m., so long as he or she has worked eight hours.

Leisure studies are often accomplished by asking people to keep a log on how they spend their time. A **log** is a record of a person's activities, such as work, school, commuting, homework, self-care, buying and preparing food, and sleeping. For a 24-hour period, total time spent in essential activities is calculated. The time left over is leisure time, **17-2**.

**17-1** The Odeon, an ancient amphitheater, is where Athenians gathered in their leisure time for theater, lectures, and discussion.

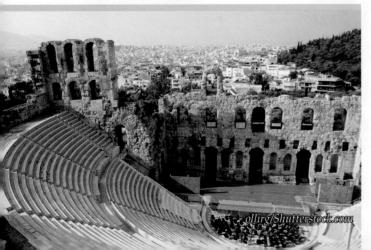

**17-2** Keeping a daily log can help people plan for leisure time.

Some people "stack" activities in order to enjoy more pleasurable experiences in their leisure time. **Activity stacking** is scheduling or dovetailing similar leisure activities throughout the day. This process allows people to spend more of their leisure time recreating with their families and friends, but still allows time for individual recreation. For example, a man may take a morning walk with his wife, coach his child's afternoon soccer game, and watch his favorite team on TV in the evening.

# Recreation

Recreation usually occurs in leisure time. Recreation is *re-creation*, when people have time to renew and restore themselves. For some people, this means doing something restful and relaxing. For others, recreation can be hard activity, such as playing sports. Many jobs today are *sedentary*, or inactive, so doing nonwork activities that are physically demanding gives people a change of pace.

Recreation occurs when a person is fully engaged in an activity. In a game that is well matched to your skill level, you might lose track of time and your surroundings. Athletes and performers often call the sensation of total involvement as being "in the groove." Most people are happiest when they are in a state of complete absorption in their activity.

Recreation activities are freely chosen and extremely varied. Some activities are individual at-home activities that cost nothing, such as reading a library book. On the other hand, participating in team sports such as baseball may require costs for uniforms and travel. Team sports also require that a player adhere to a schedule for practices and games.

## History of Public Parks and Recreation

Throughout the 1900s, the workweek gradually shortened to what it is today. As people gained more leisure time, they looked for more places to enjoy themselves. City governments began to build parks and playgrounds and develop programs. On a national level, more land and historic sites became protected through the establishment of the U.S. Forest Service in 1905, the Antiquities

Act of 1906, and the National Park Service in 1916. The **National Park Service (NPS)** is the federal agency that supervises outdoor recreation and the preservation of natural and cultural resources. The NPS is part of the Department of the Interior and manages all national parks as well as trails, national monuments, and other designated historical properties.

During the Great Depression of the 1930s, as much as one-third of the labor force were unemployed. The federal government wanted to create jobs very quickly, and at the same time, people felt a growing need for meaningful recreation. One way that President Franklin D. Roosevelt's New Deal created jobs was by building recreational facilities of all kinds, including swimming pools, park pavilions, campgrounds, and trails. One of the most popular job-creation programs was the **Civilian Conservation Corps (CCC)**. During the depression years of the 1930s, the CCC built over 800 new parks, upgraded most others, built roadways, and planted over three billion trees on government lands. The park buildings of that era tend to be of stone and timber with a distinctive architecture. CCC-era facilities can be found all over the United States, **17-3**.

## Motivations for Recreating

The main motive for taking part in recreation is pleasure, but there can be other motivations, too. A **motivation** is an *extrinsic* (external) or *intrinsic* (internal) element that moves someone toward a behavior. Motivations can be intellectual, physical, or social. People are motivated to fulfill their

**17-3** The style of architecture on this CCC meeting place at Table Rock State Park is similar to thousands of buildings from this era found across the country.

*T. Markley/Shutterstock.com*

needs, so in a particular recreation activity, they will strive to meet a certain level of need.

People's motivations for recreation can be related to Maslow's Hierarchy of Needs. For example, the first level of need, physiological, can be met when choosing fitness or sport as a recreation activity.

A simple motivation for recreation is to be social. People join hobby clubs so they can socialize with others with similar interests. Socializing can be more informal, such as when a person chooses to visit or interact with others at a coffee shop, on a walk, or at a party. In this case, the need for love and belonging is filled by associating with other people. Filling the need becomes more important than enjoying the recreational activity itself.

When playing sports, the role of competition is very clear. Many people have a competitive streak to their personalities and like to compete with peers in sports or other challenges. This form of recreation may also fill a self-esteem need. Sometimes risk is a motivator, such as for adventure recreationists who deep-water scuba dive, white-water kayak, ice climb, and bungee jump.

To meet self-actualization needs, people may seek challenges they do not find anywhere else. Competitive activities allow people to compare themselves with others or to a standard it could take a lifetime to reach. For example, mountaineers may aspire to be part of the "Seven Summits" group. The Seven Summits are the highest mountains on each of the seven continents. Fewer than 400 climbers are known to have completed this mountaineering challenge. This would definitely be associated with Maslow's highest level of self-actualization, **17-4.**

A more achievable challenge is pursued by bird watchers, also known as *birders*. Some create a "life list" of birds they have personally seen, which can involve decades and several hundred species of birds. Birding and mountaineering are examples of activities that individuals do to achieve challenging goals in their recreational time.

## Benefits of Recreation and Leisure

Recreation is highly valued in society because it benefits not only the individual, but also the

17-4  Mt. Kilimanjaro, the tallest mountain in Africa, is one of the climbs in the "Seven Summits" group.

*Mogens Trolle/Shutterstock.com*

community. City, county, state, and national governments build and support recreational facilities. Recreation offers some specific benefits.

First, recreation promotes health. Physically active recreation helps people become fit, stay fit, and maintain a healthy weight. Overweight and obesity can lead to many health problems, including greater risk of serious diseases such as diabetes and heart disease. Staying physically active helps to prevent weight gain and the serious diseases that may follow.

Physical activity is also known to improve mental health. Exercise produces chemicals called *endorphins*, which create a positive feeling in the body. Physical activity in a safe environment with others can become a positive habit that leads to both physical and mental health, **17-5**. Options are increasingly being provided for people with disabilities to exercise regularly, too.

**17-5** A person with disabilities can experience physical activity with the assistance of a therapeutic recreation specialist.

Marcel Mooij/Shutterstock.com

A second benefit of recreation is the personal development that comes from learning something new. People may want to try a new game, such as golf, to see if they like it. They can take weekly classes just to learn some basic skills and meet other people without risks. Possible risks include the expense of joining a golf club, buying golf clubs, or taking a credit course requiring a grade.

A third benefit of recreation is that people use their free time in a positive way. Unsupervised youth with a lot of energy can sometimes get into trouble. Recreation departments take credit for reducing juvenile delinquency by offering classes, programs, and events that draw teens. Sports of all types promote discipline as players need practice time and are motivated to compete to win.

Outdoor recreation in particular requires people to be more self-sufficient or independent. Have you hiked into a wilderness area and camped overnight in a tent? In such a situation, you are responsible for feeding yourself, which may require building a fire or catching a fish. To manage even 24 hours in the woods, you may be challenged to use survival skills for the first time. An organization that sponsors wilderness experiences is **Outward Bound**. Instructors consider the experience to be a kind of wilderness therapy. Many high schools, colleges, and universities offer academic credit for Outward Bound expeditions.

Socializing and making new friends is one of the most important aspects of a healthful life. Socializing comes more readily when people are relaxed and participate in activities such as bowling, ping-pong, or puzzles. When people who live alone share recreation with others, it improves their quality of life.

Recreation departments encourage cultural interaction through folk arts such as dancing, ethnic food events, and crafts. Watching or learning to dance a Bavarian folk dance will be new for some people. For others, it will be a preservation of their culture and heritage, **17-6**.

Another benefit of recreation is the opportunity to volunteer. When a community puts on a large event such as a festival or parade, organizers may need hundreds of volunteers. You may have volunteered at such an event yourself. Volunteering makes individuals feel valued and fosters a greater sense of community.

Faraways/Shutterstock.com

**17-6** These Mexican folk dancers perform in traditional costumes as an expression of their heritage.

# Public/Community Agencies

Recreation programs are offered by government-run agencies or privately run businesses. Depending on the financial status of the provider, the fee individuals pay for using of recreation facilities range from zero to all program costs to program costs plus staff and building expenses.

*Community recreation* is the term given to the work of public recreation agencies. These are owned and operated by governments to serve the public. Parks and recreation areas may be operated by governments at the municipal (city or town), county, state, and national levels.

## Municipal Departments

Municipal parks and recreation departments usually focus their mission on people, parks, and programs. They provide outdoor facilities such as parks, beaches, and sports fields. Indoor facilities include community centers and swimming pools.

Recreation professionals must be aware of people's needs and motivations for recreation before they can develop a meaningful plan. **Programming** is developing a selection and schedule of activities suitable for the demographics of the people being served. **Demographics** are statistics on groups of people about their age, ethnic background, education, or income. Programming is an essential skill of recreation professionals.

Recreation professionals develop programs for each season. They need to know if a watercolor class or a basketball tournament will serve their users, the people in their community for whom the programming is prepared. Once programmers have planned the programs, they need to recruit instructors, reserve facilities, calculate fees, and advertise. Programs for each season are usually published in booklets and advertised online, **17-7**. Regular programming generally includes the categories of games, sports, aquatics, outdoor, playground, arts, hobbies, consumer education, social events, special services, and community center activities.

Recreation professionals create programs based on age and experience from tiny tots to lifeguard training. Details include time, place, registration, and fees. In addition to regular programming, public parks and recreation departments may sponsor special events such as festivals, parades, sports tournaments, and hobby shows such as for cars or art.

## State Parks

While municipal areas manage recreation as their main purpose, state parks stress stewardship and conservation of natural resources. State park systems are responsible for protecting natural resources and landmarks while helping people learn about and enjoy them.

A state park system may have several types of land—park area, recreation area, and natural areas. You can expect to find hiking trails, picnic sites, restrooms, campgrounds, and visitor interpretation features at most parks.

# Learn-to-Swim                                      FALL

## Registration

**Register at Lions Pool one week prior to start date for fall swim lessons.**

Register in person or by phone.
No mail-in registration please.

Pay with cash, check, Visa or MasterCard.

Classes with fewer then three participants may be combined with another class or cancelled. If this happens, the Head Instructor will share options that are available.

Families registering multiple family members in the session time are eligible for a 20% discount on the third and each additional registration.

**Learn-to-Swim Fees**
$37/$30 resident discount

**Semi-Private Lessons**
$96/$80 resident discount

**Placement Tests**
Not sure of your child's skill level? Bring your swimmer to any open or recreational swim for a swim test. Staff will recommend an appropriate class level. It's FREE—unless your child chooses to participate in the session.

**Lifeguard Training Class**
This intense training class will teach you all the necessary skills to become a lifeguard. If you think you have what it takes to become a lifeguard, then register today and find out!

$80/$63 resident discount
Oct. 8–Dec. 3      M, W      6–8:00 p.m.

## Learn-to-Swim Sessions

**M / W   6–8:30 p.m.**
SESSION I      Sept. 10–Oct. 3
SESSION II     Oct. 8–Oct. 29 (*7-lesson session*)
SESSION III    Nov. 5–Dec. 3

## Children 6 months-3 years

**Tiny Tots**
This program is designed to be both fun and informative. Our instructors will work with you and your child to help them become more comfortable in the water. Tiny Tot lessons are designed to help prepare children for Preschool lessons.

## Children 3-5 years

**Preschool 1**
Front Float
Back Float
Getting face wet/bobs
Jumping in the pool unassisted
Introduction to kicking

**Preschool 2**
Freestyle unassisted
Streamline
Jumping in and swimming unassisted
Retrieve objects from the bottom of the pool
Side bobs
Introduction to backstroke
Introduction to deep water

## Placement Tests
Not sure of your child's skill level? Bring your swimmer to any open or recreational swim for a swim test. Staff will recommend an appropriate class level. It's FREE—unless your child chooses to stay and participate in the session.

## Children 6 years & older

**Level 1**
Front Float
Back Float
Getting face wet/bobs
Jumping in the pool unassisted
Introduction to kicking

**Level 2**
Freestyle unassisted
Streamline
Jumping in and swimming unassisted
Retrieve objects from the bottom of the pool
Side bobs
Introduction to backstroke
Introduction to deep water

**Level 3**
Backstroke refinement
Freestyle refinement w/side breathing
Diving basics
Introduction to dolphin kick
Elementary backstroke
Swimming strokes 30-40 feet

**Level 4**
Breaststroke
Freestyle with breathing 25 yds
Backstroke 25 yds
Elementary backstroke 25 yds
Dolphin kick refinement
Diving from the board

**Level 5**
Breaststroke refinement 50 yds
Backstroke 50 yds
Freestyle with side breathing 50 yds
Side stroke 25 yds
Butterfly 25 yds
Competitive approach and hurdle
  on diving board
Introduction to flip turns

| Lions Pool | Learn-To-Swim | Evening Lessons · M/W · I-II-III | |
|---|---|---|---|
| 6:00 | Hydrofit | Preschool | Semi-Private |
| 6:30 | Hydrofit cont. | Tiny Tots | Preschool |
| 7:00 | Level 1 | Level 2 | Level 5 |
| 7:30 | Preschool 2 | Level 1 | Level 4 |
| 8:00 | Level 3 | Level 5 | |

4

*Photo Courtesy of City of Yakima, Anton Balazh/Shutterstock.com*

**17-7** Recreation professionals create programs based on age and experience, from tiny tots to lifeguard training.

# Joanna Puthoff—Path of a Recreational Professional

Joanna Puthoff has had a long and fruitful career in the field of recreational services. She began by serving as teen assistant recreation coordinator for the city of Ellensburg, Washington, while attending school at Central Washington University. There she earned bachelor's degrees in psychology, speech communication, and recreation and tourism. She was able to put this education to excellent use when she became the youth recreation coordinator for the city of Longview, Washington, in 2002. A few years later, she was promoted to the position of athletic recreation coordinator.

Joanna is a member of the Washington Recreation & Parks Association (WRPA) and has become a Certified Recreation Professional through this organization. She has served on several WRPA committees, including the Higher Education Relations Committee (HERC) and the Facility Services Section. She has also been involved with Alturas International and Camp Fire USA, has coached a Special Olympics team, and has created a club for youth with disabilities called SOS.

Joanna has gone on to earn her master's degree in public administration from Seattle University and continues to further her education with trainings sponsored by the WRPA, the NRPA, and the International Northwest Parks and Recreation Association.

At present, Joanna is the facility coordinator for the city of Sammamish, Washington, where she manages over 15 rental facilities, oversees social media content, and works with others in the recreational field to organize community events. In 2010 she was awarded the WRPA's "Outstanding Professional"

*Photo courtesy of Joanna Puthoff (right)*

award and has also been honored with Central Washington University's "Outstanding Alum" award.

## Joanna Puthoff's Career Path

**2000–2002:** Served as teen assistant recreation coordinator for Ellensburg, WA

**2001:** Became a member of Washington Recreation & Parks Association (WRPA)

**2002:** Earned bachelor's degrees in recreation and tourism, speech communication, and psychology from Central Washington University

**2002–2005:** Served as youth recreation coordinator for Longview, WA

**2005:** Served as athletic recreation coordinator for Longview, WA

**2006:** Became a Certified Recreation Professional (CRP) through National Recreation & Parks Association

**2006:** Became current facility coordinator for Sammamish, WA

**2009:** Earned master's degree in public administration from Seattle University

**2010:** Was awarded WRPA's "Outstanding Professional" award

**2011–2012:** Continued education through trainings offered by NRPA, WRPA, and INPRA

Park sites are chosen for their natural beauty and recreational potential. All states have parks. Montana, for example, has 54 state parks. Many are in the Rocky Mountain range, but parks are located throughout the state. North Carolina has 34 state parks, 4 state recreation areas, and 19 state natural areas, as well as lakes, rivers, and state trails.

## National Parks

The 400 national parks have been called "America's Best Idea." The national park system has historic landmarks and natural landmarks in addition to parks. The mission of the National Park Service is "to preserve unimpaired the natural and cultural resources and values of the national park system for the enjoyment, education, and inspiration of this and future generations."

The parks receive about 275 million visitors a year. They are operated by the National Park Service's 27,000 full-time and temporary employees, including about 4,000 park rangers. Other employees are archeologists, botanists, ecologists, landscape architects, facility managers, historians, museum professionals, maintenance mechanics, and park police.

The exceptional scenery of the parks covers a variety of ecosystems, **17-8**. For example, Bryce and Arches are in the dry southwest mountains. Everglades National Park is a 1.5-million acre subtropical river of grass in south Florida. It protects endangered species such as the manatee and crocodile. Acadia, which was the first national park east of the Mississippi River, hugs the rugged Atlantic coast of Maine.

Besides the wonderful scenery and opportunities for interpretation and recreation offered by the NPS, the visitors to the nation's parks require lodging, food and beverage, and other amenities. In over 100 of the parks, these services are provided by private businesses or concessioners under contract. Concessions at national parks provide jobs for about 25,000 people in season.

Wherever you go, interpretation is a vital part of every park and attraction. **Interpretation** can present facts, feelings, ideas, and artistry. It is the process of helping each visitor find an opportunity to personally connect with a place. Individuals connect in different ways and in their own time.

A park ranger's discussion of a scenic vista inspires an emotional connection for some. For

National Park Service

**17-8**  These tourists are sea kayaking in Alaska's Glacier Bay.

others, intellectual connections are made through signage describing the geologic history of the same landscape. Forms of interpretation include period costumes, films, exhibits, mobile apps, signs, and artifacts. Many different job skills are required to present interpretation at a park.

The goal of all interpretive services is to increase each visitor's enjoyment and understanding of the parks and to inspire visitors to care about the future of the parks. The conservation and protection of special places depends on people caring about those places.

### World Heritage Sites

World Heritage sites are the most extraordinary natural or constructed wonders. They include places as diverse as the Galapagos Islands, the Taj Mahal, and the Great Wall of China. In the U.S., there are 21 elements within national parks that are designated World Heritage sites. These include the geyser system at Yellowstone National Park, the tallest trees at Redwoods National Park, and Hawaii Volcanoes National Park.

## Nonprofit Agencies

The segment of nonprofit agencies is growing, primarily because of cuts in publicly funded state services, **17-9**. Recently these nonprofits have also become a **hybrid**, or mix, of public and private ownership.

## Importance of Volunteers

Nonprofits are strong because of a very strong American tradition of volunteerism. When considered as a portion of total domestic output (GDP), Americans contribute the most volunteered hours of all the peoples of the world. In 2010, 62.8 million Americans volunteered a total of 8.1 billion hours to local and national nonprofit agencies.

This American spirit of volunteerism was established in the late 19th and early 20th centuries. This period of American history witnessed a tremendous growth in reform and civic spirit. The reforms were fueled by significant growth of U.S. cities as industrialization and the influx of immigrants grew. Enjoying the new freedoms of shorter

**17-9** Many state parks have instituted passes to help in the cost recovery of park operations. Here visitors are required to pay either for a one-time use or an annual pass usable throughout the state.

*Marcus Kieltyka*

hours, many citizens wanted to help their urban neighbors and share national pride with the new Americans.

Nonprofit agencies rely on volunteers to accomplish their work. Some of the main reasons why Americans volunteer include
- grassroots volunteerism spirit
- strong religious beliefs about helping others
- tax-exempt status of the nonprofit segment

### Benefits of Volunteerism

An old motto states that people help themselves by helping others. Benefits to those who volunteer proven in various studies include the following:
- *Better health.* Volunteers receive positive mental and physical health benefits from serving.
- *Civic strength.* Volunteering contributes to greater levels of trust and civility in a community.
- *Openness to travel.* In 2007, about 3.7 million U.S. volunteers travelled distances beyond 120 miles from their home and contributed to both domestic and international travel.
- *Educational success.* Student volunteers have grades about one letter-grade higher than nonvolunteers.
- *Career mobility.* Many employers report looking for volunteer activities in résumés as an early sign of leadership potential. Employers may be more inclined to hire young people with demonstrated volunteer activities over equally qualified nonvolunteers.

Where can you develop your leadership skills and gain experience for a future career in recreation? Various public and private agencies with a recreation mission can be places for personal development, **17-10**.

## Characteristics of Nonprofit Agencies

The major types of nonprofit agencies that serve the recreational needs of youth groups include secular and faith-based agencies. (**Secular** means *nonreligious.* Another word for secular is *nonsectarian.*) These groups share some common characteristics:
- Many youth leaders volunteer because of a feeling of public spirit and social obligation.

## Where Young Adults and Teens Volunteer

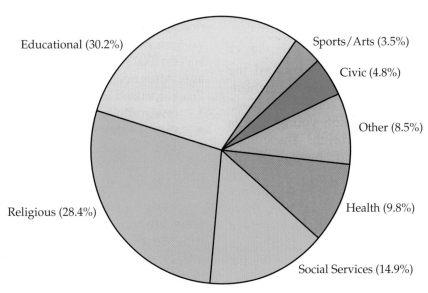

Educational (30.2%)

Sports/Arts (3.5%)

Civic (4.8%)

Other (8.5%)

Religious (28.4%)

Health (9.8%)

Social Services (14.9%)

*Volunteering and Civic Life in America*

**17-10** This graph provides insight on where young adults and teens reported volunteering in 2011.

Volunteers who benefited in their youth from similar activities believe they should likewise help younger generations.

- These nonprofit agencies seek to meet current social needs in their communities.
- Leadership may be based on a combination of professional and expert knowledge and experience.
- Funding may be through a single source or a variety of sources, including parent organizations, direct public contributions, membership fees, or competitive grants.

## Secular Youth Agencies

The secular youth-serving segment has a large recreational component. Some of the largest nationally structured organizations have broad goals of social development, good citizenship, and group recreational activities.

These youth-serving groups require the involvement of many volunteers and paid professionals with a wide variety of skills, education, and abilities. Increased education and experience are the pathways to higher levels of work within the agencies. Today, many youth-serving groups offer highly specialized or high-adventure programs that require certified, paid professional counselors and recreation activity personnel.

### Boy Scouts of America (BSA)

With over 2.7 million youth members and 1.1 million adult volunteers, the BSA partners with community organizations to provide scout troops in neighborhoods. The earliest level is the Cub Scout program. Cub Scouts range from ages 6 through 10. Oftentimes, Cub Scout "packs" rely on volunteer assistance from older scouts. The Boy Scout program is for boys ranging from 10 through 18 years of age. Boy Scouts are able to participate in a wide range of adventure training, and leadership skill development.

Between the ages of 14 and 21, Boy Scouts are eligible to join Venturing. As the fastest growing group within scouting, Venturing allows young men and women to explore a program full of challenge, adventure, and leadership training. An offshoot of Venturing is the SeaScout program, which allows this same age group to discover similar activities on ships.

### Girl Scouts of the U.S.A. (GSUSA)

With 3.2 million members and nearly 900,000 adult volunteers, GSUSA aims to empower girls and help teach values such as honesty, fairness, courage, compassion, character, sisterhood, confidence, and citizenship. Girl Scouts' achievements are recognized through rank advancement and special awards. The Girl Scouts have partnered with governmental agencies and corporations on various projects, **17-11**.

### Boys and Girls Clubs of America (BGCA)

The *Chronicle of Philanthropy* has ranked the Boys and Girls Club of America as the highest-rated organization for the 18th consecutive year. The BGCA serves over 4 million young people annually in over 3,000 chartered clubs. These clubs are located in schools, on military bases, on tribal lands, and in public housing complexes. Designed to give young people a safe and affordable place to be after school and during the summer, these clubs are led by paid trained youth development professionals.

In addition to having fun and being safe, the young people are able to build a sense of belonging, personal accountability, civility, and civic responsibility. The aim is to instill a commitment to learning, positive values, healthful habits, and high personal expectations as adults.

### Police Athletic/Activities Leagues (PALs) and Sheriff Activities Leagues (SALs)

These leagues serve more than a million youth annually through their 400 chapters located in 700 cities and towns in the United States. They developed from competitive sports leagues to groups focused on a much wider range of after-school social and academic activities for young people. Their aim is to prevent juvenile crime and violence. The agencies receive their funding primarily through grants and local contributions. The police officer staffers seek to build young members' characters, improve relations with the community, and keep young people away from illegal drugs.

**17-11** The annual Girl Scouts cookie drive gives girls experience in business, marketing, and sales—important building blocks for future careers.

*Anna Hoychuk/Shutterstock*

### Camp Fire USA

Founded in 1910, Camp Fire was the first nonsectarian, interracial organization for young women in the United States. Camp Fire annually serves 100,000 campers between 5 and 21 years of age. After becoming coeducational in 1975, Camp Fire refocused its efforts on

- environmental and camp programs
- out-of-schooltime programs
- teen service and leadership programs

## Faith-Based Youth Agencies

Early in their development, youth programs were supported by specific faiths. Today, many of these reach out beyond their traditional bases to attract youth from various faiths. While it might seem to overlap the public youth programs, this segment still has a special purpose. That purpose is to promote specific values through recreation and leisure activities, including

- day camps or week-long Bible schools with a recreational component
- year-round recreation for families, including picnics, carnivals, dances, trips, and game nights
- fellowship programs for various age levels plus discussion groups on religious themes
- various special-service programs, including child care, home visits, and activities for older adults
- sports leagues for bowling, boxing, and basketball

Figure **17-12** lists some popular religiously affiliated agencies that serve millions of young people. Many adult volunteers share their abilities with young members. Paid professional positions exist at higher organizational levels in all these agencies.

# Private Agencies

Private agencies are run by businesses. Unlike nonprofit agencies, the goal of private agencies is to make money. Private agencies may be indoor or outdoor.

## Indoor Recreation

Some recreational activities can be done both indoors and outdoors. Due to weather and time constraints, many individuals often seek the

## Religiously Affiliated Agencies

- The YMCA (Young Men's Christian Association) and YWCA (Young Women's Christian Association). The *Y* is often designated as a combination of YM and YW.
- The CYO (Catholic Youth Organization).
- The YM-YWHA (Young Men's/Young Women's Hebrew Association).
- The Islamic Society of North America (ISNA), the Muslim American Society, and the Young Muslims.

*Goodheart-Willcox Publisher*

**17-12** Do you know of any of these organizations in your area?

indoor equivalents so they can participate in the activity year-round. Many indoor places offer a variety of activities for many age groups. Some even provide child care.

### Health Clubs

Membership-based health clubs are fast-growing businesses. Some are chains that have thousands of centers open 24 hours a day, 7 days a week. Membership provides access to a secure environment at every location. The wide variety of recreation activities includes yoga and Pilates.

Some clubs offer individualized diet counseling with trained staff. Club members can track their progress online from the company's website and receive personalized coaching tips.

### Dancing

Activities such as dancing are periodically "rediscovered" by younger generations and become popular again. Ballroom dancing became a sensation after being featured on prominent television shows. Break dancing, also called *breaking* or *b-boying*, is an even more popular form of dancing worldwide. Set to a wide variety of music beats, dancers create expressive movements either individually or in groups, **17-13**.

## Outdoor Recreation

After graduation from high school, young adults have more choices in the types and level of recreational activities available. This is partially due to jobs providing the financial resources necessary to pursue individual interests. Many people immediately associate recreation with some of their favorite outdoor activities and hobbies.

### Sports

The top level of Maslow's theory of development is self-actualization and personal achievement. Young adults between the ages of 18 and 34 are seeking to develop their self-awareness. They are also at a stage of life that allows for their participation in the greatest variety of activities at the widest range of levels.

Adults discover that time for interests and abilities is limited as families and careers begin to

## *Going Green*

### NOLS

The *National Outdoor Leadership School (NOLS)* offers a complete semester of 80 days with a whole array of skills training included—backpacking, canoeing, caving, climbing, fly fishing, horse packing, mountaineering, rafting, kayaking, sailing, skiing, and wilderness medicine. The school teaches environmental stewardship throughout, emphasizing the principles of the organization *Leave No Trace Center for Outdoor Ethics*. Programs are mostly in the U.S., with several overseas.

Jose Gil/Shutterstock.com

17-13 Break dancing has become a worldwide hit.

occupy their nonwork time. Therefore, they may seek to continue their interests on a less-intensive level.

Younger people often enjoy high-impact sports that yield elevated levels of excitement. Many people refer to the physical state of excitement as an "adrenaline rush." However, less intensive sports also give participants levels of achievement and personal satisfaction.

### Spectator Sports

Spectator sports are a recreational activity in which observers pay to view a game. This includes most high school, college, semi-pro, and professional levels of spectator sports. When people cannot travel to see their favorite team, they often view the game on television or in sports clubs that televise a wide range of games. Television programming dedicated to sports coverage has provided tremendous growth in televising these events.

### Cruise Recreation

When a cruise ship docks at a port of call, passengers disembark for the day and sightsee. The cruise line offers many organized tours on land that passengers can choose at extra cost. Cruise passengers make these arrangements on board with knowledgeable staff at the shore excursions desk. Shore excursion staff coordinates with tour operators on land, **17-14**.

The ship spends some days "at sea" and does not visit a port. On sea days, cruise staff members are very busy providing a full range of recreation activities to passengers. Cruise and recreation staff, for example, coordinate bridge tournaments, karaoke events, shuffle board, yoga classes, and scuba lessons in the ship's pool.

# Specialized Recreation

Forms of recreation may be dependent on a person's current life status. For instance, those in the military or college may have a fairly limited

## *Going Green*

### The X Games

The X Game sports are an organized competition of popular recreation activities among young sports enthusiasts that do not belong in the more traditional sports groups. Some Summer X game events include motocross, skateboarding, street luge, surfing, and BMX racing. Popular Winter X games include snowboarding, snowmobile activities, ice climbing, and skiboarding. An important aspect of the X Games has been a strong "green" approach to the games' impact on the environment. Many X Games are popular with young people around the world. Some areas also include variations of games based on local interests.

Judy Tejero/Shutterstock.com

**17-14** Passengers often arrange for tours before disembarking from the cruise ship at ports of call.

selection of recreation options. However, because of its many benefits, forms of recreation are offered in the military, at colleges, and in corporate environments.

## Armed Forces Recreation

The armed forces recreation program is known as *Morale, Welfare, and Recreation (MWR)*. This program is designed to provide all military-associated individuals with a balanced lifestyle of relaxation and recreation.

Many military and civilian establishments support a wide range of fitness, athletic, travel, and entertainment activities for service personnel and their families. The U.S. Army Community and Family Support Center operates the Armed Forces Recreation Centers (AFRC). These centers are located around the world and provide a full range of resort-level services and accommodations. Many university and corporate recreation programs were built on advancements made by MWR.

## College Recreation

The variety of college sports and activities range from individual recreation interests to intramural and club sports to national or international levels of competition. College programs offer growing opportunities for recreational programmers and specialists. In addition, university recreation offers its participants

- heightened university recognition
- increased campus morale
- new paths to student development
- new opportunities for nonclass experiences

- new forms of faculty and student recruitment and retention

## Corporate Wellness

Since the 1950s, employee recreation has grown as the workplace shifted from demanding physical work to more sedentary jobs. The Employee Services Management Association is the health advocate for employees. Through research, many companies realized that major benefits could be gained by offering corporate wellness programs. These benefits included

- improved employee health and lower health costs
- decreased health-related absenteeism
- greater employee productivity
- better recruitment and retention
- improved employer-employee relations
- enhanced company image and community relations

Employees have recognized that employer-sponsored health programs

- lead to better self-image through weight loss and increased fitness
- help them find time for physical activity in their complicated schedules and long commutes
- create a sense of pride about the benefits provided by the employer over those offered by another

Due to advances in fitness equipment and a growth in the number of certified fitness specialists, companies were able to introduce wellness centers in the workplace. Employees are able to shift quickly from the work environment to physical activity or therapy held during lunch periods or longer breaks.

New services of corporate wellness now include reduced membership rates to commercial gyms, dietary counseling, health fairs, and health assessments. Corporations hire wellness coordinators and instructors. Corporate challenges between groups are designed to strengthen team building and communication.

## Residential Recreation

Some forms of available recreation are tied to a person's residence. Some examples include residential care and assisted living facilities. Owners of vacation homes or time-shares may spend a great deal of their recreation time at these properties.

## Vacation Homes

Many Americans own second homes or vacation homes, often located close to major recreational activities such as lakes, mountains, and shorelines. These homes are often built in communities that have designated recreational centers staffed by recreation programmers.

## Time-Shares

A **time-share** is part ownership in a vacation development, which gives the share owner the right to accommodations on the premises for specific periods each year. Several people will share ownership of the same property and take turns staying there at different times, **17-15**. The time-share or vacation home-sharing program has become very popular in the past 40 years. This period coincides with greater economic development and increased travel and leisure time by a growing segment of the population. In the U.S. alone, there are currently over 1,600 time-share resorts with over 150,000 units.

Many of these resorts are located at national and international tourist destinations and are often connected with popular resorts. Major hotel chains such as Marriott, Hyatt, Hilton, and Wyndam also participate in this business segment. RCI, one of the largest time-share networks in the world, facilitates exchange vacations for 4 million owners at 4,000 resorts in 100 countries.

Guests enjoy access to a wide variety of recreational activities, including swimming pools, ski slopes, tennis courts, beaches, health clubs, and golf courses. These services are staffed with a growing number of specialists, certified specialists, and trainers.

## Residential Care and Assisted Living Centers

People are not only living longer, but more importantly, they desire to be active later in life. There are over 2,500 residential care and assisted living facilities in the United States. Many older adults who seek more activity-filled days leave their homes and move to residential care facilities. These homes offer a wide range of living situations within well-maintained, well-protected environments.

To attract residents, residential care facilities compete with one another to offer an ever-growing array of activities and programs that will keep their members' days active and creative, **17-16**. Some homes include pools, health spas, golf courses, and a wide array of low-impact recreation such as walking trails and gyms. Specialized classes include yoga, Pilates, and dance. Recreation centers employ staffs that have unique skills they can share with new enthusiasts.

# Special Events

Special events are unique, singular happenings that create memories. These events might include family and friends participating in a community fun run, a neighborhood barbecue, or a birthday or anniversary celebration. The event can be active and of a personal nature, taking place at someone's home or in the community.

Businesses and corporations sponsor events as marketing to their customers. Conventions are

**17-16** Older adults remain active through recreation such as Pilates classes offered at residential care facilities.

*Robert Kneschke/Shutterstock.com*

**17-15** A Florida beachfront time-share offers a wealth of fun activities.

*Ivan Cholakov/Shutterstock.com*

a type of event that promotes business-to-business relationships. Many different positions do the work of special events, including event managers, planners, or coordinators.

# Entertainment

In the broadest sense, entertainment is an event or activity that is designed to amuse or interest an audience. As people seek to relax during their nonwork hours, they develop special interests. In the entertainment area, a person's participation is more passive. Examples include attending a music festival, viewing fireworks at a theme park, or even seeing a highly anticipated movie, **17-17**. Entertainment allows them to spend time with family and friends.

## Movie Theaters

Although many people enjoy watching movies at home, there is still a strong demand to see movies in a theater. The theater experience allows viewers to take in the full effect of a film. Many people see going to the movies as a social experience. Some families like to go to the movies on certain holidays or during a family night out.

Because there are so many other choices, theaters have started a trend of providing a more complete experience. This innovation consists of upscale dining along with more comfortable seating in family or group 'pods.' This new product creates a VIP experience, one where Maslow's needs are met. This type of theater requires a well-trained chef, exceptional waitstaff, and experienced management.

## Attractions

Many people spend their leisure time recreating by participating in local, regional, and national attractions. A temporary attraction may be a state fair. In early days, state fairs had the aim of bringing new goods and services and improved farming techniques to people who did not have the ability to travel long distances.

Another area of interest is visiting museums, which has roots in Ancient Greece. The Greeks used the word *mouseion* for a place dedicated for

**17-17** What is your favorite form of entertainment?

pjhpix/Shutterstock.com

study and the arts. Today, there are over 17,500 museums in the United States. Museums may be dedicated to a theme such as history, art, sports, people, and places.

## Gaming

Games are one of the earliest forms of relaxation. Today, games enjoyed in childhood gradually give way to more sophisticated games as people mature. Many still enjoy playing board games, with or without children, as they grow into adulthood.

### Video Games

Video games are played on consoles, handheld devices, and personal computers. The controls may be handheld with buttons for inputs, or motion detectors may be used to sense the player's movements. Some controls use a combination of the two types of inputs. Some games are played online using the Internet, either through a subscription or for free. In many types of online gaming, a player can interact with numerous other players around the world. These games are often called *massively multiplayer online (MMO)* games.

Players may set up a local area network (LAN) within one room to play an online game without using the Internet. These setups are often called *LAN parties.*

### Casinos

Games of chance are a very old form of recreation. Some people enjoy betting on all types of risks. Others play in the hope of winning more money than was used to place the bet. Today, casinos are a significant part of American entertainment. Many of the largest casino destinations, such as Las Vegas, combine entertainment, live performances, unique shopping, golf, and spa packages with gaming.

## Hobbies

The list of hobbies that people have is as long as their number of interests. Hobbies may grow into professional careers, adult interests, or stay simply lifelong hobbies. These activities help people express themselves and obtain enjoyment during their leisure time, **17-18**. Examples of hobbies include collecting, crafting, reading, and playing an instrument.

**17-18** Dancers often experience enjoyment and self-actualization from their hobby.

CREATISTA/Shutterstock.com

Less intensive yet still rewarding activities include pursuing small group interests, such as a treasure hunt based on satellite coordinates. Group interests often attract a strong following, occasionally even leading to the creation of subcultures.

## Shopping

Some people see shopping itself as a recreational activity. These people may enjoy walking around a mall, browsing, observing fashion trends, or comparing prices. Shopping may be a social activity when it is shared with friends.

Because recreation is freely chosen in leisure time, the activities become especially memorable. To add value to shared experiences, many people purchase collectibles or souvenirs at these destinations to imprint the memory. This need is apparent at all kinds of attractions where retail products are available for purchase in gift shops. Often the products are also available online.

# Careers in Recreation

Are you an active person? How active would you like to be on the job? The field of recreation often attracts people who do not want a sedentary job such as sitting at an office desk all day. They would like employment that involves more activity. Recreation professionals have the opportunity to be active. They also like to help others to be active and have a good quality of life.

Every person in the recreation area requires some similar characteristics. These include leadership qualities and the desire to be part of a team that provides memorable experiences for people, whether in the social, entertainment, or business areas.

If you are interested in a career in recreation, you could start by volunteering in your own community. Local festivals and events always require the help of volunteers. You could also gain valuable experience by volunteering with recreation agencies. The NPS offers seasonal jobs and internships that help students discover their career interests. You might also consider volunteering to work at a national park and know that you are helping to conserve lands.

## Volunteers-in-Parks

A VIP is a very important person, and in this case, one who *volunteers-in-parks*. Becoming a VIP is a great way to see if you would like to pursue a career that involves parks. More than 2.5 million people have volunteered. Below are some of the activities in which volunteers are involved:

- work at an information desk answering visitor questions
- present living history demonstrations in period costume
- give guided nature walks and evening campfire programs
- maintain trails and build boardwalks
- design computer programs or park websites
- serve on bike, horseback, or beach patrol

## Recreation Professionals

If you have ever been to summer camp or taken swimming lessons at a local pool, you have likely been supervised or instructed by a recreation professional. Recreation professionals work in a variety of settings from city parks and recreation departments to outdoor education schools.

Summer jobs as a day camp counselor or lifeguard are excellent starts to a career in recreation. While entry-level jobs in recreation do not necessarily require a degree, you will find that recreation programmers and supervisors generally need a degree, **17-19**.

### Recreation Degrees

Two-year or four-year recreation degrees are offered at many universities. Four-year degrees may be available in Parks Recreation and Tourism, Recreation and Leisure Services, or Outdoor Recreation and Tourism programs. Recreation

**17-19** Jeron Gates achieved a degree in sports management on his path to becoming Senior Coordinator for Seattle Parks and Recreation.

*Photo courtesy of Washington Recreation & Park Association*

degree programs at some universities are accredited by the *National Recreation and Parks Association (NRPA)*. Through NRPA, individuals can earn certifications such as the *Certified Parks and Recreation Professional (CPRP)*. Certifications are a combination of education and experience.

With a four-year degree and experience, you could qualify for the following types of positions:

- Recreation supervisor at the community center of a municipal parks and recreation department
- Nature center supervisor at an outdoor education center
- Special events coordinator at a tourist attraction or theme park
- Recreation programmer or assistant cruise director on a cruise ship

## Job Skills

In job ads, the skills in demand for recreation positions most often include

- ability to program recreation activities
- leadership in working with people of various ages and people with special needs
- customer-service and problem-solving skills
- certification in first aid and CPR
- knowledge of legal liability and risk-management issues
- computer skills, including Internet research and specialized software used for registering recreation users

If you wanted to work in outdoor recreation, in outdoor education, or at challenge courses, you would need additional skills. Retailers for outdoor gear and outdoor education programs are located in most states. Some retailers offer adventure travel and volunteer vacations through partnerships with volunteer programs. Instructors for outdoor education programs may also need the following:

- Applicable certification or equivalent experience in technical outdoor education
- Experience teaching or guiding outdoor education programs
- Presentation abilities
- Planning and organizational skills
- Regional knowledge of local outdoor venues and resources
- A valid driver's license with no negative incidents

## Park Staff

Park rangers and park superintendents may act as law enforcement officers, but park rangers interact more with the public. Many park maintenance workers are required since parks can receive hundreds of thousands of visitors a year. Many other types of workers operate behind the scenes. Biologists and researchers manage the natural resources. Landscape architects design parks, and trail specialists set out what visitors will see when they hike. Environmental educators and artists create exhibits that interpret the park.

## Cruise Staff

Working on a ship can be very exciting, and you can travel and see exotic ports around the world. However, you must be very adaptable, energetic, and professional to succeed at life aboard, **17-20**.

All ship staff take on extra duties that relate to safety at sea, such as complying with coast guard and public health inspections. Recreation specialists manage special programs for different age groups. Cruise lines may require their recreation specialists to have a degree in recreation, tourism, or education, and work experience with children in a recreation, education, or hospitality setting. Many cruise lines offer internships in youth programs during the busy season.

Other interesting positions on cruise ships are event staff, DJ, party planner, travel guide, and

**17-20** Cruise recreation staff program theme days, such as this Australia Day celebration on January 26.

*Dorothy Chase*

shopping ambassador. A *lifestylist* may teach fitness or offer seminars that support well-being in body, mind, and spirit. Lifestylists require a recreation and wellness background.

## Resort Recreation Staff

Land resorts need to keep their guests active and satisfied just like the "floating resorts" of cruise ships. Resorts offer activities on site as well as tours to the surrounding area. Resort recreation programmers are keenly aware that a family vacation can only be successful when children and teens have activities specially designed for them. Programming is age-appropriate with options throughout the day and evening.

A full-service resort with vacation homes and rentals, such as Sun River, Oregon, offers activities for all age groups. These may include tennis, fitness activities, golf, fishing, skiing, spa treatments, gaming, canoeing, hiking, cycling, horseback riding, and swimming. You can see that this list requires many staff members, from lifeguards to ski rental technicians to massage therapists.

## Event Planning

Event managers, event planners, or event coordinators may be hired to coordinate a complete special event. These positions are responsible for many functions. If you prefer to work with detailed planning and like to see people enjoying themselves, this career area could be for you. In addition to pay, you will be rewarded by seeing your own event produced.

The more talents and skills you develop, the more useful you can be at special events. Some training in theater, interior design, fashion, or performing arts could help you create a unique and exciting stage on which to conduct your event. Great food and drink define some events. Music and visuals are important to others. You may prefer working on informal rather than formal events. You may have a definite preference for working with clients on their family social events or in working with business people on conferences, **17-21**.

The prospects for special event careers are excellent as this is a growing field. People interested in these careers can earn a Certified Special Events Professional (CSEP) designation from the

| Positions in the Special Events Industry |
|---|
| Meeting planner |
| Caterer |
| Food and beverage manager |
| Waitstaff |
| Creative director |
| Entertainment manager |
| Event planner |
| Sponsorship |
| Manager |
| Public relations |
| Exhibit director |
| Lighting designer |
| Video director |

*Goodheart-Willcox Publisher*

**17-21** Which of these opportunities in special events would most interest you?

International Special Events Society (ISES). Certifications are also awarded by other professional associations, such as the International Festivals and Events Association (IFEA) and the Meeting Planners International (MPI).

## Other Recreation Jobs

As you can imagine, many more jobs are available in the recreation area than are discussed in this text. The following are just a few more career areas that may interest you.

- *Health club staff.* Each center has a need for various types of managers, certified personal trainers, and other special skilled employees.
- *Casino staff.* Thousands of positions are needed at casinos to ensure that patrons have an enjoyable experience. Many of these positions require advanced technical training, special certifications, and hospitality skills.
- *Museum staff.* Subject experts with advanced degrees work with museum curators to create exhibits that are informative, accurate, and interesting. Museum staff provide tours, manage ticket sales, and operate gift shops and cafés.

# Chapter 17
## Review

## Chapter Summary

- Leisure time and work-life balance is important to most people.
- Leisure and recreation are important for personal renewal and restoration.
- The National Park Service manages all national park facilities and trails, national monuments, and other designated historical properties.
- People benefit through recreation with improved physical and mental health and personal development.
- Volunteerism is a strong trait shared by many Americans and has many benefits.
- Recreation programs are offered by government-run agencies or privately run businesses.
- Categories of nonprofit, recreational youth-serving agencies are secular and faith-based.
- Private agencies offer indoor and outdoor recreation to make a profit.
- Specialized recreation focuses on offering forms of recreation for the military, on college campuses, and incorporate environments.
- Special events are unique, singular activities that take place in the home or community.

- Entertainment options allow people time to spend with friends and family.
- Recreation offers a broad range of career opportunities.

## Review

1. Contrast *leisure time* with *recreation*.
2. What is work-life balance?
3. What is activity stacking and how does it relate to leisure?
4. Name three benefits of recreation and leisure.
5. Relate programming to demographics for municipal parks and recreation programs.
6. What is the process of interpretation and how does it benefit people?
7. Name three benefits of volunteerism.
8. What are four common characteristics of nonprofit agencies?
9. How do private agencies differ from nonprofit agencies?
10. Why are specialized forms of recreation necessary?
11. How do businesses and their employees benefit from corporate wellness programs?
12. What is residential recreation? Give an example.
13. Name two special recreational events or entertainment options available in the United States.

14. Name five types of activities you could do as a volunteer-in-parks.

15. What job skills do recreation positions often demand?

# Critical Thinking

16. **Draw conclusions.** The text states that quality of life is a person's overall satisfaction with the conditions of his or her life. Draw conclusions about the way recreation influences quality of life. Discuss your conclusions in class.

17. **Assess.** Assess your personal motivations for recreation. Make a T-chart, labeling the left column *Extrinsic* and the right column *Intrinsic*. List your personal motivations for recreation in each column. Then discuss how personal motivations can influence career choices in recreation.

18. **Analyze.** Suppose you are considering a career in recreation. Analyze what activities would you like to specialize in and what recreation area captures your interest most. Write a paragraph summary of your analysis.

19. **Evaluate.** Locate a job ad for a recreation position. Note the following information from the ad: job location, skill requirements, education requirements, and benefits offered. Evaluate the position requirements against your interests and skills. In what skills requirements do you excel? What are the areas in which you need to strengthen your skills? Do the requirements of the job align with your values for work-life balance?

# Common Core

### College and Career Readiness

20. **Reading.** Further investigate the role of the Civilian Conservation Corps (CCC) in the development of public parks and recreational facilities in the United States. How did this job-creation program influence recreation

opportunities and careers available today? Use a school-approved Web-based application to create a digital poster of your findings.

21. **Speaking.** Choose a nonprofit agency (secular or faith-based) in your area that offers recreational options. Create a list of questions about the work of the agency and volunteer options. Then use the questions to interview a person who works for or volunteers with the agency.

22. **Writing.** Investigate various special events your community sponsors. Use reliable Internet and print resources such as the local newspaper, a park and recreations guide book, or your city's website. Write a summary of the events your community offers. Identify how these events meet the needs of community members for recreation.

23. **Speaking.** Visit the website for the International Special Events Society (ISES). Review the requirements for earning the Certified Special Events Professional (CSEP) designation. What is the history of the CSEP? What are the requirements for taking the CSEP examination, including eligibility and fee requirements? Give an oral report of your findings to the class.

24. **CTE Career Readiness Practice.** Use reliable Internet or print resources to investigate issues relating to *work-life balance*. Focus on information that helps people strive for and maintain work-life balance. Read two or more articles and summarize your findings in writing. When evaluating the reliability of information, remember the following:

- **Identify author/writer credibility.** Is the author or writer well-known? Is the author/writer or publisher known for reliable fact-checking?

- **Verify the details.** Can you verify the facts from other reliable sources? Is the information current?

- **Identify bias.** Is the information presented from only one point of view?

# Part Five
# The Business of Hospitality

331

332

# Chapter *18*
## Business Basics

## Chapter Objectives

After studying this chapter, you will be able to
- **describe** the three forms of business ownership.
- **explain** what a franchise is.
- **list** and describe the five functions of management.
- **assess** an organizational chart.
- **explain** the three levels of management.
- **differentiate between** revenue centers and support centers.

## Before You Read

Try to answer the following questions before you read this chapter.
- What is the difference between a partnership and a corporation?
- What functions are fulfilled by managers?

## Terms to Know

| | | |
|---|---|---|
| sole proprietorship | hired management | controlling |
| sole proprietor | planning | upper management |
| partnership | plan | supervisory management |
| partners | operations | middle management |
| corporation | operations manual | reporting relationship |
| stock | organizing | profit |
| stockholders | authority | revenue |
| manager | organizational chart | revenue center |
| management | staffing | support center |
| owner-managed business | leading | |

Hospitality businesses are like any other business. They have one or more owners. They must be managed, organized, and run efficiently. They have activities that directly bring in revenue and other activities that support the activities that bring in revenue. They must be run legally and ethically. This chapter will discuss some of the basics of business structure and organization.

# Business Structure

All businesses have structure based on the number of units, the form of ownership, and management.

## *Units*

A business can be either a single unit or multiple units. A single-unit business is called an *independent business*. Multiple-unit businesses can be either *chains* or *franchises*.

## *Ownership*

Ownership refers to who owns the business. There are only three forms of ownership: sole proprietorship, partnership, and corporation, **18-1**.

*Sole* means *only one*. A **sole proprietorship** is the form of ownership in which only one person owns the business. That one person, the **sole proprietor**, is responsible for the entire business. He or she makes all the decisions and is responsible for all the problems. The sole proprietor also gets all the profits from the business. Small businesses, such as small restaurants and bed-and-breakfasts, are often sole proprietorships.

A **partnership** is the form of ownership in which two or more people own the business. The people who are involved in a partnership are called **partners**, and they sign a legal agreement to share responsibility for the business. The partners share the profits based on the percentages in the legal agreement. Any hospitality business can be a partnership.

*Goodheart-Willcox Publisher*

**18-1** The three forms of business ownership are sole proprietorship, partnership, and corporation.

A corporation is a more complicated form of ownership. A sole proprietorship or a partnership consists of the people who own the business. A corporation is actually an artificial person created by law to act as a business. This artificial person is called a *legal entity*. A **corporation** is a legal entity established for the purpose of doing business. In order for a corporation to be established, the people who want to start the corporation apply for a legal document called a *charter* or *certificate of incorporation*. These documents are available from a state government. All corporations are established through documents from a state government, **18-2**.

As a legal entity, a corporation is responsible for all the actions of the business. A corporation can buy property, run a business, manufacture products, earn money, lose money, sue, and be sued. A corporation can even buy businesses and other corporations. As a legal entity, the corporation is separate from the people who own it. The owners are not liable for the actions of the corporation. The corporation is liable for its actions.

People who own stock in a corporation are the corporation's owners. The value of a corporation is divided into equal units called shares of stock. **Stock** is the right of partial ownership in a corporation. People who own stock in a corporation are called **stockholders**. The stockholders are the ones who actually own the corporation and get the profits from the business based on the number of shares they own.

There are several types of corporations. In a *private* (also called *closely held*) corporation, only one or a few people own the stocks. The stocks are not publicly sold. In a publicly traded corporation, the corporation's stocks are sold on the stock market to the public. Anyone can buy a share of a publicly traded corporation. For example, shares of McDonald's, which is a publically traded corporation, are sold on the New York Stock Exchange.

There are two major advantages to the corporate form of ownership. First, a corporation can raise a great deal of money by selling stock. Because it can raise a great deal of money, a corporation can grow to be very large.

Second, the stockholders are not liable for the actions of the corporation in the same way that the sole proprietor and partners are liable for their businesses. Suppose you are a customer. You eat at Restaurant X, get a foodborne illness, and sue the restaurant. You win your suit, and the court awards you *damages*—an amount of money, such as $50,000. The restaurant must pay the damages. If Restaurant X is owned by a sole proprietor, the sole proprietor is *liable* (responsible) for the damages and must pay the $50,000. If Restaurant X is owned by a partnership, the partners themselves are liable for the damages and must pay the $50,000. If Restaurant X is owned by a corporation, the corporation is responsible for the damages, which are taken from the corporation's income. The stockholders are not sued and do not pay the damages. The only money that a stockholder can lose is the money that he or she paid to buy the stock.

Businesses of all sizes can be corporations. However, the corporate form of ownership is particularly beneficial to large companies and companies that want to become large. Many hospitality businesses are among the largest corporations in the world. Examples include The Walt Disney Company, McDonald's Corporation, and Marriott International.

| Differences Among Ownership Structures | | | | |
|---|---|---|---|---|
| **Type of Ownership** | **Number of Individuals** | **Liability** | **Ease of Starting** | **Cost to Start** |
| *Sole Proprietorship* | One | Total | Easy | Low |
| *Partnership* | Two or more | Total | Easy | Low |
| *Corporation* | One or more | Limited | Complex | High |

*Goodheart-Willcox Publisher*

18-2 Each ownership structure has advantages and disadvantages.

## Management

The two basic types of work that must be done in a business are the work itself and decision making. For example, in a restaurant, the actual work includes making and serving food. Decisions about the work include what work should be done and how it should be done. In a restaurant, those decisions would include what should be on the menu, the hours the restaurant should be open, and which servers should work at what times. A person who makes decisions for a business is called a **manager**, **18-3**. The **management** of a business consists of the team of people who make decisions for the business.

Imagine a sole proprietorship in which the owner is the only worker. The sole proprietor does all the functions of a manager, makes all the decisions, and does all the work. When a business hires workers, then the business needs management.

The two basic forms of management are owner-managed and hired management. In an **owner-managed business**, the owner, whether sole proprietor, partnership, or corporation, is the manager. The owner makes all the decisions for the business. The owner will hire workers to help run the business and may even hire additional managers to help with the decision making. However, the final decisions rest with the owner.

In businesses with **hired management**, the owner hires a person or a company to manage the business. The owner may give the hired management business goals, but the hired management makes the decisions about how to reach the goals. For example, suppose you have money to invest. You decide to buy a restaurant. However, you do not know anything about running a restaurant and you are not really interested in learning. You can hire a manager to run your restaurant for you. You will still be the owner, but your manager will run the restaurant day-to-day, **18-4**.

## Chains and Franchises

Chains and franchises are multiple-unit businesses. A *chain* is a business with multiple units but one name and one owner. However, that one owner could be a sole proprietor, a partnership, or a corporation. The owner of a restaurant chain will usually hire a manager for each unit of the restaurant. This situation is considered owner-managed because the hired managers report to the owner. The owner of a hotel chain will hire either a manager or a hotel management company for each unit. The profits earned by each unit of the chain go to the chain's owner. The hotel owner who hires a hotel management company has hired management.

A *franchise* is a unit of a chain that has a different owner. The chain still has one owner, but individual units of the chain can be owned by different owners. The franchise is part of the chain, uses the chain's name, and sells the chain's products. The franchisee owns his or her unit, but is not independent. The franchisee follows the rules of the chain. The franchisor (the owner of the chain) usually has a say in most of the decisions that the franchisee makes. For example, a restaurant franchisor usually decides what menu items the franchisee can serve. The franchisee usually pays a percentage of the profits to the franchisor and keeps the rest of the profits, **18-5**.

In the lodging industry, the relationship among chain, franchise, ownership, and management can get very complicated. A brief example will give you an idea of the situation. Hilton Hotels Corporation is a corporation that owns, manages, and franchises hotels and resorts all over the world. Hilton Hotels owns resorts such as the Waldorf Astoria, the Cavalieri Hilton in Rome, the Hilton Waikoloa Village, and the Hilton Omaha. Hilton brands include Conrad Hotels, Doubletree, Embassy Suites Hotels, Hampton Inns & Suites,

**18-3** A manager has the responsibility of decision making in a business.

*Yuri Arcurs/Shutterstock.com*

| Management Structures | |
|---|---|
| **Owner** (sole proprietorship, partnership, or corporation) | |
| **Owner-Managed** | **Hired Management** |
| • Owner makes all decisions for the business.<br>• Owner hires and fires.<br>• Owner gets all profits. | • Owner determines goals.<br>• Owner gets profits.<br>• Hired management decides how to reach goals.<br>• Hired management hires and fires. |

*Goodheart-Willcox Publisher*

18-4  A business may be owner-managed or have hired management.

| Relationship of Chains and Franchises | | |
|---|---|---|
| **Chain-Owner** | **Franchisor** (owner of a chain who sells franchises) | **Franchisee** (owner of a unit of a franchise) |
| Owns all units of chain. | May or may not own some units of chain. | Owns one or a small number of units of chain. |
| Owns name, products, and services of chain. | Owns name, products, and services of chain. | Pays for the rights to use the name, products, and services of the chain. |
| Sets the procedures and standards for the chain. | Sets the procedures and standards for the chain. | Must follow the procedures and standards set by the franchisor. |
| Hires a manager for each unit of the chain. | Does not manage franchised units. May inspect units to make sure that units meet requirements of the franchise agreement. | Franchisee usually manages his or her unit. |
| Gets all profits from all units of the chain. | Does not get profits from franchised units. Gets fees from each franchisee. | Franchisee gets profits from each unit franchised. Must pay fees to franchisor. |

*Goodheart-Willcox Publisher*

18-5  Chains and franchises are both multiple-unit businesses that have some similarities, but also some differences.

Hilton Hotels, Hilton Garden Inn, and Homewood Suites by Hilton. There are over 500 Hilton hotels worldwide.

Hilton franchises buy the right to use the Hilton name, and they must meet all Hilton requirements. Some Hilton Hotels are both owned and managed by Hilton. Other hotels, such as the Red Lion Hotel in Denver, Colorado, and the Inn at Virginia Tech and Skelton Conference Center in Blacksburg, Virginia, are managed by Hilton.

Wyndham Hotels and Resorts owns and manages most of its hotels. These hotels have the Wyndham name on them. The Wyndham Cleveland is owned by the Playhouse Square Foundation, but the hotel is managed by Wyndham Hotels and Resorts, **18-6**.

| Three Management Structures of Wyndham Hotels | | |
| --- | --- | --- |
| **Wyndham Hotels** | **Wyndham Franchises** | **Wyndham Management** |
| • Owned by Wyndham<br>• Managed by Wyndham<br>• Workers report to Wyndham | • Owned by franchisee<br>• Franchisee pays for the right to use the Wyndham name<br>• Must meet Wyndham requirements<br>• Workers in the franchise report to the franchisee, not Wyndham | • Owned by non-Wyndham owner<br>• Owner hires Wyndham to manage the hotel<br>• Wyndham name on hotel<br>• Workers in the hotel report to Wyndham<br>• Owner can decide to get rid of Wyndham; then the Wyndham name and all the workers would leave, and the owner would hire another hotel management company |

*Goodheart-Willcox Publisher*

**18-6** The relationship between management and ownership structure can be complex.

# Management Functions

The major responsibility of management is to make decisions. However, there is more to management than just making decisions. Management has five major functions: planning, organizing, staffing, leading, and controlling. Decision making is part of all these functions.

## *Planning*

Planning is the foundation of any business. **Planning** consists of setting goals and developing methods to meet those goals. A **plan** is a record of the decisions made about the goals and the methods to meet them. Planning must begin before the business is even established.

Planning has three time frames: before the business is started, day-to-day, and for the future. Before a business is started, management has to decide on the concept of the business, the decor, the level and style of service, the location, and many other details. Management has to figure out how to finance the business, how many employees will be needed, and how to market the business. These decisions are recorded in a document called a *business plan*.

The day-to-day planning is the actual running of the business, which is often called **operations**. A business plan often includes an operations plan, which is sometimes called an *operations manual*. An **operations manual** is a book that includes all the details about how to run the business. It may include items such as how many servers are required for the breakfast shift.

Future planning helps the business decide how to grow and how to keep up with changes, **18-7**. Plans for the future are often made for a specific time span, such as a five-year plan and a ten-year plan.

Planning has two levels: overall and specific. Overall planning concerns goals for the entire organization. For example, an independent business will plan goals for the whole business. A corporation will plan goals for the overall corporation. A chain will plan goals for the entire chain. The overall plan for an independent restaurant might be to renovate the kitchen. The overall plan for a hotel

**18-7** Planning is an important function of the management team.

*AVAVA/Shutterstock.com*

# *Hospitality Ethics*

## Ethics and Employee Theft

How does employee theft occur in the hospitality business? The following are just a few examples:

- cheating on hours worked, such as asking another employee to log you in/out or punch your time card
- taking food, supplies, or other products from the establishment
- not charging customers for food or beverage products with the hope of increasing tips
- taking guest belongings from their rooms

In *all* circumstances, employee theft is wrong and dishonest. Theft is a violation of the employer, and also of personal ethics for right behavior and moral obligation. Employee theft is grounds for termination of employment.

chain might be to open new hotels in a foreign country. The overall plan for a restaurant might be to open franchises.

Specific plans concern how to accomplish specific goals. The overall plan to renovate the kitchen will be broken down into specific plans for how the renovation will be done, including whether to close the restaurant during the renovations. The specific plans for new hotels will include the business plan for the specific new hotel in the specific country.

## *Organizing*

Once the planning is done, organizing and staffing can take place. **Organizing** consists of designing the internal structure of the business. Sometimes staffing is considered part of organizing. Sometimes organizing and staffing are called *implementing*. Organizing and staffing involve turning the plans into reality. This text addresses organizing and staffing as two separate functions.

To organize the business, the manager will study the tasks that need to be done and decide how to use employees to do them in the most efficient way. Organizing a business often involves dividing up the tasks to be done into divisions and departments and then hiring managers to manage and organize. Managers study the tasks that need to be done and decide how to use employees to accomplish goals.

One of the most important aspects of organizing is the delegation of authority. When an independent sole proprietorship is started, one person—the owner—has all the authority. In business, **authority** is the power to make decisions and to tell other workers what to do. As the business grows, there is more and more work to do. Because the owner cannot do it all, he or she hires workers to do some of the work. To *delegate authority* means to give some of your authority to another person. The sole proprietor must delegate some authority to the workers so they can do their jobs. As the business grows larger and larger, more and more workers are hired. Eventually the owner has to organize the business into departments and hire a manager to manage each department. The owner must delegate some of his or her authority to the managers so they can do their jobs.

The organization of a business is recorded in its organizational chart, **18-8**. An **organizational chart** shows how the tasks of the business are organized and who performs these tasks. The organizational chart also shows the levels of authority and responsibility.

## *Staffing*

Once the business is organized, people have to be hired to do the jobs. **Staffing** consists of all the activities involved in hiring and keeping workers.

## Generic Organizational Chart

**General Manager**
Responsible for
whole company

**Manager Department A**
Responsible for all
Department A tasks

**Manager Department B**
Responsible for all
Department B tasks

**Manager Department C**
Responsible for all
Department C tasks

**Worker A-1**
Responsible for
all A-1 tasks

**Worker A-2**
Responsible for
all A-2 tasks

**Worker A-3**
Responsible for
all A-3 tasks

**Worker B-1**
Responsible for
all B-1 tasks

**Worker B-2**
Responsible for
all B-2 tasks

**Worker B-3**
Responsible for
all B-3 tasks

**Worker C-1**
Responsible for
all C-1 tasks

**Worker C-2**
Responsible for
all C-2 tasks

**Worker C-3**
Responsible for
all C-3 tasks

*Goodheart-Willcox Publisher*

**18-8** An organizational chart illustrates levels of authority, reporting, and task responsibility.

People often think of the staffing function when they think about what managers do. Staffing includes recruiting, hiring, training, scheduling, evaluating, and compensating. *Recruiting* is the process of looking for qualified workers. *Hiring* is the process of learning about job applicants and deciding whether to offer them a job. *Training* is providing specific education to help workers do their jobs. *Scheduling* is deciding which workers perform which tasks at what times. *Evaluating* consists of determining whether a worker is doing a good job, providing guidance to help workers do better jobs, and firing workers who are doing inadequate jobs. *Compensating* is determining how much each worker should be paid and providing a benefits package.

## Leading

**Leading** consists of influencing people to accomplish the goals of the business. The function of leading is sometimes called *directing*. The process of leading is often called *leadership*. Leading includes

motivating people, creating a positive work atmosphere, communicating clearly, and giving feedback. Leading also includes listening to coworkers and solving problems.

## Controlling

**Controlling** is making sure that the business accomplishes what it set out to accomplish. If the business is not meeting its goals, management must then take corrective steps. Controlling usually consists of five steps:
- setting measurable goals
- measuring results
- comparing results with goals
- if needed, finding out why results fall short of goals
- taking corrective action

For example, a goal might be for a room attendant to clean 20 rooms per shift. The manager counts how many rooms each attendant cleans per shift and finds that each attendant cleans only 15 rooms. The manager will then investigate why it is taking longer to clean the rooms. The manager may discover that the room attendants are spending too much time running back and forth to the supply room. The manager will then work with the room attendants and develop a way to cut down on the number of times each attendant returns to the supply room. Options might include purchasing larger, more efficient carts that hold more supplies or better planning and organizing supplies on the existing housekeeping carts.

# Management Levels

Managers have different amounts of responsibility. Some managers have more responsibility and more authority than other managers. For example, look again at the organizational chart in Figure 18-8, which shows two levels of management. The general manager has the most responsibility and authority. He or she is responsible for the whole company. The second level of management in this chart is the manager of each department. Manager A is responsible for only the tasks that department A does. Manager A is responsible for all the workers in department A and the work that they do. Manager A knows about the work in departments B and C. Manager A probably works with the managers and workers in departments B and C. However, Manager A is not responsible for these other departments. Manager A also does not have the authority to tell workers in departments B or C what to do.

In general, there are three levels of management: upper management, middle management, and supervisory management. Smaller companies have only two levels: upper and supervisory. Larger companies may have more levels of management in the middle.

**Upper management** is the top level of management. It is also called *top management*. In very large companies with many levels of management, upper management is often called *executive management* or *senior management*. Upper management is responsible for the entire company. Upper managers perform the five management functions for the whole company. In Figure 18-8, the general manager is upper management.

**Supervisory management** is the level that is closest to the workers. People in supervisory management may be called *managers* or *supervisors*. They are responsible for a specific department or area of work. They perform the five functions of management for their specific department or area. In Figure 18-8, the department managers are supervisory management.

Larger companies need more levels of management, **18-9**. **Middle management** consists of one or more levels of management between the top level and the supervisory level. For example, think of a restaurant chain that has locations around the country. Each restaurant needs a general manager and the restaurant and kitchen managers. If the restaurant is an independent business, the general manager would be the top level and the restaurant and kitchen managers would be the supervisory levels. However, a chain needs another level of management. The restaurants in the chain might be organized into regions, and each region will have a manager. This manager might be called a *regional vice president*. The regional vice president is responsible for all the restaurants in his or her region. In this situation, the regional vice presidents and the president of the company are the top management. The general managers of each restaurant become the middle level of management. The restaurant and kitchen managers are the supervisory levels. The servers, bussers, cashiers, cooks, and dishwashers are the workers.

Organizational charts show levels of management and the department for which each manager is responsible. The charts also show the reporting relationships. A **reporting relationship** specifies which manager a worker reports to. In order for business to work in an orderly way, each worker reports to only one manager. That one manager is responsible for that worker and is the only one with authority to tell that worker what to do. If the worker has a question, he or she goes to the manager he or she reports to. In Figure 18-8, workers A-1, A-2, and A-3 all report to the manager of department A. Similarly, workers B-1, B-2, and B-3 report to the manager of department B. The three managers report to the general manager. In a large corporation, there are many levels of management and many managers. Each worker must know which manager he or she reports to, **18-10**.

In addition, because large corporations are very complex, some managers may have a dotted line reporting relationship with a second manager. In a *dotted line reporting relationship*, a manager also reports to a second manager in addition to his or her main manager. For example, in a large hotel, the director of catering may be part of the banquet

## Levels of Management

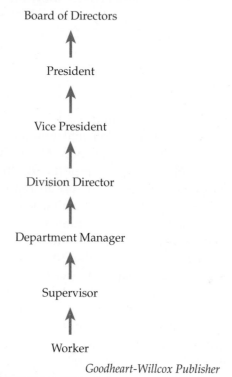

*Goodheart-Willcox Publisher*

**18-9** Large corporations have three management levels: top (executive), middle managers, and supervisors.

## Reporting Relationships in a Large Corporation

Board of Directors

↑

President

↑

Vice President

↑

Division Director

↑

Department Manager

↑

Supervisor

↑

Worker

*Goodheart-Willcox Publisher*

**18-10** This organizational chart shows the reporting relationships of a large corporation.

division and report to the banquet director. The director of catering may also have a dotted line reporting relationship with the director of sales. The reason for this extra reporting relationship is that in order to do the best job, the catering department and the sales departments must work together.

# Organization of Hospitality Businesses

Restaurants usually have two main divisions: the front-of-the-house and the back-of-the-house. Restaurants may also have a division for administrative functions. This division may include departments for human resources, marketing and sales, accounting, and engineering/maintenance.

The two main divisions in a hotel are the rooms division and the food and beverage division. A hotel may have separate divisions or departments for security, marketing and sales, purchasing and receiving, human resources, accounting, and engineering/maintenance.

A small hospitality business run by a sole proprietor, such as a travel agency, is not usually organized into departments. Larger businesses are organized into departments and divisions.

Each unit of a multiple-unit business will have its internal organization of divisions and departments. In addition, these units will be organized for easier management. Usually the organization is based on geography. The major divisions are domestic and international. The domestic division is usually divided into regions of the country or by states while the international division is divided by country.

In addition, a multiple-unit business will have a corporate headquarters. A *corporate headquarters* is the division of the company where tasks that relate to the entire company are handled. The executive managers and any divisions that do work for the entire company are located there. For example, the headquarters of McDonald's is in Oak Brook, Illinois. About 2,800 employees work there. Some of the tasks they handle include accounting, customer satisfaction, distribution, engineering, franchising, human resources, legal, marketing, media relations, product development, purchasing, quality assurance, and real estate. McDonald's headquarters is also the location of Hamburger University, McDonald's management training center. Since 1961, more than 80,000 restaurant managers, mid-managers, and owner/operators of McDonald's restaurants have graduated from Hamburger University.

# Revenue and Support Centers

Every business wants to make a profit. **Profit** is the money a business has left after all the costs of running the business are paid. Businesses have a wide variety of costs. For example, a business must pay for the building, electricity, heating, water, supplies, equipment, workers' salaries, insurance, and telecommunications services. Businesses take in money for the products they sell. All the money that a business takes in for the products and services it sells is called **revenue**. Revenue is also called *sales*.

Profit is equal to revenue minus costs. For example, suppose a restaurant sells $750,000 worth of meals in a year. The restaurant's revenue for that year is $750,000. Suppose the costs to run that restaurant for the year are $675,000. That $675,000

pays for the salaries of all the servers, bussers, hosts, cooks, dishwashers, and managers. It covers the cost of the rent or mortgage on the restaurant building, electricity, and other utilities. It also covers the costs of all food and equipment purchased to make the meals. Profit for the restaurant for that year is $75,000. Figure **18-11** shows the calculation. The profit goes to the owner of the business.

## Revenue Centers

Divisions and departments of a business are often categorized as revenue centers or support centers. A **revenue center** is a division or department that sells products that bring in revenue. In a restaurant, the front-of-the-house is the revenue center. In a hotel, the rooms division and the food and beverage division are revenue centers. In a hotel, the gift shop, golf course, and spa are also revenue centers. In a travel agency, the front office where travel packages are sold is the revenue center.

## Support Centers

A **support center** is a division or department that does not make revenue directly. Support centers are sometimes referred to as *cost centers*. Support centers provide services that enable the revenue centers to make money. Without the support centers, the revenue centers could not function. In a restaurant, the back-of-the-house is a support center. The back-of-the-house includes all the workers who make the food and the workers who handle purchasing and receiving. In a hotel, the support centers include security and housekeeping. In travel and tourism, support staff might include computer programmers who write software. Departments that support most hospitality businesses include human resources, marketing and sales, and accounting.

| What Is Profit? |
| --- |
| Profit = Revenue – Costs |
| Profit = $750,000 – $675,000 |
| Profit = $75,000 |

*Goodheart-Willcox Publisher*

**18-11** Profit is equal to revenue minus costs.

# Chapter *18*
## Review

## Chapter Summary

- The three forms of ownership are sole proprietorship, partnership, and corporation.
- Two basic types of work that must be done in a business are the work itself and decision making.
- A franchise is a unit of a chain that has a different owner.
- Management has five major functions: planning, organizing, staffing, leading, and controlling. Decision making is part of all these functions.
- In general, there are three levels of management: upper management, middle management, and supervisory management.
- A revenue center is a division or department that sells products that bring in revenue.
- Support centers provide services that enable the revenue centers to make money.

## Review

1. Explain the differences among the three forms of business ownership.
2. Who owns a corporation?
3. What are the two major advantages to the corporate form of ownership?
4. Describe the two basic types of work that must be done in a business.
5. Explain the differences between owner-managed and hired management.
6. Explain the differences between chains and franchises.
7. Describe each of the five major functions of management.
8. Why do businesses develop an organizational chart?
9. List and describe the three levels of management.
10. What is the function of a corporate headquarters in a multiple-unit business?
11. What is a revenue center?
12. What is a support center?

# Critical Thinking

13. **Predict.** If you were starting an independent restaurant, what form of ownership would you choose? Explain your reasons.

14. **Compare and contrast.** How is your school like a unit in a franchise? How are they different?

15. **Identify.** What activities are involved in staffing a restaurant?

16. **Analyze.** Why is planning the foundation of any hospitality business? Explain your reasoning.

17. **Draw conclusions.** Explain why a corporation is a more complicated form of business ownership.

18. **Determine.** If you were the new manager at a restaurant that needed to work on controlling costs, what are the first steps you would take?

 **Common Core**

**College and Career Readiness**

19. **Speaking.** Form two teams and debate the following statement: Support centers are less important to a business than revenue centers because support centers do not bring in money.

20. **Writing.** Imagine that you have just been promoted to the position of executive housekeeper in a medium-sized hotel. Write a summary of the first steps you would take to become an effective leader of your department.

21. **Speaking.** Research the franchise rules of a hotel chain of your choice. Create an electronic presentation detailing the rules that must be followed by a franchisor of the chain. Share the presentation with your class.

22. **Listening.** Interview a local hotel manager about the organization of the business's internal structure. Take detailed notes during the interview and, after the interview, prepare a written summary using the notes.

23. **CTE Career Readiness Practice.** Read the *Hospitality Ethics* features presented throughout this book. What role do you think that ethics and integrity have in decision making? Think of a time when you used your ideals and principles to make a decision. What process did you use to make the decision? In retrospect, do you think you made the correct decision? Did your decision have any consequences? How do ethics and integrity relate to decisions managers make in business?

346

# Chapter 19

## Hospitality Management

## Chapter Objectives

After studying this chapter, you will be able to

- **list** four basic duties of a hospitality manager.
- **state** the main responsibility of a general manager.
- **list** the eight tasks of managers.
- **assess** ways that managers control costs.
- **describe** the four main tasks of managing human resources.
- **list** seven management skills.
- **compare and contrast** the four styles of management.

## Before You Read

Try to answer the following questions before you read this chapter.

- What skills do effective managers need?
- What are some different styles of management?

## Terms to Know

general manager
managing director
mystery shopper
budget
employee personnel files
entry-level worker

supervisor
employee evaluation
performance review
performance appraisal
autocratic style

bureaucratic style
democratic style
laissez-faire style
motivated worker
organizational skills

Every hospitality operation has a manager who is responsible for the entire operation of the unit. Hospitality chains have district and regional managers who supervise several units.

The basic duties in hospitality management include

- welcoming customers
- producing products and services that meet customer needs
- protecting customers from being harmed while at the business
- selling products and services in a profitable and legal way

In addition, managers have many other duties and tasks. Examples include setting goals, supervising workers, cutting costs, and marketing the business.

# The General Manager

The **general manager** is the person responsible for the entire operation of one unit of a hospitality business. The general manager is also sometimes called the **managing director**. In addition to management, general managers usually have knowledge and experience in advertising, sales, marketing, design, engineering, finance, accounting, and sanitation and safety. Restaurant general managers usually have training in nutrition, a certificate in sanitation, and experience in foodservice operations. General managers of hotels often have experience in the rooms division. The general manager is usually the top level of management in a single-unit hospitality business, such as an independent travel agency. In multiple-unit businesses, there will be executive management above the general manager to manage several units.

In an independent business, the general manager is often the owner. In small businesses, the general manager usually performs all the management tasks. In a large business, the amount of work that needs to be done is too large for one manager to handle. The general manager delegates certain responsibilities to divisions or departments and their managers.

Figure **19-1** shows the organization of a typical large hotel with several divisions. The rooms division usually consists of four departments: front office, housekeeping, security, and engineering. In some hotels, each of these departments is its own separate division. Many hotels also have a foodservice division. Hotels may have several other divisions, such as human resources, marketing and sales, and accounting.

Each division is given specific management responsibilities. The divisions will each have a director, who reports to the general manager. The general manager is responsible for supervising the directors and making sure each division gets its job done.

The general manager delegates responsibilities to each division. The division directors are responsible for the tasks delegated to them and, in turn, delegate responsibility to the department managers in their division. The division directors

**19-1** A large hotel usually has at least five divisions. Sometimes the departments in the rooms division may be considered separate divisions.

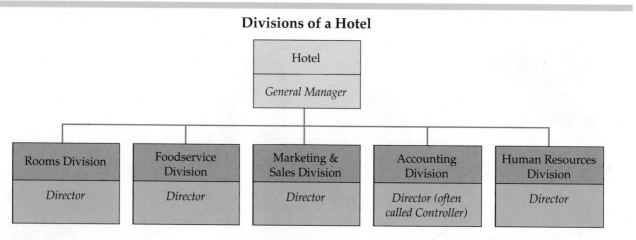

## Divisions of a Hotel

*Goodheart-Willcox Publisher*

are responsible for all the departments in their division. The division and department managers are middle level managers.

For example, the director of the rooms division will be given the responsibility for all the tasks and employees in the rooms division. In a large hotel, the amount of work that needs to be done in the rooms division is too large for one manager. To help the rooms director accomplish the tasks and supervise the employees, he or she will delegate responsibility to the departments in the rooms division. The rooms division is often divided into two departments: front office and housekeeping. The front office department and the housekeeping department will each have a manager, both of which are part of middle management. The manager of the housekeeping department is often called the *executive housekeeper*. The front office manager and the executive housekeeper report to the director of rooms. The front office manager will be responsible for all front office tasks and employees, and the executive housekeeper will be responsible for all housekeeping tasks and employees.

In a small hotel, the front office manager will directly supervise all the employees in the front office. In this case, the front office manager will be at the supervisory level of management. In larger hotels, there is too much work for the front office manager to accomplish, so he or she delegates tasks to subdepartments in the front office.

The front office is often divided into four departments: reservations, uniformed services, telecommunications, and front desk. Each department has a supervisor. The uniformed services supervisor is often called the *bell captain*. Each supervisor reports to the front office manager. Each of the supervisors supervises the employees who are doing the specific tasks. The reservations supervisor manages the reservations department and supervises the reservations agents. The bell captain manages the uniformed services department and supervises the bell attendants, door attendants, concierges, and parking valets.

The telecommunications supervisor manages the telecommunications department and supervises the operators. The front desk supervisor manages the front desk department and supervises all the front desk agents, **19-2**. The front office manager in the large hotel will be at the middle level of management. The supervisors of each subdepartment will be at the supervisory level of management.

**19-2** The front desk is just one of the departments of the front office.

*JinYoung Lee/Shutterstock.com*

# Management Tasks

Many tasks are a daily part of a hospitality manager's job. General managers and department and division managers are responsible for the following eight tasks: goal setting, customer satisfaction, cost controls, record keeping, human resources, facility maintenance, sanitation and safety, and marketing. The general manager is responsible for all these tasks for the entire operation. Division and department managers are responsible for all these tasks for their individual division or department.

## *Set Goals*

The main goal of the general manager is to make sure the business makes a profit. In order to be profitable, restaurants and hotels must meet customer expectations for quality food and quality service. The general manager must make sure that all employees—including division directors, department managers, and assistant managers—are focused on meeting the goals.

The general manager will set a goal, such as to increase profit by 1 percent. The general manager must then work with the division directors and department managers to figure out how to break that goal down for each division and department. For example, the reservations department may need to handle 20 more calls a day. The foodservice department may need to cut costs by 3 percent. The managers must figure out ways for their departments to meet these goals and set goals for their departments and each worker.

## *Oversee Customer Satisfaction*

Hospitality managers need to know if customers are satisfied with the level of service they receive. Service is increasingly becoming a method for separating the quality of one hospitality business from another.

One way to determine customer satisfaction is by the number of repeat customers the business gets. Increased sales show that customers are satisfied enough to come back again. Decreased sales show that there are problems with customer satisfaction because customers do not return.

Comment cards are another way to find out about customers' satisfaction level. Restaurants may leave comment cards on the table. Hotels often leave a comment card or a customer survey in the room, **19-3**. Many businesses now provide customer surveys on their websites.

Managers develop other ways to get feedback from their customers. One way is for the manager to talk with customers on a regular basis. Another way is to hire a mystery shopper. A **mystery shopper** is a person hired to stay anonymously at a hotel or eat at a restaurant and observe the quality. The mystery shopper then writes a detailed report on food, cleanliness, and service. The manager can use this report to see what changes or improvements are needed.

Hospitality businesses provide service to very diverse customers. In order for employees to deliver the level of service that is needed, managers must make sure that employees receive ongoing training. The training must include how to be flexible in dealing with customers and how to deal with customers from a variety of cultures. Managers also have to give employees a certain amount of authority in dealing with customer problems. For example, suppose a guest is unhappy with a restaurant meal. The server should have the authority to offer the guest another choice or take the meal charge off the bill. If the server has to get a manager's approval for every customer problem, it would take too long and be frustrating to guests.

Managers set the standards for customer service and make sure they are met. For example, a goal might be to maintain a specific score on the guest surveys. Managers should share the feedback they get from customers with employees so employees know how to improve the quality of service.

## *Control Costs*

Hospitality managers are responsible for the profitability of the hospitality business, so they seek to help increase profitability by controlling costs. Hospitality managers control costs by setting budgets; monitoring purchasing, receiving, and inventory; and looking for ways to cut costs.

### Set Budgets

The main goal of any business is to make a profit. A **budget** is a guideline for spending money. Budgets help the business monitor spending and make a profit. Each manager develops a budget for his or her departments. For example, the executive housekeeper will develop the budget for the housekeeping department and the banquet

**Holiday Inn**
HOTELS · RESORTS

**Please tell us what you think about your stay at the Holiday Inn – ANDERSON, IN**

| | Very Satisfied | Somewhat Satisfied | Neither | Somewhat Dissatisfied | Very Dissatisfied |
|---|---|---|---|---|---|
| Please rate your overall satisfaction with <u>this</u> hotel | ☐ | ☐ | ☐ | ☐ | ☐ |

| How likely would you be to... | Extremely Likely | Very Likely | Somewhat Likely | Not Very Likely | Not At All Likely |
|---|---|---|---|---|---|
| Recommend <u>this</u> hotel if you knew someone coming to this area for a similar reason? | ☐ | ☐ | ☐ | ☐ | ☐ |
| Stay at <u>this</u> hotel if you were returning to this area for a similar reason? | ☐ | ☐ | ☐ | ☐ | ☐ |

| | Much More Likely to Stay | Somewhat More Likely to Stay | No Effect | Somewhat Less Likely to Stay | Much Less Likely to Stay |
|---|---|---|---|---|---|
| How will your stay at <u>this</u> hotel influence your decision to stay at <u>other</u> Holiday Inn® hotels in the future? | ☐ | ☐ | ☐ | ☐ | ☐ |

Please rate your stay at this hotel on the following...

| | | Excellent | Very Good | Good | Fair | Poor | NOT APPLICABLE |
|---|---|---|---|---|---|---|---|
| Overall: | Overall Physical Condition of This Hotel | ☐ | ☐ | ☐ | ☐ | ☐ | ☐ |
| | Overall Service Received at This Hotel | ☐ | ☐ | ☐ | ☐ | ☐ | ☐ |
| | Value Received for Price Paid | ☐ | ☐ | ☐ | ☐ | ☐ | ☐ |
| Appearance: | Outside Appearance of Hotel | ☐ | ☐ | ☐ | ☐ | ☐ | ☐ |
| | Lobby Condition/Attractiveness | ☐ | ☐ | ☐ | ☐ | ☐ | ☐ |
| Arrival: | Service at Check-In (friendly, efficient, prompt) | ☐ | ☐ | ☐ | ☐ | ☐ | ☐ |
| | Accuracy of Room Reservation | ☐ | ☐ | ☐ | ☐ | ☐ | ☐ |
| Staff: | Responsiveness to Your Needs | ☐ | ☐ | ☐ | ☐ | ☐ | ☐ |
| | Friendliness | ☐ | ☐ | ☐ | ☐ | ☐ | ☐ |
| | Professional Attitude & Appearance | ☐ | ☐ | ☐ | ☐ | ☐ | ☐ |
| Guestroom/ Guestbath: | Overall Cleanliness | ☐ | ☐ | ☐ | ☐ | ☐ | ☐ |
| | Guestbath Facilities (amenities, hot water, etc) | ☐ | ☐ | ☐ | ☐ | ☐ | ☐ |
| | Heating/Air Conditioning (quiet, efficient, etc) | ☐ | ☐ | ☐ | ☐ | ☐ | ☐ |
| | Bed/Pillow Comfort | ☐ | ☐ | ☐ | ☐ | ☐ | ☐ |
| | Television (quality of picture, condition, etc) | ☐ | ☐ | ☐ | ☐ | ☐ | ☐ |
| | Television Channels and Movie Options | ☐ | ☐ | ☐ | ☐ | ☐ | ☐ |
| | Condition of Furniture | ☐ | ☐ | ☐ | ☐ | ☐ | ☐ |
| | Condition of Bedspread/Drapes/Carpet | ☐ | ☐ | ☐ | ☐ | ☐ | ☐ |
| | Lighting (brightness, good working order, etc) | ☐ | ☐ | ☐ | ☐ | ☐ | ☐ |
| | In-Room Working Space and Environment | ☐ | ☐ | ☐ | ☐ | ☐ | ☐ |
| | Quietness of Guest Room | ☐ | ☐ | ☐ | ☐ | ☐ | ☐ |
| Food: | Restaurant (food quality and service) | ☐ | ☐ | ☐ | ☐ | ☐ | ☐ |
| | Room Service (food quality and service) | ☐ | ☐ | ☐ | ☐ | ☐ | ☐ |
| Other: | Hotel Safety and Security | ☐ | ☐ | ☐ | ☐ | ☐ | ☐ |
| | Telephone Services (wake-up calls, messages, long distance/local services) | ☐ | ☐ | ☐ | ☐ | ☐ | ☐ |
| | Recreational Facilities (pool, fitness center, etc) | ☐ | ☐ | ☐ | ☐ | ☐ | ☐ |
| Departure: | Service at Check-Out (friendly, efficient, prompt) | ☐ | ☐ | ☐ | ☐ | ☐ | ☐ |

**What was the primary reason for this stay?**
☐ Business   ☐ Pleasure/Leisure   ☐ Both

**Were you staying at this hotel with others for a group gathering, meeting, conference or convention?**
☐ Yes   ☐ No

**During the past 12 months, how many nights have you stayed in hotels for:**

Business:   ☐ 1 - 5   ☐ 6 - 10   ☐ 11 - 20   ☐ 21 +
Pleasure/Leisure:   ☐ 1 - 5   ☐ 6 - 10   ☐ 11 - 20   ☐ 21 +

Please provide us with any additional comments you may have about your stay:

**In which hotels have you stayed in the past 12 months?**

☐ Best Western         ☐ Hilton Garden Inn       ☐ Ramada
☐ Courtyard by Marriott   ☐ Holiday Inn Express     ☐ Wingate Inn
☐ Hampton Inn          ☐ Marriott               ☐ Other

**Gender:**   ☐ Male   ☐ Female

**Age:**   ☐ Under 18   ☐ 18 - 29   ☐ 30 - 39
          ☐ 40 - 49   ☐ 50 - 59   ☐ 60+

01105611556347933-2

*Courtesy of Six Continents Hotels, Inc. (successor of Holiday Inns, Inc.)*

**19-3** Managers find customer surveys very helpful in evaluating customer satisfaction.

# *Hospitality Ethics*

## Confidentiality

As a manager, it is unethical to share personal information about an employee or job applicant. Employers may learn sensitive information about those who work for them or applicants seeking employment. It is unethical to share confidential information about employees and doing so may end in a lawsuit. Depending on the confidentiality of the topic, sharing the information may be considered slanderous.

manager will develop the budget for the banquet department. Each of these budgets is given to the general manager, who combines the departmental budgets to determine the budget for the entire business. The accounting department often works with the managers to develop budgets. The general manager may need to make some adjustments in the individual department budgets in order to make the business profitable.

## Monitor Purchasing, Receiving, and Inventory

Foodservice businesses and lodging businesses handle large quantities of supplies. Restaurants purchase food, utensils, tableware, condiments, and table linens. Hotels purchase sheets, towels, guest supplies, paper supplies, and cleaning supplies. These goods represent a major cost and investment of money for the business. Managers must make sure the business has the right amount of supplies it needs to meet customer needs and avoid customer disappointment or poor service. If the business buys too many supplies, the business will lose money due to additional storage needs and waste. Managers must also protect the supplies from theft and spoilage.

Managers control cost of supplies by approving all purchases. They also monitor the receiving and inventory processes to make sure that ordered supplies are received in good condition and stored properly. The inventory is regularly checked for accuracy and controlled for theft.

## Cut Costs

It is often necessary to cut costs in order to make a business more profitable. Managers are expected to look for ways to reduce labor, food, supply, and utility costs. The more that costs can be controlled, the better the bottom-line financial results will be. For example, the rooms manager of a hotel will know that the hotel will only be half full during a particular week. The manager can then notify the executive housekeeper that he or she will not need a full staff of room attendants. By having fewer room attendants working that week, the hotel will save the cost of their wages. This is one way to cut costs. However, it is important to maintain quality while cutting costs. Hotel guests will not be pleased if their room is not cleaned properly or in a timely manner just so costs can be cut.

Restaurants also need ways to cut costs. Restaurants can develop ways to reduce waste, such as by improving ordering and storage procedures. Menus may be modified to emphasize foods that are less expensive but just as tasty. For example, the menu might have more chicken and pasta items than beef items. Restaurants may also improve their portion control to make sure the proper amount of each food is used in each dish.

Another way managers can cut costs is to make sure the workplace is as safe as possible. When employees are injured on the job, they cannot do their work. The replacements are often less experienced. The injured employee is paid workers' compensation, which is expensive for the business.

Good security can also lower costs to a hospitality business. Security systems help reduce costs of insurance and losses due to burglary and employee theft.

## Keep Records

Hospitality businesses generate many reports and financial records. Managers are responsible for keeping these records. Records and reports are needed for tax purposes and to determine the profit or loss for the business. In a large business, the responsibility of maintaining financial records is delegated to the accounting department. The PMS provides an efficient way to keep these kinds of records and generate reports.

In addition to financial records, files must be kept for each employee, **19-4**. **Employee personnel files** contain evaluations, job descriptions, payroll, and benefit records for every employee. These confidential files should be kept locked in the human resources office.

*Goodluz/Shutterstock.com*

**19-4** An employee's personnel file begins with the job application and other documents provided when he or she interviews for the position.

Records are also needed for planning future needs of the business. The key to keeping records is to be organized at all times.

## Manage Human Resources

One of the main responsibilities of managers is to manage the people who work for the business. People who work for a company are its human resources. Management of human resources is also called *employee management* or *supervision*. The four main tasks of human resources management are hiring and training, supervising, planning shifts, and evaluating. In larger businesses, the human resources division helps managers with some of the human resources management tasks.

### Hire and Train

The key to successful hiring is finding the right person for the right job and providing training so the new employee can succeed. Hospitality managers review job applications, interview candidates, and select the best person for the job. The human resources division often helps the managers with hiring and selection, but the final decision of whom to hire usually belongs to the department manager or supervisor.

The hospitality industry hires many entry-level workers. An **entry-level worker** is a worker with no previous work experience and few skills. The hospitality manager must make sure that entry-level workers receive enough crucial training to do their jobs well.

Workers at all levels need to keep up-to-date in their knowledge and skills. Managers must make sure that workers at all levels get the ongoing training they need to do excellent work.

### Supervise

A major responsibility of managers is to supervise their employees. The word *supervise* comes from Latin words meaning to *oversee*. A **supervisor** is a manager who makes sure each employee does his or her job properly. The supervisor is the manager closest to the workers. For example, in a large hotel, the assistant housekeeper will be the supervisor of the room attendants. The assistant housekeeper will make sure the room attendants make the beds properly, leave the right number of guest supplies, clean the room thoroughly, and work quickly. If an attendant is having problems doing the job properly, the supervisor will work with that attendant to help him or her improve performance.

The supervisor is the person who trains employees on the details of their jobs, answers questions, or solves problems that occur while the employee is working. The supervisor also makes sure that his or her employees meet goals and standards set by the general manager.

## Plan Shifts

Organizing and planning each shift is an important part of the hospitality manager's job. Many hospitality businesses, especially lodging businesses, are open 24 hours, 7 days a week. These businesses need workers during all three shifts every day of the week. The hospitality manager is responsible for having enough workers for every shift. Schedules should be developed by taking the following items into consideration:

- upcoming events that are scheduled at the restaurant or hotel, such as meetings, banquets, and weddings
- the experience level of the employees
- holidays
- level of demand (usually seasonal)
- employees' requests for certain shifts

Employees are happier when they can work the shifts they prefer, and happy employees tend to work harder. As a result, managers should try to meet employees' shift requests. To accommodate requests, managers often ask employees to submit their shift requests ahead of time. The manager can then take these requests into account when he or she plans who will work during each shift.

## Evaluate

Employee evaluations are an important part of a manager's job. An **employee evaluation** is a formal review and evaluation of an employee's performance on the job. This evaluation is also called a **performance review** or **performance appraisal**. Many businesses require each employee to have an annual performance review. Evaluating employees serves two purposes. First, evaluations help improve work performance. Second, they give the manager a formal opportunity to communicate with the employee about performance, problems, training, and opportunities.

The annual review usually has two parts. The manager starts by filling out a performance review form, **19-5**. This form lists the tasks that the employee is responsible for and has a place for rating the employee's performance of each task. This review form provides legal documentation of

**19-5** The employee evaluation form is a confidential document kept in the employee's personnel file.

Ryan R Fox/Shutterstock.com

the employee's performance. It can then be used as a basis for decisions about employees, such as promotions. This formal documentation is especially important if the employee is not meeting standards and has to be terminated.

The second part consists of a meeting between the manager and the employee. During this meeting, the manager gives the employee the performance review form and they discuss the employee's performance. The purpose of this meeting is to help the employee solve any problems he or she might be having. If performance problems are serious, the manager and employee will develop a formal improvement plan.

The performance review meeting is the time to make action plans and set goals for the next evaluation period. These goals are often recorded on the review form. It is also the opportunity to plan future training and responsibilities. The performance review meeting is usually the time when employees are promoted and given raises.

Evaluation should not only be a once-a-year occurrence. Good managers meet with employees throughout the year and constantly give feedback.

## Maintain the Facility

The general manager is responsible for making sure the physical building, equipment, and grounds are properly maintained. In larger businesses, this responsibility is delegated to the engineering division. The general manager is responsible for supervising the engineering division director and the performance of his or her division. In a small business, the general manager will be responsible for engineering and maintenance.

To keep the building, equipment, and grounds in the best condition, the manager must make sure there is a schedule for regular maintenance. Preventive maintenance programs should be developed as a way of reducing maintenance and repair costs. It is best to maintain equipment and a facility on a regular basis, because waiting until something needs major repairs or replacement can be very expensive.

## Oversee Sanitation and Safety

The general manager of a foodservice business or a lodging business is responsible for the health and safety of all guests and employees. The manager is responsible for making sure employees are trained to use proper sanitation practices, **19-6**.

*Ken Hammond for U.S. Department of Agriculture*

**19-6** The general manager of a foodservice is responsible for making sure that all sanitation practices, such as wearing gloves and keeping meats at proper temperatures, are followed.

The general manager is responsible for making sure every employee understands the importance of safety and security. In most states, a foodservice manager must have a sanitation certificate.

In a large hotel, the responsibility for sanitation is delegated to the housekeeping department. In a large restaurant, the responsibility for sanitation is delegated to the kitchen manager or the chef. In either case, the general manager is responsible for making sure these departments are ensuring proper sanitation.

Managers are always concerned about the safety and security of guests, employees, and property. Safety and security are the responsibility of the general manager. In a large business, security may be delegated to the security department.

Responsibility for safety training may be delegated to the human resources department. However, the general manager is responsible for overall safety and security.

## Market the Business

Hospitality businesses need customers. Even the smallest business must find a way to let potential customers know about the business's products and services. The general manager is responsible for increasing sales. One way to increase sales is to advertise and promote the business. Another way is to make sure that you are meeting customer needs. *Marketing* includes all the tasks done to increase sales.

In an independent business, the owner or general manager will be in charge of marketing. In a larger business or a small chain, the responsibility for marketing will be delegated to the marketing department. In a large chain, the corporate headquarters will have a marketing and sales division. This division will plan and coordinate marketing for the entire chain. In each case, the general manager will be responsible for making sure all marketing efforts are successful and result in increased sales.

# Management Skills

All employees need management skills to manage themselves and their work. All employees should be able to plan their work, organize their tools and materials, and control the quality and quantity of work they complete. All employees need communication skills and work knowledge. In addition, computer skills are necessary in many areas of hospitality work.

Workers who manage people need additional skills. Some of the skills needed are listed in Figure **19-7**. Managers also need skills such as delegation, management styles, motivation, communication, technical, computer, and organizational.

## Delegation Skills

A company's organizational chart shows how the general categories of responsibility are delegated. However, managers have to know how to delegate responsibility for the specific tasks for which their division or department is responsible. Some managers want to do everything themselves and find it difficult to delegate. However, the

---

### Management Skills That Hospitality Managers Need

- Plan and organize work in a timely and efficient manner.
- Select and train workers.
- Make decisions correctly and effectively.
- Adapt their management styles to the needs of workers.
- Recognize the organizational structure and chain of command.
- Understand, interpret, and apply company policies and rules.
- Understand, interpret, and apply local, state, and federal laws and ordinances.
- Use current technology to solve problems.
- Supervise workers.

*Source: An industry survey conducted by Professor Joseph Gregg, Florida International University*

19-7 Managers need a variety of organizational, management, and people skills.

---

most efficient managers know how to delegate the right jobs to the right people. If there is a large job that needs to be done, it can often be broken up into smaller jobs. A good manager can assign the proper people to the smaller jobs in order to get the large job finished.

## Management Styles

There are four basic styles of management. These styles are sometimes called *leadership styles* or *supervision styles*. They are autocratic, bureaucratic, democratic, and laissez-faire. Good managers use a combination of these management styles and vary their style depending on the person involved and the situation.

The **autocratic style** manager gives orders to employees. The employees are expected to carry out the orders immediately and without questioning. This management style does not share power with employees. For example, an autocratic style catering manager would tell employees exactly how to set up a banquet event for 300 guests. There would be no input from the employees. Employees could not give their opinions or make suggestions. An autocratic style is often necessary when training new employees. At this time, the employees need a great deal of direction. Autocratic styles are also necessary during emergencies, when one person must be in charge and make decisions.

The **bureaucratic style** manager seeks employee input before he or she makes a final decision. The manager has the final authority, but listens to employees before making decisions. The bureaucratic style catering manager would ask the employees for suggestions in setting up the banquet. This manager would listen to the suggestions made by the employees and make the final decision based on their suggestions.

The **democratic style** manager shares the decision making with the employees. This type of manager builds trust, respect, and commitment from his or her employees. This type of manager tends to be a good communicator and team leader. "What do you think?" is the key phrase a democratic leader uses. The democratic style catering manager would hold a meeting with the staff so the group could decide together how to set up the banquet.

The fourth style of leadership is called **laissez-faire style**. The term is French for *let it be* or *hands-off*. With this style of leadership, the employer gives all the power to employees, who make all the decisions. This is also described as a "hands-off" approach to leadership. This style is appropriate when the employees are experienced and know what they are doing. For example, the laissez-faire style catering manager would turn over all control of the banquet setup to the employees.

## Motivation Skills

A manager's job includes developing a team spirit and motivating employees. A **motivated worker** is one who willingly puts forth effort on the job. Unmotivated employees do not perform their jobs well. Motivation usually comes from within, but managers can help motivate workers. The seven methods often used to motivate workers include recognition, rewards, the work itself, responsibility, advancement, professional development, and facilitating multiple roles.

Recognition is one of the easiest and best ways to motivate people. Everyone wants to be recognized for a job well done. A note of praise or a thank-you is a great motivational technique. Giving complete and fair evaluations can also motivate employees, **19-8**. Some companies have

iofoto/Shutterstock.com

**19-8** An employee evaluation filled with positive feedback can be an effective motivational tool.

an "employee of the month" program. The person who is employee of the month is recognized publicly. Recognition might take the form of an award and his or her photo posted in the lobby. He or she may be given special privileges, such as being given the best spot in the parking lot for the month.

Rewards are an essential way to motivate workers. Appropriate pay and raises based on good work performance are major ways to reward good employees. Another important way is to provide good benefits, such as paid vacation, health coverage, and retirement benefits.

The work itself can often be a motivator. The way to use the work itself is to make sure that you have the right person in the right job. Match your workers' talents to the jobs that need to be done. When workers are good at their jobs and successful, they feel better about themselves and enjoy the work. They are also motivated to work harder.

Some people are more motivated when they are given more responsibility for their work. These employees like to solve problems themselves. When possible, give these employees responsibility for an entire project from beginning to end.

Some employees are motivated by the opportunity to advance in the company. They enjoy working hard in order to receive a promotion. You can help these employees by making sure they know what they have to do in order to be promoted.

Professional development is another way to help motivate employees. Professional development can keep workers from getting bored or tired of their jobs. Managers can help workers grow professionally by sending them to training sessions; giving them memberships in professional organizations; sending them to conferences and conventions; and encouraging attendance of webinars and local training sessions. Learning new skills and meeting new people helps keep employees productive and interested in their jobs.

One more way to motivate employees is to help them meet the demands of their multiple roles in life. Each employee has a role in the business—the job he or she performs. An employee may be a server, a bell attendant, the director of security, or the general manager. However, that is not the only role that the person has in life. People may also have roles in their families, friendship groups, religious communities, social organizations, and charitable organizations. The best managers are flexible and help each employee meet the demands of the various roles.

One of the ways managers can help employees meet the demands of multiple roles is through flexible scheduling. Other ways include child care, benefits for older adults, and vacation time.

## Communication Skills

All employees need good communication skills. Managers need especially good communication skills because of their responsibilities to supervise and train their employees. Communication skills that are needed include public speaking, presentation skills, interpersonal skills, and leadership skills.

Today, managers supervise a culturally diverse workforce. It is important for managers to understand different cultures, customs, and lifestyles. If many of the managers' workers speak a foreign language, it helps if the manager can speak that language, too.

A good manager needs to know how to listen. Managers cannot be effective if they do not know the needs of the people who work for them. By listening, a manager can do what is necessary to meet the needs of the employees.

## Technical Skills

Foodservice, housekeeping, security, and engineering managers must have specialized knowledge

in their fields. Workers in these areas use sophisticated and potentially dangerous equipment. Examples include industrial ovens, washing machines, and dishwashers; building heating and cooling systems; and security alarm systems. Managers must have a basic understanding of how to operate each piece of equipment. They must also be able to read and understand equipment manuals. Equipment supply companies usually have highly skilled repair technicians to repair equipment. However, the manager must understand how to maintain the equipment to reduce repair costs.

## Computer Skills

Computer systems have been integrated into every area of the hospitality business. Today's hospitality managers must be able to use computers to help manage resources efficiently. Some of the tasks that computers help managers do include the following:
- employee scheduling
- forecasting customer counts
- ordering supplies
- managing inventory
- collecting sales information
- keeping financial records

Managers need extensive computer skills because most hospitality businesses use computer-based financial systems. Today's managers must be able to understand how to analyze a spreadsheet. They must also know how to use computers to report the financial state of their department.

## Organizational Skills

**Organizational skills** are the skills that enable you to keep your tools and information in order, **19-9**. A chef with good organizational skills organizes cooking utensils so they will be easy to find and reach. An organized linen room supervisor knows how many linens she has and where they are. An organized front desk manager can easily find each worker's shift preferences so he can give workers the shifts they prefer. Computers can be helpful with these organizational tasks.

A part of organizational skills are time-management skills. All workers need to be able to use time efficiently. Managers must be able to use their own time efficiently as well as plan their workers' time to get tasks completed efficiently.

**19-9** Many managers use organizational tools such as smartphones and digital tablets to keep track of their appointments and tasks.

# Chapter 19

## Review

### Chapter Summary

- The general manager is the person responsible for the entire operation of a single unit of a hospitality business.
- General managers and department and division managers are responsible for goal setting, customer satisfaction, cost controls, record keeping, human resources, facility maintenance, sanitation and safety, and marketing.
- Hospitality managers control costs by setting budgets; monitoring purchasing, receiving, and inventory; and looking for ways to cut costs.
- The four main tasks of human resources management are hiring and training, supervising, planning shifts, and evaluating.
- A supervisor is a manager who makes sure each employee does his or her job properly.
- Many businesses require that each employee have an annual performance review.
- The general manager of a foodservice business or a lodging business is responsible for the health and safety of all guests and employees.
- Skills that managers need include delegation, management styles, motivation, communication, technical, computer, and organizational.

### Review

1. Describe the knowledge that a restaurant or lodging general manager should have.
2. List and describe the eight tasks of a hospitality manager.
3. What is the main goal of a general manager?
4. How can hospitality managers determine if their customers are satisfied?
5. What are three ways managers can control costs in a hospitality business?
6. Describe the role of a supervisor.

7. What are the two purposes of employee evaluations?
8. Describe the role of the general manager in facility maintenance, sanitation, and safety.
9. Give an example of delegation.
10. List and summarize the four styles of management.
11. Explain seven ways that a manager can motivate an employee.
12. Why do managers need communication skills, technical skills, computer skills, and organizational skills?

# Critical Thinking

13. **Predict.** What could happen if a manager did not set goals?
14. **Create.** Use the information in this chapter to develop an organizational chart for a large, independent, single-unit hotel.
15. **Analyze.** Make a list of the stressful situations that hospitality managers could experience on the job. Write a paragraph about how you could manage each of these situations.
16. **Identify.** Imagine you are a mystery shopper for a local pizza restaurant. Make a list of items you would be observing at the restaurant.
17. **Draw conclusions.** Why should a manager's job include developing a team spirit and motivating employees?
18. **Compare and contrast.** Contact at least two hospitality businesses in your area. Find out what types of customer satisfaction surveys they use and ask for or print out copies. Evaluate the surveys for similarities and differences. Would you recommend adding anything to the surveys or deleting any existing questions? Report your findings to your class.

19. **Speaking.** Form two teams and debate the following statement: Support centers are less important to a business than revenue centers because support centers do not bring in money.
20. **Writing.** List the skills that are needed to be a hospitality manager. Then write an essay describing how you would use these skills if you were the general manager of a restaurant, or hotel, or travel agency.
21. **Listening.** Invite the general manager of a local hotel to speak to your class. Prior to this visit, develop three questions to ask about his or her position as general manager. Take good notes during the discussion. Afterwards, write a one-page report describing the general manager's job.
22. **Speaking.** In small groups, make up examples of people who demonstrate each of the four styles of management. Role-play these types of management styles in front of your class. Use any type of hospitality businesses in your examples.
23. **Listening.** Interview a person who has been a mystery shopper about the tasks involved in the role.
24. **CTE Career Readiness Practice.** You may have been taught to treat others how *you* would like to be treated. This is often referred to as *the golden rule.* Productively working with others who have a background different from yours may require that you learn to treat others as *they* wish to be treated. Conduct research on the Internet about cultural differences related to personal space, time, gestures/body language, and relationship toward authority figures. Create a T-chart that show the difference on the left and ways you would adapt your interactions to account for that difference on the right.

362

# Chapter *20*

## Human Resources

## Chapter Objectives

After studying this chapter, you will be able to

- **explain** the importance of human resources.
- **list** the eight major functions of HR.
- **summarize** the process of recruiting job candidates.
- **give examples** of compensation and benefits.
- **describe** reasons why companies must have policies and procedures.
- **list** and give examples of laws that affect HR.
- **explain** why record keeping is an important HR function.
- **summarize** requirements of HR employees.
- **analyze** issues that affect human resources management.

## Before You Read

Try to answer the following questions before you read this chapter.

- What kinds of tasks are handled by the human resources department?
- Why is employee retention important to a business?

## Terms to Know

human resources
personnel
recruitment
screening process
compensation
wage
salary
wage and salary scale
benefits
Social Security

Federal Insurance Contributions Act (FICA)
workers' compensation
sexual harassment
regulatory compliance
discrimination
Americans with Disabilities Act (ADA)
disability
minimum wage

tipped employee
job description
Human Resources Information System (HRIS)
labor union
collective bargaining
employee retention
turnover
temporary worker

Every business has resources that it uses to run the business and produce products and services. Money is one type of resource that is often referred to as a *financial resource*. Buildings and equipment are another type and are often called *capital resources*. The people who work in the business are a third type of resource, often called **human resources**. Human resources, also called **personnel**, includes everyone who works for the company—all managers and all workers, **20-1**.

The success of any hospitality business depends on the people who work for it. Human resources should be managed as carefully as financial resources or capital resources. In many ways, a business's human resources are its most valuable resource. The quality of service provided by a business separates it from other businesses. The quality of service depends on all the people who work for the company. If employees are happy with their jobs and treated well by their employer, they will do a better job.

# Human Resources Division

All managers are responsible for managing the people who report to them. Whether a company is large or small, someone must handle all the human resource management tasks. In a small company, the general manager and the other managers will handle all the human resources tasks. In a larger company, there will be a separate human resources department or division. When human resources is part of a larger division, such as Administration, then human resources will be a

department in that division. In very large companies and corporations, human resources will be a separate division.

In a company with a human resources department or division, the managers will still be responsible for a large number of human resources management tasks. Examples include hiring, training, supervising, planning shifts, and evaluating. However, many of the administrative, record-keeping, research, and program-development tasks will be handled by the human resources division or department. A human resources division or department is often called *HR* for short. HR is sometimes called the *personnel department*.

The eight major functions of HR are recruitment, compensation and benefits, policies and procedures, regulatory compliance, employee performance, record keeping, labor relations, and employee retention.

# Recruitment

**Recruitment**, also called *staffing*, is the process of finding candidates for job openings. A business has a job opening because a worker has left or because a new job has been created. The manager with the open job needs a new employee as soon as possible, so HR works with the manager to find the best worker quickly.

Recruitment is one of the major responsibilities of HR. Recruitment includes finding candidates, screening candidates, reference checking, and testing.

The traditional way to find job candidates is to place an ad in the newspaper. Today, most companies primarily advertise employment opportunities on job search websites. HR works with the manager to write the ad for the job position and uploads it to the Internet. HR then collects the résumés that are submitted. Many company websites also spotlight a special section for career opportunities, which is maintained by HR. Other ways to look for candidates include career fairs, employment agencies, and executive search firms.

Another way to recruit is to hire student interns during the summer or part-time during the school year. These students are eager to get work experience in a hospitality business and often become candidates for employment positions after they graduate.

**20-1** All employees are considered part of a company's human resources.

merzzie/Shutterstock.com

Once HR has a group or pool of candidates, the candidates must be screened. The **screening process** consists of determining which candidates are likely to be a good fit for the job. HR will perform the screening by reading the résumés and doing some phone interviews, 20-2. The résumés of the candidates with appropriate qualifications will be presented to the manager, who will then select and interview the best candidates.

When a person applies for a job, they are asked to supply references. A *reference* is a person who is willing to talk to employers about the candidate's ability to do the job and the candidate's personal qualities. HR usually checks the references for the candidates who are interviewed. Reference checking can include other checks, such as education, employment history, Social Security number, credit history, and driver's license. HR will call the appropriate offices to make sure the information that the candidate gave is correct. For example, if the candidate says he earned a college degree, HR will call the college to verify that the candidate did get that degree. Some companies check social networking pages of potential job candidates for inappropriate information or photos. In addition, HR does criminal background checks for certain jobs, such as security officer.

HR will also handle any testing that is required. For example, some jobs require certain math skills. HR will administer the appropriate math test. In addition, many companies require

20-2  This member of the HR staff is using the phone to screen candidates and check references.

Elena Elisseeva/Shutterstock.com

preemployment drug testing. HR will usually arrange for the testing process.

HR will present all information learned about the candidates to the manager. The manager makes the final decision on which candidate to hire.

# Compensation and Benefits

**Compensation** consists of the money paid and benefits provided to a person for his or her work. **Wage** is the term used for the amount of money that a person is paid per hour. A person who is paid hourly wages is eligible for overtime pay. A **salary** is an annual amount of money that a person is paid. Managers and professionals are usually paid a salary instead of an hourly wage. People who are paid a salary usually do not get overtime pay but are sometimes eligible for bonuses.

Although many people love their work, people work to earn money. In order for a business to get the best workers, the business has to pay the workers a competitive wage. For example, suppose you are applying for a job as a busser at two restaurants. The restaurants are the same in every way except for the wages offered. One restaurant is offering $9.00 an hour. The other is offering $9.75 an hour. Most people would take the job with the higher wage.

One of the responsibilities of HR is to find out through wage and salary surveys what other businesses are paying their workers. HR uses this salary information to develop a report for management and then works with management to decide what wage or salary to offer for each job in the company. A list of wages and salaries paid for each job is called a **wage and salary scale**.

Another part of compensation is benefits. **Benefits** include all forms of compensation other than salary and wages. One benefit that most employees get is Social Security. **Social Security** is a federal program that ensures workers will get some income after they retire. Social Security was established through the **Federal Insurance Contributions Act (FICA)**, which permits the federal government to take a small percentage of every worker's paycheck and put it in the Social Security fund. The benefit part is the employer's contribution. For each employee, the employer contributes to the Social Security fund an amount equal to the amount of money that the employee paid.

Another benefit that employers must offer is **workers' compensation**, which requires the employer to provide medical and salary coverage for an illness or injury that an employee experiences as a result of the job. Each state has developed its own workers' compensation laws.

Most employers provide many other benefits, which HR researches and develops. Benefits commonly offered include paid vacation, paid sick days, health insurance, life insurance, disability insurance, savings plans, and retirement plans.

Educational benefits are also common. Many companies will help employees get a college degree by paying for part of their tuition, **20-3**. Employees usually have to meet certain requirements before they are eligible for this benefit, which is called *tuition reimbursement*. In addition, many companies will pay for courses and professional training that are directly related to the worker's job.

# Policies and Procedures

Every company must have policies and procedures that ensure the safe and efficient running of the company. HR usually works with management to establish these policies and procedures, and then develop an employee handbook. An *employee handbook* is a document, usually in book or pamphlet form, that explains all company policies and procedures concerning employees. HR is responsible for making sure each employee receives a copy of the handbook and understands its contents.

Companies need policies and procedures for many areas. Examples include attendance, appropriate dress, employee conduct, personal phone calls, and smoking. For example, most companies limit the number and length of personal phone calls during work hours. Some companies do not allow employees to carry cell phones while working because they cause too many distractions and work interruptions.

In addition, most companies develop a formal discipline policy to ensure fair treatment of all employees. The discipline policy is usually used when employee behavior or performance is causing serious problems in job performance or to other employees and customers. Minor problems, including occasional lateness and small problems

**20-3** Many employers help employees get a college education.

Robert Kneschke/Shutterstock.com

in job performance, are handled by the employee's direct supervisor. The supervisor will meet with the employee to discuss the problem and develop ways to solve it.

Serious problems are covered in the discipline policy. The policy usually requires that the employee receive warnings about the problem—first a verbal warning, and then a written one if the behavior continues. There are also specific steps to be taken if the behavior is serious enough to lead to suspension or termination from the job. These steps usually include documentation by the supervisor of the employee's behavior and work. Sometimes the employee is required to undergo counseling. Often, a formal correction plan is developed for the employee to follow.

Many companies have specific policies concerning sexual harassment, 20-4. **Sexual harassment** is considered to be any unwelcome behavior of a sexual nature that creates an intimidating, hostile, or offensive work environment. Sexual harassment also includes the request or demand for sexual favors as part of the terms of employment or as a basis for employment decisions such as promotions or raises.

There are certain behaviors that a company cannot tolerate from employees while they are at work and that are usually grounds for immediate dismissal from a job. These behaviors include fighting, refusing to follow a supervisor's instructions, consuming or being under the influence of alcohol or illegal substances, possession of firearms, stealing company property, damaging company property, and violation of safety rules.

# Regulatory Compliance

The many local, state, and federal laws that employers must follow change frequently and are often very complex. In addition to the laws themselves, many regulations based on these laws must be followed. One of the major responsibilities of HR is to make sure the company knows the laws and regulations and follows them. Following appropriate laws and regulations is called **regulatory compliance**. HR works with the company lawyer or legal department for professional legal advice, especially if the company is sued.

Laws and regulations that affect HR can be organized into three groups: equal opportunity, workers' rights, and safety laws.

---

## Information on Sexual Harassment from an Employee Handbook

The Company is committed to providing a workplace that is free from all forms of discrimination, including sexual harassment. Sexual harassment is considered a form of misconduct. An employee whose behavior fits the definition of sexual harassment may be subject to disciplinary action up to and including dismissal. Sexual harassment could also subject this Company and, in some cases, the individual, to substantial civil penalties.

The Company has a detailed written policy on sexual harassment. This written policy is part of the Company's overall affirmative action efforts, pursuant to state and federal laws prohibiting discrimination based on age, disability, race, color, religion, marital status, and gender.

Each employee is responsible for refraining from sexual harassment in the workplace. Briefly, sexual harassment is defined as any unwelcome behavior of a sexual nature that creates an intimidating, hostile, or offensive work environment. No employee—male or female—should be subjected to unsolicited or unwelcome sexual overtures or conduct in the workplace. Specific definitions of sexual harassment are in the written policy.

Furthermore, it is the responsibility of all supervisors to make sure the work environment is free from sexual harassment. All forms of discrimination and conduct that can be considered harassing, coercive, or disruptive, or that create a hostile environment, must be eliminated.

Copies of the written policy are available from your supervisor.

*Goodheart-Willcox Publisher*

20-4  Why is it important for companies to have a specific policy on sexual harassment?

## Equal Opportunity

Starting with the Declaration of Independence, the United States of America has had the ideal of equality for all. Unfortunately, this ideal has not always been carried out—especially in the workplace. In the workplace, people should be evaluated based on their work performance. All workers should be treated with dignity and respect, and everyone's rights should be respected. **Discrimination** is treating people unfairly based on irrelevant characteristics. For example, people have been discriminated against in the workplace because of their race or religion.

Over the years, national, state, and local governments have passed a variety of laws to ensure that workers are treated fairly. Many of these laws prevent discrimination in the workplace based on age, disability, gender, national origin, race, and religion, **20-5**.

The **Americans with Disabilities Act (ADA)** was passed to make sure that people with disabilities are treated fairly in public places and in the workplace. According to the ADA, a **disability** is a permanent condition that limits one or more major life activities. Examples of major life activities include walking, speaking, and sleeping.

According to the ADA, each job must be analyzed for its *essential functions*—those tasks that the person in the job must be able to do. The ADA requires that if a person can perform the essential functions of a job, then the person should be given equal consideration for the job, regardless of disability. If the person hired has disabilities, the ADA requires that the company make reasonable accommodations so the person can do the job. Reasonable accommodations are accommodations that do not cost so much that the cost is detrimental to the business. The HR department analyzes jobs for essential functions and helps the company meet the ADA requirements.

For example, an essential function of a door attendant is the ability to load and unload luggage from cars and carry luggage into the hotel. A person who must use a wheelchair to get around cannot perform this essential function and therefore is not qualified for a bell attendant job. However, essential functions for a reservations agent are being

| Equal Opportunity Laws | | |
|---|---|---|
| **Year** | **Laws** | **Main Provisions** |
| *1964, 1991* | Civil Rights Act | Bans employment discrimination based on race, color, religion, sex, or national origin<br>Created the Equal Employment Opportunity Commission (EEOC), which investigates charges of discrimination<br>Allows jury trials and punitive damages in discrimination cases |
| *1967, 1990* | Age Discrimination Employment Act, Older Workers Benefit Protection Act | Bans discrimination against workers age 40 and older |
| *1986* | Immigration Reform and Control Act | Bans employment of noncitizens who are not authorized to work in the U.S.<br>Bans discrimination against citizens who may appear foreign<br>Bans discrimination against noncitizens who have legal work permits |
| *1990* | Americans with Disabilities Act | Bans discrimination against individuals with disabilities in matters of employment, government services, public accommodations, commercial facilities, and transportation |

*Goodheart-Willcox Publisher*

**20-5** Equal opportunity laws prevent unfair discrimination in the workplace.

# Juanita Nañez— Never Stop Learning

*Photo courtesy of Juanita Nañez*

Juanita Nañez was an honor student in high school. Because of family obligations, she was not able to attend college immediately after high school. Juanita put her dream of college on hold and started working.

One of her first jobs was at a bank. She worked as a part-time coordinator for college recruiting. She coordinated interview schedules and prepared information packets. In screening résumés, she learned the importance of detail and accuracy.

Juanita found the work fascinating. She enjoyed searching for the right people (recruiting) and matching them to the right jobs. She excelled in her work and was soon promoted to corporate recruiter. Her new job responsibilities included working with supervisors and interviewing.

Juanita left the human resources area to work as a bilingual office manager for an international oil and gas supply company. On this job she developed her planning, organizational, and international business skills. She also learned about compensation and benefits. The company went out of business, and Juanita was out of a job. She decided to return to the human resources field.

She saw a job ad for an assistant in the management recruiting department for T.G.I. Friday's, a popular casual dining restaurant chain. Juanita liked the idea of working for a restaurant. She knew that restaurants are fast-paced, people-oriented businesses. Juanita got the job, worked hard, and quickly moved up the career ladder. Friday's is owned by the parent company Carlson Restaurants Worldwide, Inc. (CRWW). In 1999, Juanita became the executive director of corporate human services for CRWW, and in 2003, vice president of diversity.

Juanita has won numerous awards and recognition for her performance in human resources and diversity. She is now a human resources and diversity consultant with The Hopkins Group. Her background and expertise have prepared her well for human resources consulting.

## Juanita Nañez's Career Path

**1962:** First job, server in a soda fountain/diner in a pharmacy

**1972:** Corporate recruiter, First National Bank in Dallas, Texas

**1982:** Office manager, Dallas International Supply Co.

**1983:** Assistant in management recruiting, T.G.I. Friday's

**1989:** Director of employee relations, Carlson Restaurants Worldwide, Inc. (CRWW)

**1990:** Received Professional in Human Resources certificate from the Society for Human Resource Management

**1996:** Senior director of employee relations and staffing, CRWW

**1999:** Executive director of corporate human services, CRWW

**2003:** Vice president of diversity, CRWW

**2005:** Recognized by Texas Diversity Council for outstanding service and commitment

**2011:** Joined the Hopkins Group as human resources and diversity consultant

able to answer the phone, understand customers, respond to requests, and make reservations. If a candidate can perform these reservations agents functions, using a wheelchair is irrelevant. The hotel must give the candidate who uses a wheelchair equal consideration for the reservations job with candidates who do not use wheelchairs. If the hotel hires the person who uses a wheelchair, the hotel must make reasonable accommodations. Reasonable accommodations are determined on a case-by-case basis. A reasonable accommodation may be getting a desk that accommodates a wheelchair. An unreasonable accommodation might be replacing an outdoor wheelchair ramp with an elevator.

## Workers' Rights

Workers' rights are protected by a variety of laws and regulations, 20-6. One of the major provisions of the Fair Labor Standards Act (FLSA) is the minimum wage provision. The **minimum wage** is the lowest hourly rate that a worker must be paid. The federal government sets the minimum wage. In order to raise the federal minimum wage, Congress must pass a bill and the President must sign it into law. The law also requires that a poster be visibly displayed at the worksite, 20-7.

There are many conditions and exceptions to the minimum wage laws. First, each state can make its own minimum wage laws. However, the state laws have to provide at least the minimum in the federal law. Second, certain categories of workers can receive less than minimum wages. Some of these categories include student-learners and tipped employees. HR must be up-to-date on all the details and help the company comply with the laws and regulations.

The category of tipped employees is especially important in the hospitality industry. A **tipped employee** is a worker who receives tips from customers. Most restaurant servers are tipped employees. The federal law establishes a lower minimum wage for tipped employees. However, the tipped employee must actually receive tips that make his or her minimum wage meet the federal minimum wage. If the tipped employee does not make enough in tips, the employer must make up the difference. For example, in 2012, the federal minimum wage was $7.25 per hour and the federal minimum wage for tipped employees was $2.13 per hour. A tipped employee had to earn at least $5.12 in tips each hour. Suppose the employee made only $3.00 in tips an hour. Then the employer must pay an additional $2.12 an hour. The individual states can make stricter laws.

A large number of complex laws cover benefits. The only benefits that employers are required to provide are FICA and workers' compensation. Employers often choose to provide other benefits, such as health insurance and retirement benefits. A large number of laws cover these benefits. The purpose of these laws is to protect the rights of the workers. HR is responsible for keeping up-to-date on all these laws and making sure they are followed.

| Workers' Rights Laws | | |
|---|---|---|
| **Year** | **Laws** | **Main Provisions** |
| *1938* | Fair Labor Standards Act | Minimum Wage<br>Overtime pay<br>Restrictions on employment of children<br>Record keeping |
| *1963* | Equal Pay Act | Men and women must be paid equal amounts if they are doing the same job or substantially similar jobs |
| *1993* | Family and Medical Leave Act | Entitles eligible employees up to 12 weeks of unpaid, job-protected leave in a 12-month period for specified family and medical reasons |

*Goodheart-Willcox Publisher*

**20-6** These laws ensure the protection of the rights of employees.

# EMPLOYEE RIGHTS
## UNDER THE FAIR LABOR STANDARDS ACT

THE UNITED STATES DEPARTMENT OF LABOR WAGE AND HOUR DIVISION

### FEDERAL MINIMUM WAGE
# $7.25 PER HOUR
**BEGINNING JULY 24, 2009**

**OVERTIME PAY**  At least 1½ times your regular rate of pay for all hours worked over 40 in a workweek.

**CHILD LABOR**  An employee must be at least **16** years old to work in most non-farm jobs and at least **18** to work in non-farm jobs declared hazardous by the Secretary of Labor.

Youths **14** and **15** years old may work outside school hours in various non-manufacturing, non-mining, non-hazardous jobs under the following conditions:

> *No more than*
> • **3** hours on a school day or **18** hours in a school week;
> • **8** hours on a non-school day or **40** hours in a non-school week.

Also, work may not begin before **7 a.m.** or end after **7 p.m.**, except from June 1 through Labor Day, when evening hours are extended to **9 p.m.** Different rules apply in agricultural employment.

**TIP CREDIT**  Employers of "tipped employees" must pay a cash wage of at least $2.13 per hour if they claim a tip credit against their minimum wage obligation. If an employee's tips combined with the employer's cash wage of at least $2.13 per hour do not equal the minimum hourly wage, the employer must make up the difference. Certain other conditions must also be met.

**ENFORCEMENT**  The Department of Labor may recover back wages either administratively or through court action, for the employees that have been underpaid in violation of the law. Violations may result in civil or criminal action.

Employers may be assessed civil money penalties of up to $1,100 for each willful or repeated violation of the minimum wage or overtime pay provisions of the law and up to $11,000 for each employee who is the subject of a violation of the Act's child labor provisions. In addition, a civil money penalty of up to $50,000 may be assessed for each child labor violation that causes the death or serious injury of any minor employee, and such assessments may be doubled, up to $100,000, when the violations are determined to be willful or repeated. The law also prohibits discriminating against or discharging workers who file a complaint or participate in any proceeding under the Act.

**ADDITIONAL INFORMATION**
- Certain occupations and establishments are exempt from the minimum wage and/or overtime pay provisions.
- Special provisions apply to workers in American Samoa and the Commonwealth of the Northern Mariana Islands.
- Some state laws provide greater employee protections; employers must comply with both.
- The law requires employers to display this poster where employees can readily see it.
- Employees under 20 years of age may be paid $4.25 per hour during their first 90 consecutive calendar days of employment with an employer.
- Certain full-time students, student learners, apprentices, and workers with disabilities may be paid less than the minimum wage under special certificates issued by the Department of Labor.

For additional information:
# 1-866-4-USWAGE WHD
(1-866-487-9243)    TTY: 1-877-889-5627    U.S. Wage and Hour Division
# WWW.WAGEHOUR.DOL.GOV

U.S. Department of Labor | Wage and Hour Division

WHD Publication 1088 (Revised July 2009)

*www.dol.gov*

**20-7** Workers' rights to a minimum wage are guaranteed by the federal government. (There are some exceptions.)

## Safety Laws

The major safety law is the federal *Occupational Safety and Health Act of 1970* (OSH Act). The purpose of OSH Act is to assure safe and healthful working conditions for all workers. The OSH Act also established the *Occupational Safety and Health Administration (OSHA)*, the agency that makes sure the laws and regulations in the OSH Act are carried out, **20-8**.

# Employee Performance

The manager or supervisor of each employee has the major responsibility for his or her employees' training and performance. However, HR does some training and provides support to managers.

One of the major tasks of HR is to develop a job description for each job. A **job description** is a document that lists the essential functions and requirements for a job. HR usually works with the managers to develop job descriptions. Figure **20-9** shows the information usually covered in a job description. Many companies list their job descriptions on their websites.

Another major responsibility of HR is to coordinate performance reviews. HR often uses the job descriptions to develop performance review forms and works with managers to make sure that reviews are done in a timely fashion.

HR is involved in new employee orientation and training. When new workers are hired, they need to learn many things about the company. HR usually has an orientation session to give them the information they need. For example, HR might present the employee handbook and go over it during orientation. HR also works with the managers to help them provide the training that their workers need.

# Record Keeping

Record keeping is one of the most important functions of HR. In a small business, such as a bed-and-breakfast, it is easy to keep track of information since there are few employees. In a large business, such as a 2,000-room luxury hotel, there may be hundreds of employees, including part-time workers. HR must be efficient, well organized, and computerized to keep track of the information

on all these employees. The record that is kept on each employee is called an *employee personnel file*. Personnel files contain basic information, required forms, evaluations, job descriptions, payroll, and benefit records. These files are confidential and are kept locked in the HR office.

There is a certain amount of basic information that must be kept for each employee, such as name, address, telephone number, and Social Security number. In addition, there are several forms that the federal government requires each employee to fill out. The employer must then keep these forms on file. The first form is the W-4, *Employees Withholding Allowance Certificate*. This form is used to determine how much federal tax the employer must take from each worker's paycheck.

Another required form is the I-9, *Employment Eligibility Verification*. This form is required by the Immigration Reform and Control Act. The I-9 form documents the employment status of each potential worker. Potential workers are generally in three categories: U.S. citizens, who are eligible to work; non–U.S. citizens who have received official permission to work; and non–U.S. citizens who are not permitted to work in the U.S. The purpose of the I-9 form is to keep employers from hiring non–U.S. citizens who do not have permission to work in the United States.

The FLSA also requires that employers keep records for each employee concerning the hours worked and the wages earned. These records are required so the U.S. Department of Labor can make sure employers are following the requirements of the FLSA.

Most HR departments keep additional records, such as performance reviews and benefit program enrollments, on each employee. If an employee has performance or conduct problems, these are also documented and kept in the personnel files.

HR must keep personnel files up-to-date. New files must be made for new employees. Changes in employee status must be recorded, including retirement, resignation, promotions, address changes, and changes in family status such as marriage, divorce, or new children. In addition, the FLSA requires employers to keep certain records for two to three years.

Most HR departments use computers to help with record keeping. A **Human Resources Information System (HRIS)** is the general name for a computer system that human resources departments use for personnel records. An HRIS

# Job Safety and Health

## It's the law!

**OSHA®**

**Occupational Safety and Health Administration**
**U.S. Department of Labor**

### EMPLOYEES:

- You have the right to notify your employer or OSHA about workplace hazards. You may ask OSHA to keep your name confidential.

- You have the right to request an OSHA inspection if you believe that there are unsafe and unhealthful conditions in your workplace. You or your representative may participate in that inspection.

- You can file a complaint with OSHA within 30 days of retaliation or discrimination by your employer for making safety and health complaints or for exercising your rights under the *OSH Act*.

- You have the right to see OSHA citations issued to your employer. Your employer must post the citations at or near the place of the alleged violations.

- Your employer must correct workplace hazards by the date indicated on the citation and must certify that these hazards have been reduced or eliminated.

- You have the right to copies of your medical records and records of your exposures to toxic and harmful substances or conditions.

- Your employer must post this notice in your workplace.

- You must comply with all occupational safety and health standards issued under the *OSH Act* that apply to your own actions and conduct on the job.

### EMPLOYERS:

- You must furnish your employees a place of employment free from recognized hazards.

- You must comply with the occupational safety and health standards issued under the *OSH Act*.

*This free poster available from OSHA –*
*The Best Resource for Safety and Health*

Free assistance in identifying and correcting hazards or complying with standards is available to employers, without citation or penalty, through OSHA-supported consultation programs in each state.

**1-800-321-OSHA (6742)**
**www.osha.gov**

OSHA 3165-02 2012R

*www.osha.gov*

20-8 Employers are required to display this poster about the OSH Act.

## What Goes on a Job Description

| Heading (Other terms for the heading) | Explanation | Examples |
|---|---|---|
| **Job Title** (Position Name) | Name of the job | Server |
| **Reports to** | Job title of the whom the job | |
| **Purpose** (Scope, Objective, Primary Responsibilities) | Describe the b the job | |
| **Essential Functions** (Specific Functions, Job Duties) | Describe all th a person doing perform | ls |
| **Qualification Standards** (Education and Experience) | Describe the ed experience, and requirements f | |
| **Physical Requirements** | The physical re a job may be gi separate from t and experience requirements | |

*Goodheart-Willcox Publisher*

20-9  In what ways is a job description useful?

system can keep track of employee information such as employee attendance, wage histories, anniversaries of hire date, birth dates, disciplinary records, names, addresses, and Social Security numbers. The software can then be used to quickly access information about any employee. HRIS can also be used to generate reports, such as a specific employee's work history and number of workdays the employee has missed. An HRIS can generate reports about all the employees, such as how many employees are currently on staff, the average wages, and the average workdays missed.

An important responsibility of HR is confidentiality, **20-10**. HR staff members have access to a great deal of personal, private information. All employee files are confidential, and HR staff must be able to keep all information private. Only the employee and authorized HR staff can see the whole file. The manager to whom the employee reports directly can only see items directly related

to job person

## Lab

T the p labor ring to union. ers wh labor u

fair wages, decent benefits, and safe working conditions. Labor unions achieve this purpose through collective bargaining. **Collective bargaining** is the way that labor and management discuss what they expect from each other. The union represents the workers in collective bargaining with management. Many unions also offer training and apprenticeship programs.

*[handwritten note: Employee Performance Provide Un Is orgn represen employ huelga =]*

20-10  What might happen if employee information is not kept confidential?

There are several unions active in the hospitality industry. One of the major unions, UNITE HERE, represents people who work in the hotel, gaming, foodservice, laundry, and airport industries.

At each hospitality business, it is up to the employees whether they want to be represented by a union. Many hospitality businesses have no union representation, while some hospitality businesses have several unions. Each union represents a different group of workers. In a business where there is union representation, the relationship between the labor unions and the management of the company is called *labor relations*. HR is usually responsible for labor relations.

There are many laws that govern labor relations. The main law is the federal National Labor Relations Act. Many states have developed their own laws for labor relations. HR is responsible for making sure that all labor relations laws and regulations are followed.

# Employee Retention

**Employee retention** refers to the efforts made to keep good employees and reduce turnover. **Turnover** occurs when an employee leaves the company and another employee must be hired to take his or her place, **20-11**.

Turnover is very expensive for a business. When an employee leaves a job, the job is vacant and there is no one to do the work. This situation causes the business to have trouble meeting customer needs. Second, the business must find a new employee. This process can be costly and take a great deal of time. Third, once the new employee is hired, the employee needs time to learn how to do the job. Even if the employee has a great deal of experience, he or she has never worked at this particular job for this particular company and has

Martin Novak/Shutterstock.com

20-11 Employee turnover is costly to a company in terms of both money and time.

a great deal to learn. It might take a while before the employee does his or her job well.

There is always some employee turnover. Turnover occurs when a worker is promoted within the company or when employees leave for a variety of personal reasons. Businesses learn how to deal with this type of turnover.

Turnover also occurs when employees are unhappy with their jobs, or when a competing company offers much better wages, benefits, or working conditions. Part of the function of HR is to make the workplace as positive as possible. HR researches wages and benefits that other companies

offer to make sure the business offers a competitive package. HR also develops programs such as quality of work life programs to help retain employees.

## HR Staff

The size of the HR staff depends on the size of the business. In a small business, the general manager or president of the company will handle all HR tasks. A business of 60 or more employees will often have one HR staff member. This person will be called the *director of HR*. As the number of employees increases, the number of HR staff members will increase. A large HR division will be divided into several departments: recruitment, training, labor relations, and compensation and benefits. Large HR departments often have a number of assistants and clerical staff.

Employees in HR need a variety of skills and personal qualities, **20-12**. HR staff members who interview candidates, do training, and handle labor relations must have excellent communication and interpersonal skills. Staff members who deal with compensation and benefits must have excellent math skills and be very detail oriented. HR staff who deal with regulatory compliance must also be detail oriented. All HR staff must be able to keep confidential information confidential.

## HR Issues

The HR division or department deals with many issues that concern individual employees and their problems. Other issues affect the hospitality industry more broadly, including diversity in the workforce, recruitment, family and medical leave, and quality of life programs.

### *Diversity in the Workforce*

The nature of the workforce in the United States has changed over the past 60 years and will continue to change. In the past, most of the workforce was white and male. Major changes include the increase in women and people of various ethnicities in the workforce. The aging of the workforce is another factor.

The increase in diversity of the workforce has created challenges and opportunities for the hospitality industry. The opportunity is to provide

Goodluz/Shutterstock.com

20-12 In what situations would HR staff members need excellent communications and interpersonal skills?

better customer service because the customers are more diverse than they used to be. The challenge is to create a smoothly functioning team from individuals from a variety of different backgrounds. People are usually most comfortable with people who are just like them. A diverse workforce puts people from different backgrounds together, so they need to learn to work together and understand one another's backgrounds. Issues that arise include prejudice, discrimination, sexual harassment, and communication problems.

HR helps the company deal with the issues that arise from a diverse workforce. Some companies have created a special job to deal with diversity issues. For example, many hospitality companies have a vice president of diversity.

HR develops training programs that help people work with one another. In addition, if there are any language issues, HR may develop language classes to help workers learn English. HR can also develop training programs in employees' native languages to help them with their jobs while they are learning English.

## Recruitment

Another major issue for the HR department is recruitment. Hospitality companies often have a difficult time finding enough qualified employees to fill job openings. In addition, there is competition among hospitality companies for the best workers. HR spends a great deal of time developing ways to find qualified candidates. HR also works to make

# *Hospitality Ethics*

## Business Computers

While you are at work, it is important to be respectful in your use of computer equipment. The computer is available for your use as a tool to accomplish a task. It is unethical to use the computer without permission for personal means such as playing games, shopping, or other activities that are outside of your assignments. It is also unethical to access confidential information, download copyrighted material, or harass others. Many organizations monitor users to make certain that the computer activity is ethical and legal.

its company more appealing to the candidates than the competition is.

In order to fill open positions, the company often has to hire temporary workers. A **temporary worker** is a worker who is hired for a specific, usually short, amount of time. A temporary worker is not on the regular payroll and does not receive company benefits.

Temporary workers are widely used in today's workforce. These workers do not just fill in for clerical positions. They are used at all levels of hospitality businesses to fill in for regular workers on medical leave or family leave, **20-13**. They are often used for banquet services where additional help is needed for one evening. Temporary workers are also especially useful during peak seasons. Issues with temporary workers arise because these workers do not receive benefits. They may work at several different hospitality businesses in order to work the equivalent of a full-time job.

## Family and Medical Leave

The Family and Medical Leave Act (FMLA) was designed to help workers deal with family needs and still keep their jobs. Before this law was passed, the worker would often have to quit in order to get the time needed to care for the family member.

The act entitles workers to take up to 12 weeks of leave (without pay) for certain family needs, then be able to return to their jobs. There are many details involved in meeting this law, and HR is responsible for those details. First, only employers who have at least 50 employees are required to follow this law. Smaller employers are exempt. The employee must be eligible for the leave. An eligible employee has worked for the employer for at least 12 months, and must have worked at least 1,250 hours during the 12 months before the leave starts. Family members, for the purposes of this law, are parents, children, and spouses only. Family needs, for the purposes of this law, include birth or adoption of a child or serious illness of a family member. Proof of the nature and seriousness of the illness must be provided. The leave does not have to be taken all at once. The maximum amount of leave is 12 weeks in 12 months.

**20-13** Temporary workers are widely used in the hospitality industry.

*erwinova/Shutterstock.com*

The FMLA was amended in 2008 to add care for a seriously injured or ill family member of the armed forces. For this reason, employees are allowed to take up to 26 weeks off in a 12-month period. Immediate family members of military personnel may also use FMLA for military family leave. This means they are entitled to time needed for handling issues related to a family member's deployment.

This law is very helpful to workers and their families. However, it creates problems for the company beyond the record keeping. The major issue is how the work will get done. FMLA requires that the employer hold the position or provide an equivalent position when the employee returns from leave. Arrangements must be made to accomplish the work while the employee is taking FMLA leave. For example, suppose the front office manager has to leave for 12 weeks during the peak season for maternity leave. If the company hires a new front office manager, which position will they give to their original office manager when she returns from maternity leave? HR would work on a solution to this problem.

## Quality of Work Life

*Quality of work life (QWL)* is a concept that refers to how the worker feels about the work experience itself, which depends on many aspects of the job. Some of these factors include management styles, freedom to make decisions on the job, physical surroundings of the job, job safety, work hours, and meaningful job tasks. HR may be given the task to improve QWL. The approach of a good QWL program says that a person's job and work environment should meet as many of the worker's needs as possible.

HR finds out what workers need, what makes them unhappy, and what would make them happy. HR then uses this information to develop QWL programs. One QWL program might work with managers on issues involving management style. Another might work on improving the quality of the employee cafeteria. Common QWL programs include courses on stress management and financial planning, wellness programs, health club membership, and health screenings, **20-14**. HR often organizes holiday parties, charity drives, and employee recognition programs.

QWL programs are especially important in the hospitality industry. Most businesses work Monday through Friday, from 9:00 a.m. to 5:00 p.m. In contrast, the hospitality industry runs 24 hours a day, 365 days a year. When everyone else is on vacation or out celebrating, hospitality employees are working. It is harder to keep hospitality staff feeling appreciated and motivated when all their friends have every weekend off. HR is the department that deals with these issues. HR develops QWL programs that help staff feel appreciated and motivated.

Lucky Business/Shutterstock.com

20-14 Membership in a health club is often part of a QWL program.

# Chapter 20
## Review

## Chapter Summary

- The major functions of HR are recruitment, compensation and benefits, policies and procedures, regulatory compliance, employee performance, record keeping, labor relations, and employee retention.
- Recruitment is one of the major responsibilities of HR.
- Compensation and benefits are provided to a person for his or her work.
- Companies must have policies and procedures that ensure the safe and efficient running of the company.
- Laws and regulations that affect HR can be organized into three groups: equal opportunity, workers' rights, and safety laws.
- HR develops a job description for each job in the company.
- Record keeping is an important task for HR.
- Companies work very hard to reduce employee turnover.
- Some issues affect the HR department.

## Review

1. List and describe the eight major functions of HR.
2. Summarize the four tasks that are involved in recruitment.
3. What are the differences between compensation, wages, and salaries?
4. Describe what is contained in an employee handbook.
5. Give two examples of equal opportunity laws and two examples of workers' rights laws.
6. List and explain the headings in a job description.
7. List the types of information kept in an employee personnel file.
8. What is the purpose of a labor union?
9. Why is employee retention important to a company?
10. List and describe some of today's HR issues.

# Critical Thinking

11. **Draw conclusions.** Describe what happens when turnover occurs after a busser resigns from a restaurant.

12. **Identify.** List and describe the essential functions for the position of dishwasher.

13. **Make inferences.** Why is it important for HR to know what other businesses are paying their workers?

14. **Determine.** Choose one of the laws that affect HR. Describe a situation in which that law would apply.

15. **Assess.** Why is quality of work life (QWL) important?

# Common Core

### College and Career Readiness

16. **Speaking.** Research and give an oral presentation on an HRIS system to the class.

17. **Writing.** Imagine you are the general manager of a hospitality business. Your business has just expanded from 60 employees to 200, so you decide to add an HR department. How many people would you hire for your new department? Give each one a title and write a job description.

18. **Writing.** Research one of the workers' rights laws. Write a report of the conditions that prompted the law, the efforts to make the law a reality, and the changes brought about by the law.

19. **Speaking.** With a classmate, brainstorm inexpensive ways to make reasonable accommodations for employees with disabilities.

20. **Reading.** Obtain a copy of the I-9 Employment Verification Form and the instructions for filling it out. Underline any words you don't understand and look up their definitions.

21. **Speaking.** Prepare an electronic presentation about the history of Social Security. Address the following questions:

    - What is Social Security? Why was it established?
    - How and when was Social Security established?
    - How is money collected for the Social Security fund?
    - At what age are you currently eligible to begin receiving Social Security benefits?

22. **CTE Career Readiness Practice.** Examine the issues related to the future of Social Security. In two teams, debate this question: "Will funds from Social Security still be available when we retire?" Cite reliable resources as evidence to support your position.

382

# Chapter *21*

## Marketing and Sales

### Chapter Objectives

After studying this chapter, you will be able to
- **list** the four major functions of marketing.
- **describe** the five basic areas of marketing.
- **give** the meaning of sales in the business sense and another meaning of sales in the context of promotion.
- **state** the purposes of a marketing plan.
- **list** the four main methods of promotion.
- **describe** two types of selling that are done in hospitality businesses.
- **compare** the marketing done by a small business with that done by a large chain.

### Before You Read

Try to answer the following questions before you read this chapter.
- What are the four Ps of marketing?
- What methods of promotion can you identify?

### Terms to Know

marketing
product
good
service
marketing mix
four Ps of marketing
marketing research
market segmentation
revenue management software
promotion

personal communication
nonpersonal communication
sales
repeat business
marketing plan
competitor
advertising
advertisement
commercial
print advertising

Internet advertising
billboard
reader board
public relations
press release
publicity
sales promotion
loyalty program
suggestive selling
convention and visitors bureau (CVB)

Imagine you open a restaurant serving food that very few people like. You have almost no customers, and the restaurant eventually goes out of business. Now imagine that you open a wonderful, trendy hotel. The few guests who have found it think it is great, but very few people have ever heard of it. Your hotel has very few guests, and it eventually goes out of business.

The problem of the restaurant is that it provided a product no one wanted. The problem of the hotel was that no one knew about it. The purpose of marketing is to prevent both of these problems. The following are the four major functions of marketing:

- Learn what customers want and need.
- Develop a product that meets those wants and needs.
- Make sure that potential customers know about the product.
- Persuade customers to buy your product.

# Marketing

There are many definitions for both sales and marketing. Some people think sales is the same as marketing. Some people think marketing is advertising. In the hotel industry, the director of marketing is often only in charge of sales. Sometimes the director of sales is in charge of both sales and marketing. Sometimes the director of marketing and sales only does sales. To avoid confusion, this text will use the most up-to-date definitions of marketing and sales. Marketing includes many activities involved in developing and selling products, and sales is just one type of marketing activity.

**Marketing** consists of developing products that meet customer needs and promoting those products so customers will buy them. In the marketing world, the term **product** refers to any goods and services a business sells. A **good** is an item you can touch, such as pizza and running shoes. A **service** is an activity that is done for another person, such as providing a place to sleep. The main product of the hospitality industry is service, **21-1**. Many hospitality businesses, such as restaurants, provide both goods and services. The goods are the food, and the services are the cooking, presentation, and serving of the food.

There are five basic areas in marketing: target market, product, price, place, and promotion.

lightpoet/Shutterstock.com

**21-1** When you take an airplane, you have the service of being transported from one place to another as opposed to a tangible product.

In order for marketing to be successful, decisions must be made in each of these areas. The first decision is choosing your target market. The combination of decisions made about the next four areas—product, price, place, and promotion—is called the **marketing mix**. These four areas are called the **four Ps of marketing**.

## Target Market

Before you make any other marketing decisions, you must choose your target market. Research that is done to learn about the market and potential customers is called **marketing research**. The information gathered during marketing research helps the sales department determine the target market and make decisions about product, price, place, and promotion.

Marketing research helps you understand the market and decide how to segment it. A *market* consists of all the people who could potentially buy what you are selling. In the foodservice industry, the market consists of everyone who eats and drinks. In the travel and lodging industries, the market consists of everyone who travels. In the

# Hospitality Ethics

## Copyrighted Material

It is unethical to use something created or written by another person. Under copyright law, as soon as something is in tangible form, it is automatically copyrighted. Anything in print—including music, images on television or movie screens, or the Internet—is copyrighted. If any material is copied or used without the copyright holder's permission, a theft has occurred. It is critical for a marketing professional to not use copyrighted material in print promotions.

recreation industry, the market consists of everyone. Because meeting the needs of such diverse and large markets is difficult, it is more useful to divide the market into subgroups with similar needs. These subgroups are called *market segments*. A market segment is a subgroup of a larger market and has similar needs and wants for the product you are selling.

The process of dividing a large market into market segments is called **market segmentation**. After a market has been segmented, the business will choose a segment on which to focus. The *target market* is the market segment whose needs you strive to meet.

A very useful way to segment a market is based on age. Age segments might include children, teens, adults, and older adults. Another way to segment the market is based on family size. Family segments include singles, couples, and families with children. Sometimes a market is segmented based on activities, such as businesspeople, shoppers, sightseers, and movie attendees. Another useful way is based on income, which may include segments for low, moderate, high, and very high.

There is no one right way to segment a market. A business will segment the market in the way it finds most useful. The most useful way to segment a market is the way that results in a good segment to target. A good target market is large, easy to identify, able to afford your product, and willing to buy your product.

A popular segment for a restaurant to target is families with children. The restaurant will then study these potential customers to determine what

they need and want. For example, they might discover that families need high chairs and booster seats. To meet these needs, the restaurant will make sure it has plenty of high chairs and booster seats.

A popular segment for hotels to target is business travelers. Business travelers are often on the road three to four days a week and do not want to feel like they are in a hotel. They want to feel at home and comfortable. To meet these needs, many hotels have installed more comfortable beds, ergonomic desk chairs, and décor that has a warm, homelike feeling.

A hospitality business usually decides on one or two target markets when it first opens. However, as the business develops and grows, it might decide to attract a new target market. For example, the number of female business travelers is growing, and many hotels want to attract them, **21-2**.

**21-2** Women business travelers are a specific growing market for hotels to target.

Wyndham Hotels was one of the first chains to target this market. A website and advisory board were developed to share resources and important travel tips with women travelers. As a result, Wyndham began offering a number of amenities to meet women travelers' needs. Examples include a hair dryer, iron, and ironing board in each room; complimentary "Toiletries You Forgot;" full-length mirrors; and more healthful menu choices.

## Product

As one of the Ps of marketing, product includes all activities involved in deciding what product to sell and developing the product. Will it be a restaurant or a hotel? It includes developing the *concept* for the restaurant or hotel. Will the restaurant be a casual family place or an elegant dining experience? Will the hotel emphasize lower prices with fewer amenities, or will it be a luxury resort? What will the décor be? All these questions will be answered with the target market in mind. Answering all these types of questions is part of the product task of marketing.

Part of marketing and the product decision is to look for changes in wants and needs in the target market. If a change occurs, the business investigates ways to change the product to meet those new needs and wants.

The product decision includes deciding on the general price range of the business. Price ranges might be as low as possible, budget, moderate, high, and luxury. The price range is also chosen with the target market in mind.

## Price

After the general price range is decided, the exact price to charge for each product and service must be decided. The price task of marketing consists of setting prices. Setting prices is a complex task that involves knowing your costs, profit goals, and competitors' prices. The top managers of a business usually set the prices. Setting prices can be particularly complex in the hotel and airline industries because prices vary based on demand. Many hotels use **revenue management software**, a type of software that helps calculate the best prices to charge for guest rooms.

## Place

The place task of marketing involves determining where the product will be sold. For the foodservice industry and the lodging industry, the place decision includes determining where the restaurant or hotel should be located. Location is often a key factor in determining the success of a hospitality business, **21-3**.

21-3 Do you think this business's location contributes to its success?

*Doubletree La Posada Resort. Hilton Hotels Corporation*

# *Promotion*

The fourth P, promotion, is the one most often identified with marketing. It is the most visible and often the most expensive part. Most businesses have at least one staff person who is responsible for promotion.

## Communication with Customers

Promotion is communication with customers. Specifically, **promotion** is telling customers about a product or the company that offers it. The purpose of promotion is to influence customers to buy the product while creating a positive image of the company and the brand.

Two types of communication are used in promotion: personal and nonpersonal. **Personal communication** occurs when two or more people communicate directly, either in person or by telephone. When a travel agent describes a beautiful resort to the customer sitting in front of her, she is using personal communication. **Nonpersonal communication** is a set message conveyed through mass media, including television, radio, the Internet, newspapers, magazines, fliers, pamphlets, and billboards. Imagine a print advertisement in the newspaper for the same beautiful resort. The advertisement is nonpersonal communication, **21-4**.

There are four types of promotion: advertising, sales promotion, public relations, and sales. Advertising, sales promotion, and public relations all use nonpersonal communication. For example, a Wendy's commercial on television is nonpersonal communication. Everybody who watches TV sees the exact same Wendy's commercial.

Sales uses personal communication. **Sales** is promotion that occurs when a representative of the company speaks directly with the customer about the product. The sales representative can adjust the message to meet the needs of each individual customer. Personal communication is what separates sales from other forms of promotion. In fact, sales is often called *personal selling*.

The term *sales* has several meanings. In the business sense, *sales* is the money the business takes in when it sells its product. Sales is the reason the business exists. Another word for this meaning of sales is *revenue*. A business needs sales (revenue) to run the business and make a profit. A restaurant makes sales every time a guest pays for a meal and a hotel makes sales every time a guest pays for a room.

*wavebreakmedia/Shutterstock.com*

**21-4** You may notice promotions in the form of print advertisements when you read a magazine.

The goal of the whole business is to increase sales. As a result, everything employees do can increase sales. In the hospitality industry, every member of the staff must be committed to selling the business every day, in everything they do, and with everyone they meet. A smiling greeting, quality food, gracious service, and attention to detail all contribute to increasing sales. Part of the reason HR works so hard to keep employees happy is that happy employees are more motivated to sell the business every day and in every way.

Promotion consists of those activities whose specific goal is to increase sales. In the context of promotion, *sales* refers to the process of communicating directly with customers to influence them to buy the product. In the promotion context, sales is part of a complete plan to increase sales (revenue) of the hospitality business.

Hospitality businesses need repeat business. **Repeat business** consists of satisfied customers who return to the business again and again. Hospitality businesses also need good word-of-mouth publicity. Each interaction between a hospitality employee and a guest influences the guest, so the goal of each employee is to make that influence positive, **21-5**. Then the guest is more likely to return and to tell friends good things about the business.

## Brand Identity

The development of a brand identity is an important part of marketing. Often it is considered part of promotion. However, a brand identity should represent all the decisions made about target market, product, price, place, and promotion.

A *brand* is a name, logo, tagline, or any combination of these that distinguishes a product from its competitors. When customers see the brand, they associate a certain product and type of service with it. It is very important that a brand be unique so it does not get confused with another brand.

The *logo* is the part of the brand that includes the brand name or corporate name. The logo is usually in a distinctive typeface and graphic design. Once the logo is developed, it is used on most, if not all, of the promotional materials, signs, and communications with customers and suppliers. A unique and consistently used logo creates brand recognition.

# The Marketing Plan

A **marketing plan** is a document that lists the marketing goals of the business and describes how

these goals will be achieved. Upper management develops the marketing plan using marketing research and sales data. Sales data, which tells how much money the business made in the past year, is usually obtained from the accounting department. In a hotel, management will use reports generated by the PMS. These reports might include numbers of guests from each state, amount of money each guest spent during the stay, percent of sales from conventions, and other data about guests and their stays.

The marketing plan helps the company accomplish its goals. It also helps management figure out ways to actually reach the goals. Marketing plans are extremely important for a new business. However, most companies update their marketing plans every year to make sure they are meeting both customer needs and the company's goals.

Marketing plans usually have four sections: situation analysis, goals, strategies, and evaluation, **21-6**.

## Situation Analysis

A business must understand the situation it is in. The *business situation*, sometimes called the *business environment*, includes everything that could affect the business. The two aspects of the business environment are the external business environment and the internal business environment.

The *external business environment* includes influences that are outside the business and cannot be controlled by it. Types of external influences include the status of the economy, the

21-5 Servers can encourage repeat business by being pleasant and friendly to customers.

CREATISTA/Shutterstock.com

---

### Parts of a Marketing Plan

**Situation Analysis:** analysis of all factors that could affect the business, such as economic conditions, competitors, and changes in the market

**Goals:** a statement of what the business wants to achieve in a specific time period, usually a year

**Strategies:** a detailed plan for achieving the goals

**Evaluation:** the process of determining whether the strategies achieved the goals

*Goodheart-Willcox Publisher*

21-6 A marketing plan is a document that lists the marketing goals of the business and describes how these goals will be achieved.

political situation, government regulations, competitors, and changes in the market.

One of the major components of the external business environment is competitors. A **competitor** is a business similar to yours that wants to take away your customers. In order to make good business decisions, you must know as much as you can about your competitors. The hospitality industry is very competitive. Customers have many choices of restaurants and hotels. For example, Antonio Amore opened an Italian restaurant called Amore's. Suppose a unit of the Olive Garden chain opens across the street from Amore's. The new unit of Olive Garden and its location will be an important external influence on Antonio's business. Keep in mind that competition is not necessarily bad. In Antonio's case, there may be enough demand for Italian food that both restaurants will be successful. In addition, after the Olive Garden opens, Antonio might decide to make his restaurant different from the Olive Garden to attract a different target market.

The *internal business environment* includes all influences that are inside the business. Often a business can do something about an internal influence that causes a problem. For example, one type of internal problem is a high rate of employee turnover. The business can do something to reduce the turnover rate. However, the things that need to be done to reduce the turnover rate might be expensive. Another internal problem might be the location of the business. The company could consider moving the business, but that might not be financially reasonable. Instead, the company could develop a marketing campaign that would counteract the problem of a poor location.

Another way of analyzing the business situation is called SWOT. *SWOT* stands for *strengths, weaknesses, opportunities, and threats*. The business analyzes its internal business environment for strengths and weaknesses. The business then analyzes the external business environment for opportunities and threats. As the marketing plan is developed, the business will try to take advantage of its strengths and build up its weak areas. It will also try to take advantage of opportunities and minimize threats.

For example, Amore's strength is its unique family recipes. Its weakness is the cost and amount of time needed to make the special recipes. The opportunity is the fact that the town in which Amore's is located is growing, and people are eating out more. The threat is the new Italian restaurant that opened across the street. The goal of Antonio Amore's marketing plan will be to emphasize the strengths, figure out a way to turn the weakness into a strength, and figure out a way to attract customers away from the new competitor.

## Goals

Upper management will work with marketing to develop specific goals, **21-7**. The goals will be based on the business situation. Typical marketing goals for a restaurant include the following:

- Increase the number of customers on Tuesday nights by 20 percent.
- Advertise in the local newspaper.
- Develop a promotional program to increase the number of older adult customers.

Typical marketing goals for a hotel might include the following:

- Attract 20 percent more leisure travelers on weekends.
- Sell 3,000 more rooms to groups.

## Strategies

The strategy section is the heart of the marketing plan. In this section, a detailed plan is given for achieving the goals. Specific departments and staff are assigned specific projects. Time lines are given for completion of the projects and budgets are set.

For example, suppose a hotel wants to sell 3,000 more rooms to groups. The detailed plan would include advertising to the groups, developing special room rates for groups, and assigning specific sales representatives to call on certain

**21-7** Development of a business's goals requires direction from upper management as well as input from marketing.

Yuri Arcurs/Shutterstock.com

categories of groups. A calendar for completing these activities will also be included.

## Evaluation

Every good marketing plan includes a section on evaluation. The business needs to know if the marketing plan is achieving its goals. The plan also needs to be evaluated in case there has been a change in the business situation. The marketing plan will specify times, procedures, and standards for evaluating the marketing plan.

# Promotion Methods

There are four main methods of promotion: advertising, public relations, sales promotion, and personal selling, **21-8**. These methods are often described in the strategies section of a marketing plan.

## Advertising

**Advertising** is a promotional message about a product that is paid for by an identified sponsor. Advertising is nonpersonal communication. One promotional advertising message is called an **advertisement**. Often an advertisement is referred to as an *ad*. A message is developed and then broadcast to a large number of people. Advertising takes many forms, most commonly commercials, print, Internet, billboards, and reader boards.

A **commercial** is an advertisement that is broadcast on television or radio. Commercials are often called *broadcast advertising*. Commercials are like short TV or radio shows. They usually require actors, music, scripts, and sophisticated TV or radio equipment. Many fast-food restaurants advertise on TV.

**Print advertising** consists of ads that appear on paper. Print ads appear in newspapers and magazines, **21-9**. Print advertising also includes fliers, posters, and brochures. Most hospitality businesses use some form of print advertising.

**Internet advertising** usually takes the form of the company website and ads on other websites, such as travel websites and Internet search engines. Most major hospitality businesses have a company website that provides detailed information about the business's products and services. A restaurant website usually provides a menu. A hotel website will provide photos of its rooms and facilities. A resort or entertainment website might provide a virtual tour of the facility. Airline websites will provide route and schedule information. Most hospitality websites enable customers to make reservations or order tickets over the Internet.

A **billboard** is a type of print advertising that appears on a large outdoor panel. Billboards are also called *outdoor advertising*. Lodging properties and restaurants located along highways find billboards effective in attracting guests.

A **reader board** is an announcement board located in a hotel lobby and other locations on a

---

### Promotion Methods

**Advertising:** nonpersonal promotional message about a product that is paid for by an identified sponsor

    **Commercials:** advertising that is broadcast on television or radio

    **Print advertising:** advertising that appears on paper

    **Internet advertising:** advertising on the Web

    **Billboards:** type of print advertising that appears on a large outdoor panel

    **Reader board:** an announcement board, usually located in a hotel lobby

**Public Relations:** activities performed to create goodwill between the public and the business

**Sales Promotion:** a specific offer designed to increase sales

**Personal Selling:** communication directly between the seller and potential customers

    **Suggestive selling:** recommending products or services to an individual customer

    **Group sales:** one or more salespeople selling hospitality services to groups

*Goodheart-Willcox Publisher*

21-8 The methods of promotion are often described in the strategies section of a marketing plan.

When your event is on the line, so are we.

**Bring your next event to the Hilton Pasadena.** With 296 guest rooms, 26,000 sq. ft. of meeting and event space and an award winning restaurant, your event will go exactly as planned. To book now call us directly at **626-577-1000**.

Hilton HHonors
Points & Miles

**It happens** at the Hilton.

Hilton HHonors membership, earning of Points & Miles, and redemption of points are subject to HHonors Terms and Conditions. ©2002 Hilton Hospitality, Inc.

*Hilton Hotels Corporation*

**21-9** You may see print ads such as this in travel magazines.

lodging property. The reader board lists the time, location, and sponsor of all events in the hotel for the day. In most hotels, the reader board is a TV monitor. The hotel has its own channel, which guests can also view on in-room TVs.

## Public Relations

**Public relations** consists of activities performed to create goodwill between the public and the business. *Goodwill* is a positive feeling of approval. Creating goodwill usually has two parts. The first part is doing something good or newsworthy. The second part is making sure that the public knows about it.

One of the main ways businesses do something good is to support charitable causes. Companies support a wide variety of charitable causes, including children's sports teams, reduction of environmental pollution, and research for a cancer cure. The McDonald's Corporation supports the Ronald McDonald House Charities. The purpose of the Ronald McDonald House Charities is to improve the health and well-being of children. To date, there are more than 275 Ronald McDonald Houses in 52 countries.

Public relations staff members make sure that the public knows about the good works. The main way they do this is to write a press release. A **press release** is an article written by a company for use as the basis for news in a newspaper, Internet, radio, or TV news program. Other ways to let the public know about good works include holding an event, such as a grand opening, and holding a press conference.

The result of activities by public relations staff is publicity. **Publicity** is information that appears in the media about a company or product. Publicity is not paid for by the company. As a result, the company cannot control what the media writes or says about the company or its products. The goal of the public relations staff is to get the media to give positive reports. For example, suppose your restaurant decides to serve free Thanksgiving dinners to the homeless. Your public relations writer writes press releases that are then sent to all the local newspapers and radio and TV stations. You would hope that, as a result, some news reports would mention the free dinners. Ideally, a TV station or newspaper would send a crew to your restaurant. The crew would get interviews with you and with some of your homeless guests and take photographs for the newspaper or video for the TV broadcast.

Publicity is sometimes called *unpaid promotion* because a sponsor does not pay for it. The media decides whether to write about your company at all and exactly what to say. For this reason, many people think publicity is unbiased. People trust articles in newspapers and news reports in the media more than advertising.

However, publicity is not always positive. If there is a problem at your restaurant, the media will also cover that. For example, if some people eat at your restaurant and get sick, the media will report it. Publicity that exposes problems with the company or its products is called *bad publicity*. Bad publicity can spread very quickly over the Internet. Another one of the responsibilities of public relations staff is to respond immediately to bad publicity.

## Sales Promotion

A **sales promotion** is a specific offer designed to increase sales. A sales promotion is often referred to as an *incentive*—something that attracts a person to action. An example of an incentive is a "buy one, get one free" offer. Another incentive is an offer of a free gift if you purchase something. Sales promotions include free product samples, coupons, two-for-one offers, sweepstakes, and loyalty programs.

Coupons are a popular form of sales promotion. Many fast-food restaurants print coupons in local newspapers or post them online. When the customer brings the coupon to the restaurant, they pay a lower price for the product. For example, Pizza Hut offers weekly coupons.

A **loyalty program** is a program that rewards frequent customers with free or lower-priced products, **21-10**. The program keeps track of customer purchases. When a customer reaches a certain level of purchases, he or she gets a reward. The airlines discovered the value of loyalty programs when they started their frequent flier programs in the 1980s. After a customer had flown a certain number of miles, he or she got a free ticket. Now many types of hospitality businesses have loyalty programs. In a hotel loyalty program, each hotel stay adds points to your account. After you have accumulated a specific number of points, you get a free night or a gift card. Some of these programs are set up to earn frequent flier miles on an airline as well.

A business will often look at the market segments to develop a sales promotion. The business will then design an incentive to encourage the target market to try the service or product. For example, a restaurant that wants to attract families with children might develop a kid's meal with a special price.

## Personal Selling

Two types of personal selling occur in the hospitality business. The first is suggestive selling. The second is group sales.

### Suggestive Selling

Suggestive selling can be done by any hospitality worker. **Suggestive selling** is recommending additional products or services to a customer while that customer is buying something else. For example, a restaurant server might recommend dessert. Hotel reservations or front desk agents might recommend a larger room or a longer stay.

Suggestive selling can significantly increase sales in restaurants that have seated service. Many restaurants train servers to use suggestive selling techniques. Servers are trained to present menu items in an appealing way. Servers may be instructed to recommend the more expensive items. Servers are often instructed to recommend wine, appetizers, desserts, and after-dinner drinks. Guests are often pleased with the recommendations. The more food and beverages the guest orders, the more money the restaurant makes. The server is also likely to get a larger tip due to the larger guest check.

### Group Sales

Restaurants and hotels that sell to groups will have a sales department. In a smaller business, one person, either the general manager or a salesperson, will be the sales department. Group sales consist of selling meals, lodging, and other facility services to groups, **21-11**. Groups include corporations, professional associations, charitable groups, and social groups. Job titles for people who work in sales include: salesperson, sales representative, account executive, director of catering, banquets manager, sales agent, or sales manager. These salespeople sell banquets, catering services, meeting rooms, convention services, exhibition services, and event planning services.

Many lodging properties earn a large percentage of their revenue from group sales. As a result, these properties will have a large sales department.

**21-10** A loyalty program card may be swiped when a purchase is made to add points to the account.

*Lili White/Shutterstock.com*

21-11 Group sales may include events such as conventions, meetings, and weddings.

Sales staff members are responsible for finding potential groups and contacting them. Sales staff members contact potential customers by phone, mail, and in person. Companies or professional associations that hold large conventions often visit the hotel to observe the facilities and quality of service. The sales department hosts these visitors.

The director of catering is an important part of the sales effort in a hotel. The director of catering may be part of the sales department or the banquet department. On occasion, catering is a separate department, but has dotted-line reporting relationships with the sales and banquet departments. Regardless of where in the organizational chart the catering director is, he or she must work closely with the sales department and the banquet department. The salesperson will make the initial contact with the group and sell them on the idea of using the hotel for their convention. The salesperson will also arrange for the booking of the sleeping rooms. The group representative will work with the catering manager to plan the meals and meetings. If a trade exhibit is involved, the group representative will also work with the exhibits manager to plan the exhibition hall. The catering manager will then work with the banquet department to make sure the food is ordered and prepared. The catering director or another member of the catering staff attends all the events. The catering director is responsible for making sure all aspects of each function run smoothly.

Sales representatives must have good people skills and friendly attitudes. They must also be detail oriented because arranging meetings and events requires attention to many details.

# Hospitality Marketing

All hospitality businesses market themselves. The amount and type of marketing varies with the business. A small business may do very little marketing. In these cases, the general manager or owner will handle the marketing and sales. Many larger businesses and chains have full marketing and sales divisions or departments.

Many smaller businesses do not have the expertise to carry out marketing tasks and functions. Some of the larger businesses and chains have so much marketing work that they can't do it all themselves. In such cases, the manager responsible for marketing will hire an outside agency.

## Outside Agencies

Marketing is an industry all of its own. There are companies that offer services in all areas of marketing. They will work with the managers of a business to develop a marketing plan, carry out the plan, and evaluate it.

Other companies specialize in specific areas of marketing. Some specialize in marketing research, advertising, or public relations, 21-12. Others specialize in website development and management. There are also companies that specialize in restaurant and hotel marketing, advertising, and public relations.

## Single-Unit Restaurant

A single-unit restaurant is likely to do some advertising, public relations, and sales promotion. If the restaurant is large and handles group

21-12 This advertising agency develops print ads for hospitality businesses.

functions, it might also have someone who handles group sales. The general manager or owner is likely to be in charge of all marketing and sales. The general manager may develop the marketing plan. He or she may then hire an advertising agency to carry out the advertising part of the plan and a website developer/manager to develop and manage the website. The general manager may also make sure that the servers get trained in suggestive selling.

## Single-Unit Lodging Property

The amount of marketing done by a single-unit property will depend on its size and its goals. Some very small properties may just print a brochure and rely on word-of-mouth. A small lodging property may handle marketing in a way similar to a small restaurant—the general manager or owner will be responsible for all marketing and sales. The general manager will develop a marketing plan and then hire an agency to perform parts of the plan.

A large convention hotel will have a whole division or department devoted to marketing and sales, **21-13.** The director of this department will work with the general manager and other department managers to develop the marketing plan. The director will then work with his or her department managers and staff to ensure that the goals are met.

The marketing and sales division often has three departments: sales, advertising, and public relations. The public relations manager will write press releases, plan publicity events, and develop contacts with the media. In special situations, the public relations manager might hire an outside public relations agency.

The advertising manager will handle all the advertising for the hotel. Advertising might include billboards, reader boards, ads in newspapers and magazines, and brochures about the hotel. The advertising manager might hire an outside agency for special projects. For example, a billboard will require special expertise.

The sales manager will be responsible for group sales and the sales staff. Group sales are often divided into four areas: convention services, corporate sales, catering, and reservations. Each area may have one or more staff members. The convention services sales staff will research and develop contacts with organizations that hold conventions. The goal is to convince these organizations to hold their conventions at the hotel.

The corporate sales department will target corporations with employees who must stay at a hotel when they travel for work. The sales representatives will contact corporations that need lodging for their traveling employees. The goal is to convince the corporation to always use the hotel when their employees travel.

The catering department will cover general group sales not covered by the previous two departments. These groups would include social and family groups making arrangements for weddings, reunions, and charity events.

Often, the reservations sales agents are considered part of the sales division. However, they may also be part of the front office.

**21-13** A large hotel will have a marketing and sales division.

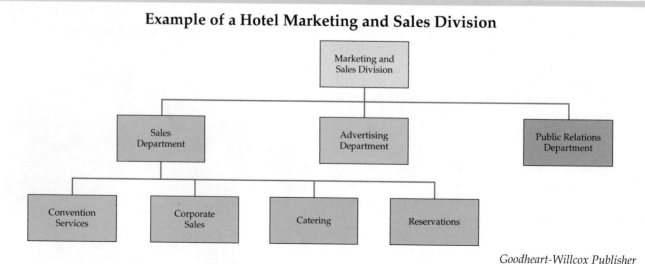

**Example of a Hotel Marketing and Sales Division**

*Goodheart-Willcox Publisher*

## Chains

One of the advantages of a chain is more resources for marketing. The corporate headquarters usually has a marketing department. This marketing department will develop a marketing plan for the entire chain. A chain will often have regional or national advertising. The corporate office will handle the national advertising. For example, Chili's is a national restaurant chain. The advertising department at Chili's national headquarters will handle development of TV commercials that promote all units of the Chili's chain.

Many chains require that each unit use only the advertising developed by national headquarters. Other chains may allow each unit to do some local advertising. However, most chains require that the national office approve any local advertising.

## Tourism Organizations

Many government and nonprofit organizations promote the hospitality industry. Governments may have departments or ministers of tourism, and many hospitality businesses have joined together to create nonprofit organizations to promote tourism. These governments and businesses realize that the hospitality industry is critical to economic success. An increase in hospitality and tourism increases jobs, incomes, and standards of living.

### International

One of the major international organizations that promote tourism is the World Tourism Organization (UNWTO). Its members include 155 countries and territories, 6 associate members, and over 400 affiliate members. This organization is a specialized agency of the United Nations. The affiliate UNWTO members are members who are not national governments. Affiliate members include local governments, tourism associations, and private hospitality businesses such as airlines and hotels.

### National

Many nations have national tourism organizations that promote their countries to the international tourist market. These organizations are part of the national government. The United States has the U.S. Office of Travel & Tourism Industries (OTTI), which is part of the Department of Commerce. China has the China National Tourism Administration. Many countries have a ministry of tourism. Mexico is one example.

### State and Local

In the United States, each state has an office of tourism, often located in the state's department of economic development. These offices carry out a great deal of advertising for their states. You can contact any state office of tourism and get maps, brochures, and lists of the attractions in the state.

In addition, many cities and regions have convention and visitor bureaus, 21-14. A **convention and visitors bureau (CVB)** is a nonprofit organization that promotes tourism and provides services to travelers. A CVB may be an independent organization, part of the city government, or part of a chamber of commerce. A CVB works to get groups to have conventions in its city. A CVB carries out many marketing activities, including marketing research and advertising. Most CVBs also help convention planners and visitors plan their visits to the city or area. Many CVBs have tourist information centers along major highways in their region. The tourist information centers are staffed with a tourism specialist, who can answer questions and help tourists plan their trips. The centers are also stocked with maps and brochures about attractions and hotels in the area.

21-14 Convention and visitors bureaus provide information for tourists and promote tourism to the area.

Lake County Indiana Convention & Visitors Bureau, Hammond, Indiana. www.alllake.org

# Chapter 21
# Review

## Chapter Summary

- The major functions of marketing are: Learn what customers want and need. Develop a product that meets those wants and needs. Make sure that potential customers know about the product. Persuade customers to buy your product.

- The basic areas of marketing are target market, product, price, place, and promotion.

- The marketing plan helps the company accomplish its goals.

- In order to make good business decisions, the business must know as much as possible about competitors.

- The four main methods of promotion are advertising, public relations, sales promotion, and personal selling.

- Two types of personal selling occur in the hospitality business: suggestive selling and group sales.

- All hospitality businesses market themselves.

- Many government and nonprofit organizations promote the hospitality industry.

## Review

1. List the four major functions of marketing.
2. List and summarize the five basic areas of marketing.
3. Describe at least two ways to segment a market.
4. What is the difference between personal communication and nonpersonal communication?
5. List the four parts of a marketing plan.
6. Give four examples of external influences on a business.
7. Give an example of each of the four main methods of promotion.
8. List five types of advertising.
9. What is the purpose of public relations?
10. Name two types of personal selling that occur in hospitality businesses.
11. When would a hospitality business use an outside marketing agency?
12. Why do governments promote tourism?
13. What are the functions of a convention and visitor's bureau?

# Critical Thinking

14. **Compare and contrast.** Compare the marketing done by a small business with that done by a large chain.

15. **Identify.** Choose a hospitality business with which you are very familiar. Describe the target market, product, and place of that business.

16. **Evaluate.** Choose a hospitality business with which you are very familiar. Select one of that business's products. Describe its price and a promotion you have seen for that product. Would you say the promotion was effective? Cite your reasons.

17. **Draw conclusions.** Explain the purposes of a loyalty program, citing five examples of loyalty programs in the hospitality industry.

18. **Make inferences.** What do you think are the target marks for each of the following hospitality venues?
    - a country club
    - a fine-dining restaurant
    - a cruise on a Disney Cruise Line ship

## Common Core

### College and Career Readiness

19. **Writing.** Imagine that you are the marketing and sales director for a convention hotel. Write a summary describing how you would promote your hotel.

20. **Speaking.** Create an electronic presentation on the four Ps of marketing and present it to the class.

21. **Reading.** Find five advertisements related to the hospitality industry. Evaluate these advertisements to see if they are adequately influencing customers to buy the product or service.

22. **Writing.** Create an Internet advertisement for a new bed-and-breakfast inn.

23. **Listening.** Interview a local hospitality manager about SWOT analyses and how they are used in the business. Report a summary of the interview to the class.

24. **CTE Career Readiness Practice.** Suppose you are interested in a career in the marketing career pathway. You have done your research in regard to educational requirements for such careers and think this fits with your personal goals and career goals. However, you feel you are missing the first-hand experiential knowledge necessary to commit to such a career. Locate a person with a local company or organization who is an expert in your career of interest. Make arrangements to job shadow or work with this individual as a mentor as you pursue your career. How can you benefit by having such a mentor in your life?

398

# Chapter 22
## Accounting

## Chapter Objectives

After studying this chapter, you will be able to
- **compare and contrast** a credit and a debit.
- **describe** the functions of the accounting department.
- **explain** the purpose of the Uniform System of Accounts.
- **identify** the responsibilities of the controller.
- **describe** the responsibilities of the five departments in a hotel accounting division.
- **explain** why the front office and accounting department must have a good working relationship.

## Before You Read

Try to answer the following questions before you read this chapter.
- What are some examples of financial statements?
- What is a night audit?

## Terms to Know

| | | |
|---|---|---|
| financial transaction | system of accounts | night audit |
| ledger | Uniform System of Accounts | night auditor |
| accounting | controller | posting charges |
| debit | accounts receivable | credit department |
| credit | accounts receivable clerk | credit history |
| payroll | accounts payable | food and beverage controller |
| taxes | accounts payable clerk | delinquent guests |
| account | audit | point of sale |

In the Middle Ages, innkeepers kept simple records of their daily financial transactions. A **financial transaction** is the process of buying something and paying for it. The innkeepers recorded each financial transaction in a book called a **ledger**. As the restaurant and hotel industry developed from single, individually owned inns to today's giant restaurant and hotel chains, the need for a more sophisticated system increased. Today, record keeping, financial analyses, budgets, and forecasts are major parts of hospitality management, **22-1**. **Accounting** is a system of recording and summarizing financial transactions and analyzing and reporting the results. An accounting department performs many functions and activities related to handling the company's finances. Examples of accounting activities include maintaining records of all financial transactions, preparing budgets, managing credit, controlling cash and costs, purchasing and receiving inventory, developing financial statements, processing payroll, and paying taxes.

Debits and credits are the basis of accounting systems. A **debit** is money that is owed or taken out of a business. A debit is subtracted from a total. A **credit** is money or payment that has been received. A credit is added to a total.

# Functions

Accounting departments have five main functions: keep track of all financial transactions, make payments and deposits, categorize transactions, control costs, and prepare financial reports and statements.

## *Keep Track of Transactions*

The accounting department keeps a record of every financial transaction that occurs in the business. Many different kinds of transactions take place in a restaurant or hotel business each day. The general categories of transactions are guest purchases, business purchases, payroll, and taxes. Guest purchases include anything a guest buys, including meals, sleeping accommodations, spa services, and gifts. Business purchases include everything the business buys to run the business, including kitchen equipment, food, linens, and outside services such as laundry and advertising. **Payroll** is a special type of purchase: the money paid to employees for their labor. **Taxes** are money paid to the federal, state, and local government as required by law.

Computer systems and software are used in many hospitality businesses to keep track of financial transactions. The software used in a lodging business is called the *Property Management System (PMS)*. The software used in a food and beverage business is called *Point-of-Sales System (POS)*. (Many hotels also have a POS system.) The PMS keeps track of each lodging guest's purchases. When the guest checks in, the front desk agent sets up a record for that guest. This record is called the *guest folio*. From that time on, every time the guest charges a good or service to the room, it is recorded in the guest folio. At the end of the stay, the PMS will generate a bill, **22-2**. The POS keeps track of the food and beverage purchases of each restaurant guest. The server will create a record in the POS for each party and record the orders of each guest. At the end of the meal, the POS will generate a bill. The information in the PMS or POS for customer transactions is then transferred to the general accounts of the business.

## *Make Payments and Deposits*

The accounting department handles all the money that flows in and out of the business. Bills are paid by the *accounts payable clerks* in the accounting department. When money has been received and needs to be deposited in the bank, the accounting department handles it. The people who handle this function are called *accounts receivable clerks*. The accounting department also handles payroll.

22-1 Accounting is an important aspect of managing a hospitality business.

*Homewood Suites by Hilton. Hilton Hotels Corporation*

## PMS-Generated Hotel Bill

**The Taylor Inn**
**1500 Mistletoe Lane**
**Corpus Christi, Texas**

| Last Name | First Name | | | | Folio | Page |
|-----------|------------|--|--|--|-------|------|
| Olivera   Rachel M. | | | | | 1 | 1 |

| Street | | | | Room | Rate |
|--------|--|--|--|------|------|
| 2019 Heatherbrook Drive | | | | 1210 | 119.00 |

| City | State | Zip Code | Arrival | Departure |
|------|-------|----------|---------|-----------|
| Chicago | IL | 60477 | 2/28/XX | 3/4/XX |
| | | | Bonuses | Type |

### CCARD

Tele- xxx-xxx-xxxx      Fax- xxx-xxx-xxxx

| Date | Rm | Description | | Charge |
|------|-----|-------------|--|--------|
| 2/28 | 1210 | ROOM SERVICE | 1210/3572/21:47/ROOM SERVICE | $13.77 |
| 2/28 | 1210 | ROOM CHARGE | #1210 OLIVERA, RACHEL M. | $119.00 |
| 2/28 | 1210 | CITY OCCUPANCY TAX - 9% | CITY OCCUPANCY TAX - 9% | $10.71 |
| 2/28 | 1210 | STATE OCCUPANCY TAX - 6% | STATE OCCUPANCY TAX - 6% | $7.14 |
| 3/1 | 1210 | ONION CREEK GRILL | 1210/1504/13:39/ONION CREEK GRILL | $5.60 |
| 3/1 | 1210 | ROOM CHARGE | #1210 OLIVERA, RACHEL M. | $119.00 |
| 3/1 | 1210 | CITY OCCUPANCY TAX - 9% | CITY OCCUPANCY TAX - 9% | $10.71 |
| 3/1 | 1210 | STATE OCCUPANCY TAX - 6% | STATE OCCUPANCY TAX - 6% | $7.14 |
| 3/2 | 1210 | ROOM CHARGE | #1210 OLIVERA, RACHEL M. | $119.00 |
| 3/2 | 1210 | CITY OCCUPANCY TAX - 9% | CITY OCCUPANCY TAX - 9% | $10.71 |
| 3/2 | 1210 | STATE OCCUPANCY TAX - 6% | STATE OCCUPANCY TAX - 6% | $7.14 |
| 3/3 | 1210 | ROOM SERVICE | 1210/3737/18:38/ROOM SERVICE | $15.21 |
| 3/3 | 1210 | ROOM CHARGE | #1210 OLIVERA, RACHEL M. | $119.00 |
| 3/3 | 1210 | CITY OCCUPANCY TAX - 9% | CITY OCCUPANCY TAX - 9% | $10.71 |
| 3/3 | 1210 | STATE OCCUPANCY TAX - 6% | STATE OCCUPANCY TAX - 6% | $7.14 |
| 3/3 | 1210 | MOVIES | 46 SERVICES | $12.71 |
| 3/4 | 1210 | ROOM CHARGE | #1210 OLIVERA, RACHEL M. | $119.00 |
| 3/4 | 1210 | CITY OCCUPANCY TAX - 9% | CITY OCCUPANCY TAX - 9% | $10.71 |
| 3/4 | 1210 | STATE OCCUPANCY TAX - 6% | STATE OCCUPANCY TAX - 6% | $7.14 |
| | | Subtotal | $731.54 | |
| 3/4I | 1210 | VISA         VISA | XXXXXXXXXXXX1205 Ex XX/XX | ($731.54) |

TOTAL DUE     $.00

I agree that my liability for this bill is not
waived and I agree to be held personally
liable in the event that the indicated person,
company, or association fails to pay for any
part or the full amount of these charges.

_____
Signature

*Goodheart-Willcox Publisher*

22-2  The Property Management System (PMS) makes it easy to provide guests with an itemized bill.

## Categorize Transactions

Another important accounting function is to categorize the transactions. Transactions are categorized by placing each transaction in its proper account.

### Accounts

An **account** is a financial record that lists transactions and shows the balance. A simple example of an account is a personal checking account at a bank. Whenever you deposit money into your account, the transaction is recorded as a credit. Whenever you take money out of the account, the transaction is recorded as a debit. You receive an account statement at the end of the month showing all the transactions that have taken place on your account during the month. In addition, the statement provides a *balance*. The balance shows the amount of money currently in the account, which is determined by subtracting all debits and adding all credits.

The accounting department will set up a separate account for each category of transaction, **22-3**. Each separate account will be used to keep track of all the transactions in one category. The account can then be analyzed to determine the expenses or revenues in that category.

For example, a hotel needs to know how much money it spends on cleaning supplies each month. The accounting department will set up an account called "Cleaning Supplies." Every time a cleaning supply is purchased, the record of that transaction goes into the "Cleaning Supplies" account. The cost of the supply and the amount

paid for it is recorded. At the end of the month, the total amount spent on cleaning supplies can be calculated. This information is needed by the executive housekeeper to determine whether the hotel is purchasing enough cleaning supplies and whether the hotel is getting the best price for them. This information is also used for budgeting.

### Universal System of Accounts

A **system of accounts** is an organized way of naming and categorizing accounts. In 1961, the American Hotel & Lodging Association asked the National Association of Accountants to develop a system of accounts for the lodging industry. The result was the Uniform System of Accounts for hotels.

The **Uniform System of Accounts** provides uniform names for each category of account for use throughout the hotel industry. It also provides a coding system for each account. The system specifies standard formats for preparing financial statements. The Uniform System of Accounts is often part of the PMS or POS. The computer system can identify and categorize each transaction as long as the transaction is given the proper name and code number when it is entered into the computer.

The Uniform System of Accounts makes it possible to compare financial data among different hotels within a company. A property can compare its own financial position and performance to other properties. Today, most businesses in the hospitality industry use the Uniform System of Accounts. There are three types of Uniform System of Accounts for the hospitality industry:

- Uniform System of Accounts for the Lodging Industry
- Uniform System of Accounts for Restaurants
- Uniform System of Accounts and Expense Dictionary for Small Hotels and Motels

## Control Costs

Another important task of the accounting department is controlling costs. The accounting department monitors the costs of items purchased by the business. If costs start rising, the accounting department notifies the appropriate manager. The manager then works to reduce costs. For example, the accounting department might notice that food costs have increased, **22-4**. Accounting will notify the manager, and together they will try to find the reason for the rise in food costs. The manager might discover that the five-ounce dinner portions

**22-3** Why is it helpful for the accounting department to set up a separate account for each category of transaction?

*Odua Images/shutterstock.com*

Kzenon/Shutterstock.com

22-4 Portion control is one way to control costs.

of chicken are being used in the lunch sandwiches, which are supposed to have the three-ounce lunch portions. The manager can now make sure that the proper three-ounce portions are used at lunch. The food costs should now drop back to normal.

## Prepare Financial Statements

The accounting department is responsible for preparing a variety of financial statements and financial reports. The preparation of these statements and reports requires analyzing the financial information that has been gathered. The financial statements help the owners assess if the business is making money or losing money.

The three basic financial statements are the balance sheet, the income statement, and the cash flow statement. The *balance sheet* is a document that shows the financial value of the company on a specific date. The balance sheet shows everything the business owns, such as a building, land, and equipment. It also shows everything that the business owes to other businesses, such as loans that must be repaid.

An *income statement* summarizes all the revenue made and all the expenses paid out during a specific period of time, such as a month or a year. Revenue is the money taken in when goods or services are sold. Expenses consist of the money paid out when the business buys things for the business and pays its employees. An income statement is also called a *profit and loss statement*.

A *cash flow statement* shows the way that cash moves in and out of the business during a specific period of time.

The accounting department is also responsible for filing tax returns to the federal, state, and local governments.

# The Controller

The top manager of an accounting department or division is called a *controller*. The **controller** oversees all the operations of the accounting department and supervises the accounting staff, **22-5**. The controller reports directly to the general manager.

One of the main responsibilities of the controller is to prepare reports based on the summaries of daily financial transactions. The reports are given to the general manager. If the hotel is part of a chain, the general manager usually sends these reports to the corporate headquarters. The reports that the controller develops include daily business reports and financial statements. The controller provides all the reports and statistics that are needed to evaluate and operate the property.

Another major responsibility of the controller is to supervise the preparation of budgets. The controller will work with other accounting staff and other department managers to develop department budgets and a total budget for the hotel. The total budget for the hotel will be presented to the general manager. In chain operations, a designated corporate officer will be given a copy of the budget for final approval. Once the budget has been approved, each department must stick to the budgeted amount.

*StockLite/Shtuterstock.com*

**22-5** The controller, the top manager of an accounting department, often works long hours.

A third major responsibility of the controller is to manage the accounting department. The controller is responsible for hiring, training, and supervising the accounting staff.

Independent restaurants typically do not have a controller. A restaurant might have only one or two people performing accounting tasks. A restaurant might also hire an accountant or accounting firm to do many of its accounting tasks. Restaurant chains will have an accounting department and a controller at the regional or corporate office.

# *Going Green*

## Green POS Systems

Many POS systems have features that prevent wasted energy and paper. For example, energy efficient terminals and computer servers reduce energy consumption and costs. These include ENERGY STAR qualified displays and back office equipment. To save even more energy, the power-management feature on terminals should be enabled.

Some POS systems offer paper-saving features, such as an electronic receipt option. Instead of printing out paper receipts, these systems can e-mail receipts to customers. This reduces paper use and allows the operation to save money. Forms and reports can also be filled out online and sent electronically.

# Departments Within Accounting

The accounting division of a large hotel is usually divided into five departments: accounts receivable, accounts payable, night audit, credit, and food and beverage controller, **22-6**. Large hotels have full accounting departments. They may have positions such as controller, accounts receivable clerks, accounts payable clerks, night auditors, cashiers, credit managers and clerks, payroll, internal controls, and a food and beverage controller.

The accounting division in a smaller hotel may be organized differently. There may not be any departments and one person may do several accounting tasks. For example, the manager or night auditor may do all of the accounting procedures at a small hotel. This person may be assisted by an outside accountant, who will analyze financial information and may also fill out the tax returns for the hotel.

## Accounts Receivable

**Accounts receivable** consists of money that is owed to a business. The department that is responsible for collecting the money owed to the business is called the *accounts receivable department*. Depending on the size of the business, there may be one or more accounts receivable clerks. If there are two or more clerks, there is usually an accounts receivable supervisor.

The **accounts receivable clerk** collects money that is owed to a business. Money that is owed should be collected as quickly as possible. The accounts receivable clerk will call or write letters to remind customers to pay outstanding bills. If a bill is not paid within ninety days, it will be sent to a collection agency. The collection agency will then be responsible for collecting the bill.

## Accounts Payable

**Accounts payable** consists of money that a business owes to other businesses. Restaurants and hotels buy equipment and supplies. They also buy outside services, such as laundry, lawn maintenance, and advertising. The bills for these items are usually not paid immediately. The *accounts payable department* is responsible for keeping track of the bills and making sure they get paid.

Depending on the size of the business, there may be one or more accounts payable clerks. If there are two or more clerks, there is usually an accounts payable supervisor. If the business is small, one person may do both accounts payable and accounts receivable.

The **accounts payable clerk** pays invoices that a business owes to other businesses, **22-7**. An *invoice* is another word for a bill. If the food and beverage department purchases tables, the table company will send an invoice to the hotel for the amount owed. The invoice is sent to the accounts payable clerk. When an invoice is received, the accounts payable clerk will check the quantity and unit cost that was billed. This will be checked against the purchase order and the receiving slip. Once the total on the invoice is checked and approved, the accounts payable clerk will initial the invoice to show that it is correct. The clerk then

**22-6** What are the responsibilities of each accounting division of a large hotel?

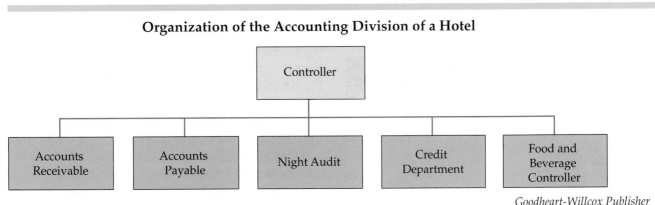

**Organization of the Accounting Division of a Hotel**

Controller

Accounts Receivable | Accounts Payable | Night Audit | Credit Department | Food and Beverage Controller

*Goodheart-Willcox Publisher*

mangostock/Shutterstock.com

22-7 The accounts receivable clerk collects all money that is owed to the business. The accounts payable clerk pays invoices that the hotel owes to other businesses. In a business, one person may handle both types of accounts.

pays the company for the tables. The purchase amount is entered as a debit to the food and beverage department in the hotel's accounting system.

Checks that are sent out from the accounts payable department to the supplier should be signed by at least two people, usually the general manager and the controller. All supporting documents, such as invoices and purchase orders, should be attached to the checks when they are presented for signatures. When the invoices have been paid, they may be voided with a "paid" stamp, 22-8. The invoices are then filed with a copy of the check.

*Payroll* is the money paid to employees. The same term is also used to refer to the process of

22-8 A "paid" stamp helps signal that an invoice is ready to be filed.

Raphael Daniaud/Shutterstock.com

paying employees. It is a separate process from accounts payable. Payroll is usually handled by a payroll clerk or a payroll department. The payroll department is responsible for making sure that each employee gets paid and the proper deductions are made for taxes and other items. It is also responsible for keeping records on each employee's payment history.

## Night Audit

An **audit** is a careful examination of the financial records of a person or company. All businesses perform audits on a regular basis to discover and correct accounting errors. Auditing is also done to make sure that proper accounting procedures are followed. Proper accounting procedures are referred to as *GAAP*, which stands for *generally accepted accounting principles*. The accounting department is responsible for making sure regular audits are done. Some businesses hire an outside accounting company to perform the audit. Regular audits show that the company is conducting business in a legal manner.

A night audit is a special type of audit that is performed nightly in a hotel. The **night audit** is the careful examination of the hotel's financial transactions for that day. The person who does the night audit is called the **night auditor**. The night auditor is usually a front desk agent on the night shift (11 p.m. to 7 a.m.). The night auditor may report to someone in the accounting department or to someone in the front office.

The night auditor performs several tasks as part of the night audit. One important task is to post room charges and taxes. Each night that a guest stays in the hotel, he or she is charged the room rate and taxes. These charges must be entered into each guest's folio, which is called **posting charges**. If the property has a PMS, the PMS automatically posts the charges.

Another task is balancing the daily financial transactions. The auditor will compare the cash, checks, and credit card receipts on hand with the records in the PMS. The two amounts should match. The purpose is to make sure no money was lost or stolen. While balancing the transactions, the night auditor may discover errors or problems. It is the night auditor's job to correct the errors and solve the problems.

The night auditor will also prepare a night audit report. This report will show the financial activities for each department for the day, total sales, and total expenses. These reports help managers with their financial planning. The night audit report is sent to the accounting department.

## Credit Department

The goal of the **credit department** is to protect the business from loss due to customers or businesses with bad credit, **22-9**. The credit department approves credit limits for each individual guest. The department also researches the credit history of businesses that want to do business with the hotel or restaurant. A **credit history** is a record that shows whether a person or a business pays its bills promptly. The credit history also shows if the person or business has failed to pay bills. If a person or a business has a poor credit history, it means that they may not pay their hotel bills.

Many businesses use the services of a particular hotel on a regular basis. In this case, the businesses may establish a credit account with the hotel so the business can charge hotel fees to the credit account. Then the hotel will bill the business once a month. Paying once a month is easier for the business than paying each time the business uses the hotel. The hotel manager has to make sure the business has a good credit history before the business can establish a credit account with the hotel.

For example, a business may want to hold regular meetings at a hotel. Employees of that business will spend about three nights at the hotel, banquets will be served, and meeting rooms will be used. The company plans to hold two of these meetings each month. The company wants to charge the expenses and be billed once a month. The credit department will check the credit history of the business to see if they pay their bills on time and if they are a good credit risk. If the business has a good credit history, the hotel will establish a credit account for the business, and the business will be billed monthly.

In large hotels, the credit department can consist of a credit manager, an administrative assistant, and a few assistants or clerks. The credit

22-9 How might a hospitality business be affected by people or businesses that do not pay bills in a timely manner?

*Marie C Fields/Shutterstock.com*

manager reports directly to the controller. In a small hotel, the general manager may designate a manager to handle credit. A small hotel may hire an outside credit management company to handle these tasks.

## *Food and Beverage Controller*

The **food and beverage controller** is the accountant for the food and beverage department of a hotel. This person is in charge of keeping all financial records for the hotel restaurants and banquet operations. The food and beverage controller reports to the financial controller.

# Personal Qualities and Skills

Accounting department employees need business accounting knowledge. They must also be able to pay attention to detail, especially when numbers are written, copied, or entered into the computer. Computing skills are important for all members of the accounting department.

Accounting department supervisors and the controller must be able to analyze financial data and write reports. They must also have good administrative skills, organizational abilities, problem-solving skills, and experience in the accounting field.

Good customer relations skills are also important for employees of the accounting department. Dealing with delinquent guests is not easy. **Delinquent guests** are guests who are late with payments that they owe the hotel. Accounting employees must have positive attitudes toward their customers at all times, even delinquent guests.

The position of controller often requires very long hours. Persistence and patience are valuable when major reports and audits are due. It is critical to have a positive attitude.

The most important personal qualities are honesty and integrity, **22-10**. Honesty is being trustworthy. Integrity is sticking to your values. Honesty and integrity are always critical personal qualities when dealing with money.

The front office is responsible for many financial tasks, including recording guest transactions,

22-10 Honesty and integrity are important qualities in people who handle money.

*Lisa F. Young/Shutterstock.com*

taking payment, and performing the night audit. The front office and accounting department must have a good working relationship to make sure all these tasks are performed properly.

# Technological Innovations

Computerization has changed the workload of the accounting department in a hotel. The PMS provides a daily list of guest account balances and can notify the front desk when a guest balance goes over a specific amount. The PMS makes it easy for the front desk agent to print out a bill for guests. Some PMSs interconnect with the hotel TV system so guests can review their bills on their room televisions. Guests can use an express checkout system, which automatically places guest room charges on the credit card that was presented at check-in. The guest does not have to check out at the front desk. Guests can also have their bills split between two or more people sharing a room. This used to be a tedious task for the front desk clerk. Now it is easy to do.

A **point of sale** is a place where goods or services are sold and money is collected. A restaurant is a point of sale. In a hotel, the front desk is a point of sale. Other points of sale in a hotel include the gift shop, fitness center, spa, room service, valet service, minibar, and in-room pay-per-view movies.

Before computers, every sale had to be written down by hand. In a hotel, these sales had to be collected from each point of sale, delivered to the accounting department, and entered into the guest's folio. A computerized point-of-sale system (POS) enables each transaction to be recorded in the computer. It is then automatically added to the guest folio. This saves time and effort for both the front desk and the accounting departments. In a hotel, a computer terminal is placed in each point-of-sale area, **22-11**. In a restaurant, the terminals are

Z-River/Shutterstock.com

**22-11** The spa is a point of sale in a hotel. A computerized POS system enables all spa charges and payments to be automatically transferred to the guest's folio.

placed throughout the restaurant where servers can enter guests' orders. The POS collects all charges from each guest in the guest folio. The POS can then print out a bill when it is needed.

POSs have reduced the workload of both restaurants and hotels. Transactions recorded in the POS are automatically added to the guest folio. Orders can be changed and corrected with very little effort. Credit card and debit card payments are entered into the POS. Hotel PMS and POS systems work together to create a smooth record of guest expenditures at the hotel.

Computerizing the payroll part of the accounting department has eliminated most accounting-related problems. When the old "paper and pencil" systems were used, a tedious review of the night audit had to be done to see which employees were on staff and how many hours they worked. Now, it is only necessary to review the night audit printout.

# Chapter 22
## Review

## Chapter Summary

- Accounting is the system of recording and summarizing financial transactions and analyzing and reporting the results.
- A debit is subtracted; a credit is added.
- The five main functions of the accounting department are to keep track of financial transactions, make payments and deposits, categorize transactions, control costs, and prepare financial reports.
- The Uniform System of Accounts makes it possible to compare financial data among different hotels.
- The controller is responsible for managing the accounting department, preparing financial reports, and preparing budgets.
- The accounting division of a hotel is usually divided into five departments: accounts receivable, accounts payable, night audit, credit, and food and beverage controller.
- Because the front office performs many financial tasks, the front office and accounting must work together.
- Computer systems such as the PMS and POS have reduced the workload in accounting departments.

## Review

1. What is the difference between a debit and a credit?
2. List the five main functions of the accounting department.
3. Name the two types of software used in the hospitality industry to keep track of financial transactions.
4. What is the purpose of the Uniform System of Accounts?
5. How does the accounting department help a business control costs?
6. List the three basic financial statements.
7. Who is the person in charge of the accounting department?
8. List the five departments within accounting.
9. Describe the tasks of each of the five accounting departments.
10. What is an audit?
11. Name four qualities that workers in the accounting department should have.
12. Why do the front office and the accounting division need to work together?

# Critical Thinking

13. **Identify.** List all the point-of-sale locations at a restaurant and a hotel.

14. **Draw conclusions.** Why is it important for a hotel to check the credit history of a company that wants to set up an account for regular billing?

15. **Assess.** Research career options in the accounting part of the hospitality industry. What types of positions are available? Make sure you think about the entire hospitality industry as you think about these career opportunities. Which opportunities might interest you most?

16. **Evaluate.** Have technological innovations reduced the workload of the accounting department in a hotel? Why or why not? Explain your reasoning.

# Common Core

### College and Career Readiness

17. **Writing.** Imagine that you are a general manager. Write a want ad for your new controller.

18. **Speaking.** Imagine that you are the controller of a hotel accounting division. Describe to the class the computer software you require.

19. **Writing.** Imagine that you are the controller of a hotel accounting division. Write a job description for each employee in your department.

20. **Reading.** Using the Internet, research information related to either a Property Management System (PMS) for hotels or a Point-of-Sales System (POS) for restaurants. Find out how these computer systems are operated and how they assist hospitality businesses. As you do this research, look up any words that you do not understand in the dictionary. If you do not understand a sentence or paragraph, reread it to try to simplify the content. Write a one-page report about the computer system that you researched.

21. **Listening.** Interview a hotel night auditor. Ask this person to explain the importance of night audits and why they must be conducted at night. What is included in the night audit?

22. **CTE Career Readiness Practice.** One way to start solving a problem or to think about a problem differently is to use *metaphors*—words or phrases that suggest a likeness or analogy to an object or idea. Presume you are an accountant whose primary responsibility is controlling costs. For the term *controlling costs*, think of as many metaphors as possible with a link. Although metaphors do not solve problems, in what way do they help you focus on the problem differently? How can this help lead to a solution?

412

# Chapter *23*

# Workplace Safety and Emergencies

## Chapter Objectives

After studying this chapter, you will be able to

- **state** the main purpose of the Occupational Health and Safety Act.
- **list** the causes of accidents.
- **describe** the parts of a prevention program.
- **evaluate** steps employees can take to prevent accidents.
- **explain** the purpose of an emergency action plan.
- **compare** a minor emergency with a major emergency.
- **explain** the fire triangle.
- **list** the steps of a general emergency procedure.
- **list** do's and don'ts while waiting for medical help.

## Before You Read

Try to answer the following questions before you read this chapter.

- What elements make up the fire triangle?
- What are some signs that a person is having a medical emergency?

## Terms to Know

safety
accident
emergency
safety procedures
emergency procedures
Occupational Safety and Health Act (OSH Act)
hazard
Occupational Safety and Health Administration (OSHA)
right-to-know

material safety data sheet (MSDS)
compliance
negligence
fatigue
emergency action plan
flammable liquid
emergency coordinator
evacuation
minor emergency
fire triangle
fire extinguisher

combustible
ABC extinguisher
minor injury
major emergency
CPR
emergency medical services (EMS)
paramedic
emergency medical technician (EMT)
first aid
abdominal thrust

You go to school or work every day. Some days, you may eat at a restaurant or stay in a hotel. You may go to a water park, slide down the water slides, and float down the lazy river, **23-1**. You expect your surroundings to be safe. However, accidents, emergencies, and disasters can happen at any time and any place.

Injuries and death at work are a major public health problem. Thousands of employees in the United States die each year from work-related accidents. Millions of nonfatal workplace injuries and illnesses are reported each year. Teens are included in these statistics. Every year, thousands of teenagers are injured on the job and some of these injuries are fatal. In addition to the tragedy and pain, injuries at work are costly to a hospitality business. When workers are ill or injured, they cannot work. Either their work does not get done or the business must hire replacement workers until the injured workers get well. The cost of work-related injuries and illness is very high. Injuries alone cost U.S. businesses billions of dollars every year.

When guests visit restaurants, hotels, and other hospitality businesses, they expect all food to be wholesome and safe. Customers expect their persons and their belongings to be safe when they stay at lodging properties. Guests expect all equipment to be in safe working order. Guests also expect hospitality businesses to be prepared for accidents and emergencies. When a fire, natural disaster, or medical emergency occurs, hospitality businesses must be ready to respond in ways that protect the lives of their employees and guests, **23-2**.

# Safety vs. Emergencies

**Safety** consists of actions taken to prevent accidents and emergencies. An **accident** is an unexpected event caused by carelessness or ignorance that results in harm to people or property. An **emergency** is an unforeseen event that can cause harm to people and property. An accident can lead to an emergency. Emergencies can result when people forget or ignore safety requirements. For example, a cook walks away from a pan of oil

**23-1** No matter where you go, you expect to be safe.

*North Dakota Tourism. Photo by David Lee.*

23-2 When an emergency occurs, hospitality businesses must be prepared to deal with it as quickly as possible.

that is heating on the range. The oil gets so hot that it catches on fire. This is an emergency that results from forgetting or ignoring safety requirements. Emergencies can also result from other unpredictable events, such as weather, industrial accidents, utility disruptions, civil disturbances, and workplace violence.

In order to protect employees, guests, and the business, each business must have safety procedures and emergency procedures. **Safety procedures** include everything done to prevent an accident or emergency. **Emergency procedures** include everything done to respond to an emergency that has already occurred.

Safety procedures include all actions taken to ensure food safety and sanitation, security, and the safe operation of equipment. In addition, safety procedures include actions taken to prevent accidents. Emergency procedures include actions such as fire alarms, building evacuations, and first aid. Emergency procedures are usually covered in an emergency action plan.

# The Role of Government

The federal, state, and local governments have passed laws and regulations to make sure that all businesses follow a minimum of safety and health procedures. The main federal law that requires businesses to follow safety and health procedures is the Occupational Safety and Health Act. State, city, and county governments also have passed a variety of health and safety laws.

## *Occupational Health and Safety*

The **Occupational Safety and Health Act (OSH Act)**, passed in 1970, requires employers to make the workplace free of hazards that might cause injury or death to employees. A **hazard** is a situation that could result in an accident or an emergency. The OSH Act states a number of safety and health requirements for employers and rights and responsibilities for employees, **23-3**.

The OSH Act also established the **Occupational Safety and Health Administration (OSHA)**. OSHA is the federal agency responsible for making sure that the laws and regulations of the OSH Act are followed. The major responsibilities of the federal OSHA are to develop mandatory job safety and health standards and to enforce those standards through inspections. If an emergency occurs, employers and employees can call OSHA's toll-free number for help. OSHA also provides training programs and works with employers to help them develop safe workplaces. Many states have their own state OSHA. The federal OSHA is responsible for approving all state occupational safety and health programs.

OSHA has developed standards for a number of workplace hazards. Examples of the hazards covered include electrical hazards, fall hazards, fire and explosion hazards, infectious diseases, machine hazards, and toxic substances. One of the important requirements of the OSH Act, the **right-to-know** requirement, states that the employer must inform all employees about any toxic or dangerous materials they use in the workplace.

For each hazardous substance used in the workplace, the employer must get a material safety data sheet from the manufacturer. A **material safety data sheet (MSDS)** is a form completed by the manufacturer for each hazardous substance it makes. The form contains information about the hazardous components, fire and explosion hazard data, health hazards, safe handling of the substance, and first aid and emergency procedures if the substance is mishandled. The employer must make these forms available to all employees. The employer must ensure that all employees who use the hazardous materials learn how to safely handle them.

In addition, the employer must make sure that each employee knows his or her rights under the OSH Act. Therefore, as part of the OSH Act requirements, the employer is required to post the OSHA poster.

## Some Key Requirements of the Occupational Health and Safety Act

| Expectations of Employers | Expectations of Employees |
|---|---|
| • Provide a safe workplace.<br>• Know and follow all OSH Act standards and requirements related to their business.<br>• Post the OSHA poster where employees can easily see it.<br>• Inform employees of potential health and safety hazards.<br>• Provide health and safety training.<br>• Make sure that employees have and use appropriate protective and safety equipment.<br>• Develop an emergency action plan.<br>• Keep OSHA-required records of job-related injuries and illnesses.<br>• Within 8 hours, report any job-related accident that results in the death of one or more employees or the hospitalization of three or more employees.<br>• Cooperate with OSHA staff during inspections.<br>• Not discriminate against any employee who reports health or safety hazards.<br>• Penalties can be imposed on employers who violate OSH Act requirements. | • Read the OSHA poster.<br>• Follow all employer health and safety rules.<br>• Report hazardous conditions to supervisor.<br>• Seek help immediately for any job-related illness or injury.<br>• Report any job-related illness or injury to supervisor.<br>• Cooperate with OSHA staff during inspections. |

*Goodheart-Willcox Publisher*

23-3 The Occupational Safety and Health Act requires employers to make the workplace free of hazards that might cause injury or death to employees.

## *State and Local Safety Regulations*

In addition to federal laws, there are state and local safety and health ordinances that must be followed. The three areas in which state and local governments make safety regulations are building codes, health inspections, and liquor licenses.

### Building Codes

Building safety codes are enforced during construction, remodeling, and operation of the business. Failure to correct building safety violations can result in fines, loss of certificate of occupancy, or jail sentences. A *certificate of occupancy* is issued by a city or county building inspector after she or he approves the building for business use. Business owners whose buildings violate safety codes are also subject to lawsuits by customers if injuries occur before the violations are corrected.

Building safety codes ensure that the foundation is prepared properly and that it can pass a stress test. The codes cover fire prevention, structural safety, the size and number of rooms allowed, and required exits. The codes also cover ventilation, refrigeration, heating, and sanitary equipment for buildings. In addition, there are usually safety code requirements such as fencing around swimming pools, 23-4.

Fire safety codes for buildings make sure that a building is constructed to minimize the chance of fire and to slow down the spread of fire. The codes cover items such as construction materials, interior fabrics, entrance and exit requirements, smoke alarm installation and maintenance, fire alarm installation and maintenance, and sprinkler system installation and maintenance. In many areas, the local fire department regularly inspects buildings for fire safety.

### Health Inspections

Health inspections are regularly conducted by the local health department. These inspections include the kitchen, storage, bar, and restaurant

Cheryl Casey/Shutterstock.com

**23-4** Fencing required around swimming pools help keep guests—especially small children—safe.

areas. Inspectors look for compliance with sanitation standards, the absence of pests, proper care and handling of food, proper food storage techniques, and correct temperature of wash water. A health inspection certificate is usually issued after each health inspection.

### Liquor Licenses

Hospitality businesses that sell alcoholic beverages to the public must have a liquor license granted by the state. Businesses that have a liquor license are required to attend safety lessons on the procedures for selling and serving alcoholic beverages. These procedures help protect the public from drunk drivers. Business owners must teach their employees how to identify drunken customers, who cannot be served more alcohol and should be prevented from driving. In addition, state laws prohibit the service or sale of alcoholic beverages to people younger than the age of 21.

# Safety and Accident Prevention

The hospitality industry is full of chances for employee accidents. Servers carry heavy trays. Kitchen staff members work with fire and knives. Housekeeping staff work with strong chemicals and a variety of equipment. Banquet staff members move heavy furniture and equipment. Maintenance staff members work with complex electrical and mechanical equipment. The most common minor accidents are cuts, falls, and burns. The most common major emergency is fire.

## Causes of Accidents

There are many causes of accidents. The four major causes are
- a poor accident prevention plan
- lack of employee knowledge and skills

- employee negligence
- employee fatigue

The first two are the responsibility of the business and are corrected through prevention programs. The last two are the responsibility of the employee. Accidents can be prevented through prevention programs and employee responsibility.

## Prevention Programs

Each business must make sure it has a strong accident prevention program. Accident prevention programs cannot stop all accidents, but they can prevent most of them. A good accident prevention program has three parts. The first part focuses on rules and policies that create a safe workplace. The second part focuses on training everyone in the rules and policies and creating an atmosphere that promotes safe behavior. The third part focuses on safety inspections.

### Rules and Policies

The best way to establish safety rules and policies is by establishing a safety committee that includes at least one representative from each department. Employees from all levels should also be represented. Managers must make sure that the rules and policies follow OSH Act requirements. Front-line employees know the details of the day-to-day risks they encounter. They deal with faulty equipment, work in crowded banquet rooms, work beside each other in poorly laid-out kitchens, clean dirty laundry, push carts through busy hallways, and hear guest complaints during checkout. The safety committee can also help develop safety training programs and safety inspection programs.

The safety rules and policies should be reviewed regularly. For example, many companies review policies every year and update them to meet new needs.

### Safety Training

Rules and policies are useless unless everyone knows them and follows them. The following of rules and policies is called **compliance**. The goal of a business should be 100 percent compliance with safety rules and policies. The main way to get compliance is through appropriate training, **23-5**. Training is also necessary because one of the major causes of accidents is lack of employee knowledge and skills.

Safety training should cover three areas: general safety rules, specific job-related safety rules,

Courtesy of the National Restaurant Association

**23-5** Safety training is often available at professional conferences. This program took place at the annual National Restaurant Show, sponsored by the National Restaurant Association.

and safety attitude. General safety rules apply to everyone in the company. Sample topics include hazards to notice and report, safe lifting, and emergency action plans. The training should include safety drills to practice evacuations and other emergency procedures. As many staff as appropriate should get certified in first aid. Some hotel companies require all managers on duty to be certified in first aid or CPR.

Specific job-related safety training should be tailored to each specific job. For example, kitchen staff must be trained in using knives safely. Room attendants must be taught the safest way to use bathroom cleaning products. Engineering staff must be trained to safely use all equipment and detect potential hazards.

# Carol Wallace— Facilities Manager Extraordinaire

Carol Wallace loves her job. As president and chief executive officer of the San Diego Convention Center Corporation, she is responsible for a 2.6 million square foot world-class facility, a budget of over $33 million a year, a staff of 560, and approximately 250 events a year.

Carol learned the value of hard work from her mother, a single parent who cleaned houses to support her family. Her mother was widely respected for her excellence and hard work. Carol decided she wanted to be part of the work world, too.

Carol attended college at Ohio State University. While working for the University and later for the Ohio Lung Association, she was given the opportunity to plan meetings. She enjoyed it, and her special events were extremely successful.

Her next major career move was an entry-level job as an event coordinator at the Dallas Convention Center. Carol describes her work there as being like an intern in a hospital, where you work hard to support the senior staff. Over the next nine years, she rose through the ranks from event coordinator to the number two position of assistant general manager.

In 1989, Carol became executive director of the brand new Colorado Convention Center in Denver. She found it gave her many opportunities to grow personally and professionally. She was responsible for hiring the staff and opening the center.

She was so successful that in 1991, she was offered another exciting job as general manager for San Diego's convention center. Carol is now the President and Chief Executive Officer of the

*Photo courtesy of San Diego Convention Center Corporation*

San Diego Convention Center Corporation. She is successful because she loves her job, has high standards, and always stays until the job is done.

## Carol Wallace's Career Path

**1948:** Born in Cincinnati, Ohio

**1967:** Graduated from Ohio State University with a degree in English

**1976:** Director of fundraising and public relations, Ohio Lung Association

**1980:** Event coordinator, Dallas Convention Center

**1984:** Promoted to assistant general manager, Dallas Convention Center

**1989:** Named Executive Director, Colorado Convention Center

**1991:** Executive vice president/ general manager, San Diego Convention Center Corporation

**1996:** President and chief executive officer, San Diego Convention Center Corporation

**2006:** Named to the "Power Pack 100" by *Trade Show Week*, recognizing her as one of America's most influential leaders in the convention and trade show industry

**2007:** Women of Influence Award from *Venues Today* magazine for outstanding leadership and lifelong volunteerism

The third area of safety training is attitude. All safety training should promote the importance of safety. Posters, speakers, videos, and other company-wide activities promote safety awareness. All managers should enthusiastically participate in safety programs. Many businesses develop incentive and reward programs for departments that have the best safety records.

Safety training should be part of each new employee's orientation and also take place regularly throughout the year. New safety training should take place whenever new rules or policies are made or new equipment or chemicals are used.

### Safety Inspections

Inspections are a part of the job descriptions of many employees in foodservice, security, and engineering. Foodservice staff members are responsible for monitoring food safety at the critical control points. Security checks the entire property for security problems and safety hazards. Engineering checks all equipment and maintains it regularly. In addition, the safety committee should perform regular safety inspections to look for situations the others may have missed.

Fire inspections should be conducted on a regular basis, preferably monthly. Inspectors look for potential fire hazards and situations that would cause difficulties if a fire were to occur. The local fire department often carries out yearly inspections and is available to help businesses with fire safety issues.

## *Employee Responsibility*

Employees have a major responsibility for safety on the job, **23-6**. Employees affect both the safety of fellow employees and the safety of guests. According to OSHA, employees have a number of important responsibilities. Refer again to Figure 23-3.

In addition to following all safety rules and policies, employees should always be alert for possible hazards. Examples include slippery floors, burned out lights, blocked fire exits, unattended open flames in kitchens, frayed or worn electrical cords, and objects or equipment left where someone could trip over them. Employees should know which hazards they can correct themselves and which hazards they should report. For example, an employee can clean up a water spill immediately. A frayed electrical cord should be reported to the proper person for repair.

*Tonis Valing/Shutterstock.com*

**23-6** All employees are responsible for safety on the job. Chefs must take special care when working with fire.

Two of the major causes of accidents are employee negligence and employee fatigue. Both are situations that employees can prevent. **Negligence** includes behaviors such as carelessness, laziness, ignoring the rules, and improper use of equipment. Employees can prevent negligence by paying attention to their work, asking questions when unsure of what to do, and following all rules and policies.

**Fatigue** is tiredness that can be caused by physical exertion, stress, or lack of sleep. Hospitality jobs are physically and mentally demanding. When people are tired, they become inattentive and do not respond as quickly. People also tend to forget or skip safety rules and procedures when they are tired. Employees can avoid fatigue by getting sufficient sleep, good nutrition, and appropriate exercise. However, fatigue can also develop due to the demands of the job. New workers should work with experienced workers to develop ways to avoid fatigue and perform jobs efficiently.

# Emergencies

OSHA requires most businesses to have emergency action plans. Most hospitality businesses develop emergency action plans that cover both employees and guests. An **emergency action plan** is a detailed, usually written, plan that describes what to do in case of an emergency. Emergency action plans are also called *emergency response plans*. Many businesses compile all emergency action plans into an *emergency manual*. A typical hotel emergency manual can be more than 100 pages, **23-7**.

Emergencies can be grouped into five general categories: fire, natural disasters, medical emergencies, industrial accidents, and civil disturbances.

Fires can result from careless handling of cigarettes and matches, faulty electrical wiring, and faulty appliances and heating equipment. Grease buildup in kitchen ventilation hoods and unattended flames in kitchens are additional causes of fires. Another cause is the careless use of flammable liquids. A **flammable liquid** is a liquid that catches fire easily and burns quickly. Kerosene—a commonly used fuel, solvent, and paint thinner—is a flammable liquid.

Natural disasters include weather emergencies such as hurricanes, tornadoes, lightning, and blizzards. Flooding and earthquakes are other natural disasters.

Medical emergencies occur when a person suddenly becomes sick or injured. A medical emergency can range from minor injuries such as a cut to a life-threatening event such as a heart attack.

Industrial accidents include a wide range of events that occur when something goes wrong with industrial equipment. Examples include chemical spills, gas explosions, toxic chemical releases, and nuclear power plant accidents. Industrial equipment in your business, such as boilers, can explode. If you are located near train tracks, trains carrying toxic substances could derail near your business. This category can also include interruptions in utility services, such as electricity, water, and gas. For example, sometimes there is a power failure and all electricity goes out. Utility interruptions can be caused by weather, but sometimes they are due to industrial accidents.

*Civil disturbance* is the term used for riots and acts of war. Workplace violence and terrorist attacks are also part of this category.

# Emergency Action Plans

Since emergencies are unforeseen, how can you protect your employees, guests, and businesses? The best way is to prepare to respond to the emergency before it happens. Few people can think clearly and logically in a crisis. Therefore, the best thing to do is to prepare an emergency action plan in advance. First, you must figure out which emergencies are the most likely. A resort in Miami Beach should prepare for hurricanes, not blizzards. Similarly, a lodge in Minnesota should prepare for blizzards, not hurricanes, **23-8**. All emergency plans should cover fires, natural disasters, medical emergencies, and civil disturbances. Most plans should cover industrial accidents.

### Table of Contents, Typical Hotel Emergency Manual

*Goodheart-Willcox Publisher*

**23-7** The table of contents for a business's emergency manual may be similar to this.

**23-8** This resort area in Michigan should have emergency plans for blizzards, but does not need emergency plans for hurricanes.

*Travel Michigan*

Emergency action plans should be as detailed as possible and tailored to the particular needs of your business. At a minimum, they should cover the following six topics: reporting, emergency coordinator, alarms, evacuation plans, rescue and medical duties, and protecting essential records. The person in charge of the emergency plans should make sure that all OSHA requirements are covered.

## Reporting

Each employee must know what to report and to whom to report it. Usually an accident or emergency, whether large or small, is reported to your direct supervisor. Your supervisor will assess the situation and decide on the next steps. There may be certain situations in which you contact emergency services directly yourself. However, in most cases, you should contact your supervisor.

## Emergency Coordinator

During an emergency, the situation can be very confusing. One person should be designated to make decisions. This person, the **emergency coordinator**, is the person given the authority to make decisions during emergencies. All employees should know who the emergency coordinator is for each shift. All employees must understand that the emergency coordinator has the authority to make decisions during emergencies. The emergency coordinator is often the manager on duty or the chief engineer.

The emergency coordinator's main responsibility is to determine the nature of the emergency. He or she decides whether the emergency action plan must be activated and if evacuation is necessary. The emergency coordinator is responsible for communicating with emergency services, such as the fire department and ambulance services. Usually the emergency coordinator is the one who calls the emergency services or directs someone else to call them. In a large hotel, the PBX operator is often the person who contacts fire, police, and ambulances. The PBX operator should have a complete list of phone numbers for people and services to contact in an emergency, **23-9**. In addition, the PBX operator should have the phone and pager numbers of the general manager, chief engineer, controller, director of human resources, and director of food and beverage.

The emergency coordinator will be responsible for all communications during an emergency.

### Sample Emergency Telephone List

| | |
|---|---|
| Fire Department | 911 |
| Ambulance | 911 |
| Police Department | 911 |
| State Police | 1-222-587-4305 |
| FBI | 1-222-522-1400 |
| Electrical Emergency | 956-1234 |
| Elevator Emergency | 1-222-717-0880 |
| Gas Service | 381-2345 |
| Sewer Service | 446-2513 |
| City Water | 446-3060 |

*Goodheart-Willcox Publisher*

**23-9** A list of emergency phone numbers should be compiled and kept for quick reference.

The emergency plan should include the designation of a specific place to be command central for an emergency. In a hotel, command central is usually the front desk. In a hotel, the emergency coordinator will work with security, engineering, and the rooms division. There should also be one person designated to talk with the media. This is usually the emergency coordinator or the manager on duty.

## Alarms

The emergency plan must include a way to alert employees and guests of an emergency. Employees are usually alerted through an audible and visible alarm system. In a hotel, staff in the rooms division may have the responsibility to alert guests.

Some hotels have sophisticated computerized smoke, fire, and flood detection systems to provide information on the safety status of each room or area of the hotel. This information is transmitted to a central control panel. When a fire is detected, the system automatically does several things. It uses the phone system to notify guests in each room that there is an emergency, calls the local fire department, and adjusts the ventilation system to push smoke out of the building. It also unlocks the fire doors located at the bottom of each stairwell. During a fire, guests will leave the building by the stairs and exit through the fire doors.

## Evacuation Plans

An **evacuation** is the orderly movement of people out of a dangerous location. A disorganized evacuation can result in confusion, injury, and property damage. Therefore, a major part of any emergency action plan is the *evacuation plan*—instructions for leaving the building entirely, **23-10**. For some types of emergencies, such as a tornado, it is safer to stay inside the building. The evacuation plan should indicate where to go within the building during these types of emergencies. An evacuation plan should cover the following six elements: conditions, chain of command, routes and exits, people with special needs, shutdown duties, and accounting for employees and guests.

**23-10** Clearly marked fire exits should be listed in the evacuation plan.

JJStudio/Shutterstock.com

### Conditions

The plan should specify the conditions that require evacuation. Any special circumstances should also be specified. For example, in case of a tornado, people should be directed to safe locations within the building.

Someone should have the responsibility to monitor news and weather forecasts. For example, in case of a hurricane, the public airwaves will be used to advise people to evacuate. In some cases, local emergency officials may order you to evacuate. Certain conditions do not require evacuation. For example, if there is a release of toxic gas in the area, it may be safer to remain in the building.

### Chain of Command

All employees should know who has the authority to order an evacuation. In addition, it may be useful to designate evacuation wardens to help guide employees and guests from danger to safe areas during an evacuation. Evacuation wardens should be trained in the layout of the workplace and all possible escape routes. All employees and especially the wardens should be made aware of employees and guests with special needs and how to help them.

### Routes and Exits

The evacuation plan should specify primary and secondary escape routes and exits. Evacuation routes and emergency exits should be
- clearly marked and well lit
- wide enough to accommodate the number of people
- unobstructed and clear of debris
- unlikely to expose evacuating people to additional hazards

Drawings showing evacuation routes and exits should be posted where employees and guests can see them. Most lodging properties post evacuation routes on the back of guest room doors.

### People with Special Needs

The evacuation plan should include instructions for meeting the special needs of people who cannot hear or see and those who have mobility difficulties, **23-11**. Employees and guests who are not fluent in English may also need special help. Some hotels keep a list of all guests with special needs so help can be provided to them during emergencies.

**23-11** The evacuation plan should include instructions for meeting the special needs of people who cannot hear or see and those who have mobility difficulties.

### Shutdown Duties

Sometimes during an emergency, local officials will request that the gas, water, and electricity be shut off. Someone, usually an engineering employee, will be designated to handle those duties.

In addition, most hospitality businesses have a variety of machinery that is running. When an evacuation occurs, someone must be in charge of shutting down appropriate equipment and machinery. For example, before evacuating the kitchen, all ovens and stoves should be turned off. In an amusement park, the rides should be shut down after all guests are off.

### Accounting for Employees and Guests

Part of the evacuation plan should include emergency meeting places. Each department or area of the building should be assigned an emergency meeting place, and employees should be informed of the location. This is the area where all employees will gather after evacuating. For fires, the meeting place must be away from the building. For a tornado, there should be designated safe areas in the building for each department and guest area.

For each meeting place, someone must be designated to account for each employee. A method must also be established for accounting for guests.

The names of anyone missing should be turned over to the emergency personnel in charge.

## Rescue and Medical Duties

Only trained personnel should engage in rescue work and emergency medical care, **23-12**. Untrained individuals may endanger themselves and those whom they are trying to rescue. Notify emergency service personnel as soon as you are aware that someone must be rescued.

Every hospitality business should have at least one person on duty at all times who is trained and certified in first aid and cardiopulmonary resuscitation (CPR). The person or persons should have an appropriate and up-to-date first aid kit available.

## Protecting Essential Records

An emergency such as a fire can result in the loss of valuable business records. The emergency action plan should include instructions for handling these records. As part of the standard operating procedures, you may want to establish a secure place to store original documents, duplicates of accounting records, and legal documents. It is advisable to have off-site backup data storage. You may also want to have an off-site location to keep your employees' emergency contact lists and other essential records.

Certain employees may also be instructed to take specific items or documents with them during an evacuation. For example, cashiers might take the cash tray with them.

**23-12** Emergency medical technicians such as these have been properly trained in emergency medical care.

# Minor Emergencies

A **minor emergency** is one that does not require the help of an expert. Minor emergencies are common in the hospitality industry. Examples include small fires and minor injuries such as small cuts, scrapes, and minor burns. If you cannot tell whether the situation is minor, assume that it is major and call for help. It is better to err on the side of getting too much help. In addition, report even minor injuries and fires to your supervisor.

## Small Fires

Small fires can start in a pan of oil on a range or in a trash can from a discarded match or cigarette. A fire needs three things to keep burning: fuel, oxygen, and heat. These three items are called the **fire triangle**, **23-13**. Removing any one part of the fire triangle will extinguish fire, so often this is the first step in extinguishing a small fire. To extinguish the fire in the pan of oil, turn off the burner to cut the heat and cover the pan with a lid to cut the oxygen. If the trash can has a metal lid, put the lid on the trash can to cut the oxygen.

### Types of Fire Extinguishers

If there is no quick, easy, and safe way to cut the oxygen, fuel, or heat, use a fire extinguisher. A **fire extinguisher** is a container filled with materials that will put out a fire. There are three basic types of fires: paper, grease, and electrical. Each type of fire requires a different type of extinguisher.

Paper fires are called *class A fires* and require class A extinguishers. Class A fires include fires burning in ordinary combustible materials such as paper, wood, cloth, rubber, and some plastics. **Combustible** means easy to burn. If a class A fire extinguisher is not available, water will work.

Grease fires are called *class B* fires and require class B extinguishers. Class B fires include flammable liquids such as grease, oil, gasoline, kerosene, and some paints. If a class B fire extinguisher is not available, baking soda will work.

Electrical fires are called *class C* fires and require class C extinguishers. Class C fires include all fires that start in electrical equipment, such as outlets, fuse boxes, wiring, electrical appliances, and electrical equipment.

Using the wrong type of fire extinguisher on a fire can make the fire worse. For example, using a type A fire extinguisher on an electrical fire might cause the fire to spread or lead to electrical shock. For this reason, there is a universal fire extinguisher called an ABC extinguisher. An **ABC extinguisher** can safely be used on class A, B, and C types of fires, **23-14**.

**23-14** An ABC extinguisher can safely be used on paper, grease, and electrical fires.

Rob Byron/Shutterstock.com

**23-13** The fire triangle consists of fuel, oxygen, and heat.

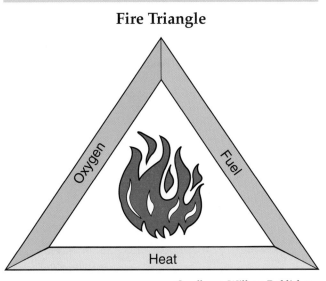

**Fire Triangle**

Oxygen

Fuel

Heat

Goodheart-Willcox Publisher

A new category of fires was established in 1998 for fires in commercial kitchens. Commercial cooking fires are called *class K fires* and require class K extinguishers. Class K fires occur in commercial cooking appliances that use new liquid cooking media. Figure **23-15** summarizes the types of fires and fire extinguishers.

### Using a Fire Extinguisher

Most fire extinguishers have the instructions on how to use them printed on the container. You should learn how and when to use a fire extinguisher before an emergency. Most fire departments will provide practice and training. The main rules to remember are to stand back 8 to 10 feet, make sure you have a clear exit path, and aim at the base of the fire. All fire extinguishers must be checked regularly to make sure they are in good working condition.

Fire extinguishers should be placed in appropriate locations throughout the hospitality business. Every hospitality worker should know where the extinguishers are located and how to use them.

## Minor Injuries

Every hospitality employee should know how to treat a minor injury. A **minor injury** is an injury that does not require the help of an expert. Minor injuries include small cuts and scrapes, bruises, and small burns. First aid kits should have basic supplies and be located where employees can easily access them, **23-16**. The supplies should be stored in a large, waterproof, brightly colored and labeled box. In addition, someone should have the responsibility to check each kit monthly to replace supplies that have been used.

All first aid treatments are complex and have many steps. Treatment also varies depending on

| Fire Types and Fire Extinguishers | | | | |
|---|---|---|---|---|
| **Type of Fire** | **Symbol** | **Examples** | **Extinguisher Class** | **Common Materials to Extinguish** |
| *Paper* | A | Paper, cloth, trash, wood, rubber, plastic | A or ABC | Water |
| *Grease* | B | Gasoline, kerosene, paint | B or ABC | Baking soda |
| *Electrical* | C | Outlets, fuses, appliances | C or ABC | Baking soda |
| *Kitchen (commercial)* | K | Liquid cooking media in commercial cooking equipment | K | None |

**23-15** Different types of fires require different types of extinguishers.

## Workplace First Aid Kit

*Note: This list does not include over-the-counter ointments, topicals, or internal medicines; consult the workplace's medical director for these.*

| Equipment | Minimum Quantity | Equipment | Minimum Quantity |
|---|---|---|---|
| 1. Adhesive strip bandages (1″ × 3″) | 20 | 14. Medical-grade exam gloves (medium, large, extra large), conforming to FDA requirements | 2 pairs per size |
| 2. Triangular bandages (muslin, 36″–40″ × 36″–40″ × 52″–56″) | 4 | 15. Mouth-to-barrier device, either a face mask with a one-way valve or a disposable face shield | 1 |
| 3. Sterile eye pads (2⅛″ × 2⅝″) | 2 | 16. Disposable instant-activating cold packs | 2 |
| 4. Sterile gauze pads (4″ × 4″) | 6 | | |
| 5. Sterile nonstick pads (3″ × 4″) | 6 | 17. Resealable plastic bags (quart size) | 2 |
| 6. Sterile trauma pads (5″ × 9″) | 2 | 18. Padded malleable splint (SAM splint™, 4″ × 36″) | 1 |
| 7. Sterile trauma pads (8″ × 10″) | 1 | | |
| 8. Sterile conforming roller gauze (2″ width) | 3 rolls | 19. Emergency blanket, Mylar | 1 |
| | | 20. Paramedic shears (with one serrated edge) | 1 |
| 9. Sterile conforming roller gauze (4½″ width) | 3 rolls | | |
| 10. Waterproof tape (1″ × 5 yards) | 1 roll | 21. Splinter tweezers (about 3″ long) | 1 |
| 11. Porous adhesive tape (2″ × 5 yards) | 1 roll | 22. Biohazard waste bag (3½ gallon capacity) | 2 |
| 12. Elastic roller bandages (4″ and 6″) | 1 each | | |
| 13. Antiseptic skin wipes, individually wrapped | 10 | 23. First aid and CPR manual and list of local emergency telephone numbers | 1 |

*Alton Thygerson, National Safety Council Essentials of First Aid and CPR, 4th edition, p. 141, ©2002. Jones and Bartlett Publishers, Sudbury, MA, www.jbpub.com. Reprinted with permission*

**23-16** What might happen if no one has the responsibility to check and restock first aid supplies?

the circumstances, the cause of the injury, and the age and general health of the injured person. General first aid for typical minor injuries in a healthy adult is presented in **23-17**. These instructions do not take the place of training or professional medical help. For the best results, take a first aid class from a qualified provider, such as the Red Cross or the National Safety Council.

# Major Emergencies

A **major emergency** is an emergency that requires professional help or is life-threatening. The first thing to do in an emergency is to assess the situation. What is the problem? What is going on? Then follow the instructions in your company's emergency manual. In most cases, the first step is to call your supervisor or the manager on duty, who will decide on the next steps.

## General Procedures

Every emergency is unique, but there are general procedures that are usually followed, **23-18**. During any emergency, quick but calm action is necessary. All employees should be familiar with the emergency and evacuation plans. Training sessions and practice drills should be carried out so employees know what they are supposed to do. Employees should be assigned specific tasks and be trained to perform them. For example, certain employees should be designated as evacuation

## General First Aid for Typical Minor Injuries in a Healthy Adult

*Note: Before treating any injury, wash your hands with soap and water if possible. If you are treating a person who is bleeding, put on vinyl or latex gloves, which should be in every first aid kit.*

| Symptom | Treatment | When to Call Doctor |
|---|---|---|
| **Bleeding** | 1. Place a sterile gauze pad over the wound.<br>2. Apply pressure directly to the wound.<br>3. If possible, elevate wounded part above the heart.<br>4. If bleeding does not stop, place more gauze pads over wound and continue applying pressure.<br>5. When bleeding stops, clean the wound with soap and water.<br>6. If bleeding starts again, apply a sterile gauze pad and direct pressure again.<br>7. Apply an antibiotic ointment.<br>8. Cover areas with a sterile and nonstick dressing or adhesive strip. | If bleeding does not stop within five minutes<br>All puncture wounds<br>All animal or human bites |
| **Bruise** | 1. Apply a cold cloth or ice pack.<br>2. If possible, elevate injured part. | If pain continues or gets worse over the next few hours |
| **Burn** | 1. Immerse burned area in cold water (not ice water).<br>2. Do not apply any ointment.<br>3. Keep area in cold water until pain is relieved. | If burn is large, deep, or oozes<br>If the burn is on the face<br>If you can see the underlying muscles<br>If the skin is charred |
| **Sprains and Strains** | Use the RICE procedure.<br>R:   rest the injured part<br>I:    apply ice or cold compress<br>C:   compress the injury<br>E:   elevate the injured part | If you suspect a broken bone<br>If pain continues and gets worse |

Goodheart-Willcox Publisher

23-17  These instructions do not take the place of training or professional medical help. For best results, take a first aid class from a qualified provider.

wardens to help employees and guests evacuate the building. Other employees should receive special training in first aid.

## Fire

In a small restaurant or bed-and-breakfast, the size of the place and the number of people are relatively small. It is fairly easy to notify everyone in case of a fire and to evacuate the building. In a hotel, the building is usually large and many people are involved. It will take time to notify everyone if the place must be evacuated. Therefore, the procedures must be more organized.

Employees in each department of the hotel have specific responsibilities during a fire emergency, 23-19. The person who discovers the fire notifies his or her supervisor. The supervisor immediately calls the manager on duty, security, and engineering and tells them the location of the fire. The manager calls the front desk and instructs the front desk agent or the PBX operator to call 9-1-1 and report the fire. The front desk will become the command center for the emergency. The manager on duty or the emergency coordinator usually meets the fire department in front of the hotel and takes them to the site of the fire.

## General Emergency Procedures

1. Assess the situation.
2. Notify your direct supervisor.
3. Remain calm.
4. Follow recommended procedures for handling the emergency. For example, use a fire extinguisher on a fire or administer first aid if you are qualified.
5. If told to evacuate, follow the evacuation procedures.
6. Walk. Do not run. Do not use elevators during a fire.
7. Know procedures for helping guests evacuate.
8. Meet at the emergency meeting place.
9. The manager in charge will take roll to make sure all employees are accounted for.
10. Do not return to the building until you are told that it is safe.

*Goodheart-Willcox Publisher*

**23-18** These procedures apply to most emergency situations.

Everyone's goal will be to notify all employees and guests, help them evacuate quickly, and make sure no one is left behind.

## Disasters

Disasters include natural disasters, industrial accidents, and civil disturbances. When a disaster occurs, you often do not know the cause of it. When a building shakes, it could be an earthquake, an explosion in a gas utility line, or a terrorist attack.

In a hotel, someone in the security department should have the task of monitoring National Weather Service reports and news reports. When severe weather is threatening, the National Weather Service will issue alerts that describe the conditions and the seriousness of the threat. News reports will describe other disasters such as earthquakes, industrial accidents, and civil disturbances. The local emergency and civil authorities will use radio and TV broadcasts to advise everyone what to do. Most cities have a civil defense warning system. Often, civil authorities will drive around with a bullhorn and announce emergency procedures.

| Responsibilities of Hotel Staff During a Fire Emergency | |
|---|---|
| **Department** | **Tasks** |
| *Managers* | Make sure your section of the hotel is evacuated. Meet employees at emergency meeting place. Account for all employees. |
| *Front Desk* | Call fire department when directed. Keep track of information and relay it to appropriate people. Prepare a list of all guests and a list of guests with special needs. Prepare to evacuate the front desk by gathering important materials: keys, portable computer storage, and credit card charge slips. Help account for guests. |
| *Room Attendants* | Inform guests of evacuation. Direct guests to safety. Make sure doors to all guest rooms are closed. Report to the emergency meeting location. Help account for guests. |
| *Foodservice Servers* | Evacuate guests from dining rooms and restrooms. |
| *Banquet Staff* | Evacuate guests from banquet rooms, meeting rooms, and restrooms. |
| *Kitchen Staff* | Turn off all stoves, ovens, and other equipment. Report to emergency meeting location. |
| *Engineering Staff* | Work with fire department. Members of the engineering staff know the location of water hydrants and hoses, the layout of the building, and the location of all electrical, heating, and plumbing systems in the hotel. |

*Goodheart-Willcox Publisher*

**23-19** Why should responsibilities be clearly designated *before* an emergency occurs?

## Weather

Potentially dangerous weather conditions include blizzards, hurricanes, lightning, thunderstorms, and tornadoes. Blizzards are most likely in the northern states; however, they do occasionally occur in central and southern states. Hurricanes are frequent in coastal areas along the Atlantic, Pacific, and Indian Oceans. Along the Atlantic Coast, hurricanes are most likely to occur between June 1 and November 30. Lightning is associated with thunderstorms, but can be dangerous even when it is not raining. Thunderstorms often lead to flooding. Tornadoes occur most often in the central states. Each type of weather situation requires specific protective actions, **23-20**.

## Other Natural Disasters

Other natural disasters include volcanoes and earthquakes. In the United States, very few volcanoes are located near hospitality businesses. Hawaii has many national parks with volcanoes. Scientists can monitor volcanic activity and can often predict when it will be dangerous. Parks can be closed to visitors at these times.

Earthquakes cannot be predicted, but scientists know where they are most likely to occur. Earthquakes occur along faults in the earth's crust and result in a violent shaking of the ground. The actual quake is usually very brief, but the results can be very destructive. Major earthquakes can destroy buildings and roads. Earthquakes can also cause fires, gas line explosions, and other dangerous situations. In the United States, serious earthquakes can occur along the San Andreas Fault in California, **23-21**.

Building codes were developed so buildings would survive an earthquake. Most public and commercial buildings along faults are built so they will survive an earthquake. When an earthquake occurs, employees should follow their earthquake emergency procedures. If possible, employees should turn off all ovens, ranges, and other equipment. The manager on duty will have to decide when and where to evacuate. After a major earthquake, buildings are often unstable and dangerous even when no damage is visible. Building engineers will have to conduct a thorough inspection of the building to make sure that it will not collapse, that all systems are in working order, and that there are no gas or water leaks. No one should enter a building after an earthquake until it has been inspected and declared safe.

| Special Instructions for Threatening Weather | |
|---|---|
| **Weather Type** | **Instructions** |
| *Blizzard* | Avoid unnecessary driving. Close ski facilities. Have backup electricity in case power lines go down. Do not touch any downed power lines. |
| *Hurricane* | National Weather Service can usually give one to two days warning. Evacuate guests from the area. Have employees follow hurricane protection procedures before evacuating themselves. These procedures include boarding up windows; bringing all outdoor tables, chairs, and other equipment indoors; turning off power and water in all buildings; and locking all buildings. |
| *Lightning* | Close all outdoor swimming pools and swimming areas. Close golf courses and other outdoor activities where guests might get struck by lightning. Avoid using landline telephones. Have staff bring guests indoors. |
| *Thunderstorm* | Follow all lightning instructions. Avoid unnecessary driving. Be alert for flooding hazards. |
| *Tornado* | Evacuate all employees and guests to appropriate tornado shelters. These areas should be designated in the emergency action plan. Safe places during a tornado are away from windows and other items that could break. Interior corridors and floors below ground level are good tornado shelters. |

*Goodheart-Willcox Publisher*

**23-20** Each type of weather situation requires specific protective actions.

## Medical Emergencies

Medical emergencies can happen any time and any place. Hospitality workers are likely to encounter many medical emergencies because customers spend a great deal of time eating, sleeping, or playing at hospitality businesses. The best thing a hospitality worker can do is become certified in first aid and CPR. **CPR** is a first aid procedure to help someone whose heart has stopped beating. CPR stands for *cardiopulmonary resuscitation*. Certification can be obtained through courses offered by the Red Cross, National Safety Council, and other medical and health organizations.

Do not perform first aid if you are not trained or have forgotten what to do. The wrong help can cause more harm than no help. If you are at all unsure, call for help. All hospitality employees should call their supervisor when a medical emergency occurs. In most hospitality businesses, there is at least one person on duty at all times who has first aid/CPR training. In many hospitality businesses, all managers and supervisors are trained.

### Signs of Medical Emergency

Not every injury or medical incident is an emergency. However, if a person is suffering significant harm or pain or might die, the situation is an emergency. Certain signs and symptoms indicate a medical emergency and that the person needs immediate medical care, **23-22**. If you are not sure how serious a situation is, get help.

### Calling for Help

Often, the best thing you can do for a person in need is to call for help. In a hospitality business, contact your supervisor. Give your supervisor as much information as you can. Important information includes the number of victims, exact location of the victims, the nature of the emergency, the type of injuries, and the suspected cause.

The supervisor will direct someone trained in first aid to go to the scene and will call 9-1-1 (or the local emergency number). The call will bring emergency medical services. **Emergency medical services (EMS)** usually consist of emergency medical professionals and medical equipment, which are brought to the scene in an ambulance. An emergency medical professional, called a **paramedic** or an **emergency medical technician (EMT)**, is a medical professional trained and licensed to perform emergency medical care.

*Andrew Zarivny/Shutterstock.com*

**23-21** Buildings in San Francisco, which is located along the San Andreas fault, must be built to withstand earthquakes.

### Signs of a Medical Emergency

- Unconscious
- Not breathing or difficulty breathing
- Chest pain
- Severe bleeding
- Severe burn
- Coughing up blood or passing blood
- Seizure
- Severe headache, distorted vision, slurred speech
- Severe or persistent vomiting or diarrhea
- Possible injury to head, neck, or back
- Sudden, severe pain
- Appears to have been poisoned
- Broken bones

*Goodheart-Willcox Publisher*

**23-22** Watch for these signs that indicate a person needs immediate medical care.

If you are not trained in first aid, there are still a number of things you should do while waiting for someone trained in first aid and the paramedics. There are also a number of things that you should not do, **23-23**.

## Going Green

### Medical Waste

Blood and other body fluids are considered hazardous waste. Gauze, needles, and other disposable supplies that come in contact with these fluids are collected separately from other trash. They are disposed of according to strict government guidelines. This helps prevent other people from coming in contact with contaminated material and possibly catching the disease.

### First Aid

First aid is treatment given to an injured or suddenly ill person before professional medical care arrives. First aid consists of a body of knowledge and skills that enable a nonmedical person to provide treatment that could save a life. First aid includes examining the victim, determining what is wrong, choosing an appropriate treatment, and carrying out that treatment. First aid is more effective if the person providing treatment has access to a first aid kit. However, the person providing treatment should know what to do if first aid equipment is not available. To be able to give first aid competently, a person should take a hands-on course from a qualified organization, such as the

American Red Cross, the American Heart Association, or the National Safety Council. These organizations also offer first aid courses online. Figure 23-24 lists common first aid procedures.

The most common first aid procedure, which all restaurant workers should know, is the abdominal thrust. (The abdominal thrust is also known as the *Heimlich Maneuver* in honor of its inventor, Dr. Heimlich.) The abdominal thrust is a first aid procedure designed to force a stuck object out of the throat. This procedure should only be performed by a trained individual when the following signals are present:

- unable to speak
- cannot breathe
- unable to cough forcefully

| Do's and Don'ts While Waiting for Medical Help | |
|---|---|
| **Do's** | **Don'ts** |
| • Keep calm. <br>• Keep the victim calm. <br>• Cover victim with a blanket unless he or she is burned. <br>• Keep others away from victim. <br>• Stay with the victim until help arrives. <br>• If victim can talk, get as much information as you can about the cause of the accident, medical history, and his or her current condition. | • Do not move the victim unless he or she is in immediate danger. <br>• Do not give the victim anything to eat or drink. <br>• Do not try to remove clothing from burned skin. <br>• Do not move or reposition a person who may have broken the neck, back, or any bones. <br>• Do not give first aid unless you are trained. |

*Goodheart-Willcox Publisher*

**23-23** If you are not trained in first aid, there are still a number of things you should do while waiting for the paramedics.

| Common First Aid Procedures | |
|---|---|
| **Procedure** | **Use** |
| *Abdominal Thrust (also known as Heimlich Maneuver)* | Remove airway obstruction (choking) |
| *Bandaging* | Hold dressing in place, control bleeding, prevent or reduce swelling |
| *Bleeding control* | Stop bleeding from cuts, gun shot, punctures, bites |
| *Burn treatment* | Treat burns due to fire, chemicals, electricity |
| *CPR* | Restart the heart beating after a heart attack, water rescue, electric shock |
| *Eye treatment* | Remove foreign object in eye; treat blow to eye, cuts, chemical burns |
| *Rescue breathing* | Restart breathing |
| *Splinting* | Keep broken bones in place |
| *Wound dressing* | Protect wounds |

*Goodheart-Willcox Publisher*

**23-24** To be able to give first aid competently, a person should take a hands-on course from a qualified organization.

- high-pitched or noisy breathing
- lips or skin are bluish in color
- holds the neck with one or both hands

The exact steps of the abdominal thrust depend on the age and the condition of the victim. The abdominal thrust should only be performed on conscious people who are over one year of age. The American Red Cross recommends the following "five-and-five" response when someone is choking and in need of assistance:

1. Ask the person if he or she is choking and if you can help. If the person gives consent, lean him or her forward and deliver five sharp back blows between the shoulder blades.
2. If the object obstructing the airway does not dislodge, give five quick abdominal thrusts using the following procedure:
   A. Stand behind the victim and wrap your arms around his or her waist.
   B. Make a fist and position the thumb side of the fist between the person's navel and rib cage.
   C. Place your other hand over your positioned fist.
   D. Give quick, upward thrusts into the victim's abdomen.
   E. Continue with short forceful thrusts until the object obstructing the airway is dislodged.
3. Repeat the cycle of back blows and abdominal thrusts until the victim is able to breathe or becomes unconscious. If the victim loses consciousness, immediately call 9-1-1 or the local emergency number.

The American Heart Association recommends that after you are given consent to help the victim, you immediately begin performing abdominal thrusts (step two above). This procedure is then performed until the object obstructing the airway is dislodged or the victim becomes unconscious.

First aid procedures are constantly being updated as new technology becomes available. For example, a victim of a heart attack needs a process called *defibrillation*. Defibrillation is the process of giving appropriate electrical shocks to the heart. Until recently, only trained paramedics or physicians could administer defibrillation. Recent advances in computer technology have led to the development of a relatively easy-to-use machine called an automated external defibrillator (AED). Nonmedical people can now be trained to use the AED in a few hours.

# Chapter 23
# Review

## Chapter Summary

- Federal, state, and local governments have laws and regulations regarding minimum safety and health procedures all businesses must follow.
- The Occupational Safety and Health Act requires employers to make the workplace free of hazards that might cause injury or death to employees.
- Workplace safety and accident prevention are the responsibility of both the employer and the employee.
- Employers are responsible for providing prevention programs and employee safety training.
- Employees are responsible for following all safety regulations and must be alert to hazards that can impact themselves, fellow employees, and guests.
- All employers are required to have a detailed emergency action plan tailored to their businesses that must meet all OSHA requirements to protect the safety of employees and guests.
- An emergency action plan describes what to do in case of an emergency.
- If you cannot tell whether a situation is a major or minor emergency, assume that it is major and call for help.
- A fire needs fuel, oxygen, and heat to keep burning.
- Assess emergency situations, follow your employer's emergency action plan, and call your direct supervisor immediately.
- For medical emergencies, do *not* perform first aid unless you are trained and certified in first aid and CPR and you know what you are doing.

## Review

1. Contrast the terms *accident* and *emergency*.
2. Why must a business have safety procedures and emergency procedures?
3. What is OSHA?
4. What is the main purpose of the OSH Act?
5. What does the term *right-to-know* mean in relationship to the OSH Act?
6. Name three areas in which state and local governments make safety regulations.
7. What are four main causes of accidents?
8. Name three parts of a good accident prevention program.

9. What is meant by the term *compliance* as it relates to safety training?

10. What six topics should an emergency action plan cover at a minimum?

11. Contrast the terms *minor emergency* and *major emergency*.

12. What actions can employees take to prevent accidents?

# Critical Thinking

13. **Predict consequences.** After reading the chapter, predict what consequences may occur if either employers or employees do not follow established emergency procedures.

14. **Identify.** Create a T-chart on a sheet of paper. Label the left side of the chart *Employer Responsibilities* and the right side *Employee Responsibilities*. Under each column, write the responsibilities of each party for workplace safety.

15. **Draw conclusions.** The text states that the two main causes of accidents are employee negligence and fatigue. Draw conclusions about the consequences of negligence and fatigue. How could lack of employee responsibility in these two areas impact a hospitality business? What preventative actions could employees take?

16. **Assess.** Suppose a guest at the restaurant at which you work shows signs of choking. Assess what to do in this situation.

17. **Writing.** Choose a cleaning product from under your sink at home. Review the information MSDS format on the OSHA website. Then develop an MSDS sheet for the identified cleaning product. Share your form with the class and identify the key parts as identified by OSHA.

18. **Writing.** Review the text material on emergency action plans. Write a summary explaining employee responsibilities for each section covered in the plan.

19. **Writing.** In your own words, write a summary about the *fire triangle* concept. Identify what the fire triangle is and what a person can do to extinguish a small fire.

20. **Speaking.** Choose a weather emergency common in your area. Imagine you are the manager of a resort hotel in your area, describe what actions you would take to protect resort guests during this weather emergency.

21. **Speaking.** Create an illustrated electronic presentation on abdominal thrust. Share your presentation to the class.

22. **Speaking.** Choose a minor injury from the list in Figure 23-17. Describe how the injury occurred. Then describe how you would treat it.

23. **CTE Career Readiness Practice.** Suppose your supervisor wants you to help reinforce the key components of the company's emergency action plan. You need to write a reminder summary for each part of the plan to present at weekly staff meetings. Choose one of the following topics included in an emergency action plan: reporting, emergency coordinator, alarms, evacuation plans, rescue and medical duties, and protecting essential records. Write the reminder summary on this topic and share it with the staff (your classmates).

The card reads "This side up · Insert and remove"

436

# Chapter 24
## Legal and Ethical Considerations

## Chapter Objectives

After studying this chapter, you will be able to

- **list** the seven categories of laws that affect hospitality businesses.
- **describe** two ways that government regulations are enforced.
- **list** the four areas in which liability issues arise.
- **list** the four common law rights of guests.
- **evaluate** seven questions that can help you make ethical decisions.
- **judge** a good work ethic.
- **determine** guidelines that will help you have a good work ethic.

## Before You Read

Try to answer the following questions before you read this chapter.

- What are zoning laws?
- How do you know if you have a good work ethic?

## Terms to Know

laws
regulation
government agency
code
ordinance
payroll deduction
Food, Drug, and Cosmetic Act

Food and Drug Administration (FDA)
zoning
zoning laws
building codes
license
permit

inspection
ethical behavior
unethical behavior
code of ethics
good work ethic
embezzlement

Ethical behavior is an important part of any hospitality business, **24-1**. Ethical behavior is doing the right thing, even when you are under pressure to do the wrong thing. Laws have been developed to protect customers, workers, the environment, and business owners against unethical practices. Following the law is the minimum requirement for ethical behavior, but true ethical behavior goes beyond that to doing what is proper and good for society.

# Laws and Regulations

**Laws** are society's rules for proper behavior. In the United States, society makes laws through local, state, and federal governments. Society often makes laws when people or businesses have not been doing what society thinks is right. For example, many industrial businesses did not protect workers from dangers in the workplace. As a result, thousands of workers died or were seriously injured on the job. The Occupational Safety and Health Act requires employers to protect the safety and health of their workers. Since then, injury and illness rates and workplace fatalities have been greatly reduced.

A **regulation** is a specific rule that is developed based on a law. A law usually has so few details that it is difficult to enforce. Some laws include the establishment of a government agency. A **government agency** is a department of government that is responsible for enforcing a law. One of the first things that an agency does is make regulations. For example, the Occupational Safety and Health Act established the basic rules

**24-1** Ethical behavior is an important part of any hospitality business.

*Blend Images/Shutterstock.com*

for occupational safety and health. The Act also established the federal agency called the Occupational Safety and Health Administration (OSHA). OSHA develops regulations based on the Act, and then enforces these regulations. Federal agencies that affect the hospitality industry include OSHA, FDA (Food and Drug Administration), USDA (U.S. Department of Agriculture), EEOC (Equal Employment Opportunity Commission), and EPA (Environmental Protection Agency).

Regulations are often organized into a list or book. A list of regulations is called a **code**. For example, the FDA has organized all the regulations and recommendations for safe handling of food into a model Food Code. Rules and regulations made by federal government agencies are recorded in the *Federal Register*. A regulation made by a local government is often called an **ordinance**. Local governments also compile codes. For example, most local governments have a building code.

Many of the policies and procedures used at hospitality businesses are based on local, state, and federal laws and regulations. Understanding these laws will help employees understand the workplace. Laws affecting hospitality can be grouped into the following seven categories: hiring and employment laws, worker safety laws, food safety laws, building and zoning laws, environmental protection, smoking ordinances, and liquor laws.

## *Hiring and Employment Laws*

Many laws have been passed to protect the rights of workers during hiring and employment, **24-2**. These laws are most relevant to the people who hire, train, and evaluate employees. There are three main areas of laws: equal opportunity, workers' rights, and taxes.

### Equal Opportunity

The equal opportunity laws require employers to treat everyone equally during the hiring process. The Civil Rights Act of 1964 and 1991 were passed to prevent discrimination against people based on their race, religion, sex, or national origin. The Age Discrimination Employment Act of 1967 and the Older Workers Benefit Protection Act of 1990 were passed to protect older workers. The Immigration Reform and Control Act of 1986 spells out the requirements concerning hiring immigrants. It also prohibits discrimination against U.S. citizens who may appear foreign. The Americans with Disabilities Act (ADA) of 1990 was passed to require

24-2 Attorneys often work together to protect the rights of workers. What areas do employment laws protect?

employers to judge people based on their ability to do the job, not any disabilities they may have. The ADA also requires employers to make reasonable accommodations for people with disabilities.

### Workers' Rights

Once a person is employed, he or she is guaranteed a number of rights. The main law is the Fair Labor Standards Act of 1938. An additional important set of laws is called *workers' compensation*. Employers must provide medical coverage for any illness or injury that an employee experiences as a result of the job. Employers must also provide income to the injured employee. Workers' compensation is a national requirement, but the states make and enforce this law. These laws vary greatly from state to state.

### Taxes

National, state, and local governments collect income taxes, mainly through payroll deduction. **Payroll deduction** is a process in which the employer subtracts taxes from each employee's paycheck and sends the taxes directly to the appropriate government agency. The national law governing income taxes is the Internal Revenue Code. States and local governments have their own tax codes. Some state and local governments do not collect income taxes.

In addition, employers are required to contribute funds for the national Social Security plan and for unemployment. Social Security is a federal program that ensures all workers will get some income after they retire. Social Security was established through the Federal Insurance Contributions Act (FICA). The employer is required to pay a certain amount into Social Security for each employee. The employee also contributes an equal amount.

The Federal Unemployment Tax Act requires employers to contribute a certain amount of money for each employee into an unemployment fund. If an employee is laid off from his or her job through no fault of the employee's, the government will then pay a certain amount of money to the employee for a limited time period while he or she is unemployed.

## Worker Safety Laws

The main federal law that protects worker safety is the Occupational Safety and Health Act (OSH Act). This act also established the Occupational Safety and Health Administration (OSHA), which enforces this act. In addition, many states have their own state occupational safety and health laws.

## Food Safety Laws

The main law that protects the safety of food in the United States is the Food, Drug, and Cosmetic Act, **24-3**. It was originally passed in 1906, revised in 1967, and revised again in 1997. The **Food, Drug, and Cosmetic Act** requires that food, drugs, and cosmetics sold to the public be proven safe and effective. This Act also established the **Food and Drug Administration (FDA)**, the government agency that makes and enforces regulations based on the Act. In addition to the Food,

24-3 Handling food safely is an important action in the hospitality industry. What U.S. laws govern food safety?

# Hospitality Ethics

## Misleading Customers

It is unethical and illegal for a business to participate in acts of collusion. Collusion occurs when competing businesses work together to eliminate competition by misleading customers, setting prices, or other fraudulent practices. Unethical businesses sometimes collude with other businesses so they can dominate the marketplace.

Drug, and Cosmetic Act, the FDA enforces numerous laws related to food, drug, and cosmetic safety.

Currently, the FDA ensures the safety and wholesomeness of almost 80 percent of the U.S. food supply. The FDA ensures the safety of all food, except for the food products monitored by the USDA. The USDA monitors the safety of meat, poultry, and some egg products. The FDA also ensures the safety and effectiveness of all drugs, biological products (such as blood for transfusion), medical devices, animal drugs, and animal feed. In the wake of the terrorist attacks in 2001, the FDA is also responsible for preventing the willful contamination of all regulated products, including food.

## Zoning and Building Laws

**Zoning** is the process of designating specific geographic areas for specific uses. Most local governments have laws concerning where businesses can be built, called **zoning laws**. Zoning laws list geographic areas and state the permitted uses for each area. Most local governments also have laws that must be followed when buildings are built. **Building codes** are rules and regulations designed to make buildings safe. Both zoning laws and building codes affect hospitality businesses.

### Zoning

Cities and counties are often zoned according to four types of uses: natural, residential, commercial, and industrial. Natural zones are not to be used for residential, commercial, or industrial uses. Residential zones are for homes and apartments. Commercial zones are for businesses that do not involve heavy industrial machinery. Industrial

zones are for heavy industries, such as mining and power plants.

Often, the purpose of zoning is to keep commercial activities out of residential areas. Many people do not want the noise, crowds, and traffic of businesses in the areas where they live. Zoning helps protect natural areas from residential, commercial, or industrial uses. Zoning also helps the local government control the number and types of businesses in its area. Hospitality businesses are usually in commercial zones, but sometimes they get special permission to locate in residential or natural zones, **24-4**.

A person who wants to build a new hospitality business will have to get approval for the project from a zoning board. The role of the zoning board is to enforce the zoning laws of the community. Owners of hospitality businesses meet with

**24-4** Zoning laws regulate the use of land and determine where hospitality businesses can be built.

*Fort Worth Convention & Visitors Bureau*

zoning boards when planning improvements or changes in their properties. Items such as a larger parking lot, the addition of a swimming pool, or the placement of a new sign may require zoning approvals. Zoning should not be thought of as an inflexible set of rules. A good manager will stay well informed about community zoning issues because many communities change their zoning laws as the community changes.

### Building Codes

Each community has its own set of building codes. A committee called the *Building and Zoning Commission* takes suggestions about building standards from community members. It also considers fire safety and construction safety. This commission evaluates each suggestion and votes on the building codes.

Building inspectors enforce building codes by checking properties to make sure the building codes have been followed. For example, most building codes require that fences around pools be designed to self-close and self-lock, **24-5**. The

purpose of the code is to prevent people, especially small children, from accidentally falling into the pool and drowning. A building inspector will occasionally inspect a hotel's pool fence to make sure this code is being followed, and the hotel may be fined if a violation is found.

## Environmental Protection

The quality of the environment has two major impacts on the hospitality industry. The first is in the area of health. Hospitality businesses need clean, safe air and water and food that is not contaminated by pesticides or other toxic chemicals. The second aspect of environmental protection is in the area of recreation. Many hospitality businesses depend on the beauty and safety of natural areas.

In 1970, President Nixon and Congress created the Environmental Protection Agency (EPA) as the lead federal agency to make and enforce environmental regulations. The mandate of the EPA is to protect human health and safeguard

**24-5** Most building codes require that fences around pools follow specific guidelines for customer safety. What safety features are most important around a public pool?

*mtr/Shutterstock.com*

the environment. The main law the EPA enforces is the National Environmental Policy Act of 1969. Additional laws the EPA enforces cover clean air, clean water, safe drinking water, cleaning up toxic wastes, protecting endangered species, protection from pesticides and other toxic substances, food quality protection, and occupational safety.

## Smoking Ordinances

Medical research has revealed that smoking and secondhand smoke can harm the human body. As a result, efforts have been made to eliminate smoking in public places. Places where smoking has been banned include government buildings, airplanes, museums, and elevators.

Many government rules and regulations have been made about smoking, most relating directly to the hospitality industry. For example, in some states smoking is banned in restaurants unless a special ventilation system is installed. Many states are passing their own smoking regulations. For example, some states have banned smoking in any public place. More and more restaurants are becoming smoke free.

Regulations have nearly eliminated smoking in the airline industry. Federal law prohibits smoking on all flights within the United States. Smoking is also not allowed on flights operated by U.S. carriers to and from Canada, Bermuda, the Bahamas, and Puerto Rico. Severe fines are given to people who smoke in airplane restrooms because of the fire hazards, **24-6**.

## Liquor Laws

Every state has a liquor authority or commission. This commission develops and enforces regulations concerning the sale and consumption of alcoholic beverages in the state. The commission usually requires all places that sell liquor get a liquor license. Many states collect taxes on liquor.

The National Minimum Drinking Age Act of 1984 required all states to raise their minimum purchase and possession age to 21. Currently, all states are in compliance. Many studies show that when the drinking age is higher, the number of fatal traffic crashes is lower among 18 to 20 year olds. The higher drinking age also reduces the incidence of other alcohol-related problems.

*l i g h t p o e t/Shutterstock.com*

24-6 Many government regulations protect customer safety during airline travel.

# Enforcing Government Regulations

Local, state, and federal governments have agencies and departments that make sure regulations are enforced. Two main ways that agencies enforce government regulations are through licenses and inspections.

## Licenses

A **license** is a document that gives the holder permission to do something. For example, a driver's license gives the holder permission to drive on public roads. Performing a licensed activity without a license is illegal. For example, if you drive without a valid driver's license, you can be fined or given other penalties.

# Gerald A. "Gerry" Fernandez, Sr.— Bringing Diversity to the Table

*Photograph by
Kris Craig, Courtesy of MFHA*

The president of an industry association must be a good problem-solver with a focus on customer needs. That describes Gerry Fernandez perfectly. Gerry learned early that everyone has roles and responsibilities. Gerry learned to cook by watching his mother prepare meals in their New England home. In high school, a teacher encouraged Gerry to enroll in the culinary program at Johnson & Wales University. Working in restaurants as a dishwasher, waiter, and cook helped Gerry pay for college.

After graduating from culinary school, Gerry worked several jobs on Long Island and in New York City before returning to Johnson & Wales University to run the Cooperative Education Program. In 1983, Gerry moved to Vermont to work under the legendary Chef Ernie Royal, who taught Gerry the importance of quality and customer service. When the Hearthside was sold, Gerry moved back to Rhode Island to open Hemenway's Seafood Grill & Oyster Bar for industry pioneer Ned Grace. After managing restaurants with the Grace organization for almost 10 years, Gerry took a job in the research and development kitchens of General Mills in 1992. He was promoted to National Account Manager three years later.

At this point in his career, something occurred to Gerry. No professional organization focused on the value of a diverse hospitality workforce. Businesses were starting to search for ways to meet the needs of workers and customers from various racial and ethnic backgrounds. Gerry put some of his thoughts on paper and began working on his idea with leaders in the industry.

In 1996, he helped found the Multicultural Foodservice & Hospitality Alliance (MFHA). Today, MFHA is the voice for multicultural issues in the food and hospitality industry. The Alliance works with employers to meet the challenges of managing a diverse workforce. MFHA also helps organizations improve their customer service and build relationships with diverse communities. As president of MFHA, Gerry Fernandez leads the organization his vision helped create.

## Gerald Fernandez's Career Path

**1956:** Born in Middleboro, Massachusetts

**1972:** Worked as a grocery bagger for Brockton Public Markets, now known as Shaw's Supermarkets

**1976:** Graduated from Johnson & Wales University; began work at The Waldorf Astoria® Hotel in New York City

**1983:** Worked at Royal's Hearthside Restaurant as a sous-chef and manager

**1984:** Opened Hemenway's Seafood Grill & Oyster Bar in Providence, Rhode Island

**1992:** Began career in the research and development kitchens of General Mills

**1995:** Promoted to National Account Manager at General Mills

**1996:** Founded the MultiCultural Foodservice & Hospitality Alliance

States and local governments often regulate hospitality businesses through licenses. The most common is the liquor license. Businesses that serve alcohol must have a license to sell alcohol. Without this license, the sale of alcohol is illegal and the owner of the business will be fined.

A permit is very similar to a license. A **permit** is written permission to do something. Building commissions give building permits to businesses that request permission to build a building. For example, when a business wants to build a new hotel, it must request a building permit from the building commission. The building commission will analyze the building permit request to make sure it meets all relevant laws and regulations. Permits are also usually required for remodeling and renovations.

## Inspections

An **inspection** is a formal visit by federal, state, and local government agencies for the purpose of making sure regulations are being followed. If they are not, the agency can impose a fine or other penalty. In extreme cases, the business can be closed down until the violation is corrected. Federal agencies that inspect hospitality businesses include OSHA, FDA, and USDA. Local health departments inspect foodservice operations.

OSHA officials can conduct workplace inspections at any time without prior notification and can also enforce the law. They make sure that all required safety and health regulations are being followed. OSHA will give a *citation* (a summons to appear in court) to any company not following

the rules. OSHA can also impose fines of tens of thousands of dollars for the violations.

The FDA regulates the production, packaging, and labeling of foods, drugs, and cosmetics. If a product is found to be unsafe, the FDA can ban the sale of the product or require the packaging to contain a warning label. The FDA also inspects manufacturers of food products to make sure the products are being made in a safe and sanitary way.

The USDA's main responsibilities are to inspect the manufacturing and processing of fresh meat and meat products. The USDA also inspects dairy farms and other food producers. Meat, poultry, and fish must all be inspected by the USDA for safety and quality.

Local health departments make sure that restaurants and health-care agencies are following health and safety regulations. For example, restaurants are inspected using a 100-point rating scale. If the restaurant fails an inspection, the health department can close the restaurant until it can successfully prove that the regulations have been met. In some cases, restaurants are permanently closed.

## Liability Issues

According to common law, people who are engaged in a public service, such as innkeepers, are responsible to the public. Common law guarantees guests certain rights such as
- decent and humane treatment
- no abusive or insulting treatment by employees

## *Going Green*

### Environmental Stewardship

Many hospitality companies today find that being good stewards of the environment can help increase sales and profits. This is because consumers often hold companies in higher regard when they act responsibly and have environmentally friendly policies. These policies are often marketed as part of public relations campaigns. Not only is good environmental stewardship good public relations, it is also an ethical responsibility.

- total use of a room, with the innkeeper's right to enter the room to clean and maintain the room
- the right to be protected from personal injury

Hospitality businesses have special liability obligations to their guests, **24-7**. *Liability* means responsibility to pay for damages or loss. There are three areas in which liability issues arise: guest injuries, property damage or theft, and guest privacy.

## Injuries to Guests

Most hospitality businesses work hard to prevent injuries to guests. However, injuries do occur. Most injury claims result from guest injuries in lobbies, hallways, guest rooms, and bathrooms. Some claims result from the consumption of food and beverage or the use of a product or service sold by the hotel. Some of these claims result in lawsuits, which determine whether the hotel is liable and the amount of liability. Hotels purchase liability insurance to help them pay for legitimate claims from guests.

## Property Damage or Theft

The general rule of common law is that innkeepers or hoteliers are liable for any losses that happen to their guests. They are liable unless the loss is caused by an act of nature or war, or if the loss was the fault of the guest. This law has been modified by some states (Illinois, Indiana, Maryland, Texas, Vermont, and Washington). Hoteliers in these states are "liable only if the loss occurs through their [the hotelier's] negligence." Laws that limit liability protect the hotel owner from losses due to the damage or theft of guest property. Signs stating the innkeeper's limits on liability are usually posted at the front desk, next to the elevator doors, and in other easy-to-see locations.

In order to protect guests' property from theft and to protect the hotel from liability for that theft, many hotels offer to place valuables in a safe deposit box. If hotels offer this service, posted signs inform guests that the hotel is not liable for any valuable *not* placed in the safe deposit box.

Hotels purchase insurance policies to protect them against a variety of risks. The types of policies that are purchased include property insurance, liability insurance, and crime insurance. The amount of insurance coverage must be reevaluated periodically. Reevaluation of policies will help hotels determine how much coverage is necessary based on past claims and future needs.

Andresr/Shutterstock.com

**24-7** What liability obligations do hospitality businesses have to their guests?

## Guest Privacy

Guests expect that their stay in a hotel will be private. Room attendants, housekeepers, or front desk agents should not allow anyone into a guest room who does not have a key. The front desk agent can verify that the person is a registered guest before issuing that person a key to the room.

Guest room numbers are not given to callers who inquire about guests, **24-8**. Instead, the hotel

**24-8** Hospitality businesses are obliged to protect the privacy of guests. What are some consequences of failing to protect guest privacy?

Ljupco Smokovski/Shutterstock.com

operator can connect the caller to the guest's hotel room. The guest can then decide whether to give the room location to the caller.

The results can be costly if hoteliers invade the privacy of a guest. For example, a front desk agent cannot ask whether a male and female are married prior to renting them a room. This is considered to be an invasion of guest privacy.

# Ethical Issues

*Ethics* is a discipline consisting of principles of conduct that govern the behavior of an individual or group. Ethics create a system of moral rules that help people decide right from wrong. The goal of ethics is **ethical behavior**—doing the right thing even when under pressure to do the wrong thing. **Unethical behavior** is doing the wrong thing. Unethical behavior is often illegal. Every person has his or her own ethics; however, in business there is a set of ethics that most people agree with. One of the primary requirements of ethics is to follow the law. Other ethical qualities include honesty, integrity, and fairness.

## Guidelines for Ethical Behavior

There are many ways to describe ethical behavior. In several cultures, the basic rule of ethics is to treat others as you would like to be treated.

Many philosophers, theologians, and others have written more detailed guidelines for ethical behavior. Most people develop their own personal rules of ethics. In business, there is general agreement about guidelines for ethical behavior. Not everyone follows them all the time. However, the eight guidelines in **24-9** are generally accepted in business.

Hospitality managers should be role models for the type of ethical behavior they want their employees to have. These eight basic ethical principles can be a guideline for ethical training and role modeling. Managers should always discourage unethical behavior.

## Code of Ethics

A **code of ethics** is a written list of rules for ethical behavior. It may also be called a *code of conduct*. Most businesses focus their codes of ethics on customers and employees. Many professional

| Eight Guidelines for Ethical Behavior ||
|---|---|
| **Ethical Quality** | **Ethical Guideline** |
| *1. Honesty* | Tell the truth, even if you may have done something incorrectly. |
| *2. Integrity* | Do not let peer pressure change your mind about what you know is right. |
| *3. Trustworthiness* | Be reliable. Be the type of person who can be trusted with valuables. |
| *4. Loyalty* | Keep confidential information confidential. Do not say bad things about your employer. |
| *5. Fairness* | Treat everyone equally. Apply the same rules to everyone. |
| *6. Concern and Respect for Others* | Care about fellow employees. |
| *7. Commitment to Excellence* | Always do your best. |
| *8. Accountability* | Be responsible for your actions. |

*Source: International Institute for Quality and Ethics in Service and Tourism (IIQUEST), Scituate, MA*

**24-9** Many businesses accept these general guidelines for ethical behavior.

organizations and other groups develop a code of ethics for their members, **24-10**.

An example of a code of ethics focusing on customers might read: "Our customers will be provided with exceptional service that is limited only by our available resources. Every complaint will be acknowledged quickly in an attempt to meet or exceed guest expectations." This type of code of ethics shows the company's interest in its customers.

An example of a code of ethics focusing on employees might read: "Our employees will be treated as well as our customers. Our company believes happy customers are the direct result of having happy employees. Happy employees are the result of careful training for every position in which they work. Our employees will receive fair benefits and wages." This type of code of ethics shows a company's interest in its workers.

## Ethical Decision Making

Employees in the hospitality industry often make decisions that involve ethics. How they handle these decisions can have a big impact on customer satisfaction, employee satisfaction, and the success of the business. The future of the hospitality industry depends on people who make ethical decisions. They must make good choices for which they take responsibility. This requires people who have strong ethics. Employees must have the courage to do what is right, even when there is pressure to do something wrong.

It often helps to ask yourself a series of questions before taking action that might be unethical. Figure **24-11** presents a list of questions commonly used to test whether an action is ethical.

Here is an example of how you could use these questions. Imagine you are on a business trip and take a taxicab to a meeting. The taxi driver gives you a blank receipt for the cab ride, which cost $5.00. You are thinking about making out the blank receipt for $10, which is $5.00 more than it actually cost. Then your company would reimburse you $10 for the cost of the cab ride, and you would have five extra dollars.

Use the seven questions to reach an ethical decision. Are your actions legal? No. Do your actions hurt anyone? Yes, your company. Are your actions fair to your company? No. Have you been

### Code of Ethics

The hospitality professional…

1. *Provides* services with objectivity and respect for the unique needs and values of individuals.
2. *Avoids* discrimination against other individuals on the basis of race, creed, religion, sex, age, and national origin.
3. *Fulfills* professional commitments in good faith.
4. *Conducts* himself/herself with honesty, integrity, and fairness.
5. *Remains* free of conflict of interest while fulfilling the objectives and maintaining the integrity of the service profession.
6. *Maintains* confidentiality of information.
7. *Assumes* responsibility and accountability for personal competence.
8. *Makes* all reasonable effort to avoid bias in any kind of professional evaluation.
9. *Voluntarily* withdraws from any substance abuse that could affect his/her organization.
10. *Accepts* the obligation to protect society and represent the profession of management by upholding these principles.

*Source: International Institute for Quality and Ethics in Service and Tourism, Ltd. (IIQUEST). (1995). Seven tests for ethics. The Voice of Excellence, 6(1).*

**24-10** A code of ethics provides specific behaviors that members of professional organizations or other groups must follow.

### Questions to Help with  Ethical Decision Making

- Is it legal?
- Does it hurt anyone?
- Is it fair?
- Am I being honest?
- Can I live with myself?
- Would I publicize my decision?
- What if everyone did it?

*Goodheart-Willcox Publisher*

**24-11** Ask yourself this series of questions before taking action that might be unethical.

honest with everyone? No, you have not been honest with your company. Can you live with the decision? Maybe. Would you publicize this decision? No. What if everyone did it? My company would have very high costs and that might lead to problems, including employees losing their jobs.

Many factors affect the ethical decisions people have to make. Family pressures, friends, school demands, money problems, and even personal goals can influence your decisions. Think about the seven ethical questions the next time you have a difficult decision to make.

# Ethics in Hospitality

We often see headlines showing questionable and sometimes criminal behavior in the hospitality industry. The following are some sample headlines:

- Hotel Investors Sue Their Accountants for $20 Million in Fraud Claims
- Restaurant Chain Sued: Former Servers Claim Sexual Harassment by Managers
- Hotel Corporation Charged with Tax Avoidance
- Restaurant Closed Because of Food Safety Violations: Health Department Fears Foodborne Illness Outbreak

Corporations that overlook their responsibilities to the environment demonstrate unethical behavior. In the hospitality industry, unethical behavior can include the lack of attention to food safety, overcharging guests, and not paying attention to the welfare of employees.

The reputation of the hospitality industry is judged by the actions of each owner, manager, and employee. The actions of everyone in the industry are important, **24-12**. The ethical action of each employee can affect the ethical reputation of the whole hospitality industry. There are three main reasons why the hospitality industry should be concerned with ethics. First, many unethical actions are also illegal and can lead to fines, penalties, and possible jail terms. Second, most people want to act ethically. Third, the teamwork style of the hospitality industry demands a great deal of integrity and honesty.

**24-12** People encounter situations that challenge their ethics every day. What ethical situations might this front desk worker encounter?

Kzenon/Shutterstock.com

For example, a person who is caught stealing from a company can be fired. If the owner presses charges against the worker, a jail term or fine can be expected. A jail term can go on a person's record, which will cause the person to have a difficult time finding a job in the future.

Most employees want to be ethical. Being ethical means doing things in an ethical way. It also involves what you do *not* do, but *should* do. If you know that someone is doing something wrong, you should report it to your supervisor. Looking the other way will just allow the problem to get worse.

All hospitality businesses require teamwork. A restaurant relies on employees in the dining room and the kitchen. A hotel relies on its front desk agents, bell attendants, and room attendants. Hospitality employees must all work together as a team for the hospitality business to be successful. When one person acts in an unethical way, it causes problems for the rest of the employees. That person is not trusted, gossip begins, and the spirit of teamwork is destroyed. The employees, the customers, and ultimately the whole business suffer.

Managers in the hospitality industry should demand a high standard of ethics. Managers must make it clear that unethical behavior is unacceptable and show by their own behavior that ethical behavior is really important.

Employees in hospitality face ethical situations every day. Some of these situations include truth-in-menu laws, sexual harassment, discrimination, and technology issues.

## Truth-in-Menu Laws

Truth-in-menu laws have been developed to protect consumers from unethical restaurant owners, **24-13**. Menus are designed to make food sound as appealing as possible. Some restaurant owners go so far as to be untruthful in their descriptions. For example, a menu might say "16-ounce sirloin steak," but the customer is served a much smaller piece of meat. The same is true of pictures of items offered on a menu. If a breakfast menu shows a picture of five pancakes and two pieces of bacon, it is telling customers that five pancakes and two pieces of bacon will be served. If less than that is served, the customer has not gotten what the menu promised. Both these cases

Blend Images/Shutterstock.com

**24-13** What consequences may occur when menu descriptions do not match the food served to customers?

are examples of unethical behavior. Many states have truth-in-menu laws that require accuracy in menus. In addition, the Federal Food and Drug Administration requires that any health claims meet the FDA standards.

## Sexual Harassment

*Sexual harassment* is illegal as well as unethical. Most businesses have written policies concerning sexual harassment. These policies specify what behavior is unacceptable and what the consequences are for anyone who engages in sexual harassment. Information about a company's sexual harassment policy is usually included in the company handbook. Any act of sexual harassment should be reported to the manager. Managers are required to investigate any occurrences of sexual harassment.

## Discrimination

Discrimination is never appropriate. *Discrimination* is showing prejudice in the treatment of a person because of his or her race, religion, age, national origin, or gender. Not only is it unethical, but it is also against the law to discriminate against a person or group of people. Most businesses have policies that prohibit discrimination.

## Technology Issues

The increase in the use of new types of technology has caused companies to watch out for unethical practices. Servers in restaurants often have access to guests' credit cards. An unethical and illegal act would be to use a guest's credit card number to make unauthorized purchases. Employees who do this are fired and prosecuted for credit card theft, 24-14.

Companies use security cameras to monitor hallways, entrances, and delivery docks to help reduce employee theft and to protect guests. It is unethical if these cameras are used improperly.

It is also unethical to use a company's computer system for nonbusiness reasons. These computers are the property of the company and should be used only for company business purposes.

24-14 Why is electronic use of credit cards a source of possible problems?

Zurijeta/Shutterstock.com

# Work Ethic

The hospitality industry is very labor intensive. This means that you, the employee, should develop a good work ethic. A **good work ethic** is an attitude that combines hard work, good performance, and dependable results, 24-15.

How do you know if you have a good work ethic? Ask yourself the following questions. Do you value your work? Do you refuse to look for the easy way out? Do you always take pride in the results of your work? Do you look for ways to make your job more efficient? Do you sometimes even work later than scheduled, if necessary? If you answered yes to these questions, you probably have a good work ethic. Following these four guidelines will also help you have a good work ethic.

## Act in a Professional Manner

While at work, make sure you always act in a professional manner. Professional behavior includes being on time and being polite, respectful, and dependable. Professionals do not use profanity on or anywhere near the job. They also avoid gossip and practice good ethical behavior. Acting in a professional manner shows your manager and coworkers that you are someone they can trust and depend on.

## Keep Your Personal Life Private

Separate your work life from your personal life. Avoid discussing personal problems at work. Your coworkers do not need to know about your personal life. Discussing your personal life at work distracts you and your coworkers from the work at hand. In other words, you should not let things that happen at home affect your work habits. Keep personal telephone calls to a minimum.

## Do Not Steal

Stealing is illegal and unethical at all times. In the hospitality business, employees are often responsible for the business's cash and property. It is illegal to take any cash or property that is not yours or has not been given to you. The temptation to steal may be great but must be avoided. Examples of stealing include

- taking office supplies or food from the storeroom
- taking cash from the cash register
- taking condiments from the table or toilet articles from guest rooms
- letting your friends eat at a restaurant or stay in a hotel room without charging them

Embezzlement is a particular type of stealing. **Embezzlement** occurs when a trusted employee takes either money or goods entrusted to him or her. For example, suppose you are responsible for taking the nightly cash deposit to the bank. You take some of the money and put it in your pocket instead of the bank. An employee can be prosecuted for this. A person caught stealing or embezzling can be punished with a fine, prison sentence, or both.

## Do Not Waste Resources

Wasting resources costs the company money and can lead to environmental problems. An example of wastefulness is restaurant managers choosing not to recycle items from their businesses. Items such as paper products, grease, and oil can easily be recycled. Managers who do not recycle are wasting valuable resources and contributing to a serious waste disposal problem.

*William Perugini/Shutterstock.com*

**24-15** A good work ethic is an attitude that combines hard work, good performance, and dependable results. What actions show a good work ethic?

# Chapter 24

## Review

## Chapter Summary

- Laws and regulations governing proper behavior in the hospitality industry are made by local, state, and federal governments.
- Two main ways that agencies enforce government regulations are through licenses and inspections.
- Hospitality businesses have special liabilities, or responsibilities to pay for damages or loss, to their guests.
- The goal of ethical behavior is doing the right thing, even when under pressure to do the wrong thing. Unethical behavior is doing the wrong thing.
- A code of ethics is a written list of rules to guide ethical behavior. In business, most codes of ethics focus on customers and employees.
- Ethics in the hospitality industry is judged by the actions of owners, managers, and employees. Many unethical behaviors are also criminal behaviors.
- A good work ethic is an attitude that combines hard work, good performance, and dependable results.

## Review

1. Contrast the terms *law, regulation, code,* and *ordinance.*
2. Under what seven categories are the laws that affect hospitality businesses grouped?
3. Name the main law that protects worker safety and the federal agency that enforces it.
4. Name the main law that protects food safety and the federal agency that enforces it.
5. What is the difference between the terms *license* and *permit*? Give an example of each.
6. What are the common law rights of guests?
7. Name the areas in which liability issues arise in hospitality.
8. Contrast *ethical behavior* with *unethical behavior*.
9. What are seven questions that can help you make ethical decisions?
10. List at least three questions you can ask yourself to judge whether you have a good work ethic.

# Critical Thinking

11. **Analyze.** The text addresses laws that protect the rights of workers. In small groups, analyze reasons why these laws exist. Make a list of potential reasons to share with the class. Discuss why these laws are most relevant to the people who hire, train, and evaluate employees.

12. **Cause and effect.** What is the cause-and-effect relationship between failure to follow food safety laws and the impact on a hospitality establishment? Why is it essential for such establishments to follow the law to the fullest extent possible?

13. **Evaluate.** Suppose you work in the housekeeping department at a lodging facility. You recently observed a coworker stealing some jewelry from a guest room. You really like your coworker. What actions would you take in this situation? What questions would you ask yourself to test whether your actions in this situation are ethical?

# Common Core

### College and Career Readiness

14. **Reading.** Read a work of nonfiction or fiction (such as Upton Sinclair's *The Jungle*) that addresses unsafe workplace conditions. Give a brief report summarizing the work, identifying its influence on workplace laws of today.

15. **Reading.** Review the text content on zoning and building laws. Then review the information on zoning and building for your community on its website. How do zoning and building laws in your community impact the local hospitality industry? Write a summary of your findings.

16. **Writing.** Presume you are a hospitality worker. Based on the definitions of ethics and ethical behavior, write your own code of ethics related to working in the hospitality industry.

17. **Speaking.** Choose one of the following text topics to further research in relationship to the hospitality industry: environmental protection, smoking ordinances, and liquor laws. Use reliable Internet or print resources to cite supporting evidence and issues related to legislation for hospitality. Create a digital presentation to enhance your findings to share with the class.

18. **Speaking.** Your work team has been asked to make recommendations for the content of the company anti-harassment and discrimination policy. In order to make recommendations, your team decides to use the *Equal Employment Opportunity Commission's* website to identify what key elements should be included in these policies. Present your findings and supporting evidence to the company (your class).

19. **CTE Career Readiness Practice.** Suppose you work in the kitchen of a well-known, high-volume restaurant. Safe and healthful actions are important to the health and safety of employees and guests. To promote safety and health, the restaurant owner strictly follows a random drug-testing policy. One of the sous chefs often brags about his off-hours alcohol and drug use—the effects of which showed in his recent near-accident with a food slicer. You question the responsibility of his actions in light of this. You go about your work without saying anything about your coworker's habits to anyone. After a few days, you learn that the sous chef has been fired. You wonder if he failed his drug test. Then you begin to examine your own ethical actions. What questions should you ask yourself in regard to your ethical actions in this situation? Write a summary.

# Part Six
# Careers

455

456

# Chapter 25
## Your Career in Hospitality

## Chapter Objectives

After studying this chapter, you will be able to

- **list** the advantages and challenges of a hospitality career.
- **describe** the steps you can take to determine whether a hospitality career is for you.
- **list** ways to learn more about hospitality careers.
- **explain** the relationship between education level, job responsibilities, and relative salary for an entry-level job, a supervisor's job, and a manager's job.
- **summarize** ways to get education or training after completing high school.
- **explain** how knowing yourself can help you find the right career.
- **describe** how a career plan helps you reach your career goal.

## Before You Read

Try to answer the following questions before you read this chapter.
- What is job shadowing?
- What is the difference between an aptitude and an ability?

## Terms to Know

entry-level job
stress
relocation
information interview
job shadowing
career ladder
cooperative education program

tech prep
postsecondary
internship
distance learning
apprenticeship
correspondence course

continuing professional education
aptitude
ability
work values
career goal
career plan

How do you picture your future? You will probably have a full-time job. Imagine that you have a job

- doing something you love
- working with a group of fun and friendly coworkers
- meeting all kinds of people
- making the best use of your talents and skills

The hospitality industry offers these types of opportunities.

The benefits of a hospitality career include working with people, traveling, and having a bright future, **25-1**. The hospitality industry is the largest service industry in the world, and it is still growing. Hospitality is one of the few industries where you can start at the bottom and work your way up to the top. Hospitality is also one of the easier industries in which to start your own business. Many hospitality professionals describe their careers as fun, rewarding, and exciting. The hospitality industry offers many advantages to employees, but it also has challenges.

# Advantages

Some of the advantages of a career in hospitality include an abundance of jobs, many opportunities for advancement, and a pleasant workplace. Fast pace and variety, opportunity to meet people, and travel are other advantages.

## Abundance of Jobs

In the hospitality industry, you can choose from an abundance of jobs. These jobs range from corporate positions to desk agent at a local lodging property. The restaurant industry alone employs millions of people. It is one of the largest employers in the United States.

## Advancement Opportunities

Salaries and wages in the hospitality industry are determined mainly by the labor supply and the level of skills required for a particular job. An **entry-level job** that requires minimum education and no experience will pay lower wages. Jobs that require education and previous experience will pay higher salaries, but will also demand more responsibility. Promotions and salary increases are based on how well you perform on the job over time. Larger companies are often able to pay their employees more than smaller companies.

What are starting salaries like in the hospitality industry? In comparison with entry-level positions in other fields, salaries are similar. Wages are often higher when there is a labor shortage or not enough workers.

One of the most important advantages of a hospitality career is the opportunity for quick advancement, **25-2**. For example, a management trainee in a restaurant could be managing a multimillion dollar operation in about two years after college graduation. Advancement depends on your willingness to learn and work hard. Employers are often willing to train employees who show promise.

25-1 The benefits of a hospitality career include working with people and traveling. Chef Martin Yan is demonstrating cooking techniques at the National Restaurant Association convention.

25-2 A young employee in the hospitality industry may move up to higher-level positions quickly.

National Restaurant Association

Minerva Studio/Shutterstock.com

Many individuals who started as entry-level employees now own franchises in the Ramada Franchise Systems. They advanced to the general manager position and later owned a franchise hotel.

## Pleasant Workplace

Working conditions in the hospitality industry are often very pleasant. Luxury hotels are beautiful and clean. Some hotels and many restaurants provide meals for their employees. Many hospitality businesses are located in exotic places with beautiful beaches or scenic mountains. Others are located in large, exciting cities. Managers often get to travel from one property to another, especially if they work for large chains. Reservations agents and travel agents often travel to the properties that they book. Some hotel and resort companies give their employees discounts when they stay at company-owned properties.

## Fast Pace and Variety

Many hospitality careers are fast-paced and provide variety. Every day brings a new set of customers and a new set of problems to solve. Often many customers arrive at once, and each one wants personal service immediately. Equipment breaks down. Kitchens run out of ingredients. The air conditioning goes out. All these problems and people provide variety and excitement.

Many hospitality jobs are not desk jobs. Some people cannot imagine sitting at a desk all day. Hospitality jobs often provide the opportunity to move around, perform physical work, and work outside. Even managers in the hospitality industry often have to walk around a great deal to oversee their businesses.

## Opportunity to Meet People

Many hospitality professionals think that meeting people is the major advantage of their careers. Every new person you meet is a new experience from which you can learn. With the great increase in world travel, many restaurants and hotels serve people from all over the world. Many luxury restaurants and hotels serve the most famous and important people in the world.

## Travel

Many careers in hospitality, especially those in travel and tourism, provide the opportunity to travel, **25-3**. In fact, many hospitality careers involve travel as part of the job. For example, regional, national, and international managers of hotel and restaurant chains often travel to their units in various locations. National and international chains often make it easy for their employees to transfer from one property to another.

25-3 What city would you most like to visit?

fstockfoto/Shutterstock.com

Mazzzur/Shutterstock.com

Suppose you work for a hotel in Cincinnati. Your hotel chain also owns hotels in Hawaii, and you would love to live there. You could apply to be transferred to a position at that hotel.

# Challenges

All jobs have both positive and negative sides, and the hospitality industry is no exception. The hospitality industry can be very demanding. It provides services to travelers who need assistance 24 hours a day, 7 days a week. Employees must be available to staff this "round-the-clock" industry. It has been said that employees in the hospitality industry work while others play. However, many people find the challenges of hospitality to be part of the industry's advantages.

## *Hours of Work*

Many hospitality employees, especially those in management, work long hours. This can limit the time employees have available to do other things, such as spending time with family and friends. It is not unusual for managers to work six days a week. They often work more than 60 hours a week. People in entry-level jobs and other nonmanagement jobs usually work 40 hours per week. If they work more, they are paid overtime. Some people think the opportunity to work overtime and earn additional money is an advantage.

In addition, many hospitality businesses are open 24 hours a day, every day. As a result, workers must be available during the night, on weekends, and on holidays. In these businesses, employees at all levels, including managers, are needed at these times. If you have a career in the hospitality industry, you will often find yourself working while your friends are playing, **25-4**.

Many hospitality employees have unusual schedules. Some employees work nights and have time off during the day. Some employees work weekends and have time off during the week. Hospitality businesses that are open on holidays usually develop a way to fairly distribute holiday work.

Some hospitality employees consider the unusual schedules a benefit of the industry. Often the schedules are flexible, so employees can choose the days and hours they work. Parents, students, and people with other obligations or interests find that flexible schedules make their lives easier.

Blend Images/Shutterstock.com

25-4  Would you enjoy a job working hours other than 9 to 5?

## *Stress*

A fast-paced career with a lot of variety also leads to stress. **Stress** is a feeling of tension that sometimes results from
- having many tasks to do at the same time
- not having enough time to complete tasks
- having many difficult tasks to do
- having dangerous tasks
- having unpredictable tasks.

A server often experiences the stress of having many tasks to do at once, especially when many parties are seated at the same time. A room attendant occasionally has an unpredictable task when he or she enters a guest room and finds a sick guest or wastebasket fire. Management jobs are usually stressful because a manager's job is to solve problems and help employees and guests with problems.

Stress is not necessarily bad. Many people who choose hospitality careers thrive on stress and say it helps them do a better job. In addition, different people experience situations in different ways. One person might find a situation stressful while another person finds the same situation exciting.

Some people do not function well under stress or experience many situations as stressful. These people can find careers in hospitality that are less stressful. For example, cooking in a commercial restaurant can be very stressful. Cooking in an institution such as a school is generally less stressful. Working at the front desk greeting new people all day is very stressful for some people. Taking reservations over the phone from customers who call might be less stressful.

## Working Conditions

Some hospitality businesses have poor working conditions. Kitchens with poor air conditioning or ventilation can be hot and uncomfortable. Some businesses may not even practice proper sanitary procedures in their kitchens. This can lead to poor health for both workers and guests. Generally, hospitality companies have good working conditions, **25-5**.

## Relocation

In some hospitality careers, advancement requires relocation. **Relocation** is the act of moving from one place to another for your job. People who have lived in one place for a long time and have many friends and family ties might consider relocation a hardship. These people can either refuse to move or search for another job in hospitality that does not require relocation. Many people find relocation exciting and a benefit of a hospitality career.

# Is Hospitality for Me?

The hospitality industry has a wide variety of career opportunities, but how can you tell if one is right for you? Steps to take include
- learn about the hospitality industry and hospitality careers
- learn about preparation requirements
- learn about yourself
- make a career plan

These steps can be done in any order. Sometimes you need to go back and forth among the steps. For example, you might want to learn about your aptitudes and abilities first. You might then learn about hospitality careers and preparation requirements. You might then match yourself to a career but go back to learn more about the career and preparation requirements before making a career plan. After you have some work experience, you will probably learn more about yourself and the hospitality industry. At that time, you might do more research and revise your career plan.

# Learn About Hospitality Careers

You have already taken the first steps to discover whether hospitality is a good career for you. By taking this hospitality course, you are learning about the industry and what hospitality professionals do.

This textbook gives you a great deal of information about the hospitality industry and careers. However, you still need to know more about what it is like to work in hospitality. You need more information about the businesses that might hire you. You also need to know about the *Occupational Outlook Handbook*.

## A Day in the Life

What is it really like to work in the hospitality industry? There are three main ways to find

**25-5** Pleasant, sanitary working conditions can have a positive impact on an employee's outlook.

ollyy/Shutterstock.com

out: talk to someone who works in the industry, observe someone who works in the industry, and get a job in the industry.

### Information Interviews

One of the ways to learn about real life in the hospitality industry is to talk to someone currently in the industry. Talking to someone to learn about his or her career is called an **information interview**. Suppose you are interested in owning your own restaurant. You could locate an independent restaurant that you like, call, and ask to speak to the owner, **25-6**. You could politely ask to do an information interview with the owner to learn about owning a restaurant. Before the interview, develop a list of questions to cover what you most want to know. Some examples include the following:

- What do you like most about your job?
- How many hours do you work a day?
- What do you like least about your job?
- What was your first job in hospitality?
- Which jobs and experiences were the most helpful in reaching your career goal?
- How much and what kind of education should I get?
- Do you have any advice for me?

### Job Shadowing

Another way to learn about a job is to watch someone doing it. **Job shadowing** is following a person while he or she does a job. Many schools arrange job shadowing for students. You could also see if you could set up job shadowing for yourself. If you are interested in hotel management, you could call the manager of a nearby hotel and explain your interest. You could then ask if you could shadow him or her for a few hours.

### Part-Time, Summer, and Co-op Jobs

The best way to learn about an industry is to actually work in the industry. As a student, you have several opportunities. You could get a part-time job at a local restaurant, hotel, or other hospitality business. You could also get a summer job in a hospitality business. In addition, your school may offer a cooperative work program (co-op program). In a cooperative work program, your school helps you find a job where you work as part of your school program. Companies are often more willing to hire an applicant who has been through such a program and has demonstrated his or her skills on the job.

## Company Research

Another way to learn about the hospitality industry is to learn about the businesses in the industry. You know many hospitality companies from using the businesses or seeing them advertised. You can learn a great deal about a company and its career opportunities by exploring its website. Most company websites include sections on careers and career opportunities that list available jobs, job descriptions, education and experience requirements, and salary.

## Occupational Outlook

The U.S. Department of Labor's Bureau of Labor Statistics compiles and publishes a great deal of information on occupations, industries,

**25-6** If you do an information interview over the phone, prepare for it as if you were going in person.

*Andresr/Shutterstock.com*

and jobs in the United States. One of the most useful documents is the *Occupational Outlook Handbook*. Additional information about hospitality occupations is available through hospitality professional associations and journals.

## The *Occupational Outlook Handbook*

The *Occupational Outlook Handbook* is available online and in most libraries, **25-7**. The web address is stats.bls.gov/oco. The *Handbook* provides information and statistics on a wide range of occupations and individual jobs. The information is revised every two years, making the *Handbook* one of the most up-to-date and comprehensive sources for this type of information.

The *Occupational Outlook Handbook* provides a detailed description of each occupation covered. The first section of this description is an overview called "Summary." This section lists

- median pay
- entry-level education
- work experience in a related occupation
- on-the-job training
- number of jobs
- job outlook
- employment change

The *Occupational Outlook Handbook* provides a great deal of additional useful information, **25-8**. The section "What They Do" describes the responsibilities and lists job titles and job descriptions. The section "Work Environment" describes the typical work hours and special stresses and pressures of the job. It also tells you how many people are currently employed in the occupation.

**25-7** The *Occupational Outlook Handbook* is available online and in libraries.

*Supri Suharjoto/Shutterstock.com*

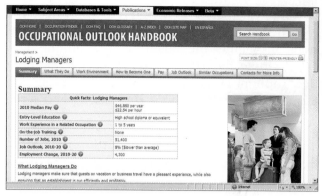

*stats.bls.gov/oco*

**25-8** This is part of the home page of the *Occupational Outlook Handbook*.

The *Occupational Outlook Handbook* also has a section called "How to Become One." This section describes what you need to do to prepare for the career. The section "Pay" lists median annual or hourly earnings. A *median earning* means that half the people employed in that occupation earned more than that amount, and half the people earned less. The earnings section also gives you some idea of the range of the earnings.

To get a picture of future employment opportunities, turn to the section titled "Job Outlook." This section details the projected employment opportunities for the next 10 years. For lodging managers, this section describes why this career will grow more slowly than others. These reasons include more limited-service hotels, fewer full-service hotels, and more streamlining of management positions.

Do not let statements that an occupation is growing slowly or declining scare you away. First, even a slowly growing occupation is growing. Second, every occupation has a certain number of people who leave the occupation or retire every year. These people must often be replaced, even when the occupation is not growing. Third, certain segments within the occupation may be growing. Fourth, even if the occupation is declining, there may be an ideal career for you in it.

The last two sections of an occupation description list similar occupations and contacts for more information. These additional sources of information are often the professional associations in the industry.

One of the challenges of using the *Occupational Outlook Handbook* is finding the occupation that interests you. The reason for this difficulty is that the U.S. Department of Labor groups occupations and names the jobs in its own unique way. For example, the website has a "Search by occupation" option. However, if you enter "server," the term used in this textbook for people who serve food in restaurants, you will get several options. In the *Occupational Outlook Handbook*, servers are called "food and beverage serving and related workers" or "waiters and waitresses." Figure **25-9** will help you find the occupation you are looking for in the *Occupational Outlook Handbook*.

| Hospitality Occupations in the Occupational Outlook Handbook | |
|---|---|
| **Occupations** | **Hospitality-related Occupation Names in the OOH** |
| (Listed on the left side of home page.) | (These terms appear when you click on the occupation in the column to the left. These are not the only terms that appear, so you may need to search for them in the list.) |
| *Management* | Accountants and auditors<br>Administrative services managers<br>Advertising, marketing, promotion, public relations, and sales managers<br>Financial managers<br>Foodservice managers<br>Human resources, training, and labor relations managers and specialists<br>Lodging managers<br>Purchasing managers, buyers, and purchasing agents<br>Top executives |
| *Service* | Building cleaning workers<br>Grounds maintenance workers<br>Chefs, cooks, and food preparation workers<br>Food and beverage serving and related workers<br>Flight attendants<br>Gaming services occupations<br>Recreation workers<br>Security guards and gaming surveillance officers |
| *Sales* | Cashiers<br>Counter and rental clerks<br>Travel agents |
| *Administrative* | Data entry and information processing workers<br>Bookkeeping, accounting, and auditing clerks<br>Payroll and timekeeping clerks<br>Procurement clerks<br>Hotel, motel, and resort desk clerks<br>Human resources assistants, except payroll and timekeeping<br>Reservation and transportation ticket agents and travel clerks<br>Shipping, receiving, and traffic clerks |
| *Production* | Stationery engineers and boiler operators |

*Goodheart-Willcox Publisher*

**25-9** These terms can help you find the hospitality occupation you are looking for in the *Occupational Outlook Handbook*.

Some hospitality jobs are not covered in the *Occupational Outlook Handbook* in detail. These are mostly jobs that do not require much education and training. Some of these jobs are covered under the heading "Occupations Not Studied in Detail," subheading "Food Preparation and Serving Occupations."

The U.S. Armed Forces is another potential employer of foodservice workers. Every day more than one million meals are prepared in military kitchens. For more information on military careers in general, see the *Occupational Outlook Handbook*, occupation "Military Careers." Additional information is available from each armed service and the Military Career Guide Online.

### O*NET Online and CareerOneStop

O*NET Online and CareerOneStop are websites sponsored by the U.S. Department of Labor. Both have unique resources to assist job seekers in finding careers that fit their needs.

O*NET Online provides tools for exploring careers, examining job trends, and assessing personal abilities and interest. It also includes options for finding jobs within a career cluster or searching for jobs related to specific skills. O*NET Online also gives you an opportunity to explore *Bright Outlook* occupations. These occupations are expected to grow rapidly in the next several years, will have large numbers of job openings, or are new and emerging occupations.

CareerOneStop offers such employment information as components to explore careers, and locating salaries, benefits, education, training, job-search tools, and other resources. CareerOneStop also links to the following tools:

- *America's Service Locator*—a website that connects people to employment and training opportunities at local American Job Centers.
- *America's Career InfoNet*—a website that helps people explore careers and make informed choices about employment and education. It includes a wide range of resources, including self-assessment tools and career exploration assistance.

### Associations and Journals

Many hospitality occupations have a professional association. Two of the major associations in the hospitality industry are the National Restaurant Association and the American Hotel & Lodging Association. Professional associations often provide continuing education and networking opportunities. Many provide information about the industry and specific jobs within it. Associations may also have a division or services specifically for students and others interested in the occupation. Many associations and career and technical student organizations provide scholarships to students.

There are also many hospitality-related journals. Many are published by hospitality-related associations and many are available online. For example, the restaurant industry's *Nation's Restaurant News* is available in print, online, and on apps.

Another very useful publication is the *Occupational Outlook Quarterly*, published by the U.S. Department of Labor, Bureau of Labor Statistics. It covers a variety of topics in job search and career development as well as ideas and information about specific careers. An online version is also available.

# Learn About Preparation Requirements

Most careers are organized into various levels. Each level has a set of jobs that require similar levels of education and experience.

The first level jobs are entry-level jobs through which you enter the career. These are often considered stepping-stones to jobs at the next levels. For example, the job of bell attendant is an entry-level job. To get this job, you need basic reading, writing, and arithmetic skills and no experience. You will be trained on the job. The job of bell attendant can be considered a stepping-stone to the next level job, bell captain. A bell captain is a supervisor of bell attendants and must have several years of experience as a bell attendant plus some supervisor training. A bell captain earns more money than a bell attendant, but also has a great deal more responsibility and job stress.

Many people are very happy in their first level jobs. They find that the jobs suit their personalities, income requirements, and other needs.

A person can turn an entry-level job into a career and perform the job with professionalism and great skill. A professional bell attendant is essential to the success of a hotel. A bell attendant might gain variety by doing the job at different businesses or in different locations. For example, a person could be a bell attendant at a luxury hotel in a big city and then at a resort in the Caribbean.

## Career Ladder

Some people are interested in moving up the career ladder. A **career ladder** is a series of related jobs at different training and education levels.

Each higher level of the career ladder requires more education or more experience or both. Each higher level of the career ladder usually involves more responsibility and more stress, but usually offers higher pay.

Each area of hospitality has suggested career ladders and education requirements. An example in the culinary area appears in **25-10**.

| Career Ladder in the Culinary Area | | | |
|---|---|---|---|
| **Career Level** | **General Description** | **Minimum Education/ Experience Requirements** | **Relative Wages/Salary** |
| *Cook's Helper* | Assist cooks and chefs by cleaning surfaces, peeling vegetables, slicing fruits, making salads, and performing other kitchen duties as needed. | No experience or specific education required. Most skills learned on the job. | $ |
| *Prep Cook* | Prepares food for line cooks and sous-chef, including cleaning, cutting, measuring, and portioning. Responsible for keeping a sanitary kitchen workstation. | No experience or specific education required. Most skills learned on the job. High school education is preferred. | $$ |
| *Line Cook* | Responsible for specific area of the kitchen such as grilled, broiled, and roasted foods or bakery items or vegetables. | Most skills are learned from being a cook's helper or prep cook. Some line cooks attend vocational programs or 2-year college programs. | $$$ |
| *Sous-chef* | Second-in-command of kitchen, directs cooks and other kitchen employees. Assumes duties of Executive Chef in the chef's absence. | Vocational programs or 2- or 4-year college education. Can receive training through combination of education and apprenticeships with chefs. | $$$$ |
| *Executive Chef* | Responsible for directing work of other kitchen employees, estimating and ordering food supplies, planning meals, and developing menus. | Many years of training and experience required. Vocational programs, professional association accredited courses, or 2- or 4-year college education. Can receive training through combination of education and apprenticeships with chefs. Some large restaurants and hotels provide their own training programs for chefs. About 8-15 years as a cook is required to become a fully qualified chef. | $$$$$ |

*Goodheart-Willcox Publisher*

**25-10** A career ladder is a series of related jobs at different training and education levels.

When you are deciding on a career, you need to know how much education and training is needed. The amount of education needed varies a great deal depending on the type and level of position that you want to have. Some careers provide training on the job. Others require that you get formal training, either in a professional school or at a college or university. For example, a person can get a job as a cook's helper and be trained on the job. However, if that person wants to become a chef or an executive chef, he or she will have to get further training at a culinary institute or college. The cook's helper will have to find out about programs, how much they cost, and how long they take. He or she will then have to decide whether to pursue the education to become a chef. Education and training requirements for various careers can be found in the *Occupational Outlook Handbook*.

## Education

Education and preparation for a career can be organized into three categories: education, training, and continuing education.

*Education* is the general process of acquiring knowledge and skills. Education can occur anywhere and continues throughout your life. However, in this context, education refers to acquiring knowledge at a school, college, or university. The level of education attained is usually confirmed by awarding the student a diploma, degree, or other document that verifies the level of education attained. Figure **25-11** shows the general order of degrees.

### High School

For most jobs, the minimum educational requirement is a high school diploma. Very few jobs are available for people without a high school diploma. To an employer, the high school diploma indicates that you have basic skills in reading, writing, and arithmetic. It also indicates that you were able to follow through on a course of study to its completion.

In addition, some high schools in the United States offer hospitality education programs. These programs include general courses about the hospitality industry, cooperative education, and tech prep. General hospitality courses provide an overview of the industry (similar to the course you are taking now). A **cooperative education program** prepares students for an occupation through a paid job and classes at school. Cooperative education programs are also called *co-op programs*. The school arranges for a local employer to provide job training. The student takes regular classes for half a day and then works during the second half of the day. After completing a cooperative program, the student is prepared for a job or for more education.

Many high schools also offer a tech prep program. **Tech prep** is a career preparation program that combines the last two years of high school with two years of postsecondary education. **Postsecondary** means after high school. Tech prep programs are also called 2 + 2 programs (2 years of high school plus 2 years of postsecondary school). The postsecondary classes are often taken at a community college or a professional

## *Hospitality Ethics*

### Ethics in Communication

Ethical communication is very important in both hospitality businesses and personal lives. Distorting information for your own gain is an unethical practice. Honesty, accuracy, and truthfulness should guide all communications. Ethically, communication must be presented in an unbiased manner. Facts should be given without distortion. If the information is an opinion, label it as such. Do not take credit for ideas that belong to someone else; always credit your sources.

| Degrees Obtained Through Formal Education | | | |
|---|---|---|---|
| **Degree** | **Description** | **Education/ Experience Examples** | **Careers that Usually Require the Degree** |
| *High School Diploma* | Obtained after completing four years of high school. | | • Entry-level hospitality positions |
| *Certificates and Diplomas* | Obtained from a career center, vocational-technical school, professional career school, or community college. Focuses on a specific vocational skill or set of skills. Usually takes a year or less. Can be taken at any point in a person's career. | • Baking and Pastry Certificate <br> • AH&LA Hospitality Skills Certifications for 17 Line-Level Staff positions <br> • Food Service Manager Certification | • Baker or Pastry Chef at a hotel <br> • Entry-level employees at a hotel <br> • Certification for food-service safety required of most foodservice workers |
| *Associate Degree* | Obtained from a community college, vocational-technical school, or professional career school. Focuses on career training. Usually takes two years. | • Baking and Pastry Arts <br> • Professional Catering <br> • Culinary Arts <br> • Hotel and Restaurant Management <br> • Travel and Tourism | • Sous-chef <br> • Executive chef <br> • Restaurant manager <br> • Hotel front desk manager |
| *Bachelor's Degree* | Obtained from a four-year college or university. Usually requires core courses such as English, math, and social sciences, followed by courses in a major subject or vocational area. Usually takes four years. | • Hotel and Restaurant Management <br> • Travel and Tourism <br> • Culinary Arts <br> • Meeting and Event Planning | • Restaurant manager <br> • Hotel manager <br> • Convention & Visitor Bureau director <br> • Human resources director |
| *Master's Degree* | Obtained from a college or university, after the bachelor's degree has been obtained. Usually intensive, advanced study in a specific area. Length of time varies, depending on whether student is going to school full-time or part-time. | • Master's in Business Administration (MBA) <br> • Master's in Hospitality Management | • Community College Instructor, Hospitality Management <br> • Many top executives have an MBA or Master's in Hospitality Management |
| *Doctorate Degree* | Obtained from a college or university, after the bachelor's degree has been obtained. Requires more courses than a master's degree. Requires a doctoral dissertation. Usually takes four or more years beyond the bachelor's degree. Often required for careers in research or college teaching. | • Doctorate in Hospitality Management (Ph.D.) | • University Professor, Hospitality Management |

*Goodheart-Willcox Publisher*

**25-11** Earning a degree can help you obtain the job you want.

career school. At the end of the program, the student has a high school diploma and an associate degree or a technical certificate. The student is prepared to enter the workforce or continue his or her education at a four-year college.

## Postsecondary School

Many careers in hospitality require more education than a high school diploma, but less than a four-year college degree. Postsecondary education is available at professional career schools, technical programs, and community colleges. These educational institutions offer education for specific careers. These programs can last from six months to two years depending on the program. They usually include a combination of classroom learning and hands-on experience. These schools offer certificates, diplomas, and associate degrees in a variety of careers. Many schools have websites that provide detailed information about the school, the courses, degrees, costs, financial aid, admissions, and student life.

Professional career schools focus on preparing students for a specific career. For example, there are a large number of culinary institutes that prepare students for culinary careers, such as the Cooking and Hospitality Institute of Chicago. This school offers an Associate of Applied Science Degree in Le Cordon Bleu Culinary Arts and a Baking and Pastry Certificate.

Community colleges are located all over the country. Most of them provide education in a variety of vocations, including hospitality. Community colleges offer certificates, diplomas, and associate of science degrees. Examples of specialized programs include Travel/Exposition/Meeting Management, Meeting and Convention Management, Travel/Tourism and Entertainment, Travel Reservations Management, Basic Culinary Skills, Food and Hospitality Service, and Hotel Management.

Many business and career colleges offer diploma, certificate, and associate degrees as well as bachelor's degrees in hospitality and master's degrees in business or hospitality management.

## College and University

Most management level positions require a bachelor's degree in the hospitality field or business, **25-12**. Bachelor's degrees can be obtained at four-year colleges and universities as well as technical and career programs. They usually provide both a theoretical background as well as some

bikeriderlondon/Shutterstock.com

**25-12** Why do you think most management level positions require a bachelor's degree?

hands-on experience. A four-year college program usually requires that you take English, math, and social science courses in addition to courses in your major. Most colleges and universities have websites that provide detailed information about the school, courses, degrees, costs, financial aid, admissions, and student life.

Many colleges and universities have departments or programs in hospitality, **25-13**. College students in hospitality usually participate in internships while they are going to school. An **internship** is supervised, on-the-job training that students do before they actually go out to work in an industry.

An internship may provide paid or unpaid work experience for a specified amount of time.

**25-13** These students are enrolled in the University of North Texas's hospitality management program.

University of North Texas Hospitality Management Program

Students participate in an internship by signing up as they would for a class. The school establishes the specific requirements for the internship. Many internship programs are available to provide a wide variety of learning opportunities.

College can be expensive. However, the U.S. Census Bureau statistics show that people with college educations earn more than people with only a high school diploma. Graduate degrees further increase the average household income.

There are many sources for money to help pay for college. Many professional organizations and career and technical student organizations offer scholarship opportunities.

A growing number of students are getting their college education over the Internet. This type of education is called distance learning. **Distance learning** uses technology so students can take courses without stepping into a classroom. Some never even visit a library because of the availability of online library materials. Students can order their textbooks online or use an electronic text.

### Graduate School

Graduate school is college or university education taken after the bachelor's degree has been received. The degrees offered are master's degrees and doctorate degrees. Many hospitality professionals who want to be top-level managers find that a master of arts degree in business administration or in hospitality management is necessary. Many universities offer these programs on a part-time basis so the student can continue working while getting the graduate degree.

## Training

Training is usually instruction on a specific skill or task needed for a job. Training often takes place on the job. However, some training programs are offered through colleges, universities, professional associations, and private companies.

### On-the-Job Training

Most entry-level jobs provide on-the-job training. Higher-level jobs expect you to have some knowledge gained in school and experience from previous jobs, but also provide some on-the-job training. Every business has its own way of providing new employees with some training. In addition, if a company gets new equipment or develops new procedures, it will usually provide training for all employees using the new equipment or procedures.

### Apprenticeships

An **apprenticeship** is the process of learning from a skilled professional. Many chefs started their careers by being an apprentice to a master chef, **25-14**. Apprenticeships are one of the oldest ways to prepare for a career. An apprenticeship is a formal program that provides instruction, training, and practice while working full-time in the career area. An apprentice is often paid a small salary. As the apprentice learns more and becomes more skilled, he or she is given more responsibility and more pay. An apprenticeship can take three to four years to complete. At the end, the apprentice will receive a certificate saying that he or she has achieved a certain level of competence.

### Certificate Programs

Universities and colleges have also developed many nondegree training programs in hospitality areas. Some of these are intended for individuals entering the field, while others are designed for experienced executives. These nondegree training programs are called *certificate programs*. Certificate programs are perfect for the busy professional who needs advanced training but has little time to spend going to school. These classes are also offered over the Internet for the convenience of the student. Certificate programs usually range from 15 to 24 credit hours of course work or approximately 5 to 8 courses.

Many professional associations have developed certificate programs, which are often offered at the annual conventions or through special classes. Colleges and universities also offer certificate programs. They may require specific work

**25-14** This apprentice is working with an executive chef (on the left) to prepare a cake.

Emily Spencer. Harvey Hotel DFW (A Six Continents Hotel)

experience in addition to courses and exams. They may be available by correspondence courses or distance learning. A **correspondence course** is a course in which the student and teacher communicate through the mail system. The teacher sends assignments to the student through the mail, and the student mails the assignments back to the teacher. (Correspondence courses were developed in the days before the Internet and are still popular.) Correspondence courses and distance learning make professional development seminars and entire degree programs accessible worldwide.

Most certification programs require students to take and pass a test. Once the certification course is completed and the test is passed, the student receives a certificate stating that he or she has mastered a certain type of knowledge or skill.

There are many examples of certification programs that are offered by professional associations. The American Hotel & Lodging Association's Educational Institute offers a certification for Certified Hospitality Educators for university professors. They also offer certification programs such as Certified Food and Beverage Executive (CFBE), Certified Hotel Asset Manager (CHAM), Certified Lodging Manager (CLM), and Certified Rooms Division Executive (CRDE). The National Restaurant Association offers ServSafe® Certification for food safety.

## Continuing Professional Education

For a professional, learning never stops. In the hospitality industry, new technology, products, and procedures require new learning, **25-15**. New trends and changes in customer wants and needs also require new learning. **Continuing professional education** is the term used to refer to education for people who have already completed their formal schooling and training. It is also called *professional development* or *ongoing education*. Continuing professional education helps managers and workers keep up-to-date on new trends and issues in the industry. Some continuing professional education is sponsored by a person's employer and takes place on the job. Some employers will provide tuition money for professional education that takes place off the job. Other professionals seek continuing education based on their own interest and commitment to their jobs. Many community colleges, business and career colleges, four-year

**25-15** Continuing professional education often takes place at meetings sponsored by professional associations. At the National Restaurant Show, chefs learn how to prepare new dishes.

colleges, and universities offer continuing professional education. In addition, many professional associations provide continuing professional education, often in the format of short courses and brief workshops and seminars. The Internet has made distance learning a very popular method for obtaining continuing professional education.

Distance education programs have been developed to allow individuals to take courses and seminars away from the campus. They can be held at off-campus locations such as at community libraries, local businesses, and public schools. Web-based courses are designed so you can take them from your personal computer at home or at work. These courses have become very popular because of their convenience for people working in the hospitality industry.

## Learn About Yourself

Now that you have all this information about hospitality careers, how do you make a career decision? The first step is to know yourself. You need to know your interests, aptitudes, abilities, and values. The second step is to match them to a career that uses your interests, aptitudes, and abilities and supports your values. The third step is to make a career plan.

There are several things you need to know about yourself in order to make a good career choice. You need to know something about the kind of work you like to do. You need to know what your aptitudes, abilities, and personal traits are. You also need to know your values, interests, and preferences.

## People, Things, Data

There are many ways to organize careers and jobs. One of the most useful ways to look at careers is to determine whether the career requires working with people, things, or data, **25-16**. Although many careers and jobs require that you work with all three, most emphasize one or two. A *people* job consists mainly of dealing with people and may involve providing a service, teaching, and helping.

**25-16** A job as a reservations sales agent consists mainly of dealing with people.

vgstudio/Shutterstock.com

A *things* job consists mainly of working with tools and objects and often involves making or repairing. *Data* jobs consist mainly of working with data or information. A data job can involve doing research, working with numbers, writing, or making long-range plans. Supervisors need to be strong in people skills and things skills. Managers need to be strong in people skills and data skills. Managers often need to have things skills, too.

For example, a job as a server is mainly a people job. Servers also work with things, such as the food and serving equipment. Servers work a little bit with data when they take orders and process them through the POS system. A job as cook is mainly a things job. Cooks work mostly with food and tools to prepare food. Cooks also work with data when they figure out quantities for recipes and purchasing. Cooks need to be able to work with the other members of the kitchen staff; however, cooking is not a people job. A job as an accounting clerk is mainly a data job. Accounting clerks work with numbers and calculations. Accounting clerks need to be able to work with the other members of the accounting department; however, accounting is not a people job.

Hospitality jobs can be organized based on whether their focus is primarily on people, things, or data, **25-17**. Most people are strongest in one of the three areas. Are you better at working with people, things, or data? Most people prefer working with one of the three.

## Aptitudes, Abilities, Personal Traits

An **aptitude** is a natural talent or natural ability to do something. If you have an aptitude for something, you can do it or learn to do it easily. For example, some people have an aptitude for cooking. They easily learn to cook, get good results, and enjoy doing it. Some people do not have an aptitude for cooking. They have a hard time learning to cook, the results are often bad, and they do not enjoy doing it. People are usually happiest in jobs and careers that use their aptitudes. A guidance counselor can give you an aptitude test to help you identify your aptitudes.

An **ability** is the knowledge and power to perform a task. Having an ability often involves learning a skill or a set of skills. For example, if you learn the skills of cooking and can perform them, you have the ability to cook. It is possible

## Hospitality Jobs Based on People, Things, or Data Focus

Note: Does not include supervisory or management jobs.

| Focus | Job Titles |
|-------|-----------|
| *People* | Bell attendants, concierges, door attendants, front desk agents, host/hostess, reservations sales agents, security officers, servers, telephone operators |
| *Things* | Audiovisual staff, banquet setup staff, bussers, cooks, dishwashers, electricians, engineers, groundskeepers, laundry attendants, maintenance workers, plumbers, room attendants, seamsters, shipping and receiving workers, storeroom workers |
| *Data* | Accounting clerks, inventory workers, night auditors, purchasers |

*Goodheart-Willcox Publisher*

**25-17** Hospitality jobs can be organized based on whether their focus is primarily on people, things, or data.

to have knowledge, but not the power or ability to perform. For example, you might learn all the steps of CPR (cardiopulmonary resuscitation), but you might not have the physical strength to do it. You would not have the ability to perform CPR.

Each job has its own set of skills and abilities. You already have some skills. For example, most jobs require that you know how to read, write, and do arithmetic. You have learned these skills at school. You will need to learn other skills before you can get a job.

Part of your career decision will be to decide whether you want to learn the skills required for a certain career. For example, in order to be a specialty cook, you must take some postsecondary training. In order to be an executive chef, you need a college or graduate degree. Part of your career decision will be how much schooling you want to do in order to reach your career goal.

Your personal traits also affect your job and career decisions. You have a variety of personal traits, including physical traits and personality traits. Physical traits include how much energy and stamina you have. Many hospitality jobs require a great deal of physical stamina, **25-18**. Personality traits include friendliness and calmness under pressure. Many hospitality jobs require these traits.

## Values, Interests, Preferences

Values, interests, and preferences all affect career choices. *Values* are your personal evaluation of what is important to you. When planning a career, you need to know your work-related values. **Work values** are the aspects of work that are the most important to you. Work values are neither good nor bad. They simply represent what you want from a job or a career. For example, some people like to work at a fast-paced job where the situation is constantly changing and there are new problems to solve every day. Other people find that a fast-paced job makes them very nervous and they cannot sleep. These people prefer a slower-paced job where they know exactly what they will be doing every day. A cook who prefers a fast-paced job would enjoy working in a commercial restaurant. A cook who prefers a slower-paced job would enjoy working in a school foodservice.

*Interests* are those things that capture your attention and that you are willing to spend time on. For example, one person might be very interested in food and food preparation. Another person might be more interested in analyzing financial data and figuring out how to price a guest room. People often develop interests in their areas of aptitude.

*Preferences* are those things you prefer to do over other things. For example, some people prefer to work with the public. Others prefer to work in an office and interact with the same people every day. Your values often lead to your preferences. If you value working out-of-doors, you may prefer a job where you can work outside.

# Make a Career Plan

Once you know yourself and you know about the industry, the challenge is to choose a career that matches your abilities, aptitudes, traits, interests, and preferences and supports your values. The career choice you make now is not necessarily permanent. Many people change careers over

Pavel L Photo and Video/Shutterstock.com

**25-18** Many hospitality employees need stamina and energy to be on their feet all day.

the course of their working life. However, making a career choice and setting a career goal in high school can be very beneficial. By making a commitment to a career, you will learn a great deal about the career and yourself. You will also have a solid way to earn a living. Once you have a career, you can always make changes along the way.

Once you have chosen a career area, it is useful to choose a career goal. A **career goal** is the highest career level that you want to reach. You should choose a career goal that makes sense to you. Some people want to own their own business or be an executive for a large corporation. Other people are happy with a career goal such as being a pastry chef at a local hotel or being a door attendant at a luxury hotel in Hawaii. People often change their career goals as they gain work experience.

A **career plan** is a list of steps that you develop to reach your career goal. It is like a map you use as a guide to your career goal. Your career plan is based on what you have learned about yourself, your career goal, and the requirements of the career. It is also based on your preferences and the opportunities you find. It is often helpful to have a school vocational counselor help you with your career plan.

A career plan usually includes education and experience. Figure **25-19** shows a sample career plan for someone who wants to be a hotel general manager. Many people can have the same career goal, but each one will develop his or her unique career plan. Also, a career plan is never final. It may change as you develop and gain experience in your career.

| Career Plan for a Hotel General Manager | | |
|---|---|---|
| **Steps** | **Education** | **Experience** |
| *High school* | Take Introduction to Hospitality course. Take co-op course. | Co-op job as front desk agent in hotel. Summer jobs as room attendant and door attendant. |
| *College* | Major in hospitality and business. | Work part-time at a hotel. |
| *First Job* | On-the-job training. | Front desk agent, limited-service property. |
| *Second Job* | On-the-job training. | Front desk agent, luxury hotel. |
| *Graduate School* | Master of Arts in Business. | Continue job as front desk agent. |
| *Third Job* | Supervisor's training on the job. | Front Office Supervisor. |
| *Fourth Job* | Workshops at AH&LA convention. | Guest Services Manager. |
| *Fifth Job* | Distance course on Rooms management. | Rooms Division Manager. |
| *Sixth Job* | Management seminar for Hotel Executives. | General Manager. |

*Goodheart-Willcox Publisher*

**25-19** A career plan may change as you develop and gain experience in your career.

As you develop your career plan and pursue your career goals, you may want to prepare a *career portfolio*. The career portfolio is a way for you to introduce yourself and present samples that highlight your school and work experience to a potential employer. The samples in your portfolio should support your job qualifications.

Your portfolio should include a cover sheet that outlines the contents of your portfolio. You should also include a letter of application and your current résumé. The main portion of your portfolio, however, should consist of your samples.

For example, if you volunteer with a group in your community, you may wish to include photographs and a written summary of your volunteer activities. This would show potential employers that you can plan projects and work as an effective member of a team.

You may also choose to include special assignments from your classes that showcase your skills and abilities. A good portfolio may take months or even years to develop. Continue to update your portfolio as you gain experience in your career.

# Chapter 25
## Review

## Chapter Summary

- Hospitality careers have many advantages and some challenges.
- To determine whether a hospitality career is for you, you need to learn about the careers and make a plan.
- The many ways to learn about hospitality jobs and careers include research and on-the-job training.
- Many jobs in hospitality require additional education or experience or both.
- Each higher level of the career ladder usually involves more responsibility and more stress, but usually higher pay.
- Postsecondary education and training are available from community colleges, business and career colleges, professional career schools, four-year colleges, and universities.
- Knowing your aptitudes, abilities, interests, preferences, and values can help you choose the right career.
- A career plan helps guide you to your career goal.

## Review

1. List three advantages and three challenges of a hospitality career.
2. What steps can you follow to help determine whether a hospitality career is for you?
3. What are three ways to find out about what it is really like to work in the hospitality industry?
4. Name at least three kinds of information you can learn from the *Occupational Outlook Handbook*.
5. What are two other online tools you can use to research career information?
6. Contrast entry-level jobs with higher-level jobs.
7. What is the difference between cooperative education programs and tech prep?
8. Name at least three ways to get education or training after completing high school.
9. What is continuing professional education and why is it necessary?
10. Contrast jobs that focus on people, things, and data.
11. What is the difference between your aptitudes and abilities?
12. How does a career plan help you achieve a career goal?

# Critical Thinking

13. **Analyze.** Analyze what you would do to learn more about a hospitality career of interest to you. Make a list and share it with the class.

14. **Compare and contrast.** What type of hospitality job environments do you think suits your aptitudes and abilities? Compare and contrast the benefits and challenges of your choices.

15. **Evaluate.** Choose two hospitality-related careers to research on O*NET or CareerOneStop. Read the summary reports for these careers. Evaluate whether your aptitudes, abilities, personal traits, values, interests, and preferences are a logical fit with one or both of these careers. Write a summary indicating why you think you are well-suited for either career.

16. **Recognize values.** Understanding your work values is key to finding meaningful employment in hospitality. Brainstorm a list of ten work values you hold. Then investigate which hospitality careers might be best suited to your work values. Which careers suit your work values best?

# Common Core

### College and Career Readiness

17. **Speaking.** Conduct an informational interview with a person who works in an area of hospitality in which you have interest. Develop your questions before the interview to be sure to get all the information you need. Share your findings with the class in an oral presentation.

18. **Writing.** Do you prefer to work with people, things, or data? Write an essay that provides information from your experiences that support your choice.

19. **Reading.** Obtain a copy of a career-research book (such as the latest edition of *What Color Is Your Parachute?*). Read the book. Then write a summary noting important guidelines the author suggests for finding meaningful employment and making a career plan. Choose two topics you found most valuable and share them with the class. Cite evidence to support your reasoning.

20. **Writing.** Take the *Interest Profiler* self-assessment on the CareerOneStop website. What were the results of your self-assessment? How can these results help you choose a hospitality-related career? Write a paragraph explaining your findings.

21. **Writing.** What samples of your work would you include in your career portfolio? Create a portfolio or digital portfolio for use in applying for internships and jobs in the hospitality industry.

22. **CTE Career Readiness Practice.** Imagine it is five years in the future and you are starting your first full-time job as a certified fitness trainer at a resort/spa that specializes in helping people become fit. Part of fitness training is learning how to balance energy requirements for a healthy lifestyle. Along with working with resort clients, part of your job involves working with staff members on maintaining fitness and a healthy lifestyle. Many coworkers have expressed interest in a class you teach on these topics. How would you develop a fitness routine for balancing energy for staff? How would you convince management to allow a certain time during the workday for staff fitness training? How would you use your leadership skills to motivate, inspire, and persuade the staff and management to make fitness and energy management a goal for life?

478

# Chapter *26*

## Skills for Success

## Chapter Objectives

After studying this chapter, you will be able to

- **explain** how the career clusters connect school preparation to career success.
- **explain** why word choice is important.
- **assess** how nonverbal communication affects communication.
- **identify** ways communication skills impact career success.
- **describe** actions to take in a job search.
- **describe** traits, skills, and actions that help you keep a job.
- **list** actions to take to advance in your career.
- **evaluate** the impact of multiple roles on your life.

## Before You Read

Try to answer the following questions before you read this chapter.
- What is the difference between verbal communication and nonverbal communication?
- What should be included on a résumé?

## Terms to Know

| | | |
|---|---|---|
| career clusters | networking | adaptability |
| communication | reference | drug abuse |
| interpersonal skills | résumé | work habits |
| nonverbal communication | cover letter | etiquette |
| body language | interview | business etiquette |
| conflict resolution | attitude | leadership |
| negotiation | self-motivation | giving notice |
| electronic communication | initiative | role |
| job lead | cooperation | |

There are many ingredients to a successful career and a successful life. Each individual chooses his or her goals, **26-1**. Each individual decides how to use his or her unique skills and abilities. However, there are many skills that are generally useful in both your work life and your personal life. These include a variety of workplace skills such as job search skills, work habits, attitudes, and maintenance of physical and mental health. They also include learning how to balance multiple roles. High school is a good place to develop many of these skills.

# Career Choices

Deciding what career you will pursue is probably one of the biggest decisions you will ever make. Most people spend a large portion of their adult life working. The average person will not stay at the same job for his or her entire work career. Knowing your strengths and interests can help you plan your future. Before you are ready to make a career decision, however, you need to learn more about different types of jobs that can be found in the work world.

## The Career Clusters

The **career clusters** are 16 groups of occupational and career specialties. Reviewing the career cluster titles is the easiest way to begin learning about the variety of career options. Each career cluster or group includes different *career pathways*, or career directions. For example, the hospitality and tourism career cluster includes four different career pathways:

- restaurants and food/beverage services
- lodging
- travel and tourism
- recreation, amusements, and attractions

Each career pathway includes a variety of occupations grouped within similar areas of knowledge and skills. The occupations in each pathway range from entry-level positions to advanced positions, **26-2**. This means you can prepare for multiple career options in similar areas

**26-1** Discussing your goals with friends can help you make plans for success.

mangostock/Shutterstock.com

## Hospitality and Tourism Careers Within the Career Pathways

| Restaurants & Food/ Beverage Services | Lodging | Travel & Tourism | Recreation, Amusements, & Attractions |
|---|---|---|---|
| • Counter server<br>• Kitchen steward<br>• Room service attendant<br>• Host<br>• Cook<br>• Caterer<br>• Executive chef<br>• Pastry & specialty chef<br>• Service manager<br>• Restaurant owner<br>• General manager<br>• Food & beverage manager | • Concierge<br>• Front desk employee<br>• Shift supervisor<br>• Laundry attendant<br>• Reservations supervisor<br>• Owner and franchisee<br>• General manager<br>• Director of human resources<br>• Housekeeper<br>• Executive housekeeper<br>• Quality assurance manager<br>• Valet | • Executive director<br>• Director of tourism development<br>• Director of visitor services<br>• Events manager<br>• Travel agent<br>• Event planner<br>• Special events producer<br>• Tour and travel coordinator<br>• Tour guide<br>• Transportation specialist<br>• Motor coach operator<br>• Interpreter | • Club membership developer<br>• Parks and gardens safety and security<br>• Parks and garden ranger<br>• Gaming and casino dealer<br>• Gaming and casino security and safety<br>• Fairs and festival promotional department<br>• Theme parks and amusement parks group events manager |

*Goodheart-Willcox Publisher*

26-2 The hospitality industry is one of the country's largest employers.

of study. If you are prepared for more than one career, you will expand your options when you begin looking for a job.

The career clusters model was developed by educators, employers, and professional groups who carefully examined what you would need to know in order to prepare for a good job. The career clusters connect your school preparation to your career success. Your parents, teachers, and guidance counselors can help you work out a study plan to match your career goals.

# Communication

**Communication** is the transmission of information and feelings from one person to another. The ability to communicate clearly and positively is one of the most important skills in work and in life. You start developing your communication skills when you are a baby and continue developing them throughout life. Good communication

skills enable you to work well with others on the job. Communication skills enable you to meet customer needs and are a very important part of interpersonal skills. **Interpersonal skills** consist of the ability to interact smoothly and productively with other people. The two types of communication skills are verbal and nonverbal.

## Verbal Communication

*Verbal* means using words. There are two aspects of verbal communication. First is the language you choose to use. The second is the choice of words in that language.

### Language

The first aspect of verbal communication is the choice of language for communication. Americans speak over 100 different languages in their homes. Many Americans who speak English use a variety of dialects of English. In order for everyone to understand one another, Standard English is the language of business communication.

Standard English includes all the rules of grammar and spelling that you learn in English classes. In most jobs in the United States, you are expected to speak and write Standard English.

However, in some hospitality businesses, you need a second language. Many Americans are not as proficient in English as they are in the language they speak at home. Many foreign visitors either do not know English or do not speak it well. Many hospitality companies are international, and you may want the opportunity to work in a foreign country. Knowing a second language can be a real benefit in the hospitality industry.

### Word Choice

The second aspect of verbal communication consists of the words you choose to use. For example, you could use a variety of different expressions to greet a customer. Your choice of words will determine the effect you have on the customer. Which of the following two greetings would have a positive effect?

- Good morning. How can I help you?
- What do you want?

Word choice is important in both spoken and written language. When you write memos and letters to coworkers, customers, and people in other businesses, you must choose your words carefully. Your words should always convey professionalism and politeness.

Word choice is extremely important when writing for marketing and advertising. Words create a feeling and pictures in a person's mind. One of the reasons for the success of the Holiday Inns is the name. What do you picture when you hear the word *holiday*? The choice of the word *inn* makes a difference, too. Compare the effect of names Holiday Inn, Holiday Hotel, Holiday Motel, and Holiday Lodge.

## Nonverbal Communication

*Nonverbal* means without words. **Nonverbal communication** is communication of information and feelings without using words, such as body language. **Body language** includes facial expressions, posture, hand gestures, and tone of voice, **26-3**. Nonverbal communication also includes color and design, which are part of written communication and media communication. Some researchers claim that over 70 percent of communication is nonverbal.

*Chef Harry Salazar demonstration, Photo courtesy of Texas Beef Council*

**26-3** What body language can you identify in this photo?

Nonverbal communication can change the meaning of words. For example, your words might be, "Good morning. How can I help you?" However, suppose you frown while you say these words, speak fast, and use a sharp tone of voice. You will communicate a very negative feeling.

Similarly, your words might be, "What do you want?" Imagine that you are talking to a child. You kneel down so that your face is at the child's level. You smile and look into the child's eyes. You say in a light, happy voice, "What do *you* want?" In this case, the feeling communicated is very friendly and happy.

Many people are not aware of their nonverbal communications. It is often helpful to practice your communication skills with another person who provides feedback on both your verbal and nonverbal communication.

## Additional Communication Skills

Additional communication skills include listening and speaking, reading and writing, arithmetic and mathematics, and electronic communication. Keep in mind that there are verbal and nonverbal aspects to these communication skills.

## Listening and Speaking

Listening and speaking are the most basic communication skills. However, that does not mean they are the easiest. Listening is an active process. You must pay attention when you listen to someone. Focus on the speaker's face and eyes. Observe their nonverbal and verbal communication. You will use your listening skills on the job whenever your supervisor or coworkers give you instructions or information. Using effective listening skills is also important when you interact with customers.

Speaking includes the words you choose, your posture, and your tone of voice. It also includes how you organize and present your thoughts. Speaking on the job ranges from formal presentations to informal conversations, 26-4.

Two very important communication skills that involve listening and speaking are conflict resolution and negotiation. **Conflict resolution** is the process of resolving a disagreement in a peaceful way. One of the main tools of conflict resolution is negotiation. **Negotiation** is a process during which two or more people talk and listen together for the purpose of resolving a disagreement or a conflict.

Conflict is a fact of life. Whether or not conflict becomes a problem depends on how people deal with it. Skillful conflict resolution requires communication skills and interpersonal skills.

## Reading and Writing

Reading is an important way to learn new information. You will have many needs for reading

26-4 Employees find that practicing ahead of time allows them to relax while giving a formal presentation.

*wavebreakmedia/Shutterstock.com*

on the job. You may be given an employee handbook to read and written guidelines for performing your job. You may have a checklist to use on the job. You may have to read labels on foods or other supplies. Whenever you use a computer, you will be reading information on the screen.

Writing is a major way to record and transmit information, which is required in many hospitality jobs. Writing includes using a keyboard to enter information into the computer. When a server takes an order, he or she either writes the order on paper or enters it into a computer system. When the executive housekeeper enters information on room status into the computer, he or she is writing. Managers often have to write reports.

## Arithmetic and Mathematics

Knowing basic arithmetic and mathematics is actually a communication skill. The business world runs on numbers. How many guests stayed at the hotel last week? How many hamburger rolls did we use? How many hamburger rolls are left? How much profit did we make? Today, computers and calculators make it faster and easier to perform calculations. However, a person needs to understand numbers and mathematics in order to use a calculator and computer properly.

## Electronic Communication

**Electronic communication** refers to the use of electronic technology for communication, including computers, smartphones, two-way radios, pagers, and tablets. The successful businessperson of today must know how to use these devices.

The hospitality industry is increasingly using wireless communication devices. Restaurants use wireless handheld computers to transmit orders to the kitchen. The kitchen uses a wireless device to notify the server when the order is ready, 26-5. Hosts and hostesses use wireless devices to alert guests when their tables are ready.

E-mail has become an important communication technology. Many businesses use e-mail in place of business letters. E-mail is also used for internal communications. In a hotel, workers from various departments communicate with each other by e-mail. Many hospitality businesses use e-mail to alert their customers to special promotions. Purchasing departments use e-mail to order supplies.

The technical aspect of e-mail involves learning how to open, address, and send an e-mail message. Once you learn these technical skills, using

## Wireless Communication in a Restaurant Operation

| Kitchen | Server |
| --- | --- |
|  |  |
| When the order is ready, the chef pages the server. There is a button for each server on duty. | When the server's pager rings, the server knows to go to the kitchen to pick up the order. |

*Photos courtesy of JTECH Communications, Inc.*

26-5 Wireless communication devices are often used in restaurant operations.

e-mail is like writing a letter or a memo. The same requirements should be followed for e-mail as for any other written business communication.

When e-mail was first used, there was a tendency to be very informal. Today, when e-mail is used for personal communication, it is still very informal. People may use abbreviations, signs, and symbols to express themselves. Personal e-mail and texting have developed a language of their own. A popular part of this language is the emoticon. An *emoticon* is a graphic symbol that conveys meaning, such as the smiley face.

Abbreviations and emoticons should not be used in business communications. Every business

e-mail should clearly indicate whom the message is for, whom it is from (name, position, and company), and the date and time the message is sent. The subject line should always be filled in with an appropriate description of the topic of the e-mail. Standard English should always be used, **26-6.**

## Job Search Skills

The first step in a job search is knowing your career goals and deciding what kind of job you want. Once you know the kind of job you want,

## Sample Business E-mail

---

From: Delores Stanley
To: Jim Houston
Date: August 13, 20XX
Subject: Candidate for Trainer Position
cc: Cynthia Whitaker


Jim,
I met with Alison Romero last Thursday (August 7). I was impressed by her background, experience, and knowledge of the restaurant business. She looks like a good candidate for our Trainer position.

I have placed her résumé, cover letter, and thank-you note in your in-box. Please review her credentials and let me know what you think of her as a new hire.


Thanks,
Delores


Delores Stanley
Human Resources Director
Restaurants Worldwide
www.xxxxxx.xxx.org
E-mail: Dstanley@provider.com
Telephone: (xxx) xxx-xxxx

---

*Goodheart-Willcox Publisher*

**26-6** Business e-mails should always be written in a professional, businesslike style.

you can start looking for it. Having good job search skills is a key to success. Most people will have to search for a job several times during their careers. Searching for a job will require excellence in all your communication skills. Three key job search skills are how to find job leads, how to fill out an application, and how to behave at an interview.

## Job Leads

A **job lead** is information that leads you to a job opening. The most popular source of job leads is the Internet. There are several websites where job openings are listed and a number of websites just for people who are searching for jobs in hospitality. Most hospitality businesses have their own websites, and many have a section for careers or career opportunities. If these headings are not immediately visible on the home page, search in the section on corporate information or "about us."

Another place to look for job leads is the want ads located in the classified section of a newspaper. Many hospitality jobs are advertised this way. Hospitality jobs can be found under the headings such as *baker, chef, cook, foodservice, hotel, manager, restaurant, servers,* and *wait staff.*

Networking is one of the best ways to find jobs. **Networking** is the process of meeting people in your profession. You may know people from organizations or meetings who are already in the profession. These people might be able to alert you to job openings. The more people you meet, the more possible contacts you have to help you in your career.

Hospitality jobs can often be found by visiting the business for which you would like to work. Many hospitality businesses post available positions in the window of their business. For example, you might see a sign that says *Waitress Wanted.* Many chain restaurants have job applications available in their restaurants. You can just walk in and pick up an application.

## Application

Once you have located a job opening, you must apply for the job. For many entry-level jobs, all you have to do is fill the application out thoroughly and neatly. When you find a job lead on the Internet, you can often fill out the application online.

Many job applications request that you list several references. A **reference** is a person who is willing to talk with employers about your job qualifications and your personal qualities. A reference should not be a person related to you. It should be an adult who knows you in a business or business-like capacity. Examples include former employers, coaches, teachers, club advisors, and other adults such as your choir director or scoutmaster. Before you start looking for a job, you should find three adults who are willing to be references for you. You should ask them for permission to use them as references. It is also a good idea to discuss with them your career goals and the type of job you want. Then write down their names, job titles, work addresses, and work phone numbers. Bring this information with you to all interviews.

Many hospitality want ads invite you to go in person to the business. The ad will specify a time,

such as *Monday afternoon, 3 p.m. to 5 p.m.* When you get there, you will usually have to fill out an application and have an interview.

Many ads will request that you e-mail a résumé. A **résumé** is a written document that lists a person's qualifications for a job, including education and work experience, **26-7**. A résumé provides a quick way for an employer to learn about the applicant's qualifications. In general, headings on a résumé include *objective*, *work experience*, *education*, *activities and interests*, and *honors*. The last line on a résumé is usually *References provided upon request*.

A résumé should be accompanied by a cover letter. A **cover letter** is a letter that introduces you, highlights your strengths, and asks for an interview, **26-8**.

## Interview

An important part of any job application is the interview. An **interview** is a formal meeting between two or more people during which questions are asked of one person. During an interview for a job, the job applicant and the employer try to get to know each other. The job applicant wants to impress the employer and learn about the job. The employer wants to learn about the job applicant and decide whether to offer the position.

# *Hospitality Ethics*

## Ethics in Applications

When applying for a job, submitting an application for acceptance into a university, or even applying for a position as a volunteer with an organization, it is important to be truthful in your application and résumé. Fabricating experience or education to gain a position is unethical and could cost you a future opportunity to be a part of that organization. This means always telling the truth about your skills, experience, and education—do not embellish. Play up your strengths without attempting to create the illusion of being someone you are not. Present your information in a positive light, but keep it honest.

Potential employers will usually uncover untruths and this will cause you to miss the opportunity you are seeking.

# Sample Résumé

**Alison Romero**

4293 Kelsey Lane

Arlington, TX 76321

Telephone: (xxx) xxx-xxxx

E-mail: aromero@provider.net

## Objective

Pursue a job/internship in the hospitality industry.

## Work Experience

<u>Good Eats Grill</u>, Lewisville, Texas: August 20XX–Present

*Hostess* - Performed all duties including training, seating guests, cleaning host area, bussing tables, answering phones, preparing host sheets.

*Server* - Performed all server duties including waiting on guests, cleaning table stations, stocking, and sidework.

<u>AMC Sundance 11 Theaters</u>, Fort Worth, Texas: May 20XX - August 20XX

*Box Office Cashier* - Performed cashier duties including selling movie tickets, registering guests for special offers, answering phones, recording daily information at closeout, filing end-of-day papers, counting banks.

*Concessionist* - Performed concession duties including opening and closing concession stand, cleaning concession area, selling concession items, stocking items.

*Usher* - Performed usher duties including cleaning movie theaters between showings, sweeping, mopping, and taking out the trash.

<u>The Disney Store</u>, Arlington, Texas: September 20XX - April 20XX

*Cast Member* - Performed cast member duties including greeting guests, assisting guests, cleaning the store, and cashier responsibilities.

<u>Subway</u>, Arlington, Texas: June 20XX - August 20XX

*Sandwich artist* - Responsible for making sandwiches while following prescribed instructions, maintained store inventory, exhibited excellent customer relations.

## Education

<u>University of North Texas</u>, Denton, Texas

School of Merchandising and Hospitality Management

Bachelor of Science, Hospitality Management

Anticipated date of graduation - December 20XX

GPA: 3.25

## Honors

Graduated with Honors from Arlington High School

Maintained a 3.25 GPA at the University of North Texas while working full-time

Excellent teamwork skills developed by working in the hospitality industry

Received recognition as Employee of the Month at Good Eats Grill

References available upon request.

*Goodheart-Willcox Publisher*

**26-7** What headings would you include on your résumé if you prepared one today?

# Sample Cover Letter

Alison Romero
4293 Kelsey Lane
Arlington, TX 76321
Telephone: (xxx) xxx-xxxx
E-mail: aromero@provider.net

August 12, 20XX

Delores Stanley
Human Resources Director
Restaurants Worldwide
Dallas, TX 79283

Dear Ms. Stanley:

Your assistant, Linda Jantzen, suggested that I contact you about the Restaurant Trainer position you have advertised in the *Dallas Morning-News*. I plan to graduate in December with a degree in Hospitality Management from the University of North Texas. I am excited about the opportunity to work for Restaurants Worldwide, especially as a trainer.

My interest in the hospitality industry and my experience in restaurants provide me with the drive and skills to make a difference in your company. At the University of North Texas, I have taken courses such as Dining Room Management, Cost Controls, Systems Analyses, Managing a Diverse Workforce, and Facilities Management.

I believe that my experience and education would make a valuable addition to Restaurants Worldwide.

My résumé provides more information about my education and work experience. I would like to discuss my qualifications for the position with you. You can reach me using the information stated at the top of this letter. I look forward to hearing from you.

Sincerely,

Alison Romero

*Goodheart-Willcox Publisher*

**26-8** A cover letter should always be set in proper business letter format.

For hospitality jobs, the interview is sometimes a little less formal. However, you should always present yourself in a professional way. One way to do this is to prepare for the interview ahead of time. Aspects of the interview to practice include the following:

- *Introducing yourself.* Prepare a strong introduction. Practice speaking slowly and clearly.
- *Shaking hands.* Practice giving a firm handshake. Use your right hand to grasp the other person's hand firmly. End the handshake after three seconds.
- *Responding to questions.* The interviewer will ask you many questions, **26-9**. Practice answering them before the interview. Never say anything negative about yourself, another person, or another company. Maintain eye contact with the person interviewing you.
- *Asking questions.* An interview is also a time for you to learn about the job. You need to

## Common Interviewer Questions

- How would you describe yourself?
- What are your greatest strengths and weaknesses?
- What do you hope to be doing five years from now?
- What is your long-term career goal?
- How do you think you can make a contribution to our company?
- What qualifications do you have to work for this company?
- Do you think your grades are a good indication of your work ability?
- Why did you decide to seek a position with our company?
- Why did you leave your last job?
- Why should I hire you?

*Goodheart-Willcox Publisher*

**26-9** Practice answering these commonly asked questions before an interview.

learn enough about the job and the work environment to determine whether you would be happy working there.

Another critical aspect of an interview is the visual impression you make. Take great care in deciding what to wear to an interview. On many hospitality jobs, you will be required to wear a uniform. However, at the interview you should look professional, clean, and well groomed.

You may be given a test as part of your interview. For example, if you are applying for an accounting job, you may have to take a computation test. In addition, bring any certificates or honors you have earned with you.

After an interview, you should always write a thank-you letter. The letter should be brief. Thank the interviewer for his or her time and interest. If you are still interested in the job, say a few words indicating your interest and your strongest qualifications for the job, **26-10**.

# Succeeding On the Job

Once you have accepted a new job, the next challenge is to keep it. It is assumed that you will learn how to do your job and do it properly. However, there are many additional traits, skills, and actions that determine your success on the job. These areas include attitude, grooming, health, work habits, and business etiquette.

## Attitude

Attitude is the second thing that is visible about a person after appearance. **Attitude** is the way you look at the world and the way you respond to things that happen. Guests and coworkers want to be around people with positive attitudes. Components of a positive attitude include friendliness, self-motivation, teamwork, and adaptability.

### Friendliness

A friendly attitude consists of a positive attitude toward yourself and others. Friendly people are generally pleasant, cheerful, and optimistic. They like other people and show it. They are polite and helpful. If you were in a restaurant, what type of server would you want—a friendly person or an unfriendly person? Friendly people are also more fun to work with.

Many advertisements for hospitality jobs mention smiles. A smile communicates an attitude of respect and caring for customers. It also communicates respect and caring for your job and your coworkers. A smile says that you have a friendly attitude, **26-11**. A smile should never be forced. It should come from your positive attitude toward life.

### Self-Motivation

**Self-motivation** is the inner urge to achieve your goals. Self-motivation includes a sense of enthusiasm about your work and your company. People who are self-motivated also have initiative. **Initiative** is the ability to get a job done without being constantly reminded by someone else. People with initiative often come up with new ideas and ways to solve problems. Self-motivated people often volunteer for the challenging assignments.

### Teamwork

An attitude of teamwork is essential to success on the job. An attitude of teamwork includes cooperation, the ability to work with others, and commitment to the team and its members. **Cooperation** is willingness to do what it takes to get the job done. A cooperative worker follows instructions and asks questions when he or she does not understand what to do.

## Sample Thank-You Letter

Alison Romero
4293 Kelsey Lane
Arlington, TX 76321
Telephone: (xxx) xxx-xxxx
E-mail: aromero@provider.net

August 12, 20XX

Delores Stanley
Human Resources Director
Restaurants Worldwide
Dallas, TX 79283

Dear Ms. Stanley:

Thank you for taking the time out of your busy schedule to meet with me last Thursday. I enjoyed meeting you and learning about Restaurants Worldwide and especially about the Trainer Position. I believe that I could make a positive contribution to Restaurants Worldwide.

During the interview, you said you were looking for two things: an ability to mentor new employees and practical restaurant experience. I feel that I have something to offer in both of these areas. My work experiences at Good Eats Grill, AMC Sundance 11 Theaters, the Disney Store, and Subway have given me the firsthand experience that is so important to success in any organization, especially restaurants. Each of these positions has taught me to be a good mentor and a role model.

Again, thank you for taking the time to visit with me. Please feel free to contact me if you need any further information.

Sincerely,


Alison Romero

*Goodheart-Willcox Publisher*

**26-10** After an interview, always write a thank-you letter.

**26-11** A smile communicates that you respect yourself, your job, and your customers.

auremar/Shutterstock.com

Someone who has the ability to work with others is pleasant, agreeable, and does not create conflict or angry situations. Such a person understands and respects diversity. He or she can work with people from all kinds of backgrounds and points of view. He or she also knows how to resolve differences of opinion or conflict in a positive way.

Commitment to the team and its members means that you feel an obligation to do your part for the sake of the team and your project. Teamwork on the job is much like being part of a basketball team or a drill team. The success of the whole team depends on your individual attendance, punctuality, good attitude, and skills. If one person does not perform well on a team, the entire team will suffer. The same is true of teamwork on the job.

## Adaptability

**Adaptability** is the ability to make changes to match new situations. The workplace is constantly changing. In the hospitality business, every day brings new challenges and problems to solve. An adaptable person can go with the flow. He or she adjusts to changes and new conditions smoothly and with a positive attitude.

## *Grooming*

Appearances do count. You may have taken special care to look good at your interview, but making a good appearance is important throughout your working life. Your appearance is the first thing that guests, coworkers, and supervisors see. People who work in foodservice have specific sanitation-related grooming and dress requirements.

## Clothing and Shoes

Find out the type of clothing you are expected to wear on the job. Many hospitality businesses require a uniform, **26-12**. Others require formal business dress, such as a business suit. Others are more casual. All clothing should be clean and neat. Uniforms should be pressed and starched if necessary.

Your shoes should be comfortable to wear and professional in appearance. Hospitality workers often spend a great deal of time on their feet. Shoes should always be clean and well maintained. Clean and polished shoes are important in achieving a professional look.

## Hygiene

*Personal hygiene* refers to keeping your body and clothes clean. Body odor will not only offend your employer and other workers, but it can also turn away potential customers. Always take a bath or shower before going to work. Use deodorant or antiperspirant. Use only a small amount of light

**26-12** Many hospitality businesses require a uniform. The uniform for this bell attendant is formal.

*Andresr/Shutterstock.com*

perfume or aftershave lotion because a strong smell can offend guests. Some guests might even be allergic to certain scents.

Fresh breath is very important, especially when dealing directly with guests. Having bad breath can offend guests and leave them with a negative impression of you and your business. Fresh breath is achieved by proper brushing of your teeth and regular visits to the dentist. Keep mouthwash or breath mints handy for freshening breath during the day.

### Hair and Nails

It is also important to have clean and well-groomed hair and nails. Maintaining these will help you keep a sharp, professional appearance. Hair should be trimmed on a regular basis. This will make it easier to style, and you will look well groomed. Nails should be trimmed to a professional-looking length. Nail polish should be clear or natural looking. Many hospitality businesses require that men be clean shaven.

## Health

Good health is the foundation for everything you do in life. Your health should never be forgotten when you are trying to achieve career success. It is difficult to concentrate or do a good job when you are not feeling your best. To stay healthy,

- get adequate sleep
- get plenty of physical activity
- eat a balanced diet
- avoid health risks
- maintain mental health

### Get Adequate Sleep

It is very difficult to work if you are tired. Well-rested people also have fewer accidents. Most people need between 7.5 and 10 hours of sleep each night. A regular schedule of going to bed and getting up at the same time will help you feel your best, **26-13**.

### Get Plenty of Physical Activity

Regular physical activity keeps your body in good condition. Physical activity can reduce stress,

**26-13** What might happen to your job performance if you do not get adequate amounts of sleep?

*Aletia/Shutterstock.com*

increase stamina, and help you stay physically fit. For example, doing a moderate activity 30 minutes every day can greatly improve physical condition. Participating in a sport or fitness classes can make physical activity more fun.

## Eat a Balanced Diet

If you eat a diet heavy in fats and sugars, your body is likely to become heavy and sluggish. The U.S. Departments of Agriculture and Health and Human Services developed guidelines for healthful eating and good health. These guidelines are MyPlate and the *Dietary Guidelines for Americans*.

The main key to a healthful diet is to eat a variety of foods. It is also helpful to eat regular meals. A good breakfast provides the body with fuel to begin the day. Other meals and healthful snacks help maintain your energy level while you work.

Drinking eight or more glasses of water a day is also a good idea. Many hospitality jobs require a great deal of running around and physical activity. It is important to drink enough water during the day.

## Avoid Health Risks

The main risks to health in America are tobacco use, drug abuse, and overweight. Tobacco is a legal drug. However, many scientific studies have shown that smoking, chewing, and inhaling tobacco can cause serious health problems. Many hospitality businesses prohibit smoking for this reason. Smoking makes rooms smell unpleasant. This is another reason that many hospitality businesses prohibit smoking or restrict smoking to specific areas or rooms. Smoking is also an expensive habit.

Alcohol is a legal drug for adults over the age of 21. However, unwise alcohol use can lead to illness and accidents. The main effect of alcohol is to slow down the body, especially the reflexes and thought processes. All workplaces prohibit employees from using alcohol while on the job. Even if you work in a place that serves alcohol, you are not allowed to drink on the job. Many companies have a *no tolerance policy*. This means that if you are found drinking or under the influence of alcohol while on the job, you may be terminated immediately.

If you become ill, your doctor may prescribe medicine for you. All medicines are powerful drugs and have a strong effect on the body. Many medicines slow down reaction times or cause drowsiness. Many hospitality jobs require you to be at your best in terms of reaction times, reflexes, and thinking. When your doctor prescribes a medicine for you, ask him or her if it will affect your ability to do your job. If your medicine will cause drowsiness or slowed reaction times, discuss this with your supervisor.

**Drug abuse** is the deliberate use of a substance in ways that harm health. Drugs prescribed by a doctor can be abused if they are used improperly. Using alcohol in harmful ways is also drug abuse. Use of any illegal drug is drug abuse. Drugs are classified as illegal because use of them harms health. Most companies have no tolerance for drug abuse. New employees are often required to take drug tests before they are hired. A person found on the job abusing drugs or under the influence may be immediately dismissed.

Being overweight is another major health risk. If you eat a balanced diet, are physically active, and get enough rest, you should be able to maintain a healthful weight.

## Maintain Mental Health

Good mental health is also important to perform effectively on the job. Figure **26-14** lists several tips for maintaining good mental health.

### Tips for Good Mental Health

- Take short relaxation breaks during the workday. Walking or stretching will help you relieve stress.

- Be organized. Keep a to-do list. This list should be arranged in the order of the importance of the task and can be kept for tasks both at home and work. A to-do list can help you limit stress by keeping you organized.

- Keep a positive attitude. Be realistic about what you can do. Give yourself credit for a job well done.

- Express your thoughts and feelings about a situation in a proper way. Keeping things bottled up on the inside is a path to disaster. It will make you unhappy with your job.

*Goodheart-Willcox Publisher*

**26-14** Good mental health is also important to perform effectively on the job.

*Stress* is a part of life. In particular, many hospitality jobs are stressful. Stress is emotional and physical. When you are feeling emotionally stressed, your body often reacts. Physical symptoms of stress include stomach upset, tension headaches, and sweaty palms. Prolonged periods of stress can contribute to a number of diseases, such as heart disease and high blood pressure. The key to good mental health is learning ways to reduce the feeling of stress.

For example, imagine that you have recently been promoted to the position of front desk manager at a hotel. If you concentrate on the enormity of your new duties, you might feel stressed. If you think you are not prepared for the new duties you might also feel stressed. However, you can choose to think about your new job in less stressful ways. You can get organized and prepare a to-do list. You can also find someone with more experience to go to with questions. You can make sure you are getting enough rest, physical activity, and eating a balanced diet. These good health habits will reduce your feelings of stress.

## Work Habits

**Work habits** are the basic routine actions that you carry out every day at work. They provide the foundation for success at work. Good work habits help you be efficient and productive. Good work habits are very similar to good study habits, **26-15**.

| **Good Work Habits** |
| --- |
| • Be on time. |
| • Be at work every day. |
| • Call your supervisor immediately if you become ill and must miss work. |
| • Complete all work in a timely fashion. |
| • Keep your work area neat and organized. |
| • Be accurate. |
| • Report mistakes or problems to your supervisor immediately. |
| • Do not make personal calls from work. |

*Goodheart-Willcox Publisher*

**26-15** What other work habits can you think of to add to this list?

## Business Etiquette

Etiquette is more than just good manners. **Etiquette** is proper behavior in social situations. Etiquette is sometimes called *manners*. There are rules of etiquette for all kinds of social situations. For example, there are rules for greeting a person and rules for using silverware while eating. Different social situations have different rules of etiquette. For example, the rules of greeting a person at a wedding are different from the rules of greeting a person at a business meeting.

**Business etiquette** is proper behavior for business situations. Examples of good business etiquette include confident handshakes, correct introductions, and appropriate attire at a business meeting. Knowing proper business etiquette can make the difference in making a sale or receiving a promotion. Proper business etiquette is seen as extremely important for people who want to climb the corporate ladder, **26-16**. Many people who want to become corporate vice presidents and presidents take special courses on etiquette.

A complicating factor is that each culture has its own rules of etiquette. For example, the rules of greeting for a business meeting in Japan are different from those in America. If you are working with Japanese businesspeople or are doing business in Japan, you must know the Japanese rules of business etiquette.

# Actions for Advancement

Many people find a job in hospitality and are happy staying in that position. Others want to advance in their careers. If you want to advance, you must take certain actions including continuing education, developing leadership skills, being active in professional organizations, and changing jobs.

## Continuing Education

In order to advance, you must continually improve your job skills. Many employers offer classes and seminars for their employees. Take advantage of them. Some employers will pay for classes at a college or professional school, especially if they are related to your job. Many professional organizations offer classes and workshops. Some also offer certification classes.

## Etiquette Quiz

How good is your etiquette? Choose the correct answers for the following questions. Answers appear below.

1. Within a standard table setting, your salad fork can be found _____.
   A. to the left of your plate, closest in
   B. horizontal and above the plate
   C. to the left of your plate, farthest out
   D. to right of your plate, next to the knife

2. When wearing a name badge, one should wear it _____.
   A. on one's left
   B. on one's right
   C. under the lapel
   D. as infrequently as possible

3. If a utensil is dropped at table, one should _____.
   A. ignore it, pick up another, and continue
   B. pick it up, wipe it off, and continue
   C. immediately call for a waiter to replace it
   D. apologize profusely and finish the meal with one's fingers

4. When asked to RSVP, one should _____.
   A. respond only if attending
   B. respond only if not attending
   C. respond promptly whether attending or not
   D. ignore the request; nobody really responds

5. Suppose you are conducting business in France, and you do not want to drink wine at meals. You should _____.
   A. drink it anyway; the host would be insulted if the wine were declined
   B. cover the glass with your hand to indicate no wine is desired
   C. turn the wine glass upside down; no one will be insulted
   D. accept a small amount but don't drink any

Answers

1. C. Since salad is usually the first course, the salad fork will be found on the left, farthest out. Use utensils from the outside first, working to the inside, by order of course served.

2. B. Name badges should be worn on one's right. During a handshake, one's eyes are naturally drawn up to the name badge.

3. A. Ignore the dropped utensil, choose a new one and continue as if nothing happened. If another is not available, quietly signal the waiter.

4. C. Always respond promptly when asked to RSVP. (RSVP stands for *Repondez s'il vous plait*. This is a French phrase that means *please respond*.) The host/hostess needs an accurate count to prepare.

5. C. Simply turn your glass upside down. No one will be insulted.

*Quiz courtesy of Nicholas & Rowe, Certified Etiquette Consultants, www.nicholasandrowe.com*

26-16 Try out your etiquette knowledge with this quiz.

## Leadership

**Leadership** is the ability to influence others and inspire excellence. Leadership is a critical skill for people who want to start their own businesses or get promoted to upper management jobs in their companies. People develop leadership skills by being in positions of leadership, such as leading work projects or involvement with social, community, civic, volunteer, and professional organizations. As a student, involvement in career and technical student organizations, student government, clubs, and extracurricular activities can also provide leadership development opportunities, **26-17**. These groups often need people to lead

*DECA–An Association of Marketing Students*

**26-17** These students are presenting a proposal for a hospitality and recreation business at a DECA conference.

their organizations and are willing to give positions to someone with little experience but a lot of enthusiasm and potential. You can usually start small, such as by agreeing to chair a committee. In addition, many groups offer leadership training. Leadership skills learned in this way are directly transferable to the job.

## Professional Associations

Involvement in a *professional association* is one of the main ways to keep up-to-date in your profession. Professional associations usually have websites, magazines, and newsletters where they publish industry and career information. Many associations have monthly meetings where you can meet people and find out about jobs. Many associations offer classes, seminars, and certificate programs. Professional associations and career

and technical student organizations offer many opportunities to develop leadership skills.

## Changing Jobs

In order to move ahead, you have to change jobs. If you like the company that you are with, you can often move up in the same company. You may still have to go through a formal process to apply for the new job. In other cases, you may want to change companies and jobs.

Whenever you are looking for a new job while still in your old job, you must have integrity. You must continue to fulfill all your obligations to your current employer. Avoid carrying out any job-hunting activities on your current employer's premises. If you need time to interview, you should take vacation time.

Once you have obtained a new job, you must be professional about leaving your old job. Most businesses require that you give at least two weeks notice before you leave a job. **Giving notice** means notifying your supervisor that you intend to leave your job. The two weeks gives the employer time to find someone to take your place, **26-18**. It also gives you time to finish up your projects and leave instructions for the next person. Giving notice is usually done by writing a letter of resignation. The letter should be addressed to your supervisor. A resignation letter should express appreciation for the time you have spent with the company, express regrets about leaving, and state your last day on the job. Then, take the letter with you when you tell your supervisor that you are leaving. Explain that you are leaving the company, express appropriate appreciation to your supervisor, and leave the letter with him or her.

auremar/Shutterstock.com

**26-18** Giving notice to your employer that you have accepted a new job allows you to finish projects and help train your replacement.

# Balancing Multiple Roles

Each person has many roles in life. A **role** is a set of responsibilities and expectations that go with an aspect of your life. For example, you currently have the role of a student. In this role, you are expected to go to school, study your subjects, and do as well as you can. You also have a role as a family member. In this role, you may have certain chores that you are expected to do. You are probably expected to follow family rules concerning things such as curfew. You also have a role as friend in which you may be expected to join your friends at parties and other social activities.

One of the challenges of life is to balance the many roles that you have. Often, the demands of different roles compete for your limited amount of time. For example, your role as student requires time for homework. Your role as friend requires time for going to the movies. Your role as family member requires time to do laundry. You must figure out a way to manage your time to meet these demands.

As you move through adulthood, you will add many roles to your life. You are likely to add the role of employee, which will require you to be at work at specific times and perform your job well. You will add the role of citizen, which requires you to be informed about current issues and vote. You may also add the roles as spouse and parent. These roles add responsibilities for relating to and taking care of others.

In the roles of community member and neighbor, you may have responsibilities for organizing and participating in community activities and volunteering your time to help others. You may also have other roles. For example, you may be a tennis player or a member of a choir. Your hobbies or special interests give you roles and responsibilities that also take up time.

When you make a career decision, you may want to consider the roles you plan to have. The role of parent is particularly demanding. One of the benefits of a hospitality career is that many of the jobs have flexible or part-time work hours.

# Chapter 26 Review

## Chapter Summary

- The career clusters include 16 groups of occupational and career specialties each of which includes different career pathways.
- Word choice determines the effect you have on the customer in both spoken and written language.
- Nonverbal communication can change the meaning of words.
- Listening is an active process that requires eye contact.
- Learning effective job-search skills helps lead to finding meaningful employment.
- Keeping a job requires many traits, skills, and actions.
- Career advancement requires taking certain actions for success.
- A challenge of adulthood is learning to balance life roles.
- Consider the life roles you plan to have when making a career decision.

## Review

1. How do the career clusters connect school preparation to career success?
2. List the four hospitality and tourism career pathways.
3. Why is word choice an important part of verbal communication? Give an example.
4. Give an example showing how nonverbal communication can change meaning.
5. Name two important communication skills that involve listening and speaking.
6. Give two examples showing how the hospitality industry uses electronic communication.
7. What are two ways to find job leads?
8. Why might you use a résumé and cover letter in your job search?
9. List four things you could practice in preparation for an interview.
10. Why is good grooming important to workplace success?
11. What health risks can impact workplace success?
12. Name three actions you can take to advance your career.
13. What is *giving notice* and when and how should you do it?
14. List four roles an adult might have.

# Critical Thinking

15. **Analyze.** According to the text, nonverbal communication can change the meaning of words. Analyze how nonverbal communication can benefit or block resolution of a conflict between two employees. Discuss in class.

16. **Predict.** Proper use of electronic communication is key to business success. Predict the consequences of failure to follow proper e-mail protocol, business communication, and use of Standard English in the workplace.

17. **Draw conclusions.** Use the text and reliable Internet or print resources to draw conclusions about the benefits of teamwork and cooperation in the hospitality workplace. Write a summary of your conclusions to share with the class.

18. **Evaluate.** All people have many life roles. Make a list of roles you might have as an adult. Evaluate how these roles could impact your work life. How might work life impact your other life roles? Write an essay about your evaluation.

# Common Core

**College and Career Readiness**

19. **Writing.** Choose a hospitality career for which you would like to apply. Write your résumé following text guidelines. Then write a cover letter that introduces you to the employer, highlights your strengths, and asks for an interview.

20. **Speaking.** With a classmate, take the roles of hospitality employer and potential employee. Make a list of potential interview questions. Then role-play an interview for the job for the class. Reverse roles and repeat the interview. Have the class provide constructive criticism of the interview. What did you do well? Where are improvements needed?

21. **Reading.** From reliable resources, read a book or several journal articles about the concept of self-motivation in the workplace. Summarize your findings in writing. When evaluating the reliability of information, remember to
    - identify the credibility of the author or writer
    - verify the details from other reliable sources (government or educational institutions)
    - identify any bias or lack of objectivity in the writer's presentation

22. **CTE Career Readiness Practice.** Careers in the hospitality industry are fast-paced and demanding. As a potential employee, take initiative to maintain your health and a healthy body weight. Use the *Choose MyPlate Super Tracker* to plan, analyze, and track your diet and physical activity. You can use these tools to plan healthful means, compare food choices for recommendations to meet nutrient needs, and identify ways to improve your fitness. After several months, assess how well you are meeting your goals for healthful eating and maintaining a healthy body weight. Write a summary of your assessment. What would you tell others about the benefits of using these tools?

500

# Chapter 27
## Starting a Business

## Chapter Objectives

After studying this chapter, you will be able to
- **state** the characteristics of successful entrepreneurs.
- **evaluate** the advantages and disadvantages of entrepreneurship.
- **describe** the advantages and disadvantages of buying a franchise.
- **describe** the three types of ownership structures.
- **summarize** the parts of a business plan.
- **identify** resources that offer help to entrepreneurs.

## Before You Read

Try to answer the following questions before you read this chapter.
- What are some advantages of buying a franchise?
- What is included in a business plan?

## Terms to Know

entrepreneurship
entrepreneur
loan

business plan
start-up costs

U.S. Small Business
  Administration (SBA)
chamber of commerce

Have you ever thought of owning your own business? For many employees, owning their own business is a dream. A hospitality business is one of the easier businesses to start. You could turn your home into a bed-and-breakfast. You could start a catering business in your kitchen. In one large hotel chain, more than 40 percent of the brand's franchises are owned by individuals who started their careers as entry-level employees. They advanced to the level of general manager and then became owners of their own hotel franchise.

# Entrepreneurship

**Entrepreneurship** is taking the risk of starting a new business. An **entrepreneur** is a person who takes that risk. Entrepreneurs started all the great businesses in the United States, **27-1**. For example, Ray Kroc started McDonald's, Conrad Hilton started the Hilton Hotels, and Walt Disney started Disneyland.

What does it take to be a successful entrepreneur? Each entrepreneur is unique. However, research has shown that successful entrepreneurs usually have a number of characteristics in common, **27-2**.

There are also advantages and disadvantages of entrepreneurship, **27-3**. Owning your own business can be both exciting and challenging.

| **Characteristics of Successful Entrepreneurs** |
| --- |
| • High energy level |
| • Like to work hard |
| • Self-confident |
| • Creative |
| • Goal-oriented |
| • Strong desire to have control over their work lives |
| • Strong motivation to succeed |
| • Willing to work when others play |

*Goodheart-Willcox Publisher*

**27-2** What characteristics do you have in common with successful entrepreneurs?

**27-1** Ray Kroc opened his first McDonald's Restaurant in 1955 in Des Plaines, Illinois. Today McDonald's is the largest restaurant company in the world.

*Used with permission from McDonald's Corporation.*

| Advantages and Disadvantages of Entrepreneurship ||
| Advantages | Disadvantages |
| --- | --- |
| • You are the boss.<br>• You might make a lot of money.<br>• You determine your work schedule.<br>• You hire the people you want. | • You are responsible for everything.<br>• You might suffer large financial losses.<br>• Income can be uncertain or irregular.<br>• You will work long hours. |

*Goodheart-Willcox Publisher*

**27-3** Owning a business is exciting and challenging. Analyze which challenges might keep you from becoming an entrepreneur. Why?

# Where to Start

Most entrepreneurs start with a great idea. Ray Kroc saw a way to make and serve food quickly. Conrad Hilton saw a need for hotel rooms. Walt Disney saw a need for an amusement park for families.

Ideas for new businesses can come from something you really love to do, such as cook. Ideas can also come from a need you observe in your neighborhood. For example, maybe you observe that there is a need for an ice cream parlor in your neighborhood. Maybe you have always dreamed of owning a bed-and-breakfast.

There are three basic ways to start a new business: buy an existing business, buy a franchise, and start from scratch.

## Buy an Existing Business

From time to time, an independent business is for sale. You can learn about businesses for sale by searching for websites that advertise businesses for sale on the Internet. You can also search newspapers under the heading "Business Opportunities." There are many advantages to buying an existing business. The business already has customers, employees, a location, business equipment, and working business operations. The business has financial records that describe its financial history. In addition, the person selling the business may be willing to act as a consultant to help you get started in the business.

The main disadvantage of buying an existing business is that you may be buying problems. The most important question to answer when buying an existing business is "Why is this business being sold?" Many businesses are sold because they are

not making a profit. However, some businesses are sold because the owner is ready to retire. Such a business might be an excellent choice.

## Buy a Franchise

Many hospitality businesses are franchises, **27-4**. Most of these businesses have websites including information about how to buy a franchise of that business. There are also franchise websites.

There are many advantages to buying a franchise. The main advantage is that you have an established product or service with an established reputation. In addition, the franchisor provides assistance with many of the aspects of starting and running the business. For example, McDonald's runs Hamburger University for training its franchisees. Another advantage of a franchise is quantity purchasing. Because your business is part of a franchise, you can place your orders for supplies with all the other franchisees. The result is that the cost of supplies is often much less than they would be for a single purchaser.

There are disadvantages to owning a franchise. The main one is that the franchisor makes many of the decisions. The franchisee must follow the rules and requirements set by the franchisor. From the beginning, the franchisor will set certain requirements that you must meet in order to be considered for buying a franchise. For example, McDonald's has a list of qualifications that they require, **27-5**. A related disadvantage is that the initial cost to buy a franchise is often high. In addition, you must pay a franchise fee (also called a *royalty fee*). A *franchise fee* is a regular payment that you make to the franchisor for the right to use the

| Some Hospitality Franchises | | | |
|---|---|---|---|
| **Food and Beverage Franchises** | | **Hotel and Lodging Franchises** | |
| Baskin Robbins | Friendly's Restaurants | AmeriHost | Econo Lodge Holiday |
| Ben & Jerry's | McDonald's Restaurants | AmeriSuites | Inn Brands |
| Bennigan's | Papa John's PIzza | Best Inns and Suites | Hilton |
| Blimpie Sub & Salads | Quizno's Subs | Comfort Inn, Suites and | Howard Johnson |
| Buffalo Wild Wings | Schlotzsky's Deli | Hotel | Microtel Inn and Suites |
| CiCi's Pizza | Steak and Ale | Crown Plaza, Crown | Motel 6 |
| Dairy Queen | Subway | Plaza Suites | Ramada Inn |
|  |  | Days Inn | Red Roof Inn |

*Goodheart-Willcox Publisher*

**27-4** Many hospitality businesses are franchises. Interview a local franchise owner to determine what it takes to become a franchise owner.

### Qualifications for a McDonald's Franchise

1. High personal integrity
2. An entrepreneurial spirit and a strong desire to succeed
3. A proven ability to motivate and train people
4. The ability to manage finances
5. A willingness to personally devote full time and best efforts to the day-to-day operation of the restaurant as an on-premise owner-operator
6. A willingness to complete a comprehensive training program and become proficient in all aspects of operating a McDonald's Restaurant business
7. Financial resources
8. Significant business experience

*Source: www.aboutmcdonalds.com*

**27-5** From the beginning, the franchisor will set certain requirements that you must meet in order to be considered for buying a franchise. For example, McDonald's has a list of qualifications they require.

franchisor's products and brand. It is usually a percentage of your profits. Another disadvantage is that the franchisor can terminate the franchise agreement for any number of reasons. If this happens, the franchisee loses all of his or her investment.

## Start from Scratch

Many entrepreneurs decide to start their businesses totally on their own. They are not interested in buying an existing business or a franchise. Starting on your own gives you the opportunity to develop the business the way you want it. You can take your own ideas and turn them into reality.

The advantage of your own business is that you get to make all the decisions. You decide on product, service, location, and concept. You will decide whom to hire, what hours to be open, and what the decor should be. You will get all the profits.

The disadvantage is that you also take on all the risk. Your new business has no track record. You may think that your new soup and salad restaurant is a great idea. However, there may not be enough customers in your area who want to buy soup and salad. Planning a new business, whether you buy one or start your own, takes a great deal of time and research. However, the existing business has already had many decisions made for it. For a new business, you have to be sure to do enough market research and financial planning to make sure the business will be financially sound.

## Ownership Structure

One of the most important decisions an entrepreneur makes is the ownership structure. The three forms of business ownership are sole proprietorship, partnership, and corporation.

There are advantages and disadvantages to each form, **27-6**.

## Cost

A new business costs money. If you buy a business or a franchise, you will need money. A restaurant might cost anywhere from $90,000 to over $2 million. Lodging properties are usually more expensive, starting around $200,000 to over $2 million.

If you start your business from scratch, you will need to buy or rent a building, buy supplies, hire and train staff, and promote the business. Money for all these items is required before the business has started to earn money.

In addition, once you have the business, you need money for the day-to-day expenses. It usually takes some time before a new business is earning enough money to cover expenses.

The amount of money needed to start a new business is usually larger than one person or a group of partners can raise. As a result, most new businesses need a loan to get started. A **loan** is money borrowed from a bank or other source, with the expectation that the money will be repaid with interest within a specific time period.

The most common source of loans is a bank. In addition, there are several government agencies that will help new businesses with financing. The U.S. Small Business Association (SBA) was established to help new businesses with financing. The SBA is the nation's single largest financial backer of small businesses. Other government sources include Small Business Investment Companies, Minority Enterprise Small Business Investment Companies, The Economic Development Administration, and state and local governments.

In order to obtain a loan, you have to prove that you know what you are doing. You also have to show that your business will earn enough money so you can repay the loan. Most banks and other lenders require you to submit a business plan. The lenders use the business plan to evaluate whether your business will be successful and to decide whether to offer you a loan.

# Business Plan

A **business plan** is a written document that describes the business and how it will operate. A business plan is a required part of a business loan application. Writing a business plan is not just a writing assignment. It is also a very valuable planning tool. Researching and writing a business plan will help you figure out how to start and run your business successfully. It is worth the time and effort to carefully and thoroughly research and write your plan. Many entrepreneurs spend between 50 and 100 hours on their business plans.

Once a business plan is written and the loan is obtained, the business plan can be used as an operating guide. Business plans should be reviewed and updated regularly.

In general, a business plan covers all the activities that go on in the business. The plan is usually divided into seven parts, **27-7**.

Some plans have an additional part called "Growth Plan." Some also have additional parts that cover specialized information. For example, a restaurant might have a separate section on sanitation and include the sanitation certificate of the executive chef. Many business plans also have an

| Ownership Structures: Advantages and Disadvantages | | |
|---|---|---|
| **Sole Proprietorship** | **Partnership** | **Corporation** |
| **Advantages**: Easy to start, minimal government regulations, owner has total control | **Advantages**: Easy to start, minimal government regulations, partners share control | **Advantages**: Limited liability, easier to raise money for the business |
| **Disadvantages**: Unlimited liability, owner has total responsibility | **Disadvantages**: Potential conflict among partners, unlimited liability | **Disadvantages**: Complicated and costly to start, many government regulations |

*Goodheart-Willcox Publisher*

**27-6** If you were an entrepreneur, which structure would be most appealing to you? Why?

## Parts of a Business Plan

- Executive Summary
- Description of Business
- Industry/Market Analysis
- Customers
- Marketing Plan
- Operations Plan
- Financial Plan
- Growth Plan

*Goodheart-Willcox Publisher*

27-7 A business plan is a written document that describes the business and how it will operate. Draw conclusions about why it is necessary for entrepreneurs to have a business plan.

appendix containing any supporting documents not included in the other sections. The appendix might include legal documents, such as a building lease, staff résumés, and letters of recommendation.

## Executive Summary

The executive summary is the first part of the business plan, but it is the last part written. After you have researched and written all the other parts, you will be ready to write the executive summary. The summary is the sales piece of the

document. In it, you should summarize the key points about your business. You should present these key points in a way that makes the reader excited about your business and its potential for success.

The executive summary is the first thing that lenders will read. If they are not impressed with the executive summary, they might not bother to read the rest of the business plan.

## Description of Business

The description of the business should include your business concept, your goals, and your ownership structure. If you are planning a restaurant or lodging business, this is the section of the business plan where you present your concept. Your restaurant concept would include the theme, target market, decor, ambiance, and service style. Your lodging concept would include the theme, target market, decor, ambiance, and level of service. A travel or tourism business would include details of what you plan to provide.

## Industry/Market Analysis

This section discusses the current state of the industry and the economy in the area where you want to start your business. This discussion should include a description of all competitors and analysis of the need for your business, 27-8.

This section should also describe the competitive edge that your business will have over

# Hospitality Ethics

## Using Social Media

Social media is commonly used by businesses to reach customers and find new ones. Because it is so available and easy to use, those who are writing communications for the organization must be prudent when using sites such as Facebook or Twitter for business purposes. Remember that it is unethical to spam customers who have not requested to be on an organization's mailing list. Keep your messages honest and return messages from those who have taken time to respond to your communication. Use good judgment and represent the organization in a professional manner.

*Jack Klasey*

**27-8** The industry/market analysis section of the business plan includes an analysis of the competitors in the area. These four lodging businesses are located in the same business park.

the other business. In other words, explain how your business will be successful in the competitive environment. You should also discuss your weaknesses and how you will overcome them.

## Customers

Customers will be crucial to the success of your business. In this section, you will describe your target market. You will need an estimate of how many customers you expect to have and how much they will spend at your business.

## Marketing Plan

The next step is to describe how you will tell your customers about your business and how you will convince them to buy your products and services. You will need to describe your four Ps of marketing: product, price, place, and promotion. In the promotion section, you will need to cover what kind of advertising you will do and whether you will have a sales force. You will also need to estimate your marketing budget and plan a timetable for your marketing program.

## Operations Plan

The operations plan discusses the nuts and bolts of the day-to-day running of the business, **27-9**. This section of the business plan is often used as the basis for the business operations manual. The operations plan should cover topics such as organizational chart, operations procedures, material resources needed (including technology), human resources needed, and the staffing plan. This section must be very detailed to show the bank that you know how to run the business. This section should also include a list of your key staff members and their résumés. The bank will want to know that the people involved in your new business have the experience and knowledge to run the business.

**27-9** Why is it important to discuss the workers you need and the equipment you will use in your business plan?

*Bonefish Grill*

## *Financial Plan*

The financial plan describes how you will fund the business and how you expect to make a profit. The purpose of this section is to show that your business will be financially healthy. It will also show that you will be able to pay back any loans that you obtain.

The first part of the financial plan is a thorough analysis of **start-up costs**. Start-up costs are all the expenses involved in getting the business started. Then you need to describe how you will get the money to cover the start-up costs. Part of this analysis can include the amount and source of any loans. When you discuss the loans, you must explain how you will pay the loans back.

This section also includes an analysis of anticipated sales and profits. This section will include many financial documents. Examples include budgets, profit and loss statements, and other financial statements.

# Resources for Entrepreneurs

The wealth of the United States was built on the energy and hard work of entrepreneurs. Small businesses create two of every three new jobs. Small businesses produce over 40 percent of the gross domestic product (GDP) and are responsible for inventing more than half the nation's new technology. Many hospitality businesses are small businesses started by entrepreneurs.

The U.S. government continues to promote entrepreneurship. The major government agency that helps new businesses and entrepreneurs is the **U.S. Small Business Administration (SBA)**. Congress created the SBA in 1953 to help America's entrepreneurs form successful small businesses. Today, the SBA has offices in every state. The SBA offers billions of dollars in business loans, loan guarantees, and disaster loans. It also offers management and technical assistance to more than one million small business owners. The SBA's website offers information on starting your business, financing, and disaster assistance, as well as information on many other business topics, **27-10**.

*www.sba.gov*

**27-10** The U.S. Small Business Administration (SBA) provides help to entrepreneurs, including business loans. Browse the SBA website. Which sections do you find most helpful as a potential entrepreneur?

Through the SBA you can reach SCORE, previously known as the Service Corps of Retired Executives. The members of SCORE are mentors and counselors who volunteer their time to help new entrepreneurs develop their business plans and their businesses.

Another good source of information is the library, which offers many books and magazines on entrepreneurship, business management, financing, marketing, and hiring and managing a staff. You will also find resources for researching the hospitality industry and specific businesses in the industry. Professional associations in hospitality and entrepreneurship can also be good sources of information.

Your local chamber of commerce will have a great deal of information on the business environment in your area. A chamber of commerce is an association of business people who work together to promote business in their area. Most states, cities, and towns have a **chamber of commerce**. The chambers may also offer programs for entrepreneurs as well as networking opportunities.

# Chapter 27
## Review

### Chapter Summary

- Entrepreneurs started all of the great businesses in the United States.
- Most entrepreneurs started their new business because they had a good idea.
- An entrepreneur can either buy an existing business, buy a franchise, or start a new business from scratch.
- There are three forms of business ownership.
- Starting a new business costs money.
- A business plan is a valuable planning tool.
- Resources exist to help new businesses and entrepreneurs.

### Review

1. Identify three characteristics of successful entrepreneurs.
2. What are the advantages and disadvantages of entrepreneurship?
3. What are the advantages and disadvantages of buying a franchise?
4. List and describe the three types of ownership structures.
5. What are the requirements for an entrepreneur to get a loan to start a business?
6. What is a business plan?
7. What are the parts of a business plan?
8. What are some resources that entrepreneurs can use to help them with their businesses?

# Critical Thinking

9. **Infer.** Describe a business that you would like to start in your area. What type of business is it? What form of business ownership would you use? How would it be different from other similar businesses? What facts support your inferences?

10. **Analyze.** Suppose you wanted to start your own business. Analyze what form of business ownership you want to use. Cite reliable resources, such as the U.S. Small Business Administration (SBA), to support your choice.

11. **Identify.** Imagine you are writing the Operations Plan section of your business plan. You need to identify the management team for your hospitality business (the human resources). What experts would you have on your team? Why do you need them? What evidence of qualifications might a lender require about these experts? How would they add to your business success? Write a summary.

12. **Assess.** Review the website for your local chamber of commerce. Assess the programs and networking opportunities offered by your local chamber for hospitality businesses. Discuss your findings in class.

## Common Core
### College and Career Readiness

13. **Reading.** Identify a successful entrepreneur who is not described in the text. Then locate and read a book or magazine article about this entrepreneur. What business did he or she begin? What characteristics does the entrepreneur possess? Why was (is) the entrepreneur's business successful? Write a summary of your findings.

14. **Writing.** Suppose you are part of a team that wants to open a "green" restaurant. You have completed the market research and have found there is a local market for such a restaurant. In order to obtain financial backing, your team needs to write a business plan. Use the *Small Business Planner* tools on the Small Business Administration (SBA) website as a guide in writing the business plan. Write the plan covering details in all specific parts of the plan. Submit your plan to your investors (the class) for review.

15. **Speaking.** As part of the business plan for your "green" restaurant, you need to develop a marketing plan that describes your four Ps of marketing. With your team, develop descriptions of your products, their prices, the place (where you will sell the product), and how you will promote the product. Give an oral presentation to share your marketing plan.

16. **CTE Career Readiness Practice.** Creativity is a skill that is often necessary in the business world. Suppose you have an opportunity to start a business, but you first need to calculate how much the start-up costs will be. Your first effort to creatively solve this problem is to ask some questions. Create a mind map like the following to dig deeper into the problem.

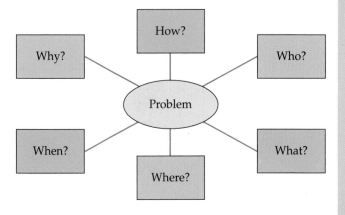

# Appendix A

## STANDARD TIME ZONES OF THE WORLD

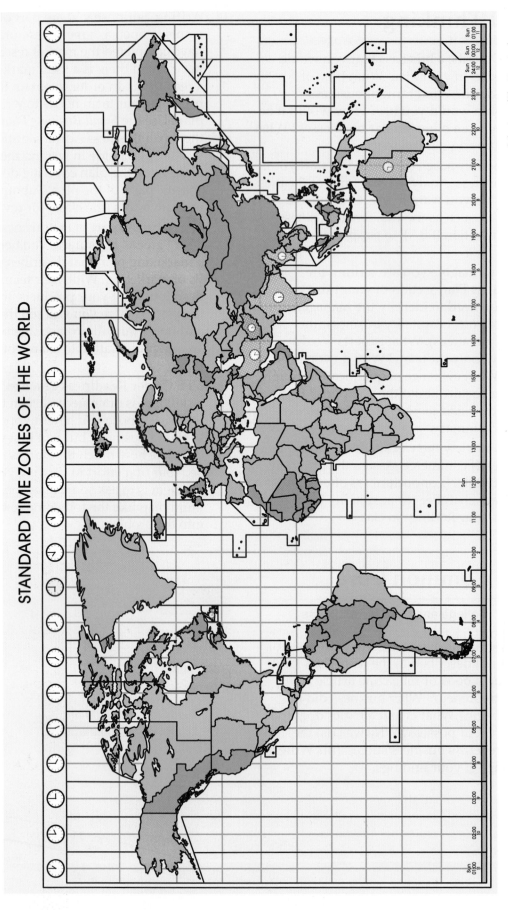

dalmingo/Shutterstock.com

# Appendix B

*Map of the Caribbean Sea*

This map can be used to identify routes commonly taken by cruise ships in the Caribbean.

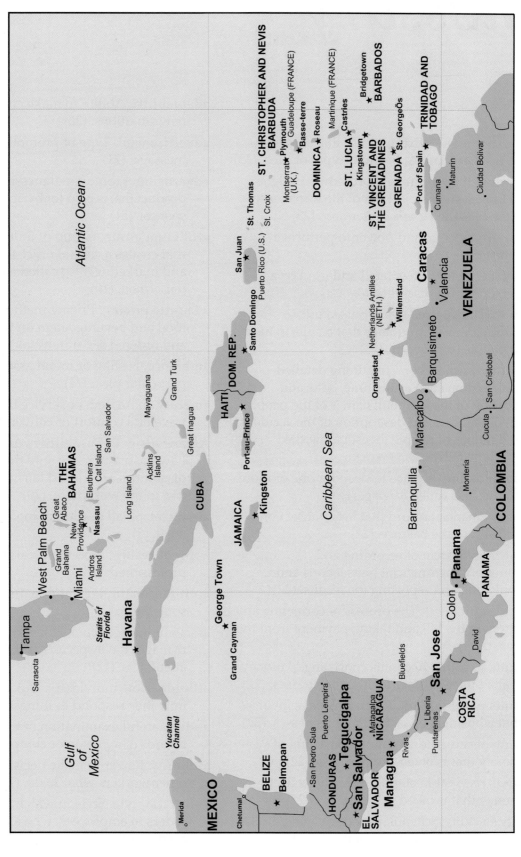

# Glossary

## A

**ABC extinguisher.** Extinguisher that can safely be used on class A, B, and C types of fires. (23)

**abdominal thrust.** First aid procedure designed to force a stuck object out of the throat; also known as the *Heimlich Maneuver.* (23)

**ability.** Knowledge and power to perform a task. (25)

**accessible.** Able to be entered and used by a person with a disability. (3)

**accident.** Unexpected event caused by carelessness or ignorance that results in harm to people or property. (23)

**accident report.** Report containing detailed information such as the time, date, and location of the accident; names of the people involved; detailed description of the accident; and names of people investigating the accident. (13)

**accommodation.** A place to sleep for one or more nights; also called *lodging.* (1)

**account.** Financial record that lists transactions and shows the balance. (22)

**accounting.** System of recording and summarizing financial transactions and analyzing and reporting the results. (22)

**account settlement.** The process of correcting any errors in the bill and taking payment from the guest. (11)

**accounts payable.** Accounts consisting of money that a business owes to other businesses. (22)

**accounts payable clerk.** Clerk who pays invoices that a business owes to other businesses. (22)

**accounts receivable.** Accounts consisting of money that is owed to a business. (22)

**accounts receivable clerk.** Clerk who collects money that is owed to a business. (22)

**activity stacking.** Scheduling or dovetailing similar leisure activities throughout the day. (17)

**adaptability.** Ability to make changes to match new situations. (26)

**advertisement.** Type of promotional advertising message. (21)

**advertising.** Promotional message about a product that is paid for by an identified sponsor. (21)

**affiliation group.** Group of independent hotels that creates a central office for reservations and marketing; also called a *referral system* or *consortium.* (10)

**à la carte pricing.** Pricing method in which every food and beverage item on the menu is priced and ordered separately. (5)

**ambiance.** Feeling or mood associated with a particular place. (4)

**amenity.** Extra item or service that adds to a traveler's comfort or convenience. (3)

**Americans with Disabilities Act (ADA).** Law passed to make sure that people with disabilities are treated fairly in public places and in the workplace. (20)

**appetizer.** Small portion of food served before a meal. (5)

**apprenticeship.** Process of learning from a skilled professional. (25)

**aptitude.** Natural talent or natural ability to do something. (25)

**assistant housekeeper.** Housekeeper who manages the inspectors and the room attendants. (12)

**attitude.** How individuals look at the world and how they respond to things that happen. (26)

**audit.** Careful examination of the financial records of a person or company. (22)

**authority.** Power to make decisions and to tell other workers what to do. (18)

**autocratic style.** Style in which the manager gives orders to employees, who are expected to carry out the orders immediately and without questioning. (19)

# B

**back-of-the-house.** Area in a hospitality business that guests usually do not see. (2)

**back-of-the-house employees.** Employees whose work rarely involves interacting with customers. (2)

**banquet.** Food served in honor of a special occasion. (7)

**banquet chef.** Chef responsible for feeding all large groups in the hotel. (7)

**banquet event order.** Written record of all the decisions that have been made about what the client wants during the banquet. (7)

**banquet manager.** Manager responsible for making sure that all aspects of each banquet run smoothly. (7)

**banquet servers.** Workers who are responsible for serving food and beverages during the banquet. (7)

**banquet setup staff.** Workers who are responsible for moving and arranging the room dividers, tables, and chairs. (7)

**bar.** Place that serves alcoholic beverages as well as nonalcoholic beverages. (7)

**bar back.** Worker who is responsible for making sure the bar is stocked with liquor, ice, glassware, and supplies. (7)

**bartender.** Worker who concentrates on alcoholic-beverage production and service to guests. (7)

**bed-and-breakfast (B&B).** Private home offering one or more guest rooms. (10)

**bell attendant.** Staff member responsible for helping guests with luggage in the hotel. (11)

**bell captain.** Staff member who supervises the uniformed services staff. (11)

**benefits.** All forms of compensation other than salary and wages. (20)

**beverage.** Liquid that is drinkable. (5)

**beverage manager.** Manger who usually oversees the hotel's front bars, service bars, special-purpose bars, room service beverage deliveries, hospitality suite bars, and minibars. (7)

**beverage server.** Worker who takes orders for beverages and gives the orders to the bartender. (7)

**bid.** Document that states what the supplier will charge for a specific product. (8)

**billboard.** Type of print advertising that appears on a large outdoor panel. (21)

**biological contaminant.** Microscopic living substance that accidentally gets into food. (9)

**biometric identifiers.** Unique, measurable characteristics that label or identify people. (16)

**body language.** Communication that includes facial expressions, posture, hand gestures, and tone of voice. (26)

**booking a reservation.** Process of taking a reservation. (6)

**brand.** A name, logo, tagline, or any combination of these that distinguishes a product from its competitors. (1)

**break down.** To clear dishes and food, clean tables and chairs, put away all furniture and equipment, and clean the floor after a banquet. (7)

**budget.** Guideline for spending money. (19)

**budget hotels.** Hotels that have the lowest rates and the least service. (10)

**buffet.** Foodservice that consists of food displayed on tables. (4)

**building codes.** Rules and regulations designed to make buildings safe. (24)

**bureaucratic style.** Style in which the manager seeks employee input before he or she makes a final decision. (19)

**business etiquette.** Proper behavior for business situations. (26)

**business plan.** Written document that describes the business and how it will operate. (27)

**business travel.** Travel done for the purpose of sales, training, and functions related to work. (15)

**busser.** Worker who assists the servers and is responsible for setup, clearing, and resetting of tables. (6)

**bussing.** Setting the place settings, clearing dirty dishes from the table, and taking the dirty dishes to the kitchen. (5)

# C

cafeteria. Foodservice in which the food is displayed along a counter called a serving line. (4)

call-ahead seating. Seating method in which customers call the restaurant and have their names added to the waiting list, in order to guarantee a place in line. (6)

career and technical student organization (CTSO). Organization for students with an interest in a career area, such as hospitality or business. (1)

career clusters. Sixteen groups of occupational and career specialties. (26)

career goal. Highest career level that a person wants to reach. (25)

career ladder. Series of related jobs at different training and education levels. (25)

career plan. List of steps that a person develops to reach a career goal. (25)

carrier. Company that transports passengers. (15)

carrying capacity. Maximum number of people that can be held in a place or on a mode of transportation. (16)

carryout restaurant. Restaurant that specializes in preparing food for customers to take with them to eat at home or elsewhere. (4)

catering. Provision of food and service for a special event. (4)

central reservations center. Office that handles reservations for all the hotels in the chain or affiliation group. (11)

chain. Business that has more than one establishment under the same name and the same ownership. (1)

chamber of commerce. Association of business people who work together to promote business in their area. (27)

charter airlines. Airlines that only fly when they are contracted by clients. (15)

check-in. Process of registering guests, assigning rooms, and distributing keys. (11)

checkout. Process of paying for rooms and returning keys. (11)

chef. Professional cook. (6)

chemical contaminant. Chemical that is toxic or not usually found in food. (9)

chief engineer. Person in charge of engineering. (14)

chlorine. Main chemical used to keep swimming pool water safe. (14)

city guide. Guide who "steps on" a coach and takes over the guiding for a city tour. (16)

Civilian Conservation Corps (CCC). Job-creation program during the 1930s that built over 800 new parks, upgraded most others, built roadways, and planted over three-billion trees on government lands. (17)

clean. State of being free of dirt and bad odors. (12)

cleaning. Physical removal of dirt and food from surfaces. (9)

cleaning cart. Doorway-sized cart that holds cleaning supplies, equipment, guest room supplies, and linens. (12)

clients. Customers. (7)

code. List of regulations. (24)

code of ethics. Written list of rules for ethical behavior. (24)

collective bargaining. Process of labor and management discussing what they expect from each other. (20)

combination pricing. Pricing method in which some food items are priced and ordered separately, and other food items are grouped together and priced as a group. (5)

combustible. Easy to burn. (23)

commercial. Advertisement that is broadcast on television or radio. (21)

commercial foodservice. Food and beverage businesses that compete for customers. (4)

commission. Percentage of the sale price that is paid to the seller. (15)

communication. Transmission of information and feelings from one person to another. (26)

compensation. Money paid and benefits provided to a person for his or her work. (20)

competitor. A similar business that wants to take away customers. (21)

compliance. Following of rules and policies. (23)

concierge. Hotel staff member who helps guests make arrangements, such as dinner reservations. (10)

**condiment.** Something that is added to food to make it taste better. (5)

**conference center.** Lodging facility where 60 percent or more of the total occupancy is generated by conferences. (10)

**conflict resolution.** Process of resolving a disagreement in a peaceful way. (26)

**consistency.** Quality of producing the same result every time. (5)

**consistent quality service.** Providing the same good service and products to customers each and every time they come to a business. (2)

**consortium.** Group of independent hotels that creates a central office for reservations and marketing; also called a *referral system* or *affiliation group*. (10)

**consulates.** Smaller diplomatic missions located in a country's regional cities. (16)

**consumables.** Products that get used up and must be replaced regularly. (12)

**contaminant.** Substance in food that does not belong in the food. (9)

**contaminated food.** Food that contains something that does not belong and can cause illness. (9)

**continental breakfast.** Breakfast consisting of breakfast foods that do not need to be cooked. (10)

**continuing professional education.** Education for people who have already completed their formal schooling and training. (25)

**contract foodservice.** Foodservice in which an outside company is hired to run a food operation. (4)

**contract housekeeping services.** Services performed by a company that is not part of the hotel. (12)

**contraction.** Period when the economy is slowing down and doing poorly; also called *recession*. (3)

**controller.** Top manager of an accounting department or division who oversees all the operations of the accounting department and supervises the accounting staff. (22)

**controlling.** Making sure that the business accomplishes what it set out to accomplish. (18)

**convention.** Large meeting, usually sponsored by a group for its members. (7)

**convention and visitors bureau.** Nonprofit organization that promotes tourism and provides services to travelers. (21)

**convention center.** Large building designed specifically to hold large meetings, conventions, and trade shows. (10)

**convention hotel.** Hotel designed to provide for the special needs of conventions and trade shows. (10)

**cook.** Person who prepares food for eating. (6)

**cooperation.** Willingness to do what it takes to get the job done. (26)

**cooperative education program.** Program that prepares students for an occupation through a paid job and classes at school. (25)

**corporation.** Legal entity established for the purpose of doing business. (18)

**correspondence course.** Course in which the student and teacher communicate through the mail system. (25)

**cost-effective buying.** Buying the most products at the best quality for the least amount of money. (8)

**country of origin.** Country from which a person's trip originates. (16)

**cover letter.** Letter that introduces you, highlights your strengths, and asks for an interview. (26)

**CPR.** First aid procedure to help someone whose heart has stopped beating; stands for *cardiopulmonary resuscitation*. (23)

**credit.** Money or payment that has been received. (22)

**credit department.** Department that protects the business from loss due to customers or businesses with bad credit. (22)

**credit history.** Record that shows whether a person or a business pays its bills promptly. (22)

**credit memorandum.** Paper that lists the products that were returned. (8)

**crime insurance.** Insurance that provides payment for losses due to crimes such as theft, arson, forgery, and embezzlement. (13)

**critical control point (CCP).** Point when a hazard can be prevented. (9)

**critical limit.** Action or a temperature required for food safety. (9)

**critical moment.** Time when the customer's experience makes a bigger impact on customer satisfaction than at other times. (2)

**cross-contamination.** Transfer of microorganisms from one food item to another. (9)

**cruise.** Pleasure trip taken by boat or ship. (3)

**culinary.** Something related to kitchens and cooking. (6)

**customer.** Someone who purchases products or services from a business. (2)

**customer-focused employee.** Employee who can anticipate customer needs. (2)

**customer satisfaction.** The positive feeling customers have about a business that meets their needs. (2)

**customer service.** The total customer experience with a hospitality business. (2)

**cycle menu.** Menu in which foods change daily for a set period of time; at the end of that period of time, the menu repeats itself. (5)

# D

**debit.** Money that is owed or taken out of a business. (22)

**deep cleaning.** More thorough cleaning that involves extra time or equipment. (14)

**delinquent guests.** Guests who are late with payments that they owe. (22)

**delivery slip.** Piece of paper prepared by the supplier that contains a complete listing of the quantity and types of items delivered. (8)

**democratic style.** Style in which the manager shares the decision making with the employees. (19)

**demographics.** Statistics on groups of people about their age, ethnic background, education, or income. (17)

**demographic trend.** Increase or decrease over time in the number of people in a demographic subgroup. (3)

**Department of Homeland Security (DHS).** Cabinet-level agency designated to protect the United States from terrorist attacks and accidents and respond quickly to natural disasters. (16)

**destination.** Predetermined endpoint to which a mode of transportation travels. (15)

**destination marketing organization (DMO).** Organization that represents stakeholders in a destination's tourism industry. (15)

**director of rooms.** Manager in charge of the rooms divisions. (11)

**disability.** Permanent condition that limits one or more major life activities. (20)

**discrimination.** Unfair treatment of people based on irrelevant characteristics, such as race or religion. (20)

**dishwasher.** Worker who operates the dishwashing machine. (6)

**distance learning.** Learning that uses technology so students can take courses without stepping into a classroom. (25)

**diversity.** Word used to describe a group of people from a variety of backgrounds, cultures, religions, beliefs, and languages. (3)

**docent.** Site guide who volunteers at a museum. (16)

**domestic independent tours (DIT).** Plans that are custom-designed for particular travelers within their own country. (16)

**domestic tourist.** Tourist traveling within his or her own country. (16)

**door attendant.** Staff member who takes care of all guest needs as guests arrive at a hotel. (11)

**drug abuse.** Deliberate use of a substance in ways that harm health. (26)

**dynamic packaging.** Process used by travel agents that allows travelers to build their own package of flights, hotels, and car rentals around their specific needs. (15)

# E

**economy of scale.** State achieved when a supplier, such as a hotel, is able to offer a reduced price because of large sales volume. (15)

**ecotourism.** Type of tourism based on observing and preserving the natural environment and culture of a destination area. (16)

**elapsed flying time.** Actual length of time that passes between departure and arrival of a flight. (15)

**electronic communication.** Use of electronic technology for communication, including computers, smartphones, two-way radios, pagers, and tablets. (26)

**embassy.** Official office of one country located in another country. (16)

**embezzlement.** Crime that occurs when a trusted employee takes either money or goods entrusted to him or her. (24)

**emergency.** Unforeseen event that can cause harm to people and property. (23)

**emergency action plan.** Detailed, usually written, plan that describes what to do in case of an emergency. (23)

**emergency coordinator.** Person given the authority to make decisions during emergencies. (23)

**emergency medical services (EMS).** Emergency medical professionals and medical equipment, which are brought to the scene in an ambulance. (23)

**emergency medical technician (EMT).** Medical professional trained and licensed to perform emergency medical care; also called *paramedic*. (23)

**emergency procedures.** Everything done to respond to an emergency that has already occurred. (23)

**empathy.** Ability of individuals to put themselves in someone else's shoes and know how that person feels. (2)

**employee evaluation.** Formal review and evaluation of an employee's performance on the job. Also called a *performance review* or *performance appraisal*. (19)

**employee handbook.** Document, usually in book or pamphlet form, that explains all company policies and procedures concerning employees. (20)

**employee personnel files.** Files containing evaluations, job descriptions, payroll, and benefit records for every employee. (19)

**employee retention.** Efforts made to keep good employees and reduce turnover. (20)

**entrée.** Main course of a meal. (5)

**entrepreneur.** Person who takes the risk of starting a new business. (27)

**entrepreneurship.** Taking the risk of starting a new business. (27)

**entry-level job.** Job that requires minimum education and no experience. (25)

**entry-level worker.** Worker with no previous work experience and few skills. (19)

**equipment.** All the devices used to prepare food. (9)

**escorted tour.** Most structured type of tour that begins and ends on a specific date and in which the itinerary is preset. (16)

**ethical behavior.** Doing the right thing even when under pressure to do the wrong thing. (24)

**etiquette.** Proper behavior in social situations. (26)

**evacuation.** Orderly movement of people out of a dangerous location. (23)

**executive chef.** Top manager in a restaurant or hotel kitchen. (6)

**executive housekeeper.** Top manager of the housekeeping department. (12)

**exhibit hall.** Space where a trade show is held. (10)

**expansion.** Period when the economy is growing and doing well. (3)

**expediter.** Member of the culinary staff who gets the orders from the servers, gives them to the station chefs or line cooks, and checks the orders before they are picked up. (6)

# F

**facility manager.** Top manager of the engineering department; also called *plant manager*. (14)

**fast-food restaurant.** Restaurant that generally has a counter where customers place their orders and wait for it. (4)

**fatigue.** Tiredness that can be caused by physical exertion, stress, or lack of sleep. (23)

**Federal Insurance Contributions Act (FICA).** Law that permits the federal government to take a small percentage of every worker's paycheck and put it in the Social Security fund. (20)

**FIFO.** Concept that the first food item received should be the first food item used; stands for *first in, first out*. (8)

**financial transaction.** Process of buying something and paying for it. (22)

**fine-dining restaurant.** Restaurant that emphasizes the highest quality in service, ingredients, décor, and atmosphere. (4)

**fire extinguisher.** Container filled with materials that will put out a fire. (23)

**fire triangle.** Three things a fire needs to keep burning: fuel, oxygen, and heat. (23)

**first aid.** Treatment given to an injured or suddenly ill person before professional medical care arrives. (23)

**fixed menu.** Menu in which the same foods are offered every day. (5)

**flammable liquid.** Liquid that catches fire easily and burns quickly. (23)

**flatware.** Knives, forks, and spoons that guests will use during a meal. (5)

**food and beverage controller.** Accountant for the food and beverage department of a hotel. (22)

**food and beverage director.** Manager in charge of all the food and beverage services in the hotel. (7)

**Food and Drug Administration (FDA).** Government agency that makes and enforces regulations based on the Food, Drug, and Cosmetic Act. (24)

**foodborne illness.** Disease that is caused by eating contaminated food. (9)

**food contact surface.** Surface that comes in contact with food. (9)

**Food, Drug, and Cosmetic Act.** Act requiring that food, drugs, and cosmetics sold to the public be proven safe and effective. (24)

**food handling.** Procedures that prevent the growth of bacteria in foods. (9)

**food presentation.** Art of making food look attractive and appetizing. (5)

**food production.** Process of changing raw foods into menu items. (5)

**foodservice.** Business of making and serving prepared food and drink. (4)

**foodservice industry.** Segment of the hospitality industry consisting of businesses that prepare food and beverages for customers. (1)

**forecasting.** Predicting the number of guests who will stay at the hotel. (11)

**foreign independent tours (FIT).** Plans that are custom-designed for particular travelers. who are traveling abroad. (16)

**four Ps of marketing.** The four essential areas of marketing: product, price, place, and promotion. (21)

**franchise.** The right to do business using the brand and products of another business; the business that is set up. (1)

**franchise agreement.** Legal document that sets up a franchise. (1)

**franchisee.** Person who buys the right to use the brand. (1)

**franchisor.** Person who owns the chain and the brand. (1)

**frequency.** Offering of several departures daily or weekly by a carrier. (15)

**front bar.** Bar that has one or more bartenders, who serve the public face-to-face. (7)

**front desk agent.** Staff member who works at the front desk and is responsible for guest check-in and checkout. (11)

**front office.** Department that handles everything related to selling sleeping rooms and interacting with guests. (11)

**front office manager.** The person who manages the front office. (11)

**front-of-the-house.** Area in a hospitality business that guests usually see. (2)

**front-of-the-house employees.** Employees whose main function is to interact with customers. (2)

**full-service hotel.** Large hotel that provides many services. (10)

**full-service restaurant.** Restaurant in which customers sit at a table and give their orders to a server, who brings their food to the table. (4)

**function.** A special event. (7)

**function room.** Room that customers rent for an activity, such as a meeting, wedding, or banquet. (11)

# G

**garnish.** To decorate a food or a plate of food; a decoration. (5)

**general manager.** Person responsible for the entire operation of one unit of a hospitality business. Also called the *managing director*. (19)

**giving notice.** Notifying your supervisor that you intend to leave your job. (26)

**glassware.** Drinking glasses that guests will use during a meal. (5)

**global economy.** Term used to refer to the worldwide economy composed of the interconnected economies of all nations. (3)

**globalization.** Process in which the economies of different nations become interconnected. (3)

**good.** Item that can be touched. (21)

**good work ethic.** Attitude that combines hard work, good performance, and dependable results. (24)

**government agency.** Department of government that is responsible for enforcing a law. (24)

**grounds.** Outside area around a building. (14)

**groundskeeper.** Person responsible for the upkeep of the grounds around a building. (14)

**groundskeeping.** Work that includes landscaping, watering, weed control, mowing, trimming, fertilizing, and trash removal. (14)

**guaranteed reservation.** Reservation that holds the room until the guest arrives, regardless of the time. (11)

**guest.** Customer who purchases products or services from a hospitality business. (2)

**guest folio.** Record of charges and payments made by a guest. (11)

**guest history record.** Record kept by a lodging property that contains information about each guest each time he or she stays at the property. (11)

**guest mix.** Percentage of each segment that is staying at a lodging property. (10)

**guest room.** Room where guests sleep for one or more nights; also called a *sleeping room*. (11)

# H

**hazard.** Situation that could result in an accident or an emergency. (23)

**Hazard Analysis Critical Control Point (HACCP).** System of assuring food safety that sets up control points to ensure the proper handling of food from the moment it enters the restaurant until it is fully prepared and served. (9)

**heritage tourism.** Tourism that involves people traveling to places that authentically represent history and culture. (16)

**hired management.** Business in which the owner hires a person or a company to manage the business. (18)

**holding.** Keeping potentially hazardous foods out of the temperature danger zone during the period while the food is waiting to be served to guests. (9)

**holding unit.** Piece of equipment that holds food at a specific temperature. (9)

**hospitality.** Meeting the needs of guests with kindness and goodwill. (1)

**hospitality industry.** Industry that provides services to people away from home. (1)

**hospitality suite.** Special room in a hotel that is reserved by a group for the purpose of serving refreshments to the group. (7)

**hosted tour.** Tour that combines together two or more elements along with the services of a local host or guide. (16)

**hostel.** Inexpensive place to stay where sleeping rooms, bathrooms, and kitchen facilities are shared. (10)

**hotel guest cycle.** Four stages of a guest visit: prearrival, arrival, occupancy, and departure. (11)

**hotelier.** Owner or manager of a hotel. (3)

**hotel management.** Day-to-day running of the hotel. (10)

**house attendants.** Workers responsible for cleaning the public areas; also called *house staff*. (12)

**housekeeping department.** Department responsible for keeping the hotel clean. (12)

**house staff.** Workers responsible for cleaning the public areas; also called *house attendants*. (12)

**hub.** Airport designated by an air carrier to serve as the point for its online connections. (15)

**human resources.** Everyone who works for the company; also called *personnel*. (20)

**Human Resources Information System (HRIS).** Computer system that human resources departments use for personnel records. (20)

**HVAC systems.** Heating, ventilation, and air conditioning systems. (14)

hybrid. Nonprofit agency that is a mix of public and private ownership. (17)

hybrid menu. Menu that is a combination of two types of menus. (5)

# I

inbound. Arriving. (16)

incentive travel. Form of reward from a company to its employees for outstanding work. (15)

independent business. Business that has only one establishment and is not connected legally or by contract to any other business; also called *single-unit business*. (1)

independent tour. Least structured type of tour that includes lodging and at least one other element from a supplier, in which the itinerary is set by the travelers themselves. (16)

information interview. Talking to someone to learn about his or her career. (25)

infrastructure. Basic physical and organizational structures needed for the operation of a society or a community. (16)

in-house foodservice. Foodservice that is run by the institution itself. (4)

in-house housekeeping services. Services done by housekeepers who are employees of the hotel. (12)

initiative. Ability to get a job done without being constantly reminded by someone else. (26)

inspection. Formal visit by federal, state, and local government agencies for the purpose of making sure regulations are being followed. (24)

inspector. Member of the team who checks the room after it is cleaned. (12)

in stock. On hand, either in the kitchen or the storeroom. (8)

insurance. Financial arrangement used to protect individuals or businesses against financial loss. (13)

insurance policy. Document in which details of an insurance arrangement are recorded. (13)

international tourist. Tourists traveling to another country, which may be few or many miles from home. (16)

Internet advertising. Company website and ads on other websites, such as travel websites and Internet search engines. (21)

internship. Supervised, on-the-job training that students do before they actually go out to work in an industry. (25)

interpersonal skills. Skills consisting of the ability to interact smoothly and productively with other people. (26)

interpretation. Process of helping each visitor finds an opportunity to personally connect with a place. (17)

interpreter. Mixture of a teacher and an actor who provides information about a destination. (16)

interview. Formal meeting between two or more people during which questions are asked of one person. (26)

inventory. Process of counting and keeping track of all the items in storage. (8)

inventory control. Process of keeping track of items in inventory. (8)

invoice. Bill that includes a complete listing of what was delivered along with the quantity and price for each item. (8)

issuing. Process of making items available to employees; also called *requisitioning*. (8)

# J

job description. Document that lists the essential functions and requirements for a job. (20)

job lead. Information that leads to a job opening. (26)

job shadowing. Following a person while he or she does a job. (25)

# K

key card. Key used in an electronic key system. (13)

key control. Knowing where all hotel keys are located at all times and knowing who has each key. (13)

kitchen manager. Top manager in the kitchen of a unit of a chain restaurant. (6)

# L

labor. Workers who are members of a labor union. (20)

**labor relations.** Relationship between the labor unions and the management of the company. (20)

**labor union.** Organization for workers who perform similar work. (20)

**laissez-faire style.** Management style in which the employer gives all the power to employees, who make all the decisions. (19)

**landscaping.** Use of trees, flowers, and shrubs in artistic ways to make a building and the grounds around it look appealing. (14)

**laundry.** Linens that need to be washed or have just been washed. (12)

**laundry attendants.** Staff members who perform all the tasks involved in washing laundry. (12)

**laundry supervisor.** Staff member who supervises the attendants and seamsters. (12)

**laws.** Society's rules for proper behavior. (24)

**leadership.** Ability to influence others and inspire excellence. (26)

**leading.** Influencing people to accomplish the goals of the business. (18)

**ledger.** Book in which financial transactions are recorded. (22)

**leisure time.** Time left over after work and other necessities. (17)

**leisure travel.** Travel for rest, relaxation, and enjoyment. (15)

**liability.** Responsibility to pay for damage or loss. (13)

**liability insurance.** Insurance that provides payment if the hospitality business is sued and the courts determine that the hospitality business is liable. (13)

**license.** Document that gives the holder permission to do something. (24)

**lifestyle trend.** Change in the way people live their lives. (3)

**limitation of liability.** Limit on the amount of money that a hotel must pay a guest for a loss of property. (13)

**limited-service hotels.** Hotels that offer a medium level of service and a midrange price. (10)

**limited-service property.** Hotel that focuses on charging lower prices, which it is able to do by providing fewer services than a full-service hotel. (10)

**linen room.** Room where clean linens are stored. (12)

**linens.** All the items in the guest room that are made of cloth. (12)

**loan.** Money borrowed from a bank or other source, with the expectation that the money will be repaid with interest within a specific time period. (27)

**lodging.** A place to sleep for one or more nights. Also called *accommodation*. (1)

**lodging concept.** Whole idea of the lodging property or chain. (10)

**lodging industry.** Industry that consists of businesses providing overnight accommodations. (1)

**log.** Record of a person's activities, such as work, school, commuting, homework, self-care, buying and preparing food, and sleeping. (17)

**loyalty program.** Program that rewards frequent customers with free or lower-priced products. (21)

**luxury hotel.** Hotel that provides the highest level of amenities, service, room furnishings, public spaces, and technology. (10)

# M

**major emergency.** Emergency that requires professional help or is life-threatening. (23)

**management.** Team of people who make decisions for the business. (18)

**manager.** Person who makes decisions for a business. (18)

**managing director.** Person responsible for the entire operation of one unit of a hospitality business. Also called the *general manager*. (19)

**market.** Group that consists of all the people who could potentially buy what a business is selling. (4)

**marketing.** Developing products that meet customer needs and promoting those products so customers will buy them. (21)

**marketing mix.** Decisions made in four essential areas of marketing: product, price, place, and promotion. (21)

**marketing plan.** Document that lists the marketing goals of the business and describes how these goals will be achieved. (21)

**marketing research.** Research that is done to learn about the market and potential customers. (21)

**market menu.** Menu that changes with the availability of food products. (5)

**market segment.** Subgroup of a larger market that has similar needs and wants for the product a business is selling. (4)

**market segmentation.** Process of dividing a large market into market segments. (21)

**material safety data sheet (MSDS).** Form completed by the manufacturer for each hazardous substance it makes. (23)

**meal plan.** Room rate that includes meals. (10)

**meetings, events, and incentive (ME&I) travel.** Type of tourism that includes a planned agenda for large groups with a similar work, educational, or recreational purpose. (15)

**mending.** Repairing, such as linens. (12)

**menu.** List of food and beverage items served in a foodservice operation. (5)

**microorganism.** Living substance so small that you must use a microscope to see it. (9)

**middle management.** One or more levels of management between the top level and the supervisory level. (18)

**mildew.** Type of fungus that grows on damp surfaces. (12)

**minibar.** Small cabinet containing small bottles of alcoholic beverages and snacks. (7)

**minimum wage.** Lowest hourly rate that a worker must be paid. (20)

**minor emergency.** An emergency that does not require the help of an expert. (23)

**minor injury.** Injury that does not require the help of an expert. (23)

**motel.** Establishment that combines basic hotel services with convenience for the automobile traveler. (3)

**motivated worker.** Worker who willingly puts forth effort on the job. (19)

**motivation.** Extrinsic or intrinsic element that moves someone toward a behavior. (17)

**multi-unit business.** Business that has two or more establishments that function as part of a chain or franchise. (1)

**mystery shopper.** Person hired to stay anonymously at a hotel or eat at a restaurant and observe the quality. (19)

# N

**National Park Service (NPS).** Federal agency that supervises outdoor recreation and the preservation of natural and cultural resources. (17)

**national tourism office.** Office that promotes tourism abroad to bring international tourists into its country. (16)

**negligence.** Behaviors such as carelessness, laziness, ignoring the rules, and improper use of equipment. (23)

**negotiation.** Process during which two or more people talk and listen together for the purpose of resolving a disagreement or a conflict. (26)

**networking.** Process of meeting and making contact with people in your profession. (26)

**night audit.** Careful examination of the hotel's financial transactions for that day. (22)

**night auditor.** Person who performs the night audit. (22)

**nonguaranteed reservation.** Reservation that expires at a specific time on the reserved date. (11)

**nonpersonal communication.** Set message conveyed through mass media, including television, radio, the Internet, newspapers, magazines, fliers, pamphlets, and billboards. (21)

**nonpotable water.** Water not clean enough to drink but still usable. (14)

**nonverbal communication.** Communication of information and feelings without using words, such as body language. (26)

**nutrients.** Chemical substances in food that help maintain the body. (5)

# O

**Occupational Safety and Health Act (OSH Act).** Act that requires employers to make the workplace free of hazards that might cause injury or death to employees. (23)

**Occupational Safety and Health Administration (OSHA).** Federal agency responsible for making sure that the laws and regulations of the OSH Act are followed. (23)

**occupied.** Room status meaning that a guest is registered to the room and that the guest or the guest's belongings or both are in the room. (12)

**off-peak seasons.** Seasons with the lowest demand. (3)

**open seating.** Policy in which customers walk in the door and expect to be seated without a reservation. (6)

**operations.** Day-to-day planning that is the actual running of the business. (18)

**operations manual.** Book that includes all the details about how to run the business. (18)

**order.** List of products that a business wants to purchase. (8)

**ordinance.** Regulation made by a local government. (24)

**organizational chart.** Chart that shows how the tasks of the business are organized and who performs these tasks. (18)

**organizational skills.** Skills that enable individuals to keep their tools and information in order. (19)

**organizing.** Designing the internal structure of the business. (18)

**outbound.** Departing. (16)

**out-of-order room.** Room status meaning that the room is being renovated or repaired; it does not need to be cleaned and is not available to sell. (12)

**outside contractors.** Outside company who provides contract housekeeping services. (12)

**Outward Bound.** Organization that sponsors wilderness experiences. (17)

**overbooking.** Making more reservations than there are tables or rooms available. (6)

**owner-managed business.** Business in which the owner is the manager and makes all the decisions for the business. (18)

# P

**paramedic.** Medical professional trained and licensed to perform emergency medical care; also called *emergency medical technician (EMT)*. (23)

**parasite.** Organism that must live in another living thing in order to survive. (9)

**par stock.** Maximum amount of a particular item that is allowed to be in storage at any one time. (8)

**partners.** The people involved in a partnership who share responsibility for the business. (18)

**partnership.** Form of ownership in which two or more people own the business. (18)

**party.** Group of people who go out to eat together. (5)

**passed-items function.** Standing buffet where servers walk around the room with food and beverages on trays. (7)

**passport.** Document issued by a national government as proof of a person's identity and citizenship. (16)

**pass-through.** Special area equipped with heat lamps to keep the food hot until served. (6)

**pathogen.** Biological contaminant that causes disease. (9)

**patrol.** Act of walking or riding around an area for the purpose of maintaining security. (13)

**payroll.** Money paid to employees for their labor. (22)

**payroll deduction.** Process in which the employer subtracts taxes from each employee's paycheck and sends the taxes directly to the appropriate government agency. (24)

**peak seasons.** Seasons with the highest demand. (3)

**performance appraisal.** Formal review and evaluation of an employee's performance on the job; also called an *employee evaluation* or *performance review*. (19)

**performance review.** Formal review and evaluation of an employee's performance on the job; also called an *employee evaluation* or *performance appraisal*. (19)

**perishable.** Product that can spoil quickly. (8)

**permit.** Written permission to do something. (24)

**perpetual inventory.** Inventory method that consists of keeping a record of the total number of each item in inventory, then adding whenever new items are received and subtracting whenever items are issued. (8)

**personal communication.** Two or more people communicating directly, either in person or through electronic mediums. (21)

**personal hygiene.** Actions a person takes to keep his or her body and clothing clean and to remove pathogens. (9)

**personnel.** Everyone who works for the company; also called *human resources*. (20)

**person-trip.** One person on a trip away from home overnight in paid accommodations, or on any trip to a place more than 50 miles (one way) away from home. (15)

**pH value.** Level of acidity or alkalinity of the water. (14)

**physical contaminant.** Item that accidentally gets into food. (9)

**physical inventory.** Inventory method that consists of actually going into the storage areas and counting every item. (8)

**plainclothes security officer.** Security officer who does not wear a uniform. (13)

**plan.** Record of the decisions made about the goals and the methods to meet them. (18)

**planning.** Setting goals and developing methods to meet those goals. (18)

**plant manager.** Top manager of the engineering department; also called *facility manager*. (14)

**plateware.** Dishes, such as plates, soup bowls, coffee cups, and saucers, that guests will use during a meal. (5)

**plating.** Placing of food on a plate. (5)

**point of sale.** Place where goods or services are sold and money is collected. (22)

**point-of-sales system (POS).** Computerized system for recording an order at the place where the order is taken (at the point where the sale is made). (6)

**portion control.** Making sure that each portion of a food item is always the correct size. (5)

**posting charges.** Guest's folio that records the room rate and taxes charged to a guest. (22)

**postsecondary.** After high school. (25)

**potable water.** Safe drinking water. (14)

**potentially hazardous foods.** Foods in which bacteria grow best. (9)

**press release.** Article written by a company for use as the basis for news in a newspaper, Internet, radio, or TV news program. (21)

**preventive maintenance.** Cleaning and repair of equipment that is in working order. (14)

**print advertising.** Advertising that consists of ads that appear on paper. (21)

**product.** Any goods and services a business sells. (21)

**professional association.** A group of people organized to improve themselves, their profession, and their industry. (1)

**profit.** Money a business has left after all the costs of running the business are paid. (18)

**programming.** Developing a selection and schedule of activities suitable for the demographics of the people being served. (17)

**promotion.** Telling customers about a product or the company that offers it. (21)

**property insurance.** Insurance that provides payment for loss or damage of property owned by the business. (13)

**property management system (PMS).** Computer software and hardware used to run lodging properties. (11)

**public areas.** Areas in a building that include hallways, stairs, lobby, lounges, public restrooms, restaurants, meeting rooms, banquet halls, and recreation areas. (12)

**publicity.** Information that appears in the media about a company or product. (21)

**public relations.** Activities performed to create goodwill between the public and the business. (21)

**purchase order.** Form used for submitting orders to a supplier. (8)

**purchaser.** Expert in buying goods and services for a business. (8)

**purchasing.** Buying of goods and services for use in a business. (8)

# Q

**quality of life (QOL).** Person's overall satisfaction with the conditions of his or her life. (17)

**quality service.** Service that meets or exceeds customer expectations. (2)

**quick-service restaurant.** Restaurant that provides customers with convenience, speed, and basic service at low prices. (4)

# R

**rack rate.** Official rate for one night's lodging at a lodging property. (10)

**reader board.** Announcement board located in a hotel lobby and other locations on a lodging property. (21)

**receiving.** Process of making sure the items delivered are the items that were ordered. (8)

**receiving dock.** Dock where deliveries are received, usually located near where the items will be stored. (8)

**recession.** Period when the economy is slowing down and doing poorly; also called *contraction*. (3)

**recipe.** Set of instructions for preparing a food item. (5)

**recreation.** Any activity that people do for rest, relaxation, and enjoyment. (1)

**recreation industry.** Industry that consists of providers of activities for rest, relaxation, and enjoyment. (1)

**recruitment.** Process of finding candidates for job openings. (20)

**reference.** Person who is willing to talk with employers about an applicant's job qualifications and personal qualities. (26)

**referral system.** Group of independent hotels that creates a central office for reservations and marketing; also called an *affiliation group* or *consortium*. (10)

**registration.** Process of keeping a list of everyone who is staying at the hotel. (11)

**registration record.** Record that contains information about the guest's method of payment, the arrival and departure dates, automobile model and license plate number, and any special requests. (11)

**regulation.** Specific rule that is developed based on a law. (24)

**regulatory compliance.** Following appropriate laws and regulations. (20)

**relocation.** Act of moving from one place to another for your job. (25)

**reorder point.** Minimum amount of an item in storage, or the point at which more of the item must be ordered. (8)

**repackaged foods.** Foods that have been partially used and not stored in their original containers after opening. (8)

**repeat business.** Occurs when satisfied customers return to the business again and again. (21)

**reporting relationship.** Relationship between a worker and the manager to whom he or she reports. (18)

**requisition form.** Form used to request items from inventory. (8)

**requisitioning.** Process of making items available to employees; also called *issuing*. (8)

**reservation.** Promise to hold something for a customer until the customer needs it. (6)

**reservation record.** Record that includes the guest's name, address, phone number, dates of the reservation, type of room assigned, and any special requests. (11)

**reservations agent.** Agent who takes guest calls and makes reservations. (11)

**residence time.** Time that it takes a party to eat a meal, pay the bill, and leave the restaurant. (6)

**resort.** Place that provides entertainment, recreation, and relaxation for vacationers. (10)

**resort hotel.** Hotel that caters to the vacationer or leisure traveler. (10)

**restaurant concept.** Whole idea of the restaurant or the restaurant chain. (4)

**restaurant manager.** Manager responsible for everything that happens in the front-of-the-house. (6)

**résumé.** Written document that lists a person's qualifications for a job, including education and work experience. (26)

**revenue.** Money that a business takes in for the products and services it sells. (18)

**revenue center.** Division or department that sells products that bring in revenue. (18)

**revenue management software.** Type of software that helps calculate the best prices to charge for guest rooms. (21)

**right-to-know.** Requirement stating that the employer must inform all employees about any toxic or dangerous materials they use in the workplace. (23)

**role.** Set of responsibilities and expectations that go with an aspect of a peron's life. (26)

**room attendant.** Person who cleans the guest rooms. (12)

**room inventory.** Count of the number of rooms sold and the number of rooms available each day. (11)

**room rate.** Price actually charged to a guest for one night's lodging. (10)

**rooms division.** Part of the hotel that handles all tasks involved in preparing and selling sleeping rooms. (11)

**room service.** Delivery of food and beverages to guests in their hotel rooms. (7)

**room service manager.** Manager who supervises all room service operations. (7)

**room temperature.** Temperature around 70°F, which is in the danger zone. (9)

# S

**safe deposit box.** Metal box that requires two keys to open. (13)

**safety.** Actions taken to prevent accidents and emergencies. (23)

**safety procedures.** Everything done to prevent an accident or emergency. (23)

**salary.** Annual amount of money that a person is paid. (20)

**sales.** Promotion that occurs when a representative of the company speaks directly with the customer about the product. (21)

**sales promotion.** Specific offer designed to increase sales. (21)

**sanitary.** State of being free from disease-causing pathogens or having a safe level of pathogens. (12)

**sanitation.** Processes of cleaning and sanitizing. (9)

**sanitizing.** Treatment of a clean surface with chemicals or heat to reduce the number of pathogens to safe levels. (9)

**scheduled airlines.** Airlines that plan flights over set routes. (15)

**scheduling.** Process of assigning staff to work at specific times. (12)

**screening process.** Determining which candidates are likely to be a good fit for the job. (20)

**seamsters.** Workers who repair worn or torn linens. (12)

**seasonality.** Fluctuations in the number of visitors, expenditures, and transportation needs. (16)

**seated banquet.** Banquet where tables are set and guests choose or are assigned a place at a table. (7)

**seated buffet.** Buffet where tables are set and guests choose or are assigned a place at a table. (7)

**seating.** Process of finding seats for customers in a restaurant. (6)

**secular.** Nonreligious. (17)

**security.** Actions taken to prevent crime and protect the safety of people and property. (13)

**security log.** Book in which all security incidents are recorded. (13)

**security officers.** Staff members who carry out the actions to prevent crime and protect the safety of people and property. (13)

**security policies.** Rules that employees must follow to ensure security. (13)

**security system.** Computerized burglar detection and alarm system. (13)

**self-motivation.** Inner urge for individuals to achieve their goals. (26)

**sense of place.** Person's subjective orientation toward a place. (16)

**servers.** Workers who serve the customers and meet all of their needs. (6)

**service.** Activity that is done for another person. (2, 21)

**service bar.** Bar where servers take customer orders and give them to the bartender, who makes the drinks, which the servers then serve to the customers. (7)

**service encounter.** Interaction between a customer and a staff member. (2)

**serving.** Delivering food to a guest. (5)

**sexual harassment.** Any unwelcome behavior of a sexual nature that creates an intimidating, hostile, or offensive work environment. (20)

**shipment.** All of the items delivered from one supplier at one time. (8)

**side dish.** Portion of food that goes with the entrée. (5)

**sidework.** Duties that servers must perform other than serving guests. (5)

**single-unit business.** Business that has only one establishment and is not connected legally or by contract to any other business; also called *independent business*. (1)

**site guide.** Guide that provides interpretation at an attraction. (16)

**skirting.** Table linen placed around buffet tables to hide the table legs and make the table look elegant. (7)

**sleeping room.** Room where guests sleep for one or more nights; also called a *guest room*. (11)

**Social Security.** Federal program that ensures workers will get some income after they retire. (20)

**social trend.** Change in the structure or beliefs of the society. (3)

**sole proprietor.** The one person owning a business who is responsible for the entire business. (18)

**sole proprietorship.** Form of ownership in which only one person owns a business. (18)

**sous-chef.** Second-in-command in the kitchen. (6)

**souvenir.** Item that reminds travelers of a place they visited. (3)

**spatial context.** Unique physical spaces that people can visit. (16)

**special-purpose bar.** Bar that is usually set up for one particular event, such as a banquet. (7)

**specialty accommodations.** Variety of accommodations that provide less personal service than a full-service hotel, but more than a motel. (10)

**specification.** Detailed description of the product that is needed. (8)

**staffing.** All activities involved in hiring and keeping workers. (18)

**standardized recipe.** Recipe that has been tested for consistency. (5)

**start-up costs.** All the expenses involved in getting a business started. (27)

**station.** Location in the room where food or beverage is available. (7)

**steward.** Worker who supervises the dishwashing, pot washing, and cleanup. (6)

**stock.** Right of partial ownership in a corporation. (18)

**stockholders.** People who own stock in a corporation and who actually own the corporation and get the profits from the business based on the number of shares they own. (18)

**storage.** Safe, secure place in which items are placed until they are needed. (8)

**stress.** Feeling of tension. (25)

**structural security.** Security features that are built into a building. (13)

**suggestive selling.** Practice of recommending additional products or services to a customer while that customer is buying something else. (21)

**suite.** Hotel accommodation that consists of more than one room. (10)

**supervisor.** Manager who makes sure each employee does his or her job properly. (19)

**supervisory management.** Level of management that is closest to the workers. (18)

**supplier.** Business from whom supplies are purchased. (8); Company that creates and provides fundamental travel products. (15)

**support center.** Division or department that does not make revenue directly and provides services that enable the revenue centers to make money. (18)

**surveillance.** Process of closely observing what is going on in an area. (13)

**system of accounts.** Organized way of naming and categorizing accounts. (22)

# T

**table d'hôte pricing.** Pricing method in which a complete meal is offered at a set price. (5)

**target market.** Market segment whose needs a business strives to meet. (4)

**taxes.** Money paid to the federal, state, and local government as required by law. (22)

**tech prep.** Preparation program that combines the last two years of high school with two years of postsecondary education. (25)

**temperature danger zone.** Temperatures in which bacteria can grow well, between 41°F to 135°F. (9)

**temporary worker.** Worker who is hired for a specific, usually short, amount of time. (20)

**theme.** Specific idea around which something is organized. (4)

**thermometer.** Tool for measuring temperature. (9)

**thermostat.** Automatic device that regulates the temperature of a piece of equipment. (9)

**time-share.** Part ownership in a vacation development, which gives the share owner the right to accommodations on the premises for specific periods each year. (17)

**tipped employee.** Worker who receives tips from customers. (20)

**tourism.** Industry that develops and organizes destinations and then markets those destinations to travelers. (15)

**tourism destination area (TDA).** Location that intentionally attracts visitors and brings in revenue through tourism. (16)

**tourism industry.** Industry consisting of businesses that organize and promote travel for business, leisure, and other purposes. (1)

**tourist card.** Identification needed to enter and exit Mexico and most other Latin American countries. (16)

**trade show.** Exhibit during which people show the goods and services they have to sell. (10)

**transmit.** To carry from one place to another. (9)

**transnational corporation.** Corporation that has major operations in several countries. (3)

**travel.** Movement of a person from one location to another location of some distance for any of several reasons. (15)

**travel agency.** Private business that promotes travel sales to the public on behalf of the travel industry. (15)

**travel agent.** Individual who works at a retail business that brings travelers and travel industry suppliers together. (15)

**travel industry.** Industry that consists of businesses that physically move travelers from one place to another. (1)

**travel package.** Package that includes trip arrangements for several segments of the hospitality industry, such as transportation, lodging, meals, and entertainment. (1)

**travel planner.** Individual with many of the same duties as a travel agent, but who usually works in-house for a large corporation. (15)

**trend.** General direction in which something is moving. (3)

**turndown service.** Housekeeping work that is performed in the evening. (12)

**turnover.** Process in which an employee leaves the company and another employee must be hired to take his or her place. (20)

# U

**United Nations World Tourism Organization (UNWTO).** Special agency of the United Nations that defines standards of tourism used in many countries. (16)

**U.S. Small Business Administration (SBA).** Government agency that helps new businesses and entrepreneurs. (27)

**unethical behavior.** Doing the wrong thing; may also be illegal. (24)

**uniformed security officer.** Security officer who wears a uniform and badge as an obvious sign of an establishment's protection. (13)

**Uniform System of Accounts.** System that provides uniform names for each category of account for use throughout the hotel industry. (22)

**upper management.** Top level of management. (18)

**utensils.** All the small pieces of equipment used in the kitchen, plus all the items used to serve food to guests. (9)

# V

**vacant.** Room status meaning that no guest is registered for that room and no guest or belongings are in the room. (12)

**vault.** Large locked room. (13)

**virus.** Microorganism that reproduces in the cells of other living things. (9)

**visa.** Permission issued by a country to a noncitizen authorizing the holder to enter, exit, or live in a country for a specific time. (16)

**visit friends and relatives (VFR).** Form of travel in which the specific purpose is to see people as opposed to the destination. (15)

# W

**wage.** Amount of money that a person is paid per hour. (20)

**wage and salary scale.** List of wages and salaries paid for each job. (20)

**wake-up call.** Phone call placed by the hotel to the guest's room at a specific time requested by the guest. (11)

**walk-ins.** Customers who arrive at a restaurant but have not made a reservation. (6)

**word-of-mouth publicity.** Informal conversation people have about their experiences with a business. (2)

**workers' compensation.** Requirement that employer provide medical and salary coverage for an illness or injury that an employee experiences as a result of the job. (20)

**work habits.** Basic routine actions carried out every day at work. (26)

**work-life balance.** Equal time spent between career or work demands and the needs of life-related activities such as home, family, friends, health, and leisure. (17)

**work shift.** Regular period of time during which work is done. (11)

**work values.** Aspects of work that are the most important to a person. (25)

# Y

**yield.** Amount of food that a recipe produces. (5)

# Z

**zoning.** Process of designating specific geographic areas for specific uses. (24)

**zoning laws.** Laws that list geographic areas and state the permitted uses for each area. (24)

# Index

## A

# C